# World
# Prehistory and
# Archaeology

## Pathways through Time

# World
# Prehistory
## and
# Archaeology

# Pathways
# through Time

## Michael Chazan
*University of Toronto*

PEARSON

Boston ■ New York ■ San Francisco
Mexico City ■ Montreal ■ Toronto ■ London ■ Madrid ■ Munich ■ Paris
Hong Kong ■ Singapore ■ Tokyo ■ Cape Town ■ Sydney

*Series Editor:* Dave Repetto
*Series Editorial Assistant:* Jack Cashman
*Development Editor:* Jennifer Jacobson
*Marketing Manager:* Laura Lee Manley
*Associate Editor:* Deb Hanlon
*Production Supervisor:* Karen Mason
*Editorial Production Service:* WestWordsPMG
*Composition Buyer:* Linda Cox
*Manufacturing Buyer:* Debbie Rossi
*Electronic Composition:* WestWordsPMG
*Interior Design:* Carol Somberg
*Photo Researcher:* Annie Pickert
*Cover Administrator:* Linda Knowles

For related titles and support materials, visit our online catalog at
**www.ablongman.com**

Between the time website information is gathered and then published, it is not
unusual for some sites to have closed. Also, the transcription of URLs can result
in typographical errors. The publisher would appreciate notification where these
errors occur so that they may be corrected in subsequent editions.

**Library of Congress Cataloging-in-Publication Data**

Chazan, Michael.
  World prehistory and archaeology : pathways through time / Michael Chazan.
      p. cm.
  Includes bibliographical references and index
  ISBN: 0-205-40621-1
  ISBN 13: 978-0-205-40621-0
    1. Prehistoric peoples. 2. Anthropology, Prehistoric. 3. Archaeology. I. Title.
  GN740.C43 2007
  930.1--dc22

                                                        2007000353

Printed in the United States of America

10  9  8  7  6  5  4  3  2       [RRD-OH]     11  10  09  08

See Figure and Photo Credits on page 486, which constitutes a continuation of the
copyright page.

For Michelle

# BRIEF CONTENTS

# CONTENTS

# CHAPTER 2

## Putting the Picture Together   36

*Building on the students' familiarity with what archaeologists do in the field and the laboratory, this chapter introduces the reader to the ways archaeologists think about the past. The major theoretical approaches to archaeology are presented within their historical context.*

*page 51*

*page 57*

*page 58*

# PART TWO
## Human Evolution  63

### Introduction: Our Place in Nature  63

*The study of human evolution draws insight from a multitude of disciplines, including paleontology, genetics, paleoclimatology, and archaeology. This section of the book synthesizes the current state of research in human evolution, strongly emphasizing the unique perspective provided by archaeology. Particular topics are the timing of hominin dispersals and changes in adaptation and technology.*

## CHAPTER 3

## Early Hominins  72

*This chapter begins by tracing the origin of tools and the way early hominins lived. It then moves on to examine the evidence for the initial spread of hominins out of Africa and the subsequent diversification of culture.*

page 72

page 77

page 90

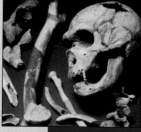
*page 102*

*page 110*

*page 128*

# CHAPTER 5

## The Origin of Modern Humans   134

*The origin of modern humans is the subject of considerable debate sparked by important archaeological discoveries. This chapter begins with a presentation of the archaeology of early modern humans in Africa, before moving on to consider the enigmatic relationship between Neanderthals and modern humans in the Middle East. The alternative hypotheses for the origin of modern humans and the fate of the Neanderthals are then discussed. The final section presents a brief overview of the European Upper Paleolithic.*

*page 134*

*page 136*

*page 154*

# CHAPTER 6

## The Peopling of Australia and the New World   164

*This chapter presents the debates over the timing of the initial human occupation of Australia and the Americas and the migration routes that were followed. These debates are tightly linked to questions surrounding the adaptations of the first peoples to arrive on these continents.*

*page 164*

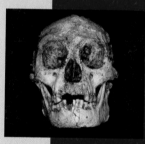

*page 171*

*page 188*

# PART THREE
## Perspectives on Agriculture 191

### Introduction: Definitions of Agriculture 192

The development of agricultural societies involved a profound reorientation of the way humans related to plants and animals, along with equally significant changes in human society and technology. Because the transition to agriculture took place independently in several distinct regions, we can take a comparative approach to the origins of agriculture in order to gain a broad understanding of the process. In doing so, we learn that the shift to an agricultural way of life often spanned a period of several thousands of years and that the details of the process differ significantly across regions.

## CHAPTER 7

### Towers, Villages, and Longhouses 202

The earliest evidence for agriculture is found in the Middle East, where settled villages preceded the domestication of plants and animals. Discussed in this chapter is the adoption of agriculture in Europe, the result of the adoption of key Middle Eastern domesticated plants and animals, including wheat, barley, sheep, goats, cattle, and pigs.

*page 202*

*page 213*

*page 216*

# CHAPTER 8

## Mounds and Maize   232

*The development and spread of agriculture had a profound effect on many societies in the Americas. This chapter examines the evidence for the initial domestication of maize and its subsequent spread into North America. Particular attention is given to the interaction between maize agriculture and the indigenous agricultural system of eastern North America.*

*page 232*

*page 236*

*page 255*

# CHAPTER 9

## A Feast of Diversity   258

*This chapter tests the paradigm for the origins of agriculture, a paradigm derived from Middle Eastern evidence against the hypothesis for the transition to agriculture from Africa, New Guinea, the Andes, and East Asia.*

*page 263*

*page 269*

*page 277*

# PART FOUR
## The Development of Social Complexity   283

**Introduction: Defining Social Complexity**   283

*In Part Three, we examined the shift to an agricultural way of life. In this final part, we visit different societies in many regions of the world and consider the increasing inequality that befell members of these ever-expanding societies. Power and access to resources came to be controlled by a smaller and smaller segment of society, leading to the emergence of state societies.*

## CHAPTER 10

# Complexity without the State   292

*This chapter presents four monumental sites constructed by societies characterized by anthropologists as chiefdoms or ranked societies. The reconstruction of these sites draws out the nature of leadership and power in complex societies that are not states.*

*page 292*

*page 304*

*page 313*

## CHAPTER 11

# Urban States   320

*The classic state is focused around large population centers or cities with elites who control considerable wealth and who have developed a writing system. This chapter presents the archaeology of three classic early state societies.*

*page 320*

*page 328*

*page 351*

# CHAPTER 12

## Enigmatic States  356

*Not all early states fit the expectations of a classic state. Cities, the control of wealth by an elite, and writing systems are not found in all state societies. This chapter presents case studies of early states that challenge expectations.*

*page 356*

*page 380*

*page 383*

## CHAPTER 13

## Empires 386

*The military expansion of the state results in the formation of empires under centralized control. This chapter considers the Inca and Aztec empires of the Americas to elicit some of the characteristics of empires and some of the challenges facing archaeologists working on such large-scale social formations.*

*page 386*

*page 396*

*page 398*

## EPILOGUE

## Bringing It Back Home   414

page 414

## TOOLBOX

# ARCHAEOLOGY IN THE WORLD

# DISCOVERING THE PAST

The world we live in is in many ways a world of our own creation. Buildings, roads, and fences structure the space we inhabit. Social institutions limit and control numerous aspects of our lives, and tools are essential to many of our activities and experiences. Yet human ancestors began to make stone tools only two-and-a-half million years ago. From the perspective of our own lives, two-and-a-half million years is a vast period of time. However, in the history of life on earth, which stretches out over three billion years, two-and-a-half million years is the blink of an eye.

Archaeology is the study of how humans have created the world we live in—a voyage of exploration into the human past. The goal of this voyage is to gain new perspectives and insights into who we are and how our world came into being. As is true of all sciences, archaeology is not a search for absolute and final answers. Archaeologists develop a knowledge of the past that can be continuously questioned and improved. The goal of this book is to involve students in the current state of archaeological research—to reveal *how* archaeologists work and *what* archaeologists know. The fascination of archaeology is found in the continual process of human self-discovery. The book will connect students to that process and make them aware not only of the discoveries that have been made, but also of the challenges that remain.

In archaeology, it is not enough simply to raise questions: One must also think of methods for providing the answers. People often think of archaeology as a random accumulation of artifacts or a series of chance discoveries. In practice, archaeology is a far more active and creative undertaking. Certainly, the excitement of discovery plays an essential role. Even in the most carefully planned project, the possibility always exists that the next shovel of dirt will lead to an unexpected revelation. However, much of the excitement of archaeology comes from asking questions about what it is we want to know and how we can find answers to those questions.

## HOW THIS BOOK IS ORGANIZED

The first section of this book, Part I, "The Past Is a Foreign Country: Getting from Here to There," presents an introduction to archaeological methods. The first chapter, "Getting Started in Archaeology," begins in the field and discusses how archaeologists find and excavate sites. From the field, we move into the laboratory to look at how the remains recovered in an excavation are analyzed. Archaeology is not only field and laboratory work, but also developing a framework for thinking about the past. In Chapter 2, "Putting the Picture Together," we consider questions of how we know the past and how much of the past can be known. This chapter presents a brief history of the ways archaeologists have thought about the past.

From here, we turn to what we currently know about prehistory. The next three sections of the text divide prehistory into three parts: human evolution, agricultural beginnings, and the development of political complexity. Part II, "Human Evolution," covers the periods from the first evidence of tool manufacture to the spread of modern humans (*Homo sapiens*) throughout the globe. Human evolution involves the interaction between the evolution of human anatomy, on the one hand, and changes in the way human ancestors lived and in the tools they used, on the other. The four chapters in this section of the book follow the process of biological evolution while tracking the geographic spread of human populations and developments in the way people lived.

Part III, "Perspectives on Agriculture" examines the shift to an agricultural way of life. The development of agricultural societies involved a profound reorientation of the way humans relate to plants and animals, along with equally significant changes in human society and technology. Because the transition to agriculture took place independently in several distinct regions, it is possible to take a comparative approach to the origins of agriculture in order to gain a broad understanding of the process. Chapter 7, "Towers, Villages, and Longhouses, " presents the archaeological record pointing to the origins of agriculture in the Middle East. Chapter 8, "Mounds and Maize," focuses on the origin of maize (corn) agriculture in Mesoamerica and the spread of maize agriculture into North America. The adoption of maize agriculture in eastern North America is particularly interesting and complex, as maize was integrated into an existing indigenous agricultural system. Chapter 9, "A Feast of Diversity," broadens the comparative perspective by briefly considering a number of other civilizations—in Africa, China, New Guinea, and Peru. The picture that emerges is that the development of agriculture often spanned a period of several thousands of years and that the details of the process differ significantly among regions.

Following their adoption of agriculture, societies in many parts of the world grew in both area and numbers, and inequality increased between members of society. Power and access to resources came to be controlled by a smaller segment of society, resulting in the emergence of state societies. The development of social complexity is the subject of Part IV, "The Development of Social Complexity." This final section covers many of the most spectacular and enigmatic archaeological sites, including Stonehenge, the pyramids at Giza, and the cities of the Maya. As with the origins of agriculture, social complexity developed independently in a number of regions. Thus, it is possible to again use a comparative approach, to gain a broad understanding of this process.

The first chapter of Part IV, Chapter 10, "Complexity without the State," considers four monumental sites—Stonehenge, Pueblo Bonito, Cahokia, and Great Zimbabwe—that were

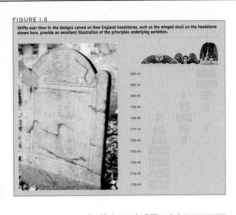

FIGURE 1.8
Shifts over time in the designs carved on New England headstones, such as the winged skull on the headstone shown here, provide an excellent illustration of the principles underlying seriation.

can be used for sites younger than 40,000 years. Accelerator mass spectrometry (AMS) radiocarbon dating is an advanced method that can date extremely small samples.
- Dendrochronology uses sequences of tree rings to date wood found on archaeological sites. In some areas of the world, the dendrochronological sequence has been established for a period of thousands of years.
- Obsidian hydration measures the decay of the surface of obsidian artifacts. Obsidian hydration is usually used on sites several thousand years old or younger.

Absolute dates can be expressed on a number of time scales. In this text, we employ a time scale that uses the birth of Christ as the point of reference. Dates after the birth of Christ can be expressed as years A.D. or years C.E. In this book, we use years A.D. Years before the birth of Christ can be expressed as years B.C. or years B.C.E. In this book, we use years B.C. When archaeologists work on early prehistoric sites, they tend to count years back from the present rather than using years B.C. In this book such dates are expressed as years before present, or years B.P.

30    PART ONE: The Past Is a Foreign Country: Getting from Here to There    www.ablongman.com/chazan

Example of a horizontal excavation: An Iroquoian longhouse at Crawford Lake, Ontario. All that remains of this structure are postholes (marked by sticks), pits, and a large sweat lodge.

to archaeology, they have led to the development of methods of archaeological stratigraphy that take into account the particular characteristics of archaeological sites.

**Stratigraphy.** When sediments are deposited in an undisturbed environment, they will develop over time. The buildup of sediment, which ... lower down ... older than the ...

localized contexts where deposition has taken place. The geological science of stratigraphy has as its goal the correlation of strata across wide areas.

In many cases, geologists drill deep into the earth to gather samples for stratigraphic analyses. Such exploratory work is essential in prospecting for minerals and oil. In other cases, such as road cuts that slice through part of a hill, it is possible to see stratigraphy directly. The exposure left by a road cut, like the one shown on page 16, is called a stratigraphic *section* or *profile*. If the rocks in the profile are sedimentary rocks—rocks that have formed from sediments in a depositional environment—we can apply the law of superposition to deduce that the rocks lower down in the sequence are older than those higher up. Often in road cuts the folding of the rocks from the processes associated with mountain building is apparent, and we can follow strata along their folds. Of course, one does need to make sure that what one is looking at is actually sedimentary rock. In many cases, what one sees in a road cut consists of either metamorphic rocks, which have formed deep in the earth's crust at high temperature and pressure, only to be thrust out onto the surface as the result of uplift, or igneous rocks, which have squeezed through the crust from the earth's mantle. The law of superposition does not necessarily apply to these kinds of rocks.

Example of vertical excavation. The stratigraphy of Tabun Cave, Israel was produced by over three hundred thousand years of human occupation.

CHAPTER 1: Getting Started in Archaeology    15

constructed by societies characterized by emerging social inequality. In Chapter 11, "Urban States," the focus shifts to three cases of classic early state formation: Uruk Mesopotamia, the Classic Maya, and Shang China. In these civilizations, the focal points of the emerging states were urban centers with large populations, and there was clear evidence for the concentration of wealth and power in a small sector of the society. In Chapter 12, "Enigmatic States," we present another three cases—Old Kingdom Egypt, the Harappan Civilization, and Jenne-Jeno—to demonstrate variations in the way that state societies developed. The final chapter of this section, Chapter 13, "Empires," considers the archaeology of empires, in which the authority of the state comes to encompass a large region. Although there are many examples of empires, we focus on the Inca and Aztec Empires. The text concludes with an epilogue entitled "Bringing It Back Home," in which we look at the traces of the past in our familiar world.

# PEDAGOGY

A number of pedagogical elements guide students through each chapter. Learning objectives help focus students in their reading of each chapter. Each chapter opener includes satellite location maps and timelines to orient students in time and place to the sites discussed in the chapter.

Within the text, key terms, concepts, and place names are defined or described when they first appear and are also defined in the margin on that page. Subsequently, they are all listed together in a "Key Terms" section at the end of each chapter, along with a "Chapter Summary," a list of "Review Questions," and a section titled "For Further Reading."

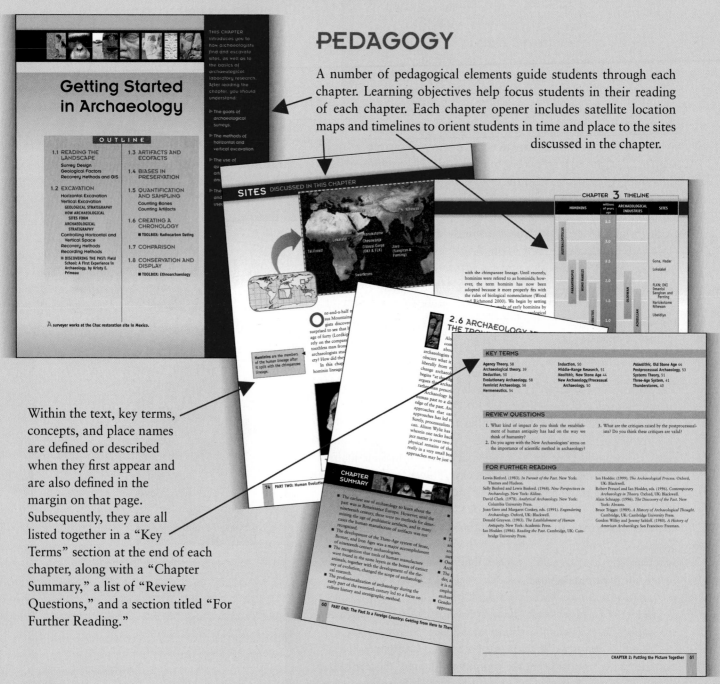

Each chapter contains dozens of stunning illustrations and photographs to engage students in the subject matter, to demonstrate key concepts, and to visually convey to them the spectacular nature of our stops along the pathways through time.

# DISTINCTIVE FEATURES OF THE TEXT

The cornerstone of this book is to present an integrated picture of prehistory as an active process of discovery. From this perspective, we cannot relegate methodological issues to the opening chapters alone: After the student is introduced to archaeological method in the first two chapters, the question of *how* we know the past comes up on numerous occasions throughout the remaining chapters. A number of features have been developed to draw together an integrated presentation of prehistory.

## TOOLBOX SECTIONS

Toolboxes, found in every chapter, introduce aspects of archaeological methods that are particularly relevant to the material covered in the chapter. For example, Chapter 1 includes two Toolboxes: "Radiocarbon Dating" and "Ethnoarchaeology." In Chapter 5, "The Origin of Modern Humans," we find three Toolboxes: "Luminescence Dating," "Use-Wear Analysis," and "Interpreting Paleolithic Art." Chapter 7, "Towers, Villages, and Longhouses," includes two Toolboxes: "Paleoethnobotany" and "Harris Matrix." Chapter 11, "Urban States," has two toolboxes: "Geophysical Methods" and "Deciphering the Mayan Hieroglyphs." Toolboxes are critical to achieving the aim of this book: to integrate prehistory with an introduction to archaeological method.

## ARCHAEOLOGY IN THE WORLD

Despite the stereotype of the archaeologist as a cloistered academic, archaeology is very much a discipline that takes place in the real world. Issues such as control over human burial remains, the antiquities trade, and the preservation of threatened cultural resources are every bit as important to archaeology as are trowels and levels. Archaeology is the study not only of what happened in the past, but also of the role of the past in the world today.

To recognize the significance of issues relating to the role of the past in the present, we have included a boxed feature that we call "Archaeology in the World." These boxes bring

out ethical issues relevant to the archaeology of the periods discussed in the chapter. Not only is the writing of the archaeological past connected with the way we know of the past, but also that writing is connected with the role of the past in the present. "Archaeology in the World" boxes include "Religion and Evolution" (Chapter 2), "Repatriation of Indigenous Burial Remains" (Chapter 6), "The Fate of Iraq's Antiquities" (Chapter 11), and "The Trade in African Antiquities" (Chapter 12).

## DISCOVERING THE PAST

A primary goal of this text is to draw students into the process of archaeological research. Rather than sitting on the sidelines observing the game, students should be on the playing field. This does not mean that this is a book only for future archaeologists; rather, it is a book meant to provide the tools to allow for a lifelong engagement with archaeology, whether through traveling, visiting museums, reading, or joining in a research project. Toward that end, we have included "Discovering the Past" boxes in nearly every chapter in which people—including students—who are actively involved in archaeological research write in a personal voice about a real archaeological project relevant to the chapter. Among these boxes are "Field School: A First Experience in Archaeology," by student Kristy E. Primeau, shown here (Chapter 1); "A Paleoepiphany," by Dr. Lynne A. Schepartz (Chapter 4); "'Towns they have none': In Search of New England's Mobile Farmers," by Dr. Elizabeth S. Chilton (Chapter 8); "Researching the Origins of Agriculture in West Africa," by Dr. Augustin F. C. Holl (Chapter 9); "Chavín de Huántar: The Beginnings of Social Complexity in the Andes," by Dr. John W. Rick (Chapter 10); and "Ancient Maya and the Medicinal Trail Site," by student David Hyde" (Chapter 11).

We hope that these sections will inspire some readers to consider volunteering on an excavation or enrolling in a field school. No words can replace the experience of uncovering the buried remains of the human past.

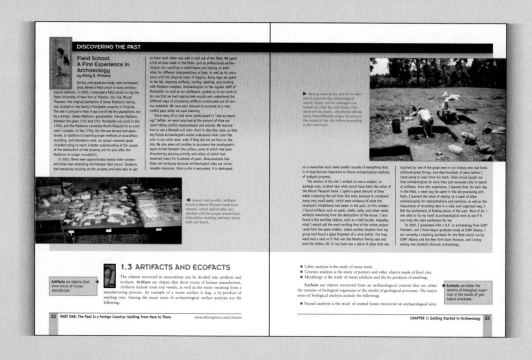

Australian aboriginal societies speak of the *dreamtime* as the time when their ancestors walked the land. The actions of the ancestors are inscribed in the land and are experienced in the landscape. Archaeology explores the "scientific dreamtime"—the time of our ancestors that we discover by archaeological research. This book is an introduction to the current state of archaeology. It is not a simple cata log of finds, but rather, is an attempt to give coherence to the vast expanses of human experience studied by archaeologists.

Our hope is that readers of the book will keep in mind the uncertainty that characterizes the study of prehistory. What is meant by "uncertainty"? Archaeology is a constant process of questioning and improving our understanding of the past. As in any science, all claims can and should be questioned. The uncertainty of archaeology is that it is a report on the current state of the human endeavor to understand our own past. We invite you into this endeavor, in which we reveal the current state of archaeological knowledge and introduce you to the methods used to gain that knowledge. We hope that these tools will enable you to actively engage in thinking about humanity from the perspective of archaeology, to think about processes that stretch over millennia and that are global in scale, and to walk the pathways of our own "scientific dreamtime."

## SUPPLEMENTS

A carefully designed supplement package supports the aims of *World Prehistory and Archaeology: Pathways through Time* and provides both students and instructors with a wealth of support materials to ensure success in teaching and in learning. Most student supplements are available for free when packaged with the textbook, so that students can benefit from them without incurring additional costs.

## STUDENT RESOURCES

**Anthropology MyKit** Replete with text-specific practice tests, learning objectives, chapter summaries, and flash cards, the Anthropology MyKit for Chazan, *World Prehistory and Archaeology: Pathways through Time* offers students a wealth of resources to test their mastery of each chapter. These online resources include access to Pearson's Research Navigator, helpful Web links related to key topics covered in the text, and a wealth of media assets such as interactive animated maps and timelines, lab exercises, and Toolbox videos based on the Toolbox sections in each chapter of the text. All of the resources reinforce the text's integration of archaeological methods with the story of our human prehistory.

**Anthropology Experience Web Site** The **Anthropology Experience** site offers online resources for the four fields of anthropology. Illustrated text is provided with introductory content that incorporates photographs and downloadable

figures and tables. PowerPoint presentations for each field serve as tutorials for students, who can use the presentations to review key concepts about that field. Instructors may wish to use these presentations in their lectures. A special video section gives students the opportunity to view footage that has been carefully selected to illustrate important anthropological concepts. Many video clips serve as "lecture launchers." Using the interactive hominin phylogeny, students can view hominin skulls in 360 degrees. In addition, an interactive glossary organized alphabetically within each field provides key terms and definitions, many in written *and* audio format. Web links organized within each field give students easy access to helpful anthropology resources—an ideal arrangement for students interested in taking more anthropology courses or considering a major in anthropology. Visit **www.anthropologyexperience.com**.

**Pearson's Research Navigator: Anthropology** Available within the Anthropology Experience, Pearson's Research Navigator™ is the easiest way for students to start a research assignment or research paper. Complete with extensive help on the research process and four exclusive databases containing credible and reliable source material (the EBSCO *Academic Journal* and Abstract Database, the *New York Times* Search by Subject Archive, the "Best of the Web" Link Library, and the *Financial Times* Article Archive and Company Financials), Research Navigator helps students quickly and efficiently make the most of their research time. A printed guide is available, together with a general introduction to the Internet, a "Virtual Tour of Anthropology" and its various subfields, and hundreds of anthropology Web links along with practice exercises.

**Careers in Anthropology** Written by W. Richard Stephens, this accessible volume contains biographies of professional anthropologists in all four fields and helps students and professors answer the often-asked question, "What can I do with a degree in anthropology?" The biographies include discussions of what can be done with a B.A., M.A., Ph.D., or a combination of degrees. The booklet also provides information about career options related to anthropology.

**Study Card for Anthropology** Colorful, affordable, and packed with useful information, the Allyn & Bacon Anthropology Study Card makes studying easier, more efficient, and more enjoyable. Course information is distilled down to the basics, helping students quickly master the fundamentals of anthropology, review a subject for understanding, or prepare for an exam. Because it's laminated for durability, students can use this Study Card in all future anthropology courses whenever they need a quick review.

# INSTRUCTOR RESOURCES

**Instructor's Manual and Test Bank** This supplement is available in print or electronic form. For each chapter of the text, the Instructor's Manual portion includes chapter summaries, learning objectives, chapter outlines, key concepts, discussion topics, classroom activities, and Internet explorations web links. The Test Bank includes between 75 and 100 questions per chapter in four formats: multiple choice, true/false, fill-in-the-blank, and essay questions.

**Computerized Test Bank** This computerized version of the test bank is available with Tamarack's easy-to-use TestGen software, making it possible for instructors to prepare tests for printing and for network and online testing. The software features full editing capability for Windows and Macintosh.

**PowerPoint Presentation** The online PowerPoint presentation for *Anthropology* combines key images from the text with chapter outlines into visual teaching modules. Using either DOS/Windows or Macintosh, a professor can easily create customized graphic presentations for lectures. PowerPoint software is not required to use the program—a PowerPoint viewer is available to access the images. Adopters may visit **www.ablongman.com/irc** to register for access to this PowerPoint presentation.

# ACKNOWLEDGMENTS

In writing this book, I have drawn on practically every experience I have had as an archaeologist. I would like to first thank some of my teachers. The late James Sauer taught me much of what I know about pottery and also showed me that archaeology has the potential to build bridges across the chasms produced by conflict. Andrew Moore and Frank Hole supported me as I stepped out of the classroom and into research and provided me with the freedom that I now try to give my own students. Learning to be an archaeologist takes place as much in the field as in the classroom. I have had the opportunity to work with project directors who somehow had the patience to put up with a novice. I am very grateful to Avi Gopher, Nigel Goring-Morris, and François Valla for teaching me how to excavate a Neolithic site; to Ofer Bar-Yosef, Liliane Meignen, and Bernard Vandermeersch for showing me why the Paleolithic is fascinating; and to Mark Lehner for the incredible experience of working at the Giza pyramids. I would also like to thank my friend Zahi Hawass for making it possible for me work in Egypt.

My views of archaeology have been greatly enriched by my association with research groups in France and Israel. Catherine Pèrles warmly welcomed me into the Prehistory and Technology Research Group of the Centre Nationale de la Recherche Scientifique that was housed in Meudon outside of Paris. During my year at Meudon, I learned from researchers Eric Boëda, Anne Delagnes, Jacques Pelegrin, and Valentine Roux, among others, how to look at technology as an aspect of human behavior. In Jerusalem, I have long enjoyed a connection with faculty at the Hebrew University, where I have been welcomed by Na'ama Goren-Inbar, Anna Belfer-Cohen, Erella Hovers, and Nigel Goring-Morris. Most recently, I have developed a number of collaborative projects with colleagues, including Joel Janetski, Liora Kolska-Horwitz, Naomi Porat, Hagai Ron, Peter Beaumont, and David Morris. I thank them for their patience, as I sometimes have had to balance my responsibilities to these projects with the excitement of writing this book.

I have been lucky to find an ideal home in the city of Toronto and wonderful colleagues and students at the University of Toronto. Much of this book stems from the courses that I teach at the university, as well as from courses I taught at Tufts and Brandeis before coming to Toronto. The dynamism of the University of Toronto is built on an appreciation of diversity that I hope is reflected in the book.

The actual process of developing the text came from the people at Allyn & Bacon who believed that we could pull it off. I had never imagined the amount of effort that goes into such a book project. My thanks go to Jennifer Jacobson, who has shepherded me through the entire project with skill and a combination of patience and enthusiasm. "Team Chazan" has grown over the years, and I have been delighted by the care this manuscript and art program has received from all involved—namely, the production team of Karen Mason and Annie Pickert at A&B; Suzanne Stradley, who cleared permissions and acquired some of the images; Brian Baker of Write With, Inc., whose excellent copyediting greatly benefited the project; and Tammy King and her colleagues at WestWordsPMG. I would like to recognize Series Editor, Dave Repetto, whose support of the project helped get us to the finish line. My thanks go to Carla Parslow who rendered the maps for each chapter. I am grateful as well to all my colleagues who provided photographs and to the professionals and students who contributed sections on their field experiences. They have provided the energy that brings this text to life.

Throughout the writing and development process, the manuscript was vigorously reviewed in various stages. Without the input from the following reviewers whom I wholeheartedly thank, we would not have been able to achieve the high level of quality in the finished product: Lisa Marie Anselmi, Buffalo State College; Mary C. Beaudry, Boston University; Charles A. Bollong, University of Arizona; Thomas H. Charlton, University of Iowa; Elizabeth S. Chilton, University of Massachusetts, Amherst; Lisa Cole, Maricopa Community College; Charles O. Ellenbaum, College of DuPage; James Fitzsimmons, University of Vermont; Charles L. Hall, University of Maryland; Bryan K. Hanks, University of Pittsburgh; Michael Heckenberger, University of Florida; Audrey Horning, College of William and Mary; Sibel Kusimba, Northern Illinois University; Randy McGuire, SUNY, Binghamton; Barbara Mills, University of Arizona; Karen Muir, Columbus State Community College; Paul Mullins, Indiana University; Mark Muniz, University of Colorado; Timothy R. Pauketat, University of Illinois at Urbana-Champaign; Bonnie Lynn Pitblado, Utah State University; Thomas J. Pluckhahn, University of Oklahoma; Mary Pohl, Florida State University; Corey Pressman, Pressman Productions; Mark A. Rees, University of Louisiana, Lafayette; Barbara Roth, University of Nevada, Las Vegas; Scott Simmons, University of North Carolina, Wilmington; Steven R. Simms, Utah State University; Alisa Strauss, University of Cincinnati; and LuAnn Wandsnider, University of Nebraska. As *World Prehistory and Archaeology: Pathways through Time* is used as a course text, I expect that instructors and students may wish to contact me. I would appreciate receiving questions, comments, and criticisms at mchazan@chass.utoronto.ca.

I would like to take the opportunity to thank my parents who have been a constant source of inspiration and support. I am delighted to have shared this project with my wife Michelle Fost and our children Gabriel and Nathan. This has been in every sense a team effort.


Michael Chazan, mchazan@chass.utoronto.ca

# ABOUT THE AUTHOR

Michael Chazan is an associate professor in the Department of Anthropology at the University of Toronto. He earned his Ph.D. in anthropology at Yale University. Before coming to Toronto, Dr. Chazan was a postdoctoral fellow with the *Centre National de la Recherche Scientifique* in Paris and at the Hebrew University in Jerusalem. Among his field experience are excavations in New Jersey, France, Israel, Jordan, Egypt, and South Africa. Dr. Chazan's publications include a monograph on the Lower Paleolithic site of Holon, Israel, coauthored with Liora Kolska-Horwitz. Dr. Chazan is currently engaged in a project on the Earlier Stone Age of South Africa. The project pulls together an international team of researchers to study a series of spectacular sites located in the Northern Cape Province.

## Conversation with the Author

**What was your motivation for writing this book? What has been your vision in writing this book?**

Archaeology is one of the most fascinating fields of human inquiry. My goal has been to bring students right up to the cutting edge of archaeological research by presenting the most recent discoveries and theoretical perspectives while showing the students *how* these discoveries are made. At the same time, I wanted to provide a sense of the relevance of archaeology in the contemporary world. The overall vision behind the book is one of integrating the multiple facets of archaeology to allow students to participate in the excitement and complexity of archaeological discovery.

> "Archaeology is one of the most fascinating fields of human inquiry."

**Why did you choose to devote two chapters to archaeological methods and then integrate those methods in the telling of the story of our human prehistory?**

The first two chapters are necessary to orient students and provide the essential fundamentals of archaeological method and theory. With this background in hand, I wanted to enable students to jump directly into learning the treasure trove of knowledge that decades of archaeological research have yielded. But I was determined not to write a text in which the facts of pre-history are narrated as omniscient established truths. I want students to see that archaeology is a dynamic field in which knowledge is continuously refined through scientific inquiry. *How* we know the past is inseparable from *what* we know of the past. Integration of method and theory with the story of prehistory is essential for communicating the dynamism of archaeology.

> "*How* we know the past is inseparable from *what* we know of the past."

**What sets your text apart from the competition?**

This book builds on generations of textbooks on world prehistory. I have adopted much of the structure from these books, particularly the focus on human evolution, the origins of agriculture, and the origins of complex society. I feel strongly that a comprehensive understanding of human prehistory is an essential element of a liberal arts education. An added benefit of its continuity with previous textbooks is that this book can be easily integrated into existing courses. However, there are elements of the book that are not found in other archaeology or prehistory textbooks. The main innovation of this text is its presentation of how we have integrated archaeological method and theory with world prehistory. Archaeology is presented as a dynamic field in which our knowledge of the past is closely linked to the methods we apply in gaining that knowledge. This integration is critical and will fit in well with the way that many instructors actually choose to teach their courses. A second innovation is the book's situation of archaeology in its contemporary context. Although previous textbooks may have touched on the ethical and political aspects of archaeology, this is the first book to integrate this material throughout the text.

**How will the way you have written and developed your text benefit students?**
For me, the hardest part of learning is assimilating large bodies of information. Ironically, even though I am a professional archaeologist, I have a tremendously hard time remembering dates! I have structured this book very carefully to help students grasp the material, and I included a range of pedagogical tools, including maps, time lines, in-text and marginal definitions, and review questions. I find that my students learn best when they understand the relevance of the material they are studying. The integration of method and theory with prehistory provides a meaningful context for the information that students are learning. It also means that technical information is broken down into small packets. I was particularly pleased with the way I was able to

> "... my students learn best when they understand the relevance of the material they are studying."

present radiocarbon dating. The basic method is presented in Chapter 1. Then, calibration is presented in Chapter 6 in the context of the peopling of Australia and the Americas, and AMS radiocarbon dating is presented in Chapter 8 in the context of the dating of the earliest domesticated maize. At each stage, the basic principles are repeated and elaborated on, allowing students to fully assimilate the material.

**What is the most rewarding part of being an archaeologist?**
I have a real love for the material aspect of archaeology. My happiest experiences range from my work at the University Museum in Philadelphia, where I had access to all the storerooms, to working in a pottery workshop in Maine. But the most rewarding part of archaeology is the human dimension. In my research project in South Africa, I collaborate with nearly 20 scientists from a wide range of disciplines. At the University of Toronto, I am able to teach students at all levels and to include students in my research projects. Over the years I have spent in South Africa, Israel, Jordan, Egypt, and France, I have had the opportunity to work with people from all walks of life. All of these strands come together in the field, along with the sheer pleasure of uncovering buried artifacts.

> "... the most rewarding part of archaeology is the human dimension."

# The Past Is a Foreign Country: Getting from Here to There

**A**RCHAEOLOGY is the study of the human past through the traces of the past that exist in the present. After reading this section, you should understand:

▶ The structure of the discipline of archaeology.

▶ The fundamental elements of archaeological ethics.

## INTRODUCTION: QUESTIONS OF TIME AND ETHICS

*The thing the Time Traveller held in his hand was a glittering metallic framework, scarcely larger than a small clock, and very delicately made. There was ivory in it, and some transparent crystalline substance . . . "This little affair," said the Time Traveller, resting his elbows upon the table and pressing his hands together above the apparatus, "is only a model. It is my plan for a machine to travel through time." (Wells 1895: 39)*

**T**ime travel, as imagined by H. G. Wells in his visionary novel *The Time Machine* and in countless subsequent films and books, remains a tantalizing impossibility.

In Boston, the Old South Meeting House stands in stark contrast to the surrounding modern city.

We cannot mount the saddle of an apparatus, or for that matter the seat of a DeLorean, that will whisk us back in time. We are rooted firmly in the present.

Archaeologists have developed a solution to the problem of time travel that is every bit as intricate as the mechanism built by Wells's hero. Archaeological excavation and analysis is a highly developed scientific discipline that allows us a means of access to the human past. Archaeology does not take us into the past, but enables us to read the traces of the past that exist with us in the present.

A simple "thought experiment" can give a sense of how archaeology works. Imagine a building that you are familiar with, perhaps your family home or a school you have attended. Picture how this structure looks today, and then attempt to remove any elements that were added in the past twenty years. If the building is old, try pushing back forty, sixty, or even a hundred years. Now extend your view to encompass a larger landscape, perhaps a neighborhood or a town. Although we cannot reenter the past, we are surrounded by the material traces of the past. Uncovering and understanding these traces is the archaeologist's task.

Because archaeological remains can take many forms—objects made or modified by people, organic material, geological features—the discipline of archaeology is diverse. As a result, archaeology is often found spread across academic disciplines. In the United States, archaeology is considered a subfield of anthropology, and departments of archaeology are rare. Anthropologists study the diversity of human experience, and archaeology provides an important bridge between biological anthropologists and anthropologists studying modern society and culture. Archaeology also provides time depth and gives a clear material focus to anthropology. Archaeologists working on the ancient civilizations of Mesopotamia, Egypt, and the biblical world are often found in departments of Near or Middle Eastern civilizations, while archaeologists of classical Greece and Rome are usually in departments of classics or art history. Archaeologists are also employed as curators in museums.

Archaeologists today tend to work outside of the university or museum setting. In the United States, most professional archaeologists are employed by private companies, dedicated to excavating and surveying areas in advance of impending construction. This type of archaeology, usually referred to as cultural resource management, or CRM, is critical to preserving our heritage in the face of development. CRM is increasingly a global enterprise and includes firms that operate internationally. Other archaeologists work in various branches of the government, particularly the National Park Service. Archaeologists working in the public sector play a critical role in both the preservation and presentation of cultural heritage. Archaeologists have also begun to find employment in law enforcement, interdicting illegally traded artifacts and halting illegal excavation. Finally, archaeologists contribute to the development of methods of forensic science and remain active in projects documenting crime scenes, both on the local level and internationally in conjunction with investigations of war crimes.

Training in archaeology is based on a combination of university course work and practical experience. Most professional archaeologists have advanced training, at least at the master's level. Archaeological research is expensive, supporting both the process of excavation and scientific analysis of the recovered materials. For CRM

**N**ational Park Service archaeologists search for archaeological evidence in the dense forest of Sitka National Historical Park, Alaska.

firms, the costs of excavation are paid by the landowner, as required by law. In most cases, the firm has to bid for a contract, the terms of which bind and limit the firm. Academic and museum-based archaeologists have the luxury of pursuing projects that develop from a program of research rather than the imperatives of development. However, to pursue research, it is necessary to raise funds from government and private agencies. In the United States, the National Science Foundation and the National Endowment for the Humanities provide critical funding for archaeological research.

Archaeology is a diverse field of study, and archaeologists follow a range of career paths. However, the discipline is bound not only by shared methods and interests, but also by a shared ethic. Archaeologists have recently begun to recognize the importance of exploring and codifying archaeological ethics. The Register of Professional Archaeologists (RPA) was founded in 1998 as a listing of archaeologists with both graduate training and practical experience who agree to abide by an explicit code of conduct and standards of research performance (http://www.rpanet.org/). The Society for American Archaeology has set out eight principles of archaeological ethics (http://www.saa.org/public/resources/ethics.html):

- **Stewardship:** The archaeological record is irreplaceable, and archaeologists are responsible for acting as stewards, working for long term conservation and protection of the archaeological record. Stewards are caretakers and advocates who work for the benefit of all people. The archaeological record includes archaeological materials, sites, collections, records, and reports.
- **Accountability:** Archaeologists are accountable to the public and must make an effort to consult actively with all groups affected by their research.
- **Commercialization:** Archaeologists should discourage and avoid the enhancement of the commercial value of archaeological objects, particularly those not curated in public institutions or accessible to the public.
- **Public Education and Outreach:** Archaeologists should reach out to, and cooperate with, interested members of the public.

In Jerusalem, the close juxtaposition of the sacred remains of the past and the modern city creates a landscape fraught with tension, highlighting the ethical dimension of archaeology.

- **Intellectual Property:** Original materials and documents from archaeological research should not be treated as personal possessions. After a limited and reasonable time, these materials should be made available to others.
- **Public Reporting and Publication:** Knowledge gained from archaeological research should be published within a reasonable time to a wide range of interested publics. If necessary for the preservation of a site, its location and nature may be obscured in publications.
- **Records and Preservation:** Archaeologists should actively work for the preservation of archaeological records and reports.
- **Training and Resources:** Archaeologists must have adequate training, facilities, and support before carrying out research.

Archaeologists study the past, but they work for the present and the future. Although we are motivated by the excitement of discovery, we are also compelled by the importance of conservation. The practical decision of how much of a site to excavate offers an example of maintaining a balance between exploration and conservation. While archaeologists might like to clean out every nook and cranny of a site as they search for critical pieces of data, such an approach is acceptable only in situations where the site faces imminent destruction. In all other cases, the desire to explore is tempered by the imperative of leaving material for future generations of archaeologists, who may arrive with new methods capable of unlocking aspects of the archaeological record that are inaccessible today.

From Indiana Jones to Lara Croft, archaeologists have become popular movie heroes. The irony is that the reality of archaeology is much closer to moviemaking than to the exploits of a movie hero. Like making a movie, archaeology involves the logistics of working with a team on location, for long hours, and with an eye toward pragmatic compromise. Like filmmakers, archaeologists do a great deal of unglamorous pre- and postproduction work. Archaeology calls less for bravery in battle than it does for the courage to take creative leaps based on intuition. The result of archaeological research is not triumphantly grasping a trophy, but rather reaching conclusions that open an entirely new vista of questions.

## PART SUMMARY

- Because archaeological remains can take many forms, including objects made or modified by people, organic material, and even geological features, the discipline of archaeology is highly diverse.
- In the United States and Canada, the academic discipline of archaeology is usually found in departments of anthropology, as well as departments of Near or Middle Eastern civilizations, classics, and fine arts.

- Most archaeologists today work outside of academia, in either cultural resource management firms or government agencies.
- Archaeological ethics are based on the idea that archaeologists should act as stewards of the archaeological record.

## REVIEW QUESTIONS

1. Can you think of a place you are familiar with where the physical remains of the past are apparent?
2. How does stewardship of the archaeological record differ from ownership?

3. In what ways do archaeologists work for the future?

## FOR FURTHER READING

Abu El-Haj, Nadia. (2001). *Facts on the Ground: Archaeological Practice and Territorial Self-Fashioning in Israeli Society*. Chicago: University of Chicago Press.

Meskell, Lynn, ed. (2005). *Embedding Ethics*. Oxford: Berg.

Scarre, Christopher. (2006). *The Ethics of Archaeology: Philosophic Perspectives on Archaeological Practice*. Cambridge, UK: Cambridge University Press.

Thomas, Julian. (2004). *Archaeology and Modernity*. New York: Routledge.

Vitelli, Karen, ed. (2006). *Archaeological Ethics*. Lanham, MD: Altamira.

# Getting Started in Archaeology

A surveyer works at the Chac restoration site in Mexico.

THIS CHAPTER introduces you to how archaeologists find and excavate sites, as well as to the basics of archaeological laboratory research. After reading the chapter, you should understand:

▶ The goals of archaeological surveys.

▶ The methods of horizontal and vertical excavation.

▶ The use of quantification in artifact and ecofact analysis.

▶ The ways comparison and analogy are used in archaeology.

We experience the past at almost every instant. Think of how you hear a piece of music. You do not simply hear a succession of notes as they unfold in time. Rather, your hearing of each note is shaped by your memory of the preceding notes and your anticipation of what is to come. The human present is created through a fusion of past, present, and future.

As humans, we live in a present shaped by our consciousness of the past. Our sense of the past exists in our memories—in our visual, auditory, and olfactory images and sensations. Athletes also speak of a "body memory" that allows them to carry out elaborate fine-tuned sequences of action. But memory goes far beyond our minds and our bodies. Writing systems and, more recently, computer technologies store memory externally. Anthropologists speak of collective memories, particularly memories of traumas, such as the events of September 11, that are held by a group rather than being the property of an individual. Objects and places can also embody memory: Most families have heirlooms that carry a memory and a direct connection to previous generations (Lillios 1999).

Archaeology is a science that probes the depths of the human past. But archaeology is not time travel: Archaeologists and the objects they study remain firmly anchored in the present. The essential trick of archaeology is how to use static objects that exist in the present to infer the dynamics of past societies (Binford 1983). Put more simply, the goal of archaeological method is to be able to use the objects we dig up to understand the lives of people who lived in the past.

The goal of this chapter is to introduce you to archaeological method—to show you how archaeologists look at the world. We begin with fieldwork, first the way that archaeologists locate sites and then how sites are excavated. Archaeological excavation draws heavily on tools used in geology, so we also take time to consider aspects of geological stratigraphy. We then move to the laboratory to see how the objects recovered in excavations and surveys are analyzed. We pay particular attention to the quantitative methods archaeologists use to glean information from the totality of the recovered material.

# 1.1 READING THE LANDSCAPE

The first challenge facing archaeologists is finding the traces of human action. The purpose of an archaeological **survey** is to map the physical remains of human activity. The scale of surveys can range from an entire region to the surface of a single site. The evidence recorded can be as fine grained as individual stone tools and pot sherds or as massive as large standing structures.

> ▶ Archaeological **surveys** map the physical remains of human activity.

## Survey Design

The most obvious reason for carrying out an archaeological survey is to discover sites, be they sunken ships, buried cities, or hunter–gatherer camps. But archaeologists also use surveys to understand the distribution of sites within a region, how sites are distributed across the landscape, or where different activities took place within a site. In some cases, the goal is to determine whether sites will be destroyed by construction projects. Often, there is pressure to gain as complete a picture as possible at the lowest possible cost.

Archaeological surveys must be designed with the goals of the project in mind (Banning 2002). Simply recording everything is rarely possible, or even necessary, so archaeologists usually determine a strategy to sample the survey area. Statistical sampling in archaeological survey works on the same basis as a public-opinion poll. In both cases, a carefully selected sample is used to represent a larger population.

## Geological Factors

It would be naïve to expect that we can simply walk across the landscape and find traces of all past human activity. Archaeological survey must take into consideration geological factors that affect the preservation and visibility of sites. Often, sites are so deeply buried that no artifacts are visible on the surface. Early prehistoric sites in East Africa, such as Olduvai Gorge, are examples of this kind of deeply buried context. At Olduvai Gorge, sites can be discovered only where natural erosion has cut through the accumulation of sediments, exposing fossil- and artifact-bearing levels.

Although erosion is often the archaeologists' indispensable ally, erosion can also complicate the interpretation of survey results. In many cases, stream channels have cut through archaeological sites and redeposited material far downstream. Archaeologists must take care to determine whether archaeological material picked up on a survey is actually in the place where it was originally deposited or whether it has been redeposited by erosion. Archaeologists refer to material that is in the place where it was originally deposited as *in situ*. It is often possible to identify archaeological material that has been transported by water on the basis of characteristic wear patterns and the absence of very small fragments.

> *In situ* material is recovered in the place where it was originally deposited.

## Recovery Methods and GIS

Most surveys involve little more than a team of archaeologists walking slowly, with heads bent, across the landscape. The problems faced in surface collection vary tremendously according to the context of the research. On the one hand, in locations where there is heavy brush coverage, actually seeing artifacts can be extremely challenging. On the other hand, there are areas where one is walking on a "carpet of artifacts"—a situation that is problematic because one has to decide what to pick up and record.

In a depositional environment, where there is a constant buildup of sediments, artifacts may not always be found on the surface. In such a context, many archaeologists rely on a strategy of digging small test pits to find buried artifacts. The type of survey and the extent of available resources together determine the placement of the test pits.

Archaeologists draw on a wide range of technologies to increase their ability to detect archaeological deposits and to collect and organize spatial information:

- Methods of remote sensing, including aerial and satellite photography, play a critical role both in discovering sites and in orienting exploration.
- Geophysical techniques are used to gain an idea of what lies below the surface of a site without having to excavate the site, allowing archaeologists to detect

Surveyors in Cyprus carefully work their way up a slope looking for archaeological remains. Compare this setting to that shown on page 3.

FIGURE 1.1

**Geographical information system (GIS) works by creating a series of georeferenced overlays.**

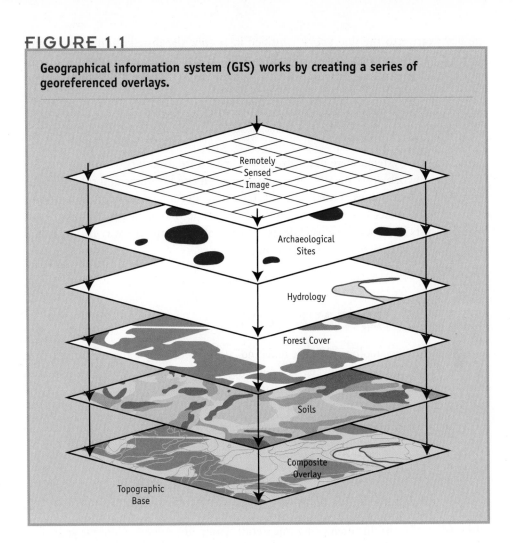

invisible features. The two main geophysical methods used in archaeological survey are magnetometry and ground-penetrating radar.

■ The precise location of archaeological sites can be determined with handheld Global Positioning System (GPS) receivers.

Archaeologists have access to a wide range of geographical information. Satellite images, aerial photographs, topographic maps, and the coordinates of locations of sites already found make up a rich body of data. **Geographical information systems (GIS)** are a suite of software applications that allow spatial data to be brought together and consolidated. GIS software works as a series of layers or overlays that the software sets to the same scale (see Figure 1.1 above). Imagine that you have a series of "documents," including an aerial photograph of a site, a topographic map of the region in which the site is located, a soil map of the same region, and, from a survey, the coordinates of archaeological finds at the site (Wheatley 2002). For any one of these documents to be used in a GIS environment, the exact longitude and latitude of two or three points in the area covered by the map must be known, allowing the document to be georeferenced. Once the image is georeferenced, it must be digitized as either a digital or a raster image. A digital image is an image, all of whose points are digitized; a raster image is simply a scanned picture. Once each of the documents is digitized and georeferenced, all of them are ready to be treated as layers by a GIS program. The program will overlay the images at a uniform scale and location. One can then see how a particular

▶ **Geographical information systems (GIS)** are software applications that allow spatial data to be brought together and consolidated.

site lies relative to the find spots identified in survey, the distribution of soils, and the topography of the area. GIS programs come with tools to both visualize and analyze these data. To help archaeologists visualize a region, topographic maps can be used to create three-dimensional models of the terrain and to statistically test the association of find spots with elevation, slope, and soils. One popular application is to analyze the "viewshed"—what would have been visible to a person from a given spot in the landscape.

When GIS systems were first introduced, they were used largely within an ecological framework, looking at relationships between site locations and the availability of natural resources. Other applications were developed to model migration routes and to predict where sites would likely be found. In recent years, a number of archaeologists have begun to use GIS as a means of exploring the way people in the past would have experienced the environment.

# 1.2 EXCAVATION

The archaeological "time machine" consists of simple tools such as trowels, screens, and levels. The fundamental characteristic of archaeological excavation is the careful attention paid to recording the context in which artifacts are discovered. Intensive documentation is what distinguishes archaeological excavation from vandalism and looting.

## Horizontal Excavation

> **Horizontal excavation** involves excavating a broad area to expose the remains of a single point in time.

In A.D. 79, the Roman city of Pompeii was rapidly buried by volcanic material from the eruption of Mt. Vesuvius. The archaeological site at Pompeii preserves the last moments of the city in often gruesome detail. Pompeii provides a unique snapshot of life in a Roman city at a single moment in time. The effort to reconstruct such a moment is one of the major goals of archaeological excavation. At most sites, time is not frozen quite as spectacularly as at Pompeii, and archaeologists must work with fragmentary remains that have been significantly altered by both subsequent occupants of the site and natural processes.

When archaeologists work to reconstruct a particular moment in time, it is necessary to excavate broad areas of a site. Such an approach is referred to as horizontal excavation and is contrasted with vertical excavation, which focuses on the sequence of occupations of the site. The photos on pages 14 and 15 show examples of horizontal and vertical excavations.

Horizontal excavations can be carried out on any type of site, from simple hunter–gatherer camps to large urban centers. The French prehistorian André Leroi-Gourhan was among the pioneers of horizontal excavation (Leroi-Gourhan 1984). At the site of Pincevent in the Paris Basin, Leroi-Gourhan excavated a hunter–gatherer encampment from the Magadalenian period (20,000–11,000 B.P.). These people left behind no traces of architecture, yet by carefully mapping every stone tool and every animal bone found on the site, Leroi-Gourhan was able to reconstruct the locations of tents and estimate the number of family groups using the site. Pincevent was a perfect site for this undertaking, because it has only one major layer of occupation, which was rapidly buried by river silts.

Another ideal setting for horizontal excavation, on a much grander scale, is offered by the city of Amarna in Egypt. A new capital city, Amarna was constructed by Akhenaton as part of his program of religious reformation (1350 B.C.). Follow-

**A** moment frozen in time. Excavation of bodies trapped in volcanic ash at Pompeii.

ing Akhenaton's death, his reforms were repudiated and his city abandoned. Amarna was never reoccupied. Excavations at Amarna have been able to expose large parts of the city plan, giving us an invaluable perspective on New Kingdom Egyptian town planning (Kemp 1989).

## Vertical Excavation

Most archaeological sites include more than a single period of occupation. Many archaeologists are drawn to sites with a lengthy history of occupation because their interest is in long-term processes of culture change. Several archaeologists have emphasized that sites such as Pincevent and Amarna are in fact quite rare and, in addition, more complex than they at first seem. Thus, for all archaeologists, an understanding of how sites develop over time is critical. Vertical excavations focus on exposing the record of a sequence of occupation. Emphasis is placed more on excavating the entire depth of deposits than on opening large horizontal areas. In vertical excavation, archaeologists analyze the sequence of deposits, or stratigraphy, of the site. The basic concepts of stratigraphy are drawn from geology; applied

▶ The goal of a **vertical excavation** is to expose the record of a sequence of occupation.

**E**xample of a horizontal excavation: An Iroquoian longhouse at Crawford Lake, Ontario. All that remains of this structure are postholes (marked by sticks), pits, and a large sweat lodge.

to archaeology, they have led to the development of methods of archaeological stratigraphy that take into account the particular characteristics of archaeological sites.

**Geological Stratigraphy.** When sediments are deposited in an undisturbed environment, a stratigraphic sequence will develop over time. The buildup of sediments is said to be stratigraphic in that it follows the **law of superposition,** which states that, in any undisturbed depositional sequence, each layer is younger than the layer beneath it. A stratigraphic sequence can be either continuous or discontinuous. In a continuous sequence, the sediments or rocks are uniform throughout, with no clear breaks. In a discontinuous sequence, there are clear breaks in either the types of rocks or the types of sediments. In a discontinuous sequence, it is possible to identify discrete layers, or, as they are often called in archaeology and geology, strata. Geological **strata** can be characterized either in terms of the type of rock or sediment they consist of or by the fossils they contain.

The surface of the earth is not an undisturbed depositional environment. The movements of the plates of the earth's crust cause mountain chains and rift valleys to form. Volcanic activity brings igneous rocks from the earth's mantle to the surface. Erosion by wind, water, and glaciers breaks down and transports rocks and sediments. As a result of all of this activity, the law of superposition applies only in

A stratigraphic sequence builds up when deposits are laid down in accordance with the **law of superposition,** which states that, in an undisturbed depositional sequence, each layer is younger than the layer beneath it.

Discrete layers in a stratigraphic sequence are called **strata.**

**E**xample of vertical excavation. The stratigraphy of Tabun Cave, Israel was produced by over three hundred thousand years of human occupation.

localized contexts where deposition has taken place. The geological science of stratigraphy has as its goal the correlation of strata across wide areas.

In many cases, geologists drill deep into the earth to gather samples for stratigraphic analyses. Such exploratory work is essential in prospecting for minerals and oil. In other cases, such as road cuts that slice through part of a hill, it is possible to see stratigraphy directly. The exposure left by a road cut, like the one shown on page 16, is called a stratigraphic *section* or *profile*. If the rocks in the profile are sedimentary rocks—rocks that have formed from sediments in a depositional environment—we can apply the law of superposition to deduce that the rocks lower down in the sequence are older than those higher up. Often in road cuts the folding of the rocks from the processes associated with mountain building is apparent, and we can follow strata along their folds. Of course, one does need to make sure that what one is looking at is actually sedimentary rock. In many cases, what one sees in a road cut consists of either metamorphic rocks, which have formed deep in the earth's crust at high temperature and pressure, only to be thrust out onto the surface as the result of uplift, or igneous rocks, which have squeezed through the crust from the earth's mantle. The law of superposition does not necessarily apply to these kinds of rocks.

Geological time in an Indiana roadcut. The colored bands are layers of sedimentary rock. Which layer is the oldest?

**How Archaeological Sites Form.** Most environments on the surface of the earth can be classified as either erosional or depositional—locations where sediment is being either carried away or deposited, respectively. Buried archaeological sites form in depositional environments. In some cases, artifacts are deposited on a surface and then, over time, become incorporated into the geological strata. Most early prehistoric sites were formed in this way. In discussing the stratigraphy of such sites, one is usually referring to the position of the archaeological deposits in geological strata.

On most archaeological sites, *stratigraphy* refers to the accumulation of strata that result from a combination of geological and anthropogenic deposits. **Anthropogenic** refers to deposits that result from human activity. Human activities range from building fires on ephemeral hunter–gatherer camp sites to erecting the palaces and fortifications of great cities. For village and city sites, it is necessary to understand the methods and materials used in their construction, and it is also important to understand how structures decay and collapse. In many areas, the main construction material used until recently has been unbaked mud brick. As mud brick structures fall out of use, they are usually eroded along the base, causing them to collapse. The resulting collapsed house forms a mound of earth that was simply leveled out before new structures were built. As layers of collapsed mud brick houses accumulate, large artificial mounds, known in the Middle East as *tels*, often develop. In areas where wood or stone was the main building material, such mounds will not form, because wood will decay and stones are liable to be reused.

> **Anthropogenic deposits** are the result of human activity.

At the site of Hammath Tiberius in northern Israel, a crude stone wall and pillars cut into an earlier mosaic floor. In most archaeological contexts it is more difficult to identify construction phases.

## Archaeological Stratigraphy.

Archaeological sites are rarely, if ever, a simple "layer cake" of strata. Archaeological layers or strata emerge only through the process of stratigraphic analysis. The basic units of archaeological sites are **depositional units**—material that was deposited at a particular point in time. In practice, depositional units go by many names, including *locus* and *stratigraphic feature*.

> ▶ A **depositional unit** is the material deposited at a particular point in time.

Any process that has led to the accumulation of material on an archaeological site is considered to be a depositional event. Because deposition is not continuous on archaeological sites, archaeologists are able to define depositional units. What makes the concept of a depositional unit confusing is that depositional units can be of many types, including walls, floors, and the infill of pits.

In practice, interpreting an archaeological sequence often hinges on paying attention to the relationships among depositional units. One example of the types of problems faced in the field is determining the date of a burial pit (see Figure 1.2 on page 18). The burial is not part of the depositional unit it cuts into. Rather, it is in superposition to the depositional unit, even though they are at exactly the same height. It is critical to find the surface of origin of the pit—the surface from which the pit was excavated.

Archaeologists use a range of methods to assist in a stratigraphic analysis:

- Soil micromorphology is used to characterize the accumulation of sediments at a microscopic scale.
- The Harris matrix is a method for placing depositional units in stratigraphic order.

FIGURE 1.2

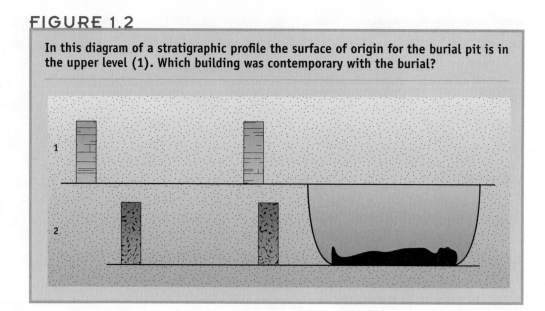

In this diagram of a stratigraphic profile the surface of origin for the burial pit is in the upper level (1). Which building was contemporary with the burial?

■ Postdepositional-process analysis examines the natural and cultural processes that have affected the formation of archaeological sites.

## Controlling Horizontal and Vertical Space

The critical task for archaeologists is to record the precise context, or provenience, of objects recovered during excavation. Control of horizontal and vertical space is essential to modern archaeological excavation. The first job on an archaeological site is to create a grid that covers the intended excavation area (see Figure 1.3 on page 19). The size of the squares forming the grid varies from 1 square meter on early prehistoric sites to 25 square meters (5 meters × 5 meters) on large excavations. In some contexts, linear trenches are used rather than squares. The size of the squares and their spacing will depend on the goals of the excavation. If the

Excavation of Tel Knedig, Syria. The excavation consists of a series of square excavation units. Most of the baulks have been removed at this stage of excavation to provide a continuous view of the architecture.

FIGURE 1.3

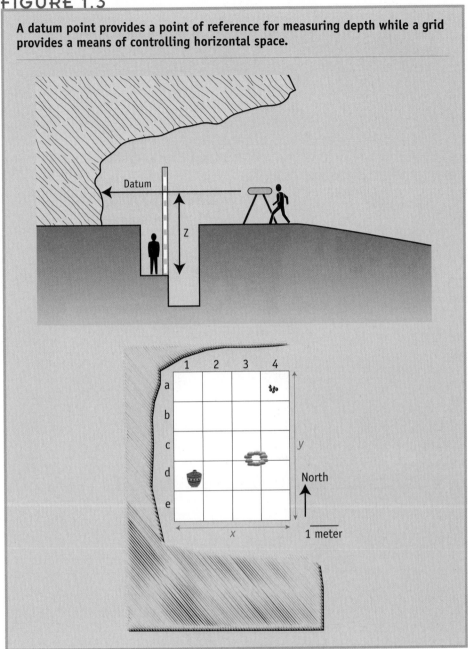

**A datum point provides a point of reference for measuring depth while a grid provides a means of controlling horizontal space.**

goal is to get a sample representing an entire settlement, small squares might be distributed randomly across the site. If the goal is to get a broad exposure, excavation squares will cover a single continuous area. The grid is usually laid out with pegs and string. However, in cave sites, the grid can be suspended from high-tension wires anchored into the walls of the cave.

Control of vertical space requires the establishment of a fixed **datum point**, or, simply, datum, that serves as a reference for all depth measurements on the site (see Figure 1.3). Ideally, this datum is at a known elevation above or below sea level. It is essential, though not always easy, for the datum to be marked on an object or a location that will not be moved or damaged in the future. The datum point is the linchpin for the control of the excavation; loss of the datum point would make it difficult to return to the site and continue the excavation.

> On archaeological sites, a fixed **datum point** is used as a reference for all depth measurements.

## FIGURE 1.4

**Stratigraphic profile from the site of Abu Hureyra, Syria. How does this differ from the geological stratigraphy shown on page 16?**

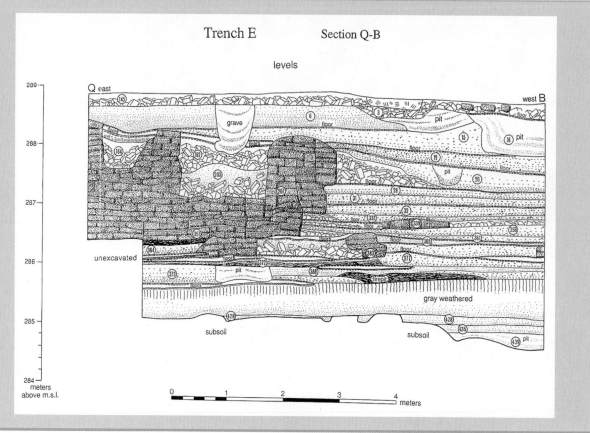

A wide range of tools is used for laying out grid squares and measuring depths relevant to the datum. Most excavations make use of a theodolite, which is able to measure both distance and elevation relative to a given point. Increasingly, archaeologists use digital surveying equipment during excavation, allowing for the precise recording and automatic storage of spatial data.

Excavating in square units makes it easier to draw plans of the layout of architectural remains and artifacts because one can measure the locations of objects and features with reference to the sides of the excavation square. The other advantage of excavating in square units is that the sides of the holes provide a record of the stratigraphic sequence. The sides of excavation units, known as stratigraphic profiles, show the stratigraphy of the site much in the way that a road cut gives a view of the geological stratigraphy (see Figure 1.4). Often, a one-half-meter area called a baulk is left standing around each excavation square to provide profiles. Baulks also facilitate movement around the excavation without trampling on newly exposed deposits. Drawings of the profiles left in baulks are critical records of a site's stratigraphy. Great care is taken during the excavation to ensure that these profiles are protected and that they are as straight as possible.

During excavation, it is necessary to keep moving between a horizontal and a vertical perspective. In excavating an urban site, it is critical that one think in terms of the architecture being excavated. However, if, at the same time, one does not keep in mind the site's stratigraphy, there is the danger of erroneously combining walls from different phases of occupation.

## Recovery Methods

The digging tools used in an archaeological excavation vary with the scale and goals of the project. Backhoes and bulldozers are often employed to dig exploratory trenches or to clear overlying deposits. Hand tools range from shovels and hoes to trowels and dental picks. Most excavations involve screening the excavated sediments to make sure that all artifacts are recovered. The size of the screen mesh is important in determining what sizes of objects will be recovered. If one of the goals of the excavation is the recovery of small artifacts and bones, then it is necessary to use a very fine mesh, together with water to break up the sediments and move them through the screen. This process, called **wet screening**, is usually carried out by spraying water onto the sieve.

The recovery of botanical material (wood and seeds) requires special methods. In many locations, the most effective method is **flotation**, which involves vigorously mixing sediments in water. In the process, charred remains of seeds and wood float to the surface while the mineral sediments settle to the bottom. The charred botanical material can then be skimmed off and dried for analysis. On sites where recovering botanical material is a high priority, it is possible to set up a system that will process sediments rapidly.

At every step of recovery, whether collecting objects while excavating, from the sieve, or from flotation, it is essential that the context from which the objects were recovered be carefully tracked. Every bucket of earth that goes to the sieve must be clearly labeled so that its precise context is known. After the earth is sieved, the label must be transferred to the bag of recovered objects. Ultimately, each object should be labeled in ink, with the label stating the exact provenience of the find.

▶ **Wet screening,** in which water is sprayed onto sediments as they pass through a screen, is often used to recover very small artifacts and bones.

▶ **Flotation** is a method used to recover charred botanical material (wood and seeds) by mixing sediments with water and allowing the charred remains to float to the surface.

## Recording Methods

Archaeological excavation is essentially a destructive act. We cannot go back and excavate an area a second time. What is destroyed in excavation is not, one hopes, archaeological objects. Rather, it is the context within which these objects are found—the matrix of depositional units—that is destroyed. The goal of recording methods is to allow archaeologists to go back and reconstruct that context on paper after excavation. Also, it is essential that all recovered objects be capable of being linked with as precise a provenience as possible.

There are almost as many recording systems as there are archaeologists. The basic unit is usually the depositional unit, also called a locus or stratigraphic feature. Each depositional unit has its own recording sheet, which includes plan maps at various stages of excavation, stratigraphic sections showing the relation of the depositional unit to other depositional units, and a description of the contents of the depositional unit. A careful description of soil color and texture is often also included.

Architectural features can be treated as depositional units. In practice, many archaeologists prefer to treat walls and buildings separately from other depositional units. On excavations of urban sites, the excavation team often includes an architect whose job is to draw plans of architectural remains. Increasingly digital media are being integrated into the process of excavation. Digital photography allows excavators to annotate photographs during the excavation and to point out significant details. Digital video allows for an ongoing recording of the excavation process.

## Field School: A First Experience in Archaeology
### by Kristy E. Primeau

During undergraduate study, most archaeologists attend a field school to learn archaeological methods. In 2003, I attended a field school run by the State University of New York at Potsdam. Our site, Mount Pleasant, the original plantation of James Madison's family, was located on the family's Montpelier property in Virginia. The site is unique in that it was one of the few plantations run by a woman, James Madison's grandmother, Frances Madison, between the years 1732 and 1761. Montpelier was built in the 1760s, and the Madisons converted Mount Pleasant to an overseers' complex. In the 1770s, the site was burned and abandoned. In addition to learning proper methods of excavation, recording, and laboratory work, our group's research goals included trying to reach a better understanding of the causes of the destruction of the property and its uses after the Madisons no longer occupied it.

In 2003, there were approximately twelve other women and three men attending the Potsdam field school. Students had temporary housing on the property and were able to get to know each other very well in and out of the field. We spent a full 40-hour week in the field—just as professional archaeologists do—working in small teams and relying on each other for different interpretations of data, as well as for assistance with the physical labor of digging. Rainy days we spent in the lab, cleaning artifacts, sorting, labeling, and working with flotation samples. Archaeologists on the regular staff of Montpelier, as well as our professors, guided us in our work to be sure that we kept appropriate records and understood the different ways of processing artifacts constructed out of various materials. We were also allowed to excavate at a very careful pace while we were learning.

Since many of us had never participated in "real archaeology" before, we were surprised at the amount of time we spent taking careful measurements and records. We learned how to use a Munsell soil color chart to describe color, so that any future archaeologists would understand what color the soils in our units were, even if they did not set foot on the site. We also drew soil profiles to document the stratigraphic layers buried beneath the surface, some of which had been disturbed by plowing activity and others of which had remained intact for hundreds of years. Measurements like these are necessary because archaeological sites are nonrenewable resources. Once a site is excavated, it is destroyed,

◄ Ceramic and metallic artifacts found at Mount Pleasant have been cleaned, sorted stylistically, and labelled with the proper provenience information showing precisely where each was found.

# 1.3 ARTIFACTS AND ECOFACTS

The objects recovered in excavations can be divided into artifacts and ecofacts. **Artifacts** are objects that show traces of human manufacture. Artifacts include tools and vessels, as well as the waste resulting from a manufacturing process. An example of a waste artifact is slag, a by-product of smelting ores. Among the major areas of archaeological artifact analysis are the following:

> **Artifacts** are objects that show traces of human manufacture.

▶ Having come to the end of the level and to preserve the archaeological record, Kristy and her colleague use trowels to clean the unit floors. Plan views will be drawn, and photos will be taken from different angles to preserve the record of the site before excavating to the next level.

so a researcher must make careful records of everything that is or may become important as future archaeological methods of analysis progress.

The section of the site I worked on was a midden, or garbage area, located near what would have been the cellar of the Mount Pleasant home. I spent a great amount of time water screening the soil from this area, because it contained many very small seeds, which were evidence of what the structure's inhabitants had eaten in the past. In this midden, I found artifacts such as seeds, shells, nails, and other metal artifacts remaining from the destruction of the house. I also found a few exciting objects, such as a belt buckle. Arguably, what I would call the most exciting find of the entire project came from the same midden, where another student from my group had found a glass fragment of a wine bottle. The fragment had a seal on it that was the Madison family seal and bore the letters JM. In my hand was a piece of glass that was

touched by one of the great men in our history who had lived, achieved great things, and died hundreds of years before I came along to learn from his trash. Field school taught me that archaeologists do more than just excavate soils in search of artifacts. From this experience, I learned that, for each day in the field, a week may be spent in the lab processing artifacts. I learned the value of relying on a team of other archaeologists for interpretations and opinions, as well as the importance of recording data in a clear and organized way. I felt the excitement of finding pieces of the past. Most of all, I was able to try my hand at archaeological work to see if it was truly the right profession for me.

In 2005, I graduated with a B.A. in archaeology from SUNY Potsdam, and I have begun graduate study at SUNY Albany. I am currently a teaching assistant for the field school run by SUNY Albany and the New York State Museum, and I enjoy seeing new students discover archaeology.

■ Lithic analysis is the study of stone tools.
■ Ceramic analysis is the study of pottery and other objects made of fired clay.
■ Metallurgy is the study of metal artifacts and the by-products of smelting.

**Ecofacts** are objects recovered from an archaeological context that are either the remains of biological organisms or the results of geological processes. The major areas of biological analysis include the following:

■ Faunal analysis is the study of animal bones recovered on archaeological sites.

▶ **Ecofacts** are either the remains of biological organisms or the results of geological processes.

- Paleoethnobotany is the study of archaeological plant remains, such as charred seeds and pollen.
- Human osteoarchaeology is the study of the biological characteristics of human skeletal material recovered on archaeological excavations.

Ecofacts are studied with an eye toward reconstructing the ecological setting of the site or looking for evidence of human activity on the site. Often, these two goals are closely linked. For example, in studying the animal bones from a hunter-gatherer site, one needs to reconstruct the ecological setting in order to understand the occupants' hunting strategies.

Archaeologists have developed conventions for representing objects in drawings. One example is the illustration of ceramic vessels, shown in Figure 1.5 on the next page. The convention is to show a view of the outside of the vessel, including any surface treatment and decoration, on one side of the drawing. The other side of the drawing reveals a section through the vessel wall, which gives a sense of the thickness of the vessel and the shape of the rim and base. This convention can be used both with complete vessels and with fragments from the rim of the vessel—what archaeologists refer to as rim sherds. In drawing a rim sherd, the original diameter of the vessel is calculated on the basis of the arc of the fragment of the rim.

# 1.4 BIASES IN PRESERVATION

Look around the room you are sitting in, and imagine what would be preserved thousands of years from now. Most organic materials, such as paper and leather, will be preserved only under remarkable conditions,

The soft tissue of this one thousand year old burial known as Lindow Man has been preserved because it was buried in a bog, resulting in a process of natural mummification.

## FIGURE 1.5

**This archaeological illustration of a ceramic vessel shows the exterior of the vessel on the left side and a section through the vessel wall on the right.**

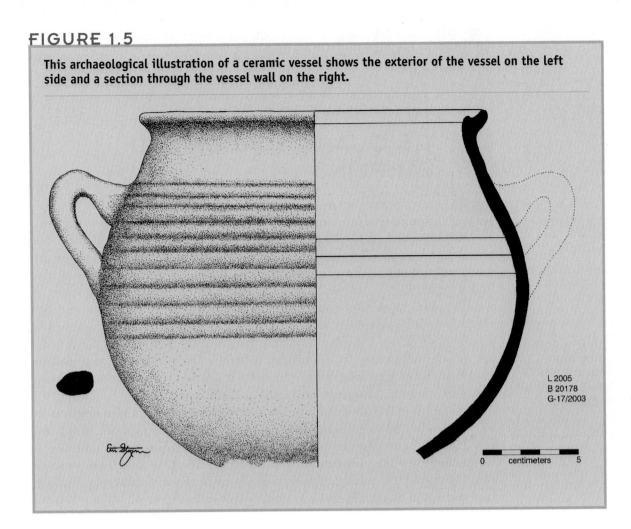

L 2005
B 20178
G-17/2003

0  centimeters  5

such as rapid burial in an environment with no oxygen (e.g., a bog). Similarly, valuable metals are likely to be reused, unless they are left behind when a site is abruptly abandoned or they are placed in a ritual context such as a tomb. Differences in preservation create a bias in what is found on archaeological sites. Archaeologists must take into consideration **postdepositional processes**—those events which take place after the site was occupied. Postdepositional processes can be caused by climate (such as frost heave) and biological agents (including termites, earthworms, and rodents), both of which can move material around the site and distort its stratigraphy. A number of archaeologists have pointed out that cultural practices, such as where garbage is disposed, will also shape the archaeological record (Schiffer 1987).

**Taphonomy** is the study of the processes that affect organic remains after death. An important line of evidence for all taphonomic studies is traces found on the surface of bones recovered on archaeological sites. The overall condition of the surface of the bone can indicate whether the bone has been transported by water or has suffered significant chemical weathering. Chew marks from animals ranging from rodents to bears often leave characteristic marks on the surface of the bone. If a bone has passed through the digestive tract of an animal such as a hyena or a dog, the surface of the bone will have characteristic etching. Human action can often be detected through the identification of cut marks left when meat was sliced off the

> ▶ **Postdepositional processes** are those events which take place after a site has been occupied.

> ▶ **Taphonomy** is the study of the processes that affect organic remains after death.

bone or the carcass was disarticulated with a stone tool. Human action can also be detected on the basis of percussion marks left when the bone is smashed open to access marrow.

# 1.5 QUANTIFICATION AND SAMPLING

In early excavations, representing what had been found was a simple process. One just took all the complete vessels and tools, placed them in a row, and snapped a photograph or made a sketch of the collection. The photo shown on page 46 provides an excellent example of this. But this approach works only so long as one recovers complete artifacts and discards everything else. Today, archaeologists recover all artifacts, including broken pieces and waste, as well as a wide range of ecofacts. Only in rare cases is it possible to present each object individually. Certainly, unique pieces and artifacts of particular historical or artistic merit receive individual attention. However, the vast bulk of the material can only be represented by quantitative methods. The methods of **quantification** used by archaeologists range from simple databases, which provide counts of various types of objects, to sophisticated statistical techniques.

> Archaeologists use **quantification** to represent the large quantities of material recovered in excavations and surveys.

In analyses of large bodies of data, it is often possible to use a sampling strategy such that only a portion of the material is analyzed. In studying artifacts and ecofacts, archaeologists often rely on statistical sampling strategies to allow a true representation of the site to emerge without having to measure or describe every single object recovered. On many sites, the number of artifacts and ecofacts recovered is in the hundreds of thousands, making sampling an essential tool.

## Counting Bones

Using quantitative methods requires that one understand the way those methods work. Problems that at first glance seem quite simple often turn out to be far more complex. For example, counting animal bones would seem to be quite a straightforward undertaking (Davis 1987). If one is able to identify the bones by species, then one should be able to make a chart illustrating the relative frequency of bones of different animals found on the site. This method of counting is known as number of identifiable specimens (NISP). Some archaeologists have argued that NISP does not provide an accurate quantitative picture of the relative frequency of different animals that make up an assemblage. To bring out this point, imagine a site that produced the complete skeleton of a rabbit and ten left tibia from cows. According to NISP, there would be more rabbits represented on the site than cows. But in fact, there are the remains of one rabbit and five cows. To get around this problem, some archaeologists prefer to use a method known as minimum number of individuals (MNI). According to that method, each skeletal element (i.e., left tibia or first upper premolar) is counted individually. The number of examples of a given element is then divided by the number of bones of that type which occur in an individual skeleton. For example, there are two first upper premolars in any individual skeleton, so the number of upper premolars found would be divided by 2. It is quite likely that not all skeletal elements will indicate the same number of animals, so the largest number is used to determine the MNI of animals at the site. In the case just

**FIGURE 1.6**

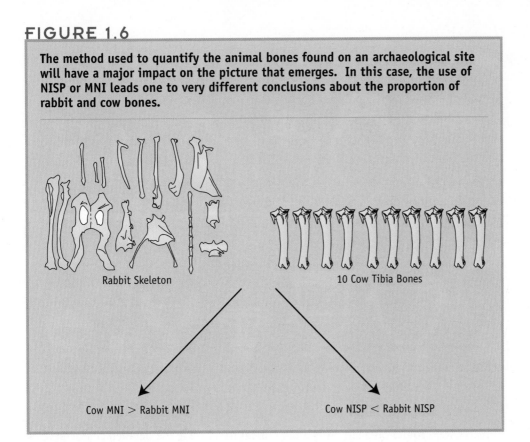

The method used to quantify the animal bones found on an archaeological site will have a major impact on the picture that emerges. In this case, the use of NISP or MNI leads one to very different conclusions about the proportion of rabbit and cow bones.

Rabbit Skeleton

10 Cow Tibia Bones

Cow MNI > Rabbit MNI

Cow NISP < Rabbit NISP

described, the MNI for rabbits would be 1 and the MNI for cows would be 5 (see Figure 1.6). Of course, we still have the problem that the meat yield of a rabbit is quite a bit smaller than the meat yield of a cow. One way to get around this problem is to multiply the number of individuals by the average weight of a carcass of the species. What this example highlights is the fact that how objects are counted will shape the picture that emerges.

## Counting Artifacts

If you were asked to go through your kitchen and inventory its contents, you would create a list of appliances, utensils, and vessels. You would be unlikely to have much difficulty coming up with names for these various objects. Archaeologists working on colonial and historical periods in the United States have access to inventories, known as probate records, drawn up by assessors who went carefully through a person's home after the person's death (Orser 2004). However, archaeologists working on prehistoric sites do not have access to lists of artifacts drawn up by the people themselves. One of the first steps of artifact analysis is to create a classification of the objects.

Most artifact classifications begin by defining major categories of objects. In your kitchen, you would be likely to separate appliances from vessels and utensils. You might then define vessels as objects used to hold food and utensils as tools used to process food by hand. It would then be rather simple to divide vessels into pots, pans, plates, and bowls and to divide utensils into forks, knives, and spoons. Archaeologists follow such a process, often sorting artifacts on the basis of their material of manufacture (bone tools, stone tools, pottery, metal).

# FIGURE 1.7

**Greek pottery vessels with their Greek names. Do we have a similar system for the vessels we use?**

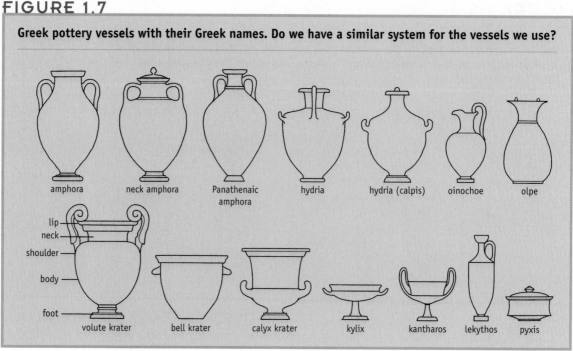

amphora  neck amphora  Panathenaic amphora  hydria  hydria (calpis)  oinochoe  olpe

lip  neck  shoulder  body  foot

volute krater  bell krater  calyx krater  kylix  kantharos  lekythos  pyxis

Archaeologists usually want to go beyond simply reporting how many bowls and plates were found on a site. It is often critical to describe the detailed characteristics of the artifacts. Including this type of information even in the inventory of your own kitchen might be challenging. How do you describe a plate, a fork, or a knife? Archaeologists often develop detailed systems of classification based on types of artifacts. A **typology** is a list of artifact types for a particular archaeological context. Archaeologists use typologies to draw up an inventory of the artifacts they have found.

A good example of a typology is the list of types of ceramic vessels used in classical Greece (see Figure 1.7). These vessel types are known by the names the ancient Greeks gave them. Most archaeological typologies, however, are far more refined than a simple description of vessel types. The purpose of detailed archaeological typologies is to register nuances of style that reflect when and where an artifact was manufactured. A modern artifact that has undergone regular changes in form is the ubiquitous Coca Cola bottle. Ever since a standard bottle was adopted for Coca-Cola in 1916, the shape and decoration of the bottle have changed regularly. These changes can be used as chronological indicators. For example, if you find a bottle with the logo "Coca-Cola" painted on it, the bottle must date to after 1958, the date when painted bottles first appeared (Orser 2004).

Archaeological typologies are often highly detailed, with dozens of types for each category of artifact. Once a typology has been developed, the number of objects belonging to each type can be counted to create a quantitative inventory of artifacts found in a particular context. Typologies are built from combinations of artifact attributes that the archaeologist intuitively selects to define the various types. An **attribute** is a particular characteristic of an artifact. For a simple ceramic bowl, one can observe a surprising number of attributes. Some of these attributes describe the clay out of which the bowl was made and the decoration applied to the bowl. Other attributes describe the shape of the bowl, including the form of the base, the curvature of the walls, and the shape of the rim. Still other attributes

> A **typology** is a list of artifact types for a particular archaeological context.

> An **attribute** is a particular characteristic of an artifact.

measure the size of the bowl. Some archaeologists see the value of typologies as limited, arguing that types can be defined only on the basis of a statistical analysis of the attributes of all of the vessels found in a context. Other archaeologists argue that the idea of vessel types should be discarded completely because they are an unjustified abstraction that distorts our picture of the archaelogical record.

# 1.6 CREATING A CHRONOLOGY

Depositional units are dated on the basis of material recovered within the unit during excavation. This is one of the reasons that it is so important to know the exact provenience of every recovered object. Objects can be dated by a variety of methods. Some artifacts are of a known date of manufacture. Coins are a good example of such artifacts. Artifacts with a known date of manufacture allow archaeologists to create an *absolute chronology* stated in terms of calendar years. Other artifacts can be placed within a regional chronology on the basis of style. Often, pottery is used to date archaeological sites because of frequent, identifiable changes in the shape and decoration of vessels. Frequently, chronologies based on artifact typology are *relative chronologies* that place assemblages in a temporal sequence not directly linked to calendar dates.

In most regional chronologies, artifacts are used to correlate the stratigraphic sequence of a site with the chronological framework for a region. In the absence of artifacts with a known date of manufacture, the relative frequency of different artifacts is used to fit a particular context into a regional chronology. The method of comparing the relative frequency of artifact types between contexts is known as seriation. The assumption behind seriation is that the frequency of an artifact form will increase gradually over time and then decline gradually after reaching a peak.

An important illustration of the principle that the frequency of an artifact form will increase gradually over time and then decline gradually after reaching a peak is found in shifting preferences for design motifs on gravestones in Colonial America like the one shown in Figure 1.8 on the next page (Deetz 1996). From 1720 to 1750, the main motif used on gravestones was the death's head. Between 1760 and 1780, the frequency of death's heads declined as cherub motifs increased. The number of cherub motifs reached a peak in 1780. Then, after 1780, the frequency of cherub motifs gradually declined as that of urn and willow motifs increased.

A number of scientific methods have been developed for determining absolute dates of material recovered from archaeological sites:

- Argon dating identifies the time of a volcanic eruption. Argon dating can be used on early hominin sites where a level of volcanic ash overlays the site.
- Paleomagnetism measures reversals in the earth's magnetic field. Paleomagnetic dating is most useful for dating early hominin sites.
- Luminescence dating methods are used to measure the uptake of radioactive material. Luminescence methods can be used to date soils (optically stimulated luminescence), animal teeth (electron spin resonance), and burnt flint (thermoluminescence) from early hominin sites. Particularly useful for the period between 300,000 and 30,000 years ago, luminescence can also be used for more recent periods to learn when pottery vessels were fired.
- Radiocarbon dating measures the decay of carbon isotopes. Charcoal, bone, and other organic material can be dated with this method. Radiocarbon dating

FIGURE 1.8

**Shifts over time in the designs carved on New England headstones, such as the winged skull on the headstone shown here, provide an excellent illustration of the principles underlying seriation.**

can be used for sites younger than 40,000 years. Accelerator mass spectrometry (AMS) radiocarbon dating is an advanced method that can date extremely small samples.

■ Dendrochronology uses sequences of tree rings to date wood found on archaeological sites. In some areas of the world, the dendrochronological sequence has been established for a period of thousands of years.

■ Obsidian hydration measures the decay of the surface of obsidian artifacts. Obsidian hydration is usually used on sites several thousand years old or younger.

Absolute dates can be expressed on a number of time scales. In this text, we employ a time scale that uses the birth of Christ as the point of reference. Dates after the birth of Christ can be expressed as years A.D. or years C.E. In this book, we use years A.D. Years before the birth of Christ can be expressed as years B.C. or years B.C.E. In this book, we use years B.C. When archaeologists work on early prehistoric sites, they tend to count years back from the present rather than using years B.C. In this book such dates are expressed as years before present, or years B.P.

The story of radiocarbon dating begins in the upper atmosphere, where neutrons from cosmic rays bombard atoms of nitrogen to produce carbon-14 atoms. Carbon-14 is an isotope of carbon, which means that it is chemically identical to other forms of carbon, including carbon-12 and carbon-13. However, because of its extra neutron, carbon-14 is unstable, or radioactive. The half-life of carbon-14 is 5,730 years. Thus, in a sample of carbon-14, half of the atoms will decay to a more stable carbon isotope over a period of exactly 5,730 years. In other words, 1% of the sample will decay every 83 years.

Once carbon-14 atoms form in the atmosphere, they rapidly form molecules of carbon dioxide ($CO_2$). These molecules then spread through the atmosphere, the oceans, and the biosphere, entering plants through photosynthesis. Remarkably, the ratio between carbon-14 and nonradioactive molecules of carbon is the same throughout the atmosphere, the oceans, and the biosphere, known collectively as the "carbon exchange reservoir."

Carbon-14 decays at a constant rate and is found in the same concentration throughout the carbon exchange reservoir. How does this fact allow us to use carbon-14 to date archaeological remains? Animals, trees, and plants are all part of the carbon exchange reservoir. While they live, these organisms maintain the same concentration of carbon-14 found throughout the reservoir. This is as true for you as it is for a tree. The tree exchanges carbon through photosynthesis, and you participate in the exchange reservoir by eating plants or by eating animals that eat plants. However, when a plant or animal dies, it ceases to exchange carbon. From that point in time, when the organism is removed from the carbon exchange reservoir, the concentration of carbon-14 begins to decay at the rate of 1% every 83 years, or 50% every 5,730 years.

Radiocarbon dating calculates the time since an organism was removed from the carbon exchange reservoir by measuring the concentration of carbon-14 relative to stable isotopes of carbon (carbon-13 and carbon-12). By calculating the amount of

carbon-14 that has decayed, it is possible to determine when the organism stopped exchanging carbon. This event usually marks the death of the organism; however, in trees it marks the end of an annual growth cycle. (See "Dendrochonology," in Chapter 10.)

The impact of radiocarbon dating on archaeology has been nothing short of revolutionary. Carbon-14 provided the first means of finding an absolute age for archaeological discoveries, an achievement that earned W.F. Libby the Nobel Prize. In later chapters, we will look at two further developments of this method: calibration (Chapter 6) and atomic mass spectroscopy (Chapter 9).

Radiocarbon dating works for samples less than 40,000 years old, although some researchers are attempting to transcend this frontier. Almost all organic materials, including bone and wood, can be dated. All radiocarbon dates are reported with an error range that reflects statistical limits of the method, as well as limits in the precision of laboratory equipment. (To simplify the presentation, the error range is not presented with dates in this book.)

REFERENCE: R.E. Taylor and Martin Aiken (1997). *Chronometric Dating in Archaeology*. New York: Plenum.

## FIGURE 1.9

**Radiocarbon dating is based on the participation of all living organisms in the Carbon Exchange Reservoir.**

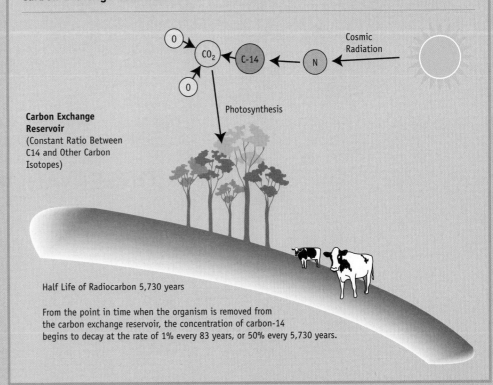

**Carbon Exchange Reservoir** (Constant Ratio Between C14 and Other Carbon Isotopes)

Cosmic Radiation

Photosynthesis

Half Life of Radiocarbon 5,730 years

From the point in time when the organism is removed from the carbon exchange reservoir, the concentration of carbon-14 begins to decay at the rate of 1% every 83 years, or 50% every 5,730 years.

# 1.7 COMPARISON

Much of the work that takes place in an archaeological laboratory involves comparison. A comparative collection, which serves as a point of reference, is an important tool in archaeological research. Faunal analysis laboratories usually have an extensive reference collection of modern skeletons from known species. Preparing these collections is a laborious process involving the collection and defleshing of carcasses. Faunal reference collections are essential for identifying the bones found on archaeological sites.

The spatial scale of comparisons can vary. **Intrasite** comparisons look at differences between contexts within a single site. Comparing the size and contents of different houses to try to determine the social structure of a society is an example of an intrasite analysis. **Intersite** comparisons examine differences between two or more sites. Comparing the number of houses between sites in a region is an example of intersite analysis.

The temporal scale of comparisons can also vary. **Synchronic studies** make comparisons within a single period. An example of a synchronic study is the comparison of burial practices from a single period. The goal of synchronic studies is to understand the workings of a society at a given point in time. A synchronic study of burial practices might indicate the presence of social inequality within a society. **Diachronic studies** make comparisons between different periods. An example of a diachronic study is a comparison of burial practices between periods. The goal of diachronic studies is to understand processes that change through time. A diachronic study of burial practices might provide evidence about the emergence of social inequality.

Archaeologists have often relied on analogies to descriptions of living cultures to help interpret archaeological remains. Some archaeologists practice "living archaeology," using observations made in the present to help interpret archaeological remains. Two such techniques are as follows:

- Ethnoarchaeology has to do with research carried out by archaeologists living with and observing communities in order to make a contribution to archaeology.
- Experimental archaeology involves attempts to replicate archaeological features or objects.

> **Intrasite** comparisons look at differences between contexts within a single site.
>
> **Intersite** comparisons examine differences between two or more sites.
>
> **Synchronic studies** make comparisons within a single period.
>
> **Diachronic studies** look at processes of change through time.

# 1.8 CONSERVATION AND DISPLAY

The process of excavation also includes the conservation of excavated areas and, in some cases, the consolidation of remains for display. At the most basic level, it is essential that excavated areas be filled back in after excavation, unless there is a clear plan for exhibition in place. When exhibition of the site is involved, the exposed remains need to be consolidated.

Recent excavations at the Neolithic site of Çatal Höyük, Turkey, directed by Ian Hodder, are unusual in that a consideration of the use of the site for exhibition is fundamental to the project as a whole (http://catal.arch.cam.ac.uk/catal/catal.html). Çatal Höyük is well known for spectacular frescoes discovered in earlier excavations. Hodder and his team have worked to develop methods of preserving these frescoes and allowing them to be viewed by the public. They are

# TOOLBOX:
## Ethnoarchaeology

*Ethnoarchaeology* refers to research carried out by archaeologists living with and observing communities in order to make a contribution to archaeology. Archaeologists bring to the study of modern cultures an intense interest in the material aspects of human lives. Ethnoarchaeological research covers a wide range of domains, including subsistence, technology, ideology, and site formation.

Much of our understanding of stone tool manufacture comes from ethnoarchaeological studies of societies that still use stone tools or have used them recently. Among the stone tool techniques studied by ethnoarchaeologists are ground stone axe manufacture in Papua New Guinea, flint knapping in Australia, obsidian tool manufacture and use in Ethiopia, and stone bead manufacture in India. All of these studies provide an insight into the process of tool manufacture and the way tools are used. Ethnoarchaeological studies have also provided an insight into how people *think* about the tools they are making. For example, on the basis of ethnoarchaeological research in Australia, Brian Hayden has questioned whether people making stone tools ever think about making a specific type of tool. Interestingly, in the group Hayden worked with, the focus of attention was on the type of edge produced, and the actual form of the tool was of little importance.

Ethnoarchaeological research also can provide a reminder of the limitations of the archaeological record. In 1974 and 1975, Robert and Priscilla Janes lived for twenty-two weeks with the Slavey Dene people in the Northwest Territory of Canada (Janes 1983). The Slavey Dene spend most of the year in Fort Norman but move to seasonal camps during the late winter or early spring. The Janes's research looked at the structure of one of these camps. Their experience living with the Slavey Dene led them to recognize the "potential immensity of the gap . . . between the results of field archaeology and the richness of a living culture" (David and Kramer 2001: 288). This gap is particularly wide in the case of hunter–gatherer societies, which made most artifacts out of perishable material.

In some cases, ethnoarchaeologists do not simply make observations, but rather collaborate with members of local communities to carry out experiments. During the 1970s, Peter Schmidt and his colleagues collaborated with members of a Haya community from northeastern Tanzania to smelt iron by traditional methods (Schmidt 1997). Because the Haya had not practiced traditional smelting for over fifty years, this project was guided by Haya elders who remembered participating in smelting operations as children. The resulting smelt was only partially successful, but did provide an opportunity to carefully document the functioning of the iron furnace, as well as the processes involved in producing charcoal and in mining the clay used to build the furnace. The furnace produced in the experiment served as an important point of reference for the interpretation of archaeologically excavated furnaces.

▶ **An ethnoarchaeologist with Hadza hunter–gatherers in Tanzania, East Africa. What kind of questions might the ethnoarchaeologist be asking?**

Despite the obvious value of ethnoarchaeological research, some archaeologists have reservations about the use of ethnographic analogies in archaeology. Martin Wobst (1978) has written of the "tyranny of the ethnographic record," which leads archaeologists to assume that the cultures they are investigating were similar to ethnographically known cultures. A slavish adherence to analogy can dull our awareness of those aspects of past societies which are unique and different from characteristics of societies living in the present. The use of ethnographic analogy is also not helpful in studying long-term processes of cultural change lasting hundreds, thousands, or even tens of thousands of years that are of particular interest to archaeologists.

REFERENCE: Nicholas David and Carole Kramer (2001). *Ethnoarchaeology in Action*. Cambridge: Cambridge University Press.

also working to integrate the archaeological process into the exhibit. In a similar vein, excavations in historical Annapolis, Maryland, aim at providing the public the opportunity to engage in the reinterpretation of the history of that city (Leone, Potter, and Shackel 1987).

**P**reparation of the natural mummy of a young girl found in a bog for exhibit. The figure to the left is a reconstructed model of the prehistoric girl. How does the model affect the way visitors will experience the mummy?

# CHAPTER SUMMARY

- Archaeological surveys involve mapping sites of the physical remains of human activity.
- Horizontal excavations have as their goal the reconstruction of a single occupation. Vertical excavations focus on exposing the record of a long sequence of occupations.
- A stratigraphic sequence develops where sediments are deposited over time. Strata can be identified when the deposition is discontinuous. The law of superposition states that, in an undisturbed depositional sequence, each layer is younger than the layer beneath it.
- Archaeological sites are made up of depositional units.

- Grids are used to control horizontal space at the site of an excavation, while measurement from a datum point is used to control the vertical dimension. Recovery methods used on excavations include sieving, wet sieving, and flotation.
- Artifacts are objects that show traces of human manufacture. Ecofacts are objects recovered from an archaeological context that are either the remains of biological organisms or the results of geological processes.
- Quantification is used to represent the large samples of artifacts and ecofacts recovered from archaeological excavations. Often, a sampling strategy is used to select a representative group of artifacts for study.

- Minimum number of individuals (MNI) and number of identifiable specimens (NISP) are two methods for quantifying animal bones.
- Quantitative studies of artifacts often rely on the use of typologies in which the artifacts are classified according to a list of discrete types.
- In some cases, archaeologists analyze artifacts on the basis of a statistical analysis of their attributes. Attributes are particular characteristics of an artifact.
- A range of scientific methods is used to date archaeological contexts. Artifact typology and seriation can also be used to date archaeological contexts.
- Synchronic studies make comparisons within a single period, while diachronic studies make comparisons across periods. Intrasite comparisons are made within a site, while intersite comparisons are made between sites.

## KEY TERMS

Anthropogenic Deposits, 16
Artifacts, 22
Attribute, 28
Datum Point, 19
Depositional Unit, 17
Diachronic, 32
Ecofacts, 23
Flotation, 21

Geographical Information
    Systems (GIS), 11
Horizontal Excavation, 12
*In Situ*, 10
Intersite, 32
Intrasite, 32
Law of Superposition, 14
Postdepositional Processes, 25

Quantification, 26
Strata, 14
Survey, 9
Synchronic, 32
Taphonomy, 25
Typology, 28
Vertical Excavation, 13
Wet Screening, 21

## REVIEW QUESTIONS

1. What is the difference between horizontal and vertical excavations? How would you decide which type of approach to choose in a given archaeological situation?
2. Are there limits to the kind of information archaeologists can recover?
3. Why do archaeologists use sampling?
4. Why is quantification important for archaeological analysis? What methods of quantification are used in the analysis of animal bones?
5. What is the difference between an analysis based on typology and an analysis based on attributes?

## FOR FURTHER READING

E.B. Banning. (2000). *The Archaeologist's Laboratory: The Analysis of Archaeological Data*. New York: Kluwer.

E.B. Banning. (2002). *Archaeological Survey*. New York: Kluwer/Plenum.

Philip Barker. (1982). *Techniques of Archaeological Excavation*. London: Batsford.

Philip Barker. (1986). *Understanding Archaeological Excavation*. London: Batsford.

James Deetz. (1996). *In Small Things Forgotten: An Archaeology of Early American Life*. New York: Anchor Books.

Colin Renfrew and Paul Bahn. (2000). *Archaeology: Theories, Methods and Practice*. London: Thames and Hudson.

Carmel Schrire. (1995). *Digging Through Darkness: Chronicles of an Archaeologist*. Charlottesville, Virginia: University of Virginia Press.

Mark Q. Sutton, Brooke Arkush, and Joan Schneider. (1998). *Archaeological Laboratory Methods: An Introduction*. Dubuque, Iowa: Kendall.

Mortimer Wheeler. (1954). *Archaeology from the Earth*. Baltimore: Penguin.

# Putting the Picture Together

Unsealing the tomb of Tutankhamon.

THE HISTORY OF archaeology has been a process of developing ideas about how we can use material remains to learn about the past. After reading this chapter, you should understand:

▶ The process by which the depth of human antiquity was recognized.

▶ The development of an explicitly scientific approach to archaeology by the "New Archaeologists," also known as processual archaeologists.

▶ The questions raised about a scientific approach by postprocessual archaeology.

In the mid-1700s, two philosophers of the French Enlightenment began one of the most audacious schemes in the history of publishing. Diderot and D'Alembert's *Encyclopedia* was to collect all human knowledge into a series of massive tomes. The resulting lavishly illustrated volumes fell far short of this goal. Today, however, the Enlightenment dream embodied in Diderot and D'Alembert's *Encyclopedia* is alive and well, particularly on the Internet, where attempts to collect massive quantities of information have reached a level unimaginable even a decade ago. Still, regardless of technological advances, the Internet is likely to fail just as the two French philosophers failed two hundred fifty years ago.

The basic flaw in Diderot and D'Alembert's plan was in failing to realize that knowledge does not emerge from a collection of facts. If nothing else, data in the absence of ideas simply overwhelms our capacity to assimilate information; nobody could actually read the entire *Encyclopedia*. This is a critical insight for archaeologists. The archaeological record includes the totality of traces left by human activity over a period of more than two million years, across almost the entire surface of the globe. If archaeology were simply the collection of data, then we would be engaged in a futile task, one in which we would rapidly drown in masses of information. Methods of recovery, recording, and analysis are not enough for archaeology to function. Archaeologists cannot simply be technicians (Taylor 1948); archaeologists must also develop the ideas that guide and give meaning to their search through the human past.

The previous chapter discussed the methods archaeologists use in the field and in the laboratory. These methods are tightly linked to ways of thinking about the past and about what we can learn about the past from the material remains found on archaeological sites. This chapter presents a brief history of the development of **archaeological theory** and method. Archaeological theory consists of the ideas archaeologists have developed about the past and about the ways we come to know the past. We begin the chapter with an examination of the origins of archaeology and the recognition of the depth of human antiquity. We then consider the growing awareness that archaeologists must develop a body of self-reflexive theory—theory that addresses the question of how we use the archaeological record to gain access to the past. We will look at the powerful set of ideas advanced by the New Archaeologists of the 1960s and the sharp reaction to their ideas developed by the postprocessual archaeologists beginning in the 1980s. We will finish by briefly surveying some of the emerging new directions in archaeological theory.

> ▶ **Archaeological theory** consists of the ideas that archaeologists have developed about the past and about the ways we come to know the past.

# 2.1 ORIGINS OF ARCHAEOLOGY

Relics of human activity have been present on the landscape for millions of years. However, the earliest evidence of a conscious recognition of ancient objects comes from the early state societies of Mesopotamia, Egypt, and China. For example, Nabonidus, who ascended to the throne of Babylon in 556 B.C., wrote about the city of Ur: "At that time Egipar, the holy precinct, wherin the rites of the high priestess used to be carried out, was an abandoned place, and had become a heap of ruin. . . . I cut down the trees, removed the rubble of its ruins, I set eyes on the temple and its foundation terrace became visible" (Schnapp 1997: 41). In Egypt, King Thutmose IV (1412–1402 B.C.) set up a monumental inscribed stone, or stela, between the paws of the great Sphinx at Giza (see photo on this page). The inscription relates a dream Thutmose had as a young man in which the sun god promises him kingship in return for freeing the sphinx from the sands that bury it (Hallo and Simpson 1971: 265). When both Nabonidus and Thutmose IV excavated antiquities, they did so out of reverence. There is no evidence in either case for the use of the physical remains they found to explore the past.

**T**he stela in front of the sphinx records a dream in which Thutmose IV was told to free the sphinx from the sands that buried it.

## FIGURE 2.1

A fifteenth-century drawing with the oldest known representation of an archaeological excavation. The accompanying text reads: "Time conquers all, it embraces all human endeavors and all human handicrafts."

The first clear evidence for the use of excavation to recover and explore the past was in Renaissance Europe. An emblem book written by Johannes Sambucus (see Figure 2.1) in 1564 provides the earliest depiction of excavation for antiquities. The interest of Renaissance antiquarians (as the early archaeologists are known) was drawn to Greek and Roman antiquities and to questions about the origins of the Celts. By the eighteenth century, there was increasing sophistication among European antiquarians in the way they drew monuments and documented and collected artifacts.

Until the nineteenth century, antiquarians struggled with a number of interrelated problems. The most striking problem was the difficulty in distinguishing objects of human manufacture from objects created by natural processes. For example, ground stone axes were known as **"thunderstones"**—objects that formed in spots where lightning struck the earth. Arrowheads were identified as fossilized serpent tongues.

Against this background of traditional beliefs, methods for recognizing objects of human manufacture emerged. Experience with societies that still used stone tools certainly had an effect on that recognition. Michele Mercati, a Vatican doctor who lived from 1541 to 1593, wrote of the thunderstones that "those who study history judge that before the use of iron they were struck from very hard flint for the

> In Medieval Europe, ground stone tools found in agricultural fields were thought to be **thunderstones** formed in spots where lightning struck.

Illustration of bronze artifacts by Davy de Cussé shows the sophisticated methods of artifact illustration developed during the 19th century.

folly of war" (Schnapp 1996: 347). In 1732, the French naturalist Antoine de Jussieu compared the thunderstones with stone tools from the American Islands and Canada. On the basis of this comparison, he wrote that "the savages of these countries have different ways of using nearly similar stones which they have fashioned by almost infinite care by rubbing them against other stones, lacking any tool of iron or steel" (Heizer 1962: 68).

However, there was still no method for determining the age of artifacts. In the absence of such a method, all prehistoric relics were assumed to have come from a fairly brief period of time. In 1797, John Frere reported on the discovery of elephant remains together with stone tools (what he called "weapons of war") at the site of Hoxne, England. His conclusion was that "the situation in which these weapons were found may tempt us to refer them to a very remote period indeed; even beyond that of the present world" (Heizer 1962: 71). This report was ignored for over fifty years.

# 2.2 THE EMERGENCE OF ARCHAEOLOGY

The development of Darwin's theory of evolution was one of the most far-reaching achievements of nineteenth-century science. That century also saw a tremendous growth in the scope of scientific research in almost every domain. The nineteenth century was the period when archaeology emerged as a clearly defined discipline. Two of the major achievements of nineteenth-century archaeologists were the creation of the **Three-Age system** and the determination of the depth of human antiquity. It is important to realize that the growth of archaeological research was closely linked to the expansion of European empires. The archaeology of the nineteenth century often reflects the ideology and biases of European colonists.

> The Danish antiquarian Christian Jürgensen Thomsen developed the **Three-Age system,** which divided prehistory into the Stone, Bronze, and Iron Ages.

## Organizing Time

Throughout the nineteenth century, prehistoric artifacts poured into museums and other collections, but nobody knew how old these objects were or how to group them. The first step taken towards solving this problem was the development of the Three-Age system by the Danish antiquarian Christian Jürgensen Thomsen (Trigger 1989). In 1816, Thomsen was given the job of cataloguing collections for the newly founded National Museum of Antiquity. His solution was to divide the collections into the relics of three periods—the Stone Age, the Bronze Age, and the Iron Age—based on the material of manufacture. Thomsen assumed that he had arranged these periods chronologically, with the Stone Age being the earliest and the Iron Age the latest. Thomsen also recognized that some stone and bronze artifacts continued to be manufactured in later periods. He therefore augmented his classification with attention to the designs found on the objects.

## The Establishment of Human Antiquity

Already in the early 1800s, scientists were beginning to talk about the evolution of life on earth and even the possibility that humanity was the product of evolution. The French zoologist Jean Baptiste Lamarck developed an evolutionary

# TOOLBOX: Thomas Jefferson, the Archaeologist

The life and career of Thomas Jefferson shaped many facets of American life. Among Jefferson's lesser known achievements is the fact that he carried out one of the first archaeological excavations in America. In 1781, he decided to excavate a prehistoric burial mound on his property. The following passage from Jefferson's *Notes on the State of Virginia* gives a sense of the goals and methods of Jefferson's research, including attention to stratigraphy, as well as of the attitudes of one of the founding fathers towards native people.

*I know of no such thing existing as an Indian monument: for I would not honour with that name arrow points, stone hatchets, stone pipes, and half-shapen images. Of labour on the large scale, I think there is no remain as respectable as would be a common ditch for the draining of lands: unless indeed it be the barrows, of which many are to be found all over this country . . . That these were repositories of the dead, has been obvious to all: but on what particular occasion constructed was a matter of doubt . . . There being one of these in my neighbourhood, I wished to satisfy myself whether any, and which of these opinions were just. For this purpose I determined to open and examine it thoroughly. It was situated on the low grounds of the Rivanna, about two miles above its principal fork, and opposite to some hills, on which had been an Indian town. It was of a spheroidical form, of about forty feet diameter at the base, and had been of about twelve feet altitude . . . . I first dug*

▶ Along with his many other achievements Thomas Jefferson carried out one of the first archaeological excavations in the Americas.

*superficially in several parts of it, and came to collections of human bones, at different depths, from six inches to three feet below the surface. These were lying in the utmost confusion, some vertical, some oblique, some horizontal, and directed to every point of the compass, entangled, and held together in clusters by the earth. Bones of the most distant parts were found together, as, for instance, the small bones of the foot in the hollow of a scull, many sculls would sometimes be in contact, lying on the face, on the side, on the back, top or bottom, so as, on the whole to give the idea of bones emptied promiscuously from a bag or basket, and covered over with earth, without any attention to the order . . . There were some teeth which were judged to be smaller than those of an adult; a scull, which on a slight view, appeared to be that of an infant, but it fell to pieces on being taken out, so as to prevent satisfactory examination; a rib, and a fragment of the under-jaw of a person about half grown; another rib of an infant; and part of the jaw of a child, which had not yet cut its teeth . . . . I proceeded then to make a perpendicular cut through the body of the barrow, that I might examine its internal structure. This passed about three feet from its center, was opened to the former surface of the earth, and was wide enough for a man to walk through and examine its sides. At the bottom, that is, on the level of the circumjacent plain I found bones; above these a few stones, brought from a cliff a quarter of a mile off, and from the river one-eighth of a mile off; then a large interval of earth then a stratum of bones, and so on. At one end of the section were four strata of bones plainly distinguishable; at the other, three; the strata in one part not ranging with those in another . . . .*

The Neanderthal skull. This fossil was the first physical evidence for a human ancestor.

framework for the history of life on earth based on the inheritance of acquired characteristics. Lamarck was not alone. Many scientists were beginning to question a strict acceptance of the biblical chronology of life on earth, which, according to the Bishop James Ussher, placed creation at 4,004 B.C. Because the early nineteenth century was a period of political struggle between Christianity and materialism, the resistance to evolution was fierce. Theologians objected strenuously to removing divinity from creation and ridiculed the idea that "man descended from the apes."

Beginning in the late 1850s, everything began to change (Grayson 1983). Within a number of years, the evidence for the existence of human remains together with the remains of extinct animals was irrefutable. In 1857, a Neanderthal skull, shown here, was discovered near Düsseldorf (Germany), providing evidence of a premodern human. In 1859, the publication of Charles Darwin's the *Origin of Species* put the theory of evolution on new and more solid ground.

The turning point in the recognition of the depth of human antiquity came from the interaction between two very different scientists (Cohen and Hublin 1989). Jacques Boucher de Perthes was a customs officer at Abbeville in northwestern France. Far from the centers of power in Paris and London, Boucher de Perthes wrote a series of idiosyncratic books describing his discovery of tools of human manufacture together with bones of extinct mammoths and rhinoceros in the deep gravel deposits of the Somme Valley. Alone, these books had little impact.

Unlike Boucher de Perthes, Charles Lyell was a powerful scientific figure, the author of authoritative works on geology. In 1859, Lyell visited Boucher de Perthes

## FIGURE 2.2

**Drawing of Paleolithic incised bones from Southern France published by Lartet and Christy in 1875.**

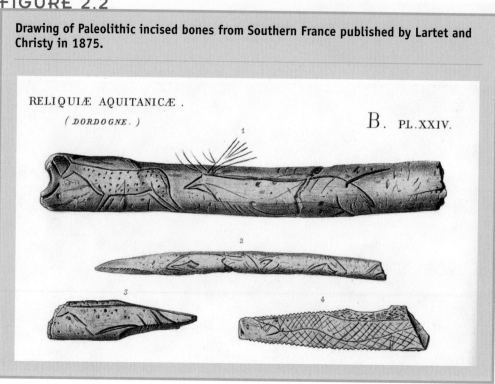

RELIQUIÆ AQUITANICÆ.

*( DORDOGNE. )*

B. PL.XXIV.

in Abbeville and became convinced of the authenticity of the association between tools that were clearly produced by humans and the remains of animals that had long been extinct. On the basis of this observation, Lyell concluded that human existence dates far back in geological time. When Lyell, who had been a critic of claims about evidence of early humans, presented his findings to the Royal Academy, the recognition of the depth of human antiquity shifted from a position held by a few mavericks to the consensus of the scientific establishment.

The vast new expanses of time opened up by these discoveries soon led to the division of Thomsen's Stone Age into two periods: In 1865, John Lubbock defined the **New Stone Age** (*Neolithic*) as the period in which there are polished stone tools and the **Old Stone Age** (*Paleolithic*) as the period during which humans lived with now-extinct animals.

> John Lubbock defined the *Neolithic* **(New Stone Age)** as the period in which there are polished stone tools and the *Paleolithic* **(Old Stone Age)** as the period during which humans lived with now-extinct animals.

## Imperial Archaeology

The nineteenth century also saw an explosion of exploration in the expanding European empires. Often, this was the work of treasure hunters with little in the way of scruples. An extreme example is Giovanni Belzoni, a circus strongman turned Egyptian explorer. Belzoni writes of moving through a passageway "choked with mummies, and I could not pass without putting my face in contact with that of some decayed Egyptian. . . . I could not avoid being covered with bones, legs, arms and heads rolling from above. . . . The purpose of my researches was to rob the Egyptians of their papyri" (Fagan 1996: 77–78). In other cases, such as Champollion's decipherment of Egyptian hieroglyphs in 1822, the motivations were more scholarly. The German archaeologist Heinrich Schliemann's identification of the site of Hissarlik, Turkey, with Troy of the *Iliad* captured the imagination of the world.

Schliemann's wife wearing treasure discovered at Troy.

Other archaeologists began to dig at the biblical-period foundations of Jerusalem and in the ancient cities of Mesopotamia. In far-flung colonies from Africa to Tasmania, archaeologists were also at work. In many areas, archaeologists created a picture of the "unchanging savage," which supported the racist underpinnings of colonial empires (Trigger 1989).

# 2.3 DEVELOPING METHOD AND THEORY

The basic tools of archaeology (including stratigraphic excavation and the quantitative analysis of artifacts) began developing during the early part of the twentieth century. Archaeological theory also began to develop during this period, particularly in the writing of V. Gordon Childe.

## Stratigraphic Method and Culture History

By the end of the nineteenth century, archaeology was an established and increasingly professional discipline. The professionalization of archaeology saw the emergence of modern methods of excavation and analysis. In Egypt and Palestine, Sir Flinders Petrie pioneered the methods of stratigraphic excavation and seriation. In North America, particular attention was given to the development of culture history through the elaboration of formal schemes for the classification of archaeological sites into culture groups. The resultant methods included the Pecos Classification in

**F**linders Petrie examining pots from an excavation. Petrie was one of the first archaeologists to use stratigraphy to create a chronology.

the southwestern United States and the Midwestern Taxonomic method. These developments were driven in part by the increasing amount of archaeological activity. In the United States, archaeology carried out under the depression-era public-works acts was a particular stimulus.

Although the focus on defining cultures generated an enormous amount of research, it also began to generate a degree of dissatisfaction. In 1948, Walter Taylor wrote, "the archaeologist, as archaeologist, is nothing but a technician" (Taylor 1948: 43). While they were focusing on classifying artifacts, archaeologists at times ignored the societies whose remains they were excavating.

In some cases, the focus on defining the extent and spread of culture took on a more insidious tone. Gustaf Kossinna used a culture history approach to reinforce German nationalism, and his work became central to the ideology of Nazi Germany (Arnold 1990).

## V. Gordon Childe

Although his only excavation was of a small village in Orkney, V. Gordon Childe is a towering figure in the history of archaeology (Harris 1994). Childe was born in Australia, but lived most of his life in England. His early work was firmly within a culture history framework. He was aided in this work by what is said to have been a near-photographic memory. A powerful visual memory allowed him to make

## Religion and Evolution

The struggle between evolution and religion predates the publication of Charles Darwin's *The Origin of Species*. Paralyzed by fear of the implications of his ideas, and of the reception they would receive, Darwin delayed the publication of his theory for years (Desmond and Moore 1992). Many of the archaeologists who first took up the study of human evolution during the late nineteenth century were motivated by an intense antipathy to religion. Perhaps the most outspoken was the French prehistorian Gabriel de Mortillet, who viewed religion as a brake on the progress of humanity.

Curiously, in the early twentieth century, prehistoric archaeology came to be dominated by a group of Jesuit priests. These priests recognized the power of evolutionary theory and enthusiastically engaged in pioneering research in all aspects of archaeology and paleontology. The most active archaeologist in this group was the Abbè Henri Breuil, who pioneered the study of Paleolithic cave art. The Jesuit prehistorians also attempted to reconcile evolutionary theory with Catholic theology. Pierre Teilhard de Chardin developed an elaborate interpretation of evolution as a process directed by divine intervention and tending towards the unity of mankind. De Chardin was "rewarded" for his creativity by a lifetime church ban on the publication of his writings.

Evolution has played a particularly central role in drawing the line between church and state in the United States. The celebrated Scopes "monkey trial" pitted Clarence Darrow in defense of the teaching of evolution against William Jenning Bryan (Larson 1997). At issue was the violation of a Tennessee law against the teaching of evolution in a public school by a schoolteacher named John Scopes. The Scopes trial became the "Trial of the Century" and inspired the play and movie *Inherit the Wind*. The fight between Darrow and Bryan resonates to this day in court cases surrounding the teaching of creationism and intelligent design in public schools. Courts have decided that both creationism and intelligent design are religious doctrine rather than science and therefore should not be taught in public schools. However, one would have to be extraordinarily naïve to think that the issue will not reappear in U.S. courts and legislative bodies.

Why has evolution attracted such conflict? After all, it is one among many scientific theories. Even within biology, other influential theories, such as the role of DNA in inheritance, have not produced similar controversy. We can trace this question back to Charles Darwin. Why did he delay publishing his breakthrough? These are difficult and profound questions that go to the very core of the nature of science and the meaning of religious belief. The power of evolutionary theory is that it provides a framework for understanding the development of the natural world without recourse to a deity. Until Darwin published his book, there was no convincing way of explaining the diversity of life on earth without

◀ Abbé Henri Breuil was a pioneering prehistoric archaeologist and a Jesuit priest.

relying on divine intervention. Darwin set out a way to look at the natural world that does not require a God. For people who draw on faith as a cornerstone of their lives, this can clearly be an unsettling concept, and the passion of the resulting debate is understandable.

As an archaeologist, I do not feel a need to struggle with these issues on a daily basis. I do not find that studying human evolution removes all meaning from the world. On the contrary, I find that the theory of evolution is a key to unlocking the complexity of the world around us. Recognizing that variability is produced by history is a fundamentally enriching insight.

comparisons and to recognize patterning in the archaeological collections across Europe.

In his later work, Childe went beyond mapping cultures to ask fundamental questions about the nature of prehistory. Archaeology showed him that across the globe societies have undergone two revolutions. The first was the Neolithic revolution, which led to the emergence of settled villages practicing agriculture. The second was the urban revolution, which led to the appearance of cities and complex forms of government. We can compare Childe's ideas with Thomsen's Three-Age system discussed earlier. Thomsen focused on the classification of objects and thus created major periods—the Stone Age, Bronze Age, and Iron Age. Similarly, Lubbock split the Stone Age into the Paleolithic and Neolithic. Childe shifted the focus from artifacts to societies of people living in a network of social and economic relations. The great changes we see in the archaeological record, Childe held, are evidence of changes in society, because the material aspects of culture are intimately connected to social and economic relations. Thus, for Childe, the presence of bronze artifacts presupposes a society that was able to gain access to tin and copper and able to support specialists with the skills necessary to practice metallurgy.

Childe was a committed and politically active Marxist. In his writing, he stressed the social organization of production and revolutionary change in human societies. His ideas were influenced by his contacts with Soviet archaeologists and also drew heavily on the U.S. ethnographer Lewis Henry Morgan.

# 2.4 ARCHAEOLOGY AS SCIENCE

Childe's work is significant in that he pushed archaeology away from defining itself in terms of the recovery and classification of artifacts and towards a focus on the study of ancient societies. This is a significant shift, and it has resulted in ongoing debates about how archaeology can go beyond describing objects to explore past societies.

## Developing Scientific Methods

Beginning in 1949, the Cambridge-based archaeologist Graham Clark brought together botanists, zoologists, and archaeologists to excavate Star Carr, a prehistoric hunter–gatherer site in East Yorkshire, England. Because the site is waterlogged, many artifacts not usually found on archaeological sites, such as wood, are well preserved. Clark opened wide excavation areas at Star Carr, with the explicit goal of gaining insight into the subsistence practices of late prehistoric hunter–gatherers. The term *subsistence* refers to the activities involved in procuring and processing food. Clark's student Eric Higgs extended Clark's emphasis on economy. Indeed, Higgs took the position that archaeology should concern itself *only* with economy. Higgs also pioneered methods for recovering botanical remains from archaeological sites.

Similar developments took place in the United States, stimulated by the work of the ecological anthropologist Julian Steward, who explored the relationship between nature and culture and developed the school of thought known as cultural ecology. In 1946, Gordon Willey carried out a pioneering survey project in the Virú Valley of Peru. The importance of this survey is that its goal was to gather evidence of settlement patterning that would provide information relevant to social organization.

Alongside the development of methodologies for the archaeology of economy and society found in the work of Clark and Willey, a number of archaeologists began to develop and stress the importance of statistical methods for archaeology. A. C. Spaulding argued on the basis of pottery studies in the Lower Mississippi Valley and the southwestern United States that archaeologists should not impose categories on material culture, but rather should discover clustering through statistical analysis of attributes. One of the important aspects of Spaulding's position is that he was championing a statistical method not because it was better for building chronologies—the goal of the culture history approach—but rather because his methods were necessary to explore how societies changed through time.

## The New Archaeology

The rumblings of discontent with the culture history approach could be heard as early as 1948, with the publication of Walter Taylor's *A Study of Archaeology*. At the same time, Clark and Willey were working to develop scientific methods for the study of the economy and organization of ancient societies, and Spaulding was urging the adoption of statistical methods. One can easily imagine these trends developing into a gradual eclipse of culture history by an increasing sophisticated social and economic archaeology—but that is not what happened.

Rather than a gradual transition, what took place in the 1960s was a fierce confrontation initiated by a group of young archaeologists: the New Archaeologists. The catalyst in this movement was Lewis Binford. In a series of fiercely polemical articles, Binford pronounced that archaeology should be a science or it should be nothing at all. Clearly, he did not view the work of traditional archaeologists as science. Why was the debate so heated? Perhaps its tone was an extension of the excitement and vitality of campus life in 1960s America. Perhaps it was the sense

Lewis Binford spearheaded the emergence of the New Archaeology in the 1960s.

that traditional archaeologists had a stranglehold on the field that could be loosened only by confrontation. It is clear that the tone of the debate reflected the fact that radically new ideas were being brought into archaeology. The **New Archaeologists** (also called **processual archaeologists**) were the first to argue that the central problem of archaeology was not the need for more data or even better methods; rather, they questioned the way archaeologists could know the past. This is essentially an intellectual, or, as it has come to be known, a theoretical, problem.

Binford was an ideal ringleader for a gang of intellectual revolutionaries. A tireless master at the cut and thrust of debate (and not shy about drawing blood), he has carried out wide-ranging research, from the midwestern United States, to the Arctic, to South Africa.

Binford set out a fundamental problem facing archaeologists. Their interest is the *dynamics* of past societies, but what they have to study is the *static* objects recovered in an excavation or a survey. Archaeologists tend to work by **induction,** drawing inferences on the basis of available data. James Deetz has described induction as "the archaeologist providing the flesh for the bare bones of his data" (quoted in Binford and Binford 1968: 17). Drawing on the philosopher of science Carl Hempel, Binford saw induction as dangerously naïve. For archaeology to be a science, it must work by **deduction** from general laws and models. The fundamental methodology of archaeology should be testing hypotheses. This stress on hypothesis testing, which was meant to ally archaeology with the hard sciences such as physics, created a breach between the New Archaeologists and the rest of the discipline.

The excitement of the New Archaeology flowed from the argument that archaeologists were not limited to describing the archaeological record. Theory and method have the potential to enable archaeological research to extend into all realms of past societies. Binford expressed this potential when he wrote that "facts do not speak for themselves . . . , data [will] tell us nothing about cultural process or past lifeways unless we [ask] the appropriate questions" (1968:13).

The key to the optimism of the New Archaeologists was the linkage they made between material remains and other aspects of society (Watson, Leblanc, and Redman 1984). To Binford, it was inconceivable that any cultural item functioned independently of nonmaterial aspects of society. Thus, the potential scope of archaeologists' knowledge of past societies would be almost limitless.

Paradoxically, processual archaeology often involved an extremely reductive view of culture. In Binford's (1962) famous formulation, "Culture is man's extrosomatic [i.e., external to the body] means of adapting to the environment," Binford's definition of culture closely echoes the writings of the cultural anthropologist Leslie White. What is striking is that, in Binford's view, all aspects of symbolic behavior are relegated to insignificance.

As archaeological theory matured, the insistence of the New Archaeologists on strict adherence to hypothesis testing and the rejection of induction tended to moderate. This trend was strongly influenced by the work of Alison Wylie, who showed, through careful analysis, that all archaeologists have to use induction at some points in their research. By 1984, Patty Jo Watson, Steven LeBlanc, and Charles Redman, important proponents of the New Archaeology, recognized that archaeological research involves a "to-and-fro" between induction and deduction (Watson, LeBlanc, and Redman 1984:60). Quoting Kent Flannery, who states that the New Archaeologists "assume that 'truth is just the best current hypothesis, and that *whatever* they believe now will ultimately be proved wrong" (Flannery 1967: 122), Watson, LeBlanc, and Redman stressed that the New Archaeology adopted a scientific approach to truth.

**A** modern salvage excavation in England. Notice the combination of heavy equipment with more traditional recovery methods.

Because the search for covering laws in archaeology yielded at best only modest results, Binford returned to his initial question about how we can know about processes that took place in the past. In the absence of covering laws, Binford emphasized the importance of **middle-range research,** which allows us to make secure statements about past dynamics on the basis of observations made on archaeological material. The key to middle-range research is to look at processes that we can observe in the present and then analyze the material patterning left by those processes. We can then develop hypotheses about the past that can be tested by reference to our observations in the present. As an example, Binford carried out a project in which he fed bones to hyenas and recorded the patterns of breakage and the markings on the bones. He could then compare these patterns with the patterns found on early human sites to test the hypothesis that these sites were produced partially by carnivore activity.

> ► **Middle-range research** looks at processes that can be observed in the present and that can serve as a point of reference to test hypotheses about the past.

The development of the New Archaeology overlapped with changes in legislation that led to a significant increase in public archaeology. New laws resulted in a demand for archaeologists who could assess the potential damage of construction projects and, when necessary, carry out excavations to salvage endangered sites. The field of public archaeology has come to be known as cultural resource management, or CRM. CRM archaeologists are found in the private sector, in government agencies, and in academia. The development of the methods of CRM archaeology has been strongly influenced by the scientific methods espoused by the New Archaeologists.

## Systems Theory

One direction pursued by the New Archaeologists is the application of **systems theory** to the study of past societies (see Figure 2.3). A system is an interconnected network of elements that together form a whole. A classic example of a system is the combination of a thermostat and the heating system in a house. The ambient

> ► **Systems theory** views society as an interconnected network of elements that together form a whole.

FIGURE 2.3

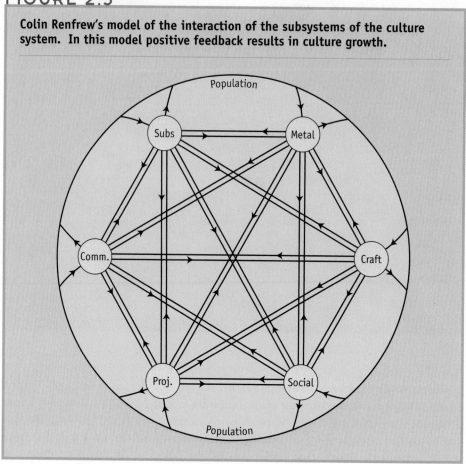

**Colin Renfrew's model of the interaction of the subsystems of the culture system. In this model positive feedback results in culture growth.**

temperature affects the thermostat, which turns the furnace on and off. The heat of the furnace raises the temperature in the house, which in turn causes the thermostat to turn off the furnace. The thermostat and furnace together control the temperature through feedback within the system. When you set the temperature in your house, this system works to produce a steady state. Archaeologists argued that societies can be viewed as systems, which normally operate at such a steady state. David Clarke and Kent Flannery were among the archaeologists who went to great lengths to try to formalize the elements of archaeological systems. One attraction of the systems approach is that it made it possible to look at periods of rapid change in the archaeological record as the result of feedback among elements of a complex system. As a result, change could be understood as the effect of internal processes—processes that took place within society. Although today formal systems theory plays a minor role in archaeology, the recognition of the complexity of social systems and the degree to which various aspects of the archaeological record are interrelated are of critical importance. Systems theory has been particularly valuable in giving archaeologists tools to integrate evidence of ecological change into models of social change.

# 2.5 ALTERNATIVE PERSPECTIVES

Lewis Binford proclaimed that archaeology should be a science based on deduction and hypothesis testing. The New Archaeologists worked to create the guidelines for an explicitly scientific approach to archaeology—

what has come to be processual archaeology—an approach strongly associated with systems theory and with an emphasis on ecology. Although the emphasis on pure deduction was gradually toned down, and the search for general laws was replaced by middle-range research, the basic premises of processual archaeology remained largely unchallenged until the mid-1980s, by which time processual archaeology had become the dominant approach to archaeological theory in the United States. Indeed, processual archaeology strongly influenced the development of public archaeology.

## Postprocessual Archaeology

The central argument of processual archaeology is that archaeology should be a science, a discipline that emulates the hard sciences such as physics. The only apparent alternative to processual archaeology was culture history based on naïve induction. It took over twenty years for this position to be effectively challenged. The challenge came from British archaeologists led by Ian Hodder, in a movement that came to be known as **postprocessual archaeology**. Hodder's challenge to Binford went to the core of processual archaeology. Why, Hodder asked, should archaeologists not choose to emulate historians rather than physicists? Perhaps archaeology is more similar to reading a text than carrying out an experiment. After all, is a science based on predicting the outcome of experiments appropriate to the study of processes that took place in the past? How can archaeologists ever replicate their results, as is expected of a laboratory scientist?

> ▶ **Postprocessual archaeology** argues that archaeologists should emulate historians in interpreting the past.

Hodder was not arguing for naïve induction or advocating a return to culture history. To parry Binford's reliance on the philosopher of science Hempel, Hodder drew on the theoretical writing of historians such as R. G. Collingwood, who espoused the idea that it is necessary for the historian to get at the "inside" of events. The historian should try to understand the past from the perspective of the people who lived through those events.

Binford had defined culture as a means of adaptation and had argued that there is no need to understand how the people themselves viewed their own culture. Following Binford, one can adopt an external, or what anthropologists term an etic, approach and still get at a true understanding of the society. Hodder argued that culture must be understood as the result of the meaningful and purposeful actions of people and that only an internal understanding of these meanings—what anthropologists call an emic approach—produces a real knowledge of the past.

The strength of Hodder's position is readily apparent. Clearly, we all experience the world as meaningful and would have a difficult time thinking of the way we live our own lives as our "extrasomatic means of adaptation." Should we not assume that that was the case for people who lived in the past? Some cultural anthropologists have argued persuasively for an etic approach to living societies. For example, Marvin Harris has studied the taboo on eating cattle in Hindu societies and has argued that the emic understanding of that taboo in religious terms hides the fact that the taboo actually serves an important ecological function. However, Harris is certainly in the minority among people who study living societies.

The problem faced by archaeologists who embrace Hodder's position is that archaeologists do not work with living societies. Archaeologists cannot simply ask their informants what something means. To meet this challenge, Hodder emphasized the importance of context in providing clues to understanding the meaning of artifacts. As he writes, "as soon as the context of an object is known it is no longer totally mute" (Hodder 1986: 4). Where objects are found and what they are found with provide the basis for making interpretations about their meaning. To use a very simple example, if a type of object is found only in a tomb setting, that fact tells us something about its meaning.

But even allowing for the use of context, it is hard to see how one could try to "work from the inside" and still meet the New Archaeologists' criteria for scientifically valid deductive research. Not surprisingly, Hodder dismissed the position that the deductive method is the appropriate framework for archaeological research.

The goal of postprocessual archaeology is not to test hypotheses, but rather to offer interpretations based on contextual data. Some have argued that this means that "anything goes," in that all interpretations are equally valid. Unlike processual archaeology, which ultimately holds that proper scientific procedure will lead archaeologists to the truth about the past, postprocessual archaeology argues that the process of interpretation is ongoing. This does not, however, mean that all interpretations are equally valid. For example, our legal system is based on the ability of a judge or a jury to reach a consensual interpretation of events. Clearly, we care very much that these interpretations be sound and well grounded.

The analogy to a jury trial is useful in introducing the concept of **hermeneutics,** which is critical to the way that Hodder views archaeology. When a jury renders its verdict, there is a degree of finality to the decision. However, the verdict is not necessarily the end of the interpretation of the past events examined in the trial; such interpretation can continue in the courts if new evidence is found or out of the courts in the investigations of reporters and historians. Hermeneutics is a theory of interpretation that stresses the interaction between the presuppositions we bring to a problem and the independent empirical reality of our observations and experiences. Rather than coming to an archaeological situation with a hypothesis, in following a hermeneutic approach we come with preexisting knowledge and questions. Hermeneutic interpre-

> **Hermeneutics** views our knowledge of the past as a continual process of interpretation.

## FIGURE 2.4

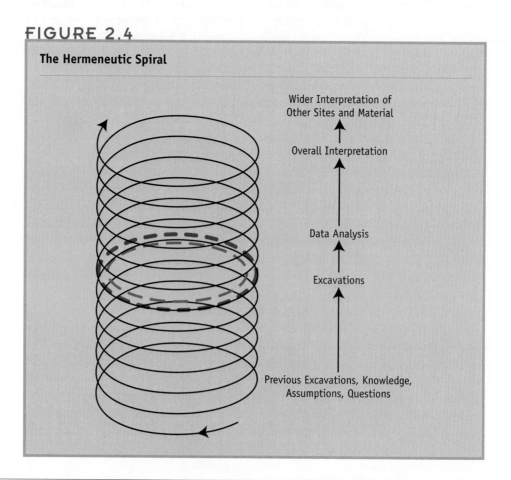

**The Hermeneutic Spiral**

Wider Interpretation of Other Sites and Material

Overall Interpretation

Data Analysis

Excavations

Previous Excavations, Knowledge, Assumptions, Questions

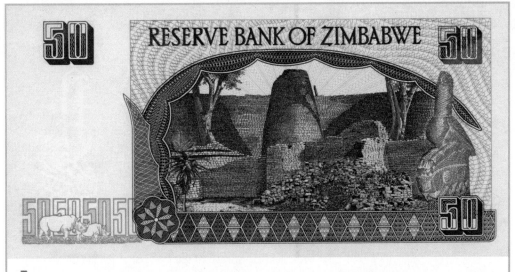

**A**n image of the archaeological site of Great Zimbabwe on a banknote from modern Zimbabwe. Why do you think this image was chosen for a banknote?

tation is an open-ended cycle of continual inquiry. Because this process results in an understanding that is continuously enriched through a confrontation with empirical reality, it is often depicted as a spiral—a process through which we arrive at a deeper understanding of the past (see Figure 2.4).

Postprocessual archaeologists have also taken the lead in seriously considering the position of archaeology in modern society. If interpretation is the continuous confrontation of presuppositions with empirical reality, then how we arrive at our presuppositions about the past becomes far more important than it would be in a processual archaeological approach. With their stress on a pure scientific method, the New Archaeologists could do little but urge their followers to do their best to separate politics from archaeology. Postprocessual archaeologists have embraced the idea that archaeology is an activity that takes place in the present and that the archaeologist is a person working in a particular historical setting. In two books published in the late 1980s, Michael Shanks and Christopher Tilley went as far as to deny that archaeologists could ever do more than simply project the present onto the past and to assert that the major role of archaeology is to legitimate the modern political order. (See, e.g., Shanks and Tilley 1987.) Although most archaeologists reject this argument, Shanks and Tilley were instrumental in spurring archaeologists to look critically at the history of archaeology in relation to factors such as colonialism, nationalism, and racism.

For processual archaeologists, archaeology should ideally be a unified science with agreed-upon procedures and standards. By contrast, postprocessual archaeology is far more open to a multiplicity of approaches and interpretations. Depending on what presuppositions one brings to a situation, the resulting interpretation will differ. At the same time, because postprocessual archaeology is supposed to work from the inside, it follows that a multiplicity of interpretations are expected, since they would reflect the diversity of perspectives held by people in the past. As a result, it is not surprising that postprocessual archaeologists have developed a number of different approaches to archaeology. In recent years, archaeological theory has been characterized by a wide diversity of approaches, ranging from those more closely allied to postprocessual archaeology to those allied with processual archaeology.

### Different Views of a Site
**by Peter Robertshaw, California State University, San Bernardino, California**

I have spent many years using archaeology to try to explain the rise of state-level societies in central Africa—in particular, the kingdom of Bunyoro in western Uganda. The best-known archaeological sites here possess extensive systems of deep ditches—as much as 15 feet deep—that usually surround a small hill. Early archaeologists considered these sites to be forts where people could defend themselves and their large herds of cattle. Radiocarbon dates indicated that the sites were inhabited in about the fifteenth century A.D.

Munsa is one of these fortified sites. I excavated here in 1995 to uncover the history of the development of the site, its functions, and its economic basis. I discovered that the hill at the center of the site was first occupied, probably as a small village, at about the tenth century. Several burials, mostly of women and children, contained scant grave goods. Among them, we discovered a few glass beads that probably came from India.

We found cattle bones, too, but stable isotopes analyses showed that women ate mostly grain rather than meat. In one corner of the site, we discovered plenty of iron slag and a furnace for the making of iron, dating to the thirteenth or fourteenth century. People dug the deep ditches that encircle the hill and enclose a large area of the adjacent small valley in the late fifteenth or early sixteenth century. An enormous grain-storage pit that we found at the center of the site leads me to believe that the people who dug the ditches were fed or given grain for their labors. The site was abandoned in the seventeenth century, although farmers continued to live in dispersed homesteads in the area up to the present day. Thus, our excavations showed that different activities took place at Munsa at different times spanning several centuries; in contrast, Munsa's modern residents tend to see the site as the remains of a single occupation.

There is only one published oral tradition about Munsa: A powerful chief named Kateboha ("he who ties up his enemies") lived there until he was killed by rebellious peasants. Historian Edward Steinhart discovered other views of Munsa. Local politicians, keen to see a revival of the old Bunyoro kingdom as a source of cultural pride and an avenue to higher status, saw the site as a military fort, pointing out locations where troops occupied barracks and the chief convened his council. These informants viewed Munsa as an important seat of power, clearly something that they wished would happen again nearby at the local town for their own economic and political benefit.

However, local farmers see Munsa as the abode of spirits, whose power might be harnessed through the intervention of a medium to promote health and a modicum of wealth. At the end of our excavations, the foreman of our local crew sacrificed a goat to appease the spirits for the disturbances that we archaeologists had caused.

◀ An excavation across one of the deep ditches surrounding the site at Munsa revealed the shape and depth of the ditch as it was originally dug in the fifteenth or sixteenth century C.E.

---

**Feminist archaeology** focuses on the way archaeologists study and represent gender, as well as bringing attention to gender inequities in the practice of archaeology. ◀

## Gender and Agency

Feminist archaeology and agency theory are two approaches that have developed out of postprocessual archaeology. **Feminist archaeology** has brought new attention both to the way that archaeologists study and represent gender and to gender inequities in the practice of archaeology (Gero and Conkey 1991). Archaeologists

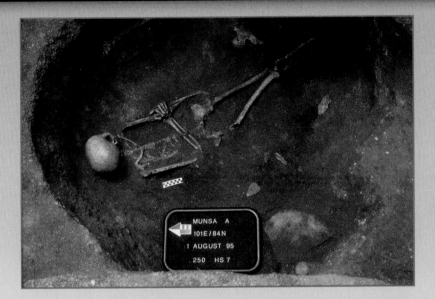

This pit at Munsa contained two burials which a local resident interpreted as the bodies of a princess and her maid. The second (later) burial is shown here. At the top of the photo you can see part of the pelvis and a femur (thigh bone) belonging to the earlier burial.

Finally, one man who perhaps stood to gain by the development of Munsa as a tourist destination was visited by a South African journalist soon after our excavations had ended. He showed this journalist the spot where he said (and the journalist recounted in his article) we had found the body of a princess whose faithful maidservant had been forced to accompany her mistress into the afterlife. The reality is that, yes, we had found two female burials, but the second one had been interred in the same pit long after the first one had decayed to a skeleton. Moreover, I rather doubt that a few glass beads are sufficient to identify a princess.

While it might be easy to dismiss the various views of Munsa as incongruous with the archaeological evidence, such a dismissal is not warranted. Munsa may at some time have been a focus of military activity, despite the absence of barracks. I suspect that Munsa was also a ritual center, although archaeological evidence for this hypothesis is elusive. If anything, archaeology reveals that Munsa has a rich history to which no single interpretation can do justice. For example, the deep ditches likely delineated the abodes of the spirits at the center of the site, served as material reminders of the organizational powers of the settlement's leadership, and kept elephants out of cultivated fields and human enemies at bay. But perhaps the real lesson to be learned here is that not only are archaeological sites repositories of potential information about the past, but they also empower the present.

Close-up of a burial at Munsa. Note the presence of iron beads and bangles next to the scale (in cm). The damage to the skull occurred after the body had been buried.

have had a tendency to treat society as homogeneous. Feminist archaeologists have drawn on studies by sociocultural anthropologists to show that the experience of individuals is shaped by their role in society. The challenge to archaeologists is how to study gender with the tools of archaeology. Studies focusing on identifying gender differences have looked at a wide range of topics, including stone tool production, textiles, and plant food processing. The difficulty is that in these realms

**A**merican archaeologist Harriet Boyd Hawes, photographed on the island of Crete in 1902. The contributions of women to archaeology is often overlooked.

identifying gender can be elusive. In cultures with written documents or art showing people at work, it has been possible to combine the information contained therein with archaeology to reach significant conclusions about gender in ancient societies. Studies of skeletal remains have also produced important insights into the relation between gender and other factors, such as diet, activity, and burial practices.

Feminist archaeology has also brought attention to the way that archaeologists represent gender. The invisibility of gender in archaeology has often masked a strong bias towards viewing men as the active and productive agents of change and women as passive "fellow travelers." One humorous example is found in the rather implausible title of one of Childe's books: *Man Makes Himself!* Feminist archaeologists have done important work in identifying the pervasiveness of gender bias in archaeology and in offering alternative images. In a number of intriguing studies, feminist archaeologists have used fiction as a way to bring attention to the active role of women in society (Spector 1991).

Feminist archaeologists have made an important contribution by demonstrating that societies are not uniform. Recently, archaeologists working with **agency theory** have taken this idea further by arguing that the basic unit of archaeology is not society, but individuals *living* in society (Dobres and Robb 2000). Based on the theory of practice developed by the sociologists Pierre Bourdieu and Anthony Giddens, agency theory emphasizes the agency of individuals—the purposeful actions of the people who lived in the past. Agency theory is a constant balancing act between the recognition that history consists of the choices and actions of individuals and an awareness that the choices people make are strongly shaped by the social world and material conditions in which they live. Archaeologists working from a foundation of agency theory have tackled a wide range of topics. One of the most interesting directions this research has taken is in reconsidering the nature of the landscape. By putting people at the center of the landscape, agency theorists have led archaeologists to investigate how ancient monuments were experienced by the people who built and lived with them (Thomas 1996).

**Agency theory** stresses the centrality of individuals living in society as the basic unit of archaeology.

## Evolutionary Archaeology

Alongside the diversification of approaches aligned with postprocessual archaeology, there has recently also been a diversification of approaches aligned with processual archaeology. **Evolutionary archaeology** was developed by processual archaeologists who stress the importance of evolutionary theory as a potential unifying theory for archaeology. Robert Dunnell pioneered this approach in his studies of archaeological systematics. In recent years, evolutionary archaeology has come to encompass a range of approaches, from ecological studies that look at changes in culture as changes in human adaptation to attempts to apply Darwinian theory to changes in the frequencies and types of artifacts found at a site.

**Evolutionary archaeology** involves a range of approaches that stress the importance of evolutionary theory as a unifying theory for archaeology.

## The Socialization of Ancient Maya Children
### by Rissa M. Trachman

As a part of my dissertation research in 2000 and 2001, I excavated three sets of multiple burials at an ancient Maya household called the Dancer group, located just outside of the site of Dos Hombres in the Rio Bravo area of northern Belize. Two of these sets of multiple burials date to the Chicanel phase (400 B.C.–A.D.100) of the Late Preclassic. The people buried in these two sets are of various ages, both children and adults, and all were accompanied in their graves by goods made of greenstone and shell and by whole ceramic vessels.

One specific shell artifact included with these goods really caught my attention. I remembered a lecture that my professor, Dr. Fred Valdez, gave regarding the everyday life of the ancient Maya. He noted that certain symbols were placed on children to identify them as to their gender. I wondered if what I had found in these burials was indeed one of these gender-specific costume elements. It sounded simple, but I had my work cut out for me. I couldn't find any archaeological documentation of the practice, so I did some research and found that, at the time of European contact in the 1500s, Friar Diego de Landa (Tozzer 1941) observed that children went through a series of life-course rituals at various ages that can be interpreted as a part of their socialization. One practice specifically identified children with their gender. When the children were very young, a bead was placed in the hair of each boy and a shell was hung from the waist of each girl. During a subsequent lifecycle ceremony called the *caput sihil,* these symbolic items were ritually taken off of the children. The ceremony was performed primarily prior to marriage.

Was this shell artifact that I found in the burials at the Dancer group household similar to the one described by Landa in the historic period? Is it possible that the ancient Maya practiced this same form of ritually identifying and socializing their children for so long? I wondered whether that kind of continuity was possible. The excavated materials from the Dancer group seemed to suggest

that it was, but I needed more evidence.

I consulted what published mortuary data I could find, looking for this pattern in other burials in the Maya lowlands. Child burials are not common, and shell beads are very common in all burials in the Maya Region. As a result, I found that the bivalve shell symbol for girls was easier to track for comparative purposes. The Maya sites of Cuello and Yaxuna both have data similar to the data pertaining to the Dancer group. At the Maya site of Cuello, Belize, two examples of the pattern sought were noted in the burial data for the Preclassic. Bivalve shell pendants were found at the pelvis in two buried children who were two to nine years at death. At Yaxuna, Mexico, as many as seven children, all in four to seven years of age at death, had the female symbol accompanying them. With one exception, these burials date to the Terminal Classic period (A.D. 800–900), a period that, interestingly, is between our Preclassic examples and the time of the historic documentation.

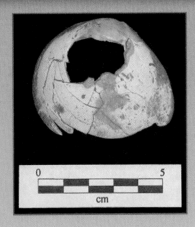

▲ The bivalve shell artifact found in the burials at the Dancer group household.

The comparative mortuary evidence from other sites in the Maya lowlands, Landa's historic writings, and the Dancer group material seemed to be adding up. Recently, another piece of the puzzle has emerged: The same symbolic costume element is depicted in a set of Preclassic murals discovered not long ago at the nearby site of San Bartolo. Given the Preclassic date of the murals, they, too, may indicate that the practice of socializing children in the manner described had a very long tenure in Maya prehistory and history. The practice of socializing to gender among the Maya may have begun as early as the Late Preclassic and lasted to the colonial period, almost 2,000 years later.

▶ Rissa Trachman excavating the burials.

# 2.6 ARCHAEOLOGY AT THE TROWEL'S EDGE

Along with the growth and diversification of archaeological theory has come a sense of a disconnection between the way archaeologists write about archaeology and what it is that archaeologists actually do. Most archaeologists would argue that the labels "processualist" and "postprocessualist" obscure what it is that they actually do. In practice, it is quite possible to borrow liberally from many theoretical perspectives. Ian Hodder has proposed that we change archaeological theory from a top-down approach to an approach that begins "at the edge of the trowel." Drawing on the theory of hermeneutics, Hodder argues that archaeological theory should build on what archaeologists *actually* do, rather than prescribing what they *should* do.

Archaeology has developed from the simple recognition of the extent of the human past to a discipline that involves intense debate about how we gain knowledge of the past. Archaeology today has a rich theoretical "tool kit"—a diversity of approaches that can be used to think about the past. This diversification of approaches has led to confusion, confrontation, and, at times, a degree of despair. Surely, processualists and postprocessualists cannot both be right! Or perhaps they can. Alison Wylie has given us a beautiful image comparing archaeology to sailing, wherein one tacks back and forth in the wind in order to make progress. Our subject matter is over two million years of human experience. Our evidence is all of the physical remains of that experience. Given the immensity of the venture, we are really in a very small boat on an enormous ocean. The ability to maneuver between approaches may be just what is needed in such a voyage.

## CHAPTER SUMMARY

- The earliest use of archaeology to learn about the past was in Renaissance Europe. However, until the nineteenth century, there were no methods for determining the age of prehistoric artifacts, and in many cases the human manufacture of artifacts was not recognized.
- The development of the Three-Age system of Stone, Bronze, and Iron Ages was a major accomplishment of nineteenth-century archaeologists.
- The recognition that tools of human manufacture were found in the same layers as the bones of extinct animals, together with the development of the theory of evolution, changed the scope of archaeological research.
- The professionalization of archaeology during the early part of the twentieth century led to a focus on culture history and stratigraphic method.

- V. Gordon Childe shifted the focus of archaeologists from changes in the material remains recovered on archaeological sites to what those remains told us about ancient and prehistoric societies.
- The New Archaeologists, also known as processual archaeologists, led by Lewis Binford, argue that archaeologists should follow an explicitly scientific method of testing hypotheses.
- One of the approaches widely used by the New Archaeologists is systems theory.
- The postprocessual archaeologists, led by Ian Hodder, argue that archaeology is closer to history than it is to the exact sciences. The postprocessualists emphasize the role of interpretation and context in archaeological research.
- Gender and agency theory are two of the approaches used by postprocessual archaeologists.

## KEY TERMS

Agency Theory, 58
Archaeological theory, 39
Deduction, 50
Evolutionary Archaeology, 58
Feminist Archaeology, 56
Hermeneutics, 54

Induction, 50
Middle-Range Research, 51
*Neolithic,* New Stone Age 44
New Archaeology/Processual
   Archaeology, 50

*Paleolithic,* Old Stone Age 44
Postprocessual Archaeology, 53
Systems Theory, 51
Three-Age System, 41
Thunderstones, 40

## REVIEW QUESTIONS

1. What kind of impact do you think the establishment of human antiquity has had on the way we think of humanity?

2. Do you agree with the New Archaeologists' stress on the importance of scientific method in archaeology?

3. What are the critiques raised by the postprocessualists? Do you think these critiques are valid?

## FOR FURTHER READING

Lewis Binford. (1983). *In Pursuit of the Past.* New York: Thames and Hudson.

Sally Binford and Lewis Binford. (1968). *New Perspectives in Archaeology.* New York: Aldine.

David Clark. (1978). *Analytical Archaeology.* New York: Columbia University Press.

Joan Gero and Margaret Conkey, eds. (1991). *Engendering Archaeology.* Oxford, UK: Blackwell.

Donald Grayson. (1983). *The Establishment of Human Antiquity.* New York: Academic Press.

Ian Hodder. (1986). *Reading the Past.* Cambridge, UK: Cambridge University Press.

Ian Hodder. (1999). *The Archaeological Process.* Oxford, UK: Blackwell.

Robert Preucel and Ian Hodder, eds. (1996). *Contemporary Archaeology in Theory.* Oxford, UK: Blackwell.

Alain Schnapp. (1996). *The Discovery of the Past.* New York: Abrams.

Bruce Trigger. (1989). *A History of Archaeological Thought.* Cambridge, UK: Cambridge University Press.

Gordon Willey and Jeremy Sabloff. (1980). *A History of American Archaeology.* San Francisco: Freeman.

# part TWO

# Human Evolution

THE STUDY OF HUMAN EVOLUTION draws insight
from a multitude of disciplines, including paleontology, genetics, the reconstruction of past climates, and
archaeology. This section of the book synthesizes the
current state of research in human evolution with a strong
emphasis on the unique perspective provided by archaeology. Particular topics are the timing of hominin dispersals and changes in adaptation and technology.

Studying the evolutionary history or phylogeny of
humans draws on a combination of anatomical, fossil,
and genetic studies. After reading this chapter, you
should understand:

▶ The place of humans in biological classification.

▶ The genetic evidence for the timing of the split between
the hominin and chimpanzee lineages.

▶ The fossil record of hominoid phylogeny.

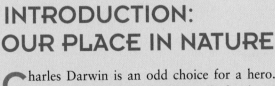

# INTRODUCTION:
# OUR PLACE IN NATURE

Charles Darwin is an odd choice for a hero. Plagued by everything
from boils to self-doubt, he hardly fits the picture of a revolutionary
figure. However, the theory of evolution developed in Darwin's *The Origin of Species* is among the cornerstones of modern science. Almost all of Darwin's
ideas were based on what he was able to observe on his voyage around the world
on the *Beagle* and on walks around his country home in England. Darwin was
obsessed by the question of how one explains the incredible variation in the living

world. The theory of evolution begins with the observation that there is significant variety within populations. Whether one is looking at a bed of roses, a flock of pigeons, or a room of people, such variation exists. Darwin suggested that if some variations offered advantages to survival, they might come to be prevalent. Drawing on an analogy to the way humans breed domesticated animals for certain traits, he proposed that natural selection would act on the variation within populations to favor organisms with traits that were adaptive. Over vast periods of time, natural selection in different settings would lead to the splitting of populations into distinct species. Darwin's conception of evolution derives much of its power from its simplicity. According to Darwin, all the spectacular variety of life on earth can be explained as the result of the action of selection on variation over very long periods of time. Thus, the emergence of new species need not be explained by an appeal to metaphysics, but rather could be rendered intelligible through a detailed understanding of shifts in environments and adaptation over time.

In *The Origin of Species*, Darwin wrote little about human evolution. Only at the end of the concluding chapter did he write that, on the basis of his theory, "light will be thrown on the origin of man and his history" (Darwin 1859). The theory of evolution is not a formulation that provides ultimate answers, but rather is a doorway to an endlessly fascinating exploration of humanity and the natural world. The next four chapters examine what we have learned in the last one hundred fifty years about the evolutionary history of humans.

## Phylogeny

Before turning to a consideration of human evolution, it is necessary to define some of the fundamental aspects of biological terminology and to situate humans within an evolutionary framework. The basic unit of biological classification is the **species,** which is defined as a group of organisms that can produce fertile offspring. A genus (plural *genera*) refers to a grouping of similar species. All living humans are members of the species *Homo sapiens,* which belongs to genus *Homo.* Similar genera are grouped into families, and similar families are grouped into orders. Humans, the great apes (orangutans, gorillas, and chimpanzees), and gibbons make up the biological family Hominoidea, or the **hominoids.** Together with monkeys and prosimians (lemurs, lorises, tarsiers, and their relatives), the hominoids belong to the order Primates. Most primates are tree-dwelling animals that live in trees. Primates rely heavily on sight in dealing with the environment and are highly social, with a tendency to live in groups.

> A **species** is a group of organisms that can produce fertile offspring.

> The **hominoids** are the biological family that includes humans, great apes, and gibbons.

## TABLE II.1

### Biological Classification of Humans

| | | |
|---|---|---|
| Species | *Homo sapiens* | All Living Humans |
| Genus (pl. *genera*) | *Homo* | Humans and Immediate Ancestors |
| Family | *Hominoidea* (hominoids) | Humans, Orangutans, Gorillas, Chimpanzees, and Gibbons |
| Order | Primates | Hominoids, Monkeys, and Prosimians |

FIGURE II.1

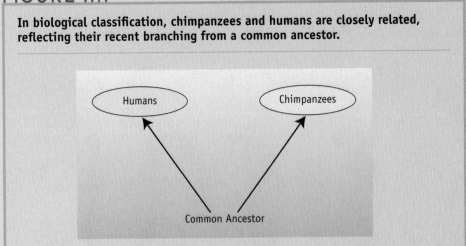

In biological classification, chimpanzees and humans are closely related, reflecting their recent branching from a common ancestor.

Table II.1 gives a biological classification of humans. Biological classifications are not based only on the degree of similarity between species; rather, they are also meant to reflect the branching pattern of evolution. Popular media often misrepresent evolution as a linear process of progress through stages (see Figure II.2). Evolution is actually a process of splitting ancestral populations into distinct lineages. A common example of the popular misconception of evolution is found in the statement, "Humans evolved from apes." The correct statement is that humans and chimpanzees share a common ancestor, as is depicted in Figure II.1.

Reconstructing evolutionary history, or **phylogeny,** is based on a combination of information from fossils and genetics. The nature of the evidence provided by each of these sources differs. Genetic evidence is derived largely from living populations of humans and animals, although in a small number of cases it is possible to recover genetic material from fossils. Genetics provides insight into the evolutionary relationship between living species and the timing of the split between the lineages leading to those species (see Figure II.2). Fossils are the physical remains of prehistoric life. It is only through fossils that we can learn about our now-extinct human ancestors.

▶ **Phylogeny** is the evolutionary history of a species.

## Genetic Evidence

The path of our growth and development as individuals (called **ontogeny**) is the result of the interaction between genetics and the environment. A copy of the DNA molecules that encode our genetic inheritance is contained in the nucleus of every one of our body cells. This **nuclear DNA** is a combination of genes inherited from each of our parents. **Mitochondrial DNA,** which is located outside of the cell nucleus, differs from nuclear DNA in that it is inherited exclusively from the maternal lineage. The DNA of all living humans is similar, so, genetically, humans are a quite homogeneous species.

Constructing a phylogeny, or evolutionary history, of the hominoids (humans, great apes, and gibbons) on the basis of genetic evidence involves comparing the degree of genetic similarity between species. Most genetic phylogenies of the hominoids emphasize the high degree of similarity between humans and chimpanzees. Chimpanzees consist of two living species: common chimpanzees (*Pan troglodytes*)

▶ **Ontogeny** refers to the growth and development of an individual organism.

▶ **Nuclear DNA,** located in the cell nucleus, combines DNA from each parent.

▶ **Mitochondrial DNA,** located outside of the cell nucleus, is inherited exclusively from the mother.

## FIGURE II.2

**Huxley's image of human evolution. This picture of evolution as a linear directional process has had a powerful influence on popular perceptions of evolution.**

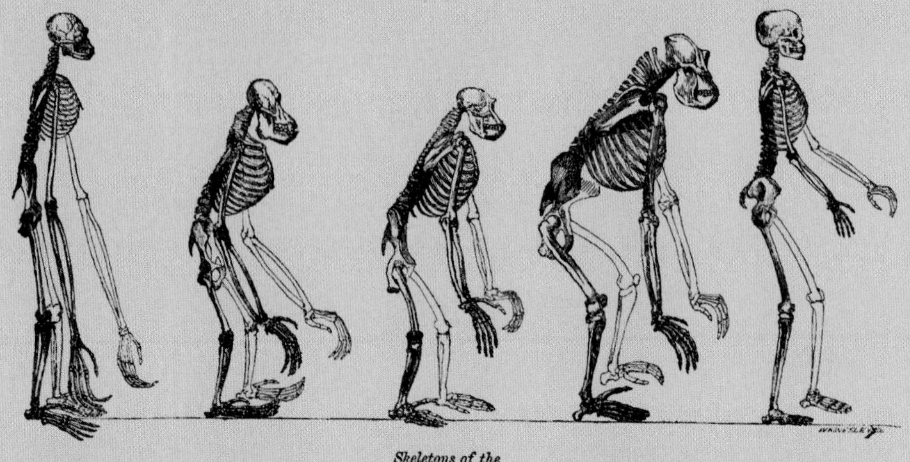

GIBBON.   ORANG.   *Skeletons of the* CHIMPANZEE.   GORILLA.   MAN.

and pygmy chimpanzees (*Pan paniscus*). The degree of similarity of humans to gorillas (*Gorilla gorilla*) is only slightly lower than the similarity of humans to chimpanzees. Orangutans (*Pongo pygmeaus*) are genetically less similar to humans than either chimpanzees or gorillas, and gibbons (*Hylobates*) are even more distantly related (see Figure II.3).

The degree of genetic similarity between species can be used to infer the timing of the split between lineages. Calculating when lineages diverged on the basis of the degree of genetic similarity rests on the concept of the **molecular clock**. The assumption underlying this concept is that genetic mutations accumulate at a constant rate. One can think of the DNA in the cell nucleus as an extremely lengthy series of coded messages. A genetic mutation is a random change in some part of this message. If one knows the degree of genetic similarity between two species, one can use the molecular clock to calculate the date when their lineages diverged. In practice, the use of the molecular clock is quite complex, and the results are controversial. However, some agreement has been reached over the timing of the divergence between the lineages of humans and the great apes. The split between the chimpanzee and human lineages is now placed between four and six million years before the present. The split between the human lineage and gorillas is said to have taken place six to eight million years before the present, and that between humans and orangutans is held to be 12 to 16 million years before the present (see Figure II.3).

> The **molecular clock** allows the timing of the split between lineages to be calculated on the basis of the degree of genetic similarity.

## The Fossil Record

Although genetic evidence provides a framework for the timing of the split of the lineages leading to living species, it does not provide information about the extinct species that make up these lineages. **Paleoanthropologists**—scientists specializing in the study of the hominoid lineage—rely on fossils to construct the evolutionary his-

> **Paleoanthropologists** are scientists who study the evolutionary history of the hominoids.

## FIGURE 11.3

**Homonoid phylogeny based on molecular data. How does this differ from Huxley's image found on page 66?**

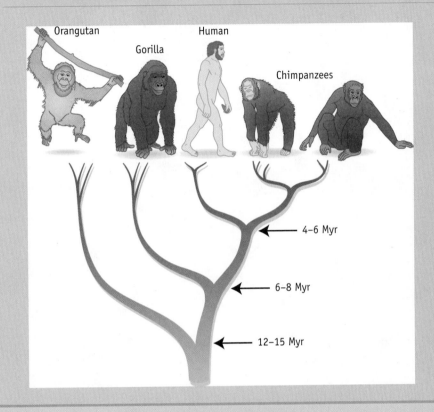

tory of humanity. As Darwin recognized in *The Origin of Species,* the study of the fossil record is like reading a book with many pages missing. Because the preservation and discovery of fossils relies heavily on chance, there are significant gaps in the fossil record. Of course, one of the exciting elements of paleoanthropology is the role new discoveries play in developing knowledge and challenging ideas.

The earliest fossils that can be attributed to the order Primates date to the Cretaceous period, ninety to sixty-five million years ago. *Purgatorius* is a late-Cretaceous primate known from fossils discovered in Montana. This small shrewlike animal subsisted on insects during the period immediately preceding the extinction of the dinosaurs. A particularly important locality for the study of early primates is the Fayum Depression, south of Cairo, Egypt. The rich fossil remains recovered from the Fayum date to the Eocene and Oligocene periods (fifty-six million to twenty-three million years ago). At that time, the Fayum, which is today a desert, was a marshland inhabited by a wide array of animals. Included in the Fayum assemblage are some of the earliest ancestors of monkeys. *Aegyptopithecus,* a fairly well represented species from the Fayum, might be the earliest member of the hominoids. If so, then the hominoid lineage dates back to the Oligocene period (thirty-five million to twenty-three million years ago).

The **Miocene era** (twenty-three million to five million years ago) saw an explosion in the number of hominoid species. During this period, hominoids filled many of the ecological niches now filled by monkeys. The range of Miocene hominoids is impressive. Species ranged from the size of a very small monkey to that of a gorilla.

> ▶ The earliest-known primate is *Purgatorius,* which lived between ninety and sixty-five million years ago.

> ▶ *Aegyptopithecus,* one of the earliest hominoids, lived between thirty-five million and twent-three million years ago.

> ▶ During the **Miocene era** (twenty-three million to five million years ago), there was an explosion in the number of hominoid species.

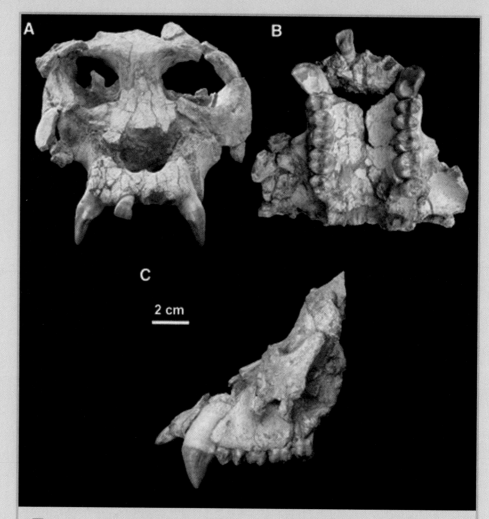

**F**ossil of a Miocene ape. Some of the important characteristics of this fossil that connect it with the ape lineage are large canine teeth and the shape of the palette.

One of the greatest challenges facing paleoanthropologists working with Miocene fossils (See Figure II.4) is to determine where they fit on the hominoid evolutionary tree. Several Miocene species show traits that are characteristic of the orangutan, to the exclusion of the other hominoids. Thus, although it is possible to identify Miocene ancestors of modern orangutans, it is still difficult to identify a clear Miocene ancestor of the chimpanzee–human lineage. One of the major gaps in the fossil record is a representative of the common ancestor of humans and chimpanzees.

## Culture and Human Evolution

One of the defining characteristics of biological evolution is that selection operates on traits that are transmitted genetically between generations. We pass our genes, not our experiences, on to our children. The early French zoologist Jean-Baptiste

Lamarck famously made the argument that giraffes evolved long necks through the inheritance of acquired characteristics. This means that as giraffes stretched their necks to reach the tops of trees, their necks grew longer, and that the lengthened-neck trait was then passed on to the next generation. A more contemporary example would be to argue that the children of fans of loud music are born partly deaf because their parents' hearing was damaged when the parents stood near loudspeakers. We now know that Lamarck had made one of the great errors in the history of science: Traits acquired during life are not transmitted genetically to the next generation.

Throughout the animal world, we often find that acquired traits are in fact transmitted. However, their transmission takes place not through genetics, but rather through learning. Learning provides a mechanism for transmitting experience from generation to generation. We frequently refer to the complex of learned behaviors found in human societies as culture. Is culture unique to humans? This is partly a matter of definition, but there is significant evidence which suggests that there is a patterning of learned behavior between chimpanzee groups that warrants the label "culture" (Whiten et al. 1999). Regardless of how one resolves this dispute, it is unquestionable that the specific nature of human culture is unique in the animal world. Change in human culture has been both rapid and cumulative. There is a clear sense that developments in human culture build on themselves, creating a kind of "ratchet" effect. When we study human evolution, we are studying not only biological evolution, but also cultural evolution. The fascination inherent in the archaeology of human origins lies in the exploration of the relationship between biological and cultural evolution. Did biological evolution drive cultural change

A teacher working with 8-9 year-old children. How does the teacher guide the children's attention?

**A** chimpanzee examining itself in a mirror. Notice that the chimpanzee uses its hands to explore, guided by the reflection in the mirror.

and innovation? Or is it possible that innovations in culture led to events in biological evolution?

Underlying these questions is one of the most engaging questions in biological science: Why is it that human culture is of a unique nature? One intriguing answer looks at the uniquely human capability to recognize others as "beings *like themselves* who have intentional and mental worlds like their own" (Tomasello 1999: 5). As far as we know, this capability is not found in any other animals, although chimpanzees can recognize themselves in a mirror (see photo). Michael Tomasello (1999) argues that the capability to see another as like oneself opens the door to powerful new mechanisms of learning, in which humans learn by identifying with another rather than simply by observation.

Language is also critical to human interaction and plays an essential role in the transmission of cultural knowledge between generations. The timing of the first appearance of language is a central topic in the archaeology of human origins. Unfortunately, language does not leave fossil evidence. We are left to infer what cultural behaviors would have required language. One intriguing idea is that the evolution of the human brain took place within the context of the evolution of language. Terrence Deacon (1997) has suggested that there was a coevolutionary relationship between language and the brain. If he is correct, the implication is that the archaeology of human origins traces the intricate give-and-take between genetic evolution and the evolution of culture. It is this interaction that makes the archaeology of human origins a unique and challenging field of study.

## SUMMARY

- Reconstructing evolutionary history (phylogeny) is based on genetic and fossil evidence.
- Genetic evidence indicates a close relationship between humans and the great apes. Chimpanzees show the greatest genetic similarity to humans. On the basis of the molecular clock, the split of the

human and chimpanzee lineages is placed at five to seven million years ago.
- The earliest fossil primate dates to the Cretaceous period. The earliest fossil ancestral to the hominoids (humans, great apes, and gibbons) lived between 35 million and 23 million years ago.

## KEY TERMS

*Aegyptopithecus,* 67
Hominins, 64
Mitochondrial DNA, 65
Miocene Era, 67
Molecular Clock, 66
Nuclear DNA, 65

Ontogeny, 65
Paleoanthropologists, 66
Phylogeny, 65
*Purgatorius,* 67
Species, 64

## REVIEW QUESTIONS

1. What is the evidence for the timing of the split between the hominin and chimpanzee lineages?
2. How would you characterize the Oligocene and Miocene hominoid fossil record?
3. What is the difference between biological evolution and cultural evolution?

## FOR FURTHER READING

Terrence W. Deacon. (1997). *The Symbolic Species: The co-evolution of language and the Brain.* New York: Norton.

John Fleagle. (1999). *Primate Adaptation and Evolution.* San Diego: Academic Press.

Mark Ridley. (1997). *Evolution.* Oxford, UK: Oxford University Press.

Michael Tomasello. (1999). *The Cultural Origins of Human Cognition.* Cambridge, Massachusetts: Harvard University Press.

# Early Hominins

THE EARLY HOMININ record includes species belonging to four distinct genera. After reading this chapter, you should understand:

▶ The hominin radiation between four million and two million years ago.

▶ The major characteristic of Lower Paleolithic stone tool industries.

▶ The evidence for the origin of tool use.

▶ The debates about hunting and food sharing by early hominins.

▶ The evidence for the first dispersal of hominins out of Africa.

Excavating an early hominin site in east Africa.

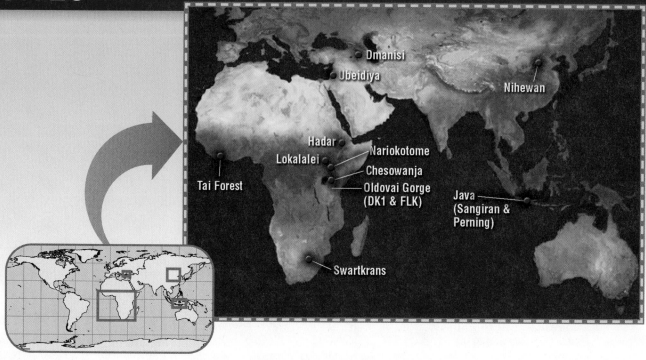

One-and-a-half million years ago, a male *Homo erectus* lived in the Caucasus Mountains, in what is today the Republic of Georgia. When archaeologists discovered his skull (see photo) at the site of Dmanisi, they were surprised to see that he had lost all but one of his teeth, years before he died at the age of forty (Lordkipanidze et al. 2005). How did he survive without teeth? Did he rely on the compassion of members of his social group for food he could eat? The toothless man from Dmanisi raises many of the fundamental questions that occupy archaeologists studying early human ancestors. What was the nature of their society? How did they get food? How did they use tools?

In this chapter, we examine the archaeology of the early members of the hominin lineage. **Hominins** include all members of the human lineage after its split

> **Hominins** are the members of the human lineage after it split with the chimpanzee lineage.

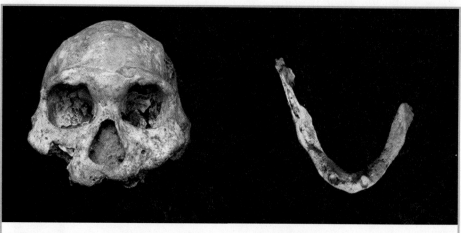

**T**he toothless Homo erectus from Dmanisi, Georgia.

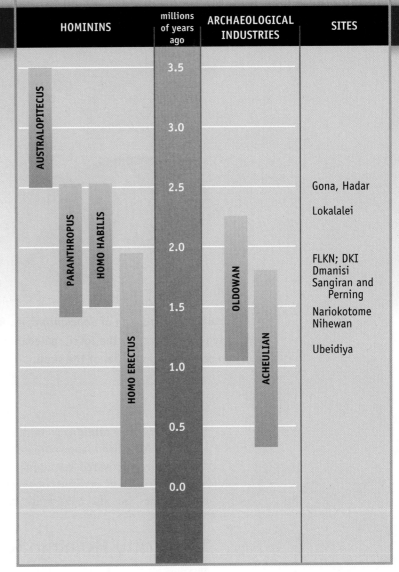

| HOMININS | millions of years ago | ARCHAEOLOGICAL INDUSTRIES | SITES |
|---|---|---|---|
| | 3.5 | | |
| AUSTRALOPITHECUS | 3.0 | | |
| | 2.5 | | Gona, Hadar |
| PARANTHROPUS / HOMO HABILIS | 2.0 | OLDOWAN | Lokalalei |
| | 1.5 | | FLKN; DKI Dmanisi Sangiran and Perning |
| HOMO ERECTUS | 1.0 | ACHEULIAN | Nariokotome Nihewan |
| | 0.5 | | Ubeidiya |
| | 0.0 | | |

with the chimpanzee lineage. Until recently, hominins were refered to as hominids; however, the term hominin has now been adopted because it more properly fits with the rules of biological nomenclature (Wood and Richmond 2000). We begin by setting the stage for the study of early hominins by examining the fossil record, the geological context of early sites, and the definition of archaeological periods. With this background, the chapter moves on to three major themes in the archaeology of early hominins: tool use, adaptation, and social organization. Tool use is often thought to be a distinctive marker of the human lineage. We consider the evidence for tool use by animals and then move on to the timing and nature of the earliest archaeological evidence for tool manufacture. Beyond tool use, we are interested in the way that early hominins lived their lives, including how they got their food and how their societies were organized. We focus on the evidence for hunting and food sharing by early hominins. Finally, the chapter turns to the archaeological evidence for the expansion of the hominin lineage beyond Africa and into Europe and Asia. One can imagine the toothless grin of the old man from Dmanisi as we struggle to understand the basic outlines of the lives of our early hominin ancestors.

# 3.1 THE FOSSIL RECORD

The earliest hominins are known from a small number of enigmatic and fragmentary remains. The oldest fossils thought to belong to the hominin lineage are of *Sahelanthropus tchadensis* (Brunet et al. 2005, Zollikofer et al. 2005). The fossils of *Sahelanthropus* have been found in Chad in levels dating to seven million years ago. A complete skull of Sahelanthropus has been discovered, but it is badly deformed, leaving room for differing interpretations of the species. Some have argued that *Sahelanthropus* is an African ape ancestor, while the discoverers of the fossil argue that it is, in fact, a hominin.

▶ *Sahelanthropus tchadensis* and *Ardipithecus ramidus* are the earliest-known members of the hominin lineage.

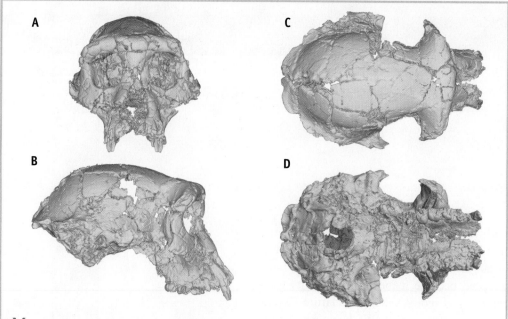

**V**irtual reconstruction of *Sahelanthropus*. By working with computerized images generated by a CT scan of the fossil, paleoanthropologists were able to correct for distortion caused by the burial of the skull.

*Ardipithecus ramidus* is another early hominin (White et al. 1994, 1995). This species, which lived approximately four-and-a-half million years ago, is known from fossils discovered beginning in 1992 at the site of Aramis in Ethiopia. The fragmentary fossil remains of *Ardipithecus* share some characteristics found in chimpanzees, but also have traits unique to the hominin lineage.

## The Early Hominin Radiation

The period between four million and two million years ago saw an explosion in the diversity of hominin species (Wood and Richmond 2000). Such an event is known in evolutionary biology as a **radiation**. The hominin radiation that took place between four million and two million years ago included three distinct genera: *Kenyanthropus*, *Australopithecus*, and *Paranthropus*.

Despite the wide variation found in these three genera, there are certain broad similarities among them. All members of the three genera appear to have been dis-

> A **radiation** is the biological term for a period when there is a rapid increase in the number of species in a single lineage.

## TABLE 3.1

| GENUS OR SPECIES | DATE | BRAIN SIZE | CHARACTERISTICS | FOUND IN |
|---|---|---|---|---|
| *Australopithecus* | 3.5–2.5 million years ago | 450–475 cc. | Bipedal | East Africa, West Africa, and South Africa |
| *Kenyanthropus* | 3.5 million years ago | 450–475 cc. | Similar to *Australopithecus* | East Africa |
| *Paranthropus* | 2.5–1.4 million years ago | 450–475 cc. | Massive molars and chewing muscles | East Africa and South Africa |
| *Homo habilis* | 2.5–1.6 million years ago | 500–800 cc. | Increased brain size | East Africa and South Africa |
| *Homo erectus* | 1.9 million–45,000 (?) years ago | 750–1,250 cc. | Further increase in brain size, dispersal out of Africa | Africa, Asia, and Europe |

tinct from living great apes in that they were adapted to walking upright. However, it is possible that some species were also adapted to move easily through trees by climbing. It is notable that these hominins lacked the pronounced canine teeth characteristic of living great apes. The mean brain size for members of the three genera was consistently between 450 and 475 cubic centimeters, at the high end of brain size for living apes. Thus, within the hominin lineage, bipedalism (walking upright) and the loss of large canines preceded a significant increase in brain size. Table 3.1 presents some important aspects of *Kenyanthropus, Australopithecus,* and *Paranthropus,* as well as of the two later species *Homo habilis* and *Homo erectus.*

### Australopithecines.

The **australopithecines** are known from as many as six distinct species. Australopithecine fossils are known from sites dating between four million and two-and-a-half million years ago (Leakey et al. 1995). Most specimens come from East Africa and South Africa; however, a new species, *Australopithecus bahrelghazali,* which lived three-and-a-half million years ago, was discovered in 1996 in Chad in Central Africa (Brunet et al. 1995). The nearly complete skeleton of an *Australopithecus afarensis* discovered by Donald Johanson in the Hadar, Ethiopia, famously nicknamed Lucy after the Beatles song "Lucy in the Sky with Diamonds," provides the first evidence that australopithecines walked on two legs. Graphic evidence that the species walked upright is found in a trail of footprints left in volcanic ash at the site of **Laetoli** in Tanzania, shown in the photo on this page (Leakey and Harris 1987). A team of excavators working with Mary Leakey in 1978 discovered fossil footprints left by three individuals walking on a surface of volcanic ash. The prints at Laetoli clearly show that these three individuals were walking upright. Because the ash dates to 3.8 million years ago, the footprints were most likely produced by members of the species *Austrolopithecus afarensis.*

### Kenyanthropus.

*Kenyanthropus,* which dates to three-and-a-half million years ago, was first discovered in 2001 by Meave Leakey and her colleagues on the shores of Lake Turkana in northern Kenya (Leakey et al. 2001). *Kenyanthropus* is still poorly understood; however, in general terms, it seems similar to the Australopithecines.

### Paranthropus.

*Paranthropus,* also known as robust *Australopithecus,* is characterized by massive molars and muscles for chewing (Wood and Richmond 2000). Lewis Leakey nicknamed the *Paranthropus boisei* skull he recovered at Olduvai Gorge in Tanzania "Nutcracker Man," and it is thought that the massive chewing mechanisms of these species is related to a diet that included seeds or fruits with a hard outer coating. The earliest-known *Paranthropus* dates to two-and-a-half million years ago, while the most recent dates to 1.4 million years ago.

> The discovery of the near-complete fossil of an Australopithicine at Hadar and **Australopithecine** footprints at **Laetoli** indicate that this species walked upright on two legs.

**T**he footsteps at Laetoli preserved in a bed of volcanic ash dated to 3.8 million years ago. Notice the hominin trackways and the tracks of other animals running off to the right.

## Fraud—Piltdown and Kama-takamori

On December 28, 1912, the *Illustrated London News* announced "a discovery of supreme importance to all who are interested in the history of the human race." The discovery, made at the site of Piltdown in East Sussex, England, included fragments of a skull and jaw that appeared to be the oldest-known fossils of a human ancestor. When the skull of Piltdown man was reconstructed, a picture emerged of an individual with a large cranium similar to the skull of living humans. However, the jaw (mandible) was in many ways apelike. The Piltdown fossils became the basis for a new genus of human ancestor: *Eoanthropus*, or "dawn man."

In 1954, forty-two years after the discovery, the fossil remains from Piltdown were unmasked as an elaborate fraud. The jaw was from a modern orangutan and had been stained to appear fossilized. The teeth had been filed down to alter their shape into a slightly more human configuration and parts of the mandible were deliberately broken off in order to make it more difficult to identify it as the mandible of an ape. The skull fragments were from a modern human of recent archaeological origin. All of the bones found at Piltdown were deliberately introduced into the site.

Of course, the intriguing question is, Who concocted and carried out this scheme? The most likely suspect is Charles Dawson, the amateur scientist and solicitor who discovered the fossils. However, Dawson did not have a clear motive, and many doubt that he had the expertise to make the fakes, as well as access to paraphernalia such as an orangutan jaw. It seems likely that Dawson was himself duped or had an accomplice. Among the list of suspects were two of the most prominent scientists of the day: Arthur Smith Woodward and Arthur Keith. Both had the expertise and access to the site, but their motive is unclear. Would they risk everything and sacrifice the most basic of scientific ethics in such an undertaking? The Catholic priest and paleontologist Teilhard de Chardin has also been implicated as a suspect, particularly given the fact that he discovered some of the Piltdown fossils himself during brief visits to the site. Even Sir Arthur Conan Doyle, the author of the Sherlock Holmes mysteries, has been suggested as a suspect. To this day, the file on the Piltdown hoax remains open.

Frauds like Piltdown are exceptionally rare in archaeology. However, a similar scandal recently rocked Japanese archaeology. In 1993, Japanese archaeologists announced the discovery of bifaces at the Kama-takamori site in a context dated to roughly 500,000 years old. The discovery was widely reported, primarily in the Japanese popular press, as the earliest evidence of human occupation of Japan. In 1995, a pit was found with fifteen tools, including ten bifaces, arranged in an oval, with two tools in the center, one made of a particularly beautiful white rock and the other from an unusual red rock.

In 2002, the archaeological community was stunned to learn that the artifacts at the Kama-takamori site had been deliberately planted by one of the excavators. Videotapes caught the excavator in the act of digging out a pit, planting the tools, covering them up, and then carefully tamping down the earth with his boot. The events at the site have cast confusion over the early prehistory of Japan, as this same excavator was involved in many projects.

It is important to distinguish between fraud, as practiced at Piltdown and Kama-takamori, and error. Fraud is inimical to scientific research, while error plays a large role in increasing our knowledge of the past. A fraud is an intentional attempt to deceive. An error is a false interpretation based on the best available evidence. Errors often form the basis for further testing and refutation of a scientific theory.

REFERENCE: Frank Spencer. (1990). *Piltdown: A Scientific Forgery*. Oxford, UK: Oxford University Press.

◀ A painting of the examination of the Piltdown skull. This painting underscores the fact that this forgery was perpetrated on the scientific establishment of the time.

*Homo habilis.* Contemporary with *Paranthropus* was a very different hominin living in East Africa. This hominin lacked the heavy chewing muscles and large teeth characteristic of *Paranthropus*. What is most remarkable about it is its brain size, which had a range of 500 to 800 cubic centimeters. This was the first primate with such a large brain and also the earliest species to be assigned to the genus *Homo*. *Homo habilis* is known from sites in East Africa dating to between 2.5 million and 1.6 million years ago, including Olduvai Gorge, Tanzania, and Koobi Fora, Kenya (Wood and Richmond 2000).

*Homo erectus.* The next member of genus *Homo* to appear in the fossil record is **Homo erectus.** The oldest evidence of *Homo erectus* dates to the period between 1.9 million and 1.5 million years ago. *Homo erectus* fossils are known from East Africa and South Africa, as well as from sites in Europe and Asia. Some paleoanthropologists separate the earliest *Homo erectus* fossils from sites in Africa into a distinct species called *Homo ergaster* (Wood and Collard 1999).

▶ *Homo habilis,* the earliest member of the genus *Homo,* is found on sites dating between 2.5 and 1.6 million years ago.

▶ *Homo erectus* is the first member of the hominin lineage to spread out of Africa.

The discovery of the complete skeleton of a juvenile adolescent *Homo erectus* at the site of Nariokotome, Kenya, has provided a unique picture of this hominin species (Leakey and Walker 1993). The fossil found at Nariokotome is the skeleton of a boy who was approximately 160 cm (5', 3") tall when he died, roughly one-and-a-half million years ago (see photo on this page). Not only was he tall, but he also was thin, with a body shape typical of tropical populations among modern humans. He lived on the rich floodplain grasslands along the banks of a channel of the Omo River, in a landscape that was mostly open grassland and swamps, with trees limited to the river's edge and high spots. It is unclear why the boy died. There is no evidence of any trauma or attack by a carnivore. The only evidence of pathology is a pocket of gum disease related to the loss of one of his milk teeth. It is possible that infection of this inflammation was the cause of death.

## 3.2 SETTING THE SCENE

The lives of early hominins left behind few traces. The only remains are the stone tools and bones discarded as they moved around the landscape. The richest context for the recovery of early hominin archaeological sites is the **East African Rift Valley.** The stone tools found on early hominin sites are grouped as belonging to the Lower Paleolithic, or, as it is known in Africa, the Early Stone Age. The Oldowan and the Acheulian are the two main industries identified within the Lower Paleolithic.

## The East African Rift Valley

The East African Rift Valley is a massive geological feature stretching from Malawi in southern Africa to Turkey and Syria in the Middle East. This formation can be thought of as an enormous trough that is in constant formation as the surface of the earth pulls apart along the rift. Three characteristics of the Rift Valley make it invaluable in the search for early hominin sites. The first is that, because it is a trough, it is filling up with sediments. It is thus a depositional environment that preserves archaeological and paleontological sites. Second, because it is tectonically active, there is a great deal of erosion. The result is the formation of badlands landscapes in which enormous deposits of earth are cut by gullies and ravines. Third, as a sort of icing on the cake, the Rift Valley is also volcanically active, so there are levels of volcanic ash that can be dated using the argon method (see Toolbox on page 88).

**Olduvai Gorge.** Of all the gullies and ravines of the East African Rift Valley, none is more impressive or more important for the study of human evolution than

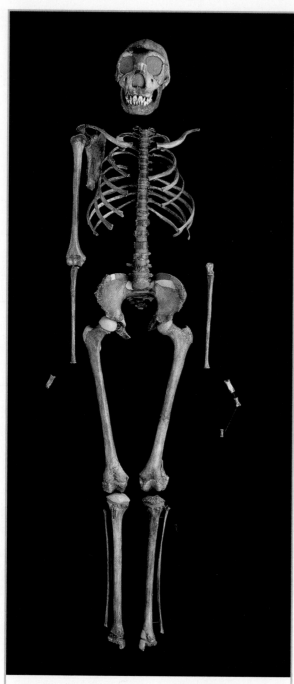

**T**he Nariokotome *Homo erectus* fossil gives a very complete picture of the anatomy of this species. Notice how low the cranial vault (forehead) is compared to modern humans.

The **East African Rift Valley** is a geological feature stretching from East Africa to the Middle East and is the location of many important early hominin sites.

**Olduvai Gorge,** Tanzania. Olduvai Gorge has come to be synonymous with the names Lewis and Mary Leakey. The Leakeys' decades of research at Olduvai revolutionized ideas of prehistory and brought attention to the tremendous potential of the East African Rift Valley for the study of early hominins. Two million years ago in the area that is now Olduvai Gorge, there was a small lake surrounded by a grassland and marsh landscape within a large basin or depression. The lake was salty, but it supported a diversity of fish and reptiles, including crocodile. The surrounding grassland and swamps of the basin supported mammals such as elephants, bovids (ancestors of cows), hippos, antelopes, and hominins. Over time, the basin filled with sediments carried by wind and water, until it was scarcely discernible on the landscape of the Serengeti Plain.

Two hundred thousand years ago, modern streams began to carve a canyon through the soft sediments filling the basin at Olduvai. Over time, this erosion created the spectacular landscape of Olduvai Gorge, a main gorge and side gorge that meet to form a Y shape. The erosion that created the Gorge provides a point of access to the fossils and stone tools deposited around Lake Olduvai. Without the erosion, this critical evidence would remain inaccessible, locked under tens of meters of accumulated sediments. Research at Olduvai first involves walking along the gorge, looking for places where tools or fossils are eroding out of the cliffs. As one walks up the walls of the gorge, one is walking up through geological time. In the spots where material is found eroding out of the sections, it is possible in some cases to dig into the cliff face to expose ancient living surfaces.

The sequence at Olduvai Gorge is based on geological rather than archaeological strata. Bed I is the earliest unit, Bed IV the latest, and overlying Bed IV is a unit known as the Masek Beds. Table 3.2 on the next page gives a timeline of the formation of the beds.

> Hominin fossils and archaeological sites have been
> ▶ discovered at **Olduvai Gorge,** Tanzania.

**O**lduvai Gorge is a deep accumulation of sediments that have been cut through by erosion. The geological stratigraphy is visible in the bands of different colored layers in the exposed cliff face.

TABLE 3.2

| Masek Beds | 0.6–0.4 million years ago |
|---|---|
| Bed IV | 0.8–0.6 million years ago |
| Bed III | 1.15–0.8 million years ago |
| Bed II | 1.7–1.15 million years ago |
| Bed I | 1.9–1.7 million years ago |

## Lower Paleolithic

The period during which early hominins began making stone tools is known as the **Lower Paleolithic**. In Africa, the Lower Paleolithic is often called the Early Stone Age. The Lower Paleolithic includes two major industries: the Oldowan and the Acheulian. An archaeological industry is a period characterized by a certain approach to making stone tools. Prehistorians working on very early periods tend to be cautious about using the term "culture," because it implies that the groups which lived during those periods resemble modern cultures in sharing a common set of beliefs and values and, in many cases, also a common language. We do not know whether that is true of the people who made Oldowan and Acheulian types of stone tools; therefore, the term "industry" is used.

**The Oldowan.** The **Oldowan** was defined on the basis of the archaeological material from Olduvai Gorge Beds I and II dated between 1.9 million and 1.15 million years ago. The question of which hominin made the Oldowan tools is not resolved.

The **Lower Paleolithic** is the period when hominins began producing stone tools. The Lower Paleolithic covers the time between two-and-a-half million years ago and roughly 200,000 years ago.

The **Oldowan** is the earliest well characterized archaeological industry dating between 1.9 and 1.15 million years ago.

**A**n archaeologist uses a chopper to break a bone for marrow.

*Paranthropus, Homo habilis,* and *Homo erectus* all lived during the time Oldowan tools were manufactured. Fossils of all these hominins are found either on or in near proximity to Oldowan archaeological sites.

Oldowan tools, like those shown in the photo on this page, have been described as a least-effort solution to creating sharp-edged tools (Schick and Toth 1993). The basic distinction is between flakes and cores. Flakes are slivers of rock that have been struck off of a stone. Cores are the pieces off of which flakes have been struck. The characteristic tool of the Oldowan is the chopper. To manufacture a chopper, one begins with a rounded stone and strikes a series of flakes off one edge. The process can be continued by flipping the stone over and striking a series of flakes along the same edge off the other side of the stone. When Mary Leakey began work at Olduvai Gorge, she identified choppers as tools and imagined them as being useful for butchering animals. When archaeologists began making Oldowan tools and using them to butcher carcasses, they found that choppers were not very useful. These experiments demonstrated that it was the sharp-edged flakes that were most useful. As a result, it has been argued that the actual desired product was the flake and that the chopper was simply waste from manufacture. An alternative is that both flakes *and* choppers were used. The choppers might have been useful for working wood or breaking bones to get at marrow, while the flakes were used for butchery. Unfortunately, we have no preserved wood from Oldowan sites.

**The Acheulian.** The earliest **Acheulian** industries in East Africa date to the period between 1.7 and one-and-a-half million years before the present. The date for the end of the Acheulian is currently unclear, but it is in the range between 400,000 and 200,000 years ago. Acheulian sites are found throughout Africa, including major sites in both eastern and southern Africa, as well as on sites in Europe, the Middle East, and India. The Acheulian appears at the same time as the first appearance of *Homo erectus* and the extinction of *Homo habilis.*

The characteristic tool of the Acheulian is the biface. Unlike the Oldowan, the Acheulian can hardly be described as a least-effort solution. The Acheulian **bifaces**

> The **Acheulian** industry in Africa dates between 1.7 million and approximately 200,000 years ago.

> **Bifaces** are the characteristic tools of the African Acheulian. Bifaces include handaxes and cleavers.

**A**n Acheulian cleaver (left) and handaxe (right). Archaeologists stress the symmetry of many Acheulian handaxes.

# TOOLBOX:
## Stone Tools

The archaeological study of stone tools is known as lithic analysis, and the manufacture of stone tools is known as knapping. When looking at stone tools, archaeologists see not only the formal properties of the artifact (color, shape, size, weight), but also evidence of how the tool was manufactured and used. To understand the process of knapping, archaeologists take great care to recover all stone artifacts, including waste products from manufacture.

Lower Paleolithic tools were made by delivering a sharp blow to a rock in order to break off a smaller piece, a technique known as percussion. The piece that is struck off is called a flake, and the piece off of which the flake is struck is the core. The goal of percussion can be to produce either flake tools or core tools. In many cases, both flakes and cores were used as tools.

Flakes have several important features. The surface that is split off of the core, known as the ventral face, has a convex feature called the bulb of percussion at the end where it was struck. This end is known as the proximal end of the flake. The bulb of percussion is produced when the force of the blow enters the rock. The force enters the rock as a cone, much like the cone produced when a bullet strikes glass or a stone is thrown into a body of water. The force from the blow ripples out from this initial cone, eventually splitting the flake from the core.

Percussion techniques can be classified on the basis of the way the blow is delivered. In *direct percussion,* the blow is delivered directly to the core. In *hard-hammer direct percussion,* the hammer used is a rock. In *soft-hammer direct percussion,* the hammer used is either an antler or hardwood. The use of a soft hammer allows the knapper to produce thin flakes with a less pronounced bulb of percussion. *Indirect percussion* involves the use of an intermediary device known as a punch between the hammer and the core. The advantage of indirect percussion is that the precise placement of the blow can be controlled. Indirect percussion is often used in making long blades or shaping arrowheads.

Pressure techniques follow the same principles as percussion, except that the force is applied by pressure rather than by a blow. In practice, the knappers press the tip of an antler or, in some cases, a copper tip against the edge of a tool to push off a flake. Pressure techniques involve the exertion of a great deal of force by the knapper, and usually the entire upper body is involved in exerting the force. Pressure techniques are usually used in the very fine shaping of tools. Because no blow is involved, the bulb of percussion is extremely diffuse, and very thin flakes can be removed.

In some cases, a flake would simply be used as struck. In other cases, however, a core or a flake was carefully modified to create a desired shape or edge. The careful secondary shaping of a core or flake is known as retouch.

It is critical that the knapper have control of the way the rock fractures. Many rocks are not suitable for these techniques, because they either fracture along cleavage planes in the rock or crumble when struck. The stones used by knappers are brittle, are fine grained, and do not have internal features that determine the direction in which they break. A wide variety of rocks, including flint (also known as chert), basalt, and obsidian, fits these criteria and can be used to make stone tools.

## FIGURE 3.1

**Cores and flakes bear traces of the manufacture process.**

Core     Retouch     Bulb of Percussion     Flake     Flake Ventral Surface

are better described as the earliest evidence of design. Bifaces can be either hand-axes, if they are pointed at the end, or cleavers, if they have a wide working end. Bifaces were carefully and skillfully fashioned tools and not simply cores. One aspect of the design of bifaces is that they are often symmetrical with reference to a central axis. The actual function of these tools has remained enigmatic. Clearly, they were highly effective tools if hominins continued to use them for over one million years. The handaxe was perhaps the most successful tool humans have ever invented. But what was it used for? Recently an archaeologist studied botanical remains known as phytoliths on handaxes from the site of Peninj, Tanzania. Phytoliths are a mineral element of plant cells that survive after the rest of the plant has disintegrated. The phytoliths adhering to the handaxes from Peninj suggest that these tools were used for woodworking. There is some evidence of worked wood at the Acheulian site of Kolambo Falls, Zambia.

# 3.3 THE ORIGIN OF TOOL USE

Tool use is often considered a trait that separates humans from animals. Research by ethologists—scientists who study animal behavior—casts doubt on tool use as a uniquely human behavior. Nonetheless, the development of stone tool technology marks an important point in human evolution. Stone tools dating to 2.4 million years ago are the earliest-known archaeological artifacts. Recent research indicates that the manufacture of these early stone tools was a more complex process than had been thought.

## Tool Use by Animals

Most evidence for tool use and manufacture comes from studies of chimpanzees and the other great apes. However, surprising evidence for tool manufacture by birds has emerged in a study of crows on New Caledonia, a string of islands approximately 900 miles northeast of Australia. While observing the behavior of the New Caledonian crows, Gavin Hunt noticed that the birds were carrying objects in their beaks and using the objects to extract insects from trees. Closer investigation showed that the objects the crows were using were strips cut out of

**A** New Caledonian crow grasps a hooked tool used to probe for insects.

leaves from pandanus trees. The edges of these leaves are spiked, so when a strip is cut off of the edge of the leaf, it has a series of hooks. It is these hooks that the birds use to search out their prey. Hunt found that the birds cut strips off the leaves such that the strips were often stepped in shape and that the hooks pointed towards the narrow end.

Jane Goodall was among the first to document tool use by chimpanzees in the wild. The chimpanzee group she studied at Gombe in Tanzania used twigs, bark, or grass to fish termites and ants out of mounds. In subsequent years, tool use was discovered in a number of distinct groups of chimpanzees. Perhaps the most dramatic of these discoveries comes from the studies of the chimpanzees in the **Taï Forest,** Ivory Coast (Boesch and Boesch-Achermann 2000). The Taï Forest chimpanzees use stone hammers and anvils to break open hard nuts. The tools are not manufactured, but rather used as found. However, the use of these tools is a skilled activity that young chimpanzees learn by observing their mothers over a period of years. The skills they learn include both the selection of appropriate hammers and anvils and the appropriate use of force.

On their own, dipping for ants and cracking nuts seem rather modest examples of tools use. However, an interesting pattern emerges when the distribution of chimpanzee tool-use behaviors is examined across Africa (Whiten et al. 1999): The tools that are used and the way they are used are not uniform across the continent, but rather are distinctive of particular groups. This pattern is true not only of tool use behaviors, but also of other behaviors, such as greeting and grooming. Ecological factors alone do not dictate where particular tools are used. For example, there are populations of chimpanzees living in West Africa with the same nuts available as

> The chimpanzees living in the **Taï Forest,** Ivory Coast, used stone hammers and anvils as tools to break open nuts.

**A** chimpanzee in Liberia, West Africa uses a hammerstone and anvil to crack nuts. Notice how the intent gaze of the chimpanzee guides its actions, much like the baseball player urged to "keep your eye on the ball."

those found in the Taï Forest, but that do not use stone hammers to break the nuts. These groups either ignore the nuts completely or break the nuts with their teeth, which is a far less efficient technique. These observations have led some ethologists to argue that chimpanzees have culture.

In 1990, a group of archaeologists and primatologists began an experiment to determine whether they could teach Kanzi, a pygmy chimpanzee born and raised at the Language Research Center at Georgia State University, to make stone tools (Toth et al. 1993, Schick et al. 1999). Kanzi was shown a box with a transparent door held closed by a piece of rope. A piece of fruit was placed inside the box, and Kanzi was shown that the rope could be cut with a stone flake struck off a rock with a hammer. Kanzi was then shown how to create sharp flakes by striking one piece of rock (a hammer) against another (a core). Kanzi was able to carry out this task; however, his preferred method was to smash a rock by throwing it onto the concrete floor of the laboratory. In all cases, the method of flake production was very crude. Still, Kanzi did manage to produce some tools bearing a resemblance to the earliest tools produced by hominins.

Kanzi's skill at breaking rocks seems to indicate that the ability of chimpanzees to manufacture tools is at best quite limited. However, this test might actually give an incomplete illustration of chimpanzees' capabilities for tool manufacture. The ability to manufacture stone tools might have more to do with the qualities of the human hand than any abstract conceptual abilities. Humans are unique in having a thumb and fingers that are able to rotate, allowing for a wide range of grips. Chimpanzee hands, like all ape hands, are largely limited to folding their fingers over objects or gripping small objects between the thumb and the index finger (Panger et al. 2002). Perhaps Kanzi's difficulties in stone tool manufacture reflect the limited range of grips he is capable of relative to the grips the human demonstrator is able to assume.

## The Archaeological Evidence

The earliest occupation at Olduvai Gorge, in Bed I, dates to approximately 1.8 million years ago. On the basis of discoveries made at **Hadar**, it is now clear that the earliest stone tools are at least half a million years older. The Hadar region, located in the East African Rift Valley in Ethiopia, has produced some of the most important fossils of australopithicines, including Lucy. In the early 1990s, two teams discovered stone tools at sites in the Hadar in levels that date to approximately two-and-a-half million years ago.

At the Gona site, close to three thousand stone tools were found in a single layer in two excavation areas covering an area of 22 square meters (Semaw 2000). The tools were discovered in a clay soil that shows no signs of river activity. Although the tools are simple, there is no question that they were manufactured by hominins. Given what is known about the geological context, it is not possible that any geological process produced the uniform patterns of flaking found on these tools. The major types of tools are sharp-edged flakes and cores, including choppers.

The archaeological horizon at the Gona site is sandwiched between layers of volcanic ash known as tuff (see Figure 3.2) (Semaw et al. 1997). Fortunately, these tuff layers are ideal for argon dating. The BKT-2L tuff, which underlies the site, dates to 2.9 million years ago, while the AST-2.75 tuff, which overlies the site, is dated to 2.3 million years ago. Therefore, the stone tools were produced and deposited sometime during the time interval between 2.9 million and 2.3 million years ago.

The oldest-known stone tools are found at the Gona site in the **Hadar** region of Ethiopia dated to two-and-a-half million years ago.

# TOOLBOX:
## Argon Dating

- Based on the decay of a radioactive isotope of argon into potassium.
- Dates the eruption of volcanic ash or lava.

Unlike paleomagnetic dating, argon dating provides a numerical date rather than assigning a deposit to an epoch or event. Argon dating works by means of an accumulation clock, where the unit that is accumulating is $^{40}Ar$, an isotope of the element argon. Isotopes are forms of a chemical element that have the same number of protons and electrons, but that vary in the number of neutrons in the nucleus. Because $^{40}K$, an isotope of the element potassium, decays into $^{40}Ar$ at a constant rate, the rate at which $^{40}Ar$ accumulates is also a constant.

The trick with any accumulation clock is that the clock must be set to zero at the point in time that is of interest. Argon diffuses rapidly at high temperatures while potassium does not. This means that when a material containing argon is heated, the argon will be diffused out of the material while the potassium remains stable. If a material containing both $^{40}Ar$ and $^{40}K$ is heated to a very high temperature, the product will be a material containing $^{40}K$ and no $^{40}Ar$. From that point on, $^{40}K$ will begin to decay, resulting in a steady accumulation of $^{40}Ar$.

Fortunately for archaeologists, the magma that explodes out of volcanoes to form ash or lava is rich in potassium. The magma is superheated until it cools after eruption. As a result, any volcanic material can be dated by determining how much $^{40}Ar$ has accumulated since cooling. Time zero is the point of eruption, and the time since eruption is determined by measuring the accumulation of $^{40}Ar$.

In potassium–argon dating, the measure of accumulation of $^{40}Ar$ is based on the ratio of $^{40}K$ to $^{40}Ar$. The development of single-crystal argon dating has significantly improved the reliability of the argon method. With the use of lasers to vaporize the sample, it is possible to date single crystals of lava or ash by measuring the ratio of $^{39}Ar$ to $^{40}Ar$. Argon dating has been critical to the study of human evolution, particularly at East

African sites such as Olduvai Gorge. Unfortunately, in areas with limited volcanic activity, it is not possible to use the method.

▲ Eruption of ash from Mount St. Helens, Washington in 1980. Such an eruption can blanket a wide area in a layer of ash that can be dated using the argon method.

Another team of researchers working near Gona at the site of A.L. 666 has found a smaller assemblage of tools from a similar context (Kimbel et al. 1996). Adding to the interest of this discovery is a hominin fossil found from the same level as that in which the stone tools were found. The fossil is a well-preserved maxilla (palate) that has been identified as belonging to genus *Homo*. It was not possible to determine what species the fossil belongs to, due to its fragmentary nature.

## FIGURE 3.2

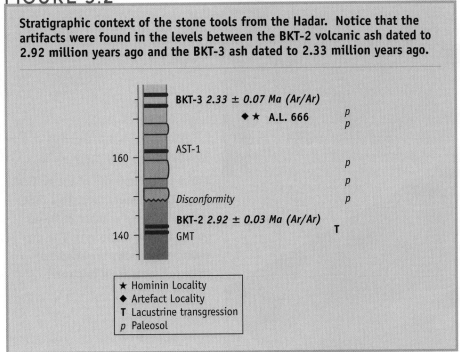

**Stratigraphic context of the stone tools from the Hadar.** Notice that the artifacts were found in the levels between the BKT-2 volcanic ash dated to 2.92 million years ago and the BKT-3 ash dated to 2.33 million years ago.

The tools from the Hadar site seem to be the simplest possible form of tools showing the least possible elaboration. Indeed, were it not for the geological context, one might even cast doubt on whether these tools even are evidence of human manufacture.

Lokalalei, located in the west Turkana region of northern Kenya, is yet another East African Rift Valley site to produce evidence of tool manufacture from an early date (Roche et al. 1999). The age of **Lokalalei,** based on the argon dating method, is approximately 2.3 million years, so the site is younger than the Hadar sites. At Lokalalei 2C, a horizontal area of 17 square meters has been excavated, and slightly over two thousand stone flakes and cores were recovered from a single surface. A wide range of animal remains was also found, including twelve mammal species as well as reptiles and fish. There is no indication of cut marks or other signs of human activity on the animal bones.

In studying the stone tools from Lokalalei, Hélène Roche and her colleagues focused on trying to understand the process through which the tools were manufactured. By carefully fitting the flakes back onto the cores from which they were struck, the researchers showed that the simple tools at Lokalalei could have been produced through a fairly elaborate process. The cores included coarse-grained cobbles from which only two or three flakes were removed, but also more fine-grained cobbles and pebbles from which up to thirty flakes were removed. The analysis of how the flakes were removed in these lengthy sequences demonstrates that the knapping was not random and haphazard, but rather followed a clear and consistent strategy. The discovery of the complexity of tool manufacture at Lokalalei demonstrates that the first stone tools were not the simplest of all possible tools, only a step removed from the hammers used by the chimpanzees in the Taï Forest and similar to the flakes produced by Kanzi. The first tools manufactured by hominins involved a sequence of manufacture more complex than any process known from studies of animal behavior (see photo on next page).

Analysis of the stone tools from **Lokalalei,** Kenya, dated to 2.3 million years ago demonstrates that the earliest tool manufacture was a complex process.

A refit core from Lokalalei, Kenya shows the complexity of the earliest stone tool manufacture. This refit includes a large number of flakes struck from a single core. The diagram below shows the stages of flake removals from this core.

# 3.4 HUNTING AND SHARING FOOD

Western philosophy has developed two opposing pictures of "man in a state of nature." For Thomas Hobbes, humans were essentially violent, and it was only through the development of institutions that it was possible for humanity to tame its destructive nature. Other philosophers, such as Jean Jacques Rousseau, imagined a life of leisure and peace that was disrupted only by the development of social inequality. Prehistorians have carried this debate into the study of early hominins. While some archaeologists view early hominins as killer apes, others envision societies of hunter–gatherers sharing meat and other food.

## Were They Hunters?

As a young professor of anatomy in South Africa, Raymond Dart was the first to identify the remains of an australopithecine. Dart subsequently became convinced that australopithecines used tools made of fractured pieces of bone. He labeled these tools the osteodontokeratic (bone, tooth, and horn) culture. The tools Dart identified included cutting tools, scoops, and spears. Dart developed a vision of australopithecines as brutal hunters "slaking their ravenous thirst with the hot blood of victims and greedily devouring livid writhing flesh" (Dart 1953: 209).

In the 1970s, archaeologists began to question Dart's interpretation with a series of studies into how bones are accumulated and what processes affect bones

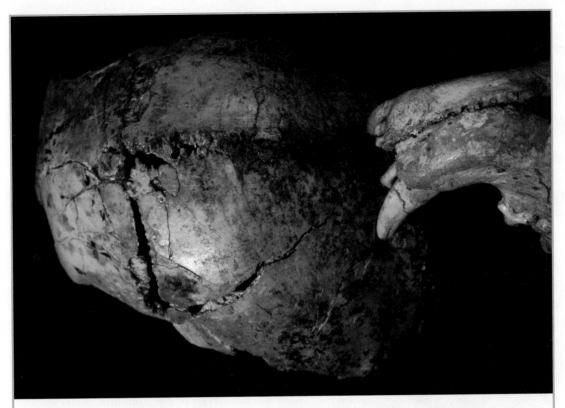

The hunted not the hunter. The skull of an *Australopithicine* from Swartkrans, South Africa, with a puncture wound that matches the spacing of the lower canines of a leopard.

after their burial. Such studies, known as taphonomic analyses, have included scrambling into hyena dens to collect bones gnawed by these carnivores. When bones from hyena dens were compared with the bones Dart had identified as tools, it became clear that the "tools" were actually produced by carnivores' gnawing. It also turns out that the hominins at these sites were not the hunters, but rather the hunted. In a particularly vivid illustration, the puncture marks on the skull of a juvenile australopithecine from the site of Swartkrans closely match the spacing of the lower canines of a leopard.

Some archaeologists began to question whether early hominins were even capable of hunting large animals. Lewis Binford vocally advanced the idea that early hominins were scavengers, living off carcasses left behind by carnivores or fallen through natural mortality. Binford left archaeologists with a tremendous challenge: Rather than being able to assume that the bones found on archaeological sites were the traces of human hunting, it now became necessary to prove that those bones were neither scavenged nor brought onto the site by geological processes.

Before looking at the archaeological evidence, it is worth considering whether it is even plausible to think that early hominins were hunters. Here again, information from the study of wild populations of chimpanzees is useful. There has long been a popular conception of chimpanzees as peaceful vegetarians, but we now know that this is far from the truth. Chimpanzees fight, often to the death, and chimpanzees hunt. The range of animals hunted by chimpanzees is quite limited, including small monkeys and very small antelope. Chimpanzees hunt without tools, but rely on cooperation to catch and kill animals. When the Taï Forest chimpanzees hunt monkeys, some members of the group chase them up a tree, while

A chimpanzee in Tanzania eating monkey meat. Notice that the adult is accompanied by a child, showing the social context of chimpanzee meat consumption.

At the **FLK North** site in Olduvai Gorge, the remains of an elephant were found together with stone tools.

others wait quietly in a strategic spot to catch the monkeys as they run away. The monkeys are usually killed by biting and then ripped apart and eaten on the spot. The hunters are males, and the distribution of meat from the hunt seems to be an important element of how particular males gain dominance in the group.

From the way chimpanzees hunt, it is safe to assume that early hominins might have hunted small animals. It should be kept in mind, however, that early hominins would have lacked the chimpanzee's prominent canine teeth and their ability to move rapidly through trees. What is most interesting about chimpanzee hunting is that it is a group activity characterized by cooperation. It is likely that early hominins were capable of similar behavior. The problem posed by Binford is that the animal bones found on early hominin sites are not only of small animals, but also of midsize animals such as antelope and very large animals, including hippopotamuses and elephants. Could early hominins armed with choppers and flakes have taken down such animals, even if the hominins were working cooperatively?

It turns out that it is very difficult to prove archaeologically that animals were hunted rather than scavenged. Perhaps the clearest evidence would be a site with the remains of a single animal carcass and stone tools. One such site is **FLK North** in Olduvai Gorge, Bed I (see Figure 3.3). FLK North is a site with six distinct occupation levels. In the lowest, the nearly complete skeleton of an extinct elephant (*Elephas recki*) was found together with a small number of choppers and flakes. At least one cut mark from a stone tool has been found on the elephant bones. Fragments of a wide range of smaller animals were also found concentrated in the area around the elephant skeleton. This is clearly a butchering site, but the Leakeys were uncertain to what degree the kill was planned. One possibility is that the elephant was "deliberately driven . . . into a swamp to be slaughtered" (Leakey 1971: 64). However, it is also possible that the hominins came upon an elephant carcass that they then scavenged for meat. Even at a site as seemingly simple as FLK North, it is not possible to determine with certainty that the hominins actually were hunting.

Although the association of stone tools with the remains of very large animals such as elephants might best be explained as the result of hominin scavenging, the same is not clearly the case for midsized to large animals. Field studies of the bones left behind after carnivores finish with a kill have raised a significant challenge to the theory that early hominins were scavengers. In general, these studies show that very little is left behind and that most of the carcass, and even many of the bones, is consumed. If the early hominins were collecting the leftovers from the meals of lions and other carnivores, their yield would have been very small.

# FIGURE 3.3

**The plan of the excavation of the elephant and associated stone tools at the FLK North site, Olduvai Gorge.**

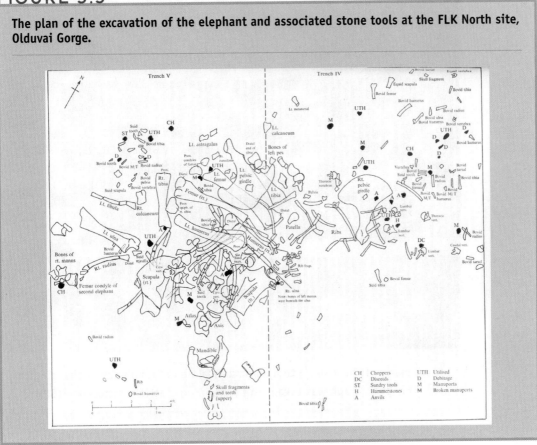

The most promising studies of how early hominins acquired meat are studies of the surface of the animal bones found on archaeological sites. If these bones are well preserved, they bear marks of three distinct processes: (1) gnawing by carnivores, which leaves characteristic pit marks and striations; (2) butchery with stone tools, resulting in clearly identifiable cut marks; and (3) smashing the bones to gain access to their marrow, which produces distinctive fracture patterns known as bulbs of percussion. By studying which bones show evidence of what kind of modification, researchers can develop a picture of meat processing that provides clues as to whether the animals were hunted or scavenged. Studies such as these point to a complex interaction among carnivores, scavengers, and early hominins.

Almost all early hominin sites with well-preserved bone surfaces produce evidence of carnivore gnawing, cut marks, and bulbs of percussion. The problem therefore is not whether both hominins and scavengers were involved in the formation of the recovered bone assemblage; rather, the difficulty lies in determining the order of events. Did carnivores kill the animals before hominins scavenged the remains, or did hominins kill animals whose remains were then scavenged? What was the role of smashing bones for marrow in this process? In the current state of research, the answer to these questions remains contentious. Some archaeologists, pointing to cut marks on the most meat-rich bones, argue that hominins had access to fresh kills. This pattern would not be expected if the hominins had access only to scraps of flesh that a carnivore left behind. However, others, emphasizing the frequency of carnivore gnaw marks on the midshaft of long bones, maintain that humans scavenged bones mostly for marrow. Such a pattern fits with studies of bone damage found when carnivores deflesh carcasses.

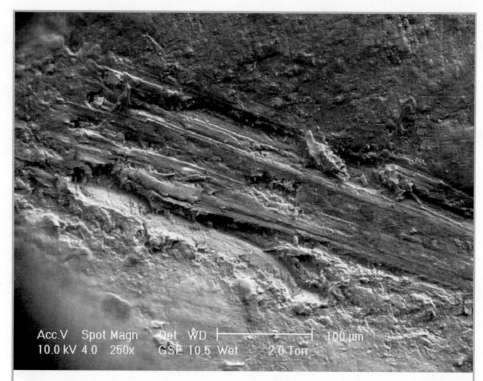

**A** cut mark left by a stone tool on an animal bone found on an archaeological site. This photograph was taken with a scanning electron microscope (SEM).

## Living Floors and Base Camps

When chimpanzees hunt, they consume the meat on the spot. They do share parts of the carcass, and as the ethologist Craig Stanford (1999: 201) has written, "meat eating is about politics as well as nutrition." For chimpanzees, the sharing of the meat plays an important role in creating the social structure of the group. Modern human groups that subsist on hunting and gathering place a great emphasis on sharing. On the basis of research on the !Kung San hunter–gatherers of Botswana, ethnographers have emphasized sharing as the fundamental ethos of such societies (Lee 2003). Unlike chimpanzee sharing, which takes place at the spot where the kill was made, sharing among hunter–gatherers takes place when meat is brought back to a camp. This distinction forms the basis of **the home-base/food-sharing model** developed by Glynn Isaac. According to this model, hominins created places on the landscape to which meat was brought for sharing among members of a community. According to Isaac, it is the ability to share and cooperate, rather than the ability to kill, that is the driving force behind human evolution.

> **The home-base/food-sharing model** developed by Glynn Isaac sees the sharing of meat at base camps as a fundamental part of the lives of early hominins.

> The stone circle found at the **DKI** site at Olduvai Gorge might be evidence of a temporary structure built on a home-base site.

**The Stone Circle at DKI.** When Isaac developed his home-base/food-sharing model, he had in mind site **DKI** in Bed I at Olduvai Gorge. Excavations at DKI in 1962 uncovered a circle of lava blocks on what the Leakeys identified as an "occupation floor"—a clearly defined level of animal bones and stone tools. The circle measures roughly 4 meters in diameter. Blocks are piled around the circumference to a maximum height of approximately 30 centimeters, and there are scattered stones on the inside of the circle. The Leakey's interpret this circle as the remains of a temporary shelter or windbreak of branches, which were then covered with

The stone circle at the DK site, Olduvai Gorge. Notice that part of the circle was destroyed in a trial excavation.

A shelter made by the Okombambi of Namibia that the Leakeys compared to the DK circle. Notice that flat stones are used at the base of the structure. How might such a construction result in the kind of circle found on the DK site?

grass or skin. In the area in and around the structure, stone tools and animal bones were found. The density of these remains was greater outside the stone circle than inside.

DKI offers a vivid picture of what an early hominin base camp would look like and suggests that these sites would have resembled the camps of modern human hunter–gatherers. However, there is some need for caution. The stone circle at DKI was found in a level immediately above the volcanic bedrock—the same material out of which the circle is constructed. The Leakeys note that "the area immediately outside the circle is relatively clear of loose stones, which become more numerous again at a distance of approximately 2 feet from the outer circumference" (Leakey 1971: 24). Thus, the possibility that the stone circle is a natural feature cannot be completely ruled out. The animal bones recovered from the DKI site included the bones of mid- and large-sized mammals, with crocodile and turtle bones predominating. This suggests that the stone circle was at the edge of a swamp or lagoon.

**Assessing the Archaeological Evidence.** As was the case with the distinction between hunting and scavenging, it appears that the answer to the question of which activities led to the concentrations of stone tools and animal bones found on archaeological sites is complex. In some cases, the association of stone tools and animal bones is the result of geological processes, primarily transport by rivers or streams. However, most other sites suggest an overlay of activities that took place at a single location. Such a situation is referred to as a **palimpsest**—an archaeological

> A **palimpsest** is an archaeological site produced by a series of distinct brief occupations.

surface that is the result of multiple distinct occupations. A palimpsest exists on a site that was revisited on at least several occasions and is distinct from a base camp that a single group continuously occupied. From this perspective, the early hominin sites were built up over time as different butchery and meat-processing events took place. For example, at FLK North, the elephant butchery was distinct from the events that led to the deposition of the fragmentary remains of other animals. It is possible that the DK site is a palimpsest site, rather than the base camp the Leakeys reconstructed. One problem with maintaining that DK is a base camp is that doubts have been raised about the evidence for the remains of shelters at the site. Equally problematic is the location of the site in close proximity to a source of freshwater. It seems unlikely that such an area, which would attract predators, would be selected as a place for sharing meat from kills.

But if these sites were not base camps, why did early hominins continuously return to the same spots on the landscape? The DK site is only one of a number of early sites with large concentrations of stone tools and animal bones. One possibility is that hominins were drawn by natural features, such as tree cover, that would have provided shelter from carnivores and scavengers. Richard Potts (1988) has suggested that stone tools might have been cached at certain locations and carcasses dragged to those locations for processing. This is certainly possible, but it does not explain every case. For example, at FLK North, only a small number of stone tools were found.

There is clear evidence that early hominins moved stone tools around the landscape, and the same appears to be true for parts of animal carcasses. However, it is still not possible to demonstrate unequivocally that the animal carcasses were coming into base camps where the members of hominin groups shared the meat in the fashion that is so characteristic of societies of modern hunter–gatherers.

## The Use of Fire

There is very little evidence for the controlled use of fire from Oldowan and Acheulian sites in Africa. At site FxJj 20 in the Okote member at Koobi Fora, two round features roughly 1 meter in diameter are thought to be evidence of the use of fire. The soil in these circles is reddish in color, and the magnetic properties of the soil suggest that it was burnt. At the site of **Chesowanja**, Kenya, dated to 1.4 million years ago, lumps of burnt clay were found in the same context as stone tools and animal bones. The excavators argue that these lumps are the remains of a hearth that has become broken up and dispersed. Because the possibility that the burnt clay was the result of natural fires cannot be ruled out, the lumps of clay from Chesowanja cannot be used as evidence that early hominins used fire.

> The site of **Chesowanja**, Kenya, dated to 1.4 million years ago, has produced tentative evidence for the use of fire by early hominins.

# 3.5 THE EXPANSION OF THE HOMININ WORLD

By 1.4 million years ago, the hominin radiation was over. Of the four genera that flourished beginning four million years ago, only genus *Homo* survived. Within genus *Homo*, there was only a single species, *Homo erectus*, and a sophisticated tool technology, the Acheulian, had developed in Africa. Overlapping with the end of the hominin radiation, the hominin colonization of areas outside of Africa began. In a **dispersal** event, a single species dramatically expands its geographic range. Dispersal, which often involves a species moving into a new ecological niche, contrasts with radiation in that it involves a single species expanding both its

> In a **dispersal** event, a single species dramatically expands its geographic range.

geographical range and the range of ecological niches it inhabits. By contrast, in a radiation event, a wide diversity of new species evolves, each of which adapts to a particular ecological niche. What took place in the hominin lineage around four million years ago was a radiation. The first event of hominin dispersal began around 1.8 million years ago, soon after the first appearance of *Homo erectus* in Africa.

What is the significance of the spread of *Homo erectus* beyond Africa? We need to take care not to view this process through the lens of the heroic modern image of the explorer. The dispersal of *Homo erectus* does not track the paths of individual wanderers; rather, it follows the expansion of populations into new ecological settings. What is it about *Homo erectus* that allowed this species to move into areas that earlier hominins did not occupy? Did *Homo erectus* possess some new ability that spurred its expansion? We will return to these questions at the end of the chapter, but first we must follow the archaeological evidence for the timing of the dispersal.

## Ubeidiya and Dmanisi

The site of **Ubeidiya** is located south of the Sea of Galilee in Israel. The Sea of Galilee is part of the northern extension of the East African Rift Valley, and the setting of the site is not very different from that at Olduvai Gorge. When the site was occupied, it was at the edge of a large freshwater lake in an area occupied by a wide diversity of mostly African species of animals. The stone tools from Ubeidiya also look much like the material from Olduvai. The lower part of the sequence includes tools characteristic of the Oldowan, including choppers and flake tools along with a small number of crude handaxes.

> ▶ The site of **Ubeidiya**, Israel, dated to between 1.4 and 1.0 million years ago, is one of the earliest archaeological sites outside of Africa.

The dating of Ubeidiya is complex and draws on a number of methods. The site can be dated to the period between 1.4 million and 1.0 million years ago, with the most likely date being 1.4 million years ago. Fragmentary hominin remains from the site are attributed to *Homo erectus*.

The prehistoric site of **Dmanisi** was discovered during the excavation of a medieval village. When the excavators were clearing out the cellars that had been dug into the ground by the site's inhabitants, they found bones eroding out of the earthen walls. A paleontologist identified the bones as fossils dating to around 1.8 million years ago. In 1994, a limited paleontological project began to recover more of these fossils, which, to the surprise of the excavators, included a *Homo erectus* mandible (jaw). This spectacular discovery was followed by the identification of stone tools on the site and the recovery of three fairly complete crania of *Homo erectus*.

> ▶ The site of **Dmanisi**, Georgia, dated between 1.7 million and 1.8 million years ago, is the oldest known archaeological site outside of Africa.

The dating of the Dmanisi site is of critical importance to understanding the initial spread of hominins out of Africa. Although dated using the argon method to 1.8 million years ago, the lava at the site is below the level in which the hominin remains were found. Accordingly, following the law of superposition, one can only assume that the hominin occupation was *later* than 1.8 million years ago. Paleomagnetic dating adds some information, constraining the hominin occupation to between 1.8 million and 1.1 million years ago. However, some animal species, including both large mammals and rodents, found with the hominin remains were either extinct or not found in the region after 1.7 million years ago. For this reason, Dmanisi is widely accepted today as the earliest evidence of human occupation outside of Africa.

The nature of the hominin activity at Dmanisi remains unclear. None of the animal bones have signs of cut marks, and it does not seem likely that the hominins had anything to do with accumulating these bones. The stone tools are found widely dispersed on the site and are not found in association with the hominin and animal fossils. The fossils and some of the tools come from irregularly shaped pits

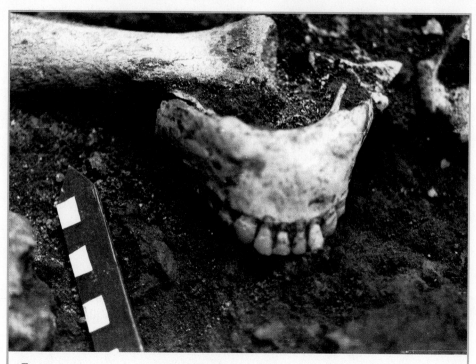
▲ *Homo erectus* mandible in its find spot at the site of Dmanisi.

in the soil. It is possible that these pits were formed by water action that created depressions into which hominin and animal carcasses tumbled. Alternatively, the pits could have been natural features altered and used as dens by carnivores.

The stone tools found at Dmanisi are mostly simple flakes (De Lumley et al. 2005). There are none of the bifaces that are characteristic of the Acheulian. A small number of choppers have been found at the site.

## East Asia

The discovery at Dmanisi of strong evidence for a hominin dispersal soon after the first appearance of *Homo erectus* in Africa is supported by recent research on sites in China and Indonesia. Like Dmanisi, the East Asian sites have produced no evidence of Acheulian technology. The early dates for sites in China and Indonesia are currently the subject of heated debate. However, if these early dates hold up to scrutiny, they suggest that the initial dispersal of *Homo erectus* was a remarkably rapid event.

**Java.** The first discovery of a *Homo erectus* fossil took place far from Africa, at the site of Trinil on the Indonesian island of Java. The Trinil fossil, discovered by the Dutch paleontologist Eugene Dubois, created a sensation and controversy when it was discovered in 1892. Many scientists were unwilling to accept Dubois's claim that he had found the "missing link" between apes and humans, arguing instead that the fossil was either an ape or a human. Dubois was so infuriated by the controversy that he stopped allowing researchers direct access to the fossils, keeping them locked in a safe in his office.

Today, controversy again surrounds the *Homo erectus* from Java. There is little controversy about the taxonomic status of the fossils; all appear to belong to the species *Homo erectus*. The subject of contention now is the dating of the fossils, specifically the fossils from the sites of **Sangiran and Perning** These fossils are found in an early geological position within the Javan sequence known as the Upper Sangiran Formation. The date of this formation was long thought to be approximately one million years ago, on the basis of paleomagnetism and the types of animal fossils found in the formation. In 1994, argon dates were published for the Upper Sangiran Formation at Sangiran and Perning that place the fossils at 1.8 million years ago. However, a number of archaeologists have questioned whether this date is accurate.

Although Java is now an island, it was not an island throughout the Pleistocene. A land bridge, known as the Sunda shelf, connected Java to mainland southeast Asia during periods of low sea level. One oddity of the early *Homo erectus* sites on Java is that none have produced evidence of stone tools. Still, it is not yet clear whether these hominins did not in fact make stone tools or whether they did but the tools have simply gone unrecognized.

Nihewan Basin. The **Nihewan Basin** in the Northern China Plain near Beijing is an area rich in paleontological sites. A number of sites with stone tools have been found at Nihewan in contexts that appear to be Early Pleistocene. Four of these sites have been dated by paleomagnetism to the period around 1.6 million years ago (Zhu et al. 2004). The stone tools from the Nihewan Basin are flakes, mostly made on poor raw material.

> The fossils of *Homo erectus* found at the sites of ▶ **Sangiran and Perning** on the island of Java have been dated to 1.8 million years ago.

> ▶ The **Nihewan Basin** in Northern China has produced solid evidence of human occupation between 1.36 million and 1.1 million years ago.

## Summing Up the Evidence

The evidence from Ubeidiya and Dmanisi makes it clear that the initial hominin dispersal took place soon after the first appearance of *Homo erectus* in Africa. If one accepts the early dates from Java, it would appear that the initial dispersal was a widespread event. Whether it is best to reconstruct a single migration or multiple migrations is open to question. It is quite possible that the dispersal of hominins to Java followed a southerly route across the Arabian Peninsula and around the Indian subcontinent. Such a route would have required crossing the minor body of water known as the Straits of Bab el Mandeb at the mouth of the Red Sea.

It is particularly difficult to try to tie the hominin dispersal in with a particular climatic event. In a general sense, climatic instability might have played a role in the dispersal. Another possibility is that some aspect of technology gave these hominins the ability to adapt to new environments. Clearly, this ability is not tied to any particular type of stone tool, as all of the early sites lack elaborate stone tools. One interesting suggestion is that it was the development of technologies of food processing, particularly the use of fire, that led to the hominin dispersal (Wrangham et al. 1999). However, to date, none of the early sites has produced evidence for the use of fire.

Some archaeologists have searched for an explanation of the dispersal in the increased cognitive capacity of *Homo erectus,* reflected in an increased brain size that might have led to the development of new forms of social organization. Clive Gamble has argued that, before *Homo erectus,* the social organization of hominins required frequent face-to-face interactions. The cognitive ability of *Homo erectus* to retain information for increased periods of time allowed for the "stretching of society in time and space," as the social group could then maintain its coherence even when individuals met infrequently (Gamble 1993: 142). As a result, *Homo erectus* social groups would be able to survive in areas where seasonal scarcity forced the group to disperse across a wide territory during parts of the year. Groups of *Homo erectus* thus were able to survive in ecological niches that could not support earlier hominin species. One can easily imagine how such wide-ranging social groups would discover new territories, perhaps as young adults explored the edges of the range of the core group, leading to its expansion into previously uninhabited areas.

# TOOLBOX:
## Paleomagnetic Dating

- Based on changes of the earth's geomagnetic field.
- Dates sediments to epochs or events.

Paleomagnetic dating is a method used to determine when sediments were deposited. The method dates the soils in which artifacts are found, rather than the artifacts themselves. To use paleomagnetism for dating artifacts or fossils, one must be confident that these objects are in the context in which they were initially deposited. If this is not the case—for example, if artifacts have been transported by water and redeposited in a new location—then the paleomagnetic date will be for the redeposition event rather than the manufacture of the artifacts.

The scientific basis for paleomagnetic dating is the observation that the earth's geomagnetic field has repeatedly switched polarity. The current state of the earth's geomagnetic field is known as normal polarity. In periods of reversed polarity the field was switched, so a compass that points north today would have pointed south then. It has been possible to build up a chronology of these switches in polarity such that geological time is divided into a sequence of epochs of normal and reversed polarity.

When any particles containing iron are deposited, these particles orient themselves in accordance with the earth's geomagnetic field. This orientation is preserved as long as the particles are not moved. Almost all soils on earth contain iron. By studying the orientation of their particles, a geophysicist can determine the direction of the earth's geomagnetic field at the time the soil was deposited. Thus, on most archaeological sites it is possible to determine whether the site formed during a normal or a reversed period.

In some cases, archaeologists working in recent periods have been able to use the paleomagnetic record of subtle shifts in the geomagnetic field to date artifacts or sites. The materials dated with these methods are usually hearths or pottery.

## FIGURE 3.4

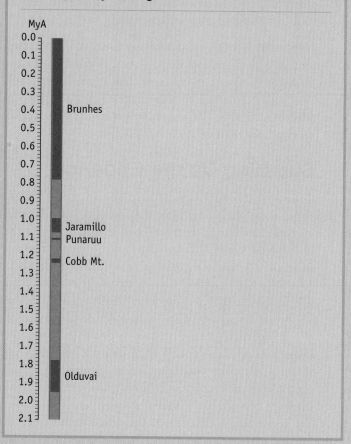

**Paleomagnetic timescale. Time in millions of years ago. Periods of normal polarity are in blue; periods of reverse polarity are in green.**

# CHAPTER SUMMARY

- The hominin radiation between four million and two million years ago included four distinct genera.
- The earliest evidence for walking upright is found in *Australopithecus afarensis*.
- *Homo habilis* is characterized by an increased brain size relative to that of other early hominins.

- The earliest known *Homo erectus* dates between 1.9 and one-and-a-half million years ago. *Homo erectus* is characterized by an increase in brain size compared with *Homo habilis*.
- Chimpanzee tool use includes fishing for termites and breaking nuts with stone hammers and anvils.

- The earliest evidence for hominin stone tool manufacture is found at the Gona site in the Hadar region of Ethiopia, dated to two-and-a-half million years ago.
- Analyses of stone tools from the site of Lokalalei indicates that the manufacture of the earliest stone tools was a complex process.
- There is debate over whether early hominins gained access to meat by hunting or by scavenging.
- The home-base/meat-sharing model suggests that meat sharing at base camps played an important role in the lives of early hominins.
- A stone circle that might be the base of a hut was found at the DK site, Olduvai Gorge. This type of site is predicted by the home-base/meat-sharing model.

- The earliest tentative evidence for the controlled use of fire was found at Chesowanja, Kenya, a site dated to 1.4 million years ago.
- The earliest archaeological sites outside of Africa are Dmanisi, Georgia (1.8 million to 1.7 million years ago), and Ubeidiya, Israel (1.4 to 1.0 million years ago).
- *Homo erectus* fossils found on the Indonesian island of Java at the sites of Sangiran and Perning have been dated to 1.8 million years ago. No other archaeological material has been found with these fossils.
- The oldest reliable evidence for human occupation of China is from the Nihewan Basin, dated between 1.36 million and 1.1 million years ago.

## KEY TERMS

Acheulian, 83
*Ardipithecus ramidus*, 75, 76
Australopithecine, 77
Bifaces, 83
Chesowanja, 96
Dispersal, 96
DKI, 94
Dmanisi, 97
East African Rift Valley, 80

FLK North, 92
Hadar, 87
Home-Base/Food Sharing Model, 94
Hominins, 74
*Homo erectus*, 79
*Homo habilis*, 79
Laetoli, 77
Lokalalei, 89
Lower Paleolithic, 82

Nihewan Basin, 99
Oldowan, 82
Olduvai Gorge, 80
Palimpsest, 95
Radiation, 76
*Sahelanthropus tchadensis*, 75
Sangiran and Perning, 99
Taï Forest, 86
Ubeidiya, 97

## REVIEW QUESTIONS

1. Why is the period between four million and two million years ago referred to as the hominin radiation?
2. Which hominin produced the earliest stone tools?
3. What is the significance of the discoveries made at FLK North, Olduvai Gorge?
4. What is the home-base/meat-sharing model? Does the archaeological evidence support this model?
5. Is the initial dispersal of *Homo erectus* best described as gradual or rapid?

## FOR FURTHER READING

Clive Gamble. (1993). *Timewalkers: The Prehistory of Global Colonization.* Cambridge, Massachusetts: Harvard University Press.

Jane Goodall. (1990). *Through a Window: My Thirty Years with the Chimpanzees of Gombe.* Boston: Houghton Mifflin.

Glynn Isaac. (1989). *The Archaeology of Human Origins: Papers by Glynn Isaac.* Edited by Barbara Isaac. Cambridge, UK: Cambridge University Press.

Virginia Morell. (1995). *Ancestral Passions: The Leakey Family and the Quest for Humankind's Beginnings.* New York: Simon and Schuster.

Kathy Schick and Nicholas Toth. (1993). *Making Silent Stones Speak: Human Evolution and the Dawn of Technology.* New York: Simon and Schuster.

Craig Stanford. (1999). *The Hunting Apes.* Princeton: Princeton University Press.

Michael Tomasello. (1999). *The Cultural Origins of Human Cognition.* Cambridge: Harvard University Press.

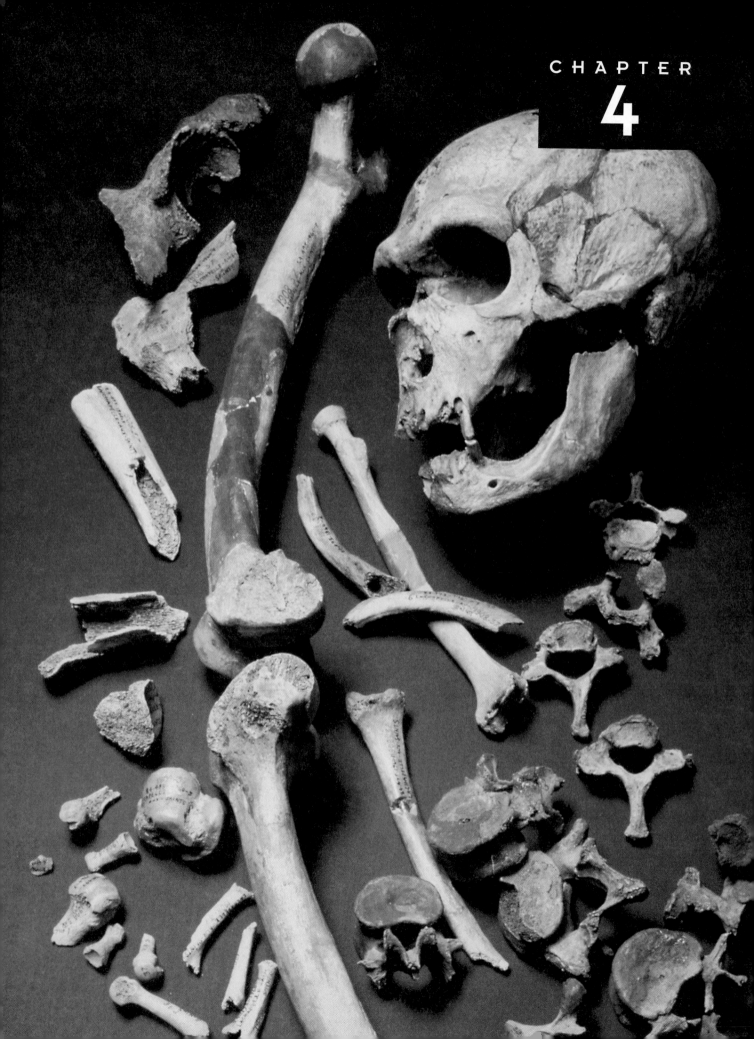

# From *Homo erectus* to Neanderthals

The Neanderthal fossil from La Chapelle-aux-Saints

NEANDERTHALS OCCUPIED Europe and the Middle East between 175,000 and 30,000 years ago. After reading this chapter, you should understand:

▶ The Oxygen Isotope glacial sequence.

▶ The spread of hominins through Europe and the characteristics of the European Lower Paleolithic.

▶ The major anatomical features that characterize Neanderthals.

▶ The three major theories of the evolution of Neanderthals.

▶ The evidence for Neanderthal hunting, use of fire, burial of the dead, and artwork.

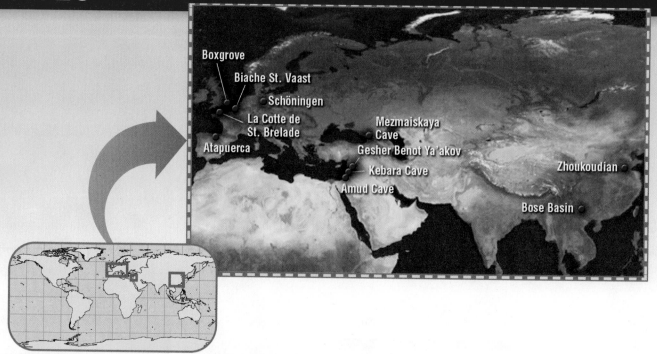

Boxgrove
Biache St. Vaast
Schöningen
La Cotte de St. Brelade
Atapuerca
Mezmaiskaya Cave
Gesher Benot Ya'akov
Kebara Cave
Amud Cave
Zhoukoudian
Bose Basin

**B**oule's reconstruction of a Neanderthal as a stooped hairy brute. Notice the club grasped firmly in the Neanderthal's right hand. Why do you think this detail is included?

The picture of Neanderthals as hulking ape-men dates back to 1908 and the discovery of the "Old Man of La Chapelle-aux-Saints." The La Chapelle fossil was the most complete skeleton of a Neanderthal ever recovered, and it provided a unique opportunity to understand the characteristics of this intriguing hominin. The task of analyzing the skeleton fell to Marcelin Boule, a prominent paleoanthropologist who came to the job convinced that Neanderthals were "a degenerate side branch of human evolution" (Bowler 1986: 88). Not surprisingly, the portrait that emerged from Boule's analysis was a hairy, stooped creature. Subsequent studies show that Boule had largely ignored the effects of arthritis and other pathologies on the posture of the fossil from La Chapelle. Contemporary studies of Neanderthals paint a far more intriguing picture of a hominin that is in numerous respects similar to modern humans, but at the same time is distinctive. In many ways, the dramatic picture of Neanderthals as our apish ancestor has been replaced by the image of Neanderthals as an enigma.

In this chapter, we begin by examining the environmental record pertaining to the Pleistocene Ice Age. We then pick up where we left off in the last chapter, to follow the record for the continued spread of populations of *Homo erectus* into Western Europe. We also look at aspects of the Lower Paleolithic archaeology of Europe and Asia that shed light on the behavior and society of *Homo erectus*. We then turn to the Neanderthal fossil record and offer

| HOMININS | thousands of years ago | ARCHAEOLOGICAL INDUSTRIES | SITES |
|---|---|---|---|
| | 800 | | Atapuerca TD-6 Bose Gesher Benot Ya'akov |
| | 700 | | Isernia de la Pineta |
| | 600 | | |
| HOMO ERECTUS | 500 | EURASIAN ACHEULIAN | Boxgrove Zhoukoudian |
| | 400 | | Schöningen |
| | 300 | | Berekhat Ram |
| | | | Atapuerca Sima de los Huesos |
| | 200 | | |
| | | MIDDLE PALEOLITHIC | Biache-Saint-Vaast La Cotte de St. Brelade |
| NEANDERTHALS | 100 | | Mauran Umm el Tlel Amud Cave Kebara Cave Mezmaiskaya Cave |

an extended consideration of the archaeological record of Neanderthal behavior and society.

## 4.1 DEFINING THE ICE AGE

The evolution of Neanderthals took place within the context of the geological period known as the **Pleistocene,** or the Ice Age. The boundary between the Pleistocene and the preceding Pliocene era is fixed at almost precisely 1.8 million years ago. The Pleistocene is characterized by periods with a significant buildup of ice sheets, known as glacial eras, and periods during which the ice sheet subsequently retreated, known as interglacial eras.

Geologists first developed a record of Pleistocene climate change on the basis of features of the landscape. One such feature is the terminal moraine, a characteristic raised ridge that formed at the point where the glacial ice sheet reached its maximum extent. Cape Cod in Massachusetts is a classic example of a terminal moraine. By looking at such features in both North America and Europe, geologists developed a glacial chronology for the Pleistocene involving four major cycles of advance and retreat of the ice sheets. In Europe, the four major glacial advances were named, from earliest to latest, Günz, Mindel, Riss, and Würm. In North America, the last two glacial advances are known as the Illinoian and the Wisconsin.

The bottom of the sea might seem to be an unlikely place to search for a record of the advance and retreat of ice sheets, but analyses of cores drilled from the ocean floor have revolutionized our view of Pleistocene climate change. The record provided by the sea cores is very different from the model of four major glacial periods. The picture that emerges is of an unstable climate with many glacial and interglacial periods over the last 1.8 million years. In the last 700,000 years, there have been eight full glacial–interglacial cycles (see Figure 4.1).

> The **Pleistocene** is the geological era that began 1.8 million years ago and is characterized by the frequent buildup and retreat of continental ice sheets.

FIGURE 4.1

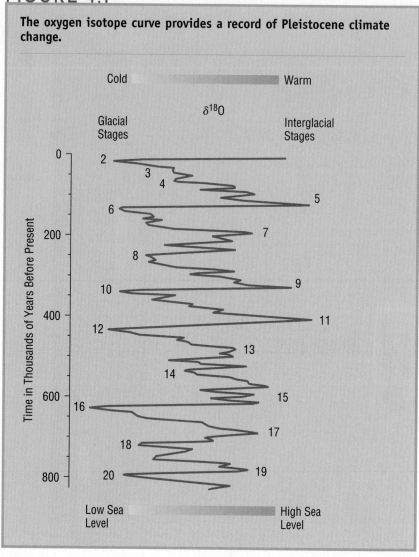

**The oxygen isotope curve provides a record of Pleistocene climate change.**

The climate record produced by the analysis of deep-sea cores is known as the oxygen isotope curve. Glacial and interglacial events are given numbers, from the most recent (we now live in Oxygen Isotope Stage 1) to the oldest (see Figure 4.1). If one looks closely at the **Oxygen Isotope Curve**, it becomes evident that the extent of glaciation and the rapidity of climate change vary considerably. For instance, the boundaries between stages 5/6 and stages 9/10 are examples of particularly abrupt climate change.

> The **oxygen isotope curve** is a record of fluctuations in global climate.

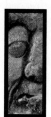

# 4.2 BEFORE THE NEANDERTHALS

In the last chapter, we examined the evidence for the initial dispersal of *Homo erectus*. To understand the evolution of Neanderthals, we need to know more about what happened after this initial dispersal. We first need to know when hominins first spread into Western Europe. We also need to know about the Lower Paleolithic cultures of Europe and Asia. We will focus on the challenge of interpreting the variability found in this period. Finally, we want to know about aspects of Lower Paleolithic culture beyond stone tools. Is there evidence for tools made from other materials? Is there artwork? Are there burials? And did hominins have control over the use of fire?

## The Initial Occupation of Western Europe

Although Dmanisi, at the eastern edge of Europe, has evidence of occupation going back approximately 1.7 million years, hominin sites older than 500,000 years ago in Western Europe are rare and often unconvincing. However, the 500,000-year barrier has been dramatically shattered by research at a system of caves located at **Atapuerca** in north-central Spain. The construction of a railroad through the hill at Atapuerca exposed a massive cave filled with 18 meters of deposits. Archaeologists perched on an elaborate system of scaffolding have swarmed over the Gran Dolina sequence, digging into eleven archaeological levels that have been dated by paleomagnetism and electron spin resonance. In the TD-6 level, dated to 800,000 years ago, a rich collection of stone tools and fossil bones were recovered along with 30 hominin fragments. TD-6 is the earliest securely dated archaeological level in Western Europe (Carbonell et al. 1999).

The stone tools from Gran Dolina TD-6 are flakes and cores. The hominin remains from TD-6 have been classified as a new species, *Homo antecessor*. Because most of the remains are fragmentary and the single fairly complete skull is of a juvenile, further discoveries are needed to confirm the identification of the species.

> The TD-6 Level of the Gran Dolina site at **Atapuerca** has produced stone tools and hominin remains dated to 800,000 years ago. These artifacts are the oldest reliable evidence for human occupation of Europe.

**E**xcavation at Atapuerca. The site was exposed by a trench dug for a railway. Because of the depth of the sequence archaeologists built a system of scaffolds to reach the excavation areas.

# TOOLBOX:
## Oxygen Isotope Curve

The development of glaciers is only one element of a global process. As glaciers build up, water is locked up in ice at the expense of water otherwise held in the oceans. When glaciers advance, sea levels drop, and when glaciers retreat, sea levels go up. During some past periods of glacial advance, the global sea level was up to 140 meters below what it is today (Rohling et al. 1998). Today's sea level reflects the fact that we are living in an interglacial period.

Analysis of cores drilled from the sea floor allows scientists to measure and date fluctuations in the amount of water in the ocean and thus develop a global "thermometer" for the Ice Age. The secret behind this thermometer is the tiny organisms known as foraminifera, which live on the surface of the ocean. The skeletons of these organisms are made of calcium carbonate, which absorbs oxygen from seawater and drifts to the sea floor

after the organism dies. Over millennia, the sea floor deposits incorporate a continuous stratigraphic sequence of foraminifera. A core drilled out of the sea floor can recover a sequence of foraminifera covering millions of years. Such sequences can be dated by the uranium series method.

Foraminifera absorb two isotopes of oxygen. $^{18}O$ is the heavier isotope and $^{16}O$ is the lighter. During periods of glacial buildup, the oceans become isotopically heavy because $^{16}O$ is drawn off with the moisture that builds the ice sheets. During glacial periods, the oceans have a high ratio of $^{18}O$ to $^{16}O$. The reverse is true during interglacial periods, when sea levels rise. Measuring the ratio of $^{18}O$ to $^{16}O$ in the foraminifera collected in deep-sea cores provides a record of the advance and retreat of glaciers during the Pleistocene.

## FIGURE 4.2

Colder Climate ⟶ More Ice on Land ⟶ Less Water in the Ocean ⟶ High Ratio of $^{18}O$ to $^{16}O$

Warmer Climate ⟶ Less Ice on Land ⟶ More Water in the Ocean ⟶ Low Ratio of $^{18}O$ to $^{16}O$

Another early site in Western Europe is Isernia la Pineta in Italy, dated to more than 700,000 years ago (Peretto 2006). In the Sett. I t.3a level, a dense occupation layer of stone tools and animal bones was found covering an area of 24 square meters. Over 1,000 stone tools were discovered, mostly simple flakes made on poor-quality stone. The animal bones include the remains of bears, elephants, rhinos, bison, and deer.

## The Acheulian Problem

In East Asia, chopper and flake tools characterize most Lower Paleolithic sites. Paradoxically, the earliest date for an Acheulian industry anywhere outside of Africa is at the site of **Bose** in China (Yamei et al. 2000). Bose is also the only site in China where handaxes have been uncovered. The artifacts at Bose are found in a river terrace in a stratigraphic unit that varies between 25 and 100 cm in thickness. Argon dating of tektites found with the tools has dated the site to 800,000 years ago. Tektites are small fragments of glass formed by meteor impacts. As with volcanic ash and lava, argon dating determines when the glass formed.

The site of **Bose** in southern China, dated to 800,000 years ago, has produced a stone tool industry that includes handaxes.

Other than Bose, the earliest well-dated Acheulian site outside of Africa is Gesher Benot Ya'akov, Israel, located to the north of the Sea of Galilee in the northern extension of the East African Rift Valley. Dated to 780,000 years ago, Gesher Benot Ya'akov is similar to the African Acheulian. Bifaces are made on very large flakes, and handaxes and cleavers are common. The excavations at Gesher Benot Ya'akov have also produced limited evidence for the use of fire and for cracking nuts.

It is only beginning 500,000 years ago that Acheulian sites became common across Europe, the Middle East, and on into the Indian subcontinent—the geographic region known as Eurasia. There is regional variation in the **Eurasian Acheulian**, but taken as a whole, these industries show some significant contrast with the African Acheulian. Cleavers are almost completely absent from the Eurasian Acheulian, and handaxes are the major type of biface.

Another characteristic of the Eurasian Acheulian is that the handaxes were often part of a tool kit that also included retouched flakes—flakes that were modified after being struck off the core. The characteristic type of flake tool is the sidescraper, in which one or two edges of the flake have been regularized and strengthened by retouching (see photo).

**Boxgrove**, located in West Sussex in southern England, is among the earliest-known Acheulian sites in Europe and one of the most extensively excavated (Roberts et al. 1999). On the basis of the animal species represented in the faunal assemblage, the site is dated to 500,000 years ago. The hominin occupation of Boxgrove appears to have been close to the shore of a small lake near the sea. The stone tools include the debris from handaxe manufacture, which, when refit, provide a detailed picture of the process involved in making these tools. The handaxes found at Boxgrove were shaped with both hard and soft hammers.

> ▶ The **Eurasian Acheulian** is found on sites across Europe, the Middle East, and the Indian subcontinent beginning 500,000 years ago. The handaxe is the characteristic tool of the Eurasian Acheulian.

> ▶ The site of **Boxgrove**, England, dated to 500,000 years ago, is among the oldest-known Acheulian sites in Europe.

Cagny-l'Epinette

0          5 cm

Level I1

Handaxe (left) and flake tool (right) from the Lower Paleolithic site of Cagny-l'Epinette, France.

Experiments in which an experienced butcher was given a replicated handaxe to use showed that these tools would have served very well to skin and butcher carcasses. Animal bones from the site, including the bones of a large horse, have traces of tool cut marks and whether or not these animals were hunted, hominins did have early access to the carcasses. No evidence for the use of fire or of a base camp has been found at Boxgrove.

Not all sites in Europe dating later than 500,000 years ago have produced handaxes. The **Clactonian** is an industry in England of simple flake tools contemporary with the Acheulian. Some have argued that Clactonian sites are simply Acheulian handaxe manufacturing sites from which the finished products are absent. This idea has been refuted, and it is now clear that the Clactonian is distinct from the Acheulian. In Eastern Europe, a number of Lower Paleolithic sites have produced flake tool industries. Vértesszölös is a particularly rich site located in Hungary and dated to 350,000 years ago. The stone tools at Vértesszölös are choppers and retouched flakes.

The variation in Lower Paleolithic industries is modest compared with the variation found in later periods, but nonetheless is real. The patterns of variation that do exist confound some of our expectations and prove difficult to explain. One would expect that all groups would rapidly adopt the Acheulian technology. However, that is clearly not the case. The site of Bose has produced the oldest-known handaxes outside of Africa. However, handaxe manufacture never became widespread among early hominins in East Asia. In Europe, Acheulian industries appeared only 500,000 years ago, hundreds of thousands of years after the first arrival of hominins. Even after the widespread appearance of handaxes in Europe

> The **Clactonian** is a simple flake tool industry contemporary with the Acheulian in England.

**E**xcavation at Boxgrove. Notice how artifacts are left in place as they are exposed providing a clear view of a broad horizontal surface.

The Zhoukoudian site, China. This massive site was formed by sediments filling gaps in a limestone mountain.

and Western Asia, there continue to be industries, such as the Clactonian, that do not involve handaxe manufacture.

One approach to this problem is to explain variation in the Lower Paleolithic as the result of ecological factors. Geoffrey Pope (1989) has proposed that the absence of handaxes in East Asia tracks the limits of the distribution of bamboo and that hominins in the region made many of their tools from bamboo. Ethnoarchaeological research with the Kuchung ethnic group in Yunan province, China, has shown that a wide range of bamboo tools could be fashioned with simple choppers and flakes. Ecological factors might also account for the differences between the African Acheulian and the Eurasian Acheulian. The African Acheulian is found in an area in which large volcanic boulders are readily available, whereas the same is not true of the Eurasian Acheulian. Perhaps the availability of types of stone accounts for the regional differences.

Another possibility is that different industries are evidence of distinct groups and that one can use the archaeological industries to track not just one hominin dispersal out of Africa, but rather several waves. Eudald Carbonell has argued that the initial dispersal was of Oldowan people pushed out of Africa by more successful Acheulian groups (Carbonell et al. 1999). In his opinion, this hypothesis would account for the absence of handaxes in the earliest hominin sites outside of Africa. Carbonell sees the widespread presence of Acheulian industries across Eurasia beginning 500,000 years ago as evidence of yet another wave of migration out of Africa.

**H**arrmut Thieme with the 400,000 year-old wooden spear he discovered at the site of Schöningen, Germany. Notice the horse skull to the right of the spear.

The stone tool industries might also reflect social factors such as group size. Steven Mithen (1994) has pointed out the importance of learning in stone tool manufacture. Elaborate stone tool manufacture involves the transmission of skills and knowledge across generations. Perhaps the size and density of the social group influenced the amount of learning that took place and thus affected the elaboration of technology. For Mithen, the elaborate technologies of the Acheulian indicate a high degree of social learning. He suggests that the context for such intensified learning was large groups of hominins living in glacial open environments with a high risk from predators and an unpredictable availability of food resources. According to this model, the far less elaborate Clactonian industries were produced by small groups of hominins living in an interglacial wooded environment with a low risk from predators and an evenly distributed availability of food resources.

## Beyond Stone Tools

The picture of Lower Paleolithic culture is limited by the nature of the available evidence. One can only wonder what we would know if we could see all the items used by early hominins, many of which might have been made of materials that rarely survive. A number of unique discoveries provide tantalizing hints of the complexity of Lower Paleolithic culture.

**Zhoukoudian** is a series of caves in Longgu-shan, or Dragon Bone Hill, outside of Beijing (Peking), China. Since excavations began at the cave known as Locality 1 in the early 1920s, the remains of more than 40 *Homo erectus* individuals and over 100,000 stone tools, all choppers and flakes, have been recovered. The hominins from Zhoukoudian, also known as Peking man, are at the center of one of the unsolved

**Zhoukoudian** is a large Lower Paleolithic site near Beijing that has produced a number of fossils of *Homo erectus*.

The Berekhat Ram figurine. The white bar is a scale of 1 cm. The groove running around the top part of the stone appears to be artificial.

mysteries of archaeology. After Japan attacked Pearl Harbor in World War II, an attempt was made to get the fossils out of Peking, which was under Japanese occupation. In the confusion of war, the fossils were lost, and no trace of them has ever appeared. Fortunately, accurate casts of most of the fossils were saved.

Locality 1 at Zhoukoudian is an absolutely massive site. The scale of the early excavations resembled a mining operation more than what we expect from a modern archaeological project. The total depth of the deposits at Locality 1 is 48 meters, which has been divided into 17 layers. The dating of the site is extremely complex; however, most studies agree on a date for the hominin occupation between 500,000 and 300,000 years before the present. The tools are restricted to flakes and simple cores.

Locality 1 at Zhoukoudian has long been thought to provide the earliest evidence for the use of fire. The most important evidence comes from Layer 10, which has been described as an ash layer. Recent research has demonstrated that there is no ash in Layer 10 and that what had been identified as ash is actually organic material brought in by a river that ran through the cave (Goldberg et al. 2001). Similar conclusions have been reached concerning the evidence of burning in Layer 4. The only evidence suggestive of the controlled use of fire by hominins at Zhoukoudian Locality 1 is the occurrence of burnt bones together with stone tools. Although evidence of fire has been identified at the Acheulian site of Gesher Benot Ya'akov in Israel, in general terms the use of fire during the Lower Paleolithic was rare.

Excavations in a coal mine at **Schöningen, Germany,** have uncovered three spruce spears together with a rich collection of stone tools and animal bones dated to 400,000 years ago (Thieme 1997). The unique context of this site allowed for the preservation of these wooden artifacts. The spears vary in length between 1.8 and 2.2 meters and between 29 and 47 mm in diameter. Another piece that is pointed on both ends, as opposed to the spears, which are pointed at only one end, is 0.8 meter long. The spears are well made and balanced, but do not appear to have had a stone tip or any decoration. The excavator interprets them as projectiles.

There is very little evidence of either artwork or ritual behavior in Lower Paleolithic contexts. Two exceptions to this generalization deserve particular mention. The first is a small pebble of volcanic rock found at the Lower Paleolithic site of

> ▶ At the site of **Schöningen, Germany,** 400,000-year-old wooden spears have been discovered.

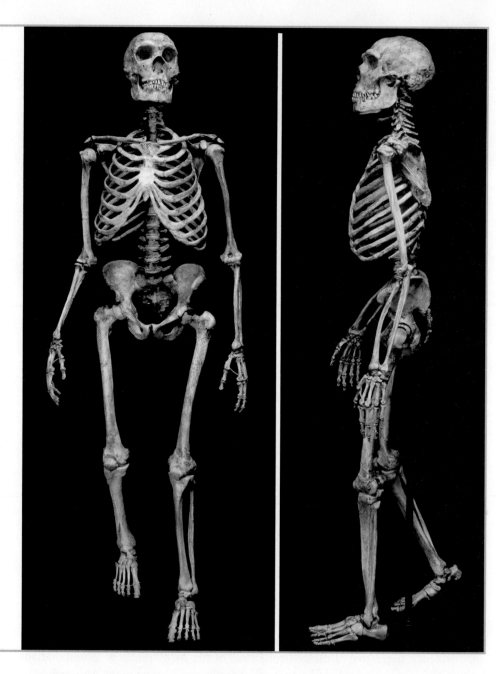

A reconstructed Neanderthal. No complete Neanderthal fossils have been found, so this model was constructed by combining elements from a number of fossils. Notice that the skull is long and the face juts forward. A chin is absent, the rib cage is broad, and the pelvis is somewhat different from the modern human pelvis.

Berekhat Ram, Golan Heights. The excavator of Berekhat Ram discerned signs of work on this stone and identified it as a representation of a human female. Because the site is older than 230,000 years, the stone is possibly the earliest evidence of a human representation. Subsequent research has confirmed that the pebble was indeed worked by the incision of a single line. Whether the intention was to create a figurine remains unclear (D'Errico and Nowell 2000).

The only significant evidence for special treatment of the dead during the Lower Paleolithic comes from a cave at Atapuerca known as Sima de los Huesos, which is dated to 300,000 years ago. In this pit, the complete remains of 27 hominin individuals were recovered (Carbonell et al. 2003). Only one stone tool, a well-made quartz handaxe, has been found in the cave. There is no evidence of human occupation of Sima de los Huesos, nor is there evidence that it was an accessible cave. It appears to have been a crevice in the rock whose only inhabitants were cave bears and other carnivores. The excavators argue that the hominins were not brought to

TABLE 4.1

| GENUS OR SPECIES | DATE | BRAIN SIZE | CHARACTERISTICS | DISTRIBUTION |
|---|---|---|---|---|
| *Homo neanderthalensis* or *Homo sapiens neanderthalensis* | 175,000– 30,000 years ago | 1,200–1,700 cc | Muscular and adapted to the cold. | Europe and the Middle East |

the cave by carnivores and that the cave was not a natural crevice into which they fell. Rather, they interpret Sima de los Huesos as a place where corpses were placed as part of a funerary ritual, and they construe the handaxe to be a funerary offering. They suggest that the large number of corpses reflects a burial of the victims of an ecological crisis. Note that there is evidence of carnivore gnawing on almost half of the human bones. These gnaw marks include the actions of a small fox-sized animal and a larger lion-sized animal. There is no evidence that the corpses were buried.

# 4.3 NEANDERTHALS

All living humans are members of the species *Homo sapiens,* also known as modern humans. Neanderthals are at once similar to modern humans and yet at the same time highly distinctive. The significance of the similarities and differences between Neanderthals and our own species is the focus of intense debate. Some argue that the similarities are so strong that Neanderthals are merely a subspecies—*Homo sapiens neanderthalensis*—of our own species. Others argue that despite the similarities, the differences warrant the creation of a distinct species—*Homo neanderthalensis*—for the Neanderthals. Table 4.1 lists some important attributes of Neanderthals.

The similarities between modern humans and Neanderthals are rooted in their shared ancestry. Unfortunately, there is some controversy surrounding the identification of the last common ancestor of modern humans and Neanderthals. Three scenarios (shown in Figure 4.3) have been posed for the evolution of Neanderthals:

1. *Neanderthals and modern humans each evolved separately from populations of Homo erectus, possibly through local intermediate species.* According to this scenario, the evolution of Neanderthals and modern humans took place in parallel in separate geographic areas. Evidence for the evolution of modern humans in Africa will be discussed in the next chapter. Neanderthals, a species (or subspecies) adapted to cold climates, evolved in Europe.

# FIGURE 4.3

**Three scenarios for the evolution of Neanderthals.**

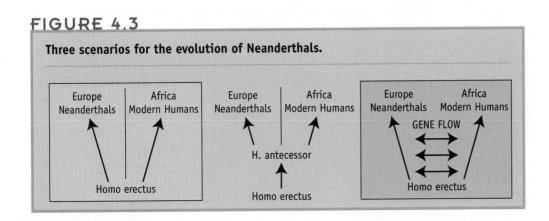

2. The common ancestor of modern humans and Neanderthals was a distinct species that itself evolved from Homo erectus and lived between 700,000 and 300,000 years ago. One candidate for this critical intermediate position is Homo antecessor, fossils of which have been obtained from Antapuerca Gran Dolina TD-6.

3. Neanderthals and modern humans did not evolve in isolation; rather, there was a constant exchange of genetic material, or gene flow, between the two populations. This possibility cannot be ruled out; however, some degree of isolation must have existed in order for Neanderthals to evolve some of their characteristic skeletal traits. According to this model, Neanderthals and modern humans are members of a single species.

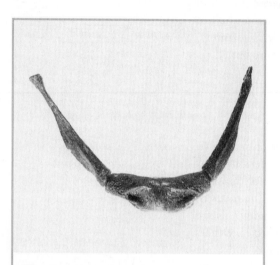

The Neanderthal hyoid bone from Kebara. The hyoid bone is found in the larynx and connects to the muscles used in producing speech. The Kebara hyoid is identical to the hyoid bone found in modern humans.

The distinctiveness of a Neanderthal skeleton is easy to identify. The skulls are elongated compared with skulls of modern humans, with an occipital bun at the back and a large, projecting nose in front. The forehead is sloping and the chin almost absent. As in *Homo erectus,* there is a brow ridge over the eyes; however, in Neanderthals, the brow ridge is double arched. The skull is not as thick as the skull of *Homo erectus* but is still thicker than is the norm among living humans. The molars of Neanderthals were large, and the front teeth show marks of wear, indicating the regular use of the incisors as tools in preparing food or gripping hides. The Neanderthal body is stocky and similar in proportions to modern humans adapted to cold climates. Particularly notable are a broad rib cage and bowed, long bones. The muscle insertions are well developed, and the bones are generally robust. Although Neanderthals were completely bipedal, the way they walked was slightly different from modern humans.

The overall impression one forms of Neanderthals is that they were very strong and well adapted to cold climates. Among the features tied to a cold-weather adaptation are the projecting face and large nose. These features distinguish Neanderthals from both *Homo erectus* and modern humans. Studies of fossil remains of Neanderthal children indicate that many of the characteristic Neanderthal features developed quite early in childhood.

The brains of Neanderthals were within the size range of the brains of modern humans, between 1,200 and 1,700 cc. This is considerably larger than the brain size of *Homo erectus.* If Neanderthals and modern humans each evolved independently from *Homo erectus,* then the increase in brain size took place as a parallel process in the two lineages. Alternatively, the large brains of Neanderthals and modern humans could be derived from a large-brained common ancestor, such as *Homo antecessor.* Or the parallel evolution of larger brains could be the product of gene flow.

The evolution of the brain in the Neanderthal lineage is critical to assessing Neanderthal behavior. If Neanderthals evolved larger brains independently from modern humans, then there is a possibility that, despite being the same size, modern human and Neanderthal brains are significantly different in organization and cognitive capacity. The idea that Neanderthals might have differed cognitively from modern humans has intrigued many researchers. One proposal is that Neanderthals lacked the cognitive capacity for language, as well as the anatomical apparatus to produce speech. Much of this argument is based on the shape of the Neanderthal cranium base, which is flat in comparison to the flexed morphology of modern human skulls. But because the soft tissue of the larynx is not preserved in the fossil record, it is difficult to make conclusive statements about Neanderthals' ability to speak. The only bone incorporated into the musculature of the larynx is a very small bone called the hyoid. The discovery of the complete hyoid of a Neanderthal at the site of Kebara Cave in Israel has produced no evidence supporting the argument that Neanderthals were physically incapable of speech (Arensburg 1989). The Kebara hyoid is identical to modern human hyoids, an unlikely coincidence if the morphology of the Neanderthal larynx had been significantly different.

## Neanderthal Genetics

In 1999, scientists announced that they had succeeded in extracting and sequencing mitochondrial DNA from a Neanderthal fossil (Krings et al. 1999). The results of this test, performed on the Neander Valley fossil from Germany, have since been replicated on a fossil from the site of Mezmaiskaya Cave in the Caucasus Mountain region of Eastern Europe.

**S**ampling of a Neanderthal bone for DNA analysis. Great care must be taken to avoid contamination by modern DNA.

The sequences of **Neanderthal DNA** that have been recovered are significantly different from the DNA sequence of living humans. This finding suggests that the divergence between the Neanderthal lineage and the modern human lineage dates back approximately 450,000 years, a date, however, that comes with a large margin of error limiting the divergence to a period of 400,000 years between 320,000 and 740,000 years before the present. The degree of difference between Neanderthal DNA and modern human DNA is less than the difference that separates the two living species of chimpanzees (*Pan troglodytes* and *Pan paniscus*), but exceeds the variation between subspecies of chimpanzees. The genetic evidence suggests that Neanderthals, whether one chooses to label them a species or subspecies, evolved separately from the modern human lineage for a considerable period of time.

> The analysis of DNA recovered from Neanderthal fossils from Neander Cave, Mezmaiskaya Cave, and Vindija Cave indicates that ▶ **Neanderthal DNA** is significantly different from the DNA of any living human.

Nuclear DNA from a Neanderthal specimen from the site of Vindija Cave, Croatia has now been extensively sequenced by two research teams (Green et al. 2006, Noonan et al. 2006). One team was able to sequence 62,250 base pairs of the Neanderthal genome and derived a date of 700,000 years ago for the last common ancestor of Neanderthals and modern humans. The other team sequenced over one million base pairs and arrived at a date of 500,000 years ago for the split between the modern human and Neanderthal lineages. The door is now open to the sequencing of the entire Neanderthal genome, perhaps as early as 2009 (Pennisi 2006).

## Chronology and Ecology

The oldest fossil that can clearly be classified as a Neanderthal was discovered at **Biache-Saint-Vaast** in northern France. Biache has been dated to 175,000 years ago by means of thermoluminescence of burnt flint. A possible older date has been proposed for a Neanderthal fossil found at the Ehringsdorf site in eastern Germany, which has been dated between 200,000 and 250,000 years ago. The Biache and Ehringsdorf fossils suggest that Neanderthals first appeared in Europe in the latter part of interglacial Oxygen Isotope Stage 7.

The most recent date for a Neanderthal fossil is roughly 30,000 years ago, from sites such as the **Mezmaiskaya Cave,** the source of one of the two Neanderthal fossils

> ▶ The oldest-known fossil of a Neanderthal is from the site of **Biache-Saint-Vaast,** France, which is dated to 175,000 years ago.
>
> ▶ **Mezmaiskaya Cave** has produced one of the most recent Neanderthal fossils, dated to 30,000 years ago.

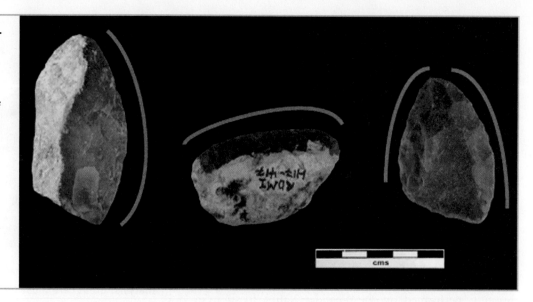

from which DNA was successfully extracted. Neanderthals thus lived through two complete glacial cycles, beginning with interglacial Oxygen Isotope Stage 7 and ending with glacial Oxygen Isotope Stage 3. Neanderthals survived through rapidly changing climatic conditions, including the deep glacial advances of Oxygen Isotope Stage 6 and the very warm conditions of the early part of interglacial Oxygen Isotope Stage 5.

Neanderthal fossils have been found across a wide area stretching from Western Europe to Central Asia. The southern limit of the distribution of Neanderthal fossils is in the Middle East. No Neanderthal fossils have been found in either Africa or East Asia. Neanderthal fossils and archaeological remains have been found in a wide range of ecological zones, including open temperate grasslands in Northern Europe and Mediterranean-climate woodlands in the Middle East.

# 4.4 ASPECTS OF NEANDERTHAL CULTURE AND ADAPTATION

Neanderthals are often portrayed as loutish brutes, and the word *Neanderthal* has become an insult indicating a lack of intelligence or culture. Fascination with Neanderthals flows from their status as both similar and different from living humans. Archaeological research presents a subtle picture of Neanderthal culture and adaptations. The archaeological period during which Neanderthals occupied Europe and the Middle East is known as the **Middle Paleolithic.**

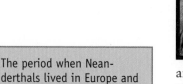

The period when Neanderthals lived in Europe and the Middle East is known as the **Middle Paleolithic.**

## Stone Tools

Neanderthals only rarely made handaxes. After having been a central part of the hominin tool kit for over a million years, handaxes rapidly disappeared from the archaeological record around 200,000 years ago. Rather than fashioning bifacial tools on cobbles or very large flakes, Neanderthals made tools by retouching the edges of flakes. The flakes used by Neanderthals as tools were not made haphaz-

# FIGURE 4.4

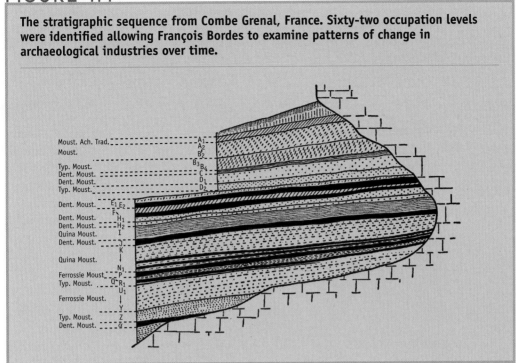

The stratigraphic sequence from Combe Grenal, France. Sixty-two occupation levels were identified allowing François Bordes to examine patterns of change in archaeological industries over time.

ardly. The dominant approach to tool manufacture during the Middle Paleolithic is known as **prepared-core technology,** a technique in which the person making the tools carefully shaped the core to control the form of the flakes produced.

Within the narrow range of Neanderthal stone tool technology, there is surprising diversity. With some important exceptions, the Lower Paleolithic is characterized as showing a great deal of uniformity across broad geographical areas and long time scales. This is not the case for the stone tool industries made by Neanderthals, known collectively as the Middle Paleolithic or Mousterian, which show a great deal of variation, both in the location and nature of the retouching and in the shape of the flakes on which the tools were made. The study of variation in Middle Paleolithic stone tools has played a critical role in developing archaeological methods of artifact analysis. Understanding these tools is key to understanding Neanderthal adaptation, culture, and cognition.

### François Bordes and Neanderthal Ethnicity.
In the early twentieth century, excavations of Neanderthal sites in Europe were undertaken on a massive scale. Layers were described on the basis of particularly characteristic artifacts that became known as "fossil directors." In most cases, the bulk of the material recovered was simply discarded as irrelevant. This approach to the excavation of Middle Paleolithic sites changed drastically due to the pioneering efforts of the French prehistorian François Bordes, who worked to improve excavation methods and to create a more fine-tuned stratigraphic division of sites. In his excavations at the sites of Combe Grenal and Pech de l'Azé, he divided the stratigraphic sequence into dozens of well-defined levels (Bordes 1972) (see Figure 4.4). He was also dissatisfied with the characterization of the archaeological content of a layer on the basis of so small a number of tools as the fossil directors. By creating a detailed list of tool types (a typology) and counting how many of each type was found in a particular level, Bordes was able to quantify the totality of the tools found in that level.

> ▶ **Prepared-core technologies** were used to make stone tools during the Middle Paleolithic.

On the basis of his excavations and quantitative studies, Bordes identified a series of distinct types of Middle Paleolithic industries. He found that in southern France these industries did not form a chronological sequence; rather, within a single site, they were found in alternating levels. Bordes interpreted the Middle Paleolithic industries as the product of distinct ethnic groups. He maintained that the stratigraphic evidence showed that these different groups lived contemporaneously in southern France.

**The Binford–Bordes Debate.** Attacking Bordes's interpretation was a temptation Lewis Binford could not resist (Binford 1983). Binford had spent time in Bordeaux while his wife, Sally Binford, worked on analyzing the stone tools from her excavations of a Middle Paleolithic site in Israel. Both Binfords had enormous respect for Bordes's analysis, but found his interpretation fundamentally flawed. Binford could not accept that variation in the types of tools found on sites was the result of ethnicity during the Middle Paleolithic. He argued that it was far more plausible that the tools found in a level reflected the activities that took place there. Different tools would be used, depending on the use of the site, whether for the preparation of hides, for butchery, or, as Bordes joked back, for peeling carrots. For Binford, the idea of Neanderthal ethnicity was an illusion built of Bordes's biases.

**Dissenting Voices.** As Binford and Bordes squared off, the study of Middle Paleolithic stone tool variability became an archaeological cause célèbre pitting the "traditional" European archaeologists against the brash American "New Archaeologists." Ultimately, it became a classic debate over the relative importance of culture and biological adaptation in archaeology. However, a number of studies emerged that undermined some of the central arguments of both Binford and Bordes.

Paul Mellars (1996) studied the sequences from southern France and reached the conclusion that the variants Bordes identified are, for the most part, found in a chronological sequence. Contrary to Bordes, Mellars did not find evidence that these variants were contemporaneous. Bordes's vision of neighboring ethnic groups is not supported by these data. Binford's picture of sites reflecting particular activity areas suffers as well, unless one imagines that a "hide-working period" was followed by a "butchery period."

Philip Chase (1986) studied the sequence of animal remains from the site of Combe Grenal. His studies failed to identify any relationship between the types of animals found or the way the bones had been processed and the type of industry. Chase's analysis further undermines Binford's position.

**The Frison Effect.** The debate between Binford and Bordes was built on the shared premise that the typology developed by Bordes was valid. On this shared basis, the two researchers went on to argue whether variation in the types of tools found was the result of ethnicity or site function. Bordes's typology is a list of tools based on subtle variations on the locations of retouching. The main type of tool is the sidescraper, which is simply a flake with retouching along the side. Sidescrapers are subdivided into flakes with retouching on one edge (simple sidescrapers), flakes with retouching on two edges (double sidescrapers), and flakes with retouching on two edges that meet (convergent sidescapers) as shown in the photo on page 118. These categories of tools are then further subdivided according to the shape of the edge.

To Bordes, tool types were fixed entities representing the goal of their manufacture. In the 1980s, an American archaeologist, Harold Dibble, developed an elegant critique of the Bordes typology (Dibble 1987). Dibble pointed out that stone tools have a lifetime of use, or use-life, that includes resharpening. This quality of stone tool

FIGURE 4.5

**The scraper reduction model proposed by Harold Dibble. As the scraper is used and resharpened, its shape and therefore its typological category changes. In this case a simple sidescraper (A) is transformed through a series of stages (B, C) into a transversal sidescraper (D).**

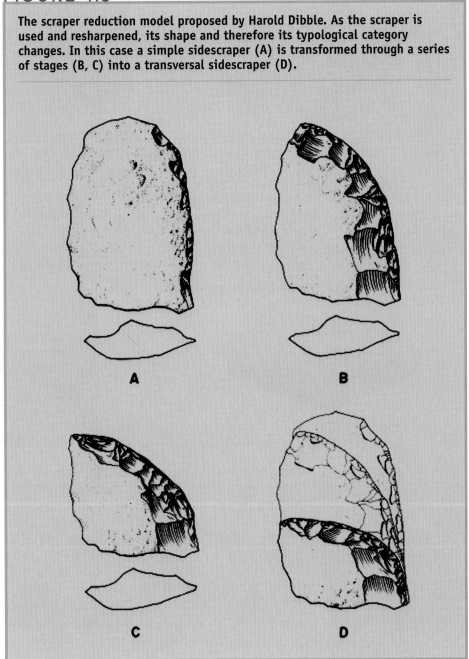

technology is known as the **Frison effect.** During its use-life, a single piece might pass through several forms as it undergoes resharpening. Dibble argued that that is exactly what happened with sidescrapers during the Middle Paleolithic. The types that Bordes saw as desired end products were actually stages in a process of a tool's use-life. A flake could begin as a single scraper, become a double scraper, and then become a convergent scraper as it passed through successive stages of resharpening; or as shown in Figure 4.5 a simple sidescraper can be transformed into a transversal sidescraper.

Dibble argued that Bordes was wrong in his view of Neanderthal society. Ethnicity was an illusion, as Binford argued. Perhaps all variability can be accounted for by the degree to which tools were exhausted. In place of Binford's site function model, Dibble proposed that variability in Middle Paleolithic stone tool industries

▶ The **Frison effect** recognizes that the shape of stone tools evolves as they are resharpened throughout their use-life.

The way Neanderthals made stone tools involved a great deal more than simply banging one rock against another. Neanderthals did use percussion methods to make stone tools. However, the process of removing flakes from cores was carefully organized, with the form of the flakes produced controlled by the knapper. It is useful to think of flint knapping as similar to a game of pool. In both pool and knapping, it is necessary to have a strategy, and this strategy involves controlling angles. In pool, it is the angles between balls on the table and between those balls and the pockets. In making stone, the control of angles allows the knapper to remove flakes of a desired shape and size.

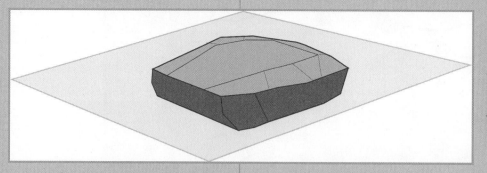

Of course, in both knapping and pool, it is also necessary to have the skill to put a plan into action!

Although Neanderthals used a number of strategies to produce flakes, the most characteristic was the Levallois method. This method can be recognized by the shape of the cores, which resemble a tortoise flipped on its back, and by the presence of flakes that are sharp edged around their entire circumference.

Recently, archaeologists have come to understand the strategy that underlies the Levallois method. In this method, the knapper conceives of the core as two surfaces that meet at a plane of intersection. The surfaces are hierarchically related, with each playing a different function. The upper surface is the surface off which the desired flakes are struck, while the lower surface provides the platforms that receive the hammer blows for the removal of these flakes. The knapper controls the shape of the Levallois flakes by shaping the convexity of the upper surface. By following these rules, a skilled knapper, whether a Neanderthal or an archaeologist, can control the form of flakes

▶ Diagram showing the organization underlying the production of flakes from a Levallois core.

produced, from the initial use of the core until it is too small to be worked. There is tremendous flexibility within the Levallois method, and the shapes of the flakes produced can include points, large oval flakes, or long, thin flakes, depending on how the knapper shapes the upper surface.

REFERENCE: Michael Chazan. (1997). Redefining Levallois. *Journal of Human Evolution* 33: 719–735.

could be explained on the basis of access to raw material and the degree of mobility of the inhabitants of the site. The further the sites were from sources of raw material, the more scrapers would be retouched. In these sites, convergent scrapers would be dominant. The more mobile a group of hunter–gatherers was, the more likely the members of the group would be to maintain their tool kit, and, in turn, the more likely there would be an increase in the number of pieces intensively retouched.

**The *Chaîne Opératoire*.** Dibble put the argument against Neanderthal ethnicity on new and more solid ground. By going to the root and challenging the very basis of Bordes's method, he managed to cast doubt on the entire theory. The French riposte came rapidly. The basis of the counterattack was the idea of the *chaîne opératoire* developed by the ethnographer and archaeologist Andrè Leroi-Gourhan. The *chaîne opératoire* looks beyond the use history of a tool to its entire life history, beginning with the gathering of raw material and ending with the spent tool finally being discarded. Leroi-Gourhan emphasized that human tool manufacture is a combination of knowledge and skill. This idea seemed intuitively true to a group of French prehistorians, who began making stone tools experimentally. To arrive at the types of flakes found on Neanderthal sites, you have to know what you are doing. The same, then, must have been true of Neanderthals. But what did they know?

The answer to this question crystallized in the study of stone tools from the site of Biache-Saint-Vaast carried out by Eric Boëda (1995). It was clear that the stone tools at Biache-Saint-Vaast were produced by a prepared-core method called the **Levallois method**, recognizable from its characteristic products. The flakes produced by the method are very large and regular and usually have a quite sharp cutting edge. The cores are asymmetrical and bifacial and bear a

**E**xperimental Levallois core (left) and flake (right). The surface of the core has been carefully shaped to allow the removal of a large sharp-edged flake.

▶ The **Levallois method** is a particular prepared-core technology used during the Middle Paleolithic, which often can be recognized on the basis of tortoise shaped cores.

striking resemblance to a tortoise flipped on its back. Because of this similarity, Levallois cores are often known as "tortoise-shaped cores." Like Dibble, Boëda was interested in getting at the process behind these types but for him the process was a process of manufacture rather than resharpening. During the study of the Biache-Saint-Vaast stone tools, Boëda realized that, to arrive at Levallois-type flakes and cores, the stone tool knappers have to respect a series of rules throughout the process. These rules are flexible, much like a strategy one might use in playing pool, and allow the knapper to respond to accidents or flaws in the material. The rules were abstract spatial concepts, such as the treatment of the block as asymmetrical and bifacial.

As Boëda and his colleagues applied this insight to Middle Paleolithic sites across Europe and the Middle East, it became apparent that there is indeed Neanderthal ethnicity, but not in the way Bordes had thought. The methods used in making flakes and the resulting types of flakes vary significantly across time and space. Researchers now realize that there is much greater diversity in the way Neanderthals made stone tools than had been thought. One important example is a group of sites in northern Europe that have produced evidence for the manufacture of elongated flake tools known as blades (Conard 1990). Nowadays, *Neanderthal ethnicity* refers to strongly held traditions in the way stone tools are manufactured. These traditions require that knowledge and skill be transmitted between generations by learning.

**Summing Up the Stones.** Dibble and Boëda have pushed the study of Middle Paleolithic stone tools into an entirely new realm, one in which the object of study is a process rather than finished objects. The stone tool analyst becomes more like an ethologist watching behavior than an art historian appreciating objects. This is not to imply that consensus reigns. Ironically, the debate between Dibble and Boëda is every bit as intense as the debate between Binford and Bordes. However, it is likely that both archaeologists have seized on a critical piece of the puzzle. Boëda has demonstrated that Neanderthal stone tool manufacture was highly sophisticated learned behavior. At the same time, Dibble has alerted us to the critical importance of raw material and mobility in identifying what tools will be found on a site.

FIGURE 4.6

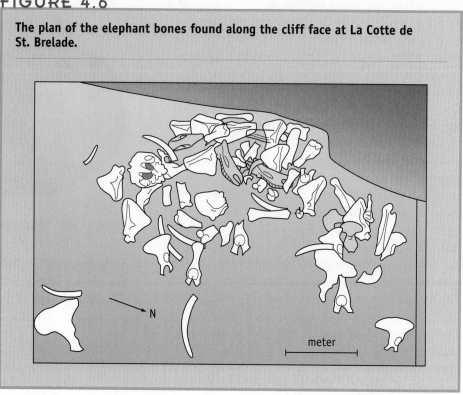

**The plan of the elephant bones found along the cliff face at La Cotte de St. Brelade.**

# Hunting

Some authors, notably Binford, have questioned whether Neanderthals were hunters. However, the discovery of a series of sites at which archaeological material is associated with a large number of animal carcasses leaves little doubt that Neanderthals were capable of hunting large game. Whether they also relied on scavenging remains an open question.

The site of **La Cotte de St. Brelade** is today located on the Jersey Islands in the English Channel. When the site was occupied during glacial Oxygen Isotope Stage 6, the Jersey Islands were connected to continental Europe due to lower sea levels. Excavations uncovered the remains of at least twenty mammoths and five woolly rhinos at the foot of a steep rock face (Scott 1986) (see Figure 4.6). These animals were deliberately stampeded over the cliff face and fell to their death in the cave below, where Neanderthal occupants butchered them.

Four Middle Paleolithic sites in southern France have produced evidence of specialized hunting of bovids, both aurochs and steppe bison. At Mauran, a 25-square-meter excavation produced a Minimum Number of Individuals (MNI) count of at least 136 bison. The excavators do not think that this was a mass kill site, but rather that it was a seasonal occupation where animals were hunted and butchered. The dating of Mauran is the subject of some controversy; however, a date of roughly 75,000 years ago, in Oxygen Isotope Stage 5, appears most likely.

There is no evidence of highly developed hunting equipment during the Middle Paleolithic. From the discovery of the wooden spear at the Lower Paleolithic site of Schöningen, we can assume that such tools were used, although they are rarely preserved. Stone tools that could have been used as spear tips are found in small numbers on most Middle Paleolithic sites in Europe. In the Middle East, such pieces are more common, and use–wear analysis of pointed Levallois flakes

**La Cotte de St. Brelade** on the Jersey Islands has produced evidence that Neanderthals hunted mammoths by stampeding them off a cliff.

from the site of Kebara Cave in Israel supports the identification of these flakes as spear tips (Shea et al. 2001).

Graphic proof that Neanderthals used stone spearpoints in hunting has been found at the Middle Paleolithic site of Umm el Tlel in Syria (Boëda et al. 1999). Umm el Tlel is an open-air site with 57 levels of Middle Paleolithic occupation and excellent preservation of animal bones. The site has not been dated exactly, but it is over 50,000 years old. At Umm el Tlel, a fragment of a Levallois point was found embedded in the cervical vertebra (neck bone) of a wild ass. The point had clearly entered the bone while the animal was alive, and the blow most likely immobilized the animal. The excavators have demonstrated that the spearpoint had to have entered the animal with considerable force and was more likely to have been thrown than thrust.

Despite the clear evidence of Neanderthal hunting, the technology used in hunting was fairly basic. The only methods available to Neanderthals were hunting with handheld and perhaps thrown spears and communal hunting by driving animals over a cliff, as occurred at La Cotte de St. Brelade. Some have argued that the high incidence of trauma, such as healed broken bones, found on Neanderthal skeletons was the result of hunting with minimal technology. One study found that the incidence of trauma among Neanderthals agrees well with the pattern found among rodeo riders (Berger and Trinkaus 1995).

**Stable-Isotope Analysis.** The evidence for Neanderthal hunting is overwhelming but provides little information about the role of meat in the Neanderthal diet. Studies of the bone chemistry of Neanderthal fossils from Belgium, France, and Croatia suggest that Neanderthals were essentially meat eaters. In ecological terms, these studies have demonstrated that Neanderthals were at the top of the food chain, or at a high trophic level. The chemical signature of Neanderthal bones matches the signature of bones of predators such as the giant lion Panthera and wolves (Bocherens et al. 2001).

Chemical evidence of the nature of the diet is based on the relative proportions of isotopes that build up in bone collagen during life. Collagen is the protein that produces the structure

A fragment of a Levallois point embedded in the vertebra of a wild ass from the site of Umm el Tlel, Syria. The upper picture shows an overview; the middle view is a detail; the bottom is a diagram showing where the Levallois point entered the animal.

of bone. The amount of $^{15}N$ in bone collagen increases between the food and the consumer. As one rises within the food chain, the amount of $^{15}N$ increases. Analyses of Neanderthal fossils from three sites in Belgium and one in Croatia show that the $^{15}N$ found in the bones of Neanderthals is equaled only by the $^{15}N$ found in the bones of predators.

A similar study of a Neanderthal fossil from the site of St. Césaire, France, examined the ratios of strontium to calcium and barium to calcium. These ratios are lower the higher one moves in the food chain. The low ratios of strontium to calcium and barium to calcium found in the St. Césaire fossil suggest that 97 percent of the diet of this individual consisted of meat (Balter et al. 2002).

Excavation at Kebara Cave.

Excavations at **Kebara Cave** have produced important evidence about the nature of Neanderthal occupation of cave sites.

## Site Organization and the Use of Fire

The evidence from animal bones and from the chemical analysis of Neanderthal fossils demonstrates that Neanderthals were hunters. Neanderthal sites include specialized kill sites, such as Mauran, but most sites appear to fit well with Glynn Isaac's concept of a base camp (see Chapter 3). These sites are sheltered locations to which meat and other resources would have been brought back for consumption. Many of the Neanderthals' base camp sites are located in caves, which serve as excellent depositional contexts with well-preserved archaeological remains. Many Neanderthal sites show evidence of intensive occupation and a deep accumulation of archaeological layers. Microscopic analysis of the sediments found in Middle Paleolithic cave sites shows that, although some of the fill is made up of sediments blown into the cave, a large number of sediments are the products of human activities, including charcoal, bone fragments, and fragments of stone tools.

Although alignments of stones are occasionally reported, there is very little evidence for any kind of construction at Neanderthal sites. A possible exception is a circle of large mammoth bones found at the site of Moldova in the Ukraine, a configuration that has been interpreted as the remains of a hut. The careful horizontal excavation of cave sites has begun to show that there is spatial organization to Neanderthal habitations. **Kebara Cave,** Israel, is a Neanderthal cave site dating to approximately 50,000 years ago (Bar-Yosef et al. 1992). The horizontal excavation of the central part of the cave indicates that the main living surface was relatively clean, while the sides of the cave were refuse areas into which bones were tossed. A

# TOOLBOX:
## Micromorphology

Soil micromorphology is a method used to make a detailed examination of the deposits that make up an archaeological site. Micromorphologists work by taking a block of sediment out of a section and then looking at microscopic traces of stratigraphy. The block is carefully removed from the section and is then encased in plaster or tape for transport to the laboratory, where it is placed in a vacuum chamber and impregnated with silicon. Once the silicon has hardened, a thin slice can be taken from the sample for examination under a microscope.

Micromorphologists have shown that a single depositional unit is in fact made up of a very large number of discrete events. The power of micromorphology is that it can tell us a great deal about how a feature formed. For example, micromorphology can identify rodent activity and the multiple events involved in resurfacing floors. In Paleolithic archaeology, micromorphology is a valuable tool for identifying the often ephemeral traces of occupation left by hunter–gatherers. At Kebara Cave in Israel, micromorphology has demonstrated that the stratigraphy of the Middle Paleolithic occupation consists of hundreds of individual hearths built up one on top of another. Micromorphological analysis at Kebara Cave has also shown that a high percentage of the sediments are anthropogenic–microscopic pieces of bone, charcoal, and stone tools brought in by the Neanderthals who occupied the site.

REFERENCE: M. A. Courty, P. Goldberg, and R. Macphail (1989). *Soils and Micromporphology in Archaeology.* Cambridge, UK: Cambridge University Press.

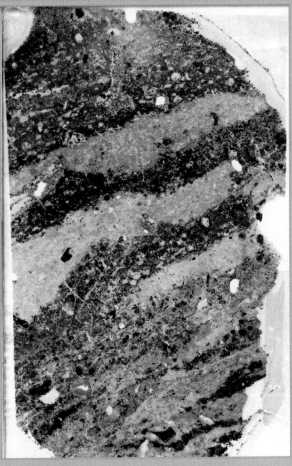

▶ **Micromorphology thin section taken from the hearth deposits of Kebara Cave. The black areas are charcoal, and the white streaks are the remains of ash.**

feature found in the central area appears to have been a pit used for the collection of discarded material.

The most significant features found at Kebara cave were hearths. In horizontal excavation, these hearths were poorly defined, and no stones were used to delimit a fireplace. Vertical excavation of the site produced a section that is striped black and white. Microscopic analyses of these deposits show that they are the remains of numerous simple fires. The black layers are charcoal, the white layers ash. Similar evidence of an extensive use of fire is found on most Neanderthal sites. Not only are there burnt sediments, but burnt flint and bone are also very common.

Neanderthal base camps are apparently modest encampments that include central living areas with hearths and peripheral areas used as dumps. There is no

The Kebara Neanderthal. This photo is of a cast made before the fossil was removed from the ground. Notice that the right arm is held close to the body, probably held in place by the limits of the burial pit.

evidence that the hearths were maintained or constructed. One significant complication in the study of Neanderthal cave sites is that the caves were shared (although not at the same time) by Neanderthals, hyenas, and, in some cases, cave bears. Distinguishing which aspects of the bone assemblage are the results of Neanderthal activity is critical.

Infant Skull

Deer Maxilla

The Amud Neanderthal child with an associated deer maxilla.

# Treatment of the Dead

The discovery of intact Neanderthal skeletons in cave sites rapidly led archaeologists to conclude that Neanderthals buried their dead, in turn leading to speculation that the Neanderthals had a concept of an afterlife. In many cases, the evidence for Neanderthal burial can be questioned (Gargett 1989). However, in a number of instances it is clear that the corpse of a Neanderthal was placed into a pit dug into the ground. Particularly clear evidence was found at Kebara Cave, where the outline of the burial pit could be traced stratigraphically. Moreover, if Neanderthals were not burying their dead, it is hard to understand why complete skeletons are recovered with no evidence of disturbance by scavengers.

At Kebara Cave, the burial pit is shallow and there is no evidence of any ritual beyond placing the body in the pit. More extravagant claims, however, have been made about a number of other sites. One such claim asserts that a Neanderthal at Shanidar Cave, Iraq, was buried with flowers (Leroi-Gourhan 1975). The claim is based on an analysis of pollen recovered from soil collected near the skeleton. However, significant questions remain about the association of the soil with the skeleton and the source of the pollen.

One of the few sites to have produced detailed evidence of an object deliberately buried with a Neanderthal is **Amud Cave**, Israel (Hovers et al. 2000). At Amud Cave, a Neanderthal infant was found in a natural niche in the side of the cave, together with the upper jaw (maxilla) of a red deer resting against the pelvis of the infant. The excavators carefully considered the possibility that the bone was found with the infant simply by chance. After all, the infant was found in a site full of animal bones and stone tools. However, the excavators concluded that such a scenario is undermined by the fact that this maxilla was the only such specimen found on the site, despite the fact that deer bones were common. They found the coincidence of a unique specimen in a clear burial context to be extremely unlikely and concluded that the maxilla was deliberately placed with the infant. The excavators did not speculate on the meaning of this gesture.

On the basis of the evidence from sites such as Kebara Cave and Amud Cave, it appears that Neanderthals did at times bury their dead in small pits, perhaps placing objects in with the deceased. However, such a reverent approach to the dead is not always to be found on Neanderthal sites. Analyses of the Neanderthal skeletal remains from the sites of Moula-Guercy, France, and Krapina, Croatia, show clear evidence of cannibalism. The Moula-Guercy Neanderthal remains were

> At **Amud Cave** in Israel, a Neanderthal child was found buried with the upper jaw of a red deer.

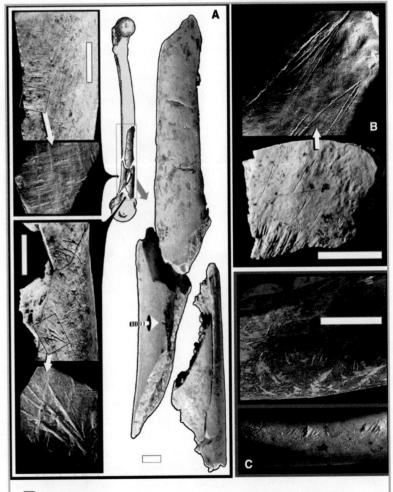

**E**vidence of cut marks on Neanderthal skull fragments from Moula-Guercy.

## A Paleoepiphany,
### by Lynne A. Schepartz,
### University of Cincinnati

I remember the feeling as if it just happened. It's not the kind of experience you forget. I had gone up to Israel from Kenya, where I had been conducting dissertation research on later Pleistocene hunter–gatherers and the biological effects of changing to herding lifeways. It was a terrific project, but like most research, it involved boring, meticulous data collection in a fascinating location. Sitting measuring teeth and bones all day for several months had burned me out. I was in serious need of a break.

And so I found myself flying up to Cairo, taking an early morning bus across the blazing Sinai Desert, and making my way to the Middle Paleolithic site of Kebara Cave. One of the project directors, Ofer Bar-Yosef, had invited me to join the excavations on my way home from Africa. I wasn't finished with my research in Africa, but I couldn't think of a better way to recharge my brain. It didn't matter that I had never been to Egypt or Israel. There were friends awaiting me there, and it was my first chance to participate in a paleoanthropological excavation.

The Kebara project was unlike any other I had ever worked on. It was run by a group of top Israeli and French Paleolithic archaeologists, paleoanthropologists, paleozoologists, and geoarchaeologists, and the diggers were all graduate students. French was the main common language, and my command of it was not stellar. But everyone was very friendly, and it was exciting to listen in on all the conversations and debates about Neanderthals and the development of the Upper Paleolithic. During the day, the cave was as quiet as a library, with all intent on their tasks. Mine was to excavate in the deepest level of the cave, expanding the 1-meter-square test pit of an earlier researcher, Moshe Stekelis. He had found the remains of a Neanderthal baby by the back wall in the 1960s. I was working with a Swiss student, and things were awfully tight in that square meter. We were only to dig another half meter to the north. Eventually, the student went to dig in another area, and I kept on in the pit. I was encountering exciting stuff: Mousterian flint artifacts, and hearths full of burnt animal remains from Neanderthal dinners. This was what I had read about in the publications of Garrod and Bate, and here I was finding it myself! Because of my inexperience and

my intense interest in bones, it was slow going. I took meticulous notes on sediment changes and called on the geologists for frequent advice, learning as I dug. I remember the French project director, Bernard Vandermeersch, coming over to visit me and exclaiming, "Enough of these animals! Find me the man!" He was not to be disappointed.

Not long before the excavation was scheduled to close, I came upon a layer of rock-hard sediments that I could not trowel through. I asked if anyone wanted to swap squares, but there were no takers, so I got a small hammer and chisel and began to break up the deposits. In them was a complete human hand bone—a metacarpal. I called the directors over, and they agreed that it could be a more recent bone that had been transported down a rodent burrow, but they suggested that I clean the area for a photo. One sweep of the brush revealed an entire mandibular tooth row in the far corner of the excavated area—and this led to more and more bones. I couldn't contain my excitement, and my shouts echoed throughout the cave. It turned out that the half meter I was excavating held most of a Neanderthal burial! It wasn't just any Neanderthal burial either: It was a very well preserved young male that mysteriously lacked the skull and one leg, but in which were spared delicate structures of the pelvis and

◀ Lynne Schepartz at Kebara (brown shirt) in 1987.

an astonishing new discovery never seen before in Neanderthals: the extremely fragile hyoid bone from the throat. I had the luck to meet this Neanderthal, nicknamed "Moshe" after Professor Stekelis, who had just barely missed discovering him two decades before, some 60,000 years after his death.

Some paleoanthropologists work all their careers to discover an important fossil or to make an exciting observation about human evolution. There seem to be two types of paleoanthropologists: those who work primarily on specimens in laboratories or museums and those who worked in the field. I wanted to be a field person, but it meant gaining experience. Kebara was my entrée to that world.

treated like all other animal bones. Evidence of butchery includes cut marks (see photo on page 129) from defleshing and percussion marks from smashing the bones to obtain marrow (Defleur et al. 1999).

## Artwork

There is currently no known artwork from Neanderthal archaeological sites. Occasionally, archaeologists have claimed to have found bones with signs of incisions. However, in every case it has been shown that the incisions were the result of gnawing by carnivores or some other natural process. One of the most spectacular recent claims was about a cave bear bone with two holes in it found at the site of Divje Babe I Cave in Slovenia. The claim was that the holes indicated that the bone was fashioned to be a musical instrument, perhaps a flute. However, a comparison of the bone in question with bones from a natural accumulation of cave bear bones shows that similar holes can occur as the result of gnawing by carnivores. Thus, it is unlikely that the piece was actually manufactured by Neanderthals.

There is evidence that Neanderthals used mineral colors. On a number of Neanderthal sites, small blocks of red ochre and black manganese are found in archaeological contexts. Some of these pieces show clear signs of being scraped by a stone tool. The function of these colorants remains enigmatic, as no painted objects have ever been found. Some have speculated that the Neanderthals would have painted their bodies or even practiced tattooing.

## Neanderthal Society

If Glynn Isaac's model is correct, then the existence of Neanderthal base camps suggests that Neanderthals, like modern hunter–gatherers, lived in societies characterized by sharing. Certainly, there is no evidence from Neanderthal sites of any markers of status or wealth. There is also almost no evidence at all, with the exception of the possible grave offering at Amud, of any kind of ritual objects.

Grasping at the structure of Neanderthal societies remains difficult. Although some evidence of reverence towards the dead exists in the form of burial, there are also clear cases of cannibalism. We can say little about gender roles in Neanderthal societies or about how a social hierarchy was established. The studies of stone tool manufacture do show that technical knowledge was passed between generations and that there is a persistence through time in local traditions of tool manufacture. Whether this translates into ethnicity is questionable. We know of no objects with which Neanderthals could have displayed their group identity. Whether the colorants found on Neanderthal sites were used for such a purpose is a matter of speculation.

There is no clear basis for determining Neanderthal group size; however, the overall sense is that, given the small size of most sites, the groups occupying them must have been relatively small. One thing that is striking is that while many sites are quite small, they show signs of intensive activity. In cave sites, this activity led to the buildup of deep stratigraphic deposits. One possibility is that Neanderthals were far more sedentary than modern human–hunter gatherers. Perhaps the reason the cave sites show such a buildup of sediments is that they were inhabited continuously. Such a pattern of occupation would be in sharp contrast to the high-mobility strategies practiced by recent hunter–gatherer groups.

Looking at the remains of small animals from the site of Hayonim Cave, Israel, Mary Stiner came up with an ingenious method of exploring Neanderthal group size and mobility (Stiner et al. 1999). Stiner found that Neanderthals at Hayonim Cave ate certain tortoises that are easy to collect, but that mature slowly. Surprisingly, she found that the tortoises were quite large and did not exhibit the reduction in size that would take place with heavy exploitation. On the basis of her observations, Stiner suggests that Neanderthal populations were "exceptionally small and that [they]. . . did not spend much time foraging in any one vicinity" (Stiner et al. 1999: 193). If there were large populations or permanent settlements, one would expect to have seen more of an impact on the tortoises. Stiner's results appear to contradict the picture of Neanderthals as quasi-sedentary hunter–gatherers in favor of a view of them as highly mobile hunter–gatherers living at an extremely low population density.

# CHAPTER SUMMARY

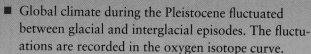

- Global climate during the Pleistocene fluctuated between glacial and interglacial episodes. The fluctuations are recorded in the oxygen isotope curve.
- The earliest evidence of human occupation of Western Europe is the TD-6 Level of the Gran Dolina site at Atapuerca, which is dated to 800,000 years ago.
- The Eurasian Acheulian is found across Europe, the Middle East, and the Indian subcontinent beginning 500,000 years ago. With the exception of Bose, China, there is little evidence of Acheulian sites east of India.
- There is little evidence of artwork or human burial during the Lower Paleolithic.
- Neanderthals share many features with modern humans, including a large brain size. There are also distinctive Neanderthal features, many of which are adaptations to cold weather.
- The pattern of similarities and differences between modern humans and Neanderthals has led to debate over the evolutionary relationship between the two groups. The main question is whether there was gene flow between populations of modern humans

in Africa and populations of Neanderthals in Europe or whether the two populations were two distinct species that evolved in isolation from *Homo erectus* or an intermediary species.
- Neanderthals occupied sites over a wide range of ecological settings, including fully glacial and interglacial Northern Europe.
- There is clear evidence that Neanderthals hunted large animals. Stable-isotope analysis indicates that meat was a major component of the Neanderthal diet.
- Neanderthal sites have no constructed features; however, the intensive use of fire is often found.
- Analyses of variability in Middle Paleolithic stone tool assemblages have produced a wide range of interpretations.
- Neanderthals appear to have buried their dead in some cases and practiced cannibalism in others. At one site, there is evidence that a Neanderthal child was buried with the jaw of a red deer.
- There is no evidence of Neanderthal (Middle Paleolithic) artwork.

# KEY TERMS

Amud Cave, 129
Atapuerca, 107
Biache-Saint-Vaast, 117
Bose, 108
Boxgrove, 109
Clactonian, 110
Eurasian Acheulian, 109

Frison Effect, 121
Kebara Cave, 126
La Cotte de St. Brelade, 124
Levallois Method, 123
Mezmaiskaya Cave, 117
Middle Paleolithic, 118
Neanderthal DNA, 117

Oxygen Isotope Curve, 106
Pleistocene, 105
Prepared-Core Technology, 119
Schöningen, Germany, 113
Zhoukoudian, 112

## REVIEW QUESTIONS

1. What are the three theories of Neanderthal phylogeny? Which view does the DNA evidence from Neanderthal fossils support?

2. How do the results of archaeological research affect the understanding of Neanderthals?

3. Why are Middle Paleolithic stone tools the subject of intense debate among archaeologists?

## FOR FURTHER READING

Juan Luis de Arsuaga, Andy Klatt, and Juan Carlos Sastre. (2002). *The Neanderthal's Necklace: In Search of the First Thinkers.* New York: Four Walls Eight Windows.

Clive Gamble. (1993). *Timewalkers: The Prehistory of Global Colonization.* Cambridge, Massachusetts: Harvard University Press.

John and Katherine Imbrie. (1979). *Ice Ages: Solving the Mystery.* Short Hills, New Jersey: Enslow Publishers.

Henri Laville, Jean Phillipe Rigaud, and James Sackett. (1980). *Rock Shelters of the Perigord: Geological Stratigraphy and Archaeological Succession.* New York: Academic Press.

Paul Mellars. (1996). *The Neanderthal Legacy.* Princeton, New Jersey: Princeton University Press.

Michael Pitts and Mark Roberts. (1997). *Fairweather Eden: Life in Britain Half a Million Years Ago as Revealed by the Excavations at Boxgrove.* London: Century Books.

Christopher Stringer and Clive Gamble. (1993.) *In Search of the Neanderthals.* New York: Thames and Hudson.

Ian Tattersall. (1999). *The Last Neanderthal: The Rise, Success, and Mysterious Extinction of our Closest Human Relatives.* Boulder, Colorado: Westview Press.

Ian Tattersall and Jeffrey Schwartz. (2000). *Extinct Humans.* Boulder, Colorado: Westview Press.

Erik Trinkaus and Pat Shipman. (1993). *The Neanderthals: Changing the Image of Mankind.* New York: Knopf.

# The Origin of Modern Humans

The view from Klasies River Mouth, South Africa.

MODERN HUMANS first appeared in Africa between 200,000 and 100,000 years ago and replaced Neanderthals in Europe between 40,000 and 27,000 years ago. The arrival of modern humans in Europe was marked by a dramatic change in material culture known as the Middle to Upper Paleolithic Transition. After reading this chapter, you should understand:

▶ The chronological and archaeological relationship between Neanderthals and modern humans in the Middle East.

▶ The major characteristics of the Middle Stone Age.

▶ The three main models for the replacement of Neanderthals by modern humans.

▶ The major characteristics of the Upper Paleolithic.

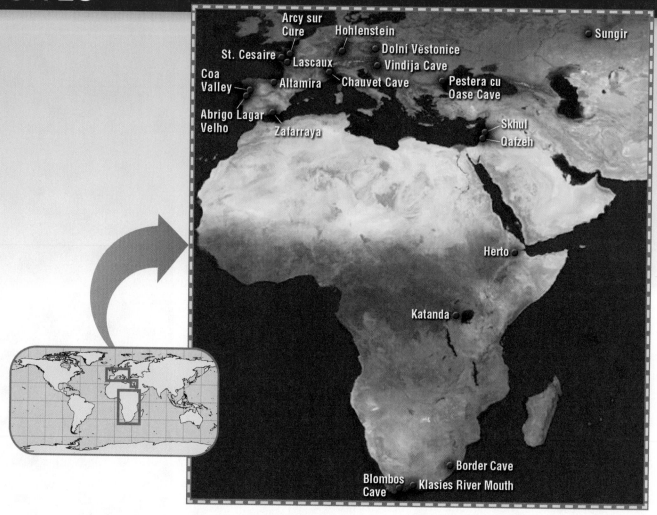

A visit to Lascaux Cave in southwestern France begins with a descent into inky blackness. Visitors, limited to a small number in order to preserve the cave, are asked to dip their feet in a pan filled with a disinfectant and then are ushered through a door into a chamber shrouded in darkness, where they wait until the guide is

**A** panoramic view of Lascaux Cave, France.

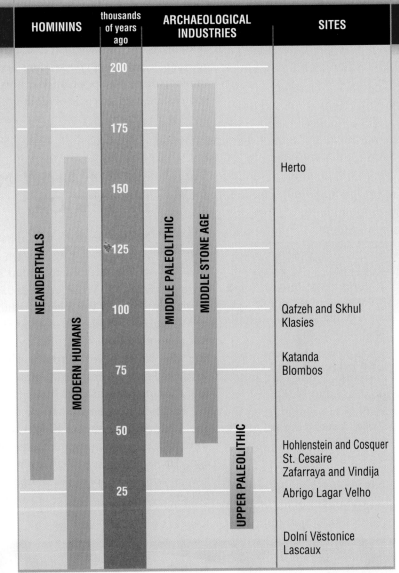

| HOMININS | thousands of years ago | ARCHAEOLOGICAL INDUSTRIES | | SITES |
|---|---|---|---|---|
| | 200 | | | |
| | 175 | | | |
| | 150 | | | Herto |
| NEANDERTHALS | 125 | MIDDLE PALEOLITHIC | MIDDLE STONE AGE | |
| | 100 | | | Qafzeh and Skhul Klasies |
| MODERN HUMANS | 75 | | | Katanda Blombos |
| | 50 | | UPPER PALEOLITHIC | Hohlenstein and Cosquer St. Cesaire Zafarraya and Vindija |
| | 25 | | | Abrigo Lagar Velho |
| | | | | Dolní Věstonice Lascaux |

ready. A switch is thrown, and in the dazzle of newly erupting light eyes are drawn upward to gaze in awe at scenes of massive bulls painted onto the cave walls 15,000 years ago. The wonder of Lascaux Cave is of such power that it stuns even the most jaded. One feels an instinctive connection to these people who shared our drive to represent the world—to make art of our experience. How did humanity move from the age of *Homo erectus* and Neanderthals to the explosion of creativity found on the walls of Lascaux Cave? This question has both inspired and vexed archaeologists for close to a century as they have struggled to understand the origin of modern humans and the fate of Neanderthals.

We begin this chapter with an examination of the biological definition of *modern humans*. We then move to Africa to trace the earliest evidence for modern human fossils and to explore what archaeology can tell us about these earliest members of our species. Next, we pause to consider the relationship between modern humans and Neanderthals in the Middle East before continuing on to Europe and the momentous question of the last Neanderthals. We will then be in a position to consider the revolution in human culture that led to the painted cave of Lascaux.

## 5.1 WHAT IS A MODERN HUMAN?

The term **modern human** refers to all members of the biological species *Homo sapiens,* including all living humans. On both genetic and anatomical grounds, some authors argue that the similarity among human populations requires that all humans be included under a single subspecies: *Homo sapiens sapiens.* Studies of the genetic diversity of living humans indicate a very low degree of species diversity. Most of the genetic variation within living humans is found within single populations rather than between populations. The low genetic variation within modern humans reflects a relatively recent common ancestry.

▶ The term **modern humans** refers to the members of the species *Homo sapiens,* which includes all living humans.

The traits found on the skull that distinguish modern humans include large brain size (1200–1700 cubic centimeters), a globular braincase, a vertical forehead, reduced brow ridges, and a pronounced chin. Modern human bodies have reduced body mass, a narrow trunk, and a unique pelvic shape. Tooth size also tends to be reduced. There is, of course, considerable variability among living humans, both as individuals and as populations; however, the anatomical traits that define *Homo sapiens* are characteristic of all living human populations.

# 5.2 EARLY MODERN HUMANS IN AFRICA

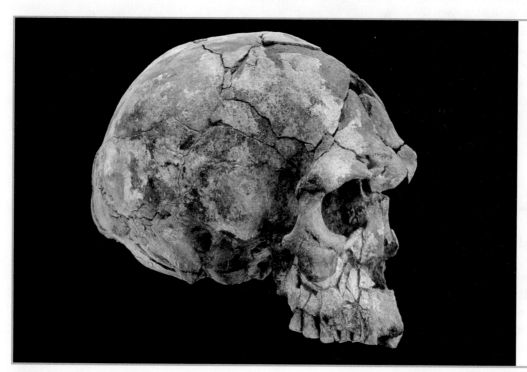

Modern humans first appeared in Africa between 200,000 and 100,000 years ago, during Oxygen Isotope Stages 6–3. The oldest known fossils clearly ascribed to *Homo sapiens* were discovered in the Middle Awash region of Ethiopia (White et al. 2003). At the **Herto** site, one adult skull, a partial juvenile skull, and a fragmentary adult skull were found eroding out of a level dated by the argon method between 160,000 and 154,000 years ago. The complete skull has a large brain, 1,450 cubic centimeters, and lacks any of the specialized traits that characterize Neanderthals. The skull has been placed within its own subspecies, *Homo sapiens idaltu*, because it retains some traits from *Homo erectus* not found among later modern humans.

Fragments of fossils that are clearly modern humans have also been found in South Africa at the sites of **Klasies River Mouth** and **Border Cave** (Deacon and Deacon 1999). In both cases, the fossils are dated to between 70,000 and 120,000 years ago. The collection of fossils from Klasies River Mouth includes bits of a skull, a jaw, an arm, and a foot. The morphology of all these fossils fits within the range for modern humans.

> The oldest known fossil of a modern human was discovered at the site of **Herto, Ethiopia,** and was dated to between 160,000 and 154,000 years ago.
>
> Fossils of modern humans dated to between 120,000 and 70,000 years ago have been discovered at the South African sites of **Klasies River Mouth** and **Border Cave.**

**T**he Herto fossil. The significant features that demonstrate that this is a modern human include the rounded form of the skull and the absence of forward projection in the face.

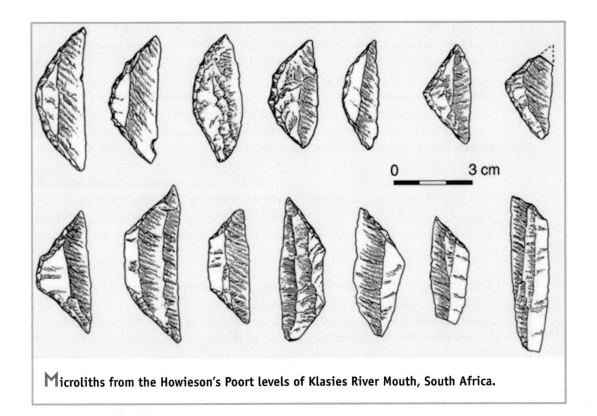

Microliths from the Howieson's Poort levels of Klasies River Mouth, South Africa.

## The African Middle Stone Age

The Acheulian industries in Africa were replaced between 300,000 and 200,000 years ago by a group of industries known as the **Middle Stone Age.** The Middle Stone Age, which ended roughly 40,000 years ago, is the archaeological context for the earliest modern humans.

**Stone Tools.** The technology of stone tool manufacture in the Middle Stone Age in Africa has many similarities to that of the European Middle Paleolithic. For example, it is now recognized that the Levallois method was widely used in Africa during the Middle Stone Age. However, when one looks at the African continent as a whole, it becomes evident that the Middle Stone Age includes a greater degree of variation than is found in the Middle Paleolithic. Also, types of tools are found in the Middle Stone Age that are absent from the Middle Paleolithic.

Across Africa, a number of distinct Middle Stone Age industries have been identified (McBrearty and Brooks 2000). The **Aterian** is a North African stone tool industry distinguished by the presence of points with a pronounced tang—a small projection located at the base of the point and used to secure the point to a spear or handle. Aterian tools also include finely made bifacial tools that served as knives or hunting points.

The **Sangoan/Lupemban** is a Middle Stone Age industry found in Central and East Africa. Characterized by very crude heavy-duty tools, the Sangoan/Lupemban might be indicative of an adaptation to a heavily wooded environment.

The **Howieson's Poort** is an industry that has been identified in South Africa. Among the sites on which Howieson's Poort tools have been discovered is Klasies River Mouth. The tools found on Howieson's Poort sites include very small crescent-shaped implements known as microliths, which had to have been used as part of a complex tool made by putting together a number of pieces. The most likely function of these tools is as an element of spears or arrows.

▶ The **Middle Stone Age** refers to the archaeological period of the earliest modern humans in Africa. The Middle Stone Age began between 300,000 and 200,000 years ago and ended around 40,000 years ago.

The Middle Stone Age includes a number of distinct industries, including
▶ the **Aterian,** the **Sangoan/Lupemban,** and the **Howieson's Poort** industries.

**Bone Tools.** **Katanda** is a site located on cliffs overlooking the Semliki River in the Democratic Republic of Congo (Yellen et al. 1995). Dating of the site has been complicated; however, all methods agree on a date that is earlier than 75,000 years ago, and the stone tools are characteristic of the Middle Stone Age (Brooks et al. 1995). The excavations at Katanda uncovered ten remarkable barbed bone points, along with a smaller number of unbarbed bone points and one piece identified as a bone knife. These are the oldest tools of those types known in the world. Although barbed points are often used on harpoons, the excavators believe that the grooves on the base of the points suggest that the points were mounted on spears.

Bone points have also been found in Middle Stone Age sites in South Africa. At the site of Blombos Cave, located at the southern tip of Africa, twenty-one bone tools were found, including two points and a number of awls (Henshilwood and Sealy 1997). The Middle Stone Age levels at Blombos Cave have been dated to 77,000 years ago by thermoluminescence.

**Adaptation.** The remains of large game are found on Middle Stone Age sites, at which it appears that hunting took place. At *Klasies River Mouth*, a stone tool was found embedded in the vertebrae of a bovid. Middle Stone Age sites, including Klasies River Mouth, also show evidence of the kind of intensive use of fire documented at Kebara Cave and other Neanderthal sites.

At Klasies River Mouth and a number of other Middle Stone Age sites, large quantities of shellfish were found, along with seal bones. In contrast, the use of marine resources is rare on Neanderthal sites. At a site on the Buri peninsula on the coast of the Red Sea in Eritrea, Middle Stone Age tools were found embedded in a coral reef deposit (Walter et al. 2000). Clearly, those who wielded these tools were people living at the edge of the sea, and it is likely that they were exploiting shellfish and other marine resources. Katanda has produced impressive evidence of fishing. Among the faunal remains recovered were many bones of large catfish weighing over 35 kg.

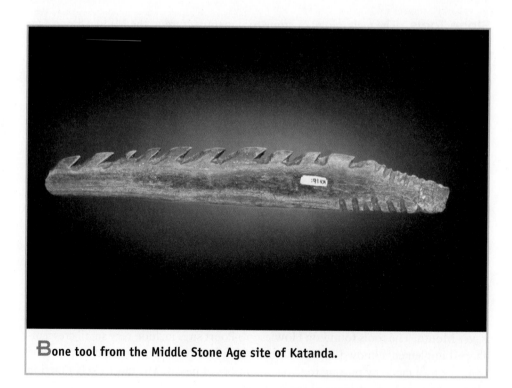

**B**one tool from the Middle Stone Age site of Katanda.

The Blombos incised ochre.

**Art.** In 1999 and 2000, two pieces of ochre with incised designs were found at **Blombos Cave,** South Africa, in a Middle Stone Age level dated to 77,000 years ago (Henshilwood et al. 2002). Ochre is a soft, red, iron-rich rock often used as a pigment. More than 8,000 pieces of ochre, many with traces of use, have been found in the Middle Stone Age levels at Blombos Cave. Both pieces of incised ochre are small—between 5 and 7 centimeters long. The incisions are a set of hatched lines on one face of the piece. These modest artifacts are the earliest evidence in the archaeological record of a hominin marking a pattern.

But what are these objects? The Blombos Cave artifacts have received considerable attention as the earliest evidence of human artwork or symbolic behavior. *Symbolic behavior* suggests that these artifacts are meant to represent something, while *artwork* implies that they were incised with an aesthetic goal in mind. This is a lot of baggage for a series of lines scratched into small pieces of ochre. Untangling the significance of the simple pattern of lines found at Blombos Cave remains one of the most difficult challenges facing Paleolithic archaeologists.

A collection of pierced shells was also found at Blombos Cave. Pierced objects have been reported from a number of Aterian sites in North Africa, and a number of late Middle Stone Age sites are reported to have included beads. A particularly interesting discovery is a painted slab with the depiction of an animal, found in the Apollo 11 Cave in Namibia. The slab is reported to come from a Middle Stone Age context, but the date provided is between 26,000 and 28,000 years old, which raises some questions about this attribution.

> ▶ At **Blombos Cave,** a piece of ochre with incised decoration was found in a Middle Stone Age level dated to 77,000 years ago.

## Comparing the Middle Stone Age and the Middle Paleolithic

A comparison of the Middle Stone Age archaeological record left by modern humans in Africa with the Middle Paleolithic record left by Neanderthals in Europe points to both similarities and differences. As regards the similarities, in both cases (1) stone

### Sibudu Cave
by Tracy L. Kivell, *Ph.D. candidate,* University of Toronto

My first archaeological field experience was in South Africa at Sibudu Cave, a Middle Stone Age (MSA) site in the KwaZulu-Natal region, about 40 km north of Durban and about 15 km inland from the Indian Ocean. Sibudu Cave is a sheltered sandstone inlet on a forested cliff overlooking the Tongati River. I was part of an international team of undergraduate students who excavated at the first Sibudu Cave field school in 1999 run by Lyn Wadley and Amelia Clarke of the University of the Witwatersrand, Johannesburg. This field school was part of the *Ancient Culture and Cognition in Africa (ACACIA)* project hoping to shed light on the origin of human cognitive modernity.

Understanding the point at which modern morphology and modern cognitive ability coincide has been a contentious issue for anthropologists. The controversy stems from the difficulty in defining "modern" behavior and then recognizing such cognitive changes in the archaeological record. Many researchers suggest that more finely worked, regionally distinct lithics or worked bone are evidence of modern behavior. This change is thought by some to have occurred during the later stages of the MSA. Therefore, Sibudu Cave is particularly important because it preserves a deep, continuous sequence of later MSA occupation. Areas that have been excavated thus far span from 26,000 to 61,000 years ago, with even earlier layers that have yet to be dated or fully excavated (Wadley 2004). Sibudu Cave is also one of only a few MSA sites in South Africa with good bone and vegetation preservation, and the only one found to date in the KwaZulu-Natal region (Plug 2004). Given the significance of this site and its period, the questions that could be answered by our excavation made this field school exciting and extremely informative.

A typical day in our field school included driving from our beach house accommodations along the Indian Ocean (we were quite spoiled!), past numerous sugarcane fields and acacia trees, to begin excavating by 7 A.M. We excavated in our

◀ A view of the countryside from the Sibudu Cave excavation area.

tools were made mostly by using a prepared core technology, (2) there is variability between stone tool industries, and (3) evidence supports both hunting and the intensive use of fire. Among the differences is the finding that the amount of variability in the Middle Stone Age stone tool industries is greater than that found in their Middle Paleolithic counterparts. Also, in the Middle Stone Age there are elaborate bone tools, as well as clear evidence of fishing and collecting shellfish, two elements that are rare in the Middle Paleolithic. Finally, there is modest evidence of artwork in the Middle Stone Age, while such evidence is absent in the Middle Paleolithic.

assigned squares and spent a large portion of the day sitting on the hillside, sorting through sediment. But this tedious task was well worth it, because there was so much to find at Sibudu Cave.

One of the most remarkable things about the cave was its abundance of stone tools; there were so many that they fairly eroded out of the hillside as one walked up to the excavation area. The most interesting MSA tools were small bifacial points made of hornfels (a coarse-grained stone that made these tools look like small Acheulean handaxes), as well as several hafted stone tools that are not common in the MSA. Residue analysis of some of these lithics revealed traces of animal tissues, blood, hair, plant tissues, grains, and ochre, indicating that the tools had a variety of complex uses (Williamson 2004).

Throughout the MSA layers, we found a consistent increase in the amount of ochre. Two ochre crayons

▶ The international ACA-CIA field school participants sort through sediment collected from each 1 x 1 meter square looking for artifacts such as stone tool flakes, charcoal, shells, or bone.

were found, but most of the ochre was in the form of natural chunks or rubbed off on various stone tools. This quantity of ochre is uncharacteristic of the MSA and may have its own implications as to the advanced cultural, and perhaps symbolic, capabilities of these final MSA occupants. Ostrich eggshell and micro- and macrofaunal bone were also common, including a massive hippopotamus canine tooth discovered on the last day of excavation and documented by the local Johannesburg television station.

More recent excavations have revealed bone artifacts, such as notched bone fragments and a bone pin (Cain 2004). The enigmatic Howieson's Poort tool industry has been uncovered in the older, as yet undated, layers (Wadley 2004). Thus, Sibudu Cave has yielded some of the earliest signs of human cognitive modernity, and I am thankful to have had a hand in uncovering some of it. There is still no indication that bedrock will be reached soon at Sibudu Cave, and future excavations will likely provide significant insights into this crucial period of modern human evolution.

The significance of the differences between the Middle Stone Age and the Middle Paleolithic remains elusive. Why didn't Neanderthals make bone tools? Carving a point out of bone appears no more complicated than chipping a point from flint. And what is the significance of the shellfish and fish remains found on Middle Stone Age sites? Why didn't Neanderthals exploit similar resources wherever they are available in Europe? The Blombos incised ochre is clearly important, but do these small pieces with their simple abstract design truly mark the entrance of humanity into the realm of symbolism?

# 5.3 EARLY MODERN HUMANS IN THE MIDDLE EAST

The Middle East is the crossroads of the continents, lying at the geographic intersection of Europe, Asia, and Africa. As a result, the Middle East plays a critical role in research on the origin of modern humans. Middle Stone Age Modern Humans in Africa were contemporaneous with European Middle Paleolithic Neanderthals. The critical problem is to determine what happened in the region where these two populations might have overlapped and coexisted.

Excavations at **Qafzeh Cave,** located in the hills of northern Israel, just outside of Nazareth, uncovered a number of skeletons in Middle Paleolithic levels (Vandermeersch 1981). Although, from their context, one might expect that these bones would be the skeletons of Neanderthals, as was the case at other Middle Paleolithic sites in the region, the Qafzeh skeletons are modern humans. A similar discovery was made at **Skhul Cave** on the Mediterranean Coast. The Skhul and Qafzeh discoveries raise several critical questions. The first is whether there are characteristics that distinguish the archaeological remains found on these sites from the remains found on Neanderthal sites. The second question is what the chronological relationship is between Neanderthals and modern humans.

> Modern human skeletons have been found in the Middle Paleolithic levels of **Qafzeh** and **Skhul Caves** in Israel.

## The Archaeological Record

Surprisingly, there is little that distinguishes the archaeological material found at Qafzeh and Skhul from the remains found on Neanderthal sites in the Middle East—sites such as Kebara Cave, Tabun Cave, and Amud Cave in Israel, Shanidar Cave in Iraq, and Dederiyeh Cave in Syria. Both Neanderthals and modern humans made stone tools typical of the Middle Paleolithic, often using the Levallois method. Neither group produced bone tools or very much in the way of art; the only exception is a piece of flint with an incised pattern found at Qafzeh cave. Both groups buried their dead in shallow pits with little in the way of burial goods. The discovery of a deer maxilla with a Neanderthal child at Amud is paralleled by the placement of a deer antler in a burial of a modern human at Qafzeh and a boar jaw found with a modern human buried at Skhul. Both groups lived in small sites at which evidence indicates the extensive use of fire.

## Chronology

Although the Middle Paleolithic cave sites in the Middle East all have deep stratigraphic sequences, none have produced fossils of both modern humans and Neanderthals. Thus, the chronological relationship between Neanderthals and modern humans in the region cannot be determined on the basis of stratigraphy. Until the 1980s, there was no method for dating the sites, and the general sense was that the Neanderthal sites must be early and Skhul and Qafzeh, with their modern human fossils, more recent. Many paleoanthropologists believed that modern humans likely had evolved from Neanderthals; therefore, Neanderthal sites must be earlier than modern human sites. With the development of electron spin resonance and thermoluminescence dating methods in the 1980s, it finally became possible to date the Middle Paleolithic cave sites. The results came as a shock: Skhul and Qafzeh date from between 120,000 and 80,000 years ago, while most of the Neanderthal

# TOOLBOX:
## Luminescence Dating

Luminescence dating methods are critical for the study of the later stages of human evolution. The luminescence methods that are most widely used are thermoluminescence, electron spin resonance, and optically stimulated luminescence. Thermoluminescence dates burnt stone tools made of flint, electronic spin resonance dates animal teeth, and optically stimulated luminescence dates either quartz or feldspar grains in sediments.

All minerals consist of atoms and molecules arranged in a three-dimensional lattice known as a crystal. Inevitably, flaws arise within the structure of a crystal. These flaws serve as traps that accumulate electrons over time. The rate at which electrons are trapped is a function of the natural background radiation. The rate at which electrons are accumulated in a year is known as the annual dose rate and is specific to a given locality. Thus, every time one uses a luminescence dating method, the annual dose rate at the precise location of the find must be measured. The annual dose rate can be measured with a tool called a dosimeter.

When a sample of a mineral is heated, the trapped light energy, or luminescence, is driven out of the crystals. The amount of this energy can be measured precisely. The measure of the trapped luminescence is known as the accumulated dose. If one knows the accumulated dose and the annual dose rate, it is fairly simple to divide the accumulated dose rate by the annual dose rate to determine how long the mineral has been accumulating light energy.

The problem is that crystals begin trapping energy the moment they are formed. Thus, as with argon dating, the critical factor is finding a mechanism that zeroes the clock at exactly the point in time we are interested in dating.

Thermoluminescence dating of flint is based on the observation that heating flint between 400 and 600 degrees centigrade effectively drives off the accumulated energy and thus resets the clock to zero. After the rock is heated to a temperature in that range, the crystals again begin to accumulate energy at the annual dose rate. When one finds a stone tool that was burnt, the equation accumulated dose rate divided by the annual dose rate will provide a measure of the date when the tool was burnt. If one is confident that the burning took place at the time the site was inhabited, usually as the result of the tool falling into a fire, then the foregoing equation yields a date for the occupation of the site. Fortunately, beginning in the Middle Stone Age and the Middle Paleolithic, burnt stone tools are common on archaeological sites.

Thermoluminescence can also be used for more recent periods to date the manufacture of pottery. The principle in the dating of pottery is that firing a ceramic vessel effectively zeroes the clock. Thermoluminescence dating of pottery has been particularly useful in detecting forged artifacts.

Optically stimulated luminescence works on the same principles as thermoluminescence. Among the grains that make up most sediments are crystals of quartz and feldspar. It has been observed that exposure of these grains to sunlight effectively drives out the trapped light energy and zeroes the clock. Thus, the relationship accumulated dose rate divided by the annual dose rate produces a date for when the sediments were last exposed to the sun, thereby effectively dating the time the site was buried.

Electron spin resonance works on the same principles as thermoluminescence and optically stimulated luminescence. The main application of electron spin resonance is dating the enamel layer of teeth. Tooth enamel is made up of the mineral hydroxyapatite. Because the mineral crystals form during the life of the animal, the accumulation of light energy begins when the animal is alive. The beauty of this method is that there is no need to reset the clock to zero, because the accumulation of light energy begins only at the point in time one is attempting to date. Electron spin resonance can be used on teeth covering the entire range of hominin evolution.

REFERENCE: R.E. Taylor and Martin J. Aitken, eds. (1997). *Chronometric Dating in Archaeology*. New York: Plenum Press.

## FIGURE 5.1

**Irregularities in the crystal structure of materials such as flint, teeth, and sand grains trap electrons that serve as the basis for the luminescence dating methods.**

sites produced dates that cluster in the range between 60,000 and 50,000 years ago (Valladas et al. 1988).

## Assessing the Middle Eastern Pattern

The Middle Paleolithic of the Middle East confounds our expectation of the relationship between Neanderthals and modern humans. There is no obvious difference in the behavior and technology of modern humans and Neanderthals living in the Middle East during the period between Oxygen Isotope Stage 5 and Oxygen Isotope Stage 3. In the current state of our knowledge, all that separates the behavior of these two species during that period is a single incised piece of flint. However, what is even more puzzling is that the fossils of modern humans are actually older than the Neanderthal fossils.

The Middle Eastern sequence provides clear evidence that Neanderthals were not a primitive precursor of modern humans, but rather a population that evolved in parallel with modern humans. Geographically, the Middle East is located between the European range of the Neanderthals and the African range of early modern humans. In ecological terms, the range of Neanderthals was centered in Eurasia, the range of modern humans in Africa. In periods when the Neanderthal range expanded, Neanderthal remains are found in the Middle East. When the modern human range expanded out of Africa, fossils of modern humans are found in the Middle East. There is no evidence that the modern human range expanded beyond the Middle East earlier than 60,000 years ago. However, sometime around 40,000 years ago, Neanderthals became extinct in the Middle East as part of a process that swept modern humans into Europe.

# 5.4 THE ARRIVAL OF MODERN HUMANS IN EUROPE AND THE FATE OF THE NEANDERTHALS

Extinction is an integral element of evolution. However, when extinction strikes a member of the hominin lineage, we often struggle to understand what happened. Nowhere is this problem more acute than in the case of the Neanderthals, who disappeared from Europe between 40,000 and 27,000 years ago and were replaced by populations of modern humans. The **Upper Paleolithic** is the archaeological period that corresponds to the first occupation of Europe by modern humans. The **Middle to Upper Paleolithic transition** is marked by a dramatic change to material culture. Three major theories relate to the replacement of Neanderthals by modern humans in Europe (see Figure 5.2 page 147).

The *multiregional hypothesis* is rooted in the idea that, beginning with the first spread of *Homo erectus* out of Africa, there was a continuous gene flow between populations. Therefore, positing Neanderthals as a discrete, isolated species is an artificial rendering of their lineage. Neanderthals evolved locally into modern humans as the result of a continuous gene flow between European and African populations. The multiregional hypothesis sees the Middle to Upper Paleolithic transition not as a local European phenomenon but rather as part of a global process in the evolution of modern humans.

The *Out of Africa hypothesis* argues that Neanderthal populations in Europe were replaced by invading populations of modern humans during the period

> The **Upper Paleolithic** is the archaeological period that saw the earliest occupation of Europe by modern humans. The **Middle to Upper Paleolithic transition** is marked by a dramatic change in material culture.

## FIGURE 5.2

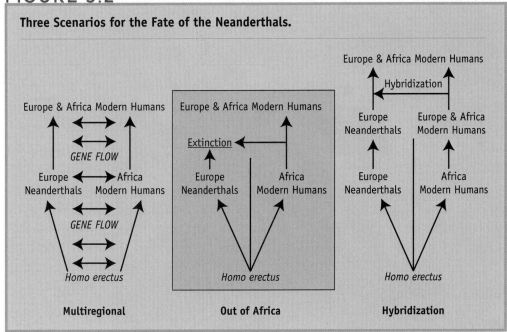

**Three Scenarios for the Fate of the Neanderthals.**

between 40,000 and 30,000 years ago. The archaeological transition is the direct result of this replacement. Neanderthals were a distinct species that evolved in parallel with modern humans and then became extinct.

The *hybridization hypothesis* proposes a middle ground by acknowledging the evidence for an influx of modern humans into Europe, but not accepting extinction of the Neanderthals as a result of that influx. Rather than becoming extinct, Neanderthals "disappeared" as a result of substantial interbreeding between populations. The archaeological transition is seen as the result of interaction between Neanderthals and modern humans.

## The Fossil Record

The fossil evidence appears to be increasingly supporting the Out of Africa position. Early fossils of modern humans have now been found in Africa at Klasies River Mouth and Herto. In Europe, there is no tendency toward modern human traits within late Neanderthal populations. The skeleton of a Neanderthal discovered at **St. Césaire** in France and dated to 36,000 years ago by thermoluminescence is in every sense a classic Neanderthal (Day 1986). The earliest well-dated modern human remains from Europe are those of a jawbone found in **Peştera cu Oase Cave** in Romania (Trinkaus et al. 2003). This mandible was collected by spelunkers among scattered bones of cave bears. The mandible itself has been dated to 36,000 years ago by accelerator mass spectrometry (AMS) radiocarbon dating.

The persistence of Neanderthal traits poses an immense problem for proponents of the multiregional hypothesis. This evidence is not problematic for proponents of the hybrid hypothesis, who expect Neanderthal traits to have persisted until there was an influx of modern humans. The hybrid hypothesis predicts that after the influx of modern humans there would be skeletons that show a mixture of Neanderthal and modern human traits. Such hybrid skeletons would be evidence of Neanderthal and modern human interbreeding.

▶ At the site of **St. Césaire** in France, a Neanderthal was found and dated to 36,000 years ago.

▶ The oldest modern human remains in Europe, found in **Peştera cu Oase Cave** in Romania, date to 36,000 years ago.

The Lagar Velho burial. Notice the red ochre stain around the skeleton, indicating that the burial was covered in ochre.

The skeleton of a modern human child discovered at **Abrigo Lagar Velho** in Portugal and dating to 24,500 years ago is thought by some to support the hybridization model.

The difficulty here with the hybrid hypothesis is that there is little agreement about how to identify a hybrid skeleton. A particularly important case is the skeleton of a child discovered in Portugal at the site of **Abrigo Lagar Velho** (Duarte et al. 2003). Dating to 24,500 years ago, the skeleton was found with Upper Paleolithic tools. The analysis of the skeleton led a group of paleoanthropologists to conclude that it "presents a mosaic of European early modern human and Neanderthal features. . . . This mosaic indicates admixture between regional Neanderthals and early modern human" (Duarte et al. 2003: 7604). However, this assessment was rapidly contested by two paleoanthropologists who concluded that "this is simply a chunky . . . child, a descendant of the modern invaders who had evicted the Neanderthals" (Tattersall and Schwartz 2003: 7119). Part of the difficulty with the Abrigo Lagar Velho skeleton is that it *is* a child. However, the fact that paleoanthropologists studying the skeleton have taken contrasting positions suggests that there is still a fundamental lack of agreement as to how to identify hybridization between Neanderthals and modern humans.

## Genetic Evidence

Another important line of evidence in the debate over the fate of the Neanderthals comes from studies of the genetic diversity of living humans. The analysis of DNA from Neanderthal fossils was discussed in the last chapter. The analysis of the DNA of living humans offers strong evidence in support of the Out of Africa hypothesis (Cann 2002). These studies work in a fashion similar to the genetic analysis of the split between the lineages of great apes and humans. Most studies look at mitochondrial DNA, which is inherited exclusively from the mother. Analyses of the mitochondrial DNA of living humans concur in identifying Africa as the place of origin of all living humans and a recent dispersal of humans out of Africa. A study published in 2000 based on the comparison of the complete DNA sequences of 53 individuals from diverse origins places the date for the spread of humans out of Africa within the last 100,000 years (Ingman et al. 2000).

Studies of the Y chromosome add important information about the male lineage. The results of these studies agree with the results of the analysis of mitochondrial DNA in identifying Africa as the region of origin for all living humans and a date for the dispersal of humans from Africa within the last 100,000 years.

The use of genetic evidence to reconstruct the later stages of human evolution is a relatively new undertaking. Several geneticists have strongly criticized the use of such evidence to support the Out of Africa model (Underhill et al. 2000). Much of their critique focuses on the statistical methods used to analyze the degree of gene flow between populations. Alan Templeton concluded a critique of the genetic evidence by stating that gene flow was common among populations and that population expansions (such as the spread of modern humans out of Africa) resulted in "interbreeding, not replacement" (Templeton 2002: 45).

## Archaeological Evidence

The fossil evidence and genetic evidence combine to strongly support the Out of Africa model. Proponents of the multiregional hypothesis are faced with the difficulty of explaining both the existence of classic Neanderthals, such as those at St. Césaire, dating to less than 40,000 years ago, and the genetic evidence from studies of both mitochondrial and Y chromosome DNA. The fossil evidence poses less of a difficulty for the hybrid hypothesis, although the genetic studies remain problematic. When we turn to the archaeological record, the balance shifts somewhat and some questions emerge for the Out of Africa model.

Before examining the archaeological data, it is important to consider the nature of archaeological evidence. In a famous debate with a French colleague, Sally Binford made the pertinent observation that "stone tools don't mate." This is a rather obvious point, but one that is nonetheless critical. The fossil record and the genetic evidence reflect patterns of mating and biological reproduction. The transmission of culture takes place, not through a process of cell replication, but through learning. Archaeology can inform us about interaction, but not about interbreeding.

European archaeologists have had a strong tendency to see the transition from the Middle to Upper Paleolithic as a local process. Several archaeological industries have been identified as transitional between the Middle and Upper Paleolithic. In Eastern Europe, the transitional industry is known as the **Szeletian** and is characterized by bifacial points. The **Ulluzian** is a transitional industry in Italy in which arched backed knives and some bone points are found.

The best-documented transitional industry is the **Châtelperronian**, found in France and northern Spain. The exact date of the Châtelperronian is the subject of debate; however, it clearly falls between 40,000 and 35,000 years ago. Châtelperronian stone tools are characterized by a type of knife known as a Châtelperronian point. Otherwise, the stone tools are similar to those found at Middle Paleolithic sites.

At the site of **Arcy-sur-Cure** in Northern France, excavators discovered a rich collection of ornaments and bone tools in a Châtelperronian level (White 1992). The ornaments include grooved and perforated canine teeth from fox, wolf, bear, hyena, and deer species and grooved and perforated incisors from bovid, horse, marmot, bear, and reindeer species. There are also small ivory beads. The bone tools include 142 items, including points, awls, and pins. The site of Quinçay is the only other Châtelperronian industry in which ornaments have been found.

A number of industries have been identified as transitional between the Middle Paleolithic and the Upper Paleolithic. These transitional industries include the ▶ **Szeletian** in Eastern Europe, the **Ulluzian** in Italy, and the **Châtelperronian** in France and northern Spain.

At the Châtelperronian site ▶ of **Arcy-sur-Cure**, France, ornaments and bone tools were found together with stone tools and a number of Neanderthal teeth.

**C**hâtelperronian carved bone bead from Arcy-sur-Cure, France.

All available evidence indicates that the Châtelperronian industry was produced by Neanderthals. The St. Césaire Neanderthal previously discussed was found in a Châtelperronian level. Identification of the Neanderthals as the hominin responsible for the Châtelperronian is supported by the discovery of several teeth identified as Neanderthal in the Châtelperronian levels of Arcy-sur-Cure.

There is considerable debate over the interpretation of the Châtelperronian industry. Critical to this debate is the chronological position of the Châtelperronian in relation to the earliest Upper Paleolithic industry, known as the Aurignacian. In all but two sites, the Aurignacian is found stratigraphically above the Châtelperronian. In the two exceptions, a Châtelperronian level is sandwiched between Aurignacian levels. This situation, described as the interstratification of Châtelperronian and Aurignacian levels, suggests that these two cultures lived at the same time in France and northern Spain.

If Neanderthals and modern humans lived in the same region at the same time, then the possibility of interaction exists. Some archaeologists suggest that the ornaments found at Arcy-sur-Cure are evidence of this interaction. They suggest also that these ornaments were made by Neanderthals copying the behavior of modern humans. Others go further and propose the possibility of exchange between Neanderthals and modern humans. Such a scenario would make the hybridization hypothesis plausible.

Although the available dates for the Châtelperronian and the earliest Upper Paleolithic intimate that these two industries overlap in time, there is room to critique those dates. A group of European archaeologists has suggested that the Châtelperronian was an independent development within Neanderthal societies that predated the arrival of modern humans in France (D'Errico et al. 1998). If they are correct, then there would not have been any sustained interactions between the two populations. These authors stress that the Châtelperronian is evidence of the culture of Neanderthals, not the influence of modern humans on Neanderthals. However, it is not clear why Neanderthals would have adopted these behaviors independently immediately before being replaced by modern humans. Why would we not see similar artifacts in earlier periods?

## The Last Neanderthals

The case of the Châtelperronian industry suggests that in some areas Neanderthals were not rapidly replaced by incoming hordes of modern humans, but rather that these two populations might have coexisted for considerable lengths of time. In other areas, it appears that Neanderthals continued to live as they had, with no evidence of interaction with or replacement by modern humans for very long periods. These areas are what biologists call refugia—isolated areas where no widespread evolutionary change has occurred. Two refugia that have been identified are the

Iberian Peninsula (Spain and Portugal) south of the Ebro River and Croatia. In these areas, Neanderthals appear to have survived in isolation from modern humans for a considerable length of time. In Spain, the site of **Zafarraya Cave** has produced Neanderthal remains and a Middle Paleolithic industry dated between 27,000 and 33,000 years ago (Hublin et al. 1995). In Croatia, two Neanderthal fossils from the site of **Vindija Cave** have been directly dated to 29,000 years ago by AMS radiocarbon (Smith et al. 1999).

## Summing Up the Evidence

Of the three models describing the fate of the Neanderthals, the multiregional hypothesis appears least likely. The absence of any trend toward modern human morphology among late Neanderthals and the genetic evidence based on both mitochondrial DNA and Y chromosome DNA argue against a local evolution of Neanderthals into modern humans.

The fossil and genetic evidence offers strong support for the Out of Africa model. Clearly, modern humans evolved in Africa long before they appeared in Europe. The fossils found with the early Upper Paleolithic industries are distinctly modern humans and could not have evolved from local Neanderthals. The genetic evidence supports Africa as the region of origin for all living humans and also supports a dispersal of modern humans after 100,000 years ago.

The archaeological evidence presents a more nuanced picture that might offer support for the hybrid theory. The arrival of modern humans was a dramatic event, but it did not signal the immediate disappearance of Neanderthals. In some areas, transitional industries such as the Châtelperronian developed that might provide evidence for interaction between Neanderthals and modern humans over a long period of time. In Spain and in Croatia, refugia areas have been identified where Neanderthals survived for thousands of years after the first arrival of modern humans in Europe. The archaeological evidence suggests that the arrival of modern humans in Europe did not spell the instant demise of Neanderthals.

> ► At **Zafarraya Cave** in Spain and **Vindija Cave** in Croatia, Neanderthal remains have been dated to between 33,000 and 27,000 years ago, suggesting that in at least these areas, Neanderthals survived long after the arrival of modern humans in Europe.

# 5.5 THE UPPER PALEOLITHIC

The first modern human hunter–gatherer societies that lived in Europe are known collectively as the Upper Paleolithic. The Upper Paleolithic is dramatically different from the preceding Middle Paleolithic.

## Chronology

The stone tool industries of the Upper Paleolithic show a clear pattern of change through time (see Table 5.1). For Western Europe, the broad chronological framework is well developed. The earliest Upper Paleolithic industry is the Aurignacian,

## TABLE 5.1

| INDUSTRY | DATE | CHARACTERISTICS |
| --- | --- | --- |
| Aurignacian | 40,000–26,000 years ago | Bladelets and split-based bone points |
| Gravettian | 26,000–23,000 years ago | Small hunting points |
| Solutrean | 23,000–20,000 years ago | Bifacial points |
| Magdalenian | 20,000–11,000 years ago | Bone harpoons |

# TOOLBOX:
## Use–Wear Analysis

Figuring out how a particular stone tool was used is not as easy as it may seem. Archaeologists have developed a method known as use–wear analysis by means of which they infer the function of a tool on the basis of microscopic traces of wear left on the edge of the tool. There are two approaches to use–wear analysis: Low-power use–wear analysis documents damage to the edge of the tool that is visible below 70-power magnification. High-power use–wear analysis examines polishes that form on the surfaces near the edge of the tool. These polishes are usually visible only at very high magnification or under a scanning electron microscope.

Use–wear analysis hinges on experiments that provide the analyst with a reference collection. The analyst uses a stone tool for a particular task, such as scraping a hide or butchering a carcass, and the wear observed on the tool can then serve as a key to understanding the wear patterns found on an archaeological sample.

One of the most compelling use–wear studies was an analysis of Solutrean points carried out by the French archaeologists Jean-Michel Geneste and Hugues Plisson. The strength of this study is that it combined multiple lines of evidence to reach the conclusion that these delicately made tools were the tips of projectiles used for hunting. The first step of the study was to produce replicas of Solutrean points and to use them for a variety of tasks, including shooting at a target with a longbow, spear thrower, and crossbow. The crossbow was particularly valuable, allowing for control of the speed of the arrow. Points were also used for a variety of other tasks, such as cutting and butchery. The patterns of breakage and wear found on the experimental tools were then compared with the assemblage of shouldered points found at the site of Combe Saunière in Southwestern France. The comparison of the experimental and archaeological tools enabled the archaeologists to identify the way the tools were used by Solutrean hunters.

REFERENCE: Jean-Michel Geneste and Hugues Plisson. (1993). Hunting technologies and human behavior: Lithic analysis of Solutrean shouldered points. In *Before Lascaux: The Complex Record of the Early Upper Paleolithic,* edited by Heidi Knecht, Anne Pike-Tay, and Randall White. Boca Raton, Florida: CRC Press.

◀ **Experimental use of stone tools provide a reference for interpreting the traces of wear found on archaeological tools.**

dated to between 40,000 and 26,000 years ago. Aurignacian sites are found throughout Europe, and later stage Aurignacian sites are also found in the Middle East. The characteristic tools of the Aurignacian are microliths known as Dufour bladelets, which would have been used as elements in complex tools, and a characteristic bone point known as a split-based point.

The Gravettian dates to between 26,000 and 23,000 years ago and is found across much of Europe. The characteristic tools of the Gravettian are small hunting points. The following period, the Solutrean, dates between 23,000 and 20,000 years ago. The latter dates correspond to Oxygen Isotope Stage 2 and the height of the Last Glacial Maximum. The Solutrean is limited mostly to France and Spain and is characterized by the presence of beautifully thin bifacial points—pieces that have been thinned by removing flakes from each face, not by striking the rock, but by applying pressure with an antler to push off remarkably delicate flakes.

The final industry of the Upper Paleolithic is the Magdalenian, which dates to between 20,000 and 11,000 years ago. The characteristic artifacts of the Magdalenian are a vast array of bone tools, including harpoons.

## Stone and Bone Tools

The Upper Paleolithic industries include microliths and bone tools, unknown in the repertoire of the Middle Paleolithic. It is interesting that both of these types of tools are known from the Middle Stone Age of Africa, bone tools from Katanda and Blombos and microliths from the Howieson's Poort.

In the Upper Paleolithic, many tools were made on blades, defined as flakes (pieces detached from a core) that are twice as long as they are wide. The dominant types of tools are endscrapers, which are blades that have been retouched at the end, and burins—flakes or blades off of which a flake, known as a burin spall, has been removed along one edge. The removal of a burin spall produces a sharp-angled bit at the end of the tool, which has been likened to the burin tools used in engraving.

Perhaps the most striking aspect of Upper Paleolithic stone and bone tool industries is the presence of sophisticated points used as light projectiles. By the Gravettian industry, there is clear evidence that an atlatl, or spear thrower, was in use. An atlatl is a hooked piece of bone, ivory, or wood used to launch a light spear.

A number of archaeologists have studied the movement of the raw materials used in stone tool manufacture. During the Upper Paleolithic, raw materials, including the famous "chocolate flint" found in Poland, were moved across long distances. This pattern is interpreted as evidence of long-distance trade networks.

Upper Paleolithic stone tools. Burins (A and B) are tools with a strong chisel-like tip created by taking long flakes off the edges. The Solutrean point (C and D) was beautifully shaped by pressure flaking, resulting in a remarkably thin cross-section (C).

**B**one tools from the site of La Madelaine, France, dating to the Magdalenian period. Notice that the tools include harpoons used for either hunting or fishing as well as awls and a sewing needle.

The bone tool industry encompasses a wide range of items, including hunting tools. In the later part of the Upper Paleolithic, there is also evidence of a well-developed tool kit for sewing, including fine bone needles.

## Human Burials

Human burials are absent from the Aurignacian. Beginning in the Gravettian, burials of individuals or groups are found with rich ornamentation. Some of these burials raise questions about the extent of inequality in Upper Paleolithic societies. At Sungir in Russia, for example, two children were found buried in a context dated to 24,000 years ago (Formicola and Buzhilova 2004). The children were buried in a large, shallow grave and covered with red ochre. The wealth of artifacts found in these burials includes thousands of ivory beads (probably the remains of beaded clothes), long mammoth tusk spears, ivory daggers, pierced fox canines, antler rods, bracelets, ivory carvings of animals, disc-shaped pendants, and ivory pins.

At the site of Dolní Věstonice in Moravia, a triple burial was discovered in a context dated to 28,000 years ago (Bahn 2002). The three individuals, all young adults between seventeen and twenty years old, face south and are positioned in a striking tableau. The central skeleton is the most gracile and is most likely female. She lies on her back and her pelvic area is covered in red ochre. To her left, a heavily built male was buried lying face down, with his head turned away from the central

The triple burial at Dolní Věstonice.

figure and his hand apparently clasping hers. His head had been smashed. To the woman's right, a second male was buried with his hands positioned on her pelvis. A large piece of wood had skewered his body through to his sacrum. Burial offerings included wolf and fox tooth pendants and small ivory beads. The excavator proposed that the triple burial reproduces the failed birth of a child, the male figure on the right being a medicine man attempting to aid in the delivery and the man on the left attempting to provide comfort.

In the Sungir burial, a tremendous wealth of objects is buried with young children who would not have had a chance to accumulate such wealth through their own efforts. The practice suggests that some individuals in that society were born into positions of high status. At Dolní Věstonice, the triple burial raises the question of the connection between the three young people and the question why they were afforded such extraordinary treatment.

Detailed analysis of the skeletal remains has uncovered a surprising link between the two sites. Both the woman from Dolní Věstonice and one of the children from Sungir show evidence of pathology. The Sungir child's skeleton displays a marked bowing and shortening of the femur, while the skeleton of the woman from Dolní Věstonice exhibits deformities to her skull and her torso. Taken together, these discoveries suggest that individuals with visible deformities might have held a particular status in some Upper Paleolithic societies.

## Artwork

The hallmark of the Upper Paleolithic industry is the dramatic appearance of a spectacular range of art objects. This richness of the repertoire of symbolic artifacts is in sharp contrast to the almost total absence of such artifacts at Middle Paleolithic sites.

**Mobiliary Art.** The earliest Upper Paleolithic artwork is found in the **Aurignacian** levels of sites in southern Germany dated between 40,000 and 36,000 years ago. The most spectacular discovery was a representation of a lion-headed man found at the site of **Hohlenstein** (see photo next page). What is particularly striking about this piece of artwork is that it is a depiction, not simply of the world as it is, but of the world of imagination. Similar carvings of animals and human figures are found at Vogelherd and Geissenklösterle, also located in southern Germany (Conard 2003).

Portable art objects such as those from Vogelherd and Hohlenstein are found throughout the Upper Paleolithic. **Gravettian-period** objects that have become known as Venus figurines are found in sites across Europe. The **Venus figurines**

► At the site of **Hohlenstein** in Germany, a lion-headed figure was found in levels with an **Aurignacian** industry.

► **Venus figurines** found with the **Gravettian** industry are portable art objects depicting the female body.

The Hohlenstein ivory figure of a human with a lion's head dating to the Aurignacian period.

A Venus figurine dating to the Gravettian period from the site of Dolní Věstonice. The schematic representation of the face, large breasts and hips, and the absence of feet are features found on many Venus figurines.

vary from a highly abstract to a more detailed representation of the female body. The faces are rarely depicted in any detail and in many cases are simply blank. The feet are always absent and in some cases have been deliberately broken off. The meaning and function of these pieces are highly enigmatic and the subject of a great deal of speculation.

Some of the Upper Paleolithic mobile art is carved onto tools. Particularly notable are Magdalenian atlatls with fine engravings. Some pieces are decorated not only with depictions of animals, but also with arrays of dots and lines. Alexander Marshack has argued that these pieces were lunar calendars (Marshack 1972). However, detailed analyses carried out by Francesco D'Errico do not support the identification of these pieces as lunar calendars but do support the idea that the incisions were not simply decorative (D'Errico 1995) (see Figure 5.3). D'Errico concludes that the marks were used to store information but does not speculate as to what that information might have been.

**Cave Art.** The spectacular cave paintings discovered at Lascaux Cave in France and other sites such as Altamira in Spain are both awe-inspiring and enigmatic. The

FIGURE 5.3

**Diagram of the La Marche antler. Capital letters indicate groups of marks made by the same tool. Small letters and arrows show where the antler was turned.**

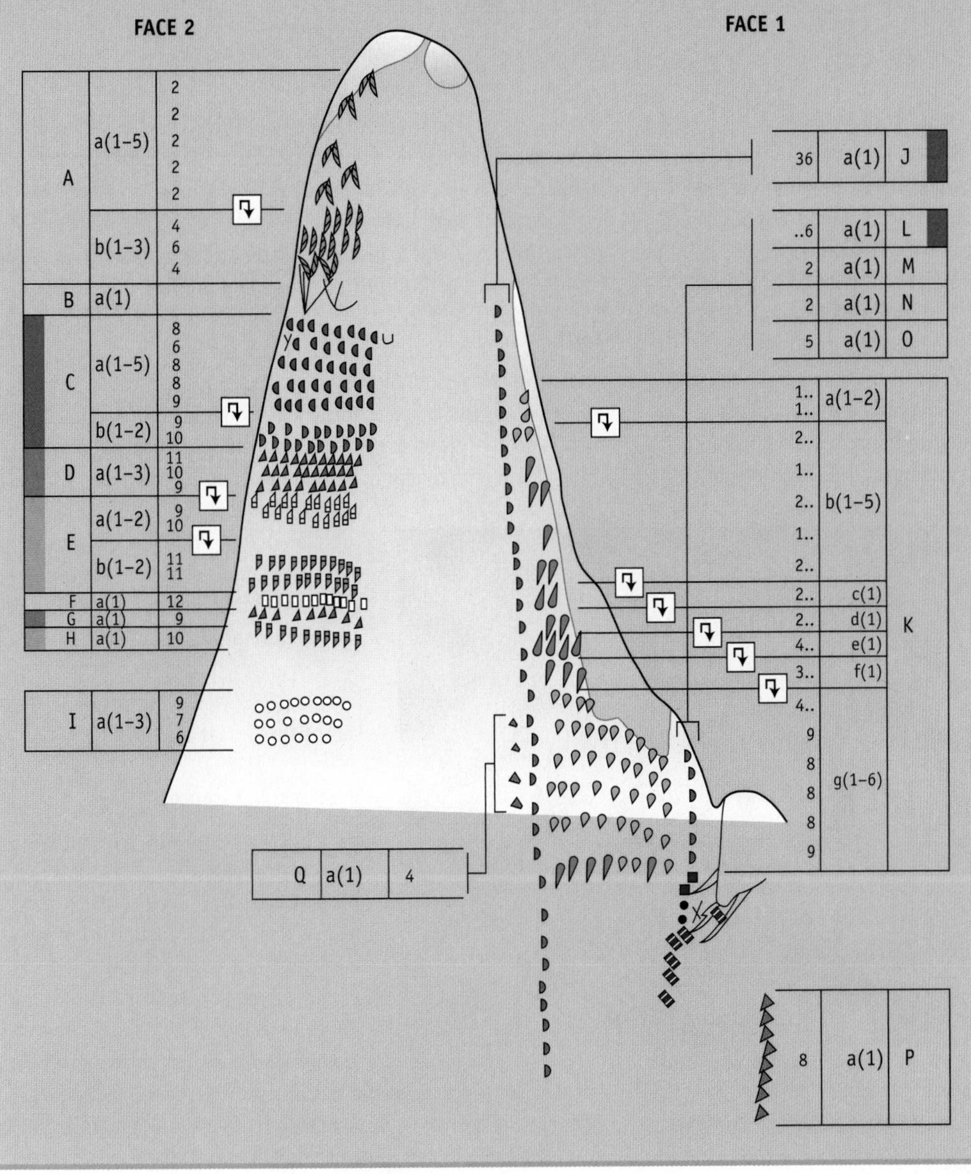

paintings were made by people who penetrated below the surface of the earth with only crude oil lamps for light. These people covered the walls of caves with sensitive depictions of the animal world, often using the irregular features of the cave to accentuate aspects of the animals' bodies. They also left stencils of their hands on the cave walls outlined by colorants they spat out of their mouths. In these handprints, fingers are often missing, most likely because they were deliberately held clenched by the artist. Not only did those people paint these caves, but also, they gauged the outlines of animals, often overlaying image over image in a dizzying mat of lines. Oddly, depictions of human figures are extremely rare in caves; most of the paintings are of animals, and abstract forms such as grids and dots are also found.

The earliest known painted cave is also one of the most recently discovered. **Chauvet Cave** was a chance discovery made by amateur spelunkers (Clottes 2003).

The earliest-known painted cave is **Chauvet Cave** in France, dated to between 38,000 and 33,000 years ago.

# TOOLBOX:
## Interpreting Paleolithic Art

When the U.S. artist Charles R. Knight depicted the painting of a Paleolithic cave, he showed the artist standing proudly before his work with a crouching assistant illuminating the scene by the light of a stone lamp. Although he wears only a simple loincloth, the artist depicted by Knight is in every other way the ideal of a Renaissance artist. One can easily imagine the same figure placed in a different setting and with a different attire representing Michelangelo himself. The painter here is pursuing art for the sake of art.

However, as one moves through a painted cave such as Lascaux, the image of the cave as a prehistoric museum begins to fade, and questions emerge. Why are paintings stacked one on top

of another? Why are paintings placed in inaccessible niches where they are hard to see? In fact, who was actually meant to see these paintings? Stripping away the electric lights and the constructed pathway, one begins to imagine the people who made the paintings, penetrating a dark realm below the earth's surface with only the light of a stone lamp to guide them. By candlelight, the walls of the caves flicker and shimmer, and the figures on the wall would seem to shift and move in the unsteady light.

Archaeologists have struggled to arrive at an understanding of the paintings in Upper Paleolithic caves. This is one of the most difficult tasks an archaeologist can undertake, because the goal is to recover the lost meaning of the paintings.

### Hunting magic

One possibility is that the paintings were elements of magic associated with hunting. Perhaps the paintings were a form of sympathetic magic, whereby the hunter would first create an

image of the animal and then be able to succeed in the hunt. Perhaps such magic even had a rational aspect: The paintings might have been plans for hunts or records of successful hunts. Proponents of the hunting magic hypothesis point to images of objects piercing the bodies of animals and to various geometric forms that can be interpreted as traps or pens.

### Fertility magic

Another explanation emphasizes aspects of the cave paintings related to fertility. Some of the arguments for this position are quite farfetched and even cite the possibility that many of the animals appear pregnant. Nonetheless, representations of females and of geometric forms resembling the vulva are found in the caves. Moreover, the female figure is frequently represented in mobiliary art, such as the Venus figurines of the Gravettian period.

◀ Charles Knight's painting of the Paleolithic artist at work.

### Shamans and trances

Both the hunting magic and fertility hypotheses emphasize the potential role of cave paintings as elements of magical practice. The conception of magic in these explanations is that it helps people arrive at an end or addresses their anxiety about the outcome of an unpredictable undertaking. Another approach to magic stresses the role of the individual mystical experience of the sorcerer or shaman, who acts as an intermediary between humans and the supernatural realm. A number of archaeologists link the practice of cave paintings to shamanism and to trances. The existence of images of humans transforming into animals, such as the figurine from Hohlenstein of a lion-headed man, suggests that shamans may have played a role in Paleolithic society. Certainly, the very act of entering caves to create a painted world suggests that the act of cave painting had a powerful spiritual component. However, whether one can explain the paintings as direct representations of what shamans visualized while in a trance or under the influence of hallucinogens remains open to question.

### Mythogram

The theories just discussed view the painted cave as the accumulation of numerous unconnected events. People went down into caves to practice magic or to experience a trance. A rather different perspective is proposed by archaeologists who see the cave as a structured whole. From this perspective, the caves, in their entirety, are to be read as a "mythogram" expressing a sophisticated metaphysical system. At first glance, such a hypothesis raises a number of questions: Why would people create a mythogram in a deeply buried cave? Why are the images overlain, sometimes many times over? Nonetheless, there is value to approaching caves as a whole entity that expresses fundamental ideas held by the groups. André Leroi-Gourhan developed an elaborate conception of the caves as expressing basic structural oppositions in the worldview of Paleolithic societies. It is not surprising that he saw the fundamental opposition as reflecting that between male and female. Leroi-Gourhan argued that the depictions on the caves were laid out to express this opposition, with certain animals associated with women and others with men.

▶ Detailed sketch of overlapping pictures of animals from the cave of Trois Frères, France.

## Information

An important approach to mobiliary art is that some pieces might have been used to store information. A particularly bold hypothesis developed by Alexander Marshack argues that some of these pieces served as lunar calendars, allowing people to predict celestial events. Although Marshack's hypothesis has been contested, there is clear evidence that in some cases markings were used to record information of some kind. Whether the painted caves could have served such a function remains to be investigated.

## The view from Les Combarelles

The meaning of cave art remains both an enigma and a topic in need of continuing research and reflection. The discovery at the Chauvet Cave of a bear skull placed on a pedestal raises the question of what types of rituals and other activities might have taken place within the caves. There is still no firm idea concerning the number of artists involved in creating the paintings and engravings found on a single cave wall. One cannot help but wonder who would have known about the paintings and who would have been able to visit the caves. Was this something everybody did in the course of a lifetime? Or was access restricted to a special group, perhaps of shamans?

The area around Lascaux, the Périgord region of southwestern France, has a large number of decorated caves. Not far from Lascaux is the less celebrated site of Les Combarelles. Because it includes few well-preserved paintings, this site is open to the public. However, a visit to Les Combarelles casts the phenomenon of cave painting in a new light. After entering the cave, you walk along a long and narrow passage. As you proceed, the guide holds up a lamp at an oblique angle to the wall, which is only inches from your face. He signals with his hand and says softly, "And here you see again, the front leg, the back leg, the back, the head." As he talks, you notice the figure of an animal engraved on the wall, and as you look up and down the passage, you realize that similar engravings run all along the walls. At Les Combarelles, we see the opposite of Knight's vision of the prehistoric artist standing and proudly considering his work. Here, the artist worked crammed up against the wall and scratched his or her design into the limestone, overlapping and cutting into existing engravings. The artists would have had little chance to gaze with satisfaction at their masterpiece, nor would others who followed. Michelangelo painting the Sistine Chapel seems a poor metaphor for what these people were doing. It would appear that the act of making the cave paintings was itself as important as regarding the finished work. As archaeologists, we are accustomed to visiting museums where objects are placed on display for us to regard. It is therefore natural that we have a tendency to treat the painted caves as museums hung with pictures. What a visit to Les Combarelles makes clear is that, to recover some of the meaning of the caves, it is essential to discard such a perspective. The caves were *not* museums; they were a part of the world in which Paleolithic people lived and experienced their lives. What is particularly fascinating is that in the process of filling the walls of these caves with paintings and engravings, these people created a world at once natural and artificial.

REFERENCE: Paul G. Bahn and Jean Vertut. (1988). *Images of the Ice Age.* New York: Facts on File.

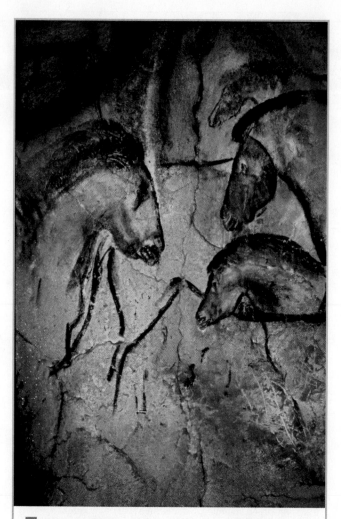

**T**hese beautiful paintings of horses from Chauvet Cave show the subtlety and expressiveness of Paleolithic cave art.

Imagine their shock when they looked around by the light of the torches and saw walls covered with panthers, battling rhinos, aurochs, and bears. The colorants used at Chauvet have been AMS radiocarbon dated to between 38,000 and 33,000 years old. The tradition of cave painting continues throughout the Upper Paleolithic. Both Lascaux and Altamira, which are among the most famous painted caves, date to the Magdalenian period.

Artwork made on objects that cannot be transported is not limited to the insides of caves. In the Coa Valley, Portugal, incised drawing of animals on exposed slabs of rock have been dated to the Upper Paleolithic (Zilhao 1998). Luckily, these unique drawings were discovered before the completion of a dam in the valley. Intense lobbying by the archaeological community led the Portuguese government to halt construction of the dam and create a park in the Coa Valley.

**Body Ornamentation.** Bone beads, pierced animal teeth, and pierced shells are found throughout the Upper Paleolithic. It is assumed that these objects were worn as necklaces or attached to clothing. Studies of impressions found on burnt clay at the site of Dolní Věstonice have identified woven textiles and basketry made from plant fibers. In an innovative study, Olga Soffer has identified depictions of headgear and other clothing on the Gravettian Venus figurines (Soffer et al. 2000).

## Site Structure

A number of open-air Upper Paleolithic sites have produced evidence of huts. Often, the existence of huts is inferred from the distribution of artifacts. At Mezherich in the Ukraine, a large circular mass of mammoth bones has been interpreted as the remains of a structure. Extensive horizontal excavations of open-air Magdalenian sites in the Paris Basin have allowed archaeologists to reconstruct the locations of tents that have left no physical trace. The distribution of animal bones and artifacts makes it possible to determine where the walls of tents once stood. In a particularly innovative study, data on the spatial distribution of artifacts and a large number of refit cores at the site of Etiolles have been combined to produce a picture of the organization of stone tool manufacture. This study demonstrated that the most experienced knappers worked on the best materials in close proximity to a central hearth, while less expert knappers worked on lower quality flint at the edges of the habitation (Pigeot 1987). At the site of Pincevent, James Enloe was able to use refit animal bones to track the sharing of meat from carcasses between habitations (Enloe 1992).

Although some Upper Paleolithic sites are quite large, there is no evidence that any of them included more than two or three structures at any given time. Margaret Conkey has interpreted some late Upper Paleolithic sites as aggregation sites where hunter–gatherer groups from a large territory would come together for a brief time (Conkey 1980).

## Subsistence

There is clear evidence that the Upper Paleolithic inhabitants of Europe were hunters. There is also limited evidence of fishing, particularly in the later part of the Upper Paleolithic. Upper Paleolithic hunters often focused on herd animals, including reindeer. Unfortunately, we know little about how plant resources were utilized during this period.

Some archaeologists see evidence that some Upper Paleolithic societies engaged in the management or control of animals. One possibility is that some groups mapped their own mobility onto the seasonal movements of a particular herd of animals; evidence of this practice is found among modern Lapp reindeer herders (Ingold 1980). There is very limited evidence to support the argument that humans controlled animals during the Upper Paleolithic in a way which anticipates their domestication. One of the most controversial pieces of evidence is an incised rock from the site of La Marche (Bahn 1978). As with many Upper Paleolithic engraved plaques, this piece is covered in a dense network of overlapping lines, so the actual depiction must be extracted by the archaeologist. The La Marche plaque clearly shows the head of a horse with a diagonal line crossing the muzzle. Paul Bahn has suggested that what is shown is a horse wearing a halter. Randall White has sharply disputed this interpretation, pointing out that similar lines are found on Magdalenian depictions of bison (White 1989). White similarly disputes the validity of the evidence in support of the view that Upper Paleolithic hunters mapped their movements onto those of particular herds.

# 5.6 EXPLAINING THE UPPER PALEOLITHIC

The richness and diversity of Upper Paleolithic material culture stands in stark contrast to that of the Middle Paleolithic. It seems obvious that this contrast must have something to do with the replacement of Neanderthals by modern humans in Europe. Many of the characteristics of the European Upper Paleolithic are anticipated by the Middle Stone Age of Africa. For example, the use of bone tools and microlithic stone tools is found in the Middle Stone Age. The discoveries at Blombos Cave demonstrate that art was not completely absent from the Middle Stone Age.

Nonetheless, nothing in the Middle Stone Age record prepares us for the cave paintings and portable art of the European Upper Paleolithic. Perhaps there simply has not been enough excavation on Middle Stone Age sites. This certainly is a possibility. New discoveries in Africa have had a tendency to bring major surprises. However, given what we know today, archaeologists are

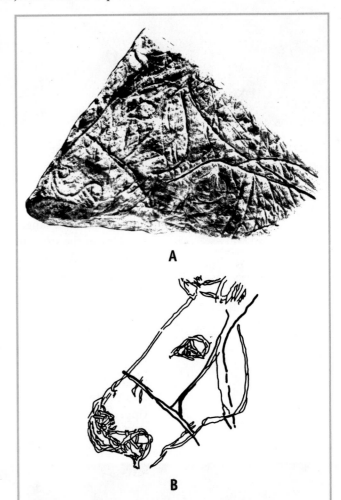

**A**

**B**

The engraved picture of a horse head from La Marche with possible evidence of a harness. A picture of the slab (A) shows the complexity of the piece. The drawing of the horse with a harness (B) was pulled out of the overlapping scenes engraved on the rock.

Later Stone Age rock art from Wildebeest Kuil, South Africa. (http://www.museumsnc.co.az/wildebeestkuil.htm).

forced to grapple with the problems posed by the Upper Paleolithic: Why did this industry appear when it did? Why did modern humans replace Neanderthals?

Because of the discoveries at Herto, Klasies River Mouth, Qafzeh, and Skhul, it is not possible to say that something about modern humans inevitably produces complex material culture. In Africa, modern humans produced Middle Stone Age industries for close to 100,000 years. In the Middle East, modern humans produced Middle Paleolithic industries for close to 50,000 years. Richard Klein has developed a bold explanation for this pattern: Klein suggest that around 50,000 years ago, there was a genetic mutation within modern human populations living in Africa. This mutation did not lead to a change in the morphology of the skeleton or the size of the brain, but it did cause changes in the organization of the brain, giving the people the cognitive capacity for language. Armed with this new capacity, the affected population experienced explosive growth and expansion. Modern humans replaced Neanderthals because modern humans had the cognitive capacity for language. Modern humans made symbolic artifacts because humans who use language will inevitably make such objects.

One of the strengths of Klein's proposal is that he sees the Upper Paleolithic as part of a global transformation of human culture. He links the Upper Paleolithic with the emergence of the African Later Stone Age, which also saw an increase in the use of clearly symbolic objects, and with the colonization of Australia and the Americas.

Klein's scenario is plausible, but difficult to prove. How does one identify a mutation that had no effect on skeletal form? How do we know that the modern humans at Herto did not have language? One of the major challenges facing Paleolithic archaeologists is to devise alternative hypotheses for the replacement of Neanderthals by modern humans and for the dramatic innovations found in the Upper Paleolithic.

## CHAPTER SUMMARY

- The earliest modern human fossil was found at the site of Herto, Ethiopia, and was dated to between 160,000 and 154,000 years ago.
- The Middle Stone Age is characterized by (1) a wide diversity of stone tool industries produced by using

prepared core technologies, (2) evidence of sophisticated bone tools, (3) hunting and the use of fish and shellfish, and (4) modest evidence of artwork.
- Modern humans are found at the sites of Skhul and Qafzeh, Israel, in layers with a Middle Paleolithic

industry dating between 120,000 and 80,000 years ago. This date is earlier than those of the Neanderthal sites in the Middle East.
- The three theories of the relationship between modern humans and Neanderthals are the multiregional hypothesis, the Out of Africa hypothesis, and the hybridization hypothesis.
- The earliest modern human fossil in Europe dates to 36,000 years ago, while the most recent Neanderthal fossil dates to between 33,000 and 27,000 years ago.

- The Middle to Upper Paleolithic transition corresponds to the appearance of modern humans in Europe and includes the development of new types of stone and bone tools and the dramatic appearance of a wide range of symbolic artifacts.
- One explanation for the Middle to Upper Paleolithic and the replacement of Neanderthals by modern humans is that modern humans were unique in possessing the cognitive capacity for language.

## KEY TERMS

Abrigo Lagar Velho, 148
Arcy-sur-Cure, 149
Aterian, 139
Aurignacian, 155
Blombos Cave, 141
Border Cave, 138
Châtelperronian, 149
Chauvet Cave, 157
Gravettian, 155
Herto, 138

Hohlenstein, 155
*Homo Sapiens*, 137
Howieson's Poort, 139
Katanda, 140
Klasies River Mouth, 138
Middle Stone Age, 139
Middle to Upper Paleolithic Transition, 146
Modern Humans 137
Peştera cu Oase Cave, 147

Qafzeh Cave, 144
Sangoan/Lupemban, 139
Skhul Cave, 144
Szeletian, 149
St. Césaire, 147
Ulluzian 149
Upper Paleolithic, 146
Venus Figurines, 155
Vindija Cave, 151
Zafarraya Cave, 151

## REVIEW QUESTIONS

1. What is the significance of the discoveries made at the Qafzeh and Skhul Caves?
2. How does the Middle Stone Age archaeological record compare with the Middle Paleolithic archaeological record?
3. Why is the modern human skeleton discovered at Abrigo Lagar Velho thought to be significant?

4. How does Klein explain the replacement of modern humans by Neanderthals and the Middle to Upper Paleolithic transition? What are the strengths and weaknesses of his hypothesis? Can you think of any alternatives?

## FOR FURTHER READING

M.J. Aitken, Chris Stringer, and Paul Mellars (Eds.). (1993). *The Origin of Modern Humans and the Impact of Chronometric Dating*. Princeton, New Jersey: Princeton University Press.

H.J. Deacon and Janette Deacon. (1999). *Human Beginnings in South Africa: Uncovering the Secrets of the Stone Age*. Cape Town: D. Phillips.

Richard Klein and Blake Edgar. (2002). *The Dawn of Human Culture*. New York: Wiley.

Heidi Knecht, Anne Pike-Tay, and Randall White (Eds.). (1993). *Before Lascaux: The Complex Record of the Early Upper Paleolithic*. Boca Raton, Florida: CRC Press.

Paul Mellars and Chris Stringer (Eds.). (1989). *The Human Revolution: Behavioural and Biological Perspectives on the Origins of Modern Humans*. Princeton, New Jersey: Princeton University Press.

Chris Stringer and Robin McKie. (1998). *African Exodus: The Origins of Modern Humans*. New York: Henry Holt.

Randall White. (1986). *Dark Caves, Bright Visions: Life in Ice Age Europe*. New York: Norton.

Milford Wolpoff and Rachel Caspari. (1997). *Race and Human Evolution*. New York: Simon and Schuster.

CHAPTER
# 6

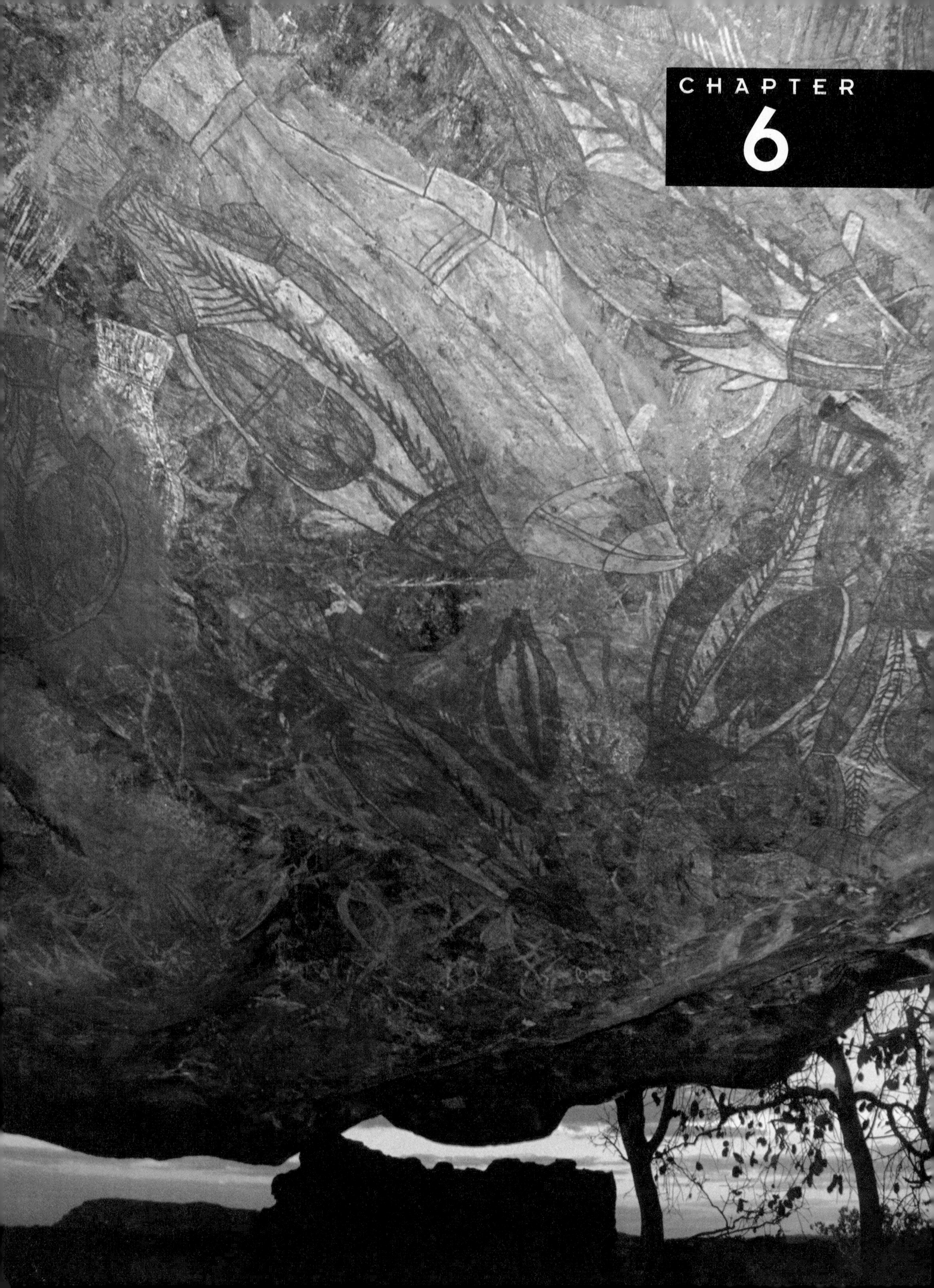

# The Peopling of Australia and the New World

Australian rock art site.

THE OCCUPATION of Australia and the Americas are major events in the global dispersal of modern humans. After reading this chapter, you should understand:

▶ The debates over the timing of the initial occupation of Australia and the Americas.

▶ The migration routes followed by the first humans moving into Australia and the Americas.

▶ The relationship between human occupation of Australia and the Americas and the extinction of megafauna.

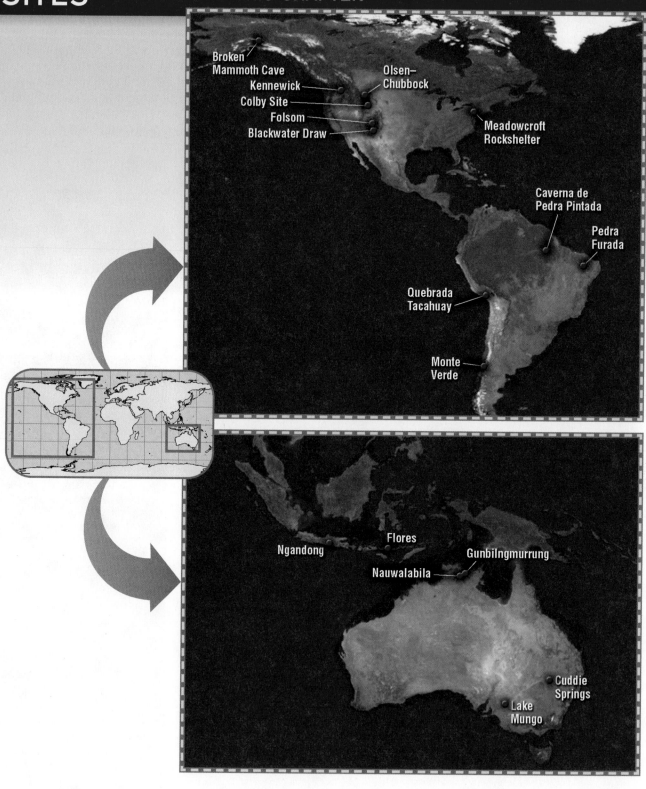

Broken
Mammoth Cave
Kennewick
Colby Site
Folsom
Blackwater Draw
Olsen–
Chubbock
Meadowcroft
Rockshelter
Caverna de
Pedra Pintada
Pedra
Furada
Quebrada
Tacahuay
Monte
Verde

Ngandong
Flores
Gunbilngmurrung
Nauwalabila
Cuddie
Springs
Lake
Mungo

| HOMININS | thousands of years ago | ARCHAEOLOGICAL INDUSTRIES | SITES |
|---|---|---|---|
| | 55 | | Nauwalabila |
| | 50 | | Lake Mungo |
| | 45 | | |
| | 40 | | Pedra Furada |
| *HOMO FLORENSIENSIS* | 35 | | |
| | 30 | | Cuddie Springs |
| | 25 | | |
| | 20 | | Meadowcroft, Rockshelter |
| | 15 | CLOVIS NENANA | Monte Verde MV II<br>Pedra Pintada<br>Quebrada Tacahuay |
| | 10 | | Olsen–Chubbock |

**G**eorge McJunkin was a quintessential scientific outsider. An African American rancher born into slavery, McJunkin became an avid amateur scientist with wide-ranging interests, including astronomy, archaeology, and fossil bones (Douglas 1997). In 1908, while fixing a fence after a storm, McJunkin noticed bones eroding out of a gully near Folsom, New Mexico. It was only in 1926, however, four years after McJunkin died, that Jesse Figgins of the Denver Museum of Natural History began excavations at Folsom. In his first season excavating there, Figgins found a distinctive spearpoint together with bison fossils. This point was thin and finely worked, with a long channel, or flute, running from the base toward the tip. Figgins's discovery was met with skepticism, but the skepticism evaporated in 1927, when another spearpoint was found lodged between the ribs of a bison skeleton. The discoveries at Folsom proved that humans had been in North America for at least 10,000 years. The discovery of a spearpoint embedded in the remains of large animals also suggested that these early occupants of the Americas were specialized big-game hunters.

In this chapter, we focus on the debates surrounding the initial human occupation of Australia and the Americas. The only hominins known from these continents are *Homo sapiens*. Migration routes into both Australia and the Americas led through East Asia, so it is important to review the current understanding of modern human origins in that area first. With this background, it is possible to move on to consider the timing of the occupation of Australia and the likely migration routes. We also consider the significance of the recent discovery of a new species belonging to the genus *Homo* on the island of Flores in Indonesia. Beyond tracking when and how people first arrived in Australia, we examine the role of humans in the extinction of megafauna on the continent and the evidence for the development of cave painting in the Australian context. We then move on to the debates concerning the timing and migration routes taken by the first people to arrive in the Americas. Here, too, we consider the role of humans in megafauna extinctions.

# TOOLBOX:
## Why Are Folsom Points Fluted?

Folsom points are among the most impressive stone tools ever made. In the first step of their manufacture, the knapper thinned the point by applying pressure along the edges with the tip of an antler and forcing off wafer-thin flakes. The process, known as pressure flaking, requires a high degree of skill and takes a significant effort to complete. However, once the point was exquisitely thinned, one step remained before it was ready. The knapper took the point and drove a long, thin flake off the base. The point was then flipped and the same procedure repeated on the other side. The result was a shallow channel, or flute, running from the base of the point to near the tip on both faces. One aspect of the process that has puzzled archaeologists is exactly how the flute was produced. Some experimental archaeologists have suggested that a lever-type device was used in fluting the point.

However, an even more puzzling issue is *why* the points were fluted. Consider that before the flute was produced, a considerable effort had been expended in carefully thinning the point with pressure flaking. All of this work was put at risk not once, but twice, as the point was subjected to the pressure required to produce the flutes. On archaeological sites, points broken during the process of fluting are common. Why take this risk with artifacts that were already suitable for use as hunting points?

A number of answers have been proposed to solve the riddle of the Folsom flute. One obvious possibility is that the flute was designed to fit a specific type of haft. Perhaps the points were designed to fit into a socket at the end of a spear shaft. Another functional explanation is that the flutes enhanced the ability of the point to penetrate an animal. However, some archaeologists question functional explanations for fluting and stress possible symbolic significance of the fluting as part of hunting rituals. None of these explanations accounts for the seeming inefficiency of investing so much energy in producing a hunting tool. One novel explanation advanced recently by Stanley Ahler and Phil Geib is that the goal of fluting was to produce a tool that could be continually resharpened as the tip was damaged during hunting. According to Ahler and Geib's theory, the investment of both effort and risk in fluting a Folsom point was balanced by the gain in efficiency from a point that could be continually resharpened.

REFERENCE: Stanley Ahler and Phil Geib. (2000). Why Flute? Folsom point design and adaptation. *Journal of Archaeological Science* 27: 799–820.

**Folsom point with associated bones from Folsom, New Mexico.**

The question of when people first arrived in Australia and the Americas is the subject of intense scientific controversy. It is important to recognize that it is also a subject of great sensitivity to indigenous people. The archaeological debate is framed entirely on the basis of scientific inquiry, which is often in conflict with native beliefs. The question of when people first arrived can conflict with native convictions that their people have been in a place since creation. Bridging these disparate worldviews requires care and respect. This is a topic archaeologists have only recently become aware of and in which great strides have already been made. The development of post-processual archaeology, which acknowledges alternative narratives and viewpoints, provides room for dialogue and constructive disagreement. Of course, issues such as the treatment of human remains that indigenous groups claim as ancestral require particular care.

## FIGURE 6.1

**Reconstruction of the components involved in Folsom point use and resharpening, A–E: The components of the hafted point including twine (A), the point itself (B), the two halves of the split wood shaft (C), a hafted point in a preliminary stage of use with minimal resharpening (D), and a hafted point that has been shortened by resharpening (E).**

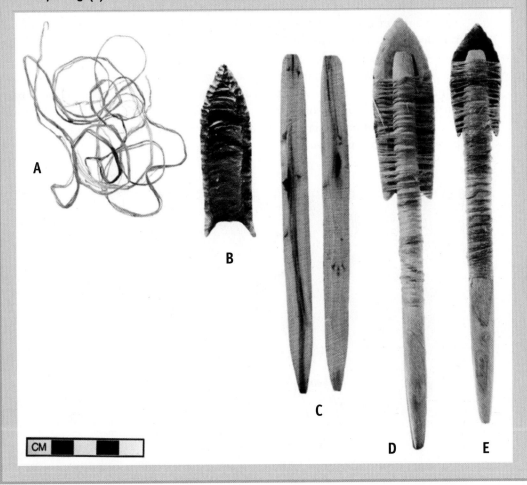

# 6.1 MODERN HUMANS IN EAST ASIA

Populations of *Homo erectus* had arrived on the Indonesian island of Java perhaps as early as 1.8 million years ago, and by 500,000 years ago *Homo erectus* was well established in China. However, what happened to East Asian populations of *Homo erectus* while modern humans were evolving in Africa and Neanderthals were evolving in Europe remains unclear. On the one hand, some paleoanthropologists argue as part of the multiregional hypothesis that there was a local East Asian evolution of modern humans from *Homo erectus* in parallel with the evolution of modern humans in Africa. On the other hand, proponents of the Out of Africa hypothesis argue vehemently that in East Asia populations of *Homo erectus* persisted until they were replaced by modern humans from Africa. Both sides of the debate recognize that they are relying on inadequate data.

The most recent known fossil of *Homo erectus* is from the site of **Ngandong** on the island of Java.

One critical piece of evidence has emerged from the dating of *Homo erectus* fossils from the island of Java. Electron spin resonance and uranium series dating of animal teeth found with *Homo erectus* fossils at the site of **Ngandong** have produced dates that range between 46,000 and 27,000 years ago (Swisher et al. 1996). If this range of dates is correct, it indicates that populations of *Homo erectus* remained in East Asia far later than anywhere else in the world. This evidence offers strong support for the Out of Africa hypothesis. However, these dates are not universally accepted, as some doubt that the animal teeth were actually found in the same deposits as the hominin fossils.

The questions concerning the fate of *Homo erectus* and the initial appearance of modern humans in East Asia provide a rather uncertain backdrop to the debates surrounding the peopling of Australia and New World (North and South America). The Paleolithic of East Asia is a critical area of research that is likely to see dramatic developments in coming years.

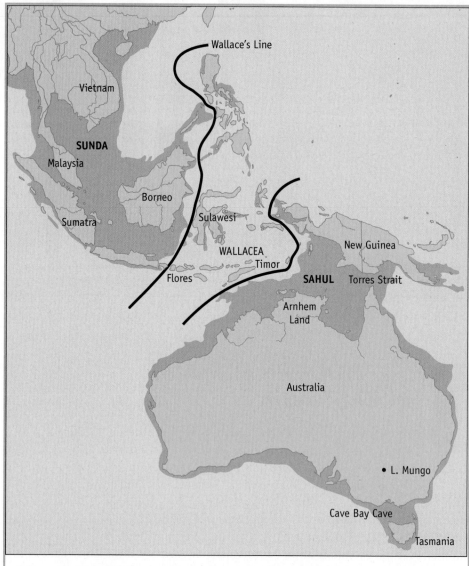

**M**ap of the landmasses of Sunda and Sahul that existed during periods of low sea level.

# 6.2 AUSTRALIA

During periods of low sea level, Australia, Tasmania, and New Guinea were linked in a landmass known as ▶ **Sahul,** and much of Southeast Asia was connected to ▶ form a landmass known as **Sunda.** Sunda and Sahul were separated by the ▶ **Wallace Line.**

During periods of glacial advance and low sea level, Australia, Tasmania, and New Guinea were connected in a landmass known as **Sahul**. A similar landmass known as **Sunda** connected much of southeast Asia, including Vietnam, Malaysia, the Philippines, and much of Indonesia. Sunda and Sahul are separated by a string of islands known as Wallacea, where the channels between the islands are too deep to have been dry land at any time for the past 50 million years. The **Wallace Line** that runs through Wallacea separates the unique animals and plants of Australia from the animal and plant communities of Southeast Asia. In order to reach Australia, humans had to cross the Wallace Line by sea.

The discovery of stone tools on the island of Flores in Wallacea suggests that *Homo erectus* was able to cross bodies of water. The levels in which stone tools are found are dated to between 800,000 and 900,000 years ago, when *Homo erectus* was the only hominin in Southeast Asia. Some authors have argued that the evidence from Flores demonstrates that *Homo erectus* was able to make and use watercraft. However, *Homo erectus* was not the only mammal species to arrive in Flores between 800,000 and 900,000 years ago. At the same time, a large elephant and a large rat also made their first appearance on the island. These animals did not arrive by a land bridge connecting Flores to the Sunda, as it is clear that no such land bridge ever existed. It is suggested that a combination of low sea level and favorable currents enabled such animals to reach Flores. It is quite likely that *Homo erectus* could have arrived through similar circumstances.

Continued excavations at Flores have stunned the scientific community with the discovery of tiny hominins who are so unique that they have been given their own

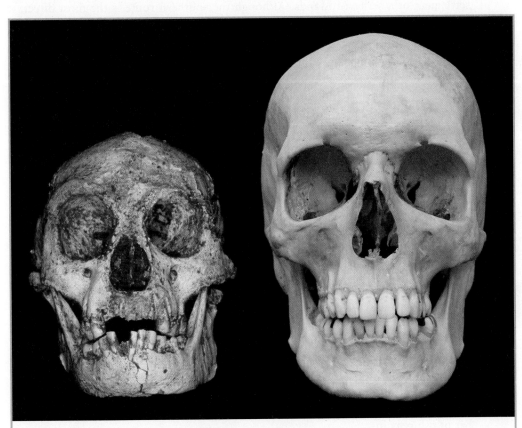

*Homo floresiensis* skull (left) next to the skull of a modern human.

species name: *Homo floresiensis* (Brown et al. 2004). The hominid remains date to the period between 38,000 and 18,000 years ago (Morwood et al. 2004). The body size of *Homo floresiensis* is quite small, and its brain size is 380 cubic centimeters, about the size of a grapefruit, which is below the range of any other member of genus *Homo*. It appears likely that the unique characteristics of *Homo floresiensis* are the result of the long-term isolation of a population of *Homo erectus* on the island of Flores for hundreds of thousands of years. There is a general tendency for isolated island populations to evolve into species with reduced body size (Van den Bergh et al. 2001). The discovery of *Homo floresiensis* raises many tantalizing issues, including the reasons for the eventual extinction of this species and the nature of their interactions with the first modern humans to arrive on the island. Initial reports suggest that *Homo floresiensis* is associated with an advanced stone tool technology, but further research is needed to understand the behavior of this unique member of genus *Homo*. Some paleoanthropologists remain unconvinced that *Homo floresiensis* is a distinct species, arguing that the fossils discovered are modern humans with a pathology known as microcephaly that results in a small brain (Martin et al. 2006).

There is no evidence that *Homo erectus* ever crossed Wallacea into Sahul. Nor is there evidence of an influx of mammals across the Wallace Line into Sahul at any time during the Pleistocene, as is found on Flores. Two possible routes for crossing Wallacea into Sahul have been identified. The northern route follows a string of small islands between the Indonesian island of Sulawesi and western New Guinea, known today as Irian Jaya. The southern route follows a series of small islands between Java and Timor, followed by a sea crossing between Timor and northern Australia. Both routes require sea voyages of greater than 10 kilometers and the settlement of a series of islands. Although the southern route is the most direct, it would have required a sea voyage of approximately 90 kilometers.

## Dating the Earliest Human Occupation

A series of sites in Australia is now well dated to the period between 60,000 and 50,000 years ago. Thus, the arrival of humans in Australia predates the arrival of modern humans in Europe by at least ten thousand years.

The earliest evidence for human occupation of Australia is found at **Nauwalabila I** and is dated to between 53,000 and 60,000 years ago.

The site of **Nauwalabila I,** located in Arnhem Land in Northern Australia, is a rock-shelter with 3 meters of archaeological deposits (Bird et al. 2002). The deepest levels have been dated by thermoluminescence and optically stimulated luminescence to between 53,000 and 60,000 years ago. Unfortunately, attempts to radio-carbon date these levels have failed. The archaeological remains from the lowest levels are mostly flake stone tools, including a thick retouched scraper. Two pieces that apparently served as grinding stones were also found.

The initial human occupation of **Lake Mungo** in southern Australia is dated to between 50,000 and 46,000 years ago.

**Lake Mungo** is one of a series of dried-out lakes known as the Willandra Lakes, located in southern Australia near the city of Canberra (Bowler et al. 2003). Two human burials and numerous stone tools have been discovered eroding out of the Lower Mungo Unit along the edge of the dried-out lake bed. The deposits in which these skeletons were found have been dated to 40,000 years ago by optically stimulated luminescence. The earliest stone tools at Lake Mungo have been dated to between 50,000 and 46,000 years ago. The stone tools found at Lake Mungo are simple flake tools and cores similar to those found at Nauwalabila I. A number of hearths were found, and the animal bones that were recovered include a large number of fish remains.

The evidence for human occupation of Australia before 60,000 years is scant. The Jinmium Cave site in Arnhem Land has produced thermoluminescence dates of

116,000 years ago for deposits with archaeological material (Spooner 1998). These dates have been contested and are not widely accepted. Current data suggest that human occupation of Australia began roughly 60,000 years ago and that the spread of humans across the continent was fairly rapid. The Lake Mungo dates indicate that humans had spread to southern Australia within ten thousand years of their initial arrival on the continent.

The current understanding of the timing of the first arrival of modern humans in Australia suggests that by 60,000 years ago they were capable of sea voyages and had already spread far beyond Africa. Some archaeologists remain skeptical about these dates and question how modern humans could have arrived in Australia before reaching Europe (O'Connell and Allen 1998). For others, the early Australian dates offer support for the multiregional hypothesis. Such an early date for modern humans in Australia might support the idea that they evolved locally in East Asia as well. Yet another possibility is that the early dates from Australia indicate that there were multiple dispersals of modern humans out of Africa. The modern human populations that arrived in Australia might have followed the same coastal route used in explaining the rapid arrival of *Homo erectus* in Java. Ultimately, we are left wondering about the voyagers who set off across the seas to arrive on a new continent. What kind of boats did they use? What compelled them to take this voyage into an unknown land?

## Megafauna Extinction

Throughout the world, there was widespread extinction of animal species at the end of the Pleistocene Ice Age. Particularly hard hit were large animals, collectively known as **megafauna.** Some have suggested that the extinction of megafauna was largely the result of hunting by modern humans; others argue that a more broadly based ecological explanation is needed.

> ▶ The Australian **megafauna** appears to have become extinct around 46,000 years ago.

The unique animal communities of Sahul fit the pattern of widespread extinction toward the end of the Pleistocene. Twenty-three of twenty-four genera of Australian land animals with a body weight greater than 45 kilograms became extinct at the end of the Pleistocene. These large animals included marsupials such as the rhinoceros-sized kangaroo *Procoptodon*, mammals, and a large flightless bird, *Genyornis newtoni.* The date of the extinction of these species is the subject of debate. The dating of 700 *Genyornis newtoni* eggshells indicates that this species disappeared suddenly around 50,000 years ago (Miller et al. 1999). A project dating paleontological sites indicates that the large placental and mammalian animals became extinct around 46,000 years ago (Roberts et al. 2001). This study restricted itself to sites in which the bones of animals were found in articulation (i.e., a part of the skeleton was found with bones in their proper anatomical positions). The reason for focusing on articulated skeletons is that in these cases there is a high degree of confidence that the bones are in their original geological context and that dating the sediments provides an accurate date for the bones. Some sites have produced unarticulated bones of megafauna in contexts dated considerably later in time. One of the most important of these sites is Cuddie Springs in southeastern Australia (Field et al. 2001). At Cuddie Springs, stone tools were found together with the bones of extinct megafauna in layers dated to between 36,000 and 27,000 years ago. There is some question as to whether these bones are in their original place of deposition, and it has not yet been possible to date the bones directly.

The preponderance of the data suggests that the extinction of Australian megafauna was an event that took place across the continent between 50,000 and 40,000 years ago. Thus, the extinction of Australian megafauna took place within

In an odd juxtaposition, a herd of sheep graze around a model reconstruction of the extinct giant marsupial.

ten to fifteen thousand years of the first arrival of humans on the continent. It is difficult to explain why an extinction took place at that time. Although there was a major climatic change in Oxygen Isotope Stage 2 (the Last Glacial Maximum) around 15–20,000 years ago, the extinction of the megafauna appears to have preceded this event by more than 20,000 years.

The fact that the megafauna extinction took place during the first ten thousand years after the first arrival of humans in Australia suggests that human activity caused the extinction. However, evidence for hunting of megafauna by humans is practically nonexistent. Cuddie Springs is one of the only sites to produce an association of stone tools and the bones of extinct animals. There is no evidence from stone tools that the first inhabitants of Australia had highly sophisticated hunting weapons. Harpoons and spear-throwers developed much later in Australian prehistory.

There is little evidence that the first inhabitants of Australia hunted large game or had a highly developed tool kit for hunting. It is therefore extremely unlikely that these people hunted the megafauna to the point of extinction. Some archaeologists have suggested that human activity altered the ecology of Australia in a manner that disrupted the highly specialized adaptations of the megafauna. One possible factor would have been human use of fire in hunting. Rhys Jones has described the aboriginal use of fire in Australia as **fire-stick farming**. Early European travelers in Australia describe the active use of fire by aboriginal societies. For example, in 1848 Thomas Mitchell wrote, "Fire is necessary to burn the grass and form those open forests in which we find the large forest-kangaroo; the native applies that fire to the grass in certain seasons; in order that a young green crop may subsequently spring up, and so attract and enable him to kill and take the

**Fire-stick farming** refers to the use of controlled burning to improve hunting conditions.

kangaroo with nets" (in Lourandos 1997: 97). If the first inhabitants of Australia used a similar strategy, then, over a period of ten thousand years, it might have resulted in the alteration of the ecology to the point where the megafaunal species became extinct.

## Rock Art

Among archaeologists, Australia is known as a continent in which a hunter–gatherer way of life persisted until contact with Europeans. This characterization of Australia does little to express the diversity and richness of aboriginal societies. Ethnographers often point to the nonmaterial aspects of aboriginal Australian culture, particularly the highly developed mythological and ritual traditions. Aspects of aboriginal mythologies have found expression in the spectacular artwork painted on thousands of rock-shelters across the continent. Many of these sites were painted recently or are still revisited and painted today. Archaeological research has begun to provide evidence that this practice is of great antiquity.

Rock art in Australia takes many forms (Chaloupka 1993). One particularly interesting approach is creating drawings by applying beeswax to a rock-shelter wall. At the site of **Gunbilngmurrung** in Western Arnhem Land, a beeswax figure of a turtle has been radiocarbon dated to 4,000 years ago (Watchman and Jones 2002). The turtle is drawn in "X-ray style," with some of the internal bone structure depicted. As at most Australian rock art sites, paintings at Gunbilngmurrung are found one on top of another. The beeswax turtle clearly lies above six older sets of figures drawn with red ochre and that must be older than 4,000 years.

In an ingenious application of optically stimulated luminescence dating, archaeologists have managed to date mud wasp nests overlying paintings on rock-shelters in Arnhem Land. In one cave, a nest overlying a mulberry-colored human figure was dated to 16,400 years ago. The human figure itself overlies a hand stencil that must be of even greater antiquity (Roberts et al. 1997).

**R**ock art from the site of Ubirr, Kakadu National Park, Australia. This figure gives a good sense of the range of equipment carried by aboriginal Australian hunter–gatherers.

► A drawing of a turtle at the **Gunbilngmurrung** rock-shelter is dated to 4,000 years ago.

► **Three Models for Human Occupation of the Americas**

- **Clovis First:** Clovis culture dated 13,500 to 12,500 years ago is the first human occupation in the Americas.
- **Pre-Clovis:** Human occupation of the Americas predates 13,500 years ago.
- **Early Arrival:** Human occupation of the Americas began as early as 30,000 to 40,000 years ago.

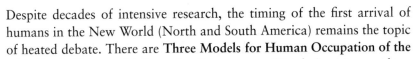

# 6.3 THE NEW WORLD

Despite decades of intensive research, the timing of the first arrival of humans in the New World (North and South America) remains the topic of heated debate. There are **Three Models for Human Occupation of the Americas.** The **Clovis First** model, long dominant among North American archaeologists, views the Clovis culture, dated to between 13,500 and 12,500 years ago, as the initial human occupation of the Americas. Recently, a large number of archaeologists have come to support the **Pre-Clovis** model, according to which the initial human occupation of the New World dates back earlier than 13,500 years ago. The **Early Arrival** model, which argues for human presence in the New World by 30,000 years ago, is a minority position.

# Clovis First

In 1932, archaeologists excavating in **Blackwater Draw** near the town of Clovis, New Mexico, discovered the remains of bison in a level with Folsom points. Below this level, evidence of an earlier occupation was found. In this earlier level, the spearpoints were slightly different from the Folsom points. Clovis points, as these earlier forms came to be known, are fluted like the Folsom points, but the resulting channel does not extend the entire length of the point. Clovis points were found together with mammoth and horse bones.

Clovis points have subsequently been found on a large number of sites across North America. These discoveries have led many archaeologists to conclude that the remains found at Clovis are characteristic of the earliest human occupation of the Americas.

Clovis points from the Lehner and Naco sites in Arizona. The point on the left is 9.7 cm long, the point on the right is 7.2 cm long.

At **Blackwater Draw**, near Clovis, New Mexico, spearpoints were found in levels below Folsom points.

**Clovis culture** is the earliest evidence of human occupation in North America. Clovis site dates to between 13,500 and 12,500 years ago.

**Clovis Culture and Chronology.** The definition of **Clovis culture** is based largely on the form of spearpoints. In the midcontinental United States and eastern Canada, Clovis points are absent, but similar pieces known as Gainey points are found on many sites. Besides spearpoints, other stone tools found on Clovis sites include blades and multifunctional tools made on flakes. Apart from these stone tools, few cultural remains are found, built features are not known, and the main features identified are hearths. A deep feature found in the Clovis levels at Blackwater Draw has been identified as a well that might have been excavated in response to drought conditions (Haynes et al. 1999).

The main type of bone tool found on Clovis sites is a rod-shaped object probably used as part of the haft of a spearpoint. A worked bone discovered at the Murray Spring site in Arizona is described as a shaft wrench due to the hole bored in one end. This is the only such object known from a Clovis site. Engraved or incised objects are rare. At the Gault site in Texas, limestone slabs with geometric decorations have been found, but it is not clear that they are from the Clovis level (Haynes 2002). The discovery of Clovis tools at a red-ochre mining site known as Powars II in Platte County, Wyoming, suggests that colorants might have been used during the period (Stafford et al. 2003).

The chronological range for Clovis sites is between 13,500 and 12,500 calendar years ago. The dates 11,500–10,500 B.P. are often given for the Clovis period; however, these are uncalibrated radiocarbon dates.

**Migration Routes.** When global sea levels dropped during periods of glacial advance, the Bering Strait that separates Siberia from Alaska was dry land. The resulting land bridge that connected Asia to North America is part of the region known as **Beringia**. It is likely that the first inhabitants of the New World crossed into North America across this land bridge. The area of Beringia includes eastern Siberia, Alaska, and parts of the Yukon, as well as the land that today is submerged under the Bering Strait. Beringia was not covered by glaciers, but was a steppe landscape with a rich cover of sage and grass that supported extensive populations of mammals, including mammoth, horse, and bison.

**Beringia** is a land bridge that connected Asia and North America during periods of low sea level.

The continental ice sheets that covered much of Canada during the last period of glacial advance (the Wisconsin glaciation, or Oxygen Isotope Stage 2) consisted of the Cordilleran glacier in the west and the more massive Laurentide glacier in the east. Proponents of the Clovis First model have argued that toward the end of the last glaciation a gap existed between the Cordilleran and Laurentide glaciers. This gap formed an **ice-free corridor** that funneled people down from Alaska to the Great Plains, from where they spread rapidly across North America. Recent research has cast doubt on whether such an ice-free corridor existed in time to serve as a migration route for the Clovis people (Mandryk et al. 2001). Even if such an unimpeded corridor did exist, it is doubtful that it would have provided conditions in which people could have survived.

**The Archaeological Evidence.** If, indeed, the Clovis people moved into Alaska from Siberia and then migrated rapidly down an ice-free corridor, one would expect to find a well-developed tradition of fluted points in Siberia and Alaska before 13,500 years ago, the date of the earliest Clovis sites.

The earliest well-dated site in Beringia is Broken Mammoth Cave, in central Alaska (Yesner 2001). The stone tools at this site are characteristic of the Nenana culture, which dates to between 14,000 and 12,800 years ago. **Nenana** stone tools include small bifacially flaked triangular points and knives. Among bone and ivory tools are an eyed needle and points. The preservation of animal remains at Broken Mammoth Cave is excellent. A wide range of species is found, including large game (bison and elk), carnivores (bear, wolf, and fox), small game (squirrel, hare, marmot, and otter), and birds (goose, duck, and ptarmigan). Stone tools similar to those uncovered at Broken Mammoth Cave are found at the site of Ushki on the Siberian side of the Bering Strait. At neither site is there evidence for fluted points. In subsequent periods, the stone tools of Siberia and Alaska are characterized by the production of very small microblades. This toolmaking tradition did not spread into areas to the south of the coast of British Columbia. Fluted points are found in Alaska; however, most do not come from sites that have been dated. It seems that the appearance of fluted points in this area is considerably later than the Clovis.

**E**ngraved stones from the Gault site, Texas.

▶ The **ice-free corridor** that formed there is a potential migration route running between the Cordilleran and Laurentide ice sheets for populations expanding out of Beringia.

▶ The **Nenana** culture dated to between 14,000 and 12,800 years ago is the earliest culture in Beringia.

## Pre-Clovis

In the years following the discoveries made at Folsom and Blackwater Draw, many claims have been made for sites predating the earliest Clovis occupation. Among the sites which have produced evidence that supports a Pre-Clovis occupation of the New World are Meadowcroft Rockshelter, Pennsylvania; Monte Verde, Chile; Pedra Pintada, Brazil; and Quebrada Tacahuay, Peru. The Pre-Clovis hypothesis also gains support from reconstructions of a possible migration route along the Pacific Coast.

# TOOLBOX:
## Radiocarbon Calibration

In Chapter 1, the basic principles of radiocarbon dating were introduced. The essential facts are that the ratio of carbon-14 to nonradioactive carbon is the same throughout the carbon exchange reservoir, which includes the atmosphere, oceans, and biosphere, and that carbon-14 decays at a constant rate. W.F. Libby, the discoverer of radiocarbon dating, thought that the ratio not only was a global constant, but also was constant through time. He has been proven wrong. Most dramatically, modern burning of fossil fuels and atomic weapons testing have increased the amount of carbon-14 in the reservoir. Also, detailed analyses of tree-ring-dated samples indicate that there have been significant fluctuations in the concentration of carbon-14 over the past 50,000 years. Apart from contributions from burning fossil fuels and testing atomic weapons, there is a gradual trend of reduction in the concentration of carbon-14 over time. Overlying this decline is an extraordinarily complex pattern of fluctuations, known as "wiggles." The long-term trend is thought to relate to a reduction in the strength of the earth's magnetic field, while the wiggles appear to be related to solar activity.

Because the ratio of carbon-14 to nonradioactive carbon is not stable over time, radiocarbon years do not map directly onto calendar years. If we think of the decay of radiocarbon as a stopwatch that begins at the death of an organism, the problem is that the starting line is set by the concentration of radiocarbon and this starting line has been redrawn over and over again.

How have archaeologists dealt with this complication? Calibration is a complex issue that ultimately draws archaeologists into realms of statistics that are beyond the scope of this text. The essential tools used to connect radiocarbon time with calendar time are calibration curves created by dating tree-ring sequences that have already been independently dated by dendrochronology (Chapter 9). Calibration curves present the radiocarbon date for samples of known calendar age. For example, a tree ring known to be 6,900 years old produces a radiocarbon date of 6,000 years. Because the carbon exchange reservoir is global, this relationship will stand for all organisms which died in that particular calendar year. Conversely, one can conclude that a sample with a radiocarbon age of 6,000 years is actually 6,900 calendar years old. The calendar age is known as the calibrated date. All dates in this book are calibrated dates.

It is important to emphasize that, in practice, calibration is extremely complex, largely because of the aforementioned wiggles, which often result in a single radiocarbon age corresponding to more than one calendar age on the calibration curve. Resolving these conflicts is among the most mathematically challenging aspects of archaeology.

## FIGURE 6.2

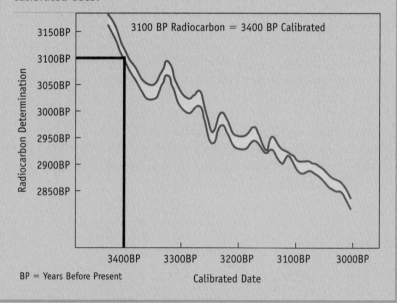

**Radiocarbon calibration diagram. To arrive at a corrected radiocarbon date, draw a horizontal line from a radiocarbon determination on the y-axis to the point where it intersects with the calibration curve (the wiggly blue line). Draw a vertical line from this point down to the x-axis to arrive at the calibrated date. How do the wiggles on the calibration curve complicate finding a calibrated date?**

3100 BP Radiocarbon = 3400 BP Calibrated

BP = Years Before Present

Calibrated Date

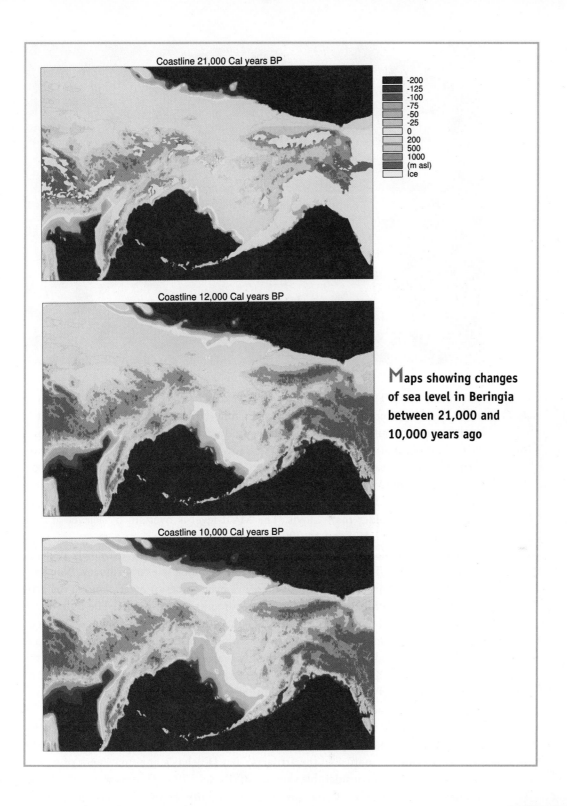

Coastline 21,000 Cal years BP

-200
-125
-100
-75
-50
-25
0
200
500
1000
(m asl)
Ice

Coastline 12,000 Cal years BP

Coastline 10,000 Cal years BP

**M**aps showing changes of sea level in Beringia between 21,000 and 10,000 years ago

**Meadowcroft Rockshelter.** One of the most compelling claims for Pre-Clovis occupation of North America comes from excavations of the Meadowcroft Rock-shelter in western Pennsylvania. Excavations have uncovered eleven natural levels in the shelter. Stratum IIa, near the base of the sequence, has produced a series of radiocarbon dates ranging between 23,000 and 15,500 years ago in association with stone tools. These dates have been disputed by archaeologists who claim that the carbon used in dating the site has been contaminated by "old" carbon carried by groundwater from coal beds in the surrounding bedrock.

> ▶ The earliest occupation of **Meadowcroft Rockshelter** is dated to between 23,000 and 15,500 years ago. These dates, however, are controversial.

Foundations of a wood structure at Monte Verde, Chile.

**Monte Verde.** The site of Monte Verde, excavated by Tom Dillehay, is on the banks of Chinchihuapi Creek in Southern Chile (Dillehay 1989). Located near the southern tip of South America, this site would seem to be an unlikely spot to find the earliest occupation of the New World. However, the discoveries made at Monte Verde pose the most serious threat to the Clovis First hypothesis. The archaeological layer at Monte Verde, which the excavators designate as the MVII level, has produced a series of radiocarbon dates that give an average date of 15,000 years ago, at least 1,500 years older than Clovis. The MVII level is overlain by a level of peat dated to between 12,500 and 14,000 years ago.

Much of the debate concerning Monte Verde is due to the extremely unusual nature of the site. The preservation of organic remains is extraordinary. Not only were the bones of animals found but there are even traces of meat. Among the artifacts are a small number of stone tools, including projectile points. The bulk of the artifacts, however, are made of organic material, including rope and wood. Much of the evidence for human occupation comes from the discovery of objects (e.g., plant remains and unmodified stones) that the excavators argue were transported to the site by humans. The excavators have also identified the remains of huts built of organic materials. Perhaps the most unusual evidence found at Monte Verde is the trace of a human footprint.

The clearly dated MVII horizon presents a significant challenge to the Clovis First model. It is not surprising, particularly given the unexpected location of the site and the unusual nature of the artifacts, that Dillehay's announcement of its discovery was met with considerable skepticism (Fiedel 1999). Doubts were raised concerning the stratigraphy of the site and the validity of the artifacts. In 1997, a prominent group of prehistorians visited Monte Verde and formed a commission to judge the validity of Dillehay's claim (Meltzer et al. 1997). Although they were not able to see the actual site, which had been destroyed by road construction, they were able to see all of the artifacts, detailed excavation records, and the regional geology. At the end of the trip, the commission published an article stating that Dillehay's identification of Monte Verde as a site of human occupation dating to 15,000 years ago was valid. The commission's report was met with criticism and even hostility, and one member of the commission recanted his support for Dillehay. In subsequent

Carbonized seeds from Pedra Pintada, Brazil.

attacks, many important questions have been raised about Dillehay's interpretation of Monte Verde. However, the existence of strong evidence that humans were in southern Chile 15,000 years ago has given new life to the idea that perhaps Clovis does not represent the initial occupation of the New World.

**Caverna de Pedra Pintada.** At present, Monte Verde remains the only site that has produced widely accepted evidence for Pre-Clovis occupation of the Americas. However, other discoveries in South America also cast doubt on the Clovis First model. Working in the Brazilian Amazon, Anna Roosevelt excavated the cave of **Pedra Pintada,** located in the Monte Alegre region of the Lower Amazon (Roosevelt 1996), a region rich in caves, many of which bear traces of decoration. Pedra Pintada has a stratigraphic sequence 2.25 meters in depth from the surface to bedrock. Fifty-six burnt remains of seeds were dated from layers 16 and 17 near the base of the deposits. The dates obtained range between 13,000 and 11,500 years ago. This occupation is thus roughly contemporary with Clovis.

2 cm

**S**tone tools from Pedra Pintada, Brazil.

The stone tools from the early levels at Pedra Pintada include triangular bifacial points, as well as tools made on flakes. Hundreds of lumps of red pigment were found in layers 16 and 17, but it was not possible to determine whether the paintings on the cave walls date to the same early period. The preservation of plant remains on the site is excellent, and there is evidence that the early occupants of the cave ate a wide range of plant foods, including fruits, palm, and Brazil nuts. The most abundant animal bones were fish, of both small and large species. There were also the remains of large and small land mammals.

The discoveries at Pedra Pintada demonstrate that, either at the same time or slightly after the Clovis occupation of North America, people lived in the Brazilian

▶ The site of **Pedra Pintada,** Brazil, shows that people were living in the tropical rain forests of South America between 13,000 and 11,500 years ago.

## FIGURE 6.3

**Stratigraphic profile and radiocarbon dates from Pedra Pintada. The diagram shows the stratigraphic context of the radiocarbon samples. Note that the dates shown are uncalibrated radiocarbon dates and are therefore younger than the dates for the occupation of the site given in the text.**

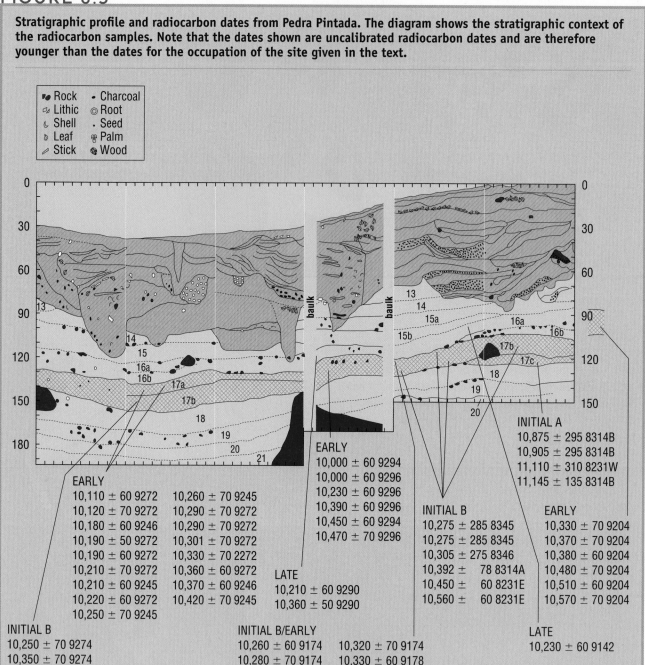

tropical rain forest, subsisting not on megafauna, but on a wide range of resources, including plants and fish. Unlike Monte Verde, Pedra Pintada does not claim to be earlier than Clovis. However, the results of this excavation cast doubts on a simple model for the initial occupation of the New World by Clovis hunters. Roosevelt concludes that the initial occupation of the Americas was more complex than the Clovis First model recognizes and that Clovis was "only one of several regional traditions" (Roosevelt 1996: 381).

**Quebrada Tacahuay.** Further support for Roosevelt's argument comes from excavations at Quebrada Tacahuay, near the coast of Peru (Keefer et al. 1998). Limited excavations at this site have produced a small number of stone tools from a level dated between 12,700 and 12,500 years ago. These stone tools were found together with a large collection of animal bones in the remnants of hearths. The dominant species are seabirds and marine fish. The dominant species of fish is the anchovy, which, due to its small size, suggests the use of nets. Some remains of marine mollusks were also found. Evidence of cut marks and burning were discovered on the bird bones, and there is some evidence for burning on the fish remains. The discoveries at Quebrada Tacahuay indicate that people in Peru were hunting seabirds and fishing, possibly with the use of netting, roughly contemporaneously with Clovis occupation of North America.

**Coastal Migration.** One obvious objection to Monte Verde is that it seems implausible that people coming from Siberia would reach Chile before they would reach the Great Plains, particularly if the ice-free corridor between the Cordilleran and Laurentide glaciers was the only route connecting Beringia with areas to the south. The discovery at Monte Verde suggests that decades of intensive research in North America have missed evidence of thousands of years of human occupation.

> Some archaeologists argue that the earliest people in the Americas moved out of Beringia along a **coastal migration** route rather than through an ice-free corridor.

In the 1970s, K.R. Fladmark advanced a model of human migration into the Americas along the West Coast rather than through an ice-free corridor (Fladmark 1979). This model has recently gained widespread attention. One attraction of a coastal migration is that it would make an early occupation of Chile more plausible. If the first occupants of the New World were adapted to coastal environments, they might have moved relatively rapidly down the coasts of North and South America. With geologists increasingly casting doubt as to whether an ice-free corridor was ever a viable migration route, interest in coastal migrations has grown.

Still, there are objections to a coastal route for human occupation of the New World. In parts of Alaska, there may have been glaciers blocking the coast, so that travel would have required the use of boats. Moreover, there is no evidence to date of any early sites on the west coast from Alaska to California.

Reconstructing the contours of the west coast of North America during the end of the Wisconsin glaciation is complex. On the one hand, the drop in sea level due to the formation of glaciers led to the exposure of extensive areas of the continental shelf. On the other hand, in the northwestern coast, the weight of the glaciers actually lowered the landmass in places, causing sea levels to be higher than would otherwise be the case. Recent studies suggest that despite the weight of the glaciers, the sea level during the end of the Wisconsin glaciation was considerably lower than it is today. The exposed coastal regions was rich in natural resources and largely free of glaciers. The difficulty is that if there was a migration along the coast, most of the relevant archaeological sites would be submerged today.

In summarizing a coastal migration model, E.J. Dixon proposes that any "human colonization of the Americas suggested by the most current data [consists of] coastal migration with inland movement and settlement within broad environmental zones . . . that extend from north to south throughout the Americas" (Dixon 2001: 292). Like Roosevelt, Dixon sees the initial occupation of the Americas as a complex process of groups of people adapting to different environments. Unlike the traditional model, which sees people moving through an ice-free corridor before being "dumped" onto the Great Plains, Dixon sees a process of people migrating along the coast and branching off to inhabit inland regions they encountered along the way. Clovis would simply be one of these branches.

# Early Arrival Model

The Pre-Clovis model differs significantly from the Clovis First model in the precise timing of the initial occupation of the New World and the migration routes used to reach the areas to the south of the glaciers. However, both models agree that human occupation of the Americas took place during the later stages of the last period of glacial advance (the Wisconsin glaciation, or Oxygen Isotope Stage 2). Thus, the consensus of the archaeological community is that, with the exception of Antarctica, the Americas were the last continents to be occupied by humans. Whether these people followed a coastal route or an ice-free corridor, their voyage breached one of the last true frontiers.

A small number of archaeologists argue that the initial human occupation of the Americas was actually much earlier in time. Proponents of an early-arrival model place the first arrival of humans in the Americas as early as 50,000 years ago, in Oxygen Isotope Stage 3. One impediment to this model is that human occupation of Beringia at that early date was extremely limited. Recent discoveries in Siberia have begun to push back the date for the initial occupation of western Beringia. The Yana River site, dated to 30,000 years ago, is the earliest evidence for human occupation of eastern Siberia. Archaeologists working in the Old Crow Basin in the Canadian Yukon claimed to have found evidence of human activity dating as far back as 40,000 years ago. However direct radiocarbon dating of a number of bone tools from the basin has shown that they are actually less than three thousand years old (Nelson et al. 1986). Currently, it is claimed that two bones found in contexts dating to 40,000 years ago at Old Crow show evidence of being cut by a stone tool, and a number of bones are held to have been flaked by humans (Morlan 2003). Neither of these claims is widely accepted, and there is as yet no clear evidence for human occupation of western Beringia (Alaska and the Yukon) before the end of the last glacial advance.

A number of claims have been made for evidence of early human occupation of South America. At Monte Verde, Dillehay found objects that might be tools in level MV I, which is below level MV II. MV I is dated to 33,000 years ago. The evidence of artifacts from that level has not been widely accepted, and Dillehay himself expresses some reservations about this claim.

At **Pedra Furada**, Brazil, evidence of human occupation is claimed to date to 48,000–35,000 years ago. This claim is highly controversial.

The boldest claim for early human occupation of the Americas comes from the excavators of the site of **Pedra Furada** in Brazil (Guidon et al. 1996). Excavations in the rock-shelter at the site uncovered burnt patches associated with pieces identified as stone tools. Radiocarbon dating placed the earliest levels at Pedra Furada between 48,000 and 35,000 years ago. The excavators argue that the burnt patches are evidence of controlled use of fire by humans. Critics have countered that these patches are equally consistent with natural bush fires. The major point of contention is whether the pieces identified as stone tools are actually the result of human manufacture. Most of the tools are very simply chipped quartzite cobbles whose source is a geological deposit found at the top of the cliff, 100 meters directly above the site. The actual sediment of the site is made up of cobbles and soil that plunged down from the top of the cliff over the course of millennia, probably during periods of heavy rainfall. David Metzer, James Adovasio, and Tom Dillehay have suggested that the chipping found on the stones recovered at Pedra Furada is the result, not of human activity, but of the impact of the cobbles as they fell down the cliff and were smashed on the ground (Meltzer et al. 1994). The researchers suggest that the cobbles are "geofacts"—objects created by geological forces—rather than artifacts made by humans. The excavators Fabio Parenti, Michel

Fontugue, and Claude Guérin have reacted with outrage to this suggestion, stating that the patterns of chipping found at Pedra Furada are too complex to have been created by a natural process. Resolving the question of whether humans were involved in the burnt features and stone tools found at Pedra Furada is of critical importance. However, it seems unlikely that a site with the geological characteristics of Pedra Furada will ever be able to provide the kind of unambiguous proof of human occupation needed for there to be widespread acceptance of the early-arrival model.

## The Solutrean Hypothesis

The lack of evidence of antecedents of the distinctive Clovis points in Siberia and Alaska casts some doubt on the Clovis First model. Added to this doubt are the aforementioned questions raised about the viability of an ice-free corridor as a migration route connecting Beringia with the regions to the south of the Cordilleran and Laurentide glaciers. Two archaeologists, Dennis Stanford and Bruce Bradley, have proposed that the origin of the Clovis people was not in Siberia, but rather in Western Europe (Stanford and Bradley 2000). This is a very unlikely scenario, as it would require a lengthy crossing of the North Atlantic. Stanford and Bradley point to similarities in the fine bifacial flaking of spear points in the Clovis of North America and the **Solutrean** period of the Upper Paleolithic of Spain and France. Their proposal, however, does not explain why these similarities could not be the result of parallel invention. As has been pointed out by Lawrence Straus, there are considerable differences between Solutrean and Clovis points, notably a lack of fluting in the Solutrean (Straus 2000). Moreover, the Solutrean industry ends around 5,000 years before the beginning of the Clovis.

> ▶ The **Solutrean hypothesis** argues that the origin of the Clovis culture lies in the Solutrean culture of the Upper Paleolithic of Western Europe.

## The Skeletal Evidence

Only a small number of human skeletal remains have been recovered from sites in the Americas that are older than 9,000 years ago. No significant human remains have been found from either Clovis or Pre-Clovis contexts. All of the human skeletal remains found in the Americas can be assigned unambiguously to *Homo sapiens*.

The small number of human skeletal remains that have been found in contexts slightly later than Clovis have recently become the focus of controversy. On the basis of analyses of the shape of the skulls of these individuals and comparisons with the shape of the skulls of modern populations, some scientists have argued that they are distinct from modern populations of Native Americans. The description of a skeleton discovered in **Kennewick**, Washington, as Caucasoid has led to an intense dispute in which the critical issue is ownership and control of the skeleton. The intensity of the political debate has clouded the question of what the recovered human remains tell us about the initial human occupation of the Americas.

> The significance of the skeleton discovered at ▶ **Kennewick,** Washington, is the subject of heated debate.

On balance, it appears that, at present, the skeletal material is too sparse to contribute significantly to models about the initial phases of occupation. There is little evidence to challenge the consensus view that the origin of the initial groups occupying the Americas was broadly Eurasian. Such a perspective does not contradict the identification of Beringia as the migration route. Several studies suggest that the skeletal evidence is consistent with multiple waves of migration into the Americas, some of which might have been relatively recent. However, this claim remains tentative (Swedlund and Anderson 2003).

# ARCHAEOLOGY IN THE WORLD

## Repatriation of Indigenous Burial Remains

*On January 9, 1877, at least 83 Northern Cheyenne were massacred by U.S. government troops near Fort Robinson, Nebraska. Remains of 17 of the Northern Cheyenne, including those of a three-year-old child, were collected for study by the U.S. Army Medical Examiner and were subsequently transferred to the Smithsonian National Museum of Natural History. Over one hundred years later, on October 9, 1993, the bones from the Fort Robinson massacre were returned to the Northern Cheyenne for reburial (Thornton 2002).*

\*

*In 1996, a human skeleton was discovered washing out of the bank of the Columbia River near the town of Kennewick, Washington. When a flint arrow was found imbedded in the pelvis, it became clear that this was not a normal forensics case. Radiocarbon dating of the bones showed that Kennewick Man was 9,200 years old, one of the earliest-known human remains in the Americas. The Army Corps of Engineers, which controls the land where the skeleton was found, decided to repatriate the bones to the Confederated Tribes of the Umatilla Indian Reservation for reburial. Outraged archaeologists filed suit in federal court to block the reburial and allow for scientific study of the skeleton. How, the archaeologists asked, could the Umatilla claim direct descent from an individual who lived over 9,000 years ago? How could the loss of such a valuable scientific specimen possibly be justified? As of 2005, the archaeologists have prevailed in court, but it is unlikely that this is the final word on disposition of Kennewick Man.*

\*

Few would dispute the right of the Northern Cheyenne to bury their dead, but at the same time many find the reburial of ancient skeletons such as that of Kennewick Man to be a tragic loss of knowledge. The scope of the problem cannot be overstated; estimates place the number of aboriginal human remains in North American institutions at between 100,000 and 200,000 individuals (Isaac 2002). Indigenous communities insist that the scientists must understand the pain and destruction caused by the excavation and collection of the remains of their ancestors. But the archaeological and scientific communities, of course, have a tremendous stake in this dispute. Claims for the reburial of human remains and restricting the study of skeletons strike at the core of the archaeological enterprise.

The dispute over repatriation is ultimately a political issue, and the U.S. government has crafted an impressive mechanism for regulating competing claims. A measure known as the Native American Graves Protection and Repatriation Act (NAGPRA) was voted into law in 1990. Senator John McCain eloquently expressed the need for NAGPRA, stating that "the subject of repatriation is charged with high emotions in both the Native American community and the museum community. I believe this bill represents a true compromise" (quoted in McKeown 2002).

NAGPRA applies to all federal agencies and all museums that receive federal funds. The basis of the law is the right of Indian tribes and native Hawaiian organizations to request the repatriation of burial remains, funerary offerings, sacred objects, and objects of cultural patrimony. There are also provisions requiring consultations with Indian tribes and Native Hawaiians concerning the disposition of human and cultural remains discovered on federal lands.

The implementation of NAGPRA is often complex. Although cases such as Kennewick Man have led to intense disputes between indigenous groups and archaeologists, such acrimony has proven to be the exception rather than the rule. The general consensus is that the impact of NAGPRA has been positive. The clear legal language provides a framework for archaeologists to redress historic wrongs. Many archaeologists have found that the implementation of NAGPRA has led to a new level of engagement between themselves and indigenous communities.

REFERENCE: Cressida Fforde, Jane Hubert, and Paul Turnbull. (2002). *The Dead and Their Possessions: Repatriation in Principle, Policy, and Practice.* (One World Archaeology volume 43). London: Routledge.

◀ Onondagas prepare ancestral remains for reburial in Jamesville, NY.

# Clovis Adaptations and Megafauna Extinction

The discovery of spearpoints together with the remains of now-extinct **megafauna** at both Folsom and Blackwater Draw suggested that the earliest inhabitants of the New World were specialist big-game hunters. It is clear from a number of sites beyond Blackwater Draw that Clovis people were able to hunt very large animals, including elephants. The Colby site in Wyoming has produced a number of mammoth bones with clear evidence that they were hunted and possibly that the meat was stored for later consumption. Because the widespread extinction of megafauna in the Americas correlates with the Clovis period, it would seem obvious that the large animals must have been killed off by Clovis hunters. Seventeen genera of North and South American megafauna, including elephants (mastodons and mammoths), horses, and camels, became extinct between 13,250 and 12,900 years ago. Other species, such as ground sloths, become extinct slightly later.

Although Clovis people hunted large animals, and many of these animals became extinct soon after the earliest Clovis sites were established, some archaeologists doubt whether overhunting by people was the cause of widespread extinction of megafauna. In examining the archaeological record, Donald Grayson and David Meltzer found that only fourteen sites show clear evidence of Clovis hunting of

> Seventeen genera of North and South American **megafauna** became extinct between 13,250 and 12,900 years ago.

**O**ne possible cause for the extinction of North American megafauna is hunting by humans. In this painting, hunters armed with spears and spear throwers stalk a mammoth mired in a bog.

Excavation of a bison mass kill at the Olsen–Chubbock site, Colorado.

megafauna (Grayson and Meltzer 2002). In every case the hunted animals were elephants, either mastodons or mammoths. In most cases, only the remains of one or two animals were found, a pattern similar to that found in Australia, where the case for human overkill of megafauna is lacking a "smoking spear." It seems implausible that human predation on a scale capable of producing a massive continentwide extinction would not leave a clearer record.

Another point of contention is whether Clovis hunters specialized exclusively in hunting large game. A number of sites have produced evidence of hunting of smaller game, including reindeer, by people using Clovis or Gainey points (Storck and Spiess 1994). Clovis people were clearly superbly equipped hunters capable of killing very large animals. The question that remains unresolved is whether this killing resulted in the widespread extinction of megafauna.

Later periods are known for massive kill sites. At the Olsen–Chubbock site in Colorado, Joe Ben Wheat excavated a continuous bed of bison bones lying in a small arroyo, or dry stream bed. The hunters had stampeded the animals into this narrow gorge, killing almost two hundred animals. Many of these animals show evidence of systematic butchery; however, the sheer mass of the kill resulted in the hunters leaving some carcasses untouched—particularly those buried in the pileup. Most of the artifacts recovered at the Olsen–Chubbock site are points. The form of the points indicate that the site belongs to the Cody Complex, which dates to approximately 10,000 years ago. It is interesting that despite the clear evidence for bison kill sites, the species did not become extinct.

- Human migration to Australia required the crossing of the Wallace Line by boat.
- The earliest evidence of human occupation in Australia is dated between 60,000 and 53,000 years ago.
- The extinction of Australian megafauna appears to have taken place approximately 46,000 years ago.
- Human occupation of the Americas followed the Beringia land bridge, which was exposed during periods of low sea level.

- There is considerable debate as to whether the Clovis Culture represents the initial occupation of the Americas or whether there was an earlier migration represented by sites such as Monte Verde.
- The first people to arrive in the Americas migrated south from Beringia either through an ice-free corridor or along a coastal migration route.
- The extinction of American megafauna took place around 13,000 years ago.

## KEY TERMS

Beringia, 176
Blackwater Draw, 176
Caverna de Pedra Pintada, 181
Clovis, 176
Coastal Migration, 183
Fire-Stick Farming, 174
Gunbilngmurrung, 175
Ice-Free Corridor, 177
Kennewick, 185

Lake Mungo, 172
Meadowcroft Rockshelter, 179
Megafauna, 173, 187
Models for Human Occupation of the Americas, 175
Monte Verde, 180
Nauwalabila I, 172
Nenana, 177

Ngandong, 170
Pedra Furada, 184
Pedra Pintada, 181
Quebrada Tacahuay, 183
Sahul, 171
Solutrean Hypothesis, 185
Sunda, 171
Wallace Line, 171

## REVIEW QUESTIONS

1. How and when did people first arrive in Australia? What is the importance of Lake Mungo in understanding the spread of humans in Australia?
2. Was the process of megafauna extinction similar in Australia and the Americas?
3. What is the significance of Monte Verde to debates about the initial occupation of the Americas? What additional information is brought by the excavations at Caverna de Pedra Pintada?
4. What are the alternative migration routes for the initial occupation of the Americas?

## FOR FURTHER READING

Tom Dillehay. (2000). *The Settlement of the Americas: A New Prehistory.* New York: Basic Books.

Brian Fagan. (1989). *The Great Journey: The Peopling of Ancient America.* New York: Thames and Hudson.

Gary Haynes. (2002). *The Early Settlement of North America: The Clovis Era.* Cambridge, U.K.: Cambridge University Press.

Bruce Huckell and J. David Kilbe (Eds.). (2004). *Readings in Late Pleistocene North America and Ealy Paleoindians: Selections from American Antiquity.* Washington: Society for American Archaeology.

Harry Lourandos. (1997). *Continent of Hunter–Gatherers: New Perspectives in Australian Prehistory.* Cambridge, U.K.: Cambridge University Press.

Tim Murray (Ed.). (1998). *Archaeology of Aboriginal Australia: A Reader.* St. Leonards, NSW: Allen and Unwin.

Peter Storck. (2004). *Journey to the Ice Age: Discovering an Ancient World.* Vancouver: UBC Press.

David Hurst Thomas. (2000). *Skull Wars: Kennewick Man, Archaeology, and the Battle for Native American Identity.* New York: Basic Books.

# part THREE

# Perspectives on Agriculture

THE DEVELOPMENT OF AGRICULTURAL SOCIETIES involved a profound reorientation of the way humans relate to plants and animals, along with equally significant changes in human society and technology. Because the transition to agriculture took place independently in several distinct regions, we can take a comparative approach to the origins of agriculture in order to gain a broad understanding of this process. In doing so, we learn that the shift to an agricultural way of life often spanned a period of several thousands of years and that the details of the process differ significantly among regions.

The development of agriculture has been linked with a trend towards the separation of humanity from nature. Recent perspectives on the domestication of plants and animals challenge this assumption. After reading this chapter, you should understand:

▶ The ideas of Lewis Henry Morgan and Gordon Childe about the origin of agriculture.

▶ The challenge to these ideas posed in the writing of David Rindos, Tim Ingold, and Marshall Sahlins.

▶ The major components of the Neoloithic Revolution.

# INTRODUCTION: DEFINITIONS OF AGRICULTURE

**A**lmost the entire evolutionary history of genus *Homo* has taken place within a hunting-and-gathering context. It was only fifteen thousand years ago that societies of modern humans in different areas of the world began to shift to an agricultural way of life. The transition from hunter–gatherer societies to agricultural societies is one of the most profound and significant events in prehistory. Early anthropologists and archaeologists saw the development of agriculture as the natural result of an inherent human tendency to move towards more advanced ways of life. Today, most archaeologists reject both the linkage between agriculture and progress and the use of progress to explain changes in prehistory. We are left with the challenge of discovering the diverse pathways taken towards agriculture in societies around the world and to grapple with the question of what caused those societies to change.

# EARLY PERSPECTIVES

*Mankind are the only beings who may be said to have gained an absolute control over the production of food.* (Morgan 1877: 24)

> **Lewis Henry Morgan** viewed the transition to agriculture as marking the boundary between the period of "savagery" and the period of "barbarism."

The pioneering American anthropologist **Lewis Henry Morgan** wrote that, through the invention of agriculture, humans placed themselves outside of the world of nature and moved towards "human supremacy on the earth" (Rindos 1984: 9). In his book *Ancient Society,* published in 1877, Morgan labeled the transition as the shift from a period of "savagery" to one of "barbarism." Morgan emphasized the invention of pottery as the defining aspect of barbarism, along with the domestication of animals and plants and the construction of buildings out of mud brick. In his writing on barbarism, Morgan emphasized that the transition was a stage in the progress of humanity.

*The escape from the impasse of savagery was an economic and scientific revolution that made the participants active partners with nature instead of parasites on nature.* (Childe 1942: 55)

> V. Gordon Childe defined the transition to agriculture as the **Neolithic Revolution.**

In the 1940s, V. Gordon Childe synthesized the existing archaeological information to reformulate Morgan's ideas about the origin of agriculture. Childe named that event the Neolithic Revolution. For Childe, the essential invention of the **Neolithic Revolution** was active control over food production. This invention led to an increase in the food supply that was able to support an increase in population, resulting in the development of settled villages.

The concepts developed by Morgan and Childe remain essential to the study of prehistory. Few archaeologists doubt the revolutionary effects of the development of agriculture on human society, and understanding the Neolithic Revolution remains central to the study of prehistory. However, although the contributions made by Morgan and Childe are widely recognized, most of their specific ideas about the nature of the shift to agriculture are the subject of debate and criticism.

# HUMANITY AND NATURE IN THE SHIFT TO AGRICULTURE

Both Morgan and Childe viewed the development of agriculture as a shift in the relationship between humanity and the natural world. To Morgan, "barbaric" society had set itself in a position of supremacy above nature. To Childe, Neolithic societies became "active partners with nature" rather than "parasites on nature." There is a sense that both Childe and Morgan imply that humans consciously removed themselves from nature by inventing agriculture. Such a conception of agricultural societies as the removal of humans from nature is today contested by archaeologists and anthropologists working from a wide range of perspectives.

> *The idea that we as a culture, a nation, or a species are in conscious control of our environment and thus of our destiny is one part truth, one part rhetoric, and two parts wishful thinking.* (Rindos 1984: 6)

For **David Rindos,** the development of agriculture was a coevolutionary process involving a symbiotic relationship between plant and animal species in which each species contributes to the other's support. Symbiotic relationships with plants and animals are not unique to humans, but rather are widespread in the natural world. For example, there is a symbiotic relationship between ants and acacia trees. Ants live in the trees and harvest sugars and leaves. The ants also remove and feed on insects that are otherwise lethal to the trees. If the ants are removed, the trees are attacked and rapidly die. The relationship is a symbiotic one in which the ants receive nutrients and shelter and the acacias receive protection from harmful insects. Nobody would argue that this biological process involves a conscious decision on the part of either the ants or the trees. Rindos argued that the domestication of plants by humans was a similar coevolutionary process.

▶ **David Rindos** saw agriculture as the result of a coevolutionary process involving a symbiotic relationship between plant and animal species.

Rock art from Valtorta, Spain. This painting illustrates Ingold's conception of hunting as a relationship of trust between the hunter and the prey.

**Tim Ingold** views the shift from hunting to agriculture as a shift from trust to domination.

Rindos based his perspective on the origins of agriculture on biological theory. Working from a different perspective, anthropologist **Tim Ingold** (2000) has also argued against the view of agriculture as the removal of humans from nature. Ingold begins by looking at the way modern hunter–gatherer societies look at the world. He finds that they do not make the kinds of distinctions between the natural and human worlds that are so critical to Childe and Morgan's account. Ingold sees the domestication of animals as a shift from a world in which relationships are based on trust to a world in which relationships are based on domination. The relationship of hunter–gatherers to the animals they hunt is based on trust in a powerful natural world that will provide for people in return for human respect and propitiation. Social relations between humans are made on the same basis of trust, because there is no essential distinction made between the human and animal worlds. A hallmark characteristic of hunter–gatherer social relations is sharing based on trust.

For Ingold, the shift from hunting to agriculture involves a shift from trust to domination, which pervades all aspects of human life. Thus, in agricultural societies, the animals are dependents of humans. Animals no longer present themselves; instead, it is the herdsman who makes life-and-death decisions. Similar concepts of domination and control pervade the social life of humans with the development of owned property and a social hierarchy. Ingold is at pains, however, to stress that the shift from trust to domination does not involve a separation of humanity from nature as envisioned by Morgan and Childe. Rather, the development of agriculture involves a "change in the terms of engagement". Not until the recent development of industrialized agriculture were animals merely objects of human control.

S<small>an</small> hunter-gatherers in the Kalahari, Botswana.

# AGRICULTURE AND PROGRESS

*There is also a Zen road to affluence. . . That human material wants are finite and few, and technical means unchanging but on the whole adequate. . . . That, I think, describes the hunter.*
(Sahlins 1972: 2)

Today it is quite jarring to read Morgan and Childe describe hunter–gatherer societies as savages. The term clearly embodies a value judgment, as does the term "barbarism" for farming societies. Both characterizations are repugnant to contemporary anthropology. Further, the entire notion of linking the transition to farming with the idea of progress has become extremely problematic. In a clever turn of phrase, the anthropologist **Marshall Sahlins** (1972) has called hunter–gatherers the "original affluent society." Through a careful comparison of ethnographic studies of hunter–gatherer and farming communities, Sahlins has shown that, contrary to our expectations, hunter–gatherers spend less time working for their food than do agriculturalists. Hunter–gatherers actually have far more leisure time than farmers. In a similar vein, on the basis of a study of human skeletal remains from prehistoric sites, Marc Cohen (1977) has demonstrated that early agriculturalists were not as healthy as hunter–gatherers. Because of increased crowding in permanent villages, agricultural societies are vulnerable to outbreaks of disease. Also, the health of agriculturalists suffered from a decrease in the quality of their diet. As a result of studies such as those carried out by Sahlins and Cohen, many archaeologists question whether the development of agriculture was the result of people choosing or inventing a "better" way of life.

> ▶ **Marshall Sahlins** described hunter–gatherers as the "original affluent society."

# SEARCHING FOR EXPLANATIONS

If agriculture is not inherently advantageous, why did it develop? Kent Flannery once crystallized the diff.iculty of answering this question, saying, "If you asked me 'Why did agriculture begin?' I'm not sure what I'd give you as a cause" (Quoted in Hayden 1990: 31). In the chapters that follow, we will pursue the trail of empirical evidence that archaeologists have uncovered and

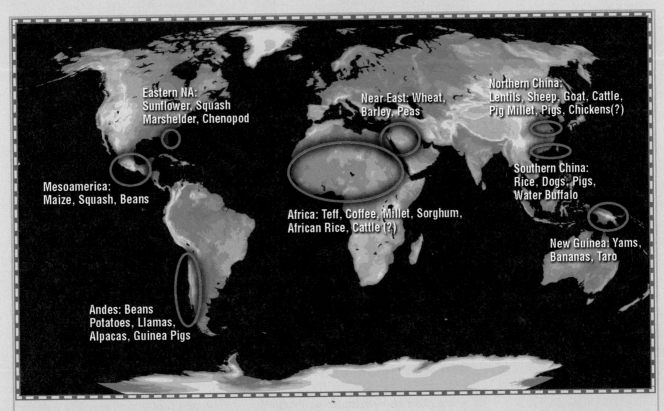

**M**ap showing major centers of domestication.

A farmer harvests maize.

continue to uncover. Central to the study of agricultural origins is the recognition that plants and animals have been domesticated independently in numerous locations. The major centers for the independent domestication of indigenous plants and animals were the Middle East, South China, North China, Africa, the Andes, and Central Mexico. Other regions in which there was a limited independent domestication of plants include Eastern North America and New Guinea. Because agriculture developed independently in at least six regions, archaeologists can explore whether there were regularities in its unfolding.

Archaeologists make a distinction between areas in which agriculture was developed independently and areas into which agriculture spread. The spread of agriculture is increasingly recognized as a process that is as complex and worthy of study as the original domestication of plants and animals. The question remains of why agriculture came to be adopted as a way of life. The origin of agriculture is a complex topic that involves both empirical and theoretical components. The essential theoretical issue that faces archaeologists is how to approach the origins of agriculture as a process. How and why did societies across the globe shift from a hunter–gatherer way of life to living in settled village farming communities?

One approach has been to look for an external trigger that played a role in the shift to agriculture. One obvious candidate for such a trigger is climate change. Another factor that might have triggered the shift to agriculture is an increase in population. Research by **Ester Boserup** suggests that population growth might actually be an underlying cause, rather than an effect, of agriculture. Boserup's (1965) studies suggest that subsistence systems—the ways people get their food—tend to be the result of population pressures.

A major breakthrough in the study of agricultural origins has been the recognition that it is unlikely that searching for a single external trigger will produce a satisfying explanation. Following an approach based on systems theory, archaeologists have shifted to developing models of how the interaction between a number of factors might have led to the adoption of agriculture (Bender 1975). For example, Lewis Binford (1968) examined the interaction between increasing population size and fluctuating climatic conditions. A particularly intriguing model developed by Brian Hayden focuses on the interaction between surplus food and social organization. Hayden begins by arguing that not all hunter–gatherer societies are the same. *Generalized hunter–gatherers* rely on scarce or unpredictable resources and, as a result, live at low population densities. In such societies, competition over food resources will be detrimental to the resources and therefore maladaptive. *Complex hunter–gatherers* use more reliable and abundant resources (such as salmon, cod, insects, rodents, grass seeds, and nuts) and therefore can live at higher population densities. Because overexploitation of these resources is practically impossible, competition can develop and will largely take the form of feasting events. It is the "competition between individuals using food resources to wage their competitive battles," says Hayden, that "provides the motive and the means for the development of food production. . . . Aspiring accumulators can be expected to exert all their ingenuity to bribe, coerce, cajole, and con other members of the community into supporting competitive feasts and

▶ **Ester Boserup** suggests that increased population size might be the cause of the shift to agriculture.

**M**anually harvesting rice in China.

**H**istoric photograph of the Walpi pueblo, Arizona.

Societies of complex hunter–gatherers that preceded the shift to agriculture and that were labeled "Archaic" in the Americas and "Epipaleolithic" or "Mesolithic" in other parts of the world, were characterized by the exploitation of a **broad spectrum** of plant and animal resources. ◀

producing as many delicacies or other high-quality foods as possible for feasts" (Hayden 1990: 35–36).

An interesting aspect of Hayden's model is that it builds on changes in hunter–gatherer adaptations, which then interact with social factors to push societies towards agriculture. In every case study that we examine in the coming chapters, we will see that increasing complexity in hunter–gatherer adaptations precedes the shift to agriculture. Such societies of hunter–gatherers are often labeled "Archaic" in the Americas and "Epipaleolithic" or "Mesolithic" in other parts of the world. Kent Flannery has emphasized that a common characteristic of these societies was that they relied on a **broad spectrum** of resources, including a wide range of plant and animal foods (Flannery 1973).

In examining the case studies presented in the coming chapters, no particular model for the origins of agriculture is adopted. We will find much support for Barbara Bender's conclusion that "there is no single hypothesis that will explain the shift to food-production in different parts of the world" (Bender 1975: 215). We will be interested in seeing the variation in the pathways different societies took in adopting farming. For this purpose, agriculture can be viewed as a broad phenomenon that can be broken into three components:

1. *Domestication.* A relationship between humans, on the one hand, and plants and animals, on the other.
2. *Technology.* The tools used for daily tasks.
3. *Community.* The development of a constructed landscape.

**Domestication** refers to a relationship between humans and plants and animals in which the humans play an integral role in the protection and reproduction of the plant or animal species. As Rindos (1984) makes clear, domestication is not necessarily the result of conscious manipulation of plants and animals by humans. Archaeologically, domestication is identified on the basis of changes in the size or shape (morphology) of plant remains or animal bones, compared with the morphology of the wild ancestors (progenitors) of the same plants or animals. Domestication is also identified when plants or animals are found outside their expected geographic distribution. With animals, domestication can sometimes be identified on the basis of the ratio of the sexes of an animal by age. Generally, an overrepresentation of young male animals is indicative of domestication.

**Technology** refers to the tools used for daily tasks, including farming, food processing, and food storage. Among the technological innovations that are often linked to agriculture are pottery, ground stone axes, and sickles.

**Community** refers to the transition to agriculture, which involves not only physical changes to the landscape through the construction of villages and monuments, but also a change in the way people view the landscape and the way ownership of the land is conceived. Agriculture involves important shifts in social organization, leadership, and the relationship between kin groups and property. The shift to agricultural society also had significant effects on cosmology—the way people saw themselves in relation to supernatural forces.

> ▶ **Domestication** refers to a relationship between humans and plants and animals wherein humans play an integral role in the protection and reproduction of the plants and animals.

> ▶ **Technology** refers to the tools used for daily tasks, including farming, food processing, and food storage.

> ▶ **Community** refers to the transition to agriculture, which involves not only physical changes to the landscape through the construction of villages and monuments, but also a change in the way people view the landscape and the way ownership of the land is conceived.

# AGRICULTURE AND PROGRESS REVISITED

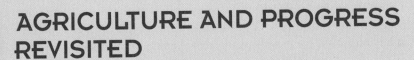

Progress has been rejected as an *explanation* for why agricultural societies came into being; however, there does seem to be an element of progress, or at least directionality, built into our conception of the origins of agriculture as a process. For example, Hayden (1990) discusses a shift from generalized hunter–gatherers, to complex hunter–gatherers, to farmers. Flannery (1973) emphasizes broad-spectrum adaptations as a precondition for agriculture.

Systems theory, as presented in Chapter 2, should not allow for such a "ratchet effect": The feedback loop between your furnace and your thermostat is a self-regulating system that has no direction; it simply adjusts to changes in temperature. The directionality inherent in the shift to agriculture poses a significant theoretical challenge. A similar challenge plagues evolutionary biologists struggling to explain how evolution can have direction without recourse to models that view progress as explaining evolution (Nitecki 1988). Several concepts from evolutionary biology are useful to our study of agricultural origins. The first is that directionality and progress are

The cathedral of San Marco in Venice. The spandrels can be seen on either side of the main arch.

distinct. Stephen Jay Gould (1988) has argued that directionality is the essential element of any historical process. Notably, Gould states that "history must be more than a string of isolated, if distinctive, events strung together one after the other" (Gould 1988: 333). The essence of historical processes is that they unfold in time. Our task in examining case studies of agricultural origins is not only to look at how various aspects of agriculture are related, but also to understand the *process* of agricultural origins. We will be interested in both the tempo of this process (e.g., was it a revolution, as Childe proposed?) and the relationships among events.

In one of the classic articles of evolution biology, Gould and his colleague Richard Lewontin used the essentially historical nature of evolutionary processes to launch an attack on what they call the "Panglossian Paradigm" (Gould and Lewontin 1979). Doctor Pangloss is a character from a satire by Jonathan Swift who elaborates ridiculous explanations of how everything in the world is for the best. Gould and Lewontin argue that evolutionary biologists think much as Dr. Pangloss does, explaining every aspect of organisms as the best possible adaptation. To counter the Panglossian Paradigm, Lewontin and Gould use an illustration from architecture. At the cathedral of San Marco in Venice, small triangular spaces between columns are used for a perfectly fitted painted scene. One might think that these triangular spaces were built for the needs of the painter, but that is not the case. The spaces, known by the architectural term *spandrels,* are created by the intersection of two rounded arches that meet at a right angle. The critical point is that the paintings in the spandrels are adapted to an existing structure. It is useful to keep Dr. Pangloss and the spandrels of San Marco firmly in mind as we move through the world of agricultural origins. We are looking at the way changes built on preexisting conditions, just as the painters of the cathedral took advantage of spaces that were structurally essential to the building; thus, we must be wary of explaining every aspect of society as adaptive.

# CONCLUSION

In the next three chapters, we will explore a series of case studies in the shift to agriculture. The focus will be on examining the relationships among domestication, technology, and community, as well as the role of external triggers, including climate changes and increases in population. The picture that emerges is one of tremendous diversity in the way agricultural societies developed. Agriculture came into being because of the actions of people, and the changes unleashed by the process shook the foundations of the world in which those people lived. The shift from hunter–gatherer societies profoundly affected every aspect of human life, from the diversity of the ecosystem to the way people experienced the supernatural. Living as we do in a rapidly changing world, we are in a good position to have some empathy and insight into such an experience. The development of agriculture is a process with immediate relevance to the upheavals that we experience today. The origins of agriculture point to the essential linkage between aspects of experience we often treat as distinct. Social change, technological innovation, ecological impact, and religious experience are all inextricably linked in a process that produced a truly revolutionary change in human societies. From thousands of years away, we look back at this process and try to piece together the evidence that survives. What was it like to be part of the generations that experienced the Neolithic Revolution? What role did individuals play in effecting the large-scale changes they lived through? Similar questions might be asked about our own experience living in a world of change.

## SUMMARY

- To many early archaeologists and anthropologists, including Lewis Henry Morgan and V. Gordon Childe, the origin of agriculture involved the separation of humanity from nature.
- More recently, anthropologists and archaeologists working from a diversity of perspectives have challenged the traditional understanding of the origins of agriculture.
- Ester Boserup has proposed that the development of agriculture was a response to an increase in population.
- Childe labeled the development of agriculture the Neolithic Revolution, a revolution that includes changes in three major aspects of human society and adaptation: domestication, technology, and community (the process of settling down).
- Plants and animals have been domesticated independently in numerous locations.

## KEY TERMS

**Ester Boserup,** 197
**Broad Spectrum,** 198
**Community,** 199
**Domestication,** 199

**Tim Ingold,** 194
**Lewis Henry Morgan,** 192
**Neolithic Revolution,** 192

**David Rindos,** 193
**Marshall Sahlins,** 195
**Technology,** 199

## REVIEW QUESTIONS

1. Why are contemporary archaeologists and anthropologists critical of Morgan's and Childe's conception of the origin of agriculture?

2. How do Rindos's ideas about the origins of agriculture differ from Ingold's ideas?

3. Why did Childe choose to describe the origin of agriculture as the Neolithic Revolution?

## FOR FURTHER READING

Peter Bellwood. (2005). *First Farmers: The Origins of Agricultural Societies*. Malden, Massachusetts: Blackwell.

Barbara Bender. (1975). *Farming in Prehistory: From Hunter–Gatherer to Food-Producer*. London: J. Baker.

Mark Cohen. (1977). *The Food Crisis in Prehistory: Overpopulation and the Origins of Agriculture*. New Haven, Connecticut: Yale University Press.

Tim Ingold. (2000). *The Perception of the Environment: Essays on Livelihood, Dwelling, and Skill*. London: Routledge.

David Rindos. (1984). *The Origins of Agriculture: An Evolutionary Perspective*. San Diego: Academic Press.

Marshall Sahlins. (1972). *Stone Age Economics*. Chicago: Aldine.

Bruce Smith. (1995). *The Emergence of Agriculture*. New York: Scientific American.

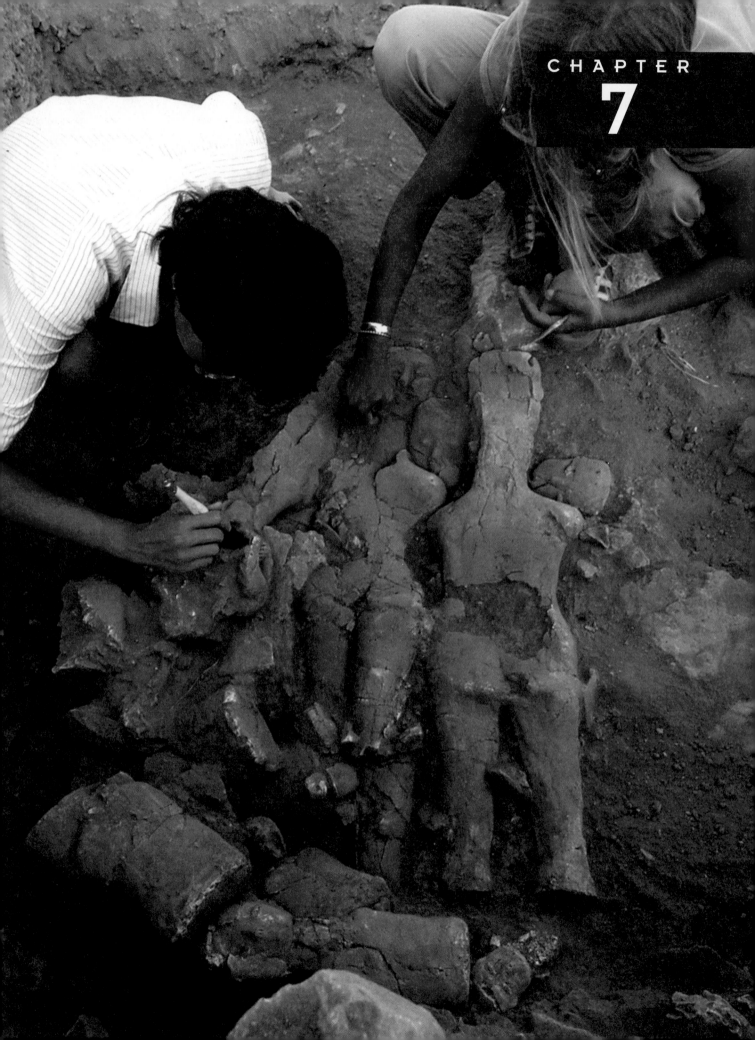
CHAPTER

7

# Towers, Villages, and Longhouses

Excavation of the plaster figures at the Neolithic site of Ain Ghazal, Jordan.

IN THE MIDDLE East the domestication of plants and animals took place within the context of large villages. After reading this chapter, you should understand:

▶ The emergence of settled villages in the Middle East.

▶ The domestication of plants and animals in the Middle East.

▶ The relationship between domestication, the villages, and technology in the development of agriculture in the Middle East.

▶ The questions surrounding the spread of agriculture to Europe.

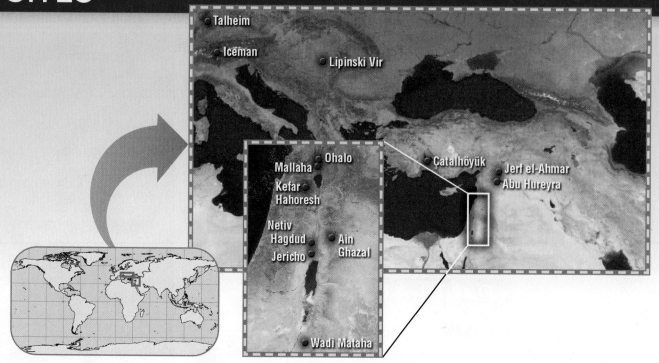

Talheim

Iceman

Lipinski Vir

Mallaha · Ohalo

Kefar
Hahoresh

Çatalhöyük

Jerf el-Ahmar
Abu Hureyra

Netiv
Hagdud · Ain
Jericho · Ghazal

Wadi Mataha

The ancient mound, or *tel,* of Jericho is a powerful lure to archaeologists. The famous walls of Jericho, toppled in the biblical book of Joshua, are exactly the type of concrete evidence archaeologists should easily be able to identify and recover. The British archaeologist Kathleen Kenyon sunk massive trenches

Photograph of the Jericho tower during excavation. Notice the opening in the top of the tower that leads to the stairway.

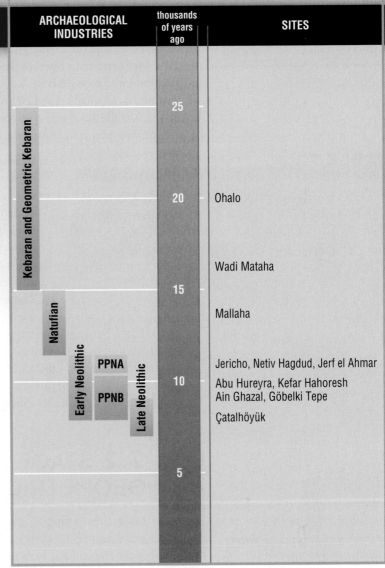

| ARCHAEOLOGICAL INDUSTRIES | thousands of years ago | SITES |
|---|---|---|
| Kebaran and Geometric Kebaran | 25 | |
| | 20 | Ohalo |
| Natufian | 15 | Wadi Mataha |
| | | Mallaha |
| Early Neolithic — PPNA / PPNB — Late Neolithic | 10 | Jericho, Netiv Hagdud, Jerf el Ahmar<br>Abu Hureyra, Kefar Hahoresh<br>Ain Ghazal, Göbelki Tepe<br>Çatalhöyük |
| | 5 | |

through the tel of Jericho, documenting the stratigraphic sequence and revealing the history of the site. Surprisingly, Kenyon recovered no evidence of a settlement dating to the biblical period. Why these remains are absent is unclear. Perhaps the story of Joshua is more myth than reality. Or the settlement of Jericho described in the book of Joshua might have been in a different, as yet undiscovered, location.

As Kenyon penetrated the deepest archaeological deposits at Jericho, she uncovered a wall and a tower that astounded the archaeological community. These constructions were far older than Joshua; in fact, they were the oldest-known monumental architecture ever discovered. The tower and wall at Jericho were built 12,000 years ago during the Early Neolithic period.

The tower of Jericho is only one of a string of discoveries that have shed dramatic light on the origins of agriculture in the Middle East. In this chapter, we examine the shift from hunter–gatherer to agricultural societies in the Middle East. The domestication of plants and animals in this region took place within the context of large and dense villages. The adoption of agriculture resulted in a transformation of all aspects of life. These profound changes affected not only social relations between people, but also the way people conceived of the supernatural. In the last section of the chapter, we explore the spread of domesticated plants and animals (domesticates) into Europe.

# 7.1 SETTING THE SCENE

The Middle East includes a wide range of climates. A ribbon of Mediterranean climate extends today from Israel and Jordan in the south, up into Turkey, Syria, and Lebanon in the north, and stretches to the east into northern Iraq and western Iran. Together, these regions form an area known as the

The **Fertile Crescent** is a ribbon of Mediterranean climate that arcs across the Middle East.

Fertile Crescent, characterized by dry summers and winter rains with enough precipitation to support vegetation ranging from woodlands to open-park woodland. Along with trees such as oak and pine, large stands of wild cereals, including wheat, barley, and rye, dot the countryside. To the south and the east of the Fertile Crescent, the Mediterranean open-park woodlands grade into steppe environments that in turn grade into true deserts.

The archaeological record clearly shows that the shift to an agricultural way of life in the Middle East was a process rather than a revolution. The transition to agriculture can be traced through a number of stages (see Table 7.1):

## TABLE 7.1

| STAGE | PERIOD | DATE (YEARS AGO) |
|---|---|---|
| 1 | Kebaran and Geometric Kebaran | 25,000-15,000 |
| 2 | Natufian | 15,000-12,000 |
| 3 | Early Neolithic | 12,000-8,500 |
| 4 | Late Neolithic | 8,500-7,000 |

1. During the Kebaran and Geometric Kebaran periods, hunter–gatherers living in the region subsisted on a wide range of plant and animal resources. There is no evidence of domesticated plants and animals during those periods, and the remains of brush huts are the only evidence of architecture.
2. During the Natufian period, constructed architecture and increased elaboration of material culture appear. There is no evidence that agriculture had yet become widespread.
3. In the Early Neolithic period, people lived in villages and began to farm a range of cereals and pulses. Subsequently, they also began to domesticate goats.
4. During the Late Neolithic period, the earliest pottery manufacture appears. In most areas, the sites of this period are smaller and less densely packed than at the end of the Early Neolithic. Sheep, goat, cattle, and pig were fully domesticated.

# 7.2 STAGE 1: KEBARAN AND GEOMETRIC KEBARAN

Most sites dating to the Kebaran and Geometric Kebaran periods are small hunter–gatherer encampments with few remains other than stone tools and animal bones. The recent discovery of **Ohalo**, a Kebaran site with excellent preservation of organic remains, has shed new light on that period.

**Ohalo** is a Kebaran site in northern Israel with the preserved remains of brush huts.

## Technology

Sites belonging to the Kebaran and Geometric Kebaran are easily identified on the basis of their characteristic stone tools (Goring-Morris and Belfer-Cohen 1998). The tools from these periods are made mostly on small blades known as bladelets. In the Geometric Kebaran, bladelets are often shaped into geometric forms such as triangles and rectangles.

## Settlements

Most sites from the Kebaran and Geometric Kebaran periods are the remains of small camps left by highly mobile hunter–gatherers who did not live all year round in one location. Ohalo, in northern Israel, has provided a unique glimpse of a Kebaran occupation site (Nadel 2002). Soon after it was abandoned, the encampment at Ohalo was submerged beneath the waters of the Sea of Galilee. Because the deposits were not exposed to air, the preservation of organic remains is

The Ohalo excavations. The huts are visible as dark stains.

extraordinary. A recent period of drought led to an unprecedented lowering of lake levels that exposed the site. Archaeologists were able to open up a large, horizontal, 2,000-square-meter area at Ohalo and unearth the remains of six brush huts that could be traced as shallow oval depressions in the ground between 3 and 4.5 meters in length.

The artifacts recovered at Ohalo include a large collection of stone tools dominated by retouched bladelets. Tools were also made of bone, mostly in the form of awls. The only personal ornaments recovered were shell beads that had been transported from the Mediterranean Sea coast. An adult male was buried near the huts at Ohalo. The skeleton was found lying on its side in a semiflexed position. No burial items were found with the skeleton; however, the excavator believes that a stone circle found near the burial might have some ritual significance.

Burials from the Kebaran and Geometric Kebaran sites are rare. A puzzling Geometric Kebaran burial was excavated by Joel Janetski at the site of Wadi Mataha in southern Jordan. Wadi Mataha was a very small campsite during that period, so the discovery of a somewhat elaborate burial feature was a surprise (Stock et al. 2005). The individual at Wadi Mataha was a young adult male buried with his face pointed down and his arms and legs "hogtied" behind his back. A stone bowl with the bottom broken out was found with the human remains, as was a long flint blade. The skull had been broken open sometime soon after death, leaving a large hole slightly above the forehead.

On the basis of the discoveries at Ohalo and Wadi Mataha, it is very difficult to understand the spiritual world of the people of the Kebaran and Geometric Kebaran periods. The burial at Ohalo, located within the camp, would fit with a burial ritual that serves to form a spiritual link between a group and their place of habitation.

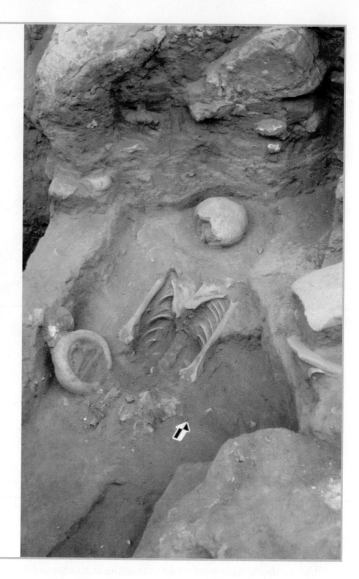

The excavation of the Wadi Mataha burial. At this stage of excavation, the legs have been removed. Note how the shoulder bones (scapula) are overlapping. What does this tell us about the way the body was buried?

The situation at Wadi Mataha is quite different, and it is difficult not to see the burial as a violent event. Art objects from either period are rare; the only known examples are two crudely incised pebbles.

## Domestication

There is no evidence of either animal or plant domestication during the Kebaran or Geometric Kebaran period. The people at Ohalo lived near the edge of a lake with access to a wide range of resources. The plant remains recovered are wild grasses—including wild barley and wild wheat—fruits, nuts, and water plants. The most common mammal bones are gazelles, but the remains of deer, wild pig, wild goat, hare, red fox, and wildcat are also found. From a single hut, nearly 10,000 fish bones, mostly of carp and cichlids, were found. The remains of over 77 species of birds, including grebes, ducks, geese, quail, and birds of prey, were also found at Ohalo.

# 7.3 STAGE 2: THE NATUFIAN

The Natufian societies of the Middle East constructed the earliest stone buildings in this area of the world and developed an impressive range of art objects and personal ornaments. However, there is no evidence that the Natufians domesticated any plants or animals. The Natufian settlements at sites such as Mallaha were small villages with up to a dozen structures.

We are still far from understanding the causes underlying the innovations found in the Natufian period. It is possible that an increase in population led to an increase in the size and complexity of settlements, but even if this was the case, we are left to question the reasons for an increase in population. Toward the end of the Natufian, coinciding with a period of climatic stress known as the Younger Dryas, there was a reduction in the size and number of Natufian settlements.

## Technology

The technology of the Natufian period shows a great deal of continuity with that of preceding periods. The stone tools continue to be made on small bladelets. The characteristic shape of tools in the Natufian is a crescent-shaped bladelet known as a lunate (Bar-Yosef and Valla 1991). It is assumed that, like the bladelet tools of the preceding periods, **lunates** served as elements in hunting tools or as parts of tools made up of many small pieces. At the site of Wadi Hammeh in Jordan, a series of lunates was found mounted in a bone haft of what appears to be a knife or a sickle (Edwards 1991). Some lunates show a type of luster known as sickle polish, formed only when stone tools are used to harvest grasses.

> ▶ **Lunates** are tiny crescent-shaped stone tools characteristic of the Natufian.

The Natufians were the first people in the Middle East to invest a great deal of energy in the manufacture of ground stone tools. Among such tools found on Natufian sites are mortars, pestles, and grooved stones known as shaft straighteners. Often, these items are decorated with a simple meander pattern. In some cases, they have been found far from the source of the stone, indicating that they were traded across long distances. Long-distance trade is also indicated by the abundance of Red Sea and Mediterranean Sea shells and shell beads found on Natufian sites, which are often quite distant from the sea.

## Settlements

The transition to village life began during the Natufian. Structures consist of undressed stones piled to form walls that are often preserved to a height of up to 1 meter. The structures are oval or open semicircles. The floors of the structures are covered with refuse, including stone tools and debris and animal bones. It is hard to imagine these surfaces being used as houses for families,

**S**mall, crescent-shaped lunates are the characteristic tool found on Natufian sites. How might such a small tool have been used?

# TOOLBOX:
## Paleoethnobotany

**P**aleoethnobotanists grasp at the most ephemeral of archaeological remains. Paleoethnobotany is defined as "the study of past cultures by an examination of human populations' interactions with the plant world" (Popper and Hastorf 1988: 1). In rare cases, plant remains are exquisitely preserved. Dry climates, such as the highland caves of Mexico, can preserve the

straws. To get around this problem, paleoethnobotanists have developed a recovery method known as flotation. The basic principle behind flotation is simple: Burnt macrobotanical remains will float in water, whereas the soil matrix will sink; therefore, if soil is vigorously mixed with water, the macrobotanicals will float free of the soil matrix. The paleoethnobotanists can then skim off the charred seeds, stalks, and wood for analysis.

◀ **Using flotation to recover charred plant remains at the site of Jerf el Ahmar, Syria.**

Paleoethnobotanists have developed elaborate floatation machines that allow large amounts of soil to be processed. After macrobotanicals are skimmed off, they need to be carefully dried and then laboriously sorted. Paleoethnobotanists can identify species of seeds and other plant parts and also can usually distinguish between domesticated and wild plants. By looking at where different types of plant remains are found, paleoethnobotanists can also contribute to understanding the spatial organization of activities on a site—for example, identifying areas where food was prepared.

desiccated remains of plants that would otherwise rapidly disintegrate. By contrast, waterlogged conditions, including bogs and deposits sealed under water, can preserve botanical remains because of the absence of oxygen. An example of such anaerobic preservation is the remains of brush huts preserved at the site of Ohalo, Israel, which was sealed below the waters of the Sea of Galilee.

▶ **Charred barley seeds recovered from the site of Tel Kerma.**

All botanical remains that can be seen without magnification are known as macro-botanicals. Most macrobotanicals are not preserved. An important exception is the charred remains of burnt seeds, plant parts, and wood found on the majority of archaeological sites. The problem for paleoethnobotanists is that these tiny fragile specimens are usually found dispersed across the site, closely bound in the soil matrix. Trying to recover such plant remains is a literal case of grasping at

although it is not clear what other function they might have had. It is usually suggested that the stone walls would have supported a superstructure made of wood and brush. At the site of **Mallaha** in Northern Israel, a tentative reconstruction of a particularly large structure has been developed.

The size of Natufian sites ranges from large villages, such as Mallaha or Wadi Hammeh, with up to a dozen structures, to much smaller sites. There is considerable debate as to whether these sites were occupied year-round.

During the later part of the Natufian, there is a marked reduction both in the number of sites and in the size of the sites. The contraction in Natufian settlements is correlated with a brief period of climatic stress known as the **Younger Dryas,** a global event often characterized as a "little Ice Age." Recent research suggests that the onset of the Younger Dryas was extremely rapid and that major shifts in climate would have taken place within a single generation. In the Middle East, the effect of the Younger Dryas was to reduce the areas suitable for human occupation. From the change in the size and density of the settlements, it is clear that the Younger Dryas had a significant effect on Natufian society.

Burials are commonly found on Natufian sites, often under the floors of houses. In some cases, in a practice that is elaborated in the subsequent Neolithic periods, the skull has been removed prior to burial. Objects found in some Natufian burials include shell necklaces and head coverings.

**P**olished stone artifact known as a shaft straightener found at the site of Wadi Mataha. Note the incised decoration.

## Domestication

Unfortunately, it has rarely been possible to recover plant remains from Natufian sites. An important exception is the site of **Abu Hureyra,** located on the Upper Euphrates River in Syria. Excavations at Abu Hureyra uncovered a culture parallel to the Natufian, but with subtle differences. For example, the houses at Abu Hureyra were found as sunken pits rather than built walls. An ambitious program of flotation for burnt seeds at Abu Hureyra was richly rewarded with a spectacular assemblage of botanical remains. The analysis of the recovered seeds indicates that the people living at Abu Hureyra, like the people at Ohalo, exploited a wide range of plants. Such a broad-spectrum strategy is not surprising, as it is an effective way for hunter–gatherers to minimize the risk that any particular resource will be temporarily scarce. Most of the plant species do not show any evidence of having been domesticated.

Paradoxically, **Natufian** hunting came to focus on a single species. With some exceptions, the animal bones found on Natufian sites are dominated by gazelle bones. At Abu Hureyra, 80 percent of the bones identified were gazelle bones. At the same time, Natufians continued to hunt a wide range of animals, including wild sheep, goats, and cattle. At sites such as Mallaha, which is located near a marsh, birds continued to be hunted as well.

▶ **Mallaha** is a Natufian site in northern Israel with the remains of oval stone structures.

▶ The **Younger Dryas** is a period of global climatic stress that had a significant impact on Natufian society.

▶ **Abu Hureyra** is a site on the Euphrates River in Syria that was occupied during the Natufian and the Neolithic periods.

▶ The **Natufians** practiced a broad-spectrum subsistence strategy that relied on a wide range of resources.

Excavation of a large Natufian structure at the site of Mallaha, Israel.

The Natufians did not domesticate any herd animals. (Gazelles have actually never been completely domesticated.) Interestingly, there is evidence that Natufians had domesticated, or at least tamed, dogs. At two sites—Hayonim Terrace and Mallaha—dog skeletons were found buried with human remains. These burials sig-

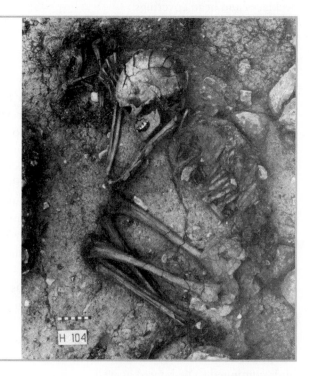

Burial of a dog together with a human from the Natufian site of Mallaha. Archaeologists have interpreted this burial as evidence that dogs were domesticated during the Natufian period.

nify that dogs were brought into human society. There is also some indication that the snouts of dogs found on Natufian sites are smaller than the snouts of wild dogs (Dayan 1994). This change in morphology is consistent with the early stages of domestication.

# 7.4 STAGE 3: THE EARLY NEOLITHIC

The Early Neolithic is divided into two major periods: the Pre-Pottery Neolithic A, which dates between 12,000 and 10,800 years ago, and the Pre-Pottery Neolithic B, which dates between 10,800 and 8,500 years ago. The beginning of the Pre-Pottery Neolithic A corresponds with the end of the Younger Dryas event, while the Pre-Pottery Neolithic B corresponds to a period of improved climate.

## Technology

For archaeologists, the major marker distinguishing the Early Neolithic from the Natufian is a gradual shift away from tools made on bladelets to a tool kit made on blades with a particular emphasis on arrowheads. By the Pre-Pottery Neolithic B, arrowheads were made on skillfully manufactured blades. Blades are also used for sickles, as is evidenced by the frequent presence of sickle polish. Ground stone axes and adzes suitable for working wood or clearing trees are an important addition to the Early Neolithic tool kit. Grinding stones used for processing grain are also found in extremely large quantities on Early Neolithic sites.

The use of plaster is highly developed during the Pre-Pottery Neolithic B period. Manufacturing plaster involves burning large quantities of limestone. Plaster was used to line the floors of houses and for ritual purposes described shortly. In some cases, plaster was used to build simple basins and bowls.

**E**arly Neolithic arrowheads and blades.

## Settlements

During the Pre-Pottery Neolithic A, the size of settlements increased and the first evidence of communal structures appeared. Houses continued to be circular, but settlements were larger than Natufian settlements. At the site of **Netiv Hagdud** in the Jordan Valley, the remains of at least three houses were found in an excavation covering 500 square meters, less than 10 percent of the total area of the settlement (Bar-Yosef et al. 1991). Although population sizes are difficult to estimate, it seems likely

**Netiv Hagdud** is a Pre-Pottery Neolithic A site in the Jordan Valley thought to have accommodated between twenty and thirty houses.

# TOOLBOX:
## Harris Matrix

Any process that has led to the accumulation of material on an archaeological site is considered to be a depositional event. Because deposition is not continuous on archaeological sites, archaeologists can define depositional units. What makes the concept of depositional unit confusing is that depositional units can be of many types, including walls, floors, and pits. The job of the archaeological stratigrapher is to place these units into a matrix of relationships. Many archaeologists use a formal system called a Harris matrix to represent the network of relationships between depositional units (Harris 1989). Much of the challenge of stratigraphy comes from the fact that we do not actually observe the creation of the site. Instead, we observe changes in the composition and color of deposits as we excavate. The excavator's art is to determine whether a change in color or soil texture represents a new depositional unit.

Building a Harris matrix is based on identifying one of three possible relationships between depositional units.

1. Units can have no stratigraphic connection. For example, if there is a floor on the inside of a wall and a road on the outside, there is no direct stratigraphic relationship between the road and the floor.
2. Units can be in superposition. For example, if a wall is built over the remains of another wall, then the two units are in superposition.

3. Units can be correlated as parts of what was originally part of a single feature. For example, if there was a large pit house that was cut in half by the excavation of a foundation trench for a wall, then the two halves of the pit (which would be identified in the field as two separate depositional units) would be correlated as part of a single feature.

On the basis of these three types of relationships, it is possible to build a formal matrix expressing the stratigraphic relationships between all of the depositional units on a site.

The life of a mud brick house provides a useful example of the range of processes that result in depositonal units.

The following is a list of depositional units that might be found in such a house:

1. The wall built into the foundation trench.
2. The fill placed between the edges of the trench and the base of the wall.
3. A pile of dirt excavated from a foundation trench of a mud brick structure and dumped in a pile outside of the house.
4. The material incorporated into the dirt floor of the house during the life of the building.
5. A hearth or cooking stove and the resulting ash deposits.
6. A pile of garbage built up outside the house.

that Netiv Hagdud housed somewhere between twenty and thirty families. Beyond the size of the settlement, there are other contrasts between Netiv Hagdud and large Natufian sites such as Mallaha. A rapid accumulation of sediments on Early Neolithic sites points to the extensive use of mud brick architecture. At Netiv Hagdud, there was a buildup of close to 4 meters of sediment over a period of two to three hundred years. The floors of the structures on Early Neolithic sites are well maintained, and debris tends to be concentrated in refuse pits. Storage pits, which are rare on Natufian sites, are common at Netiv Hagdud and other Early Neolithic sites.

The appearance of communal structures is the most striking aspect of the Pre-Pottery Neolithic A. The most spectacular of these structures is the tower discovered in the Pre-Pottery Neolithic A levels at Jericho. The 9-meter-high tower is made of undressed stones and mud brick and is attached to the inside of a massive wall. A staircase built inside the tower runs from the base to a hole in the flat platform at the top. The **Jericho tower** is the earliest-known large-scale piece of architecture in the Middle East. Estimates for the time taken to build the tower and the attached

The **Jericho tower** is a 9-meter-high structure made of undressed stone and mud brick dating to the Pre-Pottery Neolithic A.

# FIGURE 7.1

**Diagram and Harris Matrix of a mud brick house.**

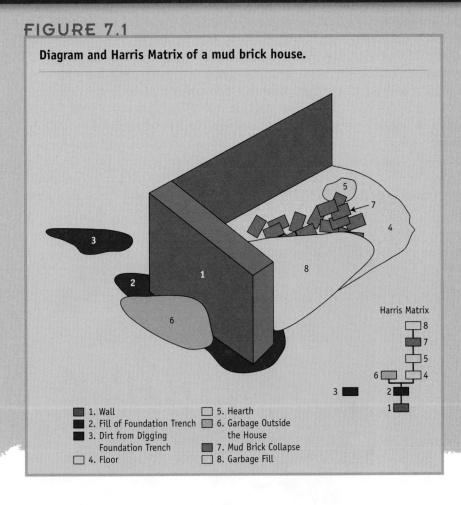

1. Wall
2. Fill of Foundation Trench
3. Dirt from Digging Foundation Trench
4. Floor
5. Hearth
6. Garbage Outside the House
7. Mud Brick Collapse
8. Garbage Fill

Harris Matrix

7. The mud bricks that have collapsed after the abandonment of the house.
8. Garbage that accumulated in the remains of the house after its abandonment.

It is possible to put all of the units of the abandoned mud brick house in superposition, except for the garbage pile outside the house and the dirt pile from the digging of the foundation trench. It is also possible to say that the garbage pile appeared later than the foundation trench and the wall. However, because there is no stratigraphic connection between the inside and the outside of the house, it is not possible to determine the stratigraphic relationship between the pile outside the house and any of the features on the inside of the house. The dirt pile from the digging of the foundation trench is in no stratigraphic relationship with any of the other depositional features.

wall range between 10,000 and 15,000 working days (Bar-Yosef 1986). Kenyon (1981) interpreted the tower as part of a defensive wall, which she thought ran around the Neolithic village. Because only a small portion of the Neolithic site was excavated, there is no way of knowing whether the bit of wall found attached to the tower does in fact run around the site. In any case, it seems extremely unlikely that the tower could have served a military purpose, as it is built on the inside of the wall. The interpretation of the tower is made more difficult by the fact that twelve skeletons were found at the base of the staircase. The skeletons were inserted when the staircase had begun to collapse. Among the suggestions as to the purpose of the tower are (1) that the tower and the wall served for flood protection and (2) that the entire installation had a cultic function, as the construction and use of the tower appears to have been a community effort.

Excavations on Pre-Pottery Neolithic A sites in Syria also have uncovered evidence of communal structures. At the site of **Jerf el Ahmar** on the Upper Euphrates River in Syria, the excavators found that although the Pre-Pottery Neolithic A houses

▶ **Jerf el Ahmar** is a Pre-Pottery Neolithic A site on the Euphrates River in Syria with the remains of a communal structure.

appear to be distributed somewhat randomly across the site, there is a sense of community planning, with groups of houses distributed around a central structure (Stordeur 1999). This central structure is larger than the other buildings and is built into the ground rather than being built on the surface. These semisubterranean buildings are round, with a large central room surrounded by a series of small cubicles. The excavators suggest that the buildings played a central communal role in the small Early Neolithic village at Jerf el Ahmar. In one case, a skeleton of an individual lying splayed on his back with his head removed was found in the central chamber of a semisubterranean house. Soon after this person died, the building was destroyed and burnt. The discoveries at Jericho and Jerf el Ahmar indicate that the organization of Pre-Pottery Neolithic A society allowed the community to act as a group. It is intriguing that much of the evidence of community level activity is found in structures with ritual functions associated with evidence of violence. We are left to question the role that ritual and violence played in knitting these early communities together.

During the Pre-Pottery Neolithic B period, there was a shift from round houses to rectangular houses and the size of settlements increased significantly. The shift to rectangular houses allowed sites to be more densely packed than they were in the Pre-Pottery Neolithic A. The villages of the Pre-Pottery Neolithic B are quite large

View of the site of Jerf el Ahmar showing houses surrounding a central circular semi-subterranean structure.

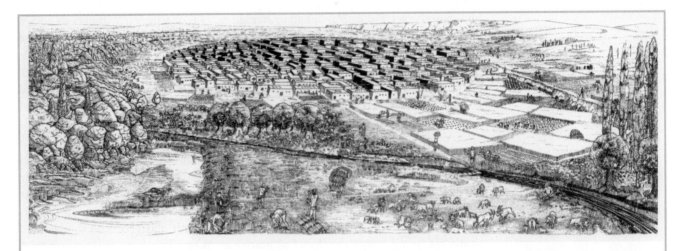

**R**econstruction of the Pre-Pottery Neolithic B village of Abu Hureyra, Syria. This picture shows the extent to which the landscape of the early Neolithic was shaped by human activity and construction.

and often show a high degree of planning. Excavators estimate that in the Early Neolithic levels of Abu Hureyra there were up to 1,440 houses with a population of about 5,000 people (Moore 2000). The houses in the areas excavated were closely packed together and had a regular orientation. There is no evidence that the site was protected by a defensive wall.

Estimates for the size of Abu Hureyra place it at the high end of Early Neolithic sites in the Middle East. However, sites that could have easily housed hundreds or even thousands of people are common. Excavations at the site of Badja in southern Jordan have shown that houses during the later part of the Early Neolithic were two or even three stories high (Gebel et al. 1997). At Badja, the size of the settlement was limited by its rather precarious setting on cliffs above a deep gully. It appears that people responded to this limitation by crowding their houses closely together and building upwards. Why people chose to live in such an inaccessible setting is an intriguing question.

During the Pre-Pottery Neolithic B, people lived in dense villages where their social life and interactions were constrained within a grid of houses. Life in these villages also required institutional structures to maintain social order. Hunter–gatherer societies, which are highly mobile, can resolve disputes simply by breaking into smaller groups, or "fissioning." The people living in villages like Abu Hureyra would not have had this option. Moreover, life in a densely packed village would have led to inevitable tensions over issues of inheritance and property rights. Discovering how Early Neolithic societies resolved these conflicts is a challenging archaeological problem, but one that is essential to resolve.

It is somewhat surprising that there is no real evidence for a social hierarchy in early Neolithic villages. Most houses look more or less the same, as do most burials. There is no sense that the regular layout of the sites reflects the decisions of a central authority.

## Ritual

Jacques Cauvin has eloquently called the Early Neolithic period the "birth of the gods," and a staggering array of symbolic artifacts has been found on Early Neolithic sites. Ritual objects appear to have operated at many levels, including everyday household objects and objects of display found in sacred precincts or temples. Within both houses and temples there was also a domain of bodies and objects built into walls and buried under floors. It seems clear that as they walked the streets of their villages, these people negotiated not only a world of constructed architecture, but also a world charged with deities, both visible and hidden. The archaeological evidence for Early Neolithic ritual activity can be broken down into three broad categories (based on ideas in Verhoeven 2002 and Naveh 2003): hidden, displayed, and daily life.

**Hidden Rituals.** Many of the ritual objects found on Early Neolithic sites are hidden away in pits or under floors. The most striking hidden objects are **plastered skulls.** The removal of skulls from human skeletons is found as far back as the Natufian. On Pre-Pottery Neolithic B sites, skulls have been discovered on which a plaster face has been modeled. Both plastered and unplastered skulls are found below the floors of houses or in small caches.

An analysis of one of the skulls from the site of Kefar Hahoresh has provided a particularly detailed picture of the process of creating a plastered skull (Goren et al. 2001). In most cases, the mandible or jawbone was removed before the face was modeled. The first stage was to plug up the recesses in the skull, including the eye sockets and nasal passages. The face was then modeled onto the skull but the position of the features was adjusted upwards. Thus, the eyes were built up on the forehead, the nose over the eye sockets, and the mouth over the nasal passage. As a result, the faces of the plastered skulls have an oddly shortened appearance. The analysis of the Kefar Hahoresh skull has shown that the process of modeling a plaster skull took place in several stages and included a range of types of plaster as well as other materials.

Careful stratigraphic analysis has indicated that in some cases plastered skulls were removed from their hiding places below the floors of houses and then carefully redeposited. Some archaeologists argue that this practice was an aspect of ancestor

> **Plastered skulls** are found buried beneath floors on sites dating to the Pre-Pottery Neolithic B period.

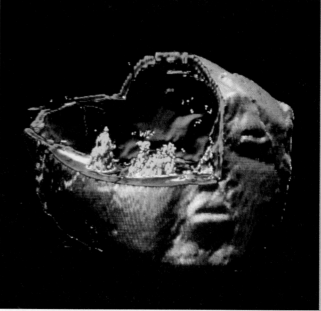

Plastered skull from the Neolithic site of Kefar Hahoresh, Israel. The image on the right was created using a CT scanner to analyze the interior structure of the skull and mask.

worship and that it was through reverence for the ancestor that Early Neolithic societies maintained cohesion. However, a number of sites appear to challenge this interpretation. At Kefar Hahoresh, much of the excavated area is taken up by a dense deposit of human skeletal remains, hardly consistent with a normal habitation site. The excavator of Kefar Hahoresh has argued that it was a ritual site serving to bring together various communities in the region.

At the site of Ain Ghazal in Jordan, a collection of plaster figures was discovered in two pits (Rollefson 1998). How these figures relate to the Pre-Pottery Neolithic B plastered skulls is an enigma. Another puzzling site is a small cave known as Nahal Hemar, located in a remote region south of the Dead Sea (Bar-Yosef 1985). In this cave, a wide range of artifacts was found, such as beads, bone tools, and arrowheads. Due to the dry conditions, textiles, including the remains of a cap and a bag, were recovered from Nahal Hemar. Along with these objects, a painted stone mask was recovered together with a skull on which the face was not decorated, but a net pattern had been applied to the cranium. What the function of this collection of artifacts was and, perhaps more importantly, how they got to where they were found are two questions that remain difficult to answer.

At the site of Badja in southern Jordan, the excavator has found a series of unused axes carefully hidden within the walls of a house. The excavator suggests that these beautifully crafted hidden objects would have had a magical function.

**Display Rituals.** The Pre-Pottery Neolithic A tower of Jericho and the special building at Jerf el Ahmar were clearly meant to be seen. It seems quite likely that, regardless of their practical functions, these structures also stood as visible symbols of the community. During the Pre-Pottery Neolithic B, visibly special buildings are found on a number of sites.

At the sites of Beidha in southern Jordan and at Kefar Hahoresh, standing stones have been found. The meaning of these objects is puzzling, but it is clear that they were meant to be visible. At the site of Göbekli Tepe on the Euphrates River in eastern Turkey, a series of buildings has been found built around monumental t-shaped pillars quarried as a single block from the bedrock. Some of these pillars are carved with either human or animal figures (Schmidt 2001). At the nearby site of Navali Çori, a series of large stone sculptures has been uncovered that includes depictions of humans, birds, snakes, and birds combined with humans. Most of these sculptures come from a structure identified as a temple.

The majority of the display items found in the Pre-Pottery Neolithic B would not have been visible from any great distance. They are thus quite different from the Pre-Pottery Neolithic A tower from Jericho. Many authors have argued that the context for display in the Pre-Pottery Neolithic B was within

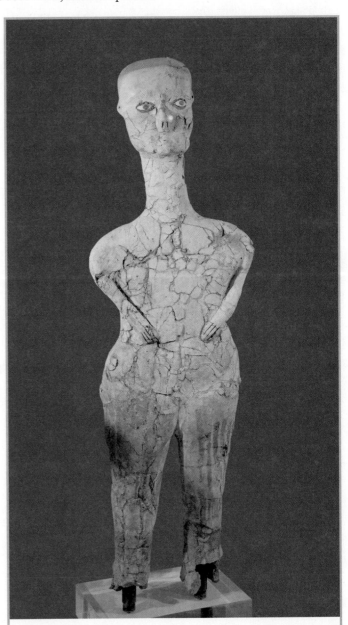

Plaster figure from Ain Ghazal after restoration.

temples or sacred precincts. This is a very important point, because it suggests that access to visible signs of divinity was controlled. Perhaps the elite of Early Neolithic society was a ritual elite.

In some cases, there is evidence for the display of skulls, objects that are normally found in hidden contexts. At the site of Çayanu in eastern Turkey, the remains of 450 individuals have been recovered from a single structure known as the skull room, mostly from pits (Schirmer 1990). However, 49 burnt skulls were also found in contexts which suggest that they fell off shelves when the building was burnt.

**Rituals of Daily Life.** On several Early Neolithic sites, a large number of simple clay figurines have been found. Although some suggest that the statuettes were children's toys, it appears more likely that they had symbolic meaning. These objects are usually found distributed among houses, together with domestic debris.

> On domesticated plants, the **rachis,** which holds the seed to the stalk, is tough so that the seed stays on the plant until it is harvested.

# Domestication

Excavations at the Pre-Pottery Neolithic A site of Netiv Hagdud recovered the remains of barley with a tough **rachis**—the part of the plant that holds the seed to the stalk. In wild grains, the rachis is brittle and shatters easily, allowing seeds to disperse.

**D**omesticated cereals such as wheat and barley develop a tough rachis which holds seeds to the plant until threshing after harvest. Wild cereals have a brittle rachis that allows for easy dispersal of the seeds.

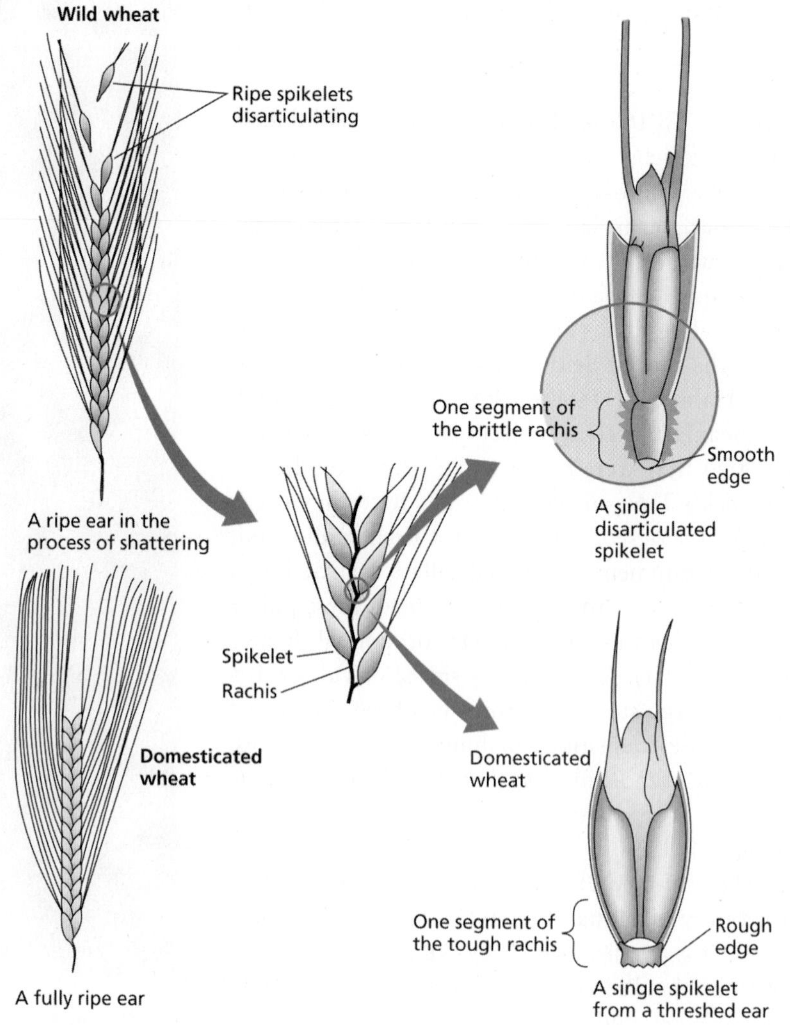

Wild wheat

Ripe spikelets disarticulating

A ripe ear in the process of shattering

One segment of the brittle rachis

Smooth edge

A single disarticulated spikelet

Spikelet

Rachis

Domesticated wheat

Domesticated wheat

A fully ripe ear

One segment of the tough rachis

Rough edge

A single spikelet from a threshed ear

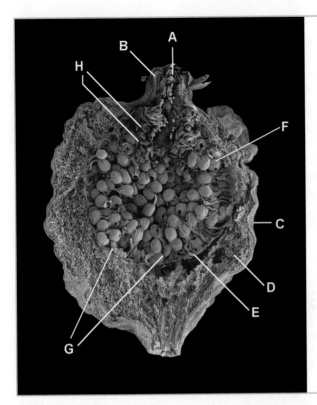

A scanning electron microscope photo of a fig from Gilgal. The letters indicate features that show that the fig was not wild. Notably, the droplets (E) are empty unlike wild figs that show evidence of wasp activity.

For agriculturalists, it is desirable to have a plant with a tough rachis so that the seed remains on the plant until it is harvested. A plant with a tough rachis is truly domesticated in that it depends on human intervention for successful reproduction.

Although the discovery at Netiv Hagdud was interpreted at first as evidence of domesticated plants in the Pre-Pottery Neolithic A, it now appears that this conclusion is not warranted (Bar-Yosef et al. 1991). Within wild populations of barley, a small percentage of plants have a tough rachis, so the small number of remains of apparently domesticated barley found at Netiv Hagdud could have been collected from wild stands along with a wide range of wild plants.

Harvesting of grains clearly did take place during the Pre-Pottery Neolithic A, as is attested to by botanical remains, grinding stones, and sickles. However, it does not appear that these plants were farmed. The wild forms of plants, including wheat and barley, were harvested, but there is no indication that seeds were stored and planted. In accordance with the criterion developed by Rindos (see page 193), cereals exploited during the Pre-Pottery Neolithic A were not domesticated, in that the plants did not depend on their relationship with humans for protection or reproduction. There is no evidence of domesticated animals other than dogs during the Pre-Pottery Neolithic A. Gazelles remained the main species hunted, together with a wide range of other animals, including fish and birds.

A series of dried figs recovered from the Pre-Pottery Neolithic A site of Gilgal, located in the Jordan Valley near Netiv Hagdud, provides the earliest compelling evidence of plant domestication in the Middle East (Kislev, Hartmann, and Bar-Yosef 2006). These figs, like modern domesticated figs, are not capable of reproduction without human intervention. Although this intervention is simple, involving merely the cutting and planting of branches, it clearly meets the definition of domestication.

Farming developed across the Middle East during the Pre-Pottery Neolithic B. A wide range of domesticated crops is found, including cereals (emmer wheat, einkorn wheat, and barley), pulses (lentil and pea), and legumes (bitter vetch and chick pea). The domesticated grains show an increase in the size of individual grains and a shift to a tough rachis.

Animal domestication developed somewhat after plant domestication. The later part of the Pre-Pottery Neolithic B affords evidence of domesticated sheep and goat. Sheep were domesticated in the northern mountainous regions of Turkey, Iraq, or Iran, their natural habitation zone. The location and timing for the domestication of goats is quite complex, as wild goats are found across the entire region. Pigs and cattle were domesticated by the end of the Pre-Pottery Neolithic B. The evidence for domesticated animals in the Pre-Pottery Neolithic B includes a reduction in the size of animals, an overrepresentation of the bones of young males, and the discovery of animals such as sheep outside of their natural range. The domestication of sheep and goat appears to have followed a falloff in gazelle populations.

# 7.5 STAGE 4: LATE NEOLITHIC

At the end of the Pre-Pottery Neolithic B, there is a sharp reduction in the number of large village sites across most of the Middle East. The reasons for the collapse of the Early Neolithic settlement system remains unclear; however, some archaeologists argue that it was the result of ecological degradation caused by deforestation. At the same time that the settlement system collapsed, there were significant changes in technology, including the introduction of pottery, and in symbolic artifacts.

## Technology

Pottery manufacture developed in the Middle East during the Late Neolithic. Among the vessels that have been found are small bowls and jars, as well as pots used for cooking. There is significant variation in the forms of vessels and in the way vessels are decorated in different regions and within different periods. Two of the main methods of decoration were burnishing the clay to produce a polished surface and using red pigments in painted designs. All pots were built by hand without the use of a potter's wheel and were fired at a low temperature. At the same time that pottery was developed, the wide-scale production of plaster was abandoned.

There was also a significant shift in stone tool manufacture during the Late Neolithic. The skillful production of blades disappeared and arrowheads became rare. Most stone tools found on Late Neolithic sites are expedient tools made on locally available materials with a minimal investment of energy. Sickle blades remain common and often have a serrated edge created by a series of notches.

## Settlement and Ritual

The end of the Pre-Pottery Neolithic saw a decline in the number and size of sites. By the end of this period, which is often labeled Pre-Pottery Neolithic C, most of the large sites in Israel, Jordan, Syria, and eastern Turkey were abandoned. The Late Neolithic in these areas is characterized by a limited number of large sites and small

**L**ate Neolithic pottery.

dispersed hamlets. The large sites differ from Pre-Pottery Neolithic B sites in that they are not densely packed with structures.

The seeming collapse of the Pre-Pottery Neolithic B settlement system presents a challenge for archaeological interpretation. One possibility is that the collapse was the result of a human-induced ecological crisis. The large populations concentrated in Pre-Pottery Neolithic B villages along with their herds of domesticated animals might have degraded their environments to the point where such population densities could no longer be supported. One important culprit in this scenario is the large-scale production of plaster, which could have led to extensive deforestation.

An alternative perspective sees the end of the Pre-Pottery Neolithic B settlement system not as a collapse, but rather as a shift toward a way of life focused on the grazing of herds of domesticated animals. The dispersed settlement system found in the Late Neolithic might reflect a population that had shifted to living scattered across the landscape rather than huddled in large villages.

The symbolic system of the Early Neolithic seems to have collapsed along with the settlement system by the time of the Late Neolithic. No longer does there appear to be any attention paid to skull removal or ornamentation. Among the most striking symbolic artifacts of the Late Neolithic are small figurines that tend to be of stylized humans rather than animals.

In Central and Western Turkey, there is a continuity in dense village settlement through the Late Neolithic. It is during this period that the spectacular settlement of **Çatalhöyük** developed on the Konya Plain of Central Turkey. Excavations at the site

The Late Neolithic site of ▶ **Çatalhöyük** includes rooms decorated with elaborate frescoes.

**F**resco painted onto a plaster wall at the site of Çatalhöyük. How would you describe the interaction between the human figures and the large bull in the center?

have revealed a densely occupied settlement dating between 9,000 and 8,000 years ago (Mellaart 1967, Cessford 2001). The excavations at Çatalhöyük uncovered a series of rooms richly decorated with frescoes depicting spectacular scenes of leopards, bulls, and goddesses, as well as geometric designs. A particularly striking image found in these rooms is that of vultures, at times depicted circling around headless human figures. Bulls' heads and other figures were often modeled in relief, and bulls' horns were set into the plaster bulls' heads. Arrangements of bulls' horns were also found on benches running through the rooms, and human burials were commonly found beneath the benches.

James Mellaart, the first excavator of the site, interpreted the decorated rooms at Çatalhöyük as shrines or temples. This interpretation is consistent with the interpretation of Pre-Pottery Neolithic B structures from sites such as Göbekli Tepe and Navali Çori. However, of the 139 rooms Mellaart excavated, more than 40 were interpreted as shrines. It appears that ritual spaces at Çatalhöyük were widely distributed. Alternatively, it could be that the structures Mellaart interpreted as shrines were actually houses and that ritual and elaborate symbolism were an integral part of daily activity rather than something set apart.

The actual interpretation of the symbolism found at Çatalhöyük has provided rich grounds for speculation. The discovery of a significant number of goddess figurines at Çatalhöyük has drawn the attention of archaeologists who argue that Neolithic society was focused on a goddess cult. Not surprisingly, Çatalhöyük has attracted the attention of Ian Hodder, who has reopened excavations at the site in order to gain a broader contextual understanding of the ritual activity and symbolism.

## Domestication

During the Late Neolithic, there is a continuous decline in the role of hunting for subsistence. Evidence of the domestication of animals during the Late Neolithic includes changes in the shape of horns in goats. A recent study has found that even at Çatalhöyük, despite the heavy symbolic emphasis on bulls, the main source of meat was domestic goat. Late Neolithic societies also continue to rely on the full range of plants domesticated during the Early Neolithic.

# 7.6 ASSESSING THE NEOLITHIC REVOLUTION

The evidence from the Middle East demonstrates that there is a great deal of value in Childe's concept of a "Neolithic Revolution." By the end of the Pre-Pottery Neolithic B, every aspect of life in the Middle East had been transformed as a result of the adoption of a village farming way of life. However, the shift to agriculture in the Middle East was not a sudden process as predicted by Childe. Rather, the beginning of the shift dates back to the Natufian period with the construction of small settlements, which then grew during the Pre-Pottery Neolithic A phase of the Early Neolithic, when there is evidence of community planning and monumental architecture. These people had begun to rely heavily on cereals, but had not domesticated either plants or animals. Plant and animal domestication began in the Pre-Pottery Neolithic B phase of the Early Neolithic, together with an increase in the size and density of settlements. Pottery was introduced only in the Late Neolithic, when there was a *decrease* in the size and density of settlements in much of the region.

The Middle East affords important insights into the causes of the adoption of agriculture. There is some evidence that the climatic stress of the Younger Dryas corresponding to the end of the Natufian and the beginning of the Pre-Pottery Neolithic A was a trigger in the development of villages. Most strikingly, agriculture developed as a consequence of people living in villages. In other words, villages preceded agriculture in the Middle East.

# 7.7 THE SPREAD OF AGRICULTURE TO EUROPE

In classic fictional mysteries, all of the clues are exposed, but the pattern stubbornly refuses to emerge. The spread of agriculture from the Middle East is as obvious and elusive as any work of fiction. The facts are clear. The origins of European domesticated plants and animals can be traced to the Middle East. There is no evidence of indigenous domestication of plants and animals. Instead, the spread of the Middle Eastern domesticates can be tracked as they move across Europe in what some archaeologists characterize as a "Wave of Advance" (Renfrew 1990). By 8,500 years ago, domesticated plants and animals had begun to spread into

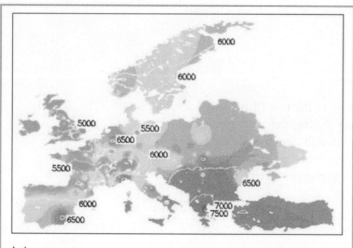

Map showing the spread of agriculture across Europe.

Southeastern Europe. Around 7,500 years ago, farming spread into Central and Western Europe. By 6,000 years ago, people in most of Western Europe, including southern Scandinavia, Britain, and Ireland, were practicing agriculture.

The clarity of the pattern has led many archaeologists to claim that a massive movement of populations is the explanation for the spread of agriculture into Europe. According to this perspective, incoming farmers gradually replaced the hunter–gatherer societies of Europe. The driving force behind the expansion is thought to be the population increase associated with farming. One fascinating line of research links the expansion of populations of farmers into Europe with the spread of the Indo–European language family. Indo–European languages include all the European romance languages, such as French, Portuguese, Italian, and Spanish; the Germanic languages, such as English, German, and Dutch; the Slavic languages, such as Russian, Polish, and Czech; Asian languages such as Farsi, Hindi, and Bengali; several Baltic and Balkan languages, such as Latvian, Lithuanian, and Albanian; and a number of more dispersed languages, such as Sanskrit and the ancient language Hittite, spoken in the area that today is Turkey. The "language dispersal hypothesis," as this idea has come to be known, views the spread of agriculture as the movement of people carrying with them an entire way of life, including farming, religion, and language (Renfrew 1990).

The language dispersal hypothesis is a bold concept, reminiscent of the Out of Africa hypothesis discussed in Chapter 5. Farming is linked with people and language. The spread of agriculture into Europe involves the replacement of hunter–gatherers by farmers. In this model, the hunter–gatherers emerge as passive and defenseless in the face of the gradual wave of advancing farmers.

However, there is increasing evidence that the millennia leading up to the shift to agriculture saw dramatic shifts in European hunter–gatherer societies that preceded the arrival of farming. These societies, collectively labeled as Mesolithic, practiced a broad-spectrum adaptation similar to that found in the Natufian of the Middle East (Perles 2001). In the Mesolithic levels of the Franchthi Cave, Greece, occupied around 11,000 years ago, there is evidence that the occupants hunted red deer, cattle, and pigs and also collected land snails and shellfish. Wild plants, including pistachios, almonds, pears, wild oats, and wild barley, were also collected. There is also evidence of long-distance sea travel. Obsidian was brought to the site from the island of Melos, a 100-km. sea voyage from the mainland. Tuna fish are also found in large quantities, indicating offshore fishing.

Paleoenvironmental studies along the coast of England are producing strong evidence that Mesolithic hunter–gatherers used fire to shape their landscape (Brown 2005). Charcoal is ubiquitous in sediment profiles dating to the period of Mesolithic occupation. The prevalence of charcoal cannot be explained on the basis of natural phenomena such as lightning strikes. Similar use of fire by Australian hunter–gatherers is known as fire-stick farming. Burning would have increased the fodder available to wild animals, which could then be hunted, and would also have increased the availability of wild plants for collecting. The evidence of burning by Mesolithic hunter–gatherers in England muddies the clarity of the division between hunter–gatherers and farmers. Clearly, the hunter–gatherers in what is now England were capable of actively manipulating aspects of their environment.

The most impressive Mesolithic site is **Lepinski Vir**, located next to a whirlpool in the Iron Gates gorges of the Danube River in Serbia. Lepinski Vir consists of a series of trapezoid-shaped structures associated with a large number of burials and sculptures that mix human and fish attributes. Untangling the relationship between sculptures, burials, and other household features such as hearths remains a major challenge (Radovanovic 2000, Boric 2005). The Danube would have been a rich source of fish, particularly sturgeon, and it is not surprising that the faunal remains from the earliest levels are dominated by fish bones. In the final stages of occupation, there appears to have been a shift to increased reliance on hunting deer. The dates for the occupation of Lepinski Vir range between 8,400 and 7,600 years ago. These dates overlap with the time of the arrival of Neolithic agriculturalists, indicating that in the later phases of the village the Mesolithic hunter–gatherers of Lepinski Vir lived alongside farming communities.

The complexity of Mesolithic hunter–gatherer societies has led some archaeologists to argue that these societies adopted domesticated plants and animals (Whittle 1996). The spread of agriculture is not seen as the result of the migration of populations from the Middle East. Rather, there was a continuity of local communities that experienced a gradual, but dramatic, shift in every aspect of their lives.

▶ **Lepinski Vir**, located along the Danube River in Serbia, is an impressive Mesolithic site with structures, burials, and sculptures.

The Iron Gates gorges of the Danube River.

# TOOLBOX:
## The Iceman

In September 1991, two hikers discovered a corpse stuck in ice in the Alps near the Austrian–Italian border. Subsequent investigation showed that their find was no ordinary corpse: It was the mummified remains of a man who had died on this spot near the end of the Neolithic period, slightly over 5,000 years ago. His body and clothing had been preserved under the ice, providing archaeologists a unique perspective on aspects of Neolithic culture that are rarely preserved. He wore a cap, a shirt, and leggings made of fur; a loincloth and shoes made of leather; and a grass cloak. He carried a bag with embers to start fires, as well as what are apparently medicinal plants. His gear included a retoucher to repair his flint tools as needed. His skin bears tattoos on his wrist, spine, knee, calf, foot, and ankle.

Since his discovery, Ötzi the Iceman, as he came to be known, has been the subject of a border dispute between Italy and Austria and what is perhaps the most detailed study any human body has ever received. Not even the single fingernail that survives has escaped scrutiny. Analysis of the fingernail found evidence of periods of stress in the months before the Iceman died.

Yet as the details build up, an air of mystery still surrounds the Iceman. Who was he and why was he up in the mountains? Was he a shepherd? A shaman? An outcast? There are many clues, but no clear answers. We do know that he experienced violence immediately before his death: An arrowhead was found lodged in his left shoulder, and he appears to have incurred deep slash wounds to his hands soon before he died (Cullen 2003). One possibility is that he fled to the mountains to escape an attack on his village, perhaps an attack like the event that produced the mass grave at Talheim.

◄ Excavation of the Iceman.

---

On the one hand, there is clear evidence that domesticated plants and animals spread into Europe from the Middle East. However, there is also little doubt that the Mesolithic societies were capable of adopting these plants and animals into their wide-spectrum adaptations. The resulting clash of ideas about the origins of agriculture in Europe—advancing populations of farmers or innovating societies of hunter–gatherers—is most clearly expressed in diverging interpretations of the earliest farming communities of Central and Western Europe known as the **Linear Band Keramik,** or LBK, culture. LBK societies cultivated Middle Eastern plants and herded Middle Eastern animals, but they lived in communities unlike any found in the Middle East. LBK villages consist of longhouses built of massive timbers. The houses reached up to 30 meters in length. Clearly, the large size of these houses must reflect the nature of the households that lived in them. It is hard to escape the conclusion that during the LBK period extended kinship groups lived together. LBK houses are evidence of far more than simply changes in technology or construction.

> The earliest farming communities of Central and Western Europe are known as the **Linear Band Keramik,** or LBK, culture. ◄

Reconstruction of a Linear Band Keramik village.

One particularly striking aspect of the LBK culture is that it is highly uniform across its entire distribution. Those who view agriculture as the spread of populations point to this feature and argue that it is best explained as the result of people moving with their way of life. However, the novelty of LBK community structure suggests that it might in fact represent a local innovation, rather than an idea that came with new groups of people.

There is a compromise position that views the shift to agriculture in Europe as the interaction between incoming populations and innovative hunter–gatherers. This perspective raises the question of the nature of the interaction between farmers and hunter–gatherers in Europe. There is some evidence of trade and exchange between LBK and Mesolithic groups. There are also some indications of violent interaction. The most graphic evidence comes from the LBK site of **Talheim** in southern Germany. At Talheim, a large pit was found with the remains of eleven men, seven women, and sixteen children. Blows to the head had killed twenty of these people, and two adults had been shot in the head by arrows. Who were the people found at Talheim? Why were they killed? How does this discovery fit with the emerging picture of the spread of agriculture into Europe? It is interesting that a detailed analysis of skeletons from the site of Lepenski Vir, where a community of Mesolithic hunter–gatherers lived alongside farming communities, did not find significant evidence of interpersonal violence (Roskandic et al. 2005)

> At the LBK site of **Talheim**, Germany, a pit containing a mass grave was discovered.

## Summing Up the Evidence

The basic facts of the spread of agriculture through Europe are clear, but their significance remains the subject of debate and research. Did populations of farmers sweep across Europe and bring new crops and a new way of life with them? Or did Mesolithic hunter–gatherers adopt domesticated plants and animals to forge a new way of life? Finding the human agents behind large-scale events such as the origins of agriculture is often a challenging undertaking. There is clearly a rupture at the beginning of the Neolithic in Europe. The problem is determining whether this rupture is the result of new people arriving or of a dramatic reorganization of local societies and economies.

# CHAPTER SUMMARY

- There is no evidence for the domestication of plants or animals during the Kebaran and Geometric Kebaran periods.
- Excavation of the waterlogged site of Ohalo in the Sea of Galilee has detected the remains of a series of brush huts.
- The characteristic stone tool of the Natufian period is the lunate, a small crescent-shaped bladelet. Some lunates have sickle polish.
- Natufian sites include the remains of circular stone built structures.
- Decorated ground stone artifacts, shell beads, and burials are frequently found on Natufian sites.
- There is no evidence for the domestication of plants from the Natufian period. Dogs were the only animal domesticated during the period.
- During the Early Neolithic, large settled villages developed. Some of these sites have evidence of large communal structures, such as the tower at Jericho and the semi-subterranean buildings at Jerf el Ahmar.

- Numerous ritual objects, including plastered human skulls, are found on Early Neolithic sites.
- Plant domestication developed sometime in the Early Neolithic during the Pre-Pottery Neolithic B period. Among the plants domesticated were wheat, barley, lentils, peas, bitter vetch, and chick peas.
- The domestication of sheep and goats developed during the Early Neolithic, after plant domestication.
- The earliest pottery is found in the Late Neolithic.
- There was a reduction in the number of large village sites across much of the Middle East during the Late Neolithic.
- In contrast to the general pattern, the site of Çatalhöyük in Turkey developed into a major center during the Late Neolithic Period.
- The origin of agriculture in Europe is based on the adoption of Middle Eastern domesticated plants and animals.
- There is considerable debate over the mechanisms underlying the adoption of agriculture in Europe.

# KEY TERMS

## REVIEW QUESTIONS

1. Can the development of agriculture in the Middle East be described as a "Neolithic Revolution"?
2. In what ways does the Natufian period differ from the preceding Kebaran and Geometric Kebaran periods?
3. What is the evidence and significance of ritual behavior during the Early Neolithic?
4. What are the opposing views of how agriculture came to be adopted in Europe? Why is the LBK significant to this debate?

## FOR FURTHER READING

Ofer Bar-Yosef and François Valla. (1991). *The Natufian Culture in the Levant.* Ann Arbor, Michigan: International Monographs in Prehistory.

Jacques Cauvin. (2000). *The Birth of the Gods and the Origins of Agriculture.* Cambridge, U.K.: Cambridge University Press.

Ian Hodder. (1990). *The Domestication of Europe.* Oxford, U.K.: Blackwell.

Steven Mithen. (2004). *After the Ice: A Global Human History, 20,000–5,000 B.C.* Cambridge, Massachusetts: Harvard University Press.

A.M.T. Moore, G.C. Hillman, and A.J. Legge. (2000). *Village on the Euphrates: From Foraging to Farming at Abu Hureyra.* Oxford, U.K.: Oxford University Press.

Alasdair Whittle. (1996). *Europe in the Neolithic: The Creation of New Worlds.* Cambridge, U.K.: Cambridge University Press.

Their greene corne

Corne newly sprong

Their sitting at meate

place of solemne prayer

# Mounds and Maize

Drawing of the Algonquian village of Secoton made by John White in 1585.

MAIZE WAS domesticated in Mesoamerica and subsequently was adopted by societies throughout the Americas. After reading this chapter, you should understand:

▶ The archaeological record of the domestication of maize, beans, and squash in Mesoamerica.

▶ The impact of the adoption of maize agriculture on the Archaic societies of the southwestern United States and northern Mexico.

▶ The complex interaction between the indigenous domestication of plants and the adoption of maize in eastern North America.

▶ The context of the mound construction of the Adena and Hopewell cultures.

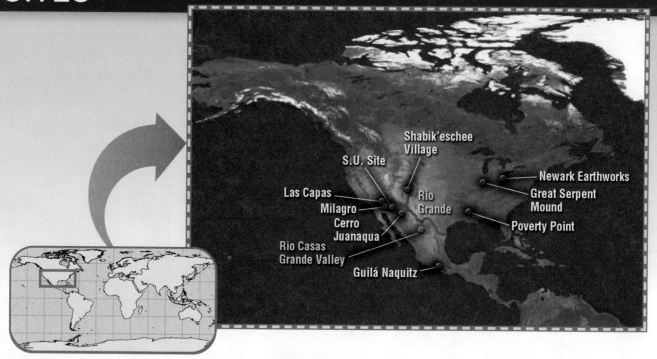

As European settlers spread westward across North America, they encountered the remains of massive artificial earthworks (Silverberg 1986). These monuments of a remote and mysterious past fired the imagination of colonial Americans. The earthworks were astonishing in their size and density. At Miamisburg, Ohio, one mound was 20 meters high and 200 meters in circumference. In the Ohio River Valley alone, there were 10,000 mounds. The earthworks were found in a wide array of forms, including flat-topped mounds, conical mounds, and enclosures. Some of the earthworks, such as the Wisconsin effigy mounds, included human and animal forms. The Great Serpent Mound in Adams County, Ohio, is the figure of an undulating snake with a curled tail stretching over 200 meters along a hill overlooking Brush Creek (Squier and Davis 1848). At the open mouth of the snake is an oval mound.

In the nineteenth century, the belief was widespread that the earthworks of eastern North America were the remains of a mysterious race of mound builders with no relation to modern Native Americans (Silverberg 1986). The mound builders were often portrayed as "civilized" in contrast to the perceived "savagery" of modern Native Americans. Theories of the origins of the mound builders ranged from the Vikings to the Lost Tribes of Israel. The fate of the mound builders was imagined as either migration to Mexico or defeat in bloody battle. The idea of a race of mound builders is now thoroughly discredited. Rather than searching for lost tribes, archaeologists today seek to trace the economic and social context of mound building among early agricultural societies.

It is difficult to organize the origins of agriculture in Mesoamerica and North America into a clear set of stages. The picture that emerges from recent research is

| thousands of years ago | ARCHAEOLOGICAL INDUSTRIES | SITES |
|---|---|---|
| 10 | | Guilá Naquiz domesticated squash |
| 9 | | |
| 8 | | |
| 7 | | |
| 6 | | Guilá Naquiz domesticated maize |
| 5 | Eastern Archaic | |
| 4 | | Poverty Point |
| 3 | SW Late Archaic / Early and Middle Woodland Adena and Hopewell | Cerro Juanaqueña Milagro Las Capas |
| 2 | SW Formative / Late Woodland | |

of regional variation in the pathways taken in the shift to an agricultural way of life. In this chapter, we begin in Mesoamerica, before moving to the American Southwest and then to eastern North America. Mesoamerica has been studied primarily as the area where major food crops, including maize, squash, and beans, were domesticated. The development of new dating methods has radically altered the chronology for the dating of these plants. Although we know quite a bit about the timing of crop domestication, many questions linger. Currently, we know little about the social context of domestication in Mesoamerica.

The uptake of maize agriculture in the American Southwest was extremely variable. In some areas, large villages with features such as terrace walls and irrigation canals appeared at the same time as the first domesticated maize. However, in other parts of the Southwest, the impact of maize agriculture was minimal. In explaining this variation, archaeologists working in the American Southwest have emphasized the ecological variability of the region and have developed models based on optimal foraging theory.

In eastern North America, we trace a complex situation involving the local domestication of plants, followed by the addition of maize to an already established farming way of life. Archaeologists in eastern North America have struggled to explain the early and pervasive appearance of earthen mounds long before the appearance of large villages. In grappling with the social meaning of these monuments, archaeologists have drawn on a variety of theoretical frameworks, including agency theory.

We end the chapter by following a debate among archaeologists working in eastern North America over the question of who actually domesticated plants. The context for this debate is feminist archaeology, but the questions raised go to the very core of the questions surrounding the origins of agriculture.

The Great Serpent Mound, Ohio.

# 8.1 PLANT DOMESTICATION IN MESOAMERICA

The Pueblo societies of the American Southwest express the centrality of maize or corn to both their subsistence and their spiritual life with the simple phrase "Corn is our mother" (Ford 1994). Maize plays a similar central role in many indigenous farming communities throughout the Americas. Archaeologists and botanists have traced the origins of maize back to **teosinte**, a wild grass found in the highlands of Mexico. Teosinte produces two rows of small triangular-shaped seeds encased in a thick glume. Maize seeds are usually several times larger than teosinte seeds and grow in four or more rows (Harlan 1995). Teosinte also differs from corn in that the rachis, the part of the plant that holds the seeds, is brittle, so the seeds disperse at maturity.

The identification of teosinte as the wild ancestor of maize has been the subject of debate. However, the genetic relation between maize and teosinte is now well established, and it is even possible that the shift from the one to the other took place rapidly (Eubanks 2001). Genetic analysis of modern populations of maize suggests that there was a single center of domestication for this crop, probably located in the highlands of Mexico (Matsuoka et al. 2002).

Archaeological research on the origins of agriculture in Mesoamerica has focused on the excavation of dry caves in the highlands of Mexico, where plant remains are well preserved. The picture that has emerged from the cave excavations is that plants, including maize, squash, and beans, were domesticated in

**Teosinte**, a wild grass found in the highlands of Mexico, is the wild ancestor of maize.

Mexico by groups of mobile hunter–gatherers. The domestication of plants appears to have had little effect on these societies beyond adding an additional resource for subsistence. However, it is possible that the archaeological emphasis on highland caves has biased our understanding of the impact of agriculture.

Excavations by Richard MacNeish in a series of caves in the Tamaulipas Mountains and in the **Tehuacán Valley** and by Kent Flannery at the cave site of **Guilá Naquitz** in the Oaxaca Valley have produced a long record of occupation by prehistoric hunter–gatherers who gradually incorporated domesticated plants into their subsistence base. It is important to emphasize that the highland valleys of Tehuacán (1,000–1,500 meters above sea level) and Oaxaca (2,000 meters above sea level) might not be the location where any of the Mesoamerican crop species were initially domesticated (Piperno and Flannery 2001). The sites were chosen for excavation because of their long sequences of occupation and excellent preservation of plant remains.

The identifiable plant remains excavated at the highland dry cave sites are too small to be dated directly with conventional radiocarbon dating methods. However, it was possible to date other organic remains, such as wood charcoal, and to build an absolute chronology of the stratigraphic sequence. Levels in the sequence were dated on the basis of the radiocarbon dating of organic remains found in the level. The age of identifiable plant remains was then determined on the basis of the date of the level in which they were recovered.

**W**ild teosinte with two rows of small triangular seeds.

It is important to emphasize that the stratigraphic sequences at Guilá Naquiz and the Tehuacán Valley sites are relatively shallow and compacted. At Guilá Naquiz, five levels were identified. The top of the sequence is Zone A, a twenty-centimeter-thick level dated to a little over 1,000 years ago. Below Zone A is a sequence of levels labeled Zone B–Zone E that date between 7,800 and 12,700 years ago. The entire thickness of Zone B–Zone E is approximately 60 centimeters, covering a period of over 4,000 years (Flannery 1986). When one considers that the plant remains are often extremely small and that the deposits are shallow, it is perhaps not surprising that stratigraphic methods of dating plant remains from dry caves have turned out not to be dependable.

The development of **accelerator mass spectrometry (AMS) radiocarbon dating** has made it possible to date identifiable plant remains directly. When plant remains are directly dated using AMS radiocarbon dating, the dates obtained are often different (in most cases, younger) from what is expected on the basis of the date of the level from which the sample was recovered. Stratigraphic context alone has proven to be an undependable method for dating identifiable plant remains on these shallow sites.

On the basis of AMS radiocarbon dating, squash was identified as the earliest plant to be domesticated in Mexico. The type of squash domesticated in Mesoamerica, *Curcubita pepo*, is the ancestor of the vast array of squashes we eat today, including pumpkins, acorn squash, zucchini, marrow squash, and spaghetti squash.

> Excavations at the highland caves of the ▶ **Tehuacán Valley** and at the site of **Guilá Naquitz** in the Oaxaca have produced the earliest evidence of domesticated plants in the Americas.

> ▶ **AMS radiocarbon dating** makes it possible to date very small samples, including plant remains.

# TOOLBOX:
## AMS Radiocarbon Dating

In previous chapters, the basic methods of radiocarbon dating and calibration were introduced. The principles of radiocarbon dating are that (1) the ratio between radioactive carbon-14 and stable carbon atoms is constant throughout the carbon exchange reservoir, which includes the atmosphere, the oceans, and the biosphere; and (2) carbon-14 decays at a known rate. When an organism dies, it is removed from the carbon exchange reservoir and the concentration of carbon-14 in the remains of the organism decreases at a fixed rate. By measuring the concentration of radiocarbon in a sample, it is possible to calculate the time since the death of the organism. Calibration becomes necessary because the concentration of carbon-14 in the global carbon reservoir fluctuates over time.

But how is the concentration of carbon-14 measured? The initial method was to measure the radioactivity of a sample as an indirect measure of its carbon-14 concentration. The problem with this method is that the concentration of carbon-14 in the carbon reservoir is very low. Therefore, in order to measure the carbon-14, large samples are needed. Thus, there was a limitation on the type of samples that could be dated. Also, very old samples in which most of the carbon-14 had already decayed could not be dated.

Accelerator mass spectrometry (AMS) dating is a solution to this problem. AMS dating combines ingenuity and power to directly count the carbon isotopes in a sample. The first step in developing AMS dating draws on the following principle of physics: When an electrically charged particle travels through a magnetic field, it follows a curved path, and the amount of curvature is related to the weight of the particle. Specifically, the lower the weight, the greater is the curvature. Using this method, a scientist should be able to take a sample of (radioactive) carbon-14 mixed with nonradioactive carbon-13 and carbon-12 isotopes (which are lighter than carbon-14), sort them into separate streams, and literally count their atoms. However, to count the small number of carbon-14 atoms, tremendous energy is needed, so an atomic accelerator is used to blast the carbon-14 atoms through the system at an acceleration of 8 million V.

The impact of AMS dating has been almost as dramatic as the initial impact of radiocarbon dating. It is now possible to directly date small samples, including seeds and residues. Samples can be dated more quickly than with conventional methods, and in some cases it is possible to date very old samples in which the surviving concentration of carbon-14 is extremely low.

## FIGURE 8.1

**Diagram of an accelerator used for AMS radiocarbon dating. Note how different isotopes of carbon are separated at the end of the line.**

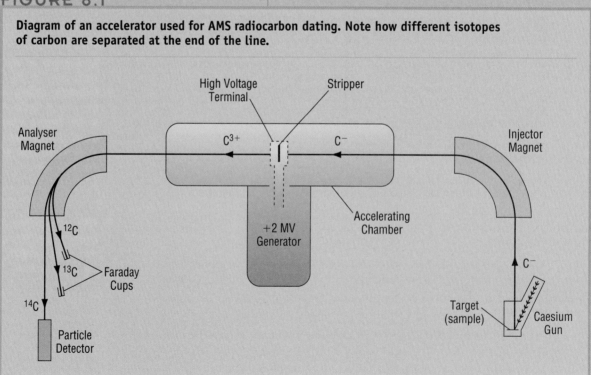

**E**arly fragments of domesticated squash from Guilá Naquiz, Mexico.

Squash seeds recovered from Zones C and B at Guilá Naquiz have been directly dated to between 10,000 and 8,300 years ago (Smith 1997). The seeds are larger than wild squash seeds. The thickness and color of the rind also distinguish domesticated from wild squash. It is only in Zone B, which dates to around 8,000 years ago, that there is an increase in the thickness of the squash rinds and a change in color from green to orange. On the basis of these results, it appears that the domestication of squash was a prolonged process that began ten thousand years ago with selection for larger seeds. Over the next two thousand years, farmers selected for an increase in the thickness of the rind and a change in its color.

The oldest directly dated maize was also found at Guilá Naquiz. The stratigraphic context for these maize samples is an ephemeral occupation between Zone B and Zone A. Two fragments of maize cobs from this context were directly dated to 6,250 years ago. The maize from Guilá Naquiz has a tough rachis and is thus clearly domesticated. It is interesting that one cob has two rows, as does teosinte, while the other has four rows, as is found in most maize.

The earliest maize from the Tehuacán Valley, directly dated to 5,500 years ago, is of the four-row variety. The long sequence from the Tehuacán Valley sites illustrates a gradual increase through time in the size of the cobs and the number of kernels.

Studies of modern domesticated beans suggest that both common beans and lima beans were domesticated independently in the Andes and Mesoamerica (Smith 1995). The oldest direct date on a domesticated bean from Mexico is approximately 2,500 years ago, for a single bean from Coxcatlán Cave in the Tehuacán Valley. It is likely that beans were domesticated at a far earlier date, possibly at the same time as maize.

# 8.2 MAIZE AGRICULTURE IN THE AMERICAN SOUTHWEST

Domesticated maize was grown in the highlands of Mexico by 6,250 years ago. Maize and squash agriculture spread to northern Mexico and the southwestern United States during the Southwestern Late Archaic Period (ca. 3,400 years ago) (Cordell 1997). The initial impact of maize and squash agriculture varied across the region. In some areas there is evidence of increased sedentism, while in other areas it appears that agriculture did not substantially alter the lives of Late Archaic hunter–gatherers.

On a steep hill overlooking the Río Casas Grande in northwest Chihuahua, Mexico, near the New Mexico border, archaeologists have found dramatic evidence that some Late Archaic farmers shifted to village life (Hard and Roney 1998). At the site of **Cerro Juanaqueña**, archaeologists have traced over 8 kilometers of terrace walls and 100 rock rings. Although the construction of these features is simple, they represent a considerable investment of energy. The excavators estimate that the construction of the walls found at the site involved moving 20,000 metric tons of rock and soil, which would have taken 16 person-years of labor.

Excavation of three of the stone circles at Cerro Juanaqueña has failed to yield evidence of their function. Excavation of the terraces has yielded a wide array of domestic debris, including ground stone and chipped stone tools, ashy soil, and burnt and unburnt animal bones. On one terrace, postholes outlining the remains of a structure were found. The excavators believe that the function of the terraces was to provide a level surface for the construction of houses. Four maize kernels from Cerro Juanaqueña have been directly AMS radiocarbon dated, with an average date of 3,070 years ago obtained. The arrowheads found at the site are forms belonging to the Late Archaic, which is consistent with the radiocarbon dates.

Although a small amount of maize has been found in excavations at Cerro Juanaqueña, seeds from wild plants, including chenopodium, gourds, and grasses dominate the plant remains found on the site. The faunal remains indicate that animals such as jackrabbit, cottontail rabbit, mule deer, and pronghorn antelope were hunted. There is no evidence of significant fishing, despite the proximity of the site to the Río Casas Grande. Almost 600 grinding slabs and basins have been found, indicating that grinding seeds or grain was a very important activity at the site. The only pottery found is from later occupations limited to two small areas of the site. Three additional large Late Archaic sites have been reported in the vicinity of Cerro Juanaqueña.

Moving to the northeast from Cerro Juanaqueña, archaeologists have found that people living in the Jornada Mogollon region along the Río Grande did not significantly engage in agriculture until A.D. 1000. There is a two-thousand-year gap in the onset of agriculture over a distance of less than 100 kilometers between the Río Casas Grande, where Cerro Juanaqueña is located, and the Jornada Mogollon region. Robert Hard and John Roney explain this pattern in terms of **optimal foraging theory** (Hard and Roney 2005), which is based on the assumption that humans act on the basis of rational self-interest to maximize efficiency in collecting and processing resources. Hard and Roney argue that, in the Río Casas Grande region, maize agriculture offered a higher rate of return than did many low-ranked resources, such as grama grass

> **Cerro Juanaqueña** is an early agricultural site in northern Mexico with extensive evidence of terracing and other stone built features.

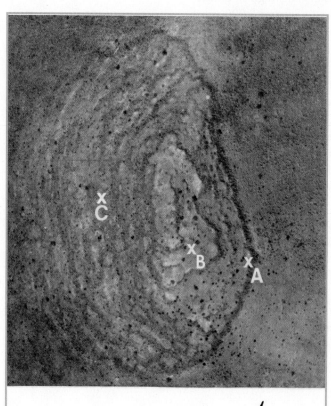

**A**erial photograph showing the terracing of the hill at Cerro Juanaqueña. Letters refer to excavation area.

and dropseed grass, that were exploited during the Late Archaic. These grasses are described as low-ranked resources because they offer little return of energy for the input of energy required to collect and process them. The Jornada region has lower rainfall than the Río Casas Grande, resulting in low returns and high risk for maize agriculture. At the same time, the availability of shrubs such as mesquite and salt-bush, as well as other plant resources, offered resources with higher rates of return. Optimal foraging explains the early uptake of maize agriculture at Cerro Jua-naqueña as the result of rational decision making based on the available resources. The delay in the development of maize agriculture in the Jornada region was the result of similar rational decisions, reflecting differences in local ecology.

Maize agriculture associated with large settlements is also found in the area around Tucson, Arizona. At the **Milagro** site, the Late Archaic people lived in pit houses and appear to have stored maize in bell-shaped pits. The plant remains recovered at Milagro include domesticated maize, along with wild plants such as amaranth, chenopod, and grass seeds. The faunal remains recovered at the site include jackrabbit and possibly deer. Two radiocarbon dates place the occupation of Milagro at 2,950 years ago.

Large-scale cultural resource management projects outside Tucson have produced spectacular insights into the agricultural settlements of the Late Archaic period (Marbry 2005). Terrace walls associated with maize remains have been excavated at the Tumamoc Hill site. At the Las Capas site, a sequence of canals was discovered dating to between 3,250 and 2,500 years ago. The canals carried water at least a mile from the Santa Cruz River to irrigated fields. These features indicate that the adoption of maize agriculture in this region involved a significant investment of labor. Ceramic artifacts, including figurines from Milagro and Las Capas and vessel fragments from Las Capas, have now been recovered from Late Archaic contexts. Some of the sites excavated in the area around Tucson include over a hundred pit houses (although not all were occupied simultaneously), as well as large communal structures.

Maize agriculture spread to the higher altitudes of the Mogollon Highlands and the Colorado Plateau at roughly the same time as the occupation of Milagro and Cerro Juanaqueña. In these regions, the adoption of agriculture did not result in the development of villages (Plog 1997). However, the storage areas, garbage pits, and

▶ **Optimal foraging theory** is based on the assumption that the choices people make reflect rational self-interest to maximize efficiency in collecting and processing resources.

▶ The **Milagro** site is an early agricultural village located outside Tucson, Arizona.

**V**iew of the Las Capas site near Tucson, Arizona. The site is located on the median strip of a highway.

**P**rofile of an irrigation ditch excavated at the Las Capas site near Tucson.

remains of fireplaces found in the excavation of cave sites indicate that the use of caves intensified with the adoption of agriculture (Cordell 1997).

Because of the dry conditions in the highland caves, the remains of basketry and other organic materials are superbly preserved. A particularly rich collection of organic remains was recovered at White Dog Cave, Arizona, named for one of the mummified dog burials found at the site (Kidder and Guernsey 1915, Cordell 1997). The organic artifacts recovered at White Dog Cave include a net made of fine fiber string that is over 200 meters long and 1 meter wide and a range of baskets decorated in woven or painted designs.

A number of human burials were excavated at White Dog Cave. Women were buried with necklaces of beads made of stones, shells, and seeds. Men were buried without clothes, while women were buried in loose-fitting aprons made of soft fiber. Both men and women were buried wearing sandals made of yucca fiber and with robes made of animal skins. Babies were found wrapped in soft rabbit-skin blankets and diapers made from juniper bark. Mobile cradles for infants were also found at the site.

## The Formative Period

The widespread introduction of pottery into the American Southwest around 1,800 years ago marks the end of the Southwestern Archaic period and the beginning of the Formative period. It is interesting that the introduction of pottery overlaps with the introduction of domesticated beans in this region. By this time, sites with architecture in the form of pit houses are common across the Southwest. The pit houses were usually square or rectangular in shape and were excavated as much as 1–2 meters below the surface (Plog 1997). The superstructure was usually built of wooden beams, brush, and soil.

The number of houses found on Formative-period sites varies from one or two to as many as twenty-five to thirty-five houses. Although storage pits are common on most sites, their placement varies (Plog 1997). The Shabik'eschee Village site in

Chaco Canyon, New Mexico, is an unusually large site in which the remains of sixty pit houses have been excavated. There is some question as to whether the entire site was occupied at any one time (Wills and Windes 1989). A large number of carefully constructed storage pits were found at Shabik'eschee, all located outside the houses.

The SU site in central New Mexico is a large Formative-period settlement with forty pit houses. At the SU site, the storage pits are located inside the houses. The contrast between Shabik'eschee Village and the SU site in the location of their storage pits has been interpreted as reflecting differences in the ownership of food stores. The placement of pits outside houses suggests communal ownership, whereas the placement of pits inside houses suggests ownership by households.

At both Shabik'eschee Village and the SU site, unusual structures were found that appear to have played a communal function. At Shabik'eschee Village, one structure was five times the size of other pit houses and was surrounded by a bench. At the SU site, one structure was unusually large and lacked the internal storage pits found in other structures.

Regional variation in the impact of maize agriculture in the American Southwest continued into the Formative period. In Utah, the Fremont Culture dated between A.D. 700 and A.D. 1200 challenges archaeologists to explain the variations in adaptation after the introduction of maize agriculture. What is particularly striking about the Fremont is "the diversity it presents in the importance of maize farming relative to hunting and gathering" (Barlow 2002: 68). Renee Barlow has analyzed the yield of maize agriculture practiced by modern Guatemalans using traditional agricultural methods and has come to the conclusion that intensive agriculture produces little food for the energy expended in growing, collecting, and processing the plants. Less formal methods of maize agriculture, in which fields rotate frequently, produce a lower total yield, but a greater yield per unit of energy expended. On the basis of optimal foraging theory, Barlow suggests that Fremont farmers adapted the intensity of their reliance on maize agriculture to the availability of other, higher ranked food resources. When food resources such as game or pine nuts were available, maize would be exploited using only low-yield methods, which require a low investment of energy. When highly ranked resources were scarce, intensive maize agriculture became worth the energy investment. The variation in the Fremont reflects the variation in rational choices made by people living in different ecological settings.

## Summing Up the Evidence

New discoveries have established the onset of intensive maize agriculture in northern Mexico and the American Southwest during the Late Archaic period, approximately 3,000 years ago. Agricultural societies lived in large villages and built large-scale features, including terraces and canals. However, the uptake of maize agriculture was not uniform across the region during the Late Archaic, and the pattern continues into the Formative period. In responding to the challenge of explaining this diversity, archaeologists have turned to optimal foraging theory to explain the variation in adaptation as a rational response to differing ecological conditions.

The AMS dating of maize from the highland caves of Oaxaca and the Tehuacán Valley has found that the gap between the domestication of maize and its spread to northern Mexico and the American Southwest is shorter than was expected. Indeed, the rapidity of the spread has led some archaeologists to argue that it was the result of the movement of populations of farmers northwards (Matson 2003). This is a controversial proposal, however, that is difficult to assess on the basis of the available data.

# TOOLBOX:
## Hand-Built Pottery

The pottery produced by the native societies of the American southwest is the antithesis of modern mass-produced ceramics. The first step in producing the pottery was to mine the clay and mix it with water. In some cases, inclusions such as sand, straw, or even crushed sherds of broken pots were added to the clay paste. Building a pot by hand often begins by making a shallow bowl from a ball of clay. The walls of the vessel are then built up with the use of either coils or slabs of clay. Next, a paddle smoothes and sometimes thins the walls of the vessel. Afterwards, the vessel is left to partially dry before surface decoration is added. Many fine-ware pots are dipped in a slip—a slurry of fine-grained clay, often mixed with iron-rich clay. A slip mixed with minerals can also be used to paint designs on pots. Pots can be polished by burnishing the semi-dry surface with a smooth stone that compresses the clay particles. After the surface of the vessel has been treated with slip, paint, or burnishing, the pot is again left to dry. Once completely dry, pots are stacked and heated in an open fire. If the fire is smothered and the pots are heated without access to oxygen, the surface will be black. If the fire is allowed to burn freely, the iron in the clay will oxidize and the surface will be red.

Over the centuries during which Southwestern potters have hand-built clay vessels, they have used these basic processes to produce a staggering array of vessel shapes and surface treatments. Many such vessels raise hand-built pottery to a fine art. The Mimbres potters created beautiful bowls with simple, yet powerful, scenes painted in black against the white surface of

▲ A pot made by Maria Martinez. The following five photographs show the process she used to make this type of vessel.

▲ A Mimbres bowl from New Mexico.

▲ 1. Preparing the clay. Notice the pots drying in the background.

the bowls. More recently, Pueblo potters have explored the range of surface treatments that can be achieved by combining burnishing with carefully controlled firing. Maria Martinez of the San Ildefonso Pueblo is among the most celebrated modern ceramic artists. Her creations include vessels with patterns formed by setting highly polished designs against a matte unpolished background. Many of these vessels are a deep black color, achieved by smothering the pot while it was firing.

▲ 4. Burnishing a pot with a smooth stone.

▲ 2. Using coils of clay to build up the vessel walls.

▲ 3. Smoothing the vessel walls.

▲ 5. Removing finished pots from the fire.

# 8.3 EASTERN NORTH AMERICA

The development of agriculture in eastern North America involved both the domestication of a wide range of local plants and the adoption of maize. The initial domestication of plants in eastern North America took place during the Eastern Archaic Period (5,800–3,800 years ago). The intensification of agriculture and the first appearance of maize in the region occurred during the florescence of the Adena and Hopewell traditions of the Early and Middle Woodland period (3,200–1,700 years ago). However, maize played a minor role in the diet, and settlements remained small and dispersed for almost a thousand years after the plant was first adopted in eastern North America. Intensive maize agriculture and large settled villages became established only at the beginning of the Late Woodland period.

## The Indigenous Domestication of Plants

A wide range of plants, including squash, chenopod, marsh elder, and sunflower, was domesticated by the Late Archaic hunter–gatherer groups of eastern North America (Smith and Cowan 2003). The domestication of squash in the region was independent of the earlier domestication of the plant in Mexico. Chenopodium was independently domesticated in South America, Mexico, and eastern North America.

Along with the presence of domesticated plants, the Eastern Late Archaic is characterized by an increasingly narrow subsistence base, particularly in areas with rich supplies of shellfish. Large accumulations of discarded shells are found on sites known as **shell middens**. Some of these sites, such as the Indian Knoll site on the Green River in Kentucky, are quite large. At the Indian Knoll site, thousands of burials were recovered, along with the traces of structures built of posts (Brose et al. 1985).

> **Shell middens** are sites built up of discarded shells.

Crude ceramic vessels first appeared in eastern North America 5,000 years ago in the Stalling Island culture of the Savannah River Valley, Georgia. The material culture of the Late Archaic also includes a wide range of ceremonial objects and ornaments. There is evidence of trade in various minerals, including galena (lead), hematite (iron oxide), jasper, native copper, and slate, over very long distances.

The Late Archaic **Poverty Point** site in Louisiana is a massive planned construction that raises many questions about subsistence and social organization during that period. The site consists of a series of six concentric embankments 2 meters high and over 20 meters across that form a semicircle more than 1 kilometer wide. Along with the embankments are a series of massive mounds, some of which appear to be in the shape of birds.

The purpose of the embankments remains unclear. If the embankments were house platforms, then Poverty Point was an extremely large, exquisitely planned village. However, plowing has largely removed any evidence that might have

**O**blique aerial view showing the semi-circular rings at Poverty Point, Louisiana.

# FIGURE 8.2

**Plan of Poverty Point.**

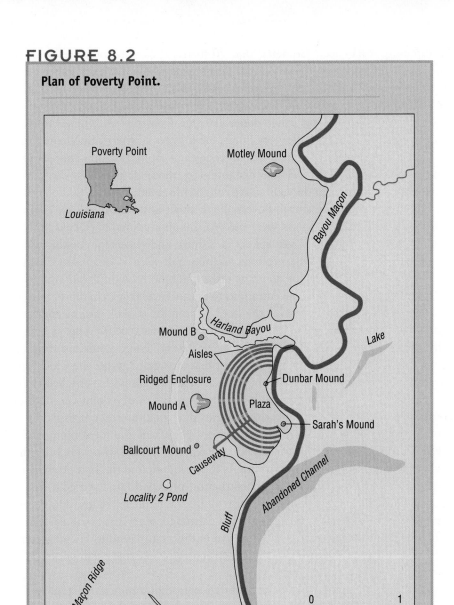

remained of houses. But is it possible that plowing obliterated all signs of the post-holes that are found on other sites of the same period? Evidence in favor of Poverty Point as a village is the density and diversity of cultural materials found on the site. Most of the finds are objects of daily life: net sinkers for fishing, stone tools for hunting animals and gathering plants, soapstone and pottery vessels, and more. But the most compelling evidence that Poverty Point was a village comes from the extensive deposits of refuse. As Jon Gibson summarizes the situation, "Claims that Poverty Point was a vacant ceremonial center are simply not tenable given the extensive midden and its secular-looking trash" (Gibson 2000: 105).

Stones for tool manufacture are not available in the area around Poverty Point. It is therefore not surprising that stone tools were brought onto the site from non-local sources. However, the quantity of material and the distance to the sources are

▶ The **Poverty Point** site is a Late Archaic site in Louisiana with a series of six concentric embankments.

astounding. It has been estimated that 70 metric tons of stone were brought onto the site. The distance of the site from the sources of the material makes this figure even more staggering: Burlington chert and galena (lead) ore were brought from quarries near St. Louis, 450 miles from Poverty Point; hematite, crystal quartz, slate, volcanic rocks, and other minerals came from the Ouachita Mountains in Arkansas, 150 miles from Poverty Point; other types of chert came from Kentucky, 365 miles from Poverty Point; and soapstone came from Alabama and Georgia, 400 miles from Poverty Point. These distances are those of the most direct route; if travel was by river, then the figures are roughly doubled.

The stones were brought to Poverty Point either as finished tools or as pieces that had been roughed out. Cherts were used for hunting points, hoes, and knives; hard minerals were used to make net sinkers for fishing; and vessels for cooking were made from soapstone. With a few exceptions, the materials were brought onto Poverty Point as finished tools or vessels for domestic tasks. But who brought them? And why were they brought in such great concentrations to that particular site? In most cases, archaeologists expect to trace a "down the line" pattern for trade items, meaning that the quantity of a given item will decrease with increasing distance from the source. Generally, this rule works for the Late Archaic, but Poverty Point stands out from the pattern. There is something about the activities that took place at that site which led to the deposition of enormous quantities of artifacts at a great distance from their source.

One possible explanation for what went on at Poverty Point can be found by returning to Hayden's model for the origins of agriculture that stresses the importance of competitive feasts. Perhaps Poverty Point was the focal point of feasting events, drawing in people from a very wide region—people who were not otherwise living together in village communities. Is it possible that in the Late Archaic of eastern North America monumental construction preceded large settled villages? The same issue will emerge when we turn to the monuments of the Hopewell. The essential question is whether the early farming communities of eastern North America could have found an alternative pathway to creating farming communities—a pathway that relied on the construction of massive earthworks instead of large villages.

Although the Late Archaic was clearly a period of significant change in the societies of eastern North America, the impact of domesticated plants on subsistence was minimal. Collecting wild plant foods and hunting wild animals continued to form the basis of subsistence. One source of evidence relevant to the role of domesticated plants in the diet is the fecal remains, or coprolites, found on archaeological sites. Although coprolites are certainly not the most glamorous aspect of archaeological research, studying them provides a unique insight into the human diet. Studies of coprolites from two sites in Kentucky dated to 3,400 years ago demonstrate a great deal of variability in the diet (Gremillion 1996). In some samples domesticated plants were dominant, whereas in others they were a minor component. These findings suggest that cultivated crops played a minor role in the diet during the initial period of plant domestication.

## The Adena and Hopewell

The **Adena** and **Hopewell** were the periods of intensive mound building in the Ohio River Valley.

Most of the mounds in Ohio and surrounding areas date to the Early and Middle Woodland period between 3,200 and 1,700 years ago (Gremillion 2003). In the Ohio River Valley, the Early Woodland corresponds to the **Adena** culture and the Middle Woodland corresponds to the **Hopewell** culture. In both the Adena and Hopewell, there is evidence of elaborate burial practices, including the construction of mounds, and extensive trade networks.

Careful excavations of Hopewell mounds have shown that some were erected over structures built of bent poles (Brown 1979). Multiple human remains were placed in these structures before the structures were filled in and then covered by a mound of earth. In some cases, bodies were laid out to decompose before burial, and the bones were either left in their original position or gathered together into bundles after decomposition. In other cases, the bodies were cremated in ceramic basins. Burials are also found in pits dug into the floors of the structures. There is evidence as well that in some cases burials were excavated into mounds while in others new structures for burial or cremation were built on top of mounds and were subsequently covered over by a secondary mound (Brose et al. 1985).

Hopewell material culture includes impressive art objects made of copper, mica, and polished stone. Expertly crafted objects that were traded over long distances are found in many Hopewell burials. It is likely that objects such as hard stone pipes in the form of animals and large plaques made of sheets of mica were produced by craft specialists. Such discoveries suggest that elite members of these societies controlled a network of trade in prestige objects.

In his classic work on eastern North American prehistory, James Griffin suggested that the Hopewell lived in villages near the massive earthworks (Griffin 1967). Griffin had in mind not only the mounds, but also the earthen enclosures found at sites such as the Liberty Earthworks near Chillicothe, Ohio. At the Liberty site, there are two circular enclosures, one over 200 meters in diameter and the other over 500 meters in diameter, as well as a square enclosure covering 27 acres (Squier and Davis 1848). However, materials collected from the farm that now includes the Liberty Earthworks have not yielded any remains of a large village until the late Middle Woodland period, toward the end of the Hopewell culture (Coughlin and Seeman 1997).

There is evidence that some of the earthworks were occupied. The massive Newark earthworks have largely been engulfed by the city of Newark, Ohio. The construction of a new highway that goes through the earthworks led to a salvage project in which the remains of two Hopewell houses were identified together with

A bird claw cut from a sheet of mica is characteristic of Hopewell art.

# FIGURE 8.3

Map of the Newark Earthworks, Ohio, published by E. G. Squier and E. H. Davis in 1848. Squier and Davis's drawings are a critical resource as many of the features they recorded have subsequently been destroyed.

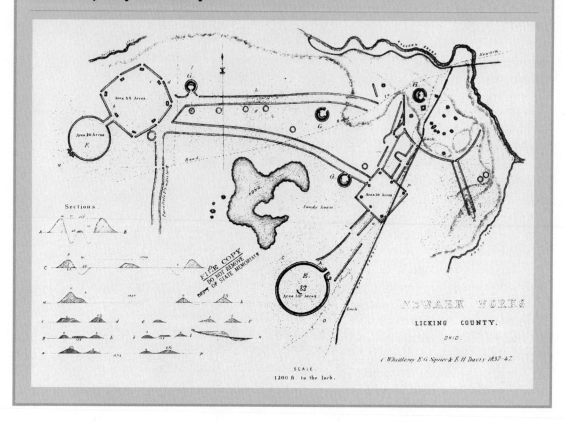

evidence of domestic activities (Lepper and Yerkes 1997). However, some archaeologists have suggested that the Hopewell did not reside in large villages, but rather that they lived dispersed across the landscape in small farmsteads (Dancey and Pacheco 1997). According to this model, known as the **vacant center pattern,** the earthworks served as the symbolic and ceremonial core of a community that lived across a wide area.

Christopher Carr and Troy Case have challenged archaeologists to think about the Hopewell phenomenon from an agency perspective. Adopting such a perspective requires that we shift our focus from the community as a whole to the individuals who make up the community. However, the conception of the individual is not the rational calculator of optimal foraging, but rather a person negotiating his or her place in the world within the context of overlapping structures of power. On the basis of careful analysis of the iconography of Hopewell figurines, Carr and Case argue that there were different types of leaders in Hopewell society, including both shamans and leaders with more secular sources of power. They raise the possibility that, rather than a series of households held together by a ceremonial core in the form of a particular earthwork, what actually existed was a situation in which each individual might have connections to multiple earthworks.

Given both the widespread modern destruction of the earthworks and their massive scale, it remains difficult to determine whether they were the locations of

> The **vacant center pattern** sees the Hopewell earthworks as the empty core of a dispersed settlement system.

large villages. Adding to the difficulty of assessing the nature of Hopewell settlements is the low archaeological visibility of many Hopewell habitation sites. Because of the massive buildup of riverborne alluvial sediments in the Ohio River valley, Hopewell sites located in the valley are deeply buried and not easily discovered by archaeologists (Stafford and Creasman 2002).

Early and Middle Woodland subsistence was based heavily on the cultivation of indigenously domesticated plants (Smith 1995). The earliest direct AMS radiocarbon dates of maize in eastern North America are between 2,000 and 1,800 years ago, from three Middle Woodland sites in Tennessee, Illinois, and Ohio. However, maize remains rare and does not appear to have played a major role in the diet. Throughout the Woodland period, hunting and collecting wild plants continued to be key elements of subsistence alongside the cultivation of domesticated plants.

## Intensification of Maize Agriculture

At the end of the Middle Woodland period, around 1,700 years ago, the extensive trade networks of the Hopewell culture and the construction of massive earthworks came to an end. At the same time, there was an increase in the number of large settled villages. By the beginning of the Late Woodland, maize is found as far north as Ontario (Crawford et al. 1997). Although maize was cultivated throughout much of eastern North America by 1,700 years ago, the **isotope analysis** of human skeletal remains affords strong evidence that maize did not come to play a major role in the diet until the period around 1,000 years ago (see Toolbox on page 252) (Katzenberg et al. 1995).

> ▶ **Isotope analysis** of bone chemistry can determine the role of maize in the diet.

## The People behind the Transition

Archaeologists studying the development of agriculture have a tendency to forget to include people in the process. The dating of the initial domestication of various crops and the description of archaeological sites provide an essential framework for understanding the transition to agriculture; however, it is necessary to go beyond this framework to consider what led people to adopt a radically new way of life.

Patty Jo Watson and Mary Kennedy have linked the seeming invisibility of people in the origins of agriculture to gender bias in our conception of the past. According to Watson and Kennedy, in the anthropological literature "men are strong, dominant protectors who hunt animals; women are weaker, passive, hampered by their reproductive responsibilities, and hence, consigned to plant gathering" (Watson and Kennedy 1991:256).

Watson and Kennedy have identified strategies that have been used by archaeologists to maintain gender bias in their explanations of the origin of agriculture. The first strategy is to view the development of agriculture as a passive process, which simply "happened" as the result of the unconscious ecological consequences of human actions. Bruce Smith's coevolutionary model for the indigenous domestication of plants in eastern North America is an example of such an approach. According to Smith, climate change led to an increased permanence of human settlements in eastern North America. This shift to more permanent settlements led to gradual ecological changes that resulted in the emergence of domesticated plants over a period of several thousand years.

# TOOLBOX: Isotope Analysis and Maize Agriculture

The bone chemistry of humans and animals is determined largely by their diet. Because of this, the chemistry of bones can be used as a source of data for reconstructing diet. However, use of the method requires the consumption of foods that have a particular chemical signature. One type of chemical signature is the relative frequency of two isotopes of the same element. Fortunately for the study of maize agriculture, the ratio of carbon-13 ($^{13}$C) to carbon-12 ($^{12}$C) differs in plants with different photosynthetic pathways. The ratio of carbon-13 to carbon-12 is expressed as the value $\delta^{13}$C, which is the deviation from an international standard. Trees, bushes, and shrubs (C$_3$ plants) have a low ratio of Carbon-13 to Carbon-12. Grasses from the tropics and subtropics, including maize, sorghum and sugar cane (C$_4$ plants), have a high ratio. The only C$_4$ plant that contributed to the diet of the Woodland-period people in eastern North America is maize. By analyzing the $\delta^{13}$C value for Woodland-period skeletal remains, it is possible to determine the role that maize played in those people's diets. The shift to a high $\delta^{13}$C value in human skeletal remains takes place only during the period around 1,000 years ago, approximately seven hundred years after the initial introduction of maize into eastern North America. This finding indicates that there was a considerable length of time between the first planting of maize in eastern North America and the adoption of maize as an essential food source.

## FIGURE 8.4

**Results of the carbon isotope analysis of human skeletal remains from Ontario. Note the elevation of δ carbon-13 around 1200 AD indicating the shift to heavy dietary reliance on maize.**

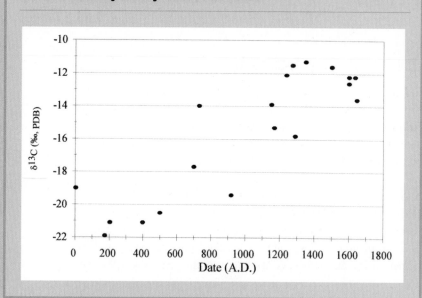

Smith outlines five major stages in the process. In the first stage, the garbage heaps around long-term human occupations provided an excellent ecological niche for weedy plants that thrived on the availability of sunlight and fertile soil. In these contexts, seeds that sprouted and grew quickly had a selective advantage. Seeds that sprout and grow quickly would be large and have a thin coat. In the second stage, people tolerated edible plants and removed useless or harmful plants. In the third stage, people began to encourage and systematically harvest useful plants while carefully weeding out useless ones. In the fourth stage, seeds of the useful plants are deliberately planted every year. In the fifth stage, plants that were clearly morphologically domesticated emerged.

Smith's model for plant domestication sets this process within a well-constructed ecological framework. The model fits with the kind of evolutionary approaches advanced by Rindos. However, Watson and Kennedy argue that "the built-in mechanisms adduced [in the model] carry plants and people smoothly and imperceptibly . . . with little or no effort on anyone's part. The plants virtually domesticate themselves" (Watson and Kennedy 1981: 262). The formulation "women = plants = passive" is maintained.

Whereas Smith views domestication as a passive process, Guy Prentice has proposed that the domestication of plants might have been the result of intentional actions by individuals. Prentice argues that the introduction of domesticated squash into eastern North America was carried out by male shamans who would have used gourds as rattles or ritual containers. Prentice writes of the shaman, "He would have the greatest knowledge of plants" (Prentice 1986: 113). Here, the domestication of plants is seen as an active process, and, tellingly, the agent is explicitly male.

As a counterbalance to existing models for the role of women in the development of agriculture, Watson and Kennedy propose a model for the adoption of maize in eastern North America that emphasizes the active role of female gardeners. The introduction of maize, which is a tropical grass, into the northern latitudes of North America is a truly impressive event. The spread of maize into northern latitudes involved a transition from midwestern twelve-row maize to a variety known, due to the smaller number of rows per cob, as eastern eight-row, or Northern Flint, maize. Watson and Kennedy propose that the women in eastern North America, who already had extensive experience growing indigenous cultivated plants, actively experimented with the midwestern twelve-row maize to develop a variety that was better suited to the soils and climates of their region. The result was the development and spread of eastern eight-row maize. According to this proposal, then, the adoption of maize agriculture in eastern North America was an achievement of the active intervention of women.

## Summing Up the Evidence

The transition to agriculture in Mesoamerica and North America was a complex process. In the southwestern United States, maize agriculture was either adopted by groups of Archaic hunter–gatherers who appear to have had no previous experience with domesticated plants or possibly spread by populations of farmers moving in from the south. The impact of the adoption of agriculture on these societies varied. In some cases, notably at Cerro Juanaqueña and the sites around Tucson, large villages developed, while in other areas people continued to live in temporary camps. This regional variability continued into the Formative period. Archaeologists have tried to explain the pattern that formed in terms of optimal foraging theory.

In eastern North America, hunter–gatherer groups had domesticated a number of plant species long before the introduction of maize agriculture. Intensively occupied sites are already found in the Late Archaic and, in the case of the Poverty Point site, had reached an impressive size and degree of planning. In the Early and Middle

## "Towns they have none": In Search of New England's Mobile Farmers

**by Elizabeth S. Chilton, University of Massachusetts, Amherst**

I am an associate professor and chair of the Department of Anthropology at the University of Massachusetts at Amherst. I returned to UMass in 2001, after completing my doctoral work here and spending five years at Harvard University as an assistant, and then associate, professor of anthropology.

When I began my graduate studies at UMass Amherst, I was very interested in the Late Woodland (A.D. 1000–A.D. 1600) and Contact (A.D. 1600–A.D. 1700) periods in the Massachusetts portion of the Connecticut River Valley in the western part of the state. In particular, archaeologists had long been looking for large Late Woodland-period villages. On the basis of expectations from the neighboring Iroquoian tribes, archaeologists expected to find large sedentary villages as a result of the adoption of maize horticulture around A.D. 1000. Nevertheless, when I came to UMass in 1988, no large Late Woodland villages had yet been found in the region.

In 1989, a local farmer reported that he had found a large number of ceramics on a forested hill surrounded by a floodplain in the valley of the Deerfield River, a major tributary of the Connecticut River. Subsequent excavation at the Pine Hill site in 1989, 1991, 1993, 1995, and 1997 as part of the UMass Amherst Archaeological Field School revealed that this was, indeed, an important Late Woodland site. We uncovered fragments of more than 300 Late Woodland–period vessels, a large number of lithic artifacts, and 22 large pit features, which likely served for food storage and/or refuse disposal. Radiocarbon dates firmly placed most of the activity at the site during the Late Woodland period.

Despite the fact that we had excavated quite a few of these Late Woodland pit features and had identified food remains (e.g., small and large mammal bones, charred nutshells and seeds), until 1995 we had not found one single kernel of maize. This surprised us, since elsewhere in New England maize had been dated to the start of the Late Woodland period. One day at the site, a student was excavating the plow zone from a 2 × 2-m test unit and suddenly said, "Hey Elizabeth, I found a weird blueberry thing." I looked at it and immediately recognized it as a charred maize kernel! Later that summer, we discovered the first pit feature on that site to produced maize kernels, approximately 200 in all! Still, 200 maize kernels are

◀ Pine Hill Site, UMass Amherst Archaeological Field School 1993 (Elizabeth Chilton, shown left).

equivalent to only about one cob of Northern Flint, eight-row maize (Chilton et al. 2000). We have many more nutshells and small animal bones than we do maize kernels.

Digging conditions on this site were quite grueling, despite the fact that we were in Massachusetts. I had done some work in Belize after graduating from SUNY Albany in 1986. There was standing water in an oxbow near the Deerfield site; therefore, the mosquitoes were far more intense than any pest that I encountered in Belize. We were bitten through our clothes, on our lips and eyelids, and on our fingers. On top of that, we did not have ready access to rest rooms, and there was a fair bit of poison ivy at the site. Digging itself was quite easy: The soils are sandy from the postglacial lake deposits. But digging in a forested environment provides its own challenges, in the form of tree roots and rodent activity.

After several years of excavating the Pine Hill site, and after conducting a detailed analysis of the attributes of the ceramics for my dissertation, we came to the conclusion that it was a Late Woodland–period site that was repeatedly occupied on a seasonal basis, primarily in the late summer to early

▶ Late Woodland period maize kernels from the Pine Hill Site, Massachusetts.

fall (Chilton 1999, 2002). This conclusion dovetails nicely with archaeological evidence from throughout the Connecticut River Valley, which suggests that, although New England peoples had adopted maize by A.D. 1000, it did not significantly alter their seasonal mobility, nor did it significantly change their diet. Archaeological evidence indicates that maize may have become more important across New England around A.D. 1300. Nevertheless, year-round villages like those of the Iroquois have not been found in New England. Instead, New England peoples offer us a clear example of mobile farming.

▶ Profile of possible food storage or trash pit, Pine Hill Site, Massachusetts.

Woodland Adena and Hopewell cultures, massive earthworks were constructed and there is evidence for specialized craft manufacture and long-distance trade in luxury items. However, the nature of the settlement systems remains poorly understood. The possibility remains that in eastern North America monumental architecture preceded settled villages. The initial introduction of maize at the beginning of the Late Woodland period had little impact on the diet or society. Studies of bone chemistry indicate that it took approximately 700 years before maize came to play a major role in the diet.

The spread of agriculture is as complex a process as the initial domestication of plants and animals. It is clear from the study of North America that local societies adapted agriculture into their lives in different ways. Rarely did the initial introduction of agriculture have an immediate transformative effect on those societies. As discussed in the last chapter, research in other areas, such as Europe, where agriculture was introduced rather than developed indigenously, similarly points to the active role played by the indigenous societies of hunter–gatherers in the adoption of agriculture.

# CHAPTER SUMMARY

- The wild ancestor of maize is teosinte, a wild grass found in the highlands of Mexico.
- The three major crops domesticated in Mesoamerica are maize, squash, and beans. No animals were domesticated in the region.
- Evidence for the domestication of plants in Mesoamerica comes mostly from excavations of highland caves in the Tehuacán and Oaxaca Valleys.
- The earliest domesticated squash dates between 10,000 and 8,300 years ago. The earliest domesticated maize dates to 6,250 years ago.
- Cerro Juanaqueña, in northern Mexico, is a large Archaic-period site with evidence of extensive terrace walls and maize agriculture.
- The site of Milagro, Arizona, is a small Archaic-period village with evidence of maize agriculture.
- Archaic-period sites in the Mogollon Highlands and the Colorado Plateau have also produced evidence

of domesticated maize. However, there is no evidence of Archaic-period villages in these areas.
- Pottery first appeared widely in the American southwest during the Formative period around 1,800 years ago.
- Among the plants that were domesticated indigenously in eastern North America were squash, chenopod, marsh elder, and sunflower. The domestication of these plants took place between 5,000 and 3,500 years ago.
- Extensive earthworks were built in Ohio and surrounding areas during the Early Woodland (Adena Culture) and Middle Woodland (Hopewell Culture) periods.
- The earliest maize in eastern North America dates to the Middle Woodland Period. However, there is evidence that maize did not play a major role in the diet until about 700 years after its introduction.

# KEY TERMS

Adena, 248
AMS Radiocarbon Dating, 237
Cerro Juanaqueña, 240
Guilá Naquitz, 237
Hopewell, 248

Isotope Analysis, 251
Milagro, 241
Optimal Foraging Theory, 241
Poverty Point, 247

Shell Middens, 246
Tehuacán Valley, 237
Teosinte, 236
Vacant Center Pattern, 250

## REVIEW QUESTIONS

1. What is known about the initial domestication of squash and maize?
2. What impact did the spread of maize have on southwest Archaic societies? Was the effect the same throughout the region?
3. What was the social and economic context surrounding the construction of the Adena and Hopewell mounds?
4. What is the basis for Watson and Kennedy's critique of models for the origin of agriculture in eastern North America? What model do they propose?

## FOR FURTHER READING

David S. Brose and N'omi Greber. (1979). *Hopewell Archaeology*. Kent, OH: Kent State University Press.

Linda Cordell. (1997). *Archaeology of the Southwest*. New York: Academic Press.

William S. Dancey and Paul J. Pacheco. (1997). *Ohio Hopewell Community Organization*. Kent, OH: Kent State University Press.

George Milner. (2004). *The Moundbuilders: Ancient Peoples of Eastern North America*. London: Thames and Hudson.

Paul Minnis. (2003). *People and Plants in Ancient Eastern North America*. Washington, DC: Smithsonian Books.

Stephen Plog. (1997). *Ancient Peoples of the American Southwest*. London: Thames and Hudson.

Bruce Smith. (1995). *The Emergence of Agriculture*. New York: Scientific American Library.

Bradley J. Vierra. (2005). *The Late Archaic: Across the Borderlands*. Austin, TX: University of Texas.

# A Feast of Diversity

BY COMPARING CASE studies, it is possible to learn whether the shift to agriculture always followed a single path. This chapter examines the origins of agriculture in Africa, New Guinea, the Andes, and East Asia. After reading this chapter, you should understand:

▶ The role of pastoralism and the timing for the introduction of pottery in Africa.

▶ The nature and significance of the archaeological site at Kuk Swamp, New Guinea.

▶ The relationship between the origin of village life and domestication in the Andes.

▶ The evidence from the two centers of domestication in China.

The bounty of domestication.

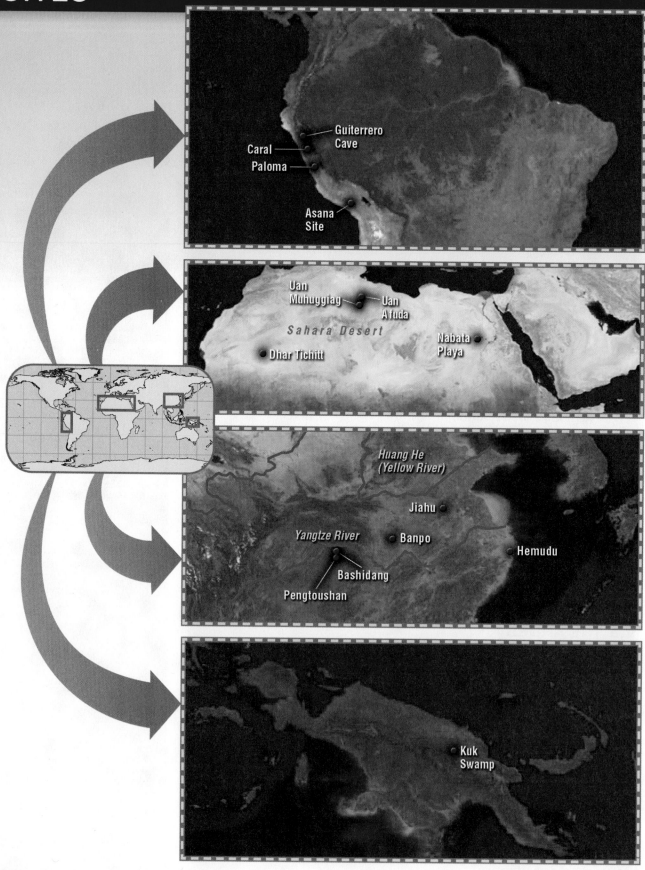

Guiterrero
Cave

Caral

Paloma

Asana
Site

Uan
Muhuggiag

Uan
Afuda

*Sahara Desert*

Dhar Tichitt

Nabata
Playa

*Huang He
(Yellow River)*

Jiahu

*Yangtze River*

Banpo

Hemudu

Bashidang

Pengtoushan

Kuk
Swamp

| thousands of years ago | AFRICA | NEW GUINEA | ANDES | EAST ASIA |
|---|---|---|---|---|
| 13 | | | | |
| 12 | | | | |
| 11 | | | | |
| 10 | | Kuk Swamp Phase 1 | | |
| 9 | Nabta Playa E-775-6 Uan Afuda | | | Pengtoushan Jiahu Bashidang Peiligang Culture |
| 8 | Uan Muhuggiag Nabta Playa | | | |
| 7 | E-75-8 | | Paloma | Yangshou Culture |
| 6 | | Wanlek | | |
| 5 | | | Caral Aspero | |
| 4 | | | Asana | |
| 3 | | | Guiterrero Cave domesticated bean | |
| 2 | | | | |

East Asia column also labeled: **Jomon**

A visit to the supermarket is also a trip around the world. In the produce section, we find corn and squash, plants domesticated in Mesoamerica; the bakery section is filled with breads baked from wheat, domesticated in the Middle East; at the butcher, we find the meat of cattle and pig (as well as the occasional sheep and goat), also domesticated in the Middle East; and down another aisle, we find sunflower seed oil, a crop first domesticated in eastern North America. As we wander through the aisles, we also come across foods, such as potatoes, yams, rice, and coffee, that point to other centers of domestication.

In this chapter, we briefly examine four additional case studies in the origins of agriculture:

- In Africa, pastoral societies based on domesticated animals developed without plant domestication.
- In New Guinea, domestication focused on plants that involve transplanting suckers, cuttings, or shoots, rather than planting seeds.
- In the Andes, there was a complex interplay between the domestication of plants and animals, on the one hand, by mobile societies living in the highlands, and, on the other hand, by village societies living on the coast, which depended heavily on marine resources. When agriculture was adopted on the coast, the main focus was a nonfood crop: cotton.
- The early agricultural societies of China might offer the strongest support available for Childe's concept of the origins of agriculture as a rapid and revolutionary event. However, this picture might be the result of limitations of the archaeological record, rather than a reflection of the actual historical process. Resolving the problem is an exciting and active area of research.

When we broaden our focus, what emerges is a great deal of flexibility in the sequence of events leading to the shift from hunting and gathering to farming. We find tremendous variation in the pathways leading from the one to the other. As we fill our shopping carts, we are not only sampling the global diversity of agricultural crops, but also enjoying the fruits of a cornucopia of social transformation.

# 9.1 AFRICA

The development of agriculture in Africa involved the indigenous domestication of plants and possibly animals, as well as the adoption of domesticated plants and animals from the Middle East. There are three major regions where plants were indigenously domesticated in Africa:

- In Ethiopia and Eritrea in northeast Africa, a wide range of plants was domesticated, including grains such as tef and finger millet, which are essential to the local diet (D'Andrea et al. 1999). A local domesticate that has had a more global impact is coffee. Unfortunately, the timing and process of the domestication of these plants is poorly understood.
- In central Africa, two critical cereals—pearl millet and sorghum—were domesticated. Most likely, pearl millet was first domesticated in the Sahara, but the location in which sorghum was first domesticated is not known.
- In West Africa, African rice (*Oryza glaberrina*) was domesticated (Linares 2002).

In addition to these indigenously domesticated plants, African agricultural systems incorporated domesticated plants introduced from the Middle East, including wheat, barley, and lentils. Among the domesticated animals introduced to Africa from the Middle East were sheep and goats. However, there is considerable debate over the origin of domesticated cattle on the continent. Although there is some genetic evidence supporting the argument that cattle were independently domesticated in Africa, the preponderance of evidence is that domesticated cattle were introduced from the Middle East.

The **Sahara desert** is the most dominant feature of the North African landscape today. The current arid environment in the Sahara developed only within the last four to five thousand years. Between 14,000 years ago and 4,500 years ago, there was considerably more rainfall in the Sahara, allowing for extensive human occupation (Muzzolini 1993).

> Between 14,000 and 4,500 years ago, there was increased rainfall in the area that is now the **Sahara Desert.**

## Villages of Hunter–Gatherers

There is widespread evidence of small villages of hunter–gatherers across northern Africa during the period of increased rainfall in the Sahara. The sites resemble the Natufian societies of the Middle East in several ways: their size, the nature of the structures on them, the exploitation of a wide range of resources, and the use of grinding stones. However, there are also significant differences between the African

Grinding stone on dry lake bed deposits in the Libyan desert, Eastern Sahara.

www.ablongman.com/chazan

sites and the Natufian. The most striking difference is that pottery is commonly found on the African sites. In the Middle East, pottery was developed only during the Late Neolithic. Another feature found on African sites that is lacking from the Natufian is a large number of storage pits.

One of the most complete pictures of an early village of hunter–gatherers in North Africa comes from excavations at **Nabta Playa** in the Egyptian Western desert (Wendorf and Schild 1998). This area is a barren desert today, but when it was occupied, it was a small lake surrounded by grasslands. Site E-75-6 was a village of 15 square or circular huts built in two rows that was occupied 9,000 years ago. Storage pits are found next to the remains of each structure. Pottery in the form of small jars with impressed designs also is present, although rare. A large range of plant remains has been recovered from this site, where the inhabitants focused particularly on the collection of wild sorghum.

Excavations at the cave site of **Uan Afuda** in Libya have given a unique perspective on the preagricultural societies of the Sahara. Uan Afuda was occupied between 9,000 and 8,000 years ago. The spectacular preservation on the site has allowed the excavators to recover wooden artifacts, basketry, and a rich array of charcoal and seeds. The botanical remains at the site indicate that the people living there were exploiting a wide range of resources. One of the most interesting discoveries was a

▶ The **Nabta Playa** in the Egyptian Western desert was the location of a series of early agricultural and preagricultural sites located along the edge of a lake.

▶ **Uan Afuda,** Libya, is a cave site that has produced the well-preserved remains of preagricultural occupation.

**R**ock art painted by pastoralists in the Sahara showing cattle.

## Researching the Origins of Agriculture in West Africa
### by Augustin F. C. Holl, University of Michigan

My research project was a move away from the current standard field practices that consisted of setting small archaeological probes in search of well-stratified deposits. I intended to rely on an "open-area" approach based on a large horizontal exposure of the features under excavation. The goal was to investigate the social context of the emergence of early West African food production. Delineating the key characteristics of Late Stone Age households was a fundamental step in that attempt. The range of variation of household installations would then be examined. At the regional level, the focus would be placed on the size and location of the site, viewed as patterned adjustment to demographic, subsistence, and environmental fluctuations.

The Dhar Tichitt is part of the extensive sandstone cliffs located in southwestern Sahara, in south central Mauritania. It is a remote area with hundreds of Late Stone Age villages more than 1,000 km from the Atlantic coast. Away from the major towns, there are no roads. One has to hire a guide to travel the last 300-km stretch. The travel, one way or the other, lasts for three days. Fine sand (fetch-fetch), windblown sand, and shifting dunes make the travel slow and demanding for both humans and machines. The expedition, which had to be self-sufficient for two months, was composed of 10 graduate students, the director, a soils scientist, drivers, mechanics, and cooks, as well as 50 workmen hired from the nearest oasis. All in all, some 70 individuals had to live for two full months in complete autarky.

Four high-range four-wheel-drive convertible trucks and two land-rover station wagons carried the crew, research equipment, gas, and supplies. It goes without saying that fresh food was not an option after the first few days. Three advanced medical students took care of health issues. The expedition was equipped with a radio transmitter powered by a generator. It was used once a week on an agreed-upon schedule to report to the capital city, Nouakchott. In case of a life-threatening emergency, a light rescue plane was supposed to come from the nearest landing strip at Tidjikja, 300 km away.

The base camp, made of a maze of tents, was set at the cliff's foot, next to the site of Akhreijit, the hub of the 1981 archaeological campaign. This site was inhabited from the

beginning to the end of the Dhar Tichitt Late Stone Age occupation (ca. 2000–500 B.C.). Built on the cliff top along the escarpment, the site measures 12 hectares and is delimited on the north by a thick 1.5–2.00-meters-high stone wall. The village consists of 200 compounds built with dry-stone masonry techniques, with a dense network of narrow alleys and open plazas. Excavation took place from 6:00 to 12:00 A.M.

◀ View of the central part of Akhreijit after restoration of the compound's walls.

▶ Dr. Holl in the Field

and 4:00 to 6:00 P.M. The heat from the sun and the sandstone bedrock was difficult to handle after 12:00 noon. One has to take a sodium pill once a day and rehydrate constantly. One day, in April, I was awed to realize that my water intake peaked to 10 liters. At least twice during the same month, we were confined to the base camp by sandstorms. Such days were spent listening to workmen's stories and drinking mint tea in endless sets of three small glasses.

The material collected, basically ceramics and lithics, was processed on a daily basis. Pollen samples and faunal remains were studied later in laboratories in Paris and Marseille. Our research ranged over a broad array of topics, including geomorphology and paleoclimatology, rock art, architecture, lithic technology, and ceramics, as well as the restoration of the village center. My work, framed in prehistoric economy terms, overlapped with all the others, but focused on a well-delineated 450-square-meter habitation unit. It was of crucial importance to understand the organization of Later Stone Age domestic space to infer the structures of household units. Faunal remains, collected from this secure context, consisted predominantly of cattle, sheep, and goat bones, along with a low frequency of wild game, large and small antelopes, and large and small gazelles, as well as fish from the nearby lakes and ponds. Flotation techniques developed to retrieve plant remains could not be fully applied for lack of water. Each crew member was allocated a third of a 10-L bucket for daily bathing and doing laundry. Limited and selective trials with a fine-mesh tea sieve of ash fills from the excavated deposits were unsuccessful. Grain impressions in pottery provided important clues, but could hardly be used to monitor changes in subsistence through time. The livestock component of the Late Stone Age subsistence was generally overlooked. Pollen analyses helped flesh out the broad characteristics of the Dhar Tichitt Late Stone Age landscape. The wild fauna provided additional and complementary insight. Food procurement equipment, grindstones, grinders, pestles, and mortars, along with storage facilities and domestic pottery, opened a vista on ordinary daily life. Images pecked on rock surfaces depicted cattle herds, sheep, and goats, as well as wild animals.

With evidence of domesticated bulrush millet dating right from the beginning of the Dhar Tichitt Late Stone Age, and with the overlooked importance of livestock husbandry, the long, gradualist model that was offered to explain the genesis of the whole agropastoralist system appeared less and less reliable. The dynamics of

▶ The base camp of the Dhar Tichitt Archaeological Mission in 1981.

agropastoralism differs considerably from that of exclusively agricultural systems. The domestication of pearl millet was very likely a rather rapid outcome of the sustained intensification of the exploitation of local resources in this relatively circumscribed region. Patches of wild millet may have been protected from livestock for human use, harvested before shattering. The genes triggering the shattering became dormant, leading to remarkable morphological changes. Domesticated bulrush millet grains are considerably bigger than those of their wild progenitors.

An arid spell at about the middle of the first millennium B.C. triggered the abandonment of the Dhar Tichitt and a southward movement of Late Stone Age agropastoralists. These peoples' societies were organized into large household units consisting of extended or polygamous families. They practiced short range nomadism and "Decrue agriculture," taking advantage of the receding summer floods to sow their millet seeds on humid soil. The millet adapted to this rather short growing season and turned into a fast-growing species with a short maturation cycle. Cultivated plots were likely located along the foot of the cliff and the shallow depressions of the cliff's top, gaining moisture from the water seeping through the cracks in the sandstone bedrock.

The last two weeks of the field season were difficult. The crew was exhausted. The field doctors prescribed a daily intake of vitamin C pills. The field effort was nonetheless intensified, to record and collect as much data as possible. Even the unbearable April heat did not preclude work in the afternoon, following a short lunch break. Everyone shed considerable weight. Pants had to be set tighter around the waist. The excitement and wonder of a fabulous expedition did it all. On the way back, with the permission of the director, we drove directly to the beach and dove into the Atlantic Ocean fully dressed—a bath at last!

10-centimeter bed of animal dung and plant remains found in the back of the cave. Analysis of the dung indicates that it is from wild barbary sheep, a North African sheep that was never domesticated. The excavators argue that such an accumulation of dung does not form simply from sheep visiting a cave site. It appears that the early occupants of Uan Afuda were keeping wild sheep in a pen at the back of the cave. This discovery suggests that although these people had not domesticated sheep, they were practicing a form of animal management by capturing animals alive and keeping them corralled in a cave.

## Pastoralists

**Pastoral societies** are mobile societies with an economy based on herds of domesticated animals.

In much of North Africa, domesticated animals were introduced before domesticated plants. Domesticated animals such as cattle, sheep, and goats appear to have been incorporated into mobile hunting-and-gathering societies. Mobile societies with an economy focused on maintaining herds of domesticated animals are known as **pastoral societies** (Holl 1998).

Fred Wendorf and his colleagues have argued on the basis of excavations at Nabta Playa that cattle might have been domesticated independently in Egypt as early as ten thousand years ago. This argument has not been widely accepted. However, it is clear that by 8,000 years ago, domesticated cattle, sheep, and goats had been introduced into societies that still did not exploit domesticated plants. Site E-75-8 at Nabta Playa has produced vivid evidence of the reliance on cattle roughly 7,500 years ago. At this site, a series of cattle burials was found under piles of stones known as tumuli (Wendorf and Schild 1998).

The earliest evidence of domesticated animals in the Central Sahara, at the site of Uan Muhuggiag, was dated to 8,500 years ago (Holl 1998). As with Nabta Playa, there is no evidence of domesticated plants at Uan Muhuggiag.

## The First Farmers

Unfortunately, the development of village farming communities in Africa is poorly understood. In Egypt, the earliest evidence for domesticated plants dates to approximately 5,000 years ago. Wilma Wetterstrom has suggested that these resources were at first adopted by hunter–gatherers to provide a "backup" for brief periods of drought or low Nile floods. Once domesticated plants were introduced, large villages developed rapidly in the rich environment of the Nile valley.

In Western Africa, the earliest evidence of plant domestication is the imprint of domesticated millet grains found in the village sites of the Dhar Tichitt region of Mauritania around 3,500 years ago. Sorghum appears to have been introduced at a somewhat later date.

## Summing Up the Evidence

There is a great deal that we still need to learn about the origins of agriculture in Africa. However, even given the preliminary nature of the archaeological record, there are some interesting patterns. Pottery was introduced at the beginning of the sequence in Africa, whereas it is found only in the Late Neolithic in the Middle East. Pastoral societies in Africa developed thousands of years before fully agricultural villages did. In Africa, as in the Middle East, small villages predate the domestication of plants and animals. The evidence for a particular focus on wild sorghum at Nabta Playa and the penning of wild sheep at Uan Afuda is particularly intriguing.

# 9.2 NEW GUINEA

During glacial periods, New Guinea, Australia, and Tasmania formed a single landmass known as Sahul. Today, New Guinea is a large island divided into the independent country of Papua New Guinea in the east and the Indonesian province of Irian Jaya in the west. The New Guinea highlands run the length of the island at an elevation between 1,300 and 2,500 meters.

Ethnographers studying the modern agricultural societies of New Guinea have emphasized the centrality of pigs and sweet potatoes not only for subsistence, but also in developing a social hierarchy. The exchange of pigs is an essential element of political power. Sweet potatoes are an important part of the diet of pigs; therefore, accumulating sweet potatoes is an essential element in gaining political power (Golson and Gardner 1990). Surprisingly, neither sweet potatoes nor pigs were domesticated indigenously in New Guinea, and both were introduced fairly recently. Sweet potatoes were domesticated in South America and were probably introduced into New Guinea after they were brought to the Philippines by Spanish sailors sometime in the sixteenth century (Gichuki et al. 2003). The timing of the introduction of domesticated pigs to New Guinea is poorly understood.

Recent genetic research indicates that a wide number of plant species were domesticated indigenously in New Guinea. These crops include yams, bananas, taro, and possibly sugarcane (LeBot 1999). None of these crops are cereals, and traditional agricultural processes in New Guinea involve transplanting suckers, cuttings, or shoots, rather than planting seeds.

## Clearing Forests and Draining Swamps

The earliest evidence of human occupation of New Guinea is found at coastal sites on the Huon peninsula, dated to 40,000 years ago (Groube et al. 1986). The earliest occupation of the highlands is found at the sites of Kosipe and Yuku, which are dated to approximately 30,000 years ago (Bulmer 1975). Animal bones recovered

Sweet potato farming in New Guinea.

from these sites indicate that a wide range of animals was hunted. There is no evidence of domesticated plants or animals. The exact date for the introduction of ground stone tools in the highlands is unclear; however, polished axes dating to 10,000 years ago are found on a number of sites.

Most of the archaeological sites in the highlands are cave sites. However, at Wanlek, the remains of a 6,000-year-old village, including remains of circular houses and a large central structure, were excavated. The artifacts recovered at Wanlek include polished stone axes, but no pottery. On archaeological sites in the highlands, no pottery is found that dates to earlier than 800 years ago.

> The **Kuk Swamp** site in highland New Guinea has produced early evidence of agriculture.

The main evidence for the development of agriculture in highland New Guinea comes from the excavation of ancient field systems at the **Kuk Swamp** in the Wahgi Valley (Denham et al. 2003). The major features found at Kuk Swamp are drainage canals, pits, and earth mounds. These features are the result of efforts to drain the swamp and create beds for planting crops. The age of the features at Kuk Swamp is based on radiocarbon dating of wood charcoal found in the fills of channels. Canals from the earliest phase at Kuk Swamp, radiocarbon dated to approximately 10,000 years ago, are limited in size and extent. In the second phase, dated to

# FIGURE 9.1

Maps showing the development of agricultural ditches and mounds at Kuk Swamp, New Guinea.

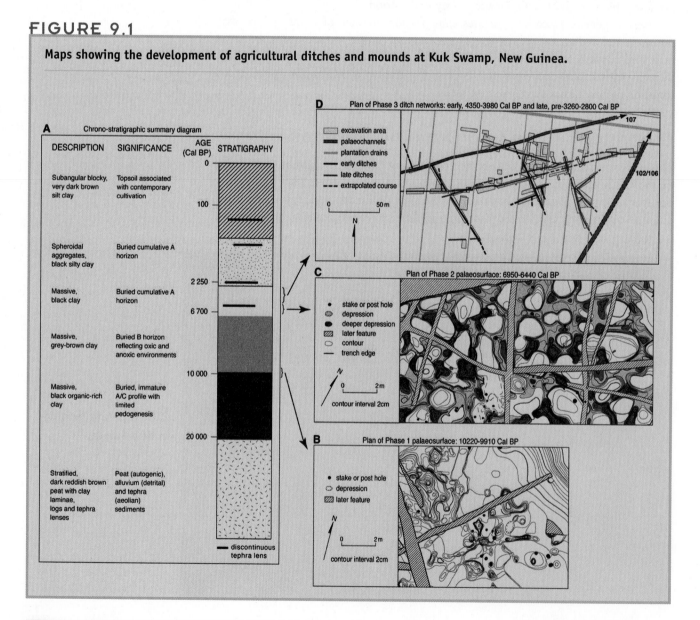

# TOOLBOX: Pollen, Phytoliths, and Starch Grains

Paleoethnobotanists are not limited to the macrobotanical remains recovered through flotation. In their efforts to understand human interactions with plants, paleoethnobotanists also draw on microbotanicals, the preserved microscopic remains of plant material.

Pollen grains, produced by the male reproductive organs of plants and trees, can be used to reconstruct past climate conditions. Pollen is best preserved in freshwater lakes and ponds, where the grains are embedded in the continuous buildup of sediments on the lake bottom. The continuous sequences recovered from these contexts allow botanists to track changes in the makeup of plant communities over time. One major change that can be tracked is the shifting frequency of pollen from trees and pollen from grasses. By looking at changes in this relationship, it is possible to determine periods when local ecology shifted from woodlands to open grasslands. Often, pollen can also be recovered from archaeological sites, providing a window into the ecological setting.

Phytoliths are silica structures that build up along plant cell walls. The source of the silica is groundwater that is pulled into the plant during its life. The form of the phytolith is shaped by the morphology of the plant; as a result, it is possible to identify types of plants on the basis of their phytoliths. Commonly preserved on archaeological sites, phytoliths can be used to reconstruct the ecological setting of a site. Sometimes phytoliths are found adhering to arti-

facts, and in these cases the phytoliths can provide an insight into how a tool was used.

Paleoethnobotanists have begun to explore starch grains found adhering to artifacts. In some cases, the grains have been shown to be remarkably resilient, surviving for thousands of years. Starch grain analysis has the potential to provide critical data about how tools were used. In one instance, the analysis of starch grains on pottery vessels recovered in Egypt allowed archaeologists to trace the process of beer production.

REFERENCE: Dena F. Dincauze. (2000). *Environmental Archaeology: Principles and Practices*. (Cambridge, U.K.: Cambridge University Press).

▲ Scanning electron microscope photograph of pine pollen.

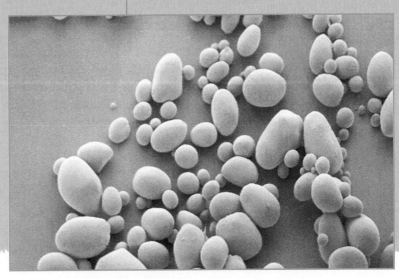

▶ Scanning electron microscope photograph of potato starch grains.

---

6,500 years ago, there are regularly distributed earth mounds and channels across the site. In the third phase, dated to 4,000 years ago, a network of drainage ditches was excavated through the site. Subsequently , the network of channels became denser and more regular. Around 3,000 years ago, the maintenance of agricultural fields at Kuk Swamp appears to have come to an end (see Figure 9.1).

Starch grains on stone tools from the first two occupations have been identified as taro, which does not grow naturally in the highlands and therefore must have been planted at Kuk Swamp. There is also evidence of banana cultivation beginning around 6,500 years ago. Phytoliths of bananas are found throughout the Kuk Swamp sequence. Phytoliths are mineral structures that build up on plant tissue. In the early phase of the occupation of Kuk Swamp, the presence of banana phytoliths is expected, because wild banana trees would have grown in the forest environment that was found in the region at that time. However, around 6,500 years ago, the environment around Kuk Swamp changed to grassland, in which a high percentage of banana phytoliths would not occur without human intervention. Therefore, the presence of large quantities of banana phytoliths in the swamp deposits after 6,500 years ago is evidence that people were planting banana trees. Features similar to those found at Kuk Swamp have been found on other sites, such as Kana, which is also located in the Wahgi Valley (Muke and Mandui 2003). However, as there is very little evidence from the excavation of village sites from these early periods in highland New Guinea, there is little basis for reconstructing the social context of plant domestication on the island (Ballard 2003).

In comparison to other cases of indigenous domestication of plants and animals, New Guinea is poorly understood. It appears that the transition to agriculture was quite gradual and that only plants were involved. New Guinea is unique in that no cereal crops were domesticated. The development of ground stone tool technology appears to be related to agriculture; however, pottery was introduced quite late and did not have any role in early agricultural systems.

# 9.3 THE ANDES

The Andes are the second-highest mountain chain in the world, with peaks reaching close to 7,000 meters above sea level. The Andean highlands can be divided into four zones based on altitude (Quilter 1989) (see Figure 9.2). The Quechua zone, between 2,300 and 3,500 meters above sea level, is where corn grows well. The Suni zone, between 3,500 and 4,000 meters, is the region in which a range of crops indigenous to the Andes are grown. The most important of these crops are a cereal called quinoa and root crops, including potatoes, oca, and olluco. The Puna zone, between 4,000 and 4,800 meters, is an open grassland used for grazing llamas and alpacas. The high peaks of the Cordillera zone, above 4,800 meters, are not exploited for agriculture. To the east, the Andean

## FIGURE 9.2

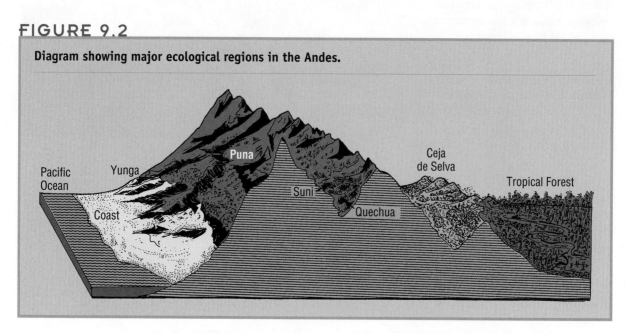

Diagram showing major ecological regions in the Andes.

highlands drop off rapidly into the Amazon rain forest, the archaeology of which, unfortunately, remains poorly understood (Raymond 1988).

To the west, the Andes descend gradually to the Pacific coast. The coastal region is a barren desert bisected by numerous rivers running down from the mountains (Burger 1992). Agriculture is limited to the river valleys. The desert is also broken by llomas—patches nurtured by mist from coastal fog in which dense vegetation grows during the winter. The coast itself is remarkably rich in marine resources, including small fish such as anchovies, large fish, ocean birds, marine mammals, and shellfish, such as clams and mussels. The wealth of the Andean coast is due to the **Humboldt Current,** which sweeps cool waters up the coast of South America, bringing nutrients to the surface.

## Domestication in the Andean Highlands

Excavations at **Guitarrero Cave** in the Andean highlands of Peru uncovered domesticated beans, which subsequently were dated to approximately 10,000 years ago (Smith 1980). The beans themselves were not dated; rather, what was dated was charcoal recovered from the same level as the beans. When one of the beans was dated directly with AMS radiocarbon, it turned out to be only 4,300 years old (Kaplan and Lynch 1998). Apparently, the beans came from a higher level in the stratigraphic sequence at Guitarrero Cave and were perhaps moved by burrowing animals.

The redating of the beans from Guitarrero Cave has thrown all early dates for domesticated plant in the Andean highlands into question. At Panaulauca Cave, a small number of quinoa seeds have been found in layers dating to between 5,700 and 4,500 years ago (Smith 1995). Until these seeds are dated directly, the timing for the domestication of quinoa remains open to question. The earliest evidence for domesticated potatoes from sites on the Peruvian coast dated to between 4,000 and 3,000 years ago. It is unlikely that these are the earliest domesticated potatoes, as the coast is not the region where wild forms of potatoes grow. An added problem is that distinguishing domesticated quinoa and potatoes from wild forms is difficult. With quinoa, a thin seed coat is used to identify a seed as domesticated. For potatoes, it is the shape and size of starch grains that are used to distinguish between wild and domesticated forms.

The domestication of **llamas** and **alpacas** in the Andean highlands is fairly well documented (Lavallée 2000). Both animals are camelids. The ancestral species of llamas are guanacos and the wild ancestors of alpacas are vicuñas. It is difficult to distinguish between domesticated and wild camelids on the basis of the shape and size of their bones. However, at a number of cave sites in the Andean highlands, the percentage of camelids relative to deer increases steadily through the period between

> ▶ The **Humboldt Current** accounts for the remarkable wealth of marine resources along the Andean coast.

> ▶ Domesticated beans from **Guitarrero Cave** in the Andean highlands have been directly dated to 4,300 years ago.

> ▶ **Llamas** and **alpacas** were domesticated in the Andean highlands.

**I**nca farmers digging up potatoes, from a Spanish sixteenth century document.

A herd of llamas in the highlands of Peru.

10,000 and 5,000 years ago, a trend that appears to indicate a gradual shift toward camelid domestication. Beginning around 7,000 years ago, the number of very young camelids increased sharply. This pattern is interpreted as the result of disease, which struck closely packed herds of domesticated animals. Another line of evidence for domestication is found at the Asana site near Lake Titicaca. In a level dated to 4,500 years ago, chemical analysis of the soils indicated that there had been a high concentration of dung in an area surrounded by postholes. The excavators interpret this feature as the remains of a corral for domesticated camelids. The other domesticated animal in the Andes is the guinea pig. Little is known about when guinea pigs were first domesticated, but it appears to have been considerably later than the domestication of camelids.

No village sites have been excavated in the Andean highlands from these early periods. Currently, it appears that the domestication of plants and animals took place in the context of mobile hunter–gatherer societies.

## Coastal Villages

By eight thousand years ago, small settled villages developed in the lloma fog meadows on the Peruvian coast (Pineda 1988). The inhabitants of these villages were hunter–gatherers who relied heavily on the rich coastal marine resources.

The village of **Paloma**, which was inhabited intermittently between 8,000 and 5,000 years ago, provides a broad view of one of these early preagricultural villages (Quilter 1989). Houses were built of reeds and grasses over a structure of wooden poles. The total population of the villages is unclear, but it appears to have been in the range of ten families at any given time. A large number of burials were excavated

**Paloma** is a preagricultural village site on the coast of Peru.

at Paloma, mostly in pits dug into the floors of houses, with grave offerings placed near the skeleton. An analysis of the burials demonstrated an overall uniformity in the treatment of the dead, with no evidence that some members of the community had a higher status than others. Males tended to be buried toward the center of houses, suggesting that they might have had a higher status than females.

The Paloma site provides a vivid demonstration of the centrality of marine resources to these early village communities. Analysis of the faunal remains from the site showed that 98% of the individuals recovered were marine animals and shellfish (Reitz 1988). The dominant species were anchovies. Only a small number of land mammals were found, including spider monkeys, camelids, and deer.

The skeletal remains also afford evidence of the intensive exploitation of marine resources at Paloma. Eight skeletons were found with auditory exostoses, a growth in the inner ear caused by spending long periods in cold water. Burial 159 at Paloma presents particularly graphic evidence of the relation these people had with the sea. Burial 159 is a young man in excellent health, except for

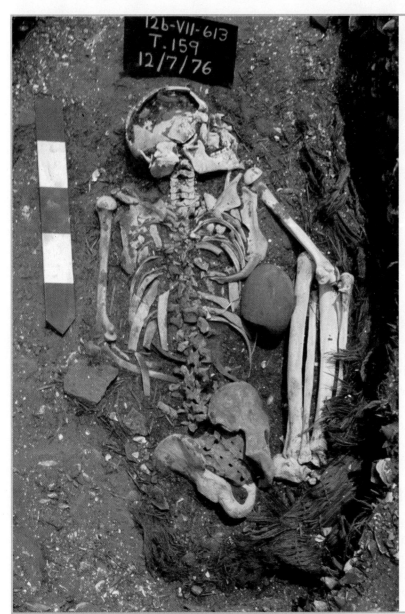

**B**urial 159 from the Paloma site, Peru. The left leg is missing and the pelvis shows marks consistent with attack by a shark.

The Cotton Preceramic mounds at the Caral site.

missing a leg. This man was buried in an elaborate cane structure tied with cord, along with a number of burial offerings. A series of cut marks was found on the man's pelvis, indicating "the likelihood that his leg was removed by a shark" (Quilter 1989: 59).

A wide range of plant resources from the llomas, including seeds, fruits, and tubers, was exploited by the people living at Paloma. The only clearly domesticated plants were cultivated gourds. Beans and squash might have been cultivated, but there is no evidence that they played a significant role in the diet.

## The Cotton Preceramic

> The sites of the **Cotton Preceramic** are often quite large and contain evidence of monumental architecture.

Approximately 5,700 years ago, large sites with monumental architecture began to appear on the coast of Peru. These sites belong to a period called the **Cotton Preceramic** in recognition of the prevalence of cotton seeds and the absence of pottery. The sites from the Cotton Preceramic reach up to 58 hectares at El Paraíso and 65 hectares at Caral (Quilter et al. 1991, Solis et al. 2001). At the site of Aspero, a large flat-topped pyramid known as Huaca de los Ídolos dated between 5,500 and 4,500 years ago is the earliest known monumental architecture in the New World. At Caral, there are six large artificial mounds, the largest of which measures 160 meters by 150 meters and is 18 meters high, dated between 4,000 and 3,500 years ago (Solis et al. 2001).

There has been considerable debate concerning the economic basis of the large Cotton Preceramic sites. Because the site of Aspero is located on the coast, it was suggested that these sites were based on fishing and collecting marine resources, rather than on agriculture. Subsequent studies have shown that, in fact, the bulk of the diet of Cotton Preceramic sites consisted of fish and shellfish. Even at the site of Caral, located 23 kilometers from the coast, almost all of the faunal remains were of clams, mussels, anchovies, and sardines (Solis et al. 2001). However, at both Caral and the coastal site of El Paraíso, a wide range of domesticated plants, including gourds, squash, chili pepper, and beans, as well as the tubers achira and jicama, were grown. The dominant crop species was cotton, which was used for making nets and textiles.

## The Role of El Niño

The Humboldt Current, which brings cool waters from the south up along the Andean coast, is responsible for the wealth of marine resources that allowed villages such as Paloma to thrive without agriculture. The large centers of the Cotton Preceramic also relied heavily on the rich marine resources brought by the Humboldt Current. **El Niño** is a severe reversal of the Humboldt Current that occurs every twenty-five to forty years. When major El Niño events strike, there is a massive decline in the fish and shellfish populations on the coast, as well as torrential rains on the shore that cause massive flooding and mud slides (Burger 1992). It is hard to imagine how villages like Paloma would have survived such events.

▶ **El Niño** is a severe reversal of the Humboldt Current that causes a massive decline in marine resources along the Andean coast.

Studies of the shellfish found on archaeological sites have led archaeologists to argue that El Niño events began only around 6,000 years ago (Sandweiss et al. 2001). According to this model, El Niño events between 6,000 and 3,000 years ago were less frequent than they are today. The onset of El Niño appears to correlate with the beginning of the Cotton Preceramic. It is possible that the climatic uncertainty of the arrival of El Niño played a role in pushing the development of large centers with a partial reliance on agriculture.

## Summing Up the Evidence

The domestication of plants and animals in the highlands of the Andes appears to have had little impact on the way people lived. Early agricultural sites are either small cave sites or open-air sites, with little evidence of architecture. However, the absence of early agricultural villages in the highlands might be the result of a bias in the types of sites that have been excavated. Archaeologists have focused largely on dry cave sites with well-preserved organic remains.

On the coast, settled villages preceded the adoption of agriculture. These villages were small collections of huts showing little evidence of social inequality. The adoption of domesticated plants took place on the coast in the context of increased settlement size and the emergence of monumental architecture. Because of the availability of rich coastal marine resources, agriculture played only a minor role in the subsistence of Cotton Preceramic settlements. The dominant crop was cotton, used for making fishing nets and textiles. The adoption of agriculture on the Andean coast might have been a reaction to the climatic uncertainty introduced by the onset of El Niño.

# 9.4 EAST ASIA

**Rice** was domesticated along the **Yangtze and Huai River Valleys** in southern China.

The two most significant plants domesticated in East Asia are **rice** and millet. Today, rice feeds half of the world's population. The wild ancestor of rice is the species *Oryza rufipogon,* and all domesticated Asian rice belongs to the species *Oryza sativa.* (Note that this species is distinct from African rice and from the plant we call wild rice.) *Oryza rufipogon,* the wild ancestor of rice, was a plant that thrived in seasonally flooded areas. The earliest stages of domestication might have involved the construction of temporary dams to expand the lands that were seasonally inundated (Smith 1995).

One strain of rice, *Oryza sativa japonica,* was domesticated in southern China in the **Yangtze and Huai River Valleys.** Other plants domesticated in southern China include water caltrop and fox nut, both of which grow, like rice, in inundated fields. Among the domesticated animals in southern China are dogs, pigs, and water buffalo. Genetic evidence suggests that another strain of rice, *Oryza sativa indica,* was independently domesticated in the region between India and Tailand (Londo et al. 2006). There is not yet any archaeological evidence for rice domestication from this region.

**Millet** was domesticated around the **Yellow River Valley** in northern China.

The **Jomon** were Japanese preagricultural societies that lived in large villages and produced elaborate pottery.

Two types of **millet**—broomcorn and foxtail millet—were both domesticated in northern China in the region around the **Yellow River Valley.** Both species of millet are highly drought resistant cereals. Animals domesticated in northern China include pigs and, possibly, chickens.

## Early Pottery

By ten thousand years ago, societies of hunter–gatherers across East Asia were utilizing a wide range of wild resources and living in permanent or semipermanent settlements. Many of these groups produced pottery. The **Jomon** societies of Japan, dated to between 13,000 and 2,500 years ago, produced elaborate pottery and lived in villages that included as many as fifty pit houses (Imamura 1996). The subsistence of the Jomon was based on hunting and gathering, with a particular emphasis on fish and shellfish. Rice and millet agriculture was introduced into Japan only during the Late Jomon period, around 3,000 years ago (D'Andrea et al. 1995).

In the Yangtze Valley, pottery has been discovered at a number of sites dating to earlier than ten thousand years ago (Higham and Lu 1998). The people who produced this pottery subsisted on wild plants and animals. It is interesting that wild rice was among the plants they collected. Because the excavated sites from this period are mostly caves, it is not possible to say whether these people lived in large settlements like those found during the Jomon period in Japan.

In northern China, little is known about preagricultural societies. The reason

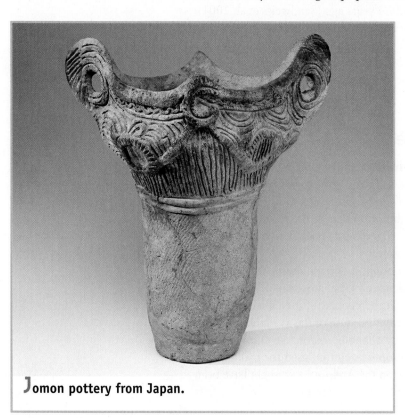

**J**omon pottery from Japan.

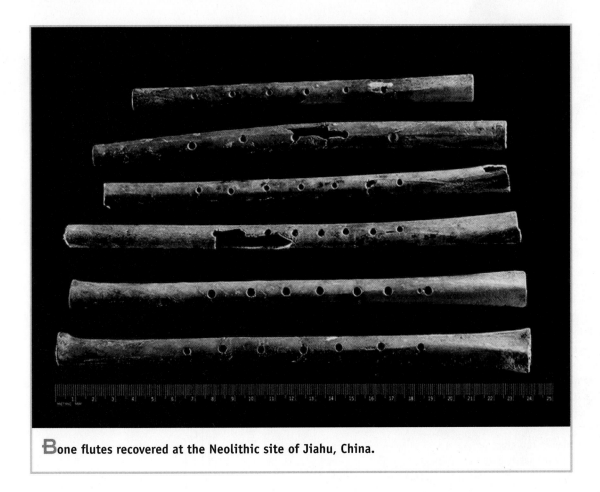

**B**one flutes recovered at the Neolithic site of Jiahu, China.

for this paucity of knowledge is a massive buildup of windblown sediments known as loess, which has buried sites from these periods deep underground.

## The First Farmers

The earliest evidence of rice farming is found on village sites in the Yangzte and Huai River valley. The site of **Pengtoushan** is a village dated to approximately 9,000 years ago that has produced evidence of domesticated rice (Higham and Lu 1998). The excavations at Pengtoushan recovered traces of houses surrounded by a protective ditch. The neighboring site of Bashidang has also produced a large quantity of charred rice (Pei 1998). Bashidang appears to have been occupied slightly after Pengtoushan. The village at Bashidang covered an area of 30,000 square meters. A wide range of wild animal bones were recovered at Bashidang, indicating that hunting continued to be important for subsistence.

In the Huai River region, the village site of Jiahu, occupied between 9,000 and 8,000 years ago, covered an area of roughly 55,000 square meters (Zhang et al. 1999). Excavations have uncovered a total of 45 houses, storage pits, and graves. As at Bashidang, a range of wild animals was hunted. Six complete flutes made from the long bones of the red-crowned crane have been found at Jiahu. These flutes are excellently preserved, so that a musician was able to use one of them to play a Chinese folk song, "The Chinese Small Cabbage." The excavators point out that in ancient China music was a part of nature and was associated with government.

The initial stages of millet farming in the Yellow River region date to approximately 8,000 years ago in what is known as the Peiligang culture.

> The **Pengtoushan** site has produced some of the earliest evidence of domesticated rice.

# TOOLBOX:
## Residue Analysis

When animals are exploited for milk and wool, they are more than just a source of meat. Andrew Sherratt has argued that the exploitation of domesticated animals for secondary products such as milk and wool transformed the economy of early farming societies. Herds of animals became a walking source of wealth.

But how can we tell whether an animal was milked? One approach is to look for evidence of dairying in the population structure of the herd. If dairying was economically significant, one would expect a culling of young males. However, this approach provides evidence that is at best indirect. In 2003, a group of biochemists published dramatic results of a new method that allowed them to identify the biochemical traces of milk residues on pottery sherds from the Neolithic in Britain (Copley et al. 2003). These results provide direct evidence that milk was an important aspect of the early farming communities of Britain.

The milk residues found in this study are lipids that have survived for approximately 6,000 years. The first stage of analysis is to get the lipids out of the pot sherd. Sherds are cleaned thoroughly, and then a sample weighing 2 grams is ground to a powder and soaked in a solvent in an ultrasonic bath. Next, the solvent, which now contains the lipids, is evaporated, leaving the lipids behind. The chemical composition of the lipids is determined with a mass spectrometer. The critical step in developing this method was finding a signature that would distinguish between adipose (body) fat and milk fat. Fortunately,

such a marker, based on differences in ratios of carbon isotopes, was found.

Biochemical methods have also been used to identify the processing of plants. In one notable study, a chemical analysis of

► **Neolithic storage jar from the site of Jiahu with the result of a mass spectrometry analysis of the chemical composition of the residues found inside the vessel.**

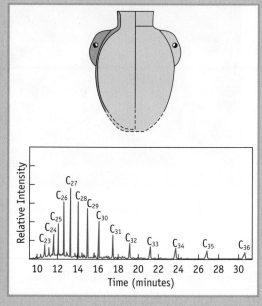

pottery sherds from the Neolithic site of Jiahu, China, found evidence of a fermented beverage made of rice, honey, and fruit (McGovern et al. 2004).

# The Development of Farming Societies

**Banpo** village is a large farming village dating to the **Yangshou culture.**

The Peiligang culture of the Yellow River developed into the **Yangshou culture** 6,500 years ago (Debaine-Francfort 2000). The Yangshou culture is particularly well represented at **Banpo**, a village site that consisted of both round semisubterranean houses and rectangular houses built on the surface. A range of wild plants and animals, including fish, fruits, and nuts, was exploited. Millet was fully domesticated, as were dogs and pigs. The repertoire of pottery vessels found at Banpo is particularly impressive and includes vessels with elaborate painted decorations.

**Hemudu** is a well-preserved rice-farming village.

In southern China, the **Hemudu** site provides a picture of a village based on rice cultivation and contemporaneous with Banpo (Smith 1995). The excavations at Hemudu have uncovered 4 meters of superbly preserved archaeological deposits. The houses at Hemudu were skillfully built of wood and raised on piles above the waters of a river or pond that existed on the spot. Because the site is waterlogged, the wooden houses are well preserved. Enormous quantities of domesticated rice, along with the bones of domesticated dogs, pigs, and water buffalo, were also recovered at Hemudu.

Chinese archaeologists have been particularly interested in understanding the social life of early farming villages (Pearson and Underhill 1987). As a result, many of the early village excavations are on a very large scale. The tendency in China is to view early agricultural societies as matrilineal clans organized around maternal lineages. Over time, these societies are seen as having evolved into patrilineal property-owning families. The logic behind this argument is that women played a decisive role in raising and tending plants and would therefore have wielded power in early agricultural societies. Attempts have been made to use the distribution of burial practices within village sites to gain a fuller understanding of their social organization. One of the burial features that have been emphasized is that young girls found buried in Yangshao cemeteries were richly adorned.

## Summing Up the Evidence

In China, as in Africa, pottery manufacture predates the development of agriculture. Hunter–gatherers living in large settlements with constructed houses are found in Japan, as they are in both the Middle East and Africa. Although the earliest stages of agriculture in China are poorly understood, it appears that the domestication of both plants and animals happened at the same time. As in the Middle East, the adoption of agriculture was accompanied by an increase in the size of sites. In China, domestication took place independently in two centers, with rice domesticated in the south and millet in the north. The overlap in animal species domesticated suggests that there was some connection between these two centers of domestication.

**P**ottery vessels found in situ on the floor of hut structure at the Banpo village site, China.

The earliest agricultural sites in China are large sedentary villages. The excavations at Pengtoushan, Bashigan, and Jiahu have uncovered the remains of large settlements with some evidence of defensive ditches. If these sites were inhabited soon after the initial domestication of rice, then southern China would provide a case in which domestication is linked directly with the formation of large villages. However, research on the preceding periods is in its early stages, so the validity of this conclusion remains open to question.

# 9.5 QUESTIONING THE NEOLITHIC

Julian Thomas has written, of the origins of agriculture, that it was a "messy and fragmented series of developments, and that any attempt to define a particular set of attributes as constituting the Neolithic will be arbitrary in the extreme" (Thomas 1999: 13). The evidence presented in this chapter supports the view presented by Thomas and contrasts sharply with Childe's view of the Neolithic Revolution as a sudden transformation of human society that took place in much the same way around the globe.

In all regions, the transition to agriculture was a gradual process. This fact has led Bruce Smith (2001) to argue that it is necessary to consider a territory "in between" hunting and gathering, on the one hand, and farming, on the other. The route taken in traversing this intermediate territory was extremely varied. Settled villages preceded agriculture in the Near East, China, Africa, and the Andean Coast, but, apparently, not in New Guinea, the Andean highlands, or Mesoamerica. Pottery can develop very early in the process, as it did in Africa and China, or very late, as it did in the Middle East, New Guinea, the Andes, and Mesoamerica. Plants can be domesticated before animals (Middle East, New Guinea), after animals (Africa and the Andes), at the same time as animals (China), or not at all (Mesoamerica).

The development of agriculture is a complex process involving changes in the biology of plants and animals, human subsistence strategies, human social organization, and the way people think about their place in the world. Perhaps it should not come as a surprise that this transition can follow many trajectories, depending on the plant and animal species involved, the characteristics of the local environment, and the particularities of cultural practices. In a sense, the diversity found in the archaeological record forces us to recognize the need for multiple perspectives on the origins of agriculture.

# CHAPTER SUMMARY

- Indigenous plant domestication in Africa took place in three major regions: Ethiopia and Eritrea, Central Africa, and West Africa.
- At Nabta Playa, a village of circular huts with storage pits and pottery vessels is dated to 9,000 years ago.
- Pottery developed in North Africa before the domestication of plants and animals.
- Domesticated animals were introduced into North Africa by pastoral societies before the adoption of domesticated plants.
- Yams, bananas, and taro were domesticated indigenously in New Guinea.
- The main evidence for the development of agriculture in New Guinea comes from the excavation of ancient field systems at the Kuk Swamp site. There is evidence of artificial drainage systems at Kuk Swamp beginning 10,000 years ago.
- Because of the Humboldt Current, the Andean coast is extraordinarily rich in marine resources.
- Domesticated beans from Guitarrero Cave, Peru, have been directly dated to 4,300 years ago. The earliest evidence for domesticated potatoes is between 4,000 and 3,200 years ago.

- There is evidence for the domestication of llamas and alpacas beginning 6,000 years ago.
- By 8,000 years ago, small villages relying on marine resources had developed along the Andean Coast.
- During the Cotton Preceramic, large sites, including monumental mounds, were built on the Andean coast. Among the domesticated crops from these sites were gourds, squash, and beans. The most significant crop was cotton.
- Rice was domesticated in southern China in the Yangtze and Huai River Valleys. The Pengtoushan site has produced the earliest evidence of domesticated rice.
- Millet was domesticated in northern China in the region around the Yellow River.
- The Jomon societies of Japan were hunter–gatherers who lived in small villages and made pottery.
- The Banpo site in northern China and the Hemudu site in southern China are large villages with extensive evidence of both plant and animal domestication.

## KEY TERMS

## REVIEW QUESTIONS

1. Do any aspects of the pattern of domestication in the Middle East fit in with the case studies in this chapter?
2. In what ways was the origin of agriculture in New Guinea unique?
3. What does Bruce Smith mean by a territory "in between" hunting and gathering, on the one hand, and farming, on the other? What are some examples of such "in-between" societies?
4. What generalizations can be made about pottery and the origins of agriculture?

## FOR FURTHER READING

Peter Bellwood. (2005). *First Farmers: The Origins of Agricultural Societies*. Malden, MA: Blackwell.

Richard Keatinge. (1988). *Peruvian Prehistory*. Cambridge, U.K.: Cambridge University Press.

Thurstan Shaw. (1993). *The Archaeology of Africa: Food, Metals, and Towns*. London: Routledge.

Bruce Smith. (1995). *The Emergence of Agriculture*. New York: Scientific American Library.

# part FOUR

# The Development of Social Complexity

IN THE PREVIOUS SECTION, we examined the shift to an agricultural way of life. In this final section, we visit different societies in many parts of the world and consider the increasing inequality among members of these societies that resulted as they grew in size. Power and access to resources came to be controlled by a smaller segment of society leading to the emergence of state societies. After reading this chapter you should understand:

► Fried and Service's categories for the forms of social organization.

► Childe's ten criteria that define urban societies.

► Explanations for the emergence of social complexity.

## INTRODUCTION: DEFINING SOCIAL COMPLEXITY

In the modern world, institutionalized power is a basic fact of life. With the exception of a small number of disputed territories, the deep oceans, and Antarctica, the entire globe is carved up into sovereign entities in which a central government holds authority. The degree to which this authority is exercised and the way in which it is exercised vary considerably; however, the existence of centralized authority is a global phenomenon.

The Canadian-American border between Maine and Quebec.

Centralized government or authority is a relatively recent development in human society. Gaining an understanding of how these institutions came into being is one of the central themes of archaeological research. Through much of the early history of archaeology, this problem was couched within the broader framework of the progress of humanity. Lewis Henry Morgan and V. Gordon Childe considered what was often called the origin of civilization to have been the inevitable next step in the upward movement of humanity following on the origins of agriculture. From such a perspective, the origin of central authority explains itself: People would naturally aspire to live within more advanced and highly developed societies.

Today, most archaeologists have a more subtle understanding of the development of politically complex human societies. Although it is recognized that the existence of centralized authority was essential for people to live in large urban centers and for significant developments to occur in culture and technology, there is also a clear sense of the costs of such authority. Political complexity is inevitably linked with increased social inequality and with limitations on personal autonomy. While early archaeologists might have questioned what allowed societies to "advance" to civilization, archaeologists today are more likely to ask about the forces that pushed societies towards increasing social inequality. The critical issue underlying much contemporary research is how centralized authority gained legitimacy within the societies over which they exercised control. An authority has **legitimacy** when its right to power is accepted. In the study of the development of centralized authority, one question is, To what degree was the legitimacy of authority the result of consensus or coercion? A system grounded in consensus operates on the basis of members of society believing in the rights of the centralized authority, while a system based on coercion forces people to accept the centralized authority. In most archaeological cases, legitimacy is the result of a combination of consensus and coercion.

**Legitimacy** is achieved when the right of a centralized authority to have power is accepted. Legitimacy can be based on consensus or coercion.

# Categorizing Political Complexity

A number of anthropologists have developed schemes for categorizing the types of social organization found in human societies around the world. These schemes provide an essential framework for guiding research endeavors dealing with the development of political complexity. The goal of such schemes is not to encompass the tremendous variation that characterizes human societies, but rather to provide a model to help bring out regularities in the way that political complexity develops.

Morton H. Fried (1967) defined four types of societies: egalitarian, ranked, stratified, and state. In *egalitarian* societies, the only differences in status between members of society are based on their skill at subsistence activities (such as hunting), their age, and their gender. The status of a person is determined by a combination of these factors. Production in egalitarian societies takes place within households, and all households carry out more or less the same task. Exchange tends to be casual and based on reciprocity.

In an egalitarian society, there are as many positions of prestige as there are people to fill those positions. A *ranked* society is defined as a society in which there are fewer positions of prestige than there are people to fill the positions. In a ranked society, there is a hierarchy of prestige that is not linked to age, gender, or ability. The basis for access to prestige is often a simple attribute, such as order of birth. In such a society, the firstborn son might have higher prestige than his siblings. Although there is a hierarchy in a ranked society, there is no real political power or exploitation. The role of a person occupying a high-status position is to collect, not to expropriate, to redistribute, rather than consume.

In ranked societies, there are individuals with high prestige, but little real power. These "big men" or "chiefs" serve as the focal point of a system of collecting and redistributing resources, but they do not expropriate or consume more than their neighbors with lower prestige. By contrast, in a *stratified* society, not all people have equal access to key resources. Access is tightly linked to prestige: People of high prestige have unimpeded access to these resources, while people of low prestige encounter impediments. In stratified societies, as in ranked societies, the number of high-prestige positions is limited on the basis of criteria other than age, gender, and ability. Because of the unequal access to key resources, including food and shelter, one characteristic of stratified societies is the growth of exploitation, which can take the form of demands on labor, institutional slavery, or more complex systems based on a division of labor among groups of specialists. In stratified societies, organization is based, not only on the household and kin group, but also on communities of people drawn from different households and kin groups.

Fried defined **states** as societies in which power is organized on a supra-kin basis (Fried 1967). The essential task of the state is to use this power to maintain the social hierarchy that has escaped from its grounding in the kin group. Characteristics of state societies include population control through the fixing of boundaries, the development of a legal system, the maintenance of military and police forces, taxation, and conscription. For Fried, the evolution of political complexity is a gradual process in which the basic unit of organization shifts from the family and kin group to large "supra-kin" communities. This process also sees increasing control of access to key resources and an increase in centralized political power.

A similar scheme developed by Elman Service (1971) divides societies into bands, tribes, chiefdoms, and states. Service's definition of *band* and *tribe societies* corresponds roughly to Fried's egalitarian and ranked societies. For Service,

> In **egalitarian societies** the only differences in status are based on skill, age, and gender.

> In a **ranked society** there is a hierarchy of prestige not linked to age, gender, or ability.

> In a **stratified society** access to key resources is linked to prestige.

> **States** can be defined as societies in which power is organized on a supra-kin basis or as a society integrated by a bureaucracy that uses force.

Maori women from New Zealand. The high status of these women is indicated by their feather cloaks and jade pendants.

chiefdoms are societies characterized by an intermediate level of social complexity. In chiefdoms, there is centralized leadership based on heredity. However, leaders in these societies have little ability to use force to maintain order, relying on religious authority as their source of power (Service 1975). State societies are sharply different from chiefdoms in that government and law are backed by force. Service summarizes his view of the state as a society integrated by a bureaucracy that uses force (Service 1971: 167). The state has a legitimate monopoly over the use of force. This does not mean that state societies are inherently violent. Rather, it is through the monopolization and controlled use of force that the rulers of state societies are able to maintain peaceful order among a large population. The role of force is to allow the bureaucratic elite to integrate society.

Both Fried and Service see the development of political complexity as the movement of authority from the kin group to a government that is not based on kinship. Fried tends to emphasize the emergence of inequality as high status becomes increasingly concentrated in the hands of a smaller number of people. Service highlights the emergence in state societies of a control over the legitimate use of force.

## Defining Cities

> In **urban societies** people live in large cities. V. Gordon Childe developed ten criteria to define urban centers.

V. Gordon Childe chose to sidestep the search for the early state by shifting the emphasis from political institutions to the definition of *urban,* or city-based, societies. Childe developed ten criteria that archaeologists could use to identify urban societies in the archaeological record: urban centers, surplus production and storage, taxes to a deity or king, monumental architecture, a ruling class, writing systems, exact and predictive sciences, sophisticated art styles, foreign trade, and specialist craftsmen. In the same way that he saw the origins of agriculture as the Neolithic Revolution, Childe saw the development of state societies as the Urban Revolution. Once again, all aspects of human life were transformed by interlocking changes in economy and society.

Midtown Manhattan. This picture illustrates the density and regularity that characterizes urban centers.

The advantage of Childe's list of criteria is that they are likely to leave visible traces in the archaeological record. However, a number of the criteria are poorly defined. For example, how big does a settlement have to be to count as an urban center? Furthermore, Childe did not make it clear why these criteria are relevant, other than the fact that they are archaeologically visible. One solution to this problem is to define the urban center in terms of its place in a regional settlement system. Henry Wright and Gregory Johnson (1975) have emphasized that, in urban societies, there is a hierarchy with at least three different levels of settlement size. This hierarchy is significant because it reflects a differentiated administrative structure. In a clever turn of phrase, Norman Yoffee (2005) points out that the birth of the city was also the origin of the countryside. The movement of people and power into cities inevitably restructured the lives of people living in towns and villages.

## A Comparative Approach to State Formation

Inequality is an essential element of all human societies. Even in those societies which Fried describes as egalitarian, there are differences in status based on skill, age, and gender. The categories developed by Fried and Service are useful tools, but they should not trick us into believing that the emergence of social inequality followed a single trajectory in all societies. For example, the societies of the northwest coast of North America offer a fundamental challenge to our expectation that the emergence of political complexity builds on the economy of a village farming way of life. The societies of the northwest coast, complex hunter–gatherers with a subsistence base that included a broad range of marine and terrestrial resources, lived in villages and had a complex social hierarchy that included the institution of slavery. Perhaps any attempt to shoehorn societies into a category such as a chiefdom or a state is misguided. One could argue that it would be better to study social

Northwest coast village near Bella Coola, British Columbia.

complexity as a continuum or, alternatively, that it is better to focus on the internal logic of each individual society.

There certainly are dangers to taking a comparative approach to the emergence of political complexity. While recognizing these dangers, Bruce Trigger has written an eloquent defense of comparative studies. Trigger writes, "The most important issue confronting the social sciences is the extent to which human behavior is shaped by factors that operate cross-culturally as opposed to factors that are unique to particular cultures. . . . Given the biological similarities and the cultural diversity of human beings, how differently are they likely to behave under analogous circumstances? The answer to this question is crucial to understanding human behavior and cultural change and for shaping the future course of human development" (Trigger 2003: 3). Adopting a comparative approach allows archaeologists to explore the regularities associated with the formation of states, regardless of the context in which that formation occurs, and at the same time to appreciate the unique features of the process in particular regions.

State societies can be divided into secondary states, which form under the influence of neighboring state societies, and primary states, which form without external influence from neighboring state societies. As with the origins of agriculture, the transition to state societies is a process that took place independently in a number of regions. Increasingly, archaeologists are paying close attention not only to the processes leading to the formation of states, but also to what causes states to collapse (Diamond 2005).

## Ecology and Society

Karl Wittfogel proposed a theory of early state formation that emphasized the importance of large-scale irrigation processes. Wittfogel (1957) argued that the need to organize large groups of workers to build and maintain irrigation canals allowed the formation of a hierarchical form of government he labeled "oriental despotism."

Wittfogel's model is an example of a prime-mover model—a model in which a single factor is seen as the cause of a phenomenon. In this case, the organization of large-scale agriculture leads to the formation of a centralized bureaucratic government. Robert Carneiro (1970) has proposed a model of state formation that considers the interaction among geography, population increase, and violence. Carneiro emphasizes that early state societies tend to develop in circumscribed areas—that is, areas which are surrounded by natural barriers or frontiers with neighboring groups. A population increase in a circumscribed area leads to increasing pressure for resources that, in turn, will lead to increased violence between communities. Carneiro argues that it is within the context of this competitive violence that power will become increasingly centralized. Unlike Wittfogel's model, the "circumscription model" proposed by Carneiro suggests that it is the interaction among multiple factors that leads to the development of state societies.

## The Source of Power

Exploring early state societies is essentially a search for the roots of power—the glue that held these large-scale, highly differentiated societies together. How did some people gain the ability to control the actions of others? The critical characteristic of power in state societies is that it comes to reside in institutions as well as developing around charismatic individuals.

A number of archaeologists have suggested that the control of information was a major element in the formation of state societies. The rise of a centralized bureaucracy rested on the ability to gather, control, and record information. The development of specialized craft production involved the transmission of elaborate technical skill and knowledge among a small group of people. The development of writing systems and mathematical knowledge gave the centralized government the ability to control resources and people.

Theories of the origin of the state tend to focus on factors drawn from Western economics. Access to resources, control of labor, population size, competition, access to information, and bureaucracy are among the factors that are often stressed as underlying the power of the centralized government of early states. Balancing such an external perspective on the process of state formation is the way the people themselves saw the world in which they lived. From this perspective, it is clear that part of the power of rulers flowed from their possession of unique symbols of power and an intimate connection to the gods. The power of special objects, be they banners, thrones, or scepters, to invoke fear, awe, or loyalty is a force that must be kept in mind in trying to understand how centralized bureaucracies came to have legitimacy in the eyes of their subjects.

In the coming chapters, we will explore the emergence of state societies from a comparative perspective. We will begin with four societies that afford clear evidence of a complex social organization, but without the institutionalization of power that is characteristic of state societies. From this foundation, we will move on to three classic state societies—the Maya, ancient Mesopotamia, and Shang China—in which urbanism and the rise of a powerful political elite are closely linked. Although these three civilizations meet many of the expectations about the characteristics of early state societies, the subjects of the next chapter—Egypt, the Indus Valley, and Jenne Jenno—do not. In Egypt the state arose without a clear

**M**odern symbols of power. Queen Elizabeth II and Prince Phillip open Parliament.

focus on urban centers, while in the Indus Valley large cities arose without leaving clear evidence of a ruling elite. It has been argued that the early West African city of Jenne Jenno developed without a rigid hierarchy. Finally, we will examine two empires: the Inca and Aztec empires of the Americas. Empires represent the expansion of the state to incorporate larger and more heterogeneous territories. Our own experience living in a world structured by complex local and global political interrelationships serves as the backdrop to all of these case studies. We are essentially examining how the world we inhabit came into being.

## PART SUMMARY

- Archaeologists today see the development of political complexity as a process that requires explanation and that cannot be viewed as the natural result of progress. Political complexity is linked with increased social inequality and limitations on personal autonomy.
- An authority has legitimacy when its right to power is accepted. Legitimacy can be based on coercion or consensus (or both).
- Morton Fried developed a system of classifying human societies into egalitarian, ranked, stratified, and state societies. For Fried, state societies are defined as the organization of society on a "supra-kin" basis.

- Elman Service divides human societies into bands, tribes, chiefdoms, and states. For Service, state societies are defined as a system that implements bureaucratic government by force.
- Gordon Childe developed a definition of urban societies based on ten criteria.
- Karl Wittfogel explained the emergence of states as a response to the need to organize large groups of workers for public-works projects.
- Robert Carneiro argued that states developed in circumscribed settings as a response to the warfare generated by population growth.

## KEY TERMS

Egalitarian Societies, 285
Legitimacy, 284

Ranked Society, 285
States, 285

Stratified Society, 285
Urban Societies, 286

## REVIEW QUESTIONS

1. How does Fried's system for classifying societies differ from Service's system?

2. Why is it important for archaeologists working on state societies not to focus exclusively on the excavation of tombs and palaces?

3. How do Wittfogel and Carneiro explain the development of state societies? Why is such an explanation needed?

## FOR FURTHER READING

Morton H. Fried. (1967). *The Evolution of Political Society: An Essay in Political Anthropology.* New York: Random House.

Elman Service. (1975). *Origins of the State and Civilization.* New York: Norton.

Bruce Trigger. (2003). *Understanding Early Civilizations: A Comparative Study.* New York: Cambridge University Press.

Norman Yoffee. (2005). *Myths of the Archaic State*, New York: Cambridge University Press.

## CHAPTER 10

# Complexity without the State

SOME OF THE MOST impressive archaeological sites in the world were produced by societies that Morton Fried would describe as ranked or stratified and Elman Service would describe as chiefdoms. After reading this chapter, you should understand:

▶ The development of Stonehenge and the social and economic context surrounding the construction of this monument.

▶ The evidence for the function and political organization of Pueblo Bonito and Cahokia.

▶ The current theories of the organization of the society of Great Zimbabwe.

Stonehenge from above.

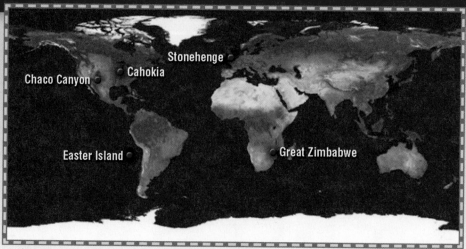

Easter Island is a speck of land thousands of miles from any other inhabited island. The monumental stone heads known as Moai that dot the island embody the enigma which is at the heart of this chapter. Easter Island has never had large cities or even large populations. The island has no particular material wealth, and its inhabitants were not in contact with any of its neighbors until European contact in 1722. So how—and perhaps more importantly, why—did the people of Easter Island construct these massive monuments? What motivated them to quarry the rock laboriously and then drag the massive stones across the island, where they were set up on elaborate platforms? Archaeological research on Easter Island has gone a long way towards providing an answer to these questions. Competing leaders erected the Moai during periods of prosperity. Competition between chiefs fueled a cycle of construction of monuments on the island. Some archaeologists argue that in the fragile island ecology of Easter Island this competitive cycle had disastrous consequences, resulting in deforestation and the decimation of resources (Flenley and Bahn 2003). During the subsequent period of ecological distress, the construction of Moai ceased and appears to have been replaced by increased levels of violence.

Societies that have developed a degree of political complexity, but lack a fully developed state bureaucracy, often produce archaeological sites that strike us as enigmatic or even mysterious. These sites are frequently characterized by elaborate and well-planned construction, yet yield little evidence of a ruling elite. In this chapter, we examine the archaeological record of Stonehenge, Chaco Canyon, Cahokia, and Great Zimbabwe. All of these sites are the ruins of structures built by societies that Fried would define as ranked or stratified and Service would describe as chiefdoms. None produce evidence of the centralized bureaucracy that characterizes the state. We explore these spectacular sites in order to gain insight into the social life of prestate complex societies.

**P**artly finished Moai statues on Easter Island.

| thousands of years ago | SITES | PHASES |
|---|---|---|
| 5 | | Phase 1—Late Neolithic |
| | STONEHENGE | Phase 2—Late Neolithic |
| | | Phase 3—Early Bronze Age |
| 4 | | |
| 3 | | |
| 2 | | |
| 1 | PUEBLO BONITO / CAHOKIA / GREAT ZIMBABWE | |
| Present | | |

## 10.1 STONEHENGE

**Stonehenge,** a ring of massive standing stones on the Salisbury Plain in southern England, has been the subject of contemplation and wonder for centuries. William Wordsworth wrote about the site in a poem:

> Pile of Stone-henge! so proud to hint yet keep
> Thy secrets, thou that lov'st to stand and hear
> The Plain resounding to the whirlwind's sweep,
> Inmate of lonesome Nature's endless year;

The construction of Stonehenge has been variously attributed to Romans, Druids, Danes, and Greeks (Castleden 1993). For some, Stonehenge is the product of mystical forces or "earth mysteries" (Chippindale et al. 1999). Archaeological research has demonstrated that Stonehenge is not a single monument, but rather the site of a sequence of monuments built over a period of more than one thousand years. Research on the region surrounding Stonehenge has documented an entire landscape upon which monuments were constructed. As a result, Stonehenge can now be grounded within a long process of development and within a broad regional context. Still, the wealth of archaeological research at Stonehenge and in the surrounding region has not dispelled all the enigmas surrounding the site. Understanding the social and economic organization of the people who built Stonehenge still poses significant challenges.

▶ **Stonehenge** is a ring of massive standing stones on the Salisbury Plain, England, that was constructed beginning in the Early Neolithic and ending in the Early Bronze Age.

## The Development of Stonehenge

Archaeological research at Stonehenge has demonstrated that the site developed through a series of stages beginning in the Late Neolithic (5,000 years ago) and ending in the Early Bronze Age (3,500 years ago) (Souden 1997, Cleal et al. 1995). Understanding Stonehenge requires an understanding of the long process through which the site came into being.

Sketch of Stonehenge by the British artist John Constable. How did Constable choose to represent this monument?

### Phase 1: The Earthwork Circle.

The first monument at Stonehenge was a round ditch excavated to enclose an area 110 meters in diameter. Slight embankments were built up on both the inside and outside of the ditch. Wooden posts were erected in a ring of holes known as the Aubrey holes, which were dug along the inside of the ditch. Animal bones, including a cattle jaw and ox skull dating to Phase 1, were found buried in the ditch. Phase 1 dates to the Late Neolithic, roughly 5,000 years ago.

### Phase 2: Burials and a Timber Structure.

During Phase 2, the ditch and the Aubrey holes were largely filled in. Human remains dating to Phase 2, including remains from cremated burials, are found in the fill of both the ditch and some of the Aubrey holes. A structure of standing timber posts was constructed near the center of the monument. Phase 2 dates to the Late Neolithic, between 5,000 and 4,500 years ago.

### Phase 3: Stone Monument.

The monumental standing stones that are the most impressive aspect of Stonehenge were erected in a series of six subphases during the Early Bronze Age between 4,500 and 3,500 years ago.

**Phase 3a: The Bluestones.** The **bluestones** were set up in either a circular or semicircular formation at the center of the monument in a series of holes known as the Q and R holes. The bluestones, which stand between 2 and 2.5 meters in height, are not the most impressive stones at Stonehenge, but they do raise many questions. The geological source of these stones is not in the vicinity of Stonehenge, but rather lies in the Preseli Mountains in Wales, over 240 kilometers away. Moving these stones from Wales to the Salisbury Plains would have required an enormous effort.

> The **bluestones** are a ring of standing stones at the center of Stonehenge. The source of the stones is over 240 kilometers from Stonehenge.

# The major stages in the development of Stonehenge

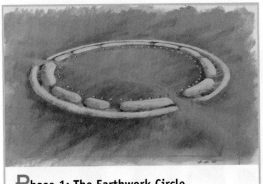

Phase 1: The Earthwork Circle.

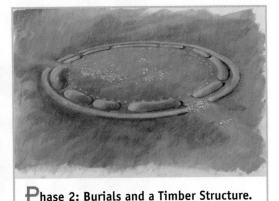

Phase 2: Burials and a Timber Structure.

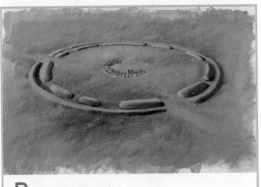

Phase 3a: The Bluestones.

Phase 3b: Sarsen Circle and Trilithons.

Some archaeologists have argued that the bluestones had been transported to southern England by glacial activity during the Pleistocene. However, it remains possible that the stones were transported from Wales as part of the construction of Stonehenge. Why these particular stones would have had a value to justify such an effort remains an open question.

**Phase 3b: Sarsen Circle and Trilithons.** In this phase, a circle of massive sandstone blocks was set up around the perimeter of the site. The blocks were of sarsen stone, a very hard sandstone found 30 kilometers from Stonehenge. In a staggering triumph of engineering, the circle of sarsen stones was capped by lintels made of solid blocks. These lintels and their supporting stones were fit together with carved joints. Inside the Sarsen Circle, another set of sarsen monoliths known as the trilithons were set up in a horseshoe arrangement oriented towards the northeast. The trilithons were set up in five pairs, each capped by a lintel. The trilithons are truly massive, reaching a maximum height of 7 meters.

**Phases 3c–f: Rearranging Bluestones and Digging Holes.** The construction of the Sarsen Circle and the trilithons was the most intensive phase of construction at Stonehenge. There followed a series of three phases in which the bluestones were reorganized and a series of holes was dug in concentric circles around the site. In the final configuration, a set of bluestones was set up in the shape of a horseshoe on the inside of the trilithons and another set of bluestones was erected between the trilithons and the Sarsen Circle. Two concentric rings of pits were excavated around the outside of the monument.

The bluestones are the smaller standing stones in the inner circle surrounded by the far larger Sarsen Stones.

## A Constructed Landscape

Stonehenge was not an isolated monument. Numerous different types of earthen mounds and enclosures were built on the Salisbury Plain during the Late Neolithic and the Early Bronze Age. One of the most impressive features is the Avenue, a

Satellite photo of the area surrounding Stonehenge. Large earthen features including the Avenue and the Cursus are clearly visible in this image.

The Cursus

The Avenue

Stonehenge

www.ablongman.com/chazan

path bounded by ditches and embankments that runs for over a kilometer between the River Avon and Stonehenge. Although the function of the Avenue appears to have been to guide people towards Stonehenge, other features on the site have a less clear function. The most massive of these is the Cursus, a slightly raised earthen platform that runs for almost 3 kilometers in an east–west alignment. The entire landscape of the Salisbury Plain was sculpted by these massive earthen constructions (Thomas 1991).

## The Context of Stonehenge

Stone monuments constructed during the Late Neolithic and Early Bronze Age are found in many parts of Western Europe. However, even within this context, Stonehenge stands out as a marvel of engineering and as a true enigma. What was the

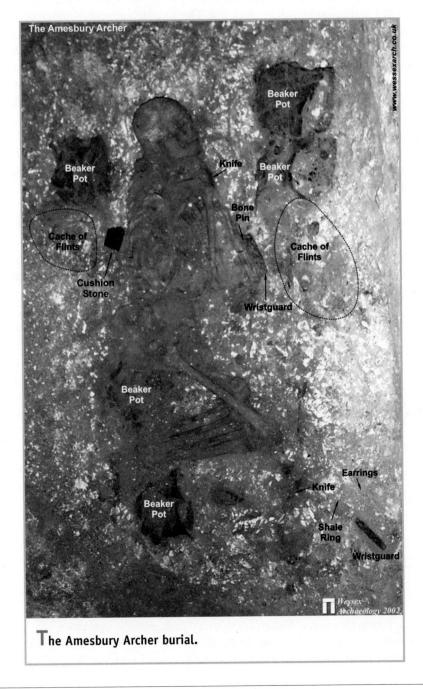

The Amesbury Archer burial.

function of this monument within the lives of the people who built it? Many have argued that the monument is aligned to allow for the prediction of celestial events. It seems beyond question that it was a construction of religious significance. Almost no domestic remains have been discovered during excavations at the site. Moreover, in the region as a whole, domestic remains are limited to small pits with artifacts and refuse and the faint traces of houses built of wooden posts (Hunter and Ralston 1999). The people who built Stonehenge were agriculturalists who raised crops of wheat and grazed cattle. There is botanical evidence that in the Late Neolithic the Salisbury Plain became an increasingly open landscape used mostly for grazing. Recent excavations at the site of Durrington Wall located 2.8 kilometers from Stonehenge have made the exciting discovery of a series of houses that appear to be part of a village dating to the Late Neolithic (Pearson et al. 2005).

The construction of Stonehenge required the ability to organize a large group of people for work beyond their basic subsistence activities. This labor force had to be coordinated and guided by clear planning. The accomplishment of transporting and erecting the 7-meter-high trilithons and then capping them with a lintel stone is quite impressive. These feats of engineering and organization were achieved by people who did not live under a state bureaucracy. The leaders who directed these projects are invisible to us today. Their authority would have rested not on an absolute control based on force, but rather on the "soft power" that comes from the redistribution of surplus goods and the status that comes from holding an inherited position in society.

Colin Renfrew (1984) has argued that Stonehenge was built by people living in chiefdoms and that the increasing scale of the monument over time reflects the increasing size of territories controlled by a single chief. Renfrew recognizes that a critical weakness in his argument is the absence of "direct evidence among the artifacts found for personal ranking, as indicated by distinctive dress, ornament, or possessions" (Renfrew 1984: 243). However, in 2002, archaeologists working on a rescue excavation before a housing development was to be constructed found a pair of burials that fulfill Renfrew's prediction: The people who built Stonehenge did include elites marked by ornaments and possessions.

The Amesbury Archer, as the main burial came to be known, was found 3 miles from Stonehenge. He lived during the Early Bronze Age, corresponding to Phase 3 in the construction of Stonehenge. Objects found with the burial include two slate wrist guards, a bone pin, two copper knives, five pots, boar tusks, a cache of flints, arrowheads, a shale belt ring, and two gold earrings. No other burial with a similar wealth of grave goods has been discovered from this period. Nearby, a second burial was found of an individual with more modest grave goods that include gold earrings. The goods found with these two burials are precisely the kind of display items that Renfrew would expect to find in the burials of the leaders of a chiefdom. However, the Amesbury Archer also raises questions. Isotopic analyses of the skeletal remains indicate that the Archer grew up, not in the vicinity of Stonehenge, but rather far off in the Alps. Why did he move such a long distance? How did he gain status in a society he was not born into?

## What Did Stonehenge Mean?

It might seem that Stonehenge must have an explanation—that Stonehenge is a mystery waiting to be unlocked. There is no lack of explanations for the monument; they range from the construction of a "prehistoric observatory" to fantasies of a Druid sanctuary (Chippendale et al. 1990). Certainly, there is some truth behind these ideas: Stonehenge must have had a ritual function, and many aspects of the arrangement of the standing stones correspond to celestial orientations. However, Barbara Bender (1992) has criticized such explanations as attempts to "freeze" the past that lack a sense of an ongoing historical process. Bender's critique is particularly relevant to the site of Stonehenge, a monument that came into being as part of a process lasting over 1,500 years. As Julian Thomas argues, "Stonehenge never had *a* meaning" (Thomas 1996:62). Over more than 80 generations, Stonehenge became the landscape within which people lived their lives. The essential explanation of Stonehenge is that it does not have a single explanation; rather, it must be understood as the long-term unfolding of a society's relationship to the landscape.

But can we say *anything* about what Stonehenge meant? Reading the meaning of ancient monuments is treacherous terrain, as we are essentially trying to gain insight into prehistoric beliefs. Ian Hodder has placed Stonehenge within the broader context of monument building in the Neolithic of Western Europe. Hodder sees the emergence of large monuments as part of the expansion of the household to include a larger group of people spread over a wider area. For Hodder (1990), Stonehenge is one of many monuments that re-create the household at the level of a regional landscape. Bender (1992) takes a somewhat different approach, seeing the scale of construction at Stonehenge and the surrounding area producing a fusion of nature and culture. Over the generations, the constructions at Stonehenge became elements of a developing landscape, where the lines between nature and culture were blurred. One intriguing idea is that, for Stonehenge and the surrounding earthworks, such as the Avenue, it was the act of producing and experiencing the landscape that was as important as the enduring monument. Bender points to the digging and refilling of holes and the way the earthworks would have channeled peoples' movements. She also suggests that the shaping of the landscape might have expressed and strengthened conceptions of gender and power in society.

## Summing Up the Evidence

Archaeological research has demonstrated that Stonehenge came into being over a period of more than 1,500 years. It is therefore very unlikely that Stonehenge has a single meaning or explanation. The cultural context of Stonehenge remains poorly understood, as there are no large preserved settlements in the vicinity. The source of power that underlies the construction of Stonehenge did not rest on control based on force, as is often found in state societies. The Amesbury Archer provides the first direct evidence of the elites of Early Bronze Age society in the region. The writing of Bender and others on the meaning of Stonehenge offers a strong reminder that Stonehenge might have been not only the product of the ability of a leader to organize large-scale labor, but also one of the leader's sources of power.

 # 10.2 PUEBLO BONITO, CHACO CANYON

Beginning around A.D. 700, there is evidence for an increased level of social complexity across the American southwest (Plog 1997). In the arid deserts of southern Arizona, sites with platform mounds and ball courts are attributed to the Hohokam culture. The largest Hohokam site is Snaketown, located in the Phoenix Basin. At the height of its development in the eleventh century,

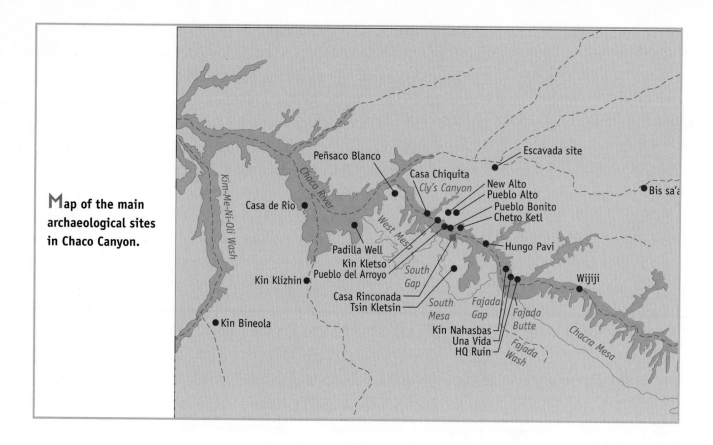

**M**ap of the main archaeological sites in Chaco Canyon.

Snaketown had a population of 300–600 people and two large ball courts. The Hohokam developed large-scale irrigation projects to pull water from the Salt and Gila Rivers to agricultural fields.

The ancestral Puebloan cultures flourished in what is now the Four Corners region, where Arizona, New Mexico, Utah, and Colorado meet. Beginning around A.D. 800, **Chaco Canyon** in the San Juan Basin of New Mexico became the center of a regional settlement network and the site of the construction of spectacular multi-storied structures known as **Great Houses.** Understanding the organization of Chaco society and the function of the Chaco Great Houses is one of the most exciting challenges in the prehistory of North America.

The current environment of Chaco Canyon "does not exactly correspond to most people's concept of Eden" (Sebastian 1992: 9). Chaco Canyon covers an area 30 kilometers long and between 0.5 and 1 kilometer wide. The canyon is between 90 and 180 meters deep. Rainfall, vegetation, surface water, and game are all sparse. The inhabitants of Chaco Canyon responded to this challenging environment by developing dams and canals to control runoff water from torrential summer rains.

> Beginning around A.D. 800, **Chaco Canyon,** New Mexico became the center of a regional settlement network and the site of the construction of large multi-storied structures known as **Great Houses.**

## The Development of Pueblo Bonito

> **Pueblo Bonito,** a massive 650-room complex, is the largest Great House in Chaco Canyon.
>
> **Kivas** are subterranean circular chambers.

**Pueblo Bonito,** a massive multistory complex of 650 rooms covering almost 2 acres, is the largest Great House in Chaco Canyon. The rooms are arranged in a semicircle enclosing a central plaza, which is divided roughly in half by a wall running in a north–south direction. The rooms that make up the Great House include a large number of subterranean circular chambers known as **kivas,** which are known from the special religious significance they have in modern Pueblo villages.

# DISCOVERING THE PAST

## Why Do I "Do" Archaeology?
### by Joe Watkins, University of New Mexico

Many of you who read this book will wonder how an American Indian became an archaeologist. Initially, I wanted to be a paleontologist and work in China with Roy Chapman Andrews, digging up dinosaur egg nests. Then, one fateful day, I was walking with my Choctaw grandmother. I was ten years old, and I found a projectile point about 6,000 years old made of milky quartz. My grandmother spoke at the most a hundred words of English, and I spoke fewer than a hundred words of Choctaw. I showed the projectile point to my grandmother, and she told me, as my cousin translated, that it represented the unwritten history of the people who had lived there before the Choctaw were moved into Oklahoma. She said that, even though it wasn't our history, it was important that we save that unwritten history for the sake of our ancestors and for the descendants of the people who would come after us.

From then on, I was interested in trying to find ways of connecting the people from the past to those alive today. Archaeology has allowed me not only to maintain that connection between the present and the past, but also has cemented my connections with the generations who lived in southeastern Oklahoma thousands of years ago.

I have been involved in all facets that archaeology offers. I have excavated archaeological sites in Europe, Oklahoma, Texas, and New Mexico; I have worked for the federal government to record sites in danger of being lost due to erosion and neglect; and I have trudged ahead of a bulldozer, building fire lines during a forest fire in the Black Hills of South Dakota.

I currently teach at the University of New Mexico, and now I'm more interested in looking at how archaeology affects indigenous populations: the descendants of the people who produced the locations archaeologists excavate and study. My research takes me to far-off places such as Australia, New Zealand, and Sweden and to some not so far-off places like Taos, Oklahoma, and Georgia. These are places where the people who have ties to the archaeological past are not necessarily the people who control the land where those sites are located.

There are often conflicts between archaeologists and the descendants of the people archaeologists study. Many descendant populations are concerned about archaeologists digging up the graves of people of the past and placing them in museums or in storage. Archaeologists are not as likely to dig up peoples' graves as they were in the past, and chief among the reasons for this are that people have complained about such actions and archaeologists are now more aware of the ways their study of past peoples affects existing populations.

I do archaeology because it helps me connect with the people who have lived in the past and with those who live today. It helps me understand the ways that we are tied to the people who have lived and died throughout written and unwritten history. Archaeology has given me a depth of experience that mere written history cannot, and it has given me the desire not only to learn more, but to share what I have learned with those around me. I am an archaeologist, and I am an American Indian. While there might still be times when I am in conflict about being both, there is rarely a time when I am disappointed that I have chosen this field. And when I do question why I became an archaeologist, I remember my grandmother's words.

◀ Professor Joe Watkins in the field.

Archaeological research at Pueblo Bonito has demonstrated that the massive Great House was built up over a period of over two hundred years in "complex stages of use and deterioration" (Windes 2003). The excellent preservation of wooden beams in the dry environment of Chaco Canyon has allowed archaeologists to develop a tight chronology based on dendrochronology, or tree ring dating. The construction of Pueblo Bonito began around 1,200 years ago (A.D. 800), and the complex reached its current extent between 1,000 and 900 years ago (A.D. 1000–A.D. 1100). Subsequently, there was a reduction in the extent of occupation of the site, and building activity slowed before the site was abandoned about 750 years ago (A.D. 1,250).

## The Function of Pueblo Bonito

Archaeologists working at Pueblo Bonito have struggled to determine the function of this impressive site (Neitzel 2003). The construction of a complex of hundreds of rooms suggests that the site was a very large settlement, perhaps occupied by an elite group in Chaco society. Population estimates for the site have ranged as high as 1,200 people. However, excavations at the site have uncovered a surprisingly small number of fireplaces and few remains of domestic activities. These observations, along with the layout of the site and the large number of kivas, have led some to argue that Pueblo Bonito was essentially a ceremonial center and that it rarely had a population of much more than 100 people.

Two large mounds of cultural debris and earth reaching 6 meters in height and located in front of the plaza are an important source of information on the function of Pueblo Bonito (Cameron 2002). Similar mounds, known as berms, are a common

**A**erial view of Pueblo Bonito. This photograph shows the semi-circular plan of the site with a central plaza divided by a wall and flanked by rooms and circular kivas.

Reconstruction of Pueblo Bonito drawn in 1878.

feature of Great Houses from the Chaco period. A unique feature of Pueblo Bonito berms is that they were plastered, so they could have served as a platform for ceremonies. Excavation of the berms at Pueblo Bonito and other sites has produced massive quantities of ceramics, suggesting that they are the refuse of ceremonial feasting rather than of normal daily activities.

The function of Pueblo Bonito might have changed over time (Neitzel 2003). The initial occupation of the site conforms to the size and organization of a residential site. It is possible that between A.D. 800 and A.D. 1000 the site was the residence of an elite group. With the expansion around A.D. 1000, the site shifted towards a greater focus on ceremonial function. Of course, it might have been that throughout the occupation Pueblo Bonito served as both an elite residence and a ceremonial center. What appears to have occurred at A.D. 1000 is that the balance of activity shifted towards the ceremonial aspect. The connection between an elite residence and a ceremonial center indicates that the power of the elite might have been partly the result of their special role in religious ceremonies.

## Evidence for Elites

The sheer scale of the construction at Pueblo Bonito suggests some form of political leadership. To get a sense of the size of the undertaking, it is necessary only to consider that over 200,000 trees were used to make the floors and roofs of the Great House. One estimate places the amount of labor involved in the construction of the Great House at 800,000 person hours (Metcalf 2003).

Archaeological evidence for social inequality at Pueblo Bonito is restricted largely to the finds made in two small rooms at the north end of the site. Although a number of rooms at Pueblo Bonito included burial remains, the burials at Room 33 are unique (Akins 2003). In this room, the disarticulated remains of sixteen individuals were found above a wooden plank floor. Below the plank floor, two

**CHAPTER 10: Complexity without the State** 305

Jet stone frog with inlaid turquoise from Room 38 at Pueblo Bonito.

male burials were found together with lavish offerings. Altogether, the burial offerings found in Room 33 included over 50,000 pieces of turquoise, including beads, pendants, and mosaic inlays. Such a concentration of turquoise is unknown in any contemporary context. Not far from Room 33, a rich deposit of beads, pendants, and mosaic pieces made of jet, a hard black stone, were found in Room 38. Although no burials were found in that room, other unusual finds included fourteen macaw skeletons. These colorful birds are native to the Gulf Coast of Mexico.

The discoveries in Rooms 33 and 38 at Pueblo Bonito make it clear that wealth was not equally distributed among members of society. It is interesting that turquoise, jet, and macaws were traded over very long distances. The concentration of large quantities of these objects in two rooms suggests that the elite of Pueblo Bonito society exercised some degree of control over trade networks.

## The Chaco Network

The large number of trade items found in Rooms 33 and 38 at Pueblo Bonito indicate that the site was part of a larger network. Within Chaco Canyon, archaeologists have identified a system of roads connecting the Great Houses.

Research using satellite imagery has provided clear evidence that the system of roads stretched far beyond the limits of Chaco Canyon (www.ghcc.msfc.nasa .gov/archeology/chaco.html). A series of photographs taken by NASA with a thermal infrared multispectral scanner (TIMS) detected over two hundred miles of roads radiating out from Chaco Canyon.

The road system links Chaco Canyon with sites covering a large part of what is today the Four Corners region of the U.S. Southwest. Sites in this region tend to share similarities in architecture which, together with the road system, suggest that they were linked into what has been called the **Chacoan Network.** Although Chaco was clearly the center of this network, there is no evidence that the people living at Chaco had control over the outlying settlements. However, more than just high-status trade items such as turquoise, jet, and macaws flowed into the Great Houses at Chaco. It has long been recognized that much of the pottery recovered at Chaco Canyon was not produced locally, but rather was brought to the site from outlying areas in the Chacoan Network. A study of maize kernels suggests that some of the food consumed at Chaco Canyon was not grown locally. By looking at the isotopes of the element strontium in maize kernels found at Chaco, researchers have shown that at least some of the maize was grown in areas over 80 kilometers from Chaco Canyon (Benson et al. 2003).

The riddle of the Chacoan Network is what made it run. What compelled people to bring food and pottery into Chaco Canyon from surrounding areas? What gave the people living at Pueblo Bonito the ability to control large quantities of high-status trade items? One possibility is that these items were brought to Chaco Canyon as taxes collected by a central authority backed by the threat of force. The problem with such a scenario is that there is no evidence of such an authority or even of very large populations in Chaco Canyon. Another possibility is that the power of the people living at Chaco Canyon was the result of the centrality of the canyon in the ritual and religious life of the people living within the greater Chacoan Network. The flow of goods into Chaco Canyon might have been the result of cycles of ceremonial feasting in which large groups of people congregated in the canyon for very brief periods, bringing from their homes food

The **Chacoan Network** links Chaco Canyon with sites in the surrounding region through a system of roads.

# TOOLBOX:
## Remote Sensing

Methods of remote sensing, including aerial and satellite photography, play a critical role both in discovering sites and in orienting exploration. Satellite imagery can cover large geographical regions. In recent years, methods of satellite imagery have come to rely heavily on sensors that detect features invisible to the human eye. Radar imaging from satellites is able to detect large-scale buried features. In research in the eastern Sahara desert, archaeologists have used space shuttle radar images to trace the remains of buried river systems associated with Paleolithic sites. Some sensors can detect minute variations in the surface temperature of the earth that provide an index of the characteristics of the soil. In Chaco Canyon, New Mexico, a thermal infrared multispectral scanner (TIMS) flown by NASA was used to detect a road system dated to between A.D. 900–A.D. 1000 (http://www.ghcc.msfc.nasa.gov/archeology/chaco.html).

Photography from aircraft or balloons can reveal buried features, raised mounds, or wall systems. Most aerial photographs used by archaeologists are taken at an oblique angle to further enhance the visibility of features. Aerial photographs are particularly useful in giving a view of an area that would be too large to excavate. Photographs of ancient cities often reveal the complete urban plan, including roads and fortification walls. Aerial photographs have even been successful in making the outlines of ancient field systems visible to archaeologists. In a small number of cases, aerial photography has revealed construction on a scale

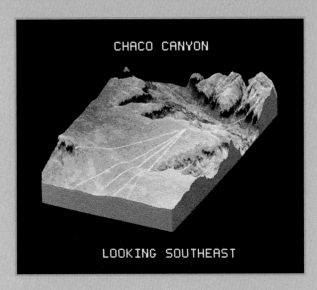

▲ Photograph taken by NASA using a Thermal Infrared Multispectral Scanner (TIMS) showing roads radiating out from Chaco Canyon.

that is too large to be seen from the ground. The most spectacular of these are the Nazca lines in Peru, which consist of representations of animals made by clearing paths on the desert floor. The form of these alignments is visible only from the air.

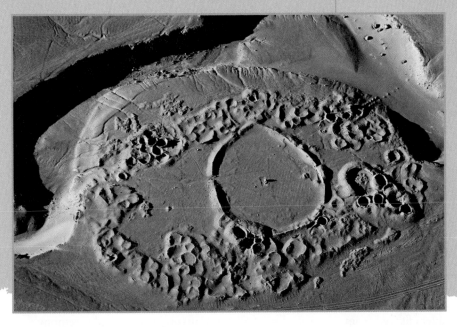

◀ Aerial photograph of Guatacondo in the Atacama Desert of Chile, second-fifth century AD. Notice how structures that have not been excavated are visible in this photograph.

and utensils that were then discarded in the refuse piles such as the berm in front of Pueblo Bonito.

## The Rise and Fall of Chaco Canyon

The location of the elaborate structures of Pueblo Bonito in the highly arid environment of Chaco Canyon has led many archaeologists to look for a connection between fluctuations in climate and the rise and fall of the Great Houses. The relationship between climate and the end of the occupation of the Great Houses is clear and direct (Sebastian 1992). A devastating drought beginning in A.D. 1130 made continuing intensive occupation untenable. As a result, construction of the Great Houses came to an end and occupation was abandoned. By the time the drought had ended, the Chacoan Network had collapsed and Chaco Canyon never regained its central role.

The link between climate and the rise of Chaco Canyon is more complex. A number of archaeologists have suggested that the Chacoan Network developed as a means of buffering risk in an uncertain environment. The idea is that, given the low rainfall in the region around Chaco Canyon, there was always a risk of local crop failure. If each group lived in isolation, then crop failure would lead to starvation. However, if groups were linked through a network in which exchange regularly took place, any group that experienced a failure of its crops could trade for food with other members of the network whose crops had not failed. The existence of a network for the redistribution of food and other goods thus acted as a buffer between the uncertain environment and local communities.

Lynne Sebastian (1992) has argued that this explanation for the rise of Chaco Canyon is wrong. She points out that the Great Houses were built during a period with relatively high rainfall. Why would a buffering mechanism be developed when climate pressures were reduced? As an alternative, Sebastian suggests that, during the periods beginning around A.D. 1000, there was an increase in annual rainfall, which allowed for an agricultural surplus. The accumulation of surpluses in the hands of local elites led to a cycle of competition. The elaborate construction at Pueblo Bonito and the concentration of rare trade goods such as turquoise and jet are expressions of this competition. For Sebastian, it is the existence of an agricultural surplus, rather than the threat of agricultural failure, that led to the spectacular developments in Chaco Canyon.

## Summing Up the Evidence

The Great Houses of Chaco Canyon were the hub of an extensive Chacoan Network. Whether this network was a buffer against stress or the result of surplus production remains the subject of debate. Excavations at Pueblo Bonito have demonstrated that there was a considerable concentration of wealth in the hands of an elite. This wealth included trade goods drawn from a very large area. At the same time, excavations indicate that the Great Houses were not densely settled towns, but rather ceremonial centers that were probably permanently occupied only by a small group. Given the effort expended in the construction of the Great Houses, the concentration of wealth in burials, and the evidence for the influx of goods to Chaco Canyon from the Chacoan Network, it is clear that the leaders of this society were extremely powerful. However, there is no evidence that their power rested on the monopolization of force. One possibility is that the power of the leaders flowed from the centrality of Chaco Canyon in ritual and ceremony.

# TOOLBOX:
## Dendrochronology

Almost all archaeological dating methods provide a date with a margin of error. Dendrochronology, tree ring dating, is the only method capable of absolute precision. Dendrochronologists use the annual rings laid down by trees as they grow to build a clock that today reaches back ten thousand years. How does this clock work? The principles are simple. Each year, as trees grow, they add on a single ring of new wood immediately under the bark. These annual rings are clearly visible in sections cut through a tree trunk. As the rings accumulate, they form a pattern that we can think of as the tree's fingerprint.

The ring pattern of a tree is a record of the fluctuating climatic conditions experienced as the tree grew. Within the same climatic region, trees of the same species experience similar growth conditions. This uniformity allows dendrochronologists to match up the ring patterns from different trees. Ultimately, by overlapping the ring patterns of trees stretching back in time, it is possible to build up a long-term chronology. The first tree used is a living tree, anchoring the chronology in the present. The beginning of the growth of this tree might overlap with a beam found in a historic house, allowing the chronology to be pushed back. This historic beam might be found to overlap with the ring pattern of a tree recovered from an ancient bog, pushing the chronology still further back in time. Once a chronology has been built up, any new piece of wood can be precisely dated by finding the closest match between its ring pattern and the fluctuating pattern found in the long-term chronology.

Dendrochronology has played a critical role in dating the prehistory of the U.S. Southwest. Dendrochronology has also provided the essential scale for calibrating radiocarbon dates. Although dendrochronology does achieve absolute precision, that does not mean that archaeologists do not need to be very careful in using the data from tree ring dating. The ring pattern of a tree can be fit into a long-term chronology to anchor the growth and death of a tree precisely in time. However, archaeologists need to be certain that the wood from the tree was used soon after its death. If, for example, wood was salvaged from an old building, the dates provided by dendrochronologists could be far older than the date of the archaeological occupation. As with all dating methods, knowledge of the context in which the sample is found is critical to the use of dendrochronology.

▲ Dendrochronologist measuring tree rings in the cross section of the trunk of a Douglas Fir.

REFERENCE: Baillie, M.G.L. (1995). *A Slice Through Time: Dendrochronology and Precision Dating.* London: Batsford.

# 10.3 CAHOKIA

Two hundred years ago, while traveling along the Mississippi River near what is now St. Louis, the explorer Henry Brackenridge encountered the great mound at **Cahokia** and was led to exclaim, "What a stupendous pile of earth!" (Brackenridge 1814) The principal mound at Cahokia is spectacular. **Monk's Mound,** as it has come to be known, rises over 30 meters in height in a series of four terraces, covers an area of more than 60,000 square meters, and contains over 600,000 cubic meters of earth.

Exploring the area around Cahokia, Brackenridge found that the "great number of mounds, and the astonishing quantity of human bones . . . announce that this valley was at one period, filled with habitations and villages" (Brackenridge 1814).

▶ **Cahokia** is a large settlement dating to the Mississippian Period and located just outside of St. Louis.

▶ **Monk's Mound,** a massive earthen pyramid, occupies the core of the ancient settlement of Cahokia.

**A**erial view looking from the back of Monk's Mound, Cahokia, across the Great Plaza.

The site at Cahokia is the largest-known settlement of the Mississippian Period in eastern North America (A.D. 1000–A.D. 1400). Archaeologists now understand Monk's Mound to be the center of an enormous site covering roughly 4.5 kilometers. It takes about an hour to walk across the site at a very brisk pace.

## The Layout of the Site

Cahokia is located in the floodplain of the Mississippi River near St. Louis. This area, known as the American Bottom, is rich in meandering stream channels, wetlands, and swamps. Monk's Mound is located to the south of Cahokia Creek, forming the northern limit of a large flat area known as the **Plaza,** which was cleared and leveled to create an open area at the core of the site. Smaller mounds are found bounding the eastern, southern, and western edges of the Plaza. Both geophysical survey and excavation have demonstrated that a wooden wall known as a palisade surrounded the Plaza and mounds.

> Located just to the south of Monk's Mound is an artificially leveled area known as the **Plaza.**

The settlement at Cahokia consisted of a series of small clusters, with the Plaza and the mounds of "Downtown Cahokia" at the center. It is likely that swamps and wetlands broke up the landscape of the settlement. Unfortunately, due to the size of the site and the poor preservation of domestic structures, it is difficult to determine the density and distribution of houses at Cahokia. As a result, estimates of the population of Cahokia range anywhere from 4,000 to 40,000 (Milner 1998). Although Cahokia was a large population center, it is not clear that the term "city" or "metropolis" accurately describes the nature of the site. More likely, Cahokia was a series of dispersed living areas centered on the monumental core of Monk's Mound and the Plaza.

FIGURE 10.1

**Map of Cahokia.**

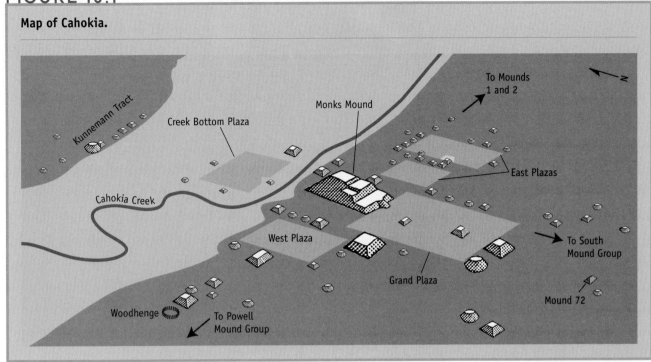

## Evidence of Inequality

Understanding the political organization of Cahokia poses an enormous challenge. Clearly, there was some mechanism in society that made it possible to construct a mound on a scale unparalleled anywhere else in eastern North America. Just as clearly, a large number of people, whether in the thousands or tens of thousands, lived at the site. For some archaeologists, Cahokia was a chiefdom on the verge of becoming a state (Young and Fowler 2000). From this perspective, the elite of Cahokia ruled not only over Cahokia itself, but also over the surrounding settlements in the American Bottom (Pauketat 2004). Others argue that the elite of Cahokia were simply the most powerful among many competing chiefdoms and that their power was limited.

The most vivid evidence of social inequality within Cahokia society comes from the excavation of **Mound 72,** located to the south of "Downtown Cahokia." Mound 72 is a relatively unimpressive mound, but what brought it to the attention of archaeologists is the fact that it is aligned directly with the western edge of Monk's Mound. Students excavating the mound were surprised to come across a cache of hundreds of complete arrowheads (Young and Fowler 2000). As they continued excavating, they found that the arrowheads were part of a spectacular burial complex. The central figure was a man laid face up on a bird-shaped platform made of over 20,000 cut shell beads. A number of other people were buried alongside this individual, together with a rich array of burial goods, including hundreds of arrowheads and polished granite discs. Other discoveries in Mound 72 suggest the possibility of victims killed to accompany the main burial. In one area, the bodies of four men were laid out with overlapping arms. All four skeletons were missing their heads and hands. In a nearby pit, the skeletons of over fifty young women were found. The discoveries made at Mound 72 show that wealth was concentrated in the hands of a small number of people within the community living at Cahokia. Twenty thousand shell beads and hundreds of arrowheads represent an enormous amount of skilled workmanship. The

> ▶ Excavation of **Mound 72** uncovered an individual buried on a bird-shaped platform made of shells, as well as mass burials of apparently sacrificial victims.

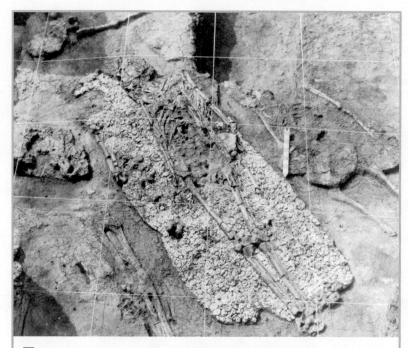

The main burial in Mound 72 at Cahokia laid out on a bed of 20,000 shell beads in the shape of a bird.

mass burials of young women and the series of headless and handless males buried raise the possibility that the elite of Cahokia had control not only over material wealth, but also over the lives of their subjects.

## Feasting

Excavations below Mound 51, located to the east of the Plaza, provide a different perspective on the social life of Cahokia that complements the dramatic discoveries from Mound 72 (Pauketat et al. 2002). Mound 51 was excavated in 1961 when it was in the process of being destroyed by residents of a nearby subdivision. Below the mound archaeologists found a well-stratified sequence rich in pottery, botanical remains, and faunal remains. This material is not ordinary residential debris, but rather the refuse from large-scale feasting that took place in the Plaza. The quantity of material found suggests that these feasting events were massive. The excavators have extrapolated the amount of material in the pit by multiplying the density of objects per cubic meter in the excavated unit by the estimated volume of the entire pit. They calculate that there were over 18,000 ceramic vessels, more than 5,000 deer, and over a half million tobacco seeds within one stratigraphic zone (G).

The excavations below Mound 51 indicate that the Plaza at Cahokia was the site of massive feasting events. The number of people who could have fit within the palisades has been estimated at 30,000 (Dalan 2003). The Plaza appears to have served as the site of communal feasts involving people from Cahokia and the surrounding region. If so, then the power of the elite of Cahokia might have stemmed from their ability to organize large numbers of people through feasting events rather than through a bureaucracy exercising the threat of force. One interesting possibility is that the Plaza served as the setting for sporting events. The polished granite discs found in Mound 72 fit with ethnographic descriptions of a game known as chunkey played with discs that were rolled along a line and struck with thrown spears (Young and Fowler 2000).

Two discoveries in the Mound 51 excavations cast light on the religious system of Cahokia. Among the bird bones, those of swan and prairie chickens are most common. Both species are rarely found in excavations of sites contemporary with Cahokia. The burial of the main individual in Mound 72 on a shell platform in the shape of a bird also suggests that birds had particular significance in Cahokia society. This interpretation is supported by the discovery during excavations in Monk's Mound of a small sandstone plaque showing a birdman.

The excavations in Mound 51 also produced a significant amount of red cedar branchlets and cypress wood chips. It has been suggested that both of these types of wood had ritual significance. Large poles of red cedar, including an enigmatic ring of poles known as "woodhenge," were used at Cahokia in special buildings.

## Summing Up the Evidence

The elites of Cahokia were able to mobilize large numbers of people. The bulk of Monk's Mound and the expanse of the Plaza are evidence of large-scale work parties. The burial goods in Mound 72 are the product of a great deal of effort by skilled artisans. The remains found below Mound 51 indicate that there were feasting events in the Plaza involving thousands or even tens of thousands of people. The political force that made this organization possible remains unclear. Was it the "soft power" of the chief, or did the elites of Cahokia also have recourse to the controlled use of force that characterizes the state? Many archaeologists see Cahokia as a society on the verge of forming a state. Unlike the societies that built Stonehenge and Pueblo Bonito, the people who built the monuments at Cahokia lived in a large, densely populated center. The sacrificial victims in Mound 72 also seem to indicate a degree of power that goes a long way towards the kind of authority found in the hands of the rulers of state societies.

**T**ablet of the 'birdman' found at Cahokia.

# 10.4 GREAT ZIMBABWE

When early European explorers visited **Great Zimbabwe,** they were convinced that they had found the palace of the Queen of Sheba. It has taken decades of archaeological research to firmly discredit such fantasies that "sustain a 'colonial' interest in denying the local people a claim in their history" (Pikirayi 2001: 24). Great Zimbabwe is now understood as evidence of local development of political complexity in southeast Africa during the period between A.D. 1300 and A.D. 1450.

> ▶ **Great Zimbabwe** is a large settlement located in modern Zimbabwe built between A.D. 1300 and A.D. 1400 that includes the remains of impressive stone enclosures.

## Chavín de Huántar: The Beginnings of Social Complexity in the Andes
### by John W. Rick, Stanford University

I fell in love with archaeology at the age of six, while accompanying my parents on a year-long plant collecting trip to Peru. Staring into the face of a 1500-year-old mummy we happened upon on the dry desert coast fired my imagination, and now, 50 years later, I am an archaeologist in the Department of Anthropological Sciences at Stanford University. I began my Peruvian work by excavating 14,000-foot-altitude cave sites for 15

terns of leadership develop, and how did people come to accept the idea of priest-leaders who could impose their will, demanding resources and undertaking massive temple projects? My project at Chavín attempts to connect the unusual features of the site with the rituals and other activities that early cult leaders used to convince converts that their emerging authority was not only legitimate, but inevitable. Ceremonies involving the reflection of sunlight on to idol-like sculptures deep in the temples, the use of psychoactive drugs, and the extensive manipulation of loud, imposing sounds in closed architectural space argue that the temples created a new world for inductees in which the priests' connection to strong natural powers would have been clear.

◀ Excavations in Chavín's Circular Plaza in 2004. Peruvian and U.S. students, together with local workers are excavating post-Chavín structures to reach the original Plaza floor. In the background are the cut stone engraved plaques showing jaguars and ritual personages, and a cut granite staircase.

years, but since 1995 I have been working at the World Heritage site of Chavín de Huántar, a complex of monumental structures—the ruins of some of the world's most fascinating temples.

Chavín de Huántar consists of roughly 3,000-year-old major temple platforms, decorated with strange rock sculptures, and containing many labyrinth-like underground passages. The site is nestled in a very narrow valley in the north-central Andes Mountains of Peru, close to some of the highest snowcapped peaks of South America. Chavín is intriguing to me because it comes early in the process of the development of Andean political authority, which culminates 2,500 years later in the incredibly powerful Inca state. Not long before Chavín's time, most Andean people were living in independent, egalitarian groups, so how did the strong pat-

Nearly every year since 1995 our research team has converged on Chavín, now growing to more than 100 students, professional archaeologists, and specialists of many nationalities, along with numerous local workers and trained site conservators. The small town of Chavín at times seems overrun by our personnel, and we add a major economic input for the local economy. We take over one or more local hotels, and lead a modest but comfortable existence, sharing rooms but enjoying frequent hot water and electricity most of the time. My team shares my feeling of awe as every day we work in the shadow of ancient monumental mounds, finding evidence of the complex engineering and the religious activity that made Chavín so successful in converting the very idea of what was human social organization. The strategies that the priests of Chavín implanted in their architecture are still effective, and

we are constantly impressed by the remaining evidence of the grandeur that fueled ancient conversion. But another feeling we have is gratefulness for the privilege of working in such an important site, an opportunity generously given to us by modern Peruvian cultural authorities. We experience, as well, the life of a traditional little Andean town, and are usually in Chavín for their patron saint fiesta—a week-long blowout of music and celebration, dancing and sporting events. Some years we are even asked to put on a show in the town's plaza, ranging from break dancing to folk singing and even bagpipe-playing on one of the fiesta evenings.

But the most overwhelming experiences are the discoveries and realizations we have in our excavations and later analyses, as we find major clues to the very different world of ritual and belief that Chavín represents. A special moment came in 2001, when we excavated in one of the underground passages of Chavín, hoping against hope that the contents of this gallery might still be intact. In late July we revealed the first of 20 perfectly intact conch shell trumpets resting on the gallery floor, instruments still capable of emitting the same deafening but haunting bellow that ancient ears heard eons ago. These massive shells had been brought at least 1000 km from the ocean waters of Ecuador, far to the north.

Unbeknownst to us, on the same days we were recovering these beautifully engraved trumpets, Dr. Alejandro Toledo, President-elect of Peru was being inaugurated in Machu Picchu to the sound of identical conch shells. When we heard of this coincidence, we were amazed at the continuity of the role these instruments played and still play in establishing and reinforcing authorities of South America.

▶ (Left to right) David Chavez, Helene Bernier, Rosa and John Rick examine a highly decorated conch shell trumpet at the moment it is extracted from the Gallery of the Conches in 2001. These instruments can still produce the same deafening noise they did 2500 years ago.

## The Layout of the Site

Great Zimbabwe is located in the modern state of Zimbabwe. The region around Great Zimbabwe is agriculturally productive and capable of supporting large herds of cattle. Great Zimbabwe also sits within an area rich in mineral resources, particularly gold.

The architecture of Great Zimbabwe consists of large enclosures surrounded by walls built of carefully dressed granite blocks and standing up to 10 meters in height. Circular huts built of a mixture of clay and gravel known as **dhaka** were built inside the enclosures. Unfortunately, early excavations at the site focused on the search for evidence of the supposed foreign origin of the builders of Great Zimbabwe, resulting in the destruction of much of the archaeological sequence of the dhaka structures built within the enclosures. Careful excavations of some of the remaining deposits have shown that the structures were frequently rebuilt, leading to the rapid buildup of deposits that reach a depth of 5 meters.

Great Zimbabwe stretches across two hills and an intervening valley. The earliest occupation of the site was on the northern hill, known as the Hill Complex, which consists of a large enclosure on the western end and a series of smaller enclosures to the east. The western enclosure is roughly 50 meters across. It is estimated that there was space for around twenty dhaka huts within the enclosure. The eastern enclosure in the Hill Complex appears to have had a ritual function. A series of tall monolithic stones were found in this area, along with stone sculptures of birds.

When the site expanded, a new enclosure, known as the Great Enclosure, was built on the southern hill. The Great Enclosure is approximately 100 meters across and could have contained over forty dhaka huts. The most striking architectural feature of the Great Enclosure is a conical stone tower 5 meters in diameter and 10 meters in height. Probes into the tower proved that it is solid.

The enclosures running down the sides of the hills and into the valley are smaller and more modest in construction than in the Hill Complex and the Great

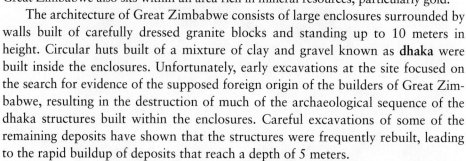

**Dhaka** is a mixture of clay and gravel that was used for building huts at Great Zimbabwe.

**V**iew of Great Zimbabwe from the Hill Complex across to the Great Enclosure.

Enclosure. It is estimated that they could each have contained about 10 dhaka huts.

## The Function of the Enclosures

There is no evidence that the walls of the enclosures at Great Zimbabwe served a defensive function. There is no source of water within the Hill Complex, and there is no sign that the walls were damaged in a conflict. The walls appear to have been built to screen the activities of elites from the view of people outside the enclosure. The enclosure walls on the Hill Complex and the Great Enclosure would have been visible from a distance. In some cases, the visibility of the enclosures was enhanced by mounting monolithic stones on the tops of the walls.

## The Organization of Great Zimbabwe Society

Many questions remain to be answered about Great Zimbabwe. As with Cahokia, there is considerable controversy over the size of the population at Great Zimbabwe. Low estimates put the population between 1,000 and 2,500 people, while others claim a population between 11,000 and 18,000.

The degree to which the elite of Great Zimbabwe had control over the rest of society is unclear, as is the extent to which Great Zimbabwe ruled over the surrounding region. More trade items, including glazed pottery from Iran and China and glass beads from Syria, are found at

The tower in the Great Enclosure at Great Zimbabwe. Note that during occupation the enclosure was filled with dhaka huts.

One of the bird sculptures from Great Zimbabwe.

Great Zimbabwe than at any other site in the region. These artifacts indicate that the elite of Great Zimbabwe played a critical role in the trade networks that stretched from the gold mines of southern Africa as far as China.

## Summing Up the Evidence

Great Zimbabwe emerged as an important node in a far-flung trade network that tied the gold mines of Africa with markets as distant as China. The elite of Great Zimbabwe lived within great enclosures that screened their lives from the rest of society and sent a visible message of their power and standing.

# 10.5 COMPARATIVE PERSPECTIVES

A comparison of Stonehenge, Pueblo Bonito, Cahokia, and Great Zimbabwe brings out the diversity of societies that Fried would define as ranked or stratified and Service would describe as chiefdoms. Stonehenge was built by people who lived in small, dispersed hamlets that have left little archaeological trace. Pueblo Bonito was at the core of a settlement network that stretched across a wide region of what is today the U.S. Southwest. Both Cahokia and Great Zimbabwe were large population centers inhabited by thousands, if not tens of thousands, of people.

These case studies also bring out the difficulty of understanding the political organization of nonstate complex societies. The prestige of the elites is clear in most cases. At Pueblo Bonito and Cahokia, the burial of individuals with large quantities of goods presents a vivid picture of the social inequality in these societies. At Great Zimbabwe, the height of the walls of the enclosures projects the power of the elite, as well as their separation from the rest of society. The monumental nature of these four sites also leaves no doubt about the ability of the elites to organize labor on a massive scale. However, the source of the power of the elites remains less clear. The critical question is the degree to which the elites had control based on the use of force or whether they managed society by other means, such as religious authority or the organization of ceremonies and feasting. The enigma of Stonehenge, Pueblo Bonito, Cahokia, and Great Zimbabwe is a question, not only of engineering, but also of social organization. One ultimately asks how and why a group of people came together to create these structures. In each case, this is a question that will continue to motivate archaeological research well into the future.

## CHAPTER SUMMARY

- Stonehenge is located on the Salisbury Plain in Southern England. This impressive monument was built up in stages beginning in the Late Neolithic and ending in the Early Bronze Age.
- Stonehenge was part of a landscape marked by many monumental constructions, including earthen mounds and enclosures.

- Stonehenge was built by people who practiced shifting agriculture without long-term year-round settlements.
- Beginning around A.D. 800, Chaco Canyon, New Mexico, became the center of a regional network and the site of the construction of multistoried structures known as Big Houses.

- Pueblo Bonito is the largest of the Chaco Canyon Big Houses, with 650 rooms covering almost 2 acres.
- Population estimates for Pueblo Bonito range between 100 and 1,200 people. It is possible that the site's primary function was as a ceremonial center and that only a small number of people lived there permanently.
- A small number of rooms in Pueblo Bonito have a concentration of high-prestige items.
- Chaco Canyon was connected by roads to a network of sites, known as the Chacoan Network, that covered a large part of the Four Corners region of what is today the U.S. Southwest.
- Cahokia is the largest-known settlement dating to the Mississippian Period (A.D. 1000– A.D. 1400) in eastern North America.

- Monk's Mound is a massive mound that lies at the core of Cahokia, overlooking a large open area known as the Plaza.
- Excavations at Cahokia have uncovered evidence of human sacrifice and material wealth in a burial mound and the remains of large-scale feasting near the Plaza.
- Great Zimbabwe was a large settlement built between A.D. 1300 and A.D. 1450.
- Large enclosures that appear to have housed the elite of Great Zimbabwe are located on hills on the east and west ends of the site. The power of the elite of Great Zimbabwe was derived from their control over long-distance trade routes.

## KEY TERMS

Bluestones, 296
Cahokia, 309
Chaco Canyon, 302
Chacoan Network, 306
Dhaka, 316

Great Houses, 302
Great Zimbabwe, 313
Kiva, 302
Monk's Mound, 309
Mound 72, 311

Plaza, 310
Pueblo Bonito, 302
Stonehenge, 295

## REVIEW QUESTIONS

1. How did Stonehenge fit into the surrounding landscape? Is it associated with a large settlement or other monuments?
2. What similarities and differences are there between Pueblo Bonito and Cahokia?

3. What evidence is there that part of the power of elites in the complex societies discussed in this chapter rested on their control over trade routes? What other sources of power emerge from these case studies?

## FOR FURTHER READING

Rinita A. Dalan. (2003). *Envisioning Cahokia: A Landscape Perspective*. DeKalb, Ill.: Northern Illinois University Press.

Jared Diamond. (2005). *Collapse: How Societies Choose to Fail or Succeed*. New York: Viking.

Peter S. Garlake. (1973). *Great Zimbabwe*. London: Thames and Hudson.

Ian Hodder. (1990). *The Domestication of Europe: Structure and Contingency in Neolithic Societies*. Cambridge, Mass: Blackwell.

George R. Milner. (1998). *The Cahokia Chiefdom: The Archaeology of a Mississippian Society*. Smithsonian Series in Archaeological Inquiry. Washington: Smithsonian Institution Press.

Jill E. Neitzel. (2003). *Pueblo Bonito: Center of the Chacoan World*. Washington, D.C.: Smithsonian Institution Press.

Timothy R. Pauketat. (2004). *Ancient Cahokia and the Mississippians*. Cambridge: Cambridge University Press.

Innocent Pikirayi. (2001). *The Zimbabwe Culture: Origins and Decline in Southern Zambezian States*. Walnut Creek, Calif.: AltaMira Press.

Stephen Plog. (1997). *Ancient Peoples of the American Southwest*. London: Thames and Hudson, 1997.

Lynne Sebastian. (1992). *The Chaco Anasazi: Sociopolitical Evolution in the Prehistoric Southwest*. Cambridge: Cambridge University Press.

David Souden. (1997). *Stonehenge Revealed*. London: Collins in association with English Heritage.

Biloine W. Young and Melvin L. Fowler. (2000). *Cahokia, the Great Native American Metropolis*. Urbana: University of Illinois Press.

# Urban States

IN MESOPOTAMIA,
MESOAMERICA, AND
CHINA, the emergence
of the state and urban
centers are closely
linked. After reading
this chapter, you should
understand:

▶ The characteristics of
the urban centers of
the three civilizations
studied.

▶ The nature of the
social organizations
of these three early
states.

▶ The development of
Mesopotamian
cuneiform, Mayan
hieroglyphs, and
early Chinese writing.

Recording Maya glyphs.

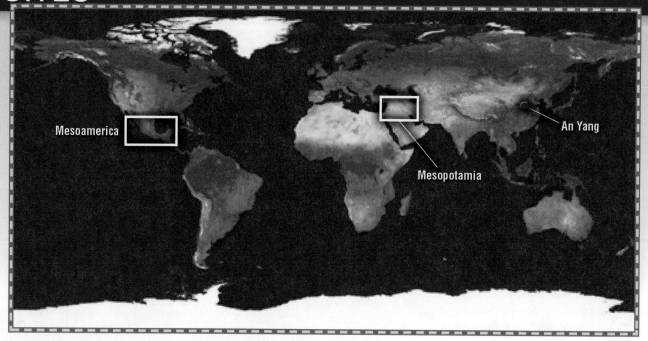

Mesoamerica

Mesopotamia

An Yang

**C**uneiform tablet of the Epic of Gilgamesh. Although the epic is set in the Uruk period, all known copies come from later contexts. The text was preserved partly because it was used as an exercise for students learning cuneiform writing.

**T**he Epic of Gilgamesh is a poem recounting the exploits of Gilgamesh, king of the city Uruk, located in ancient Mesopotamia. Gilgamesh is a partly historical and partly mythical figure whose adventures carry him through a world of both gods and humans. The core of the tale is Gilgamesh's search for the source of eternal life, triggered by his grief over the death of his companion Enkidu. Gilgamesh's quest takes him to Utnapishtim, the survivor of the great flood, who gives him a plant that grants immortality. Gilgamesh then tragically loses this plant and is left to struggle with his own mortality. It is telling that in this story Gilgamesh, the king of a great city, is left to struggle with the inevitability of death. Gilgamesh is a human king. The epic of Gilgamesh is also the story of the friendship between Gilgamesh and Enkidu. Gilgamesh embodies the power of the city, while Enkidu is a wild man, a man living outside of civilization.

Did Uruk need Gilgamesh? Did Gilgamesh need Uruk? Or did both hero and city emerge as one? Many archaeologists argue that cities require the organization provided by state bureaucracy. In large population centers, roads need planning, laws need enforcement, and violence must be controlled. Some claim that state bureaucracy developed only in response to the organizational challenges of urban life.

In this chapter, we explore cases in which state bureaucracy emerged together with cities. We begin in

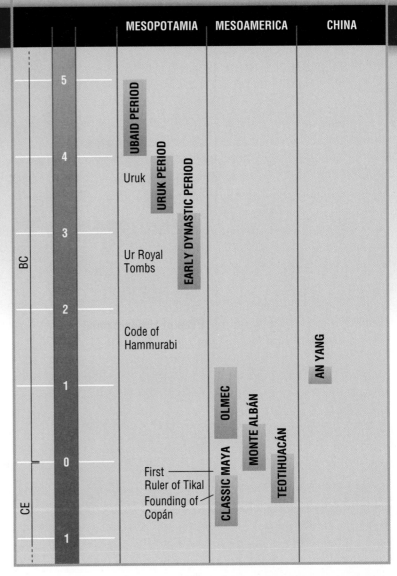

| | MESOPOTAMIA | MESOAMERICA | CHINA |
|---|---|---|---|

Gilgamesh's homeland, **Mesopotamia**, which saw the emergence of the first state societies in the world. We then move to Mesoamerica, focusing on the Mayan civilization. In the last section, we briefly consider the archaeological evidence for state formation in China.

# 11.1
# MESOPOTAMIA

Mesopotamia, the land between the two rivers, covers the region along the course of the **Tigris and Euphrates Rivers.** The heartland of Mesopotamia is in southern Iraq, where the Tigris and Euphrates flow into the Arabian Gulf. However, Mesopotamia extends to the north into Syria and Turkey and to the east into Iran. Archaeologists working in Mesopotamia have recovered a rich and complex archaeological record, as well as documents that include the earliest written epics and legal systems in the world. The earliest stages of state formation appear to have been focused in southern Mesopotamia, also known as Sumer.

▶ **Mesopotamia** is the region along the course of the **Tigris** and **Euphrates Rivers** centered in modern Iraq.

## The Physical Setting

The Tigris and Euphrates Rivers flow through a geological depression formed where the Arabian Shield ploughs into and under the Asian Shield. This powerful geological process has pushed up the Zagros Mountain chain that runs along the eastern edge of the Tigris floodplain. As they flow through the area defined by the geological depression, the Tigris and Euphrates dump their load of waterborne silts on the valley floor.

There are three important consequences of the geological position of Mesopotamia. The first is that many early sites are deeply buried by the deposit of river silts. As a result, little is known about the Paleolithic and Neolithic periods of the Tigris and Euphrates River Valley. The second consequence is that there are no mineral resources in southern Mesopotamia. The only locally available building

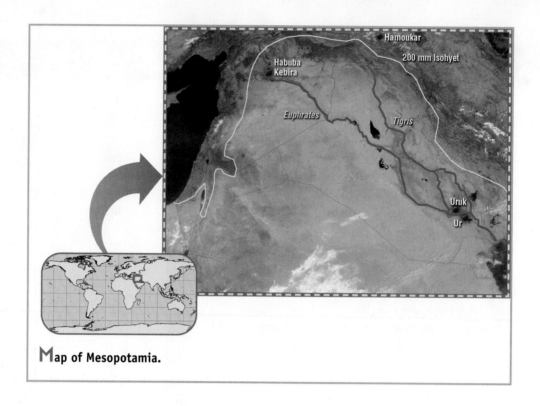

**M**ap of Mesopotamia.

**P**hotograph of marsh settlement in southern Iraq. The setting of many of the early cities of southern Mesopotamia resembled this marsh.

materials are reeds from marshes and the ubiquitous mud. The third consequence of the geological situation of the Tigris and Euphrates Rivers is that the soils of Mesopotamia are extremely fertile. This fertility is in sharp contrast to the desert regions along the western edge of the Euphrates River floodplain.

In southern Mesopotamia, crops can be grown only with irrigation, which draws water from the rivers out onto agricultural fields. Dry farming, which depends on rainfall, is possible just in areas with over 200 mm of rain per year. The 200-mm isohyet (a line on a map that connects areas of equal rainfall) defining the limit of the dry farming region runs through northern Iraq and Syria.

Many of the early cities of southern Mesopotamia today lie in what appears to be a desert wasteland. Archaeological surveys, along with aerial photographs, have shown that when these sites were occupied, they lay either within or at the edges of extensive marshlands. However, as the Euphrates River has shifted course, ancient cites have been left isolated far from the river channel. The degraded state of the modern landscape is also the result of the farming practices of the early cities, which caused salt to be concentrated in soils near the surface. As a result of this process of salination, crops can no longer be grown in the fields that once supported great cities.

## The Fate of Iraq's Antiquities

The devastation of the Iraq Museum in the days following the U.S.-led invasion of Iraq was a traumatic event. Pictures of looted storerooms and display cases provoked fears that the cultural heritage of Iraq had been irreparably damaged. The exact extent of the loss and the precise sequence of events is still being determined years after the event. It is likely that the repercussions of this event will shape the field of archaeology for decades to come.

Before trying to assess the implications of the events in Iraq, it is important to give some details of what happened to the Iraq Museum. Press stories have varied enormously and much remains unknown. However, Matthew Bogdanos, the U.S. Marine charged with investigating the events, has presented a useful time line and parameters of the looting. U.S. forces entered the area around the museum on Tuesday, April 8, 2003, three days after first reaching Baghdad. At that point, the museum became a battleground as Iraqi troops took up positions in it and the staff was forced to leave. With two exceptions, U.S. troops refrained from shelling the museum, and damage to the museum from military operations was minimal. The museum staff returned on April 12, and after that time no further looting took place. U.S. forces entered the museum on April 16. The looting appears to have taken place between April 8 and April 12. There were three separate lootings. In the public galleries, forty objects were stolen, and the looters were organized and careful in their choice of objects. In the aboveground storage rooms, there was extensive looting, apparently carried out by a disorganized mob. The number of objects stolen from these storage rooms is hard to calculate but is in the thousands. In the basement, a collection of small valuable objects, including thousands of cylinder seals, were stolen. This appears to have been an inside job, and the objects chosen were both valuable and easy to transport. Close to 10,000 objects were stolen from the basement storage.

Colonel Bogdanos, together with Italian and Iraqi colleagues, set up a combination of an amnesty program and the seizure of objects, resulting in the return of close to 2,000 objects, mostly from the aboveground storage and the gallery. The objects returned include many of the most famous pieces, including the Warka vase. Sadly, the devastation of Iraq's antiquities goes beyond the museum: There are extensive reports of large-scale looting of archaeological sites and of regional museums.

The events in Iraq highlight the political significance of archaeological remains and force archaeologists to reconsider the degree to which they can sequester themselves from current events. Archaeologists are left with a number of troubling questions. Perhaps the most important is the need to examine the role that archaeologists play in the international antiquities market and how archaeologists can help in the fight against this growing illegal market. Although the looting was carried out locally in Iraq, the devastation of the museum ultimately points to a network of dealers in antiquities who

◀ U.S. tank stationed in front of the Baghdad Museum.

are able to move objects across international borders and into the hands of collectors.

One interesting idea which emerges is that cultural heritage should be treated as a fundamental human right—that the protection of our past is a basic element of freedom.

# Chronology

Most Paleolithic and Neolithic sites in southern Mesopotamia are inaccessible to archaeologists because they are deeply buried by the accumulation of river silts. The earliest well-represented period in southern Mesopotamia is the Ubaid period, 5000 B.C.–4000 B.C. The first urban sites appeared in the subsequent **Uruk period,** 4000 B.C.–3200 B.C. The Uruk period is followed by the Early Dynastic period, during which a series of city–states developed in southern Mesopotamia. The rulers of

> The first cities in Mesopotamia developed ▶ during the **Uruk period,** 4000 B.C.–3200 B.C.

these city–states are known from written documents recovered on archaeological sites. The Early Dynastic period drew to a close when Sargon of Akkad unified southern Mesopotamia under his rule in 2350 B.C.

## Uruk

The site of **Uruk** in southern Iraq is the oldest known city in the world. The city grew from the unification of two towns dating to the Ubaid period built along opposite banks of a channel of the Euphrates River. During the Uruk period, the city grew to cover an area of 2.5 square kilometers with an estimated population between 20,000 and 40,000 (Nissen 2002). Surveys in the area around Uruk show that the city was by far the largest site in a landscape densely settled with smaller towns and villages.

> The site of **Uruk** is the oldest known city in the world.

Excavations at Uruk have focused on the two massive temple precincts located in the center of the city, where a sequence of temple structures stretching back to the Ubaid period has been uncovered. The city of Uruk grew around this central temple precinct. Among the materials the temples were built of were limestone and bitumen, both of which had to have been imported from outside of southern Mesopotamia. Many of the temple structures were built on platforms, evidently the precursor of the stepped pyramid or **ziggurat** that is at the center of Mesopotamian temple precincts from later periods. The temples were often elaborately decorated. One method of decoration was the use of colored cones inserted into mud brick walls to form a mosaic.

> **Ziggurats** are stepped pyramids found at the center of many Mesopotamian temple precincts.

Unfortunately, we know little about the organization of the city of Uruk outside of the temple area. From excavations at other sites, we know that houses were usually built around a central courtyard and were sometimes grouped together into large enclosures (Postgate 1994: 91). It is likely that they were the houses of extended families. Surprisingly, few palace structures have been found from early cities in southern Mesopotamia. Extensive surveys around Uruk have provided some information about the regional setting of this city. On the basis of these surveys, it appears that the growth of the urban center took place at the expense of rural villages. By the Early Dynastic period, there was a sharp drop-off in the number of village sites, suggesting that a migration occurred from rural villages to the urban center.

## Government

Mesopotamian society revolved around three sources of authority: the temple, the palace, and the city council. The temple was a permanent installation at the heart of the city, and the deity to which the temple was dedicated was a basic element of the identity of the city. The temple compounds were quite large, and the temples owned land and fulfilled economic functions. Excavations of temple complexes have uncovered the remains of both workshops and storage rooms.

The ziggurat at Ur, Iraq. This massive brick structure acted as the support for a temple.

The relationship between the palace and the temple in Mesopotamia was complex and, for the Uruk and Early Dynastic periods, poorly understood. It is possible that during these periods, the chief priest of the temple was the ruler of the city. The duties of the king, or *ensi,* included maintenance of the temple and military leadership of the city. Kingship was not determined strictly by descent, and there is evidence that the king was selected by a city council. Unfortunately, little is known about the powers of this council.

During the Early Dynastic period, there were over thirty independent cities in southern Mesopotamia. Although the cities cooperated on military and economic ventures, there were also rivalries between cities, and not all rulers were equal.

The Code of Hammurabi, which dates to the period around 1800 B.C., is the most extensive of a series of early Mesopotamian legal documents. The laws set out in the code of Hammurabi cover a wide range of domains, including penalties for perjury, robbery, and murder; the regulations surrounding adoption, marriage, and the ownership of slaves; and more mundane issues, such as the cost of hiring an ox or an ass. From the Code of Hammurabi, it appears that the king had jurisdiction over the regulation of commercial activities, punishment for violent acts, and aspects of family life.

## Surplus and Specialization

The growth of the cities of Mesopotamia was based on the production of agricultural surplus. This surplus depended on irrigation agriculture, which required the organization of large work crews to build and maintain canals. Already by the Uruk period, there were people who specialized in various aspects of craft production. One of the most interesting artifacts found on Uruk sites is also one of the most modest. **Bevel-rim bowls** are small, undecorated bowls made of a very coarse clay fabric (see Figure 11.1). Both complete and broken sherds of bevel-rim bowls are found in enormous quantities on Uruk-period sites. It is possible that these bowls were simply the "styrofoam cups" of the Uruk period, cheap and easy-to-manufacture containers that were rapidly discarded. However, archaeologists have puzzled about their function and particularly why the size of the bowls is very regular. Why would such simple vessels be consistently made the same size?

One proposal is that bevel-rim bowls were vessels in which grain rations were distributed to workers. The standardized vessel size would then reflect the standard ration for a day of work. If this proposal is correct, it implies that the rulers

The Warka vase showing a procession of offerings being brought to the temple.

▶ **Bevel-rim bowls** are small, undecorated bowls made of coarse clay fabric that are ubiquitous on Uruk-period sites. Theories of the function of these bowls hold that they served to distribute rations or as molds for baking bread.

## FIGURE 11.1

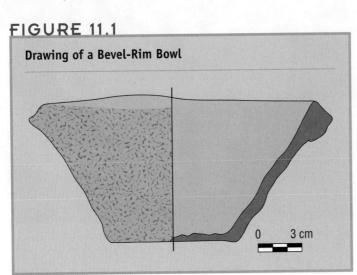

**Drawing of a Bevel-Rim Bowl**

0    3 cm

had tight control over the distribution of agricultural surplus to workers. Some archaeologists have pointed out that the shape of the bowls is not appropriate for carrying around a ration of grain: One is forced to imagine thousands of laborers carefully trying to avoid having any grain spill from their bowls as they carried their rations home. An alternative is that these vessels were used as molds for baking bread. If this is the case, then the bevel-rim bowls indicate that baking in the Uruk period was carried out by specialists who produced bread in very large quantities, perhaps to be paid out as a ration for work.

## Inequality

Mesopotamian society included kings, priests, craft specialists, merchants, laborers, and slaves. There were clear disparities in wealth and privilege among the various members of society. It appears that clothing and hairstyle were often used to mark status. The king in the Uruk period is often shown wearing a flat hat and a netted skirt. Slaves are described as bearing a distinguishing mark known as an *apputum*, which might have been a particular hairstyle.

In the 1920s, Leonard Wooley excavated a cemetery at the site of Ur that provides a vivid picture of the wealth and power of the rulers of an Early Dynastic city.

Queen Puabi's headdress from the Royal Tombs at Ur, Iraq.

**R**econstruction of a death pit at Ur just before the attendants and animals were killed.

The cemetery includes hundreds of burials, most of which are simple interments of individuals with a few pottery vessels. The chambers known as the **Royal Tombs** present a startling contrast. These tombs contain staggering deposits of wealth, including tools, jewelry, musical instruments, and vessels made from a wide range of metals (gold, silver, copper, and electrum) and precious stones (lapis lazuli, carnelian, steatite, and calcite). These materials were brought to Ur from considerable distances: Lapis lazuli comes from Afghanistan, carnelian from Pakistan. The Royal Tombs are associated with chambers Wooley called death pits that contained the skeletons of men and women together with the remains of oxen attached to carts. These people and animals appear to have been slaughtered as part of the burial ritual. Many of the skeletons are still adorned with lavish jewelry and ornaments; many clutch weapons in their hands. Among the most famous objects is the headdress of one of the main figures buried, which consists of leaves made of thinly hammered gold. Other impressive artifacts include a series of lyres inlayed with elaborate scenes and a sculpture of a ram peering out from behind some branches.

It is probable that the rich burial goods found in the Royal Tombs and the sacrificial victim were meant to accompany the deceased to the afterlife; perhaps the goods were used to provide offerings to the gods. The woman buried with an elaborate headdress appears to be a queen by the name of Puabi. Another tomb is thought to have been the burial chamber of a king.

The Royal Tombs illustrate the wealth concentrated in the hands of the king and his close family. This wealth included access to large quantities of precious materials imported from a wide geographical region outside of the areas directly controlled by the Mesopotamian state. How did the king come to be the focal point of such an extensive trade network? One possibility is that the king controlled the production of textiles in Mesopotamia and that the surplus textiles produced were traded for the precious material that the king used as the expression of his power.

> ▶ In the **Royal Tombs** at Ur, dated to the Early Dynastic period, the dead were buried with a spectacular array of precious artifacts and sacrificial victims.

The king not only controlled the flow of precious materials, but also was able to sponsor the highly skilled artisans who produced the spectacular objects found in the burials. The sacrificial victims point to another facet of the ruler's power: the ability to control the life and death of his subjects. It is hard not to conclude from the Ur burials that Mesopotamian rulers had immense power. The riddle remains why so much wealth was buried with the dead. Such a squandering of resources seems at odds with the accumulation of power found in Mesopotamian kingship. Why sacrifice not only people, but also prestigious objects? One possibility is that the destruction of wealth fueled the continuing effort to accumulate wealth and that this effort was the key to the ruler's power. The king's power might have been based, not simply on a wealth of goods, but on the ability to maintain a system of trade, tribute, and specialized craft production that continuously created wealth.

Perhaps it is wrong to see the Royal Burials from only an economic perspective. If we look back to the Epic of Gilgamesh, we see that despite his power as the ruler of Uruk, Gilgamesh struggled with his own mortality. It seems likely that the elaborate rituals of the Ur Royal Burials tapped into the same desire for immortality.

## The Development of Writing

> The **cuneiform** writing system, in which signs were impressed in clay, were used to write a range of languages, including Sumerian and Akkadian.

The origins of some of the symbols used by Mesopotamian scribes have been traced to clay tokens found on Neolithic sites in the Zagros Mountains. The **cuneiform** writing system in Mesopotamia first developed during the Uruk period. Mesopotamian scribes wrote on clay tablets, using a stylus to impress the signs into the wet clay. The cuneiform writing system originated as a pictographic script in which each "picture" represented a term or concept. By the Early Dynastic, the

Early cuneiform tablet. The dots and semicircles are numbers and most individual compartments refer to a quantity of a commodity. The signs are still visibly pictographic, some showing bowls or jars. Note the compartment in the right hand corner that includes a series of signs with no numbers. What do you think this could be?

symbols were increasingly stylized and were used to represent syllables. The cuneiform script was used to write several different languages. During the Uruk and Early Dynastic periods, the main written language was Sumerian. The cuneiform script was also used to write texts in Akkadian, a Semitic language related to modern Arabic and Hebrew, and Hittite, an Indo-European language.

Mesopotamian scribes also developed elaborate methods for making seals. The seals were carved in hard stone, which could then be pressed onto clay or mud to mark ownership by a person or a group. An important function of seals was to ensure that a room or vessel once closed remained undisturbed. These early precursors of our "tamper-proof lids" were frequently applied to clay plugs sealing vessels and to closures on doors. **Cylinder seals** first appear in the Uruk period. The seals were made by carving a scene onto cylinders of stone. The cylinder seal was then rolled across fresh clay or mud, leaving behind an impression. The carving of cylinder seals rapidly became a highly developed art. Working on a miniature scale, Mesopotamian seal carvers brought to life vivid scenes from daily life and mythology.

▶ **Cylinder seals** were one of the methods developed by Mesopotamian scribes to mark ownership.

The earliest cuneiform documents were developed to record ownership and economic transactions, not unlike our receipts and contracts. On sites dating to early in the Uruk period, hollow clay balls filled with small clay tokens are found. The surface of the clay balls, known as bullae (singular: bulla), is covered with impressions from seals and with marks recording numbers. In at least one case, the number on the bulla is known to correspond to the number of tokens in the interior.

Bullae were a concrete method of recording a transaction. Each object is represented by an actual token, and the tokens are enclosed in a clay "envelope" that was then sealed. The earliest written documents, which date to the end of the

**B**ullae are clay envelopes that enclose small tokens like those shown on the right. The surface of the bulla was marked with seals before the clay dried.

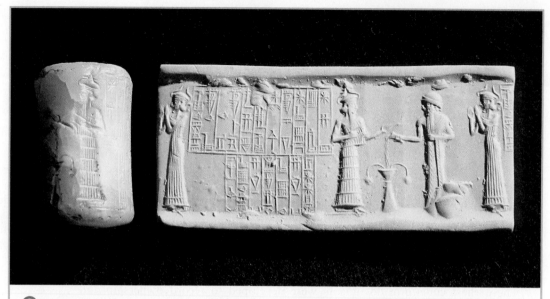

Uruk period, mirror the function of the bulla, but discard the need for the concrete tokens. If bullae are one level of abstraction from reality—the sealed tokens representing real objects—the earliest written documents take this abstraction one step further to replace the tokens with marks in clay. The development of syllabic script extended the economic functions that texts could fulfill still further. One of the most interesting types of documents from the Early Dynastic period is the kuduru texts that record transactions involving the exchange of land for goods such as bread, oil, beer, cloth, and silver. The kuduru make it clear that land was privately owned in Early Dynastic Mesopotamia and give insight into the relative values of commodities. The economy of early Mesopotamian cities included the wealth of the king and the temple, as well as private wealth. Written documents played an essential role in the operation of this complex system of ownership and exchange.

Over the course of over two thousand years, the use of the cuneiform writing system was expanded to include texts as varied as epics, histories, dictionaries, and mathematical treatises, as well as letters, treaties, and accounts.

## Warfare and Expansion

From the wealth and power displayed in the Royal Tombs of Ur, one might assume that early Mesopotamian cities were highly militaristic societies. Archaeology and texts combine to suggest that, although warfare between cities was common, the extent of the violence was quite limited. Cities were walled and the texts often speak of wars between cities. Perhaps even more telling are cylinder seals from the Uruk period depicting bound prisoners. However, the tools of war were limited, and the wars described in the texts appear to be more a display of power than conflicts resulting in massive numbers of casualties. The main tools of war were axes, spears, arrows, and carts drawn by asses or oxen. The earliest mention of a standing army comes from the time of Sargon, when there is mention of an army of over 5,000 soldiers. In later periods, the power of the Mesopotamian military expanded significantly, allowing for far-ranging campaigns of conquest in foreign lands.

Given the apparently limited extent of military might during the Uruk and Early Dynastic periods, the discovery of Uruk colonies far from southern Iraq has come as a surprise. The most completely excavated Uruk colony is the site of **Habuba Kebira,** located on the upper reaches of the Euphrates River in northern Syria (see Figure 11.2) (Algaze 1993). Habuba Kebira was occupied only during the Uruk period, and there has been very little subsequent accumulation of sediments. As a result, archaeologists have been able to open up a large horizontal excavation, uncovering an almost complete plan of the settlement. The site of Habuba Kebira is a walled town of densely packed houses running for about half a kilometer along the banks of the Euphrates. All of the artifacts found on the site are made in the styles found in the Uruk heartland in southern Iraq. Bullae with Uruk seal impressions and a temple in classic Uruk style have also been found on the site. There is very little evidence of artifacts made in the styles of the surrounding local communities. Habuba Kebira and similar sites present a challenging enigma. They are clearly evidence of the expansion of people out from the Uruk heartland, but there is no evidence that the expansion was a military one. Some archaeologists have argued that Habuba Kebira was a trading post or a settlement built to protect trade routes for critical mineral resources coming from northern Syria and Turkey. However, it remains unclear whether the people coming from southern Iraq actually dominated and controlled these exchange routes or whether there was a more subtle relationship between the people coming from the southern cities and local groups.

Recent excavations at the Uruk-period site of Hamoukar in Syria provide some of the first evidence that the Uruk expansion involved violent conflict. The excavators have found evidence for the bombardment of the site by clay sling stones leading to the collapse of walls and an ensuing fire.

## Summing Up the Evidence

The development of state societies in southern Mesopotamia is closely linked with the emergence of large urban centers. The Royal Tombs at Ur give a sense of the extensive power of the ruler of the early Mesopotamian cities. The rapid expansion of Uruk-period settlements into northern Mesopotamia provides an indication of the dynamism of these early cities. Much of the power of the cities and their rulers can be linked to economic factors, the organization of large-scale irrigation systems, and the control of surplus production of textiles. The development of the cuneiform writing system served the need of this economy to control and regulate trade and ownership. However, the growth of the Mesopotamian cities was not simply the product of economic forces. In fact, the core around which the city grew was not the palace, but the temple precinct. Still, in ancient Mesopotamia the boundary between the temple and the palace is difficult to draw. Ultimately, the power of the early

▶ The site of **Habuba Kebira** is an Uruk colony located on the upper reaches of the Euphrates River in northern Syria.

## FIGURE 11.2

**The town of Habuba Kabira, Syria. The Euphrates runs along the east side of the site; the other sides were fortified by a city wall. Notice the major road running north-south through the site and the crossroad running from the city gate.**

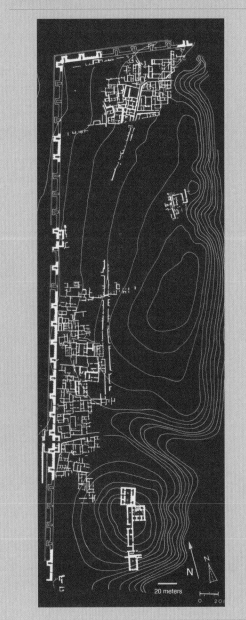

Mesopotamian state seems to flow from a blending of the power of the temple and the power of the palace.

## 11.2 THE MAYA

The modern Maya live in an area stretching from southern Mexico through Guatemala and Belize, as well as parts of Honduras and El Salvador. Beginning around 2,000 years ago, the Maya developed a state society with a complex writing system and large urban centers. Much of the rich history of the Maya was lost under Spanish rule, which brought with it devastating disease and the systematic imposition of European culture, including the burning of most Mayan books (Coe 1999). However, archaeology has made major strides in reconstructing the Mayan past. The decipherment of Mayan hieroglyphics has afforded a spectacular insight into the detailed history of the early Mayan cities. The study of modern Mayan oral traditions and cultural practices also plays a significant role in understanding the remains of the Mayan past.

The Mayan region is part of Mesoamerica, which covers the area from northern Mexico through Honduras. Mesoamerica is not a geographically defined region, but rather a region whose indigenous inhabitants share a number of cultural traits, including a complex calendar, a ball game played on a special court with a rubber ball, and an emphasis on bloodletting (Coe 1993).

## Chronology

The earliest evidence of emerging political complexity in Mesoamerica is found on **Olmec** sites along the Gulf Coast of Mexico.

The Maya were not the first state society in Mesoamerica. The earliest evidence of emerging political complexity in Mesoamerica is found on **Olmec** sites along the Gulf Coast of Mexico (Benson et al. 1996). Between 1200 B.C. and 300 B.C., the

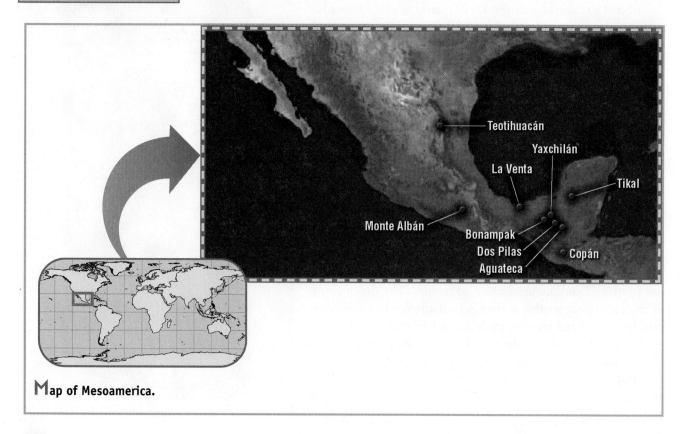

Map of Mesoamerica.

## Río Azul
### by Fred Valdez, University of Texas, Austin

I am Fred Valdez, an archaeologist with a research focus on Mesoamerican/Mayan civilizations. My current status is professor of anthropology at the University of Texas at Austin. Between 1983 and 1991, Dr. R.E.W. Adams of the University of Texas at San Antonio was directing the Río Azul Project in northeastern Guatemala and invited me to participate. At the time, I was a graduate student and saw the project as a way to contribute to original research and expand my archaeological experiences.

The Río Azul project was located in an isolated area in Guatemala that required traveling a very long, rough road that passes the great sites of Tikal and Uaxactún. The project was studying the site in part because of extreme looting there in the early 1980s that exposed significant architecture and painted tombs of the Classic Maya.

During the first phase of the project, a large truncated "pyramid"—a pyramidal building that is flat topped—was mapped and numbered G-103. I was asked to test (conduct small excavations into) the building. In

doing so during the 1986 season, I found what I thought were several well-preserved plaster-faced buildings. In the 1987 season, I expanded the research into larger excavations and found that there were not several small structures on the pyramidal platform, but rather one very large building measuring approximately 30 meters on each side. The style and construction of the building allowed for an interpretation that this monument dated to the Late Preclassic, about 200 B.C.–A.D. 200. This was a very exciting find!

The size of G-103 suggested that there might be an earlier building within it. In 1990 I placed an excavation unit behind

◀ The architecture exposed is the northeast corner of G-103 Sub 1. It has thick smooth plaster as a surface over stone blocks. This building is one of the best examples of Late Preclassic Maya architecture. The structure was painted red as evidenced by traces.

▶ Part of the central staircase of G-103 Sub 1. The excavation into G-103 Sub 1 removed three steps and tunneled into the building. G-103 Sub 2 is located immediately within the tunnel and heading down. Note the red paint on several of the stair faces. Fred Valdez is to the left of the opening, looking into the tunnel. The excavation (tunnel) is exactly at the centerline of the building (G-103 Sub 1).

the staircase, and at 3 meters deep we came upon a plastered surface that I believed to be the top of an earlier building. Our season ended, and I was able to persuade Dr. Adams that G-103 needed more work. He agreed, but made it clear that 1991 would be our last season at Río Azul (G-103). Towards the end of the season, with time running out, I decided to tunnel into G-103. By chance, and perhaps with a little luck, we came down a face of an interior structure. This earlier building was stuccoed and modeled with an incised decoration reminiscent of earlier styles. Indeed, we had found the earliest decorated building in the Mayan lowlands. I estimate the date of this early decorated building to be about 400 B.C.–500 B.C.

Monumental Olmec sculpture from San Lorenzo, Mexico.

Olmec constructed a series of major ceremonial centers in towns with populations numbering in the thousands. The Olmec developed a highly sophisticated artistic tradition that included monumental sculptures of human heads carved out of volcanic rock. These sculptures give a vivid sense of the power of the leaders of Olmec society. Particularly significant is the headgear found on the sculptures, possibly related to competition in a ball game. Hollow clay sculptures of infants with what appear to be adult heads are often found on Olmec sites. These disconcerting figures stand in sharp contrast to the raw power expressed in the monumental stone sculpture, raising the question of whether they depict leaders or divinities. The Olmec also produced spectacular sculptures from jade and other hard stones. At the site of La Venta, a cache was found of sixteen male figures carved from jade and serpentine, standing in front of a series of polished stone axes (Lauck 1996). It is possible that this scene represents a town council, a balance to the power of the rulers depicted on the monumental sculptures.

**Monte Albán,** located in the Oaxaca Valley, is the oldest city in Mesoamerica.

The first city in Mesoamerica was located at the site of **Monte Albán** in the Oaxaca Valley in the Mexican highlands. Between 500 B.C. and 350 B.C., the population of Monte Albán grew first to 5,000 and then 17,000 people living in neighborhoods built around a central plaza (Blanton et al. 1993). In the period between 350 B.C. and 250 B.C., Monte Albán was surrounded by a defensive wall. The central plaza became the focus of monumental construction, including a ball court.

**Teotihuacán** was an enormous city with a population of over 80,000 people.

Beginning around two thousand years ago (A.D. 1–A.D. 100), **Teotihuacán**, in the highland Valley of Mexico, grew into an enormous city covering an area of twenty square kilometers with a population of more than 80,000 people (Sugiyama 2004). Teotihuacán was built along a north–south orientation and housed up to twenty temple complexes. Extensive fieldwork at the site has

The center of Teotihuacán, Mexico, showing the scale of the city and the regularity of the city plan. The Pyramid of the Sun is on the left side.

uncovered evidence of large-scale specialized craft production. Three massive stepped pyramid structures were built in the center of the city. The largest, the Pyramid of the Sun, rises to a height of 64 meters and encompasses a volume of over one million cubic meters.

The Mayan cities developed during the Classic period, which dates to between 250 A.D. and 900 A.D. Around 900 A.D., many of the large Mayan cities were abandoned in what is known as the Maya Collapse. During the subsequent Postclassic period, which lasted from 900 A.D. to the arrival of the Spanish in 1519, most large Mayan sites were located in the northern Yucatán peninsula.

## The Setting

The Mayan cities developed in the lowland zones that run from the foothills of the Sierra Madre Mountains in the south to the Caribbean Sea in the north. The Mayan lowlands are divided into the tropical rain forests of the southern zone and the flat scrublands of the Yucatán in the northern zone. Most of the early cities developed along rivers and swamps in the southern zone. The northern zone became the dominant focus of Mayan settlement in later periods. Mayan sites in the northern zone are located near *cenotes*—sinkholes that were a critical source of water.

The main agricultural method used in the Mayan region is slash-and-burn cultivation, in which the forest is cleared by burning. After a number of growing seasons, the field is abandoned and the forest is allowed to regenerate. Slash-and-burn cultivation is a shifting system of agriculture in which field systems move over time as fields are cleared, exploited, and then left fallow. The Maya also developed methods for growing crops on extensive raised fields in swamps. The use of raised fields

## Ancient Maya and the Medicinal Trail Site
### by David Hyde

I started college in my midtwenties at a community college in Seattle and then transferred to the University of Texas at Austin to complete my B.A. During my first semester at UT, Austin, I enrolled in "Introduction to Archaeology." A requirement of the course was to complete a certain number of hours excavating at a prehistoric hunter–gatherer site. I loved the work and was invited to help process artifacts. At the laboratory, I noticed a long table covered with hundreds of stone tools, grouped into various clusters. The clusters, I was informed, represented change through time, reflecting the different people that had moved through the area, adapting their tools to changes in the resources they were utilizing. I was amazed by the depth of information that could be derived from stone tools, and that experience led me to pursue that type of material as a focus of my future research.

That summer, I enrolled in a Maya archaeology field school. Maya archaeology was completely different from everything I had done before, and I knew immediately that the subject was for me. For the first time, I was excavating the ruins of a complex society. I was struck by the fact that constructing the masonry architecture, modifying the landscape, cutting stone out of the bedrock, shaping stone, digging the fields, felling trees, and more were all accomplished with stones, as the Maya lacked metal tools. I have returned every year since my first visit as an undergraduate ten years ago. For the past few years, I have been the field director for the field school, teaching the students who come in as I did years before.

▲ David M. Hyde examines an excavation profile.

Having worked so many years at a number of large ceremonial centers in the same area, I became interested in the hinterland settlement.

was a critical component of the intensified agriculture needed to support large population centers. There is little evidence that Mayan agriculture rested on the kind of large-scale irrigation projects essential to the cities of southern Mesopotamia. However, some evidence exists for large-scale projects, particularly poorly understood canal systems found around some cities (Demarest 2004).

## The City

The ruins of Classic-period Mayan cities are covered by dense forest undergrowth. On many excavations, machetes are as important as trowels. Steep pyramids, their apexes often visible above the forest canopy, are the defining feature of Mayan cities. These pyramids sit in the central area of the city together with royal residences, ball courts, and open plazas. Extensive survey work and excavation on Mayan sites has demonstrated that these cities stretched far beyond the central area

▲ Late Preclassic ceremonial round structure at the Medicinal Trail site.

FIGURE 11.3

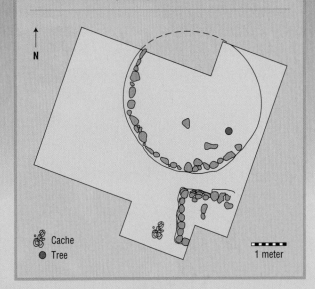

**Plan map of the Late Preclassic round structure (that is shown in the photo to the left), an associated square platform, and the cache.**

N

🐚 Cache
🔴 Tree

1 meter

Since so little work has been done in the hinterlands, some of our preconceived ideas of what to expect are constantly being reevaluated. There are always expectations of what will be found when digging, and I was pleasantly surprised to uncover a Late Preclassic round structure in the excavation of the rural Medicinal Trail site. This type of structure is generally found in much larger centers. The work at the Medicinal Trail site gives us a much different perception of the social organization of these hinterland groups. Maya society is more complex than a simple dichotomy of elites and commoners.

As a field archaeologist, I spend a considerable amount of my time away from home in a very challenging working environment. In the field, there is no electricity or running water. There are lots of biting bugs, and I am isolated from the rest of the world for extended periods. The counter to

that, however, is the excitement of unearthing something for the first time, knowing that no one has seen this building, ceramic pot, or plaster floor for more than a thousand years. Understanding ancient Maya society is not about marveling over the plaster floor or the beautiful ceramic vessel, but rather about finding out who walked on that plaster floor, what the pot was used for, and how those individuals made their living.

to include large residential areas with populations of up to 20,000 people living on small house mounds.

The central area of **Copán**, Honduras, has been the focus of intensive research. The center of Copán includes two large pyramids and an elaborate ball court. An inscription recounting the dynastic history of Copán runs down the entire face of the northern pyramid in what is known as the hieroglyphic stairway (see Figure 11.5 page 341 and photo page 342). This feature led from an altar at the base of the pyramid to a temple structure at the top. The inscription of the history of Copán in such a powerful setting has been interpreted as an effort to connect the troubled rulers of the late periods with the glorious achievements of the great ancestral kings (Fash 1991).

The Mayan pyramids were built up over centuries as new rulers tore down and built over the temples of their predecessors. The top of the pyramids served as temple platforms, while the rulers and their families were buried within the expanding structures. Research on the Mayan pyramids involves not only mapping the surface,

▶ **Copán,** Honduras, was a large Mayan city with two large pyramids and an elaborate ball court at its center.

## FIGURE 11.4

The central area of the Maya city of Copán in a reconstruction by Tatiana Proskouriakoff. This drawing places the core within an empty jungle setting. Today we know that the city of Copán covered a wide area beyond the pyramids and palaces.

but also tunneling into the pyramid to find the earlier structures that were encased as the pyramid was expanded and rebuilt. At the southern pyramid of Copán, the archaeological tunneling has resulted in the discovery of a completely intact temple from the early stages of the city's history. Unlike other structures that were destroyed before being built over, this structure, known as Rosalila, appears to have been so revered that it was encased in pristine condition. Rosalila was a rectangular edifice elaborately decorated with painted stucco figures. These sculptures present fantastic depictions of gods, birds, and snakes. In the floor of one of the rooms in Rosalila, a cache of spectacular flint artifacts chipped in the shape of a deity were found. These objects, known as eccentric flints, are among the finest objects of chipped stone ever made.

## Government

Mayan cities were ruled by dynasties of powerful kings. The exact timing of the emergence of kingship among the Maya is the subject of debate. The earliest king documented at the site of **Tikal** is Yax Ehb' Xook, who appears to have lived around A.D. 100 (Martin 2003). However, it is not clear that Yax Ehb' Xook was the ruler of a city. He might well have been the head of a society that anthropologists would classify as a chiefdom or a stratified society. It appears that the year 378 marked a major change in the history of Tikal. The glyphs speak of the arrival

The first true king of **Tikal** appears to have had links to Teotihuacán. He established his rule in A.D. 378.

# FIGURE 11.5

Cross section of Pyramid 10L-26 at Copán. In the final stage of construction the hieroglyphic stairway was built on the western face of the pyramid, but the cross section shows that there were several earlier phases that included burials, each encased within a later construction.

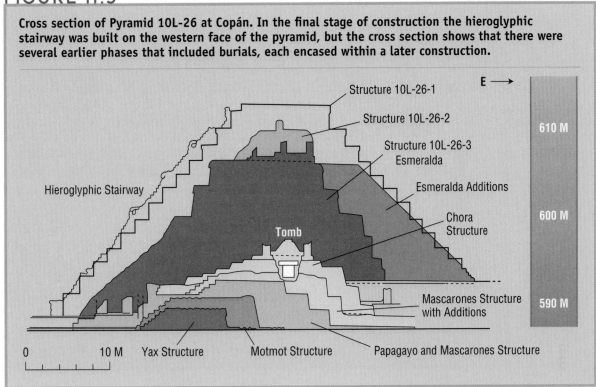

of a new ruler coming from outside and ending the dynastic line. This new ruler either came from the highland Mexican city of Teotihuacán or was in some way heavily influenced by Teotihuacán. This break in the history of Tikal also appears to mark the emergence of a state.

The foundation of the royal dynasty at the city of Copán dates to A.D. 426. The first king of Copán, named Yax K'uk' Mo', came from outside of Copán, possibly with links to Teotihuacán. One of the burials at Copán appears to be the remains of Yax K'uk' Mo'. Skeletal analysis has shown that this individual had suffered several traumas during his life, perhaps as the result of warfare or participating in ball games (Buikstra et al. 2004).

On the basis of the evidence from Tikal and Copán, the founding of the Mayan cities was linked in some cases with the arrival of a ruler connected to Teotihuacán. Once established, the ruling dynasties maintained their power for generations, often hundreds of years. Monuments were frequently used to connect the ruler with the prestige of the dynasty. The hieroglyphic staircase at Copán is the most spectacular example of such monuments. The rulers of the Mayan cities only rarely claimed to be gods themselves; however, they were viewed as uniquely sacred individuals (Houston 2000). There is no sense of a strong distinction between the palace and the temple. The dynasty was closely identified with the temple complexes at the core of the Mayan city.

Eccentric flint from Rosalila, Copán.

## FIGURE 11.6

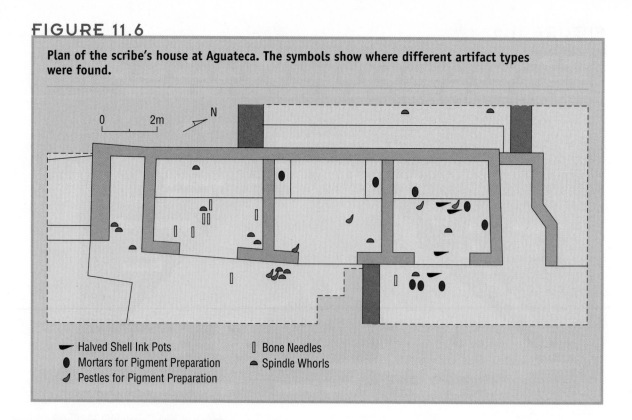

**Plan of the scribe's house at Aguateca. The symbols show where different artifact types were found.**

0    2m    N

- Halved Shell Ink Pots
- Mortars for Pigment Preparation
- Pestles for Pigment Preparation
- Bone Needles
- Spindle Whorls

**T**he Hieroglyphic Stairway at Copán.

Although the rulers of Mayan cities were able to draw on the prestige of their dynastic lineage and the sacred aspect of their office, their power was not absolute or unchallenged. There is evidence that, particularly during the later part of the Classic period, a broader aristocracy came to challenge the power of the ruler. A particularly intriguing discovery made at Copán was a building known as Popol Na, literally a mat house, which appears to have been the locale for meetings of a council of aristocrats. The tension between the power of the aristocracy and the royal lineage appears to have been a critical dynamic in the history of Mayan cities.

## Inequality

The burials of Mayan royalty do not contain large quantities of elaborate goods. The tomb of Yax K'uk Mo', the founder of the Copán dynasty, included jade and shell ornaments, the remains of a headdress made of shells, a number of pottery vessels, and a cache of eccentric flints. These are clearly high-status objects, but they are not an overwhelming display of wealth. It is possible that much greater wealth, including textiles and feathers that have not survived, were originally buried with Yax K'uk Mo'.

The development of household archaeology has begun to make an important contribution to understanding the structure of Mayan society. By moving away from the monuments of the center, household archaeologists cast light on the lives of ordinary people and of diversity among households (Robin 2003). Excavations of Mayan houses have found that not all people had equal access to high-status objects. Particularly as one moves out to small agricultural hamlets, the range of artifacts becomes limited mostly to locally produced objects used in daily life. However, household archaeologists have also found evidence that high-status trade items were not restricted to elite residences.

At the site of **Aguateca**, Guatemala, archaeologists have discovered a unique window into the lives of the Maya at the very end of the Classic period (Inomata and

**P**hotograph of the excavation of the scribe's house at Aguateca.

Stiver 1998). The town of Aguateca was burned and abandoned, most probably the result of a military attack. The people were forced to flee their homes, leaving behind much of what they owned. After the houses burned, their walls collapsed, sealing the floors under rubble. In one of the houses, the tools of a scribe were discovered, providing a vivid picture of the position of scribes in Mayan society (see photo above and Figure 11.6, page 342). The scribe's room included a large number of high-status artifacts, indicating that scribes were members of the Mayan elite. It is interesting that the scribe's room contrasts with the southern part of the building, where cooking vessels and tools used in weaving were found. The excavators suggest that this was the home of a nuclear family in which the male was a scribe and the female, probably his wife, carried out tasks related to food preparation and weaving in the southern part of the building. The excavation of the house at Aguateca points to the many levels of differentiation found in state societies. On a broad scale, there are significant differences between groups within society; however, on a smaller scale, there is also differentiation within households.

One aspect of wealth that is largely invisible archaeologically is richly woven cloth and other elaborate items of clothing. The contemporary Maya are renowned for their colorful clothing containing many design elements that can be found on Classic Mayan sculptures and paintings. Depictions of the Mayan rulers show that, in addition to wearing beautifully woven garments, they donned highly elaborate headdresses made of flowers and feathers (see the Yaxchilán lintel, page 347).

> ▶ The town of **Aguateca**, Guatemala, was compeletely burned and rapidly abandoned, preserving a picture of daily Mayan household life.

## Mayan Hieroglyphics

Like the cuneiform writing system of Mesopotamia, the **Mayan hieroglyphic** writing system developed from pictographic signs that represent concepts to a system that uses these same signs to represent syllables (see Toolbox, page 348). However, Mayan scribes never discarded the pictographic meaning of signs, resulting in a highly complex writing system in which the same sign could represent either a

> ▶ The **Mayan hieroglyphs** were developed to record the timing of ritual events in the lives of rulers.

# TOOLBOX:
## Geophysical Methods

Geophysical methods are used to gain an idea of what lies below a surface without excavating that surface. In effect, geophysical methods allow archaeologists to detect invisible features. The two main geophysical methods used by archaeologists are magnetometry and ground-penetrating radar.

Magnetometry works by detecting magnetic anomalies in the soil. These anomalies are often evidence of buried features such as tombs, pit houses, channels, and roadways (Pasquinucci and Trément 2000). In practice, a magnetometry survey involves walking along a landscape with an instrument that records magnetic readings. The data obtained are collated by computer to present a picture of subsurface anomalies that are interpreted by the archaeologist and used to guide further research.

Ground-penetrating radar (GPR) involves transmitting an electromagnetic pulse into the ground (Conyers 1997). Depending on what the pulse encounters as it travels through the ground, either it is reflected back to the surface or it continues to travel until it is completely dissipated. The analyst uses GPR instruments to build up a reflection profile that provides a picture of any variation in the sediments below the ground. The reflection profile can provide information about the depth and extent of anomalies that might indicate buried archaeological features.

At the Mayan site of Kaminaljuyu, Guatemala, GPR was used as a response to the pressures of excavating under salvage conditions (Valdes and Kaplan 2000). The site today is in a modern urban setting that has been heavily affected by development.

concept or a syllable. The development of Mayan script was not purely the outgrowth of economic functions. The major drive behind the development of written script was recording the timing of ritual events in the lives of rulers. Whereas cuneiform developed out of the economic needs of the ruling elite of the cities of Mesopotamia, the Mayan hieroglyphic writing developed out of the connection between rulers and ritual.

Mayan script first appeared during the Early Classic period through the coalescence of three distinct traditions dating back to the end of the Olmec period (Houston 2000). The first tradition was the use of a segment of an image to represent the whole. An example found in Olmec art is the use of the eye of a jaguar to represent the animal. The progressive abstraction of these forms lies behind many of the Mayan hieroglyphs.

The second tradition was the recording of a complex calendar (Fash 1991). The earliest-recorded calendar date comes from Stela C from the Olmec site of Tres Zapotes, dated to 300 B.C. The Mayan calendar was an extraordinarily complex system of multiple overlapping systems. The Long Count records time from a zero date (August 13, 3114 B.C. according to our calendar). In place of days, weeks, and years, the Maya used a series of four units for measuring time:

1 kin = 1 day

20 kins = 1 uinal = 20 days

18 uinals = 1 tun = 360 days

20 tuns = 1 katun = 7,200 days

20 katuns = 1 baktun = 144,000 days

The Maya also used a 260-day ritual calendar with 23 numbers and 20 named days, a 365-day solar calendar, and at least two other systems. The complexity of the

## FIGURE 11.7

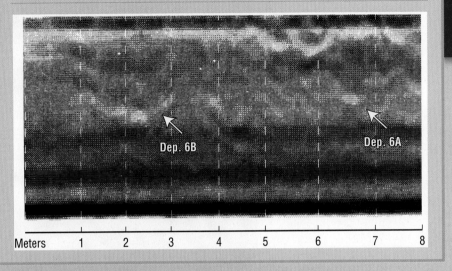

**GPR thermal printout from Kaminaljuyu showing the location of buried features.**

Plans to build a shopping complex and a hotel in the area led to urgent salvage excavations. The GPR survey allowed archaeologists to rapidly survey areas that they would not have had time to test by excavation. The survey succeeded in locating a series of buried objects, ranging from a car muffler to significant archaeological features, including the floor of a house and two ritual caches.

Mayan calendar reflects the centrality and significance the Maya attached to measuring time, matched by an intense interest in recording astronomical events.

There is very slight evidence that Mayan script might also have developed out of a tradition of using written records in economic transactions. If such records existed, they must have been written on perishable materials that have not survived. One of the main sources of evidence for the use of writing to record transactions comes from drawings of a deity writing numbers on leaves.

The Mayan documents that survive deal largely with the recording of events in the lives of the rulers of cities, particularly the dates when the rulers performed significant rituals. Most of the texts that have survived are monuments carved in stone or inscriptions on clay vessels. More complex religious and historical documents were probably written in books known as codices, only a small number of which have survived. A unique expression of the wealth of Mayan mythology is found in the **Popol Vuh,** which was transcribed following the Spanish conquest (Coe 1993). The Popol Vuh tells the epic tale of the hero twins Hunahpu and Xbalnque and their battle with the lords of the underworld, known as Xibalbá. The tale hinges on the skill and trickery of the twins, which together allow them to vanquish the lords of the underworld before rising up through the surface of the earth and into the sky, where they became the sun and moon. A ball game played to the death is central to the story of the Popol Vuh.

▶ The **Popol Vuh** is a Mayan myth written after the Spanish conquests. It tells the epic tale of the hero twins and their battle with the lords of the underworld.

## Ritual, Violence, and Warfare

Rituals of bloodletting and sacrifice were central to Mayan kingship (Schele and Miller 1986). Some of the most vivid scenes of bloodletting are found on a series of carvings from the site of Yaxchilán. In these scenes, the ruler and his wife are seen

A

B

**P**ainted Maya pot. (A) The scene on this pot shows the presentation of tribute to a seated lord (B) and a rolled out view of the scene painted on the vessel. How does this vessel compare to the Warka vase?

drawing blood from their tongues and collecting the dripping blood on special paper (see photo on page 347). The bloodletting brings on spectacular visions of enormous snakes with the heads of gods.

The ball game also played a central role in Mayan society. The epic battle between the hero twins of the Popol Vuh and the lords of the underworld appears to be at the heart of much of Mayan ritual practice. Echoing the centrality of the ball game to Mayan ritual is the position of the ball court at the core of the Mayan city. The ball courts consist of a bare patch of ground, flanked on either side by a banked structure. The game was played with a heavy rubber ball that, apparently, had to be shot through a ring without the use of the hands. Some archaeologists have argued that, as it was in the myth of the Popol Vuh, in real life the ball game was played to the death.

However, violence in the Mayan world went beyond ritual and sport. From sites such as Aguateca, there is clear evidence that cities were conquered and

Limestone lintel from Yax-chilán, Mexico. Lady Wak Tuun is shown during a bloodletting ritual. She holds a stingray spine and rope used in bloodletting and bloodied paper. In front of her, a vision serpent emerges from a bowl containing strips of paper.

burned. Inscriptions record the capture of cities and the death of their rulers, and a vivid series of murals from the site of Bonampak shows scenes of prisoners being tortured and killed. It is not clear how the Maya carried out their warfare. There is no evidence of standing armies, and Mayan weaponry appears to have been limited to flint spears and armor made from skins.

## The Mayan Collapse

In the period around A.D. 870, the cities of the southern Mayan lowlands collapsed. New construction ended and the cities were gradually deserted. The collapse of the classic Mayan cities was the result of a combination of factors internal to Mayan society and external environmental factors. One factor that played a role in weakening

A panel from the Bonampak mural showing tortured prisoners.

# TOOLBOX: Deciphering the Mayan Hieroglyphs

The decipherment of the Mayan hieroglyphs is a triumph of modern scholarship. As with many such ventures, breaking the Mayan code was the result of the combined efforts of numerous scholars. Ironically, one of the most despised figures in colonial history provided the essential key. Bishop Landa is known for the brutality of his term in the Yucatán in the mid-sixteenth century, a term that featured the notorious burning of many Mayan books and codices. However, Bishop Landa also recorded the history of the Maya, including a list of signs and their phonetic readings that turned out to be the key to unlocking the Mayan script.

The discovery that Mayan inscriptions recorded historical events was a major breakthrough in the path to deciphering Mayan hieroglyphs. In an article published in 1961, Tatiana Proskouriakoff presented a reading of stelae from the site of Piedras Negras. Proskouriakoff noticed that a series of stelae had one sign, known as the "toothache sign," associated with a particular date, and another sign, the "upended frog," associated with a date twenty to thirty years earlier. On the basis of this observation, she came to the conclusion that the toothache sign actually indicated that the date which followed was the date a ruler ascended to the throne and that the upended frog indicated that the date which followed was the ruler's birth date. Using this principle, she was able to find the glyphs that were the names of the rulers of Piedras Negras.

Proskouriakoff then turned to three stelae, known as stelae 1–3. On the front of these stelae the inscription is badly eroded, but on the back there is the well-preserved carving of a figure wearing a robe. Proskouriakoff found that stelae 1 and 2 showed the upended-frog glyph (indicating the date of birth), followed by the name of a woman. It was clear that the name was a woman's name

## FIGURE 11.8

**The back of Stela 3 from Piedras Negras showing a woman sitting on a throne with a child beside her.**

the power of the Mayan rulers was the ratcheting up of cycles of violence and warfare. By the end of the Classic period, warfare was widespread and its consequences often catastrophic. The burned town at Aguateca shows these consequences. Excavations at the large urban center of Dos Pilas have uncovered a radical transformation of the site beginning in A.D. 761, when a defensive palisade was built around the central area with stones ripped from the temples and pyramids (see Figure 11.9 on page 350). The residents built a tightly packed siege village in the open plazas and began living in the because it was prefixed by a face in profile with a crosshatched oval or lock of hair on the forehead, the prefix used to indicate that the person named is a woman. The date and the name were the same on both stelae.

The third stela clinched Proskouriakoff's argument. In the carving on this stela, a small figure is shown kneeling below the main figure. The upended-frog-glyph date for this figure is thirty-three years later than the birth date of the main figure. As Prosk-

ouriakoff concluded, "How can one reasonably doubt that both robed figures are portraits of the same person, that person is a woman, and that her little daughter, not yet born when Stela 1 was erected, is shown on Stela 3?" (Proskouriakoff 1961: 16). Proskouriakoff had succeeded in reading a small piece of Mayan history.

REFERENCE: Michael Coe. (1999). *Breaking the Maya Code*. New York: Thames and Hudson.

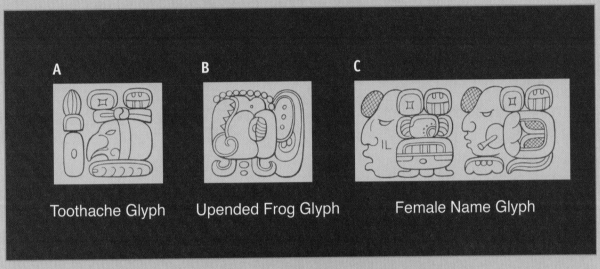

**A**

Toothache Glyph

**B**

Upended Frog Glyph

**C**

Female Name Glyph

▲ A: The toothache glyph indicating that the date that follows is the date a ruler took the throne.

▲ B: The upended frog glyph indicating that the date that follows gives a birth date.

▲ C: The name glyph of the woman on Stela 3. The profile face with a crosshatched oval over the forehead indicates that the person named was a woman.

area once reserved for ritual and ceremony (Demarest 2004). A number of archaeologists argue that the increasing power of the nobility led to a further weakening of the power of the rulers or even resulted in a "nobles revolt" (Fash 1991).

External environmental factors also contributed to the Mayan collapse. The need to feed the large populations of the Mayan cities led to damage to the agricultural lands, and the resulting decrease in agricultural productivity put stress on the cities. Also, a series of severe droughts occurred during the period of the Mayan collapse (Haug et al. 2003). It is likely that these intense short-term climatic events played a role in the abandonment of the Classic Mayan cities.

# FIGURE 11.9

**Reconstructions of the ceremonial core of Dos Pilas before 761 A.D. (bottom) and after 761 A.D. when the area was encircled by a palisade and houses built in the central plaza.**

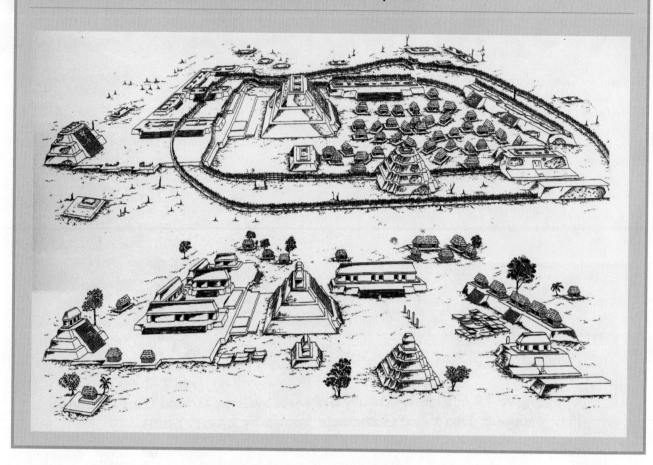

## Summing Up the Evidence

Mayan kings ruled over large urban centers. The emergence of both cities and state society among the Maya is closely linked with external influences, particularly from the highland city of Teotihuacán. The power of the Mayan kings was based on the prestige of the royal lineage and was reinforced by the critical ceremonial role of the king. The prestige of the royal lineage was literally built into the city in the form of monumental inscriptions and the pyramids that encased the burials of the kings. The hieroglyphic writing system was developed as a central tool in recording the timing of ritual events in the lives of rulers. The eventual collapse of the Mayan cities appears to have been the result of a number of factors, including warfare, ecological degradation, and external climatic events. Of these factors, the emergence of warfare between cities seems to have played a decisive role.

## 11.3 SHANG CHINA

According to Chinese historical texts, three powerful dynasties—the Hsia, the Shang, and the Zhou—emerged in northern China during the period between 2000 B.C. and 500 B.C. Unfortunately, it is difficult to trace the archaeological record of the Hsia and early Shang dynasties. Some archaeologists have gone as far as to argue that the Hsia dynasty never really existed. The oldest archaeological site that can be securely correlated with the historical documents is the impressive site of An Yang, the capital of the Late Shang dynasty (1200 B.C.–1045 B.C.).

**An Yang** was discovered when inscribed bones began to appear on the antiquities market and the source of the bones was tracked to a small village in northern China. Intensive excavations at the site recovered the remains of an immense city. The inscribed bones that first led archaeologists to the site are **oracle bones,** which were used to predict the outcomes of events ranging from battles to the weather. After a question was posed in an oracle bone ceremony, the bone was burned and the king interpreted the meaning of the resulting crack. Beginning in the late Shang period, the question posed, the divination, and the eventual outcome were carefully inscribed on the bone. In total, over 150,000 inscribed oracle bones have been recovered, providing a unique perspective on the lives of the rulers of the Shang dynasty (Keightley 2000).

It is likely that historical records and economic transactions were recorded on silk and bamboo slips; however, none of these documents have survived from the Shang period. The other source of inscriptions from An Yang is elaborate bronze vessels that often bear inscriptions. The richly decorated bronze vessels of the Shang dynasty have been described as "the politically all-important ritual symbols" (Chang 1994: 68). The importance of these vessels went beyond the considerable effort involved in acquiring tin and copper and the skill needed to cast such elaborate forms. The bronze vessels were of central importance in carrying out rituals that were the exclusive domain of royalty and nobility. The significance of bronze vessels is expressed in the legend of the Nine Bronze Tripods first cast by Yu, the founder of the Xia dynasty. These tripods became the essential symbols of royalty transferred to the Shang after the fall of the Xia and later passed along to the Zhou dynasty.

The legitimacy of the rulers of the Shang dynasty rested on the unique role they fulfilled in the performance of rituals. The power of divination was reserved for the ruler, and the ruler possessed the vessels necessary for such performance. The power of the rulers flowed not from their identification with a god, but with their essential role in connecting the human world with the divine world.

It is interesting that the Shang used bronze for ritual vessels and for weapons. Bronze was not used for agricultural implements or the tools of daily life. Shang warfare involved the use of horse-drawn chariots, and one oracle bone

▶ **An Yang** was the capital of the Late Shang dynasty (1200 B.C.–1045 B.C.) and is the oldest-known Chinese city.

▶ **Oracle bones** used in divination ceremonies are a rich historical source of information on Shang society.

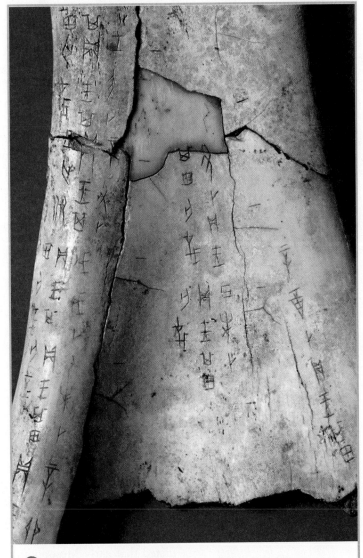

**O**racle bone from An Yang, China. The inscription records the prediction made as well as the actual course of events.

**S**hang bronze vessel from An Yang, China.

records a fighting force 13,000 strong. Clearly, the power of the ruler in Shang society also involved military strength.

The excavations at An Yang have uncovered the remains of a massive burial ground with over 1,000 simple burials and eleven deep burial pits reached by ramps. Large numbers of sacrificial victims, some with their heads buried separately from their bodies, are found in the pits. In the one tomb that had not been robbed in antiquity, an enormous quantity of burial goods, including 440 bronzes and almost 600 jades, were discovered.

An Yang was a large city with a palace area surrounded by neighborhoods and areas with workshops and tombs. The elite area of the site consists of large structures built on platforms of stamped earth laid out on a clear grid. The buildings themselves were made of very simple materials. The excavators believe that some of the structures are divided into a residential area, a temple area, and a ceremonial area. In contrast to the elite houses built on platforms, most of the people lived in small houses dug into the ground.

The power of the rulers of An Yang stretched far beyond the city. It is estimated that the Shang state controlled an area of about 230,000 square kilometers (Trigger 2003). There appears to have been another center near Shangqiu, in eastern Henan province, 215 kilometers from An Yang. The Shang ruler appears to have moved around the kingdom, journeying for business transactions, hunting, feasting, rituals, and warfare against local rebellions and foreign groups.

##  11.4 THE URBAN STATE

In Mesopotamia, Mesoamerica, and China, state societies emerged as part of the same process that led to the emergence of large urban centers. We go back to the image of Gilgamesh and the emergence of the hero together with the city. Civilization and the city are here one and the same. However, using the term "hero" for Gilgamesh raises some questions about the rulers of these early cities. Can we really picture them as the heroes of their societies, or did they sit at the top of a chain of exploitation causing misery for the people living under their control? In Mesopotamia, the despotic ruler is visible in the Ur burials, the seemingly senseless waste of resources and human lives speaking volumes about the power of the elites of Early Dynastic society. However, governmental institutions such as the Code of Hammurabi attest to the ability of the elites to provide justice to a society that thrived at an unprecedented scale. Certainly, few would have predicted that early Mesopotamia had a dynamic economy that involved the private sale of lands recorded in the Kuduru texts.

The Mayan elite ruled over thriving cities and impressive developments in the arts and sciences. However, the horror of warfare shown on the Bonampak murals depicts another side of the activities of these elites. The elites of these early states made possible a degree of social complexity and concentrations of populations that were unprecedented. Yet they did so through a system that involved the control of violence and through the exploitation of the labor of those over whom they ruled.

Mesopotamian and Mayan cities developed around a sacred core. However, there was a significant difference between the sacred cores of the cities in those two areas. The Mesopotamian temple was identified with a deity, who was the source of identity and power for the city. The relationship between the palace and the temple was often ambiguous. In the Mayan cities, the sacred core was closely associated with the ruling dynasty and included the physical remains of rulers buried within the accreting levels of pyramids, as well as their deeds, recorded in carved stone monuments.

In all three civilizations, writing played a critical role in society. On the basis of the available evidence, it appears that, for the Maya and in Shang China, writing was used primarily in a ritual context and to record the actions of the rulers. By contrast, in Mesopotamia, writing was essential to the economy. It is likely that some economic texts were kept by the Maya on organic materials that have not survived. Similar documents written on fragile organic material might have also existed in Shang China.

A critical distinction emerges in comparing the Maya and Mesopotamia with Shang China. For the Maya and in Mesopotamia, each city was an individual polity, a state in and of itself. We refer to cases in which the state is identical to the individual city as city–states. The rivalry between the Mayan city–states evidently contributed to the Mayan collapse. In Mesopotamia, warfare between cities existed but appears to have never reached the magnitude found among the Maya. The tensions between Mesopotamian cities were balanced by a loose confederacy with paramount rule circulating between cities. It is possible that the differences between the Maya and Mesopotamia can be traced back to the sacred spaces at the core of their cities. Among the Maya, the prestige of the city was the expression of the power of the ruling dynasty. It was perhaps inevitable that competition would emerge between dynasties and, as a result, between the cities that were in a sense the incarnation of the dynasty. In Mesopotamia, the temple was dedicated to a divinity rather than a lineage. The city in Mesopotamia was the incarnation of the power and benevolence of a god, and the gods of each city–state made up a part of the Mesopotamian pantheon, providing a divine model for the rulers to follow in developing a system of confederation.

Shang China appears to have been starkly different from the Mayan and Mesopotamian civilizations. An Yang was not one among several city–states, but rather one of perhaps two cities at the core of a large area controlled by a single ruler who traveled frequently across the kingdom. Shang China is an example of a territorial state, a state in which the ruler controls a large territory through provincial and local administrators. It is interesting that the picture in Shang China of the ruler was as the intermediary between the divine and the earthly realms. Through divination rights and the possession of sacred symbols such as bronze tripods, the ruler took the position as the connection between heaven and earth. The power of the ruler flowed not from a place in the city, but from his place in the cosmos.

In all three cases considered in this chapter, states, cities, and clearly marked and powerful elites are closely connected. All of these societies fit well with V. Gordon Childe's (1942) definition of the "Urban Revolution." However, taking up the questions posed by Bruce Trigger about the regularity of the transition to urban state societies, we find significant variation among the cases despite some very general similarities. In the next chapter, we consider three cases that do not fit in easily with the idea of an "Urban Revolution." By casting our net more broadly, we find an even wider diversity of pathways taken in the transition to state society.

- Mesopotamia covers the region along the course of the Tigris and Euphrates Rivers, a region where large-scale agriculture is possible only with irrigation.

- Urban sites appear in Mesopotamia during the Uruk Period, 4000 B.C.–3200 B.C. These cities were developed around temple precincts dating back to the earlier Ubaid period.

- The cuneiform writing system developed in Mesopotamia to record economic information. Cuneiform came to be used for a wide variety of texts, including epics and legal codes.

- The Royal Tombs at Ur demonstrate the power and wealth of early Mesopotamian kings.

- There is little evidence of extensive warfare in early Mesopotamia; however, Uruk sites such as Habuba Kebira, did develop far to the north on the Euphrates River.

- The Olmec sites of 1200 B.C.–300 B.C. on the Gulf Coast of Mexico are the earliest evidence of political complexity in Mesoamerica.

- By 500 B.C., the site of Monte Albán in the Oaxaca Valley had grown into a large city with a population of 5,000 people. Beginning around two thousand years ago, Teotihuacán, in the Valley of Mexico, had grown into a city with a population of more than 80,000 people.

- The Mayan hieroglyphic writing system developed out of the connection between rulers and rituals.

- The core of the Mayan city included royal residences, open plazas, pyramids, and ball courts.

- Mayan cities were ruled by powerful dynasties. The power of the king derived from the prestige of the dynasty and the sacred aspect of kingship.

- Violence and warfare in Mayan society were closely linked to rituals of bloodletting. There is clear evidence of warfare between Mayan cities.

- Around 870 A.D., cities in the southern Mayan lowlands collapsed.

- The emergence of state societies in China is linked to three dynasties known from historical texts: the Hsia, the Shang, and the Zhou.

- The site of An Yang was the Shang capital. Excavations at An Yang have uncovered a large city laid out on a grid. The royal tombs at An Yang include evidence of human sacrifice and a great wealth of burial goods.

- The power of the rulers of the Shang dynasty rested on their role in performing rituals.

## KEY TERMS

## REVIEW QUESTIONS

1. What are the reasons for the development of writing systems in the three civilizations studied? Are there similarities between the civilizations, or is each unique?

2. How does the role of violence in Mayan society compare with that in Early Mesopotamia?

3. Is the association of the Shang ruler with the performance of rituals unique, or are there similarities to the roles of the rulers of Mesopotamian and Mayan cities?

G.L. Barnes. (1993). *China, Korea, and Japan: The Rise of Civilization in East Asia.* London: Thames and Hudson.

K.C. Chang. (1980). *Shang Civilization.* New Haven, Connecticut: Yale University Press.

Arthur Demarest. (2004). *Ancient Maya: The Rise and Fall of a Rainforest Civilization.* Cambridge, U.K.: Cambridge University Press.

William Fash. (1991). *Scribes, Warriors and Kings: The City of Copán and the Ancient Maya.* London: Thames and Hudson.

Susan Pollock. (1999). *Ancient Mesopotamia: The Eden That Never Was.* Cambridge, U.K.: Cambridge University Press.

J.N. Postgate. (1992). *Early Mesopotamia: Economy and Society at the Dawn of History.* London: Routledge.

Linda Schele and M.E. Miller. (1986). *The Blood of Kings: Dynasty and Ritual in Maya Art.* New York: Braziller.

Norman Yoffee. (2005). *Myths of the Archaic State.* Cambridge, U.K.: Cambridge University Press.

# Enigmatic States

IN THE THREE CASE studies presented in this chapter, no consistent association exists between the state, urban centers, and elites. After reading this chapter, you should understand:

▶ The nature of kingship and the role of monumental architecture in ancient Egypt.

▶ The evidence for social organization and the role of the bureaucracy in the Indus Valley civilization.

▶ The characteristics of the urban center and Jenne-Jeno.

Statue of Pharaoh Menkaura, found at Giza.

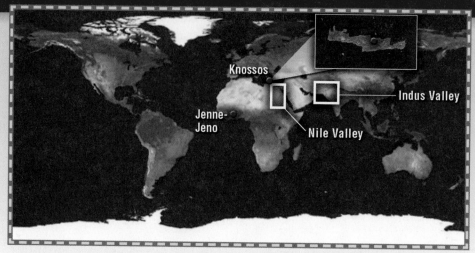

On a spring day in 1900, Arthur Evans stood on the hill of Knossos on the island of Crete and began the excavations that were to transform our knowledge of ancient Greece. As Evans directed his crew digging into the hill of Knossos, he was hunting for a myth. Greek mythology told the story of King Minos of Crete and the terrible secrets of his labyrinth, where the minotaur, a man-eating monster who was half man and half bull, lived imprisoned in the twisted complex built by Daedalus. Perhaps Evans imagined Daedalus and his son flying away from Knossos on wings made of wax and feathers before Icarus, flying too

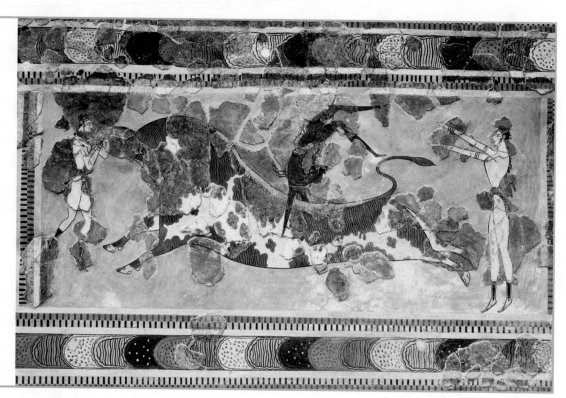

Fresco of a bull leaper from the palace at Knossos. Notice that the scene was reconstructed from fragments visible as darker colored areas in the image.

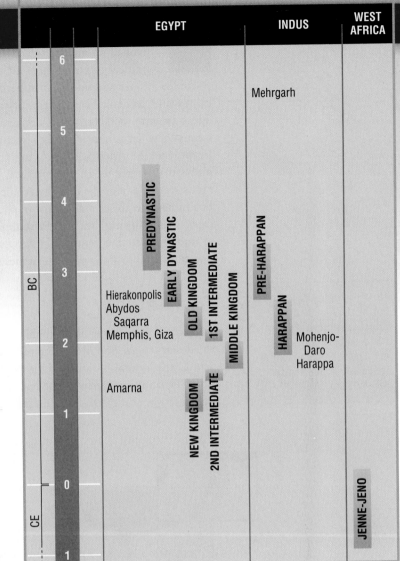

close to the sun, melted his wings and plunged to his death.

Evans's experiences at Knossos lived up to his expectations. He indeed uncovered a large palace adorned with frescoes showing incredible scenes of bull-leaping festivals. However, today some archaeologists question whether the discoveries Evans made at Knossos actually confirm the historical reality of the Greek myth of Minos (MacGillivray 2000). What remains beyond question is that Evans, together with other archaeologists, raised the curtain on a previously unknown civilization: the Minoan civilization of Crete. Over a century after Evans sunk his first pit at Knossos, the Minoans remain an enigmatic counterpart to the walled city–states of mainland Greece. Minoan centers are palaces, like the palace at Knossos, characterized by large reception areas and storage facilities. Much of the functioning of Minoan society remains the subject of ongoing research. However, it is clear that the Minoans had a form of social organization that allowed for the development of social complexity without the emergence of urban centers.

In the civilizations discussed in the last chapter, state bureaucracies developed in the context of emerging urban centers with clearly identified ruling elites. This chapter examines three cases in which the association between the state, urban centers, and elites is less clearly defined. In Egypt, the state developed around the figure of the divine king. The core of the Egyptian state was not an urban center, but rather the monumental mortuary temples that reached colossal form in the pyramids at Giza. In the Indus Valley the state emerged in the context of large urban centers. However, the evidence for a clearly defined elite is ephemeral. The monumental architecture and rich burials characteristic of other early states are absent from the Indus Valley. Finally, the recently discovered city of Jenne-Jeno in West Africa raises the question of whether the development of urban centers is necessarily the expression of a rigidly hierarchical state. Together, all these case studies give a sense of the diversity of pathways followed in the emergence of the state.

# 12.1 EGYPT

The splendor of the temples and tombs of ancient Egypt have long invoked an air of both wonder and mystery. Some have even been led to mystical interpretations of ancient Egypt, seeing monuments such as the pyramids at Giza as evidence of supernatural or extraterrestrial activity. Archaeological research has uncovered a very different perspective on ancient Egypt. As archaeologists unearth potsherds and domestic remains and trace the processes by which monuments were constructed, a picture of the intensely human aspect of ancient Egypt emerges. Ancient Egypt is not the product of otherworldly forces. The monuments that amaze us are the products of human effort and imagination on an enormous scale. Perhaps the most awesome feature of the pyramids is not their sheer size, but rather the chisel marks left on the stones over four thousand years ago. These chisel marks open up the real mysteries of the pyramids: How were people motivated to undertake such a venture? How were they organized? How were they fed? These questions lead to the core of the issues surrounding the origin of the state.

> The **Nile Valley** descends out of the highlands of Ethiopia and cuts through the deserts of the Sudan and Egypt before reaching its outlet in the Mediterranean Sea.

## The Setting

The Nile descends out of the highlands of Ethiopia to cut a dramatic swath through the deserts of the Sudan and Egypt. Until the construction of the Aswan Dam in the 1960s, the annual flooding of the Nile deposited rich alluvial silts across the valley floor. The contrast between the lush vegetation of the **Nile Valley** and the surrounding desert is stark. One can literally place one foot in agricultural fields and the

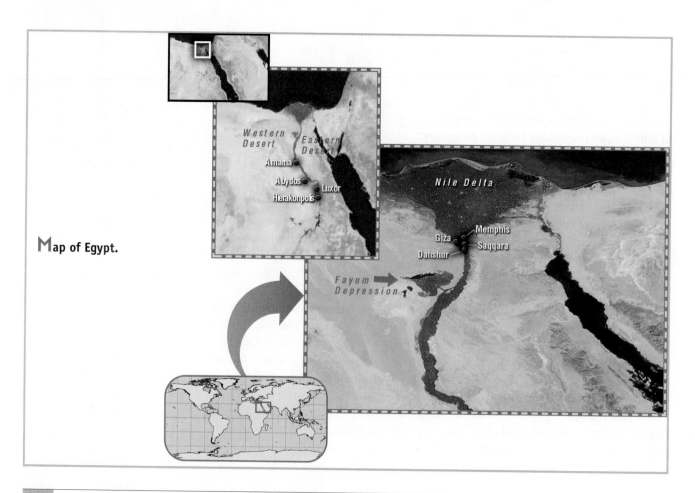

Map of Egypt.

The lush Nile Valley contrasts sharply with the surrounding desert.

other in desert sand. Egypt is thus an extreme case of circumscription, in which the limits of inhabitable land are clearly defined.

Egypt is divided into **Upper Egypt** in the south and **Lower Egypt** in the north. To the north of Cairo, the Nile Valley spreads into several branches, forming the Delta region as it flows towards the Mediterranean Sea. To the south, the limit of Upper Egypt is defined by a series of cataracts or rapids in the area around the modern border between Egypt and Sudan. Aside from the Nile Valley and the Delta, the major inhabitable areas in Egypt are a number of small oases in the Western Desert and the Fayum Depression located just south of Cairo.

The unusual geography of Egypt played a major role in defining the nature of ancient Egyptian society. Because Egypt was protected by deserts to the east and west and by the cataracts to the south, the threat of foreign invasion was minor. Almost all human settlement was located along the Nile Valley. The Nile served as a means of transportation allowing for the easy movement of people and goods north and south along the river. The annual flooding of the Nile served to replenish the soil, so the problems of salination found in southern Mesopotamia are not endemic to Egypt. The richness of the flood also meant that massive irrigation projects were not necessary. The Nile River valley, like Mesopotamia, is completely lacking in mineral resources. However, the surrounding deserts contain sources of metals, including copper and gold, and building materials—including limestone, alabaster, and granite—that the Egyptians exploited heavily.

> ▶ **Upper Egypt** refers to the southern part of the Egyptian Nile Valley. **Lower Egypt** refers to the northern part of the Egyptian Nile Valley.

## Chronology

The shift towards state society in Egypt began during the Predynastic period, the political organization of which remains poorly understood. However, it appears that by the late Predynastic period three kingdoms had formed along the Nile Valley. The earliest evidence for the unification of Egypt under a single ruler is a slab of

## TABLE 12.1

### Chronology of Ancient Egypt (Lehner 1997)

| PERIOD | DATES | DYNASTY | MAJOR SITES |
|---|---|---|---|
| Predynastic | 4500 B.C.–3000 B.C. | | |
| Early Dynastic | 3000 B.C.–2575 B.C. | 1–3 | Hierakonpolis, Abydos, Saqqara |
| Old Kingdom | 2575 B.C.–2134 B.C. | 4–8 | Giza, Memphis |
| First Intermediate | 2134 B.C.–2040 B.C. | 9–11 | |
| Middle Kingdom | 2040 B.C.–1640 B.C. | 12–14 | |
| Second Intermediate | 1640 B.C.–1532 B.C. | 15–17 | |
| New Kingdom | 1532 B.C.–1070 B.C. | 18–20 | Thebes, Amarna |
| Third Intermediate | 1070 B.C.–712 B.C. | 21–25 | |

> The **Narmer Palette** discovered at the site of Hierakonpolis shows the unification of Upper and Lower Egypt under king Narmer.

carved slate known as the **Narmer Palette,** discovered at the site of Hierakonpolis in Upper Egypt.

The Narmer Palette shows vivid scenes of conquest by a king named Narmer (see photo page 364). The rule of Narmer marks the end of the Predynastic period and the beginning of the Early Dynastic period. Significantly, on one side of the pallet Narmer is shown wearing the white conical crown of Upper Egypt, while on the

The Narmer Palette shows Narmer wearing the crowns of Upper and Lower Egypt. How is the power of Narmer shown on this artifact?

other he is shown wearing the red crown of Lower Egypt. The depiction of Narmer with these two crowns indicates that he ruled the entire Nile Valley.

The chronology of Egyptian kings (Table 12.1) is known from historic documents and monuments. The classical historian Manetho (300 B.C.) devised the system of grouping kings into dynasties. Egyptian dynastic history can be divided into three cycles of integration and collapse (Hallo and Simpson 1971). During periods of integration (Early Dynastic/Old Kingdom, Middle Kingdom, New Kingdom), Egypt was controlled by a single centralized authority. During periods of collapse (First Intermediate, Second Intermediate, Third Intermediate), competing centers of authority emerged and competing dynasties, with control over only a part of the country, ruled simultaneously.

A constant dynamic in Egyptian dynastic history is a struggle for dominance between Upper and Lower Egypt. The **First Dynasty** was based in **Hierakonpolis** and **Abydos** in Upper Egypt. The Second Dynasty offers the first evidence for a shift to the Royal Cemetery of Saqqara in Lower Egypt, and during the Old Kingdom kingship was firmly established at Memphis in Lower Egypt. In the New Kingdom, the center of power shifted to Luxor in Upper Egypt.

▶ **Hierakonpolis** and **Abydos** in Upper Egypt were centers of the **First Dynasty.**

Although Egypt was relatively well protected from foreign invasion, incursions from the north and south did take place, particularly during the periods of collapse. During the Middle and New Kingdoms, Egypt embarked on ambitious military campaigns in the north, ultimately coming into conflict with Mesopotamian powers. During those same kingdoms, Egypt also came to play an active role in trade networks connecting the lands of the eastern Mediterranean.

**S**ection of the bakery scene in the Tomb of Ty, Saqqara. This register shows the integral role scribes played in the economy of the Old Kingdom.

# TOOLBOX:
## Tracking Trade Routes

Tracking trade routes is essential to understanding how politically complex societies interact with their neighbors. In some cases, it is possible to find the physical traces of trade. A stunning example is the discovery at the site of Ulu Burun off the southern coast of Turkey of the wreck of a shipwreck dating to the Egyptian New Kingdom (Bass 1986). Excavations at Ulu Burun recovered a rich assemblage of trade items, including copper, tin, and glass ingots, storage jars containing traces of organic products, and more exotic items such as gold and ivory.

Archaeologists can also trace trade routes on the basis of the physical properties of artifacts. For example, on Egyptian sites dating to the New Kingdom, pottery vessels from Cyprus and Greece can easily be identified on the basis of their distinctive shapes and surface finish. However, in many cases, it is necessary to employ more complex methods to identify the source of archaeological artifacts.

For objects made of clay, petrographic analysis is often used to identify the place where the artifact was produced. Petrography is a branch of geology that focuses on the identification of minerals and rocks on the basis of their physical properties. Archaeological petrographers identify the minerals that have been added to clay during its manufacture. Petrographic analysis involves taking a very thin slice from a piece of pottery and then polishing it until it is so thin that light can travel through it. The "thin section" is then studied under a petrographic microscope that allows light to pass through the section. By combining evidence having to do with size, color, and the way light is refracted through the thin section, the petrographer can identify the mineral component of the pottery vessel. By referring the mineral composition of the specimen to geological maps, the petrographer will often be able to determine where a pot was manufactured.

▲ Excavation of the shipwreck at Ulu Burun, Turkey. Shown in this picture are stacks of copper ingots that made up an important part of the ship's cargo.

## Government and Writing

The ultimate source of the power of the Egyptian king was his identification as a divinity. The king in Egypt was the human incarnation of the falcon god Horus, the paramount god in the Egyptian pantheon. Upon his death, the king became the incarnation of the god Osiris, the god of the dead. The king also had a special relationship to the sun god Ra; however, the way this relationship was expressed varies among documents.

The power of the king was tightly linked to the critical Egyptian concept of *ma'at,* which combines the virtues of balance and justice. In Egyptian thought,

◄ The concept of *ma'at* combines the virtues of balance and justice.

Petrographic analysis has been applied to the study of diplomatic letters discovered in the New Kingdom Egyptian city of Amarna (Goren et al. 2004). Although found in Egypt, these documents were written on clay tablets in Akkadian, the language of Mesopotamia, using cuneiform script. During the New Kingdom, cuneiform was used as the medium for diplomatic communication. The letters are from neighboring kings seeking alliances with Egypt. The Amarna letters provide a unique insight into the diplomatic world of the New Kingdom. However, some information about the geographical location of the kings sending the letters is unclear. A petrographic analysis project treated these tablets as clay artifacts and managed to link some tablets to the places they were made on the basis of the mineral component of the clay.

Neutron activation analysis is another method for finding the source of ceramic artifacts. Rather than looking at the mineralogy of materials added to the clay, neutron activation focuses on the chemical characteristics of the clay itself. With the help of a nuclear reactor, it is possible to create a profile of the rare elements that are present at very low levels in the clay. This profile can serve as a chemical fingerprint for the clay a pot was made from that can be matched with the fingerprint of known geological clay sources. Neutron activation analysis was used to trace a unique pot known as the "Dolphin Vase" found on the Middle Kingdom Egyptian site of Lisht back to its place of manufacture near the modern city of Gaza (McGovern et al. 1994).

◄ One of the Amarna letters. Although written in cuneiform, these are letters between the Egyptian ruler and vassal states to the north.

chaos and disorder were viewed as catastrophic and the role of the king was to ensure the preservation of *ma'at*. The breakdown of centralized rule during periods of collapse is described in Egyptian documents as a fundamental, even cosmic, calamity.

It is quite a distance from the lofty concepts of divine kingship and *ma'at* to the more mundane business of organizing a large kingdom. It is clear, for example, that the divine status of the ruler did not prevent palace intrigue and, in some cases, even murder. The king controlled the state through the agency of armies of scribes (Kemp 1991). In the harvesting and processing of cereals, scribes intervened at every stage to measure output and deter theft. The yield of the harvest was measured in the field, during transport, and at delivery. The quantities of bread and beer produced from grain were carefully measured before being distributed as rations.

A vivid picture of the role of the scribe is found on the bottom register of a scene painted in an Old Kingdom tomb from Saqqara. Egyptian tombs were often painted with detailed depictions of daily life meant to magically provide for the deceased in the afterlife. The Tomb of Ty at Saqqara gives particularly detailed pictures of a bakery/brewery. In the bottom register, a line of scribes is shown at work.

Scribes are depicted as an integral element of the operation of a bakery. An individual on the left side of the scene is shown being brought to the scribes for discipline.

There is a clear sense that in ancient Egypt the extended family remained an essential social unit. Some even go as far as to suggest that the conception of kingship was based on an extension of the household. A study of graffiti left by workers on blocks in the Giza pyramids affords a unique insight into the organization of labor in the Old Kingdom (Roth 1991). Workers were organized into large labor groups, perhaps organized by clan or extended family. This evidence offers a challenge to the idea that the state represents a rupture with social organization based on kinship.

The Egyptian bureaucracy often operated by breaking tasks into equivalent parts. The practice of dividing tasks into parts is vividly preserved in an unfinished chamber located below the pyramid of Cheops at Giza. The chamber is reached by climbing down a long descending passageway that stretches deep below bedrock. For reasons that are not clear, this chamber was abandoned in the midst of quarrying and was never completed. Walking around the room, one can follow the hammerblows of the workers as they labored to hollow out the subterranean room. One can see that the room has been divided in half and then in half again, with two sets of two teams working in parallel. This simple organizational tactic appears to have been widely used by Egyptians to organize large-scale construction projects.

The hieroglyphic writing used by Egyptian scribes is based on a combination of logograms (signs that represent a whole word), phonograms (signs that represent sounds), and determinatives (signs that indicate the exact meaning of a word). Documents were written in ink on paper made of papyrus, a reed native to the Nile Valley. Unfortunately, few of these documents survive from early periods. Because hieroglyphics were not suited for rapidly writing administrative documents, an alternative script known as hieratic was developed by the Fourth Dynasty. Hieroglyphics remained in use primarily for inscribing monuments.

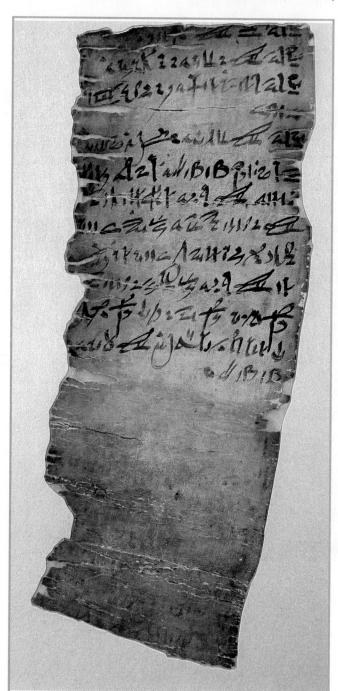

**P**archment in Egyptian hieratic script from the Third Intermediate period.

# The Pyramids

In the early Mesopotamian and Mayan cities, temples were located at the core of large urban centers. In Mesopotamia, the temple was kept separate from the palace, and it was the temple as the home of the god that gave the city its sense of permanence and identity. The pyramids and temples of Mayan cities were closely identified with the rulers of the city, with the pyramids often encasing the tombs of deceased royalty. Monumental inscriptions such as the hieroglyphic staircase at Copán recorded the history of the ruling dynasty.

The pyramids of Old Kingdom Egypt are among the most impressive monuments ever built. These spectacular structures were constructed on the desert fringe at a distance from major settlements. The pyramids were temples to the deceased king, who was the incarnation of the god Osiris. Veneration of the king required both the preservation of his corpse and provision for his needs in the afterlife. The mortuary temples of Egypt were not the core around which the city developed, but rather were a distinct center of power.

### The Development of Mortuary Architecture.
The development of royal mortuary architecture in Egypt has its roots in the Predynastic period. By the Early Dynastic period, elaborate royal burial structures were built at the site of Abydos. The first pyramid was the stepped pyramid at Saqqara built in the Third Dynasty. This pyramid was soon followed by the construction of true pyramids, culminating in the great pyramid at Giza.

### Hierakonpolis and Abydos.
The earliest structure identified as a royal tomb is Tomb 100 from the site of Hierakonpolis, which dates to the end of the Predynastic period. Tomb 100 is a mud brick structure with crude wall paintings that include

## FIGURE 12.1

The painted wall of Tomb 100 at Hierakonpolis. Can you find any scenes like those on the Narmer Palette?

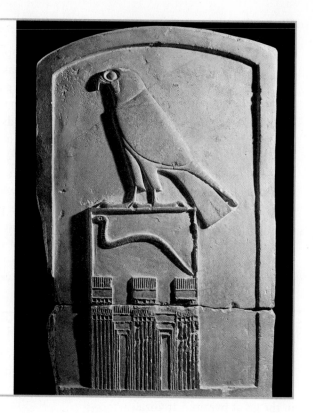

**S**tone tomb marker of Djet from Abydos, First Dynasty. The snake hieroglyph, *djet,* is framed within a depiction of a royal palace façade.

depictions of a figure smiting an enemy. It is interesting that the wall paintings of Tomb 100 include depictions of two boats, possibly reflecting the beliefs that led later kings to bury boats next to their tombs.

During the First and Second Dynasty, the royal burial ground moved to the desert cemetery of Abydos (Kemp 1991). The tombs at Abydos are simple brick chambers built into pits dug into the ground. Above the burial chamber, a square

**P**lan of the Djoser complex. The pyramid complex is contained within an enclosure wall.

mud brick enclosure was erected and then filled in with earth and gravel. A pair of stone markers inscribed with the name of the king was placed in front of the tomb, and a separate small temple was built close to the valley floor. Recent excavations of the burial remains of King Aha at Abydos have made some surprising discoveries. The burial enclosure appears to have been purposefully destroyed shortly after construction. Outside the enclosure, a number of subsidiary burials have been excavated that appear to provide evidence of human and animal sacrifice to accompany the deceased king to the afterlife (http://www.museum.upenn.edu/new/research/ Exp_Rese_Disc/AfricaEgypt/abydos/release.shtml). Archaeologists have also recently uncovered an enigmatic fleet of buried boats at Abydos.

**Saqqara and Dahshur.** By the Third Dynasty, the royal burial site had shifted to **Saqqara**, located outside of Cairo. The first pyramid is the stepped pyramid constructed by **King Djoser** of the Third Dynasty (Lehner 1997). At Saqqara, an enclosure wall surrounds a large open-air courtyard in the middle of which stands the stepped pyramid. The royal tomb is located in a granite vault in an elaborate network of chambers branching off from a central shaft below the pyramid. The pyramid itself was built in a series of stages. It appears to have been originally conceived as a simple, if massive, filled enclosure like those found at Abydos. Only after building was underway did the project evolve into the construction of a pyramid.

Three engravings found in the Djoser complex depict the Sed festival, an event during which the king would run a course in an important ritual of renewal. In this festival, a performance by the king is essential to maintaining order in the world. The architecture of the Djoser complex actually replicates in stone the field that the living king would have run during the Sed festival. It is notable that because of the high enclosure walls, this symbolic ritual ground was hidden from view. Although the portion of the stepped pyramid visible beyond the enclosure would have been impressive, the fundamental characteristic of the Djoser pyramid complex is that it encloses and hides sacred space.

▶ The stepped pyramid of **King Djoser** at **Saqqara** is located within a walled complex.

**V**iew of the stepped pyramid at Saqqara. Early construction phases are visible in the bottom level of the pyramid.

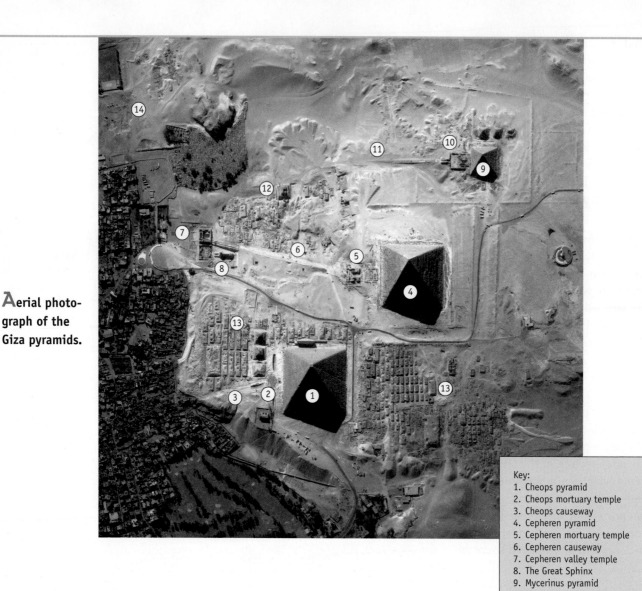

**Aerial photograph of the Giza pyramids.**

Key:
1. Cheops pyramid
2. Cheops mortuary temple
3. Cheops causeway
4. Cepheren pyramid
5. Cepheren mortuary temple
6. Cepheren causeway
7. Cepheren valley temple
8. The Great Sphinx
9. Mycerinus pyramid

The first true pyramid was built by King Snefru of the Fourth Dynasty at the site of Dahshur just south of Saqqara. Snefru actually attempted to build a pyramid three times before succeeding in constructing a true pyramid on the third try. The first attempt, at the site of Meidum, appears to have collapsed during construction. Snefru then moved to Dahshur, where he built the bent pyramid that began at a very steep slope of approximately 60 degrees (Lehner 1997). Midway through construction, the slope was decreased to approximately 44 degrees, resulting in a pyramid with a pronounced "bend." The final pyramid built by Snefru was the Red Pyramid, a true pyramid 105 meters in height.

> The apex of pyramid building was reached in the Fourth Dynasty pyramids of **Cheops, Cepheren,** and **Mycerinus** at **Giza.**

**Giza.** Pyramid building reached its apex with the Fourth Dynasty kings who built their pyramids at **Giza, Cheops, Cepheren,** and **Mycerinus.** Subsequent dynasties put far less effort into the construction of monumental pyramids, although the tradition persisted well into the Middle Kingdom. The Giza pyramids are very different in conception from the Djoser pyramid complex. At Giza, there is no enclosure wall hiding the sacred ground. The Giza pyramids are one element of a pyramid complex made up of four parts. The first element of the complex was a temple constructed near the

View of the Cepheren (left) and Cheops (right) pyramids from the south.

Nile Valley. The second element was a massive causeway connecting the valley temple to the desert plateau on which the pyramids were built and to the third element of the pyramid complex, the mortuary temple, which itself is built up against the pyramid. The pyramid itself was the final and most visible element of the complex. The three royal pyramids at Giza are surrounded by subsidiary structures, including secondary pyramids, massive fields of bench-shaped "mastaba" tombs of nobility, and long pits in which boats were buried.

The first pyramid built at Giza is also the largest pyramid ever built. The pyramid of Cheops rises to a height of 146 meters and contains an estimated 2,300,000 blocks of stone. This monumental building task appears to have been accomplished during a reign that lasted 32 years. Ironically, the only royal statue that remains of Cheops is a crude stone figure less than eight centimeters in height. Originally, the pyramid was sheathed in a casing of fine polished limestone. It is hard to imagine the effect this massive gleaming edifice would have had, emerging from the flat, dull landscape of the desert plateau. The burial chamber of the Cheops pyramid is hidden within the body of the pyramid at the top of a massive ramp. The actual burial chamber is constructed of massive granite monoliths transported from Upper Egypt. Standing in the burial chamber today, one is struck by the complete absence of ornamentation. The body of the king, presumably wrapped in a shroud, was laid to rest in a sarcophagus embedded in the floor of the burial chamber. The sarcophagus was then enclosed in the massive granite walls of the chamber, which itself is buried deep within the mass of the pyramidal structure.

The Cepheren pyramid is slightly smaller than the Cheops pyramid. Some of the original casing stones have survived on the upper part of the Cepheren pyramid, providing an idea of what these monuments looked like when they were first constructed. Cepheren's image is well preserved in a series of powerful sculptures discovered in his pyramid's valley temple. One of the most famous features at Giza is the Great Sphinx, the figure of a cat with a human head carved into the bedrock of a small hill adjoining the Cepheren valley temple.

The Great Sphinx was carved from a small limestone hill. The layers of rock vary in hardness resulting in unequal weathering of the body of the Sphinx.

# TOOLBOX:
## Excavating Giza

How can an archaeologist hope to understand monuments as overwhelming as the pyramids of Giza? Mark Lehner has approached this problem in a unique fashion. Rather than choosing to focus on one particular monument or tomb, Lehner has taken on the daunting task of exploring the Giza Plateau as a unified landscape. One of his first insights came from working with a geologist. Together, they were able to show that the pyramids were built at the edge of a limestone plateau. For the bulk of the pyramids, the builders were able to use rocks quarried from the edge of the plateau.

Lehner then began to ask questions about how the construction of the pyramids was organized. How were blocks brought up to the plateau? Where were the ramps located to drag blocks up the rising pyramids? Perhaps most importantly, where did the builders live? After over a century of exploration, there was only scant evidence for a workers village at Giza, a circumstance that seems quite odd, given that the labor force must have been in the thousands or even tens of thousands.

In 1988, Lehner began a project to answer the latter question. He drew on his intimate knowledge drawn from over a decade of experience at Giza and tried to figure out where on the crowded Giza Plateau there might be space for a settlement. The first location he examined was a bowl-shaped depression to the south of the pyramids. Examination of this area quickly showed that it had never been inhabited. He then turned to a second area behind the Cepheren pyramid, where the archaeologist Flinders Petrie had found a series of large rectangular rooms or galleries. Lehner's excavations uncovered the same galleries found by Petrie and showed that this was a truly massive structure that was over a football field long. However, there was no trace of habitation in the rooms—only scant traces of manufacturing. It appears that these rooms were storerooms and workshops.

Lehner then turned to a third area near the shallow depression where he had begun his search. Here, a massive wall separated the sacred space of the plateau from the area beyond. Excavations quickly began to pick up the traces of occupation, particularly vessels used for brewing beer and baking bread. By the end of the second season, Lehner had uncovered a bakery and his Egyptian colleagues, led by Zahi Hawass, had found a large burial ground.

Once the bakery was excavated, Lehner was faced with a problem: He could continue to excavate, structure by structure, but using traditional archaeological methods, he would never get an idea of the area as a whole. So he launched a bold campaign of horizontal excavation, stripping the overlying sands from a massive area with the help of heavy equipment. These excavations are still in progress, but already the traces of a palace and workshop complex have been uncovered. These traces provide a picture of the royal establishment at Giza and the workshops that would have produced the food to supply a large workforce. But what of a workers' village? One possibility is that such a village lies below the modern town Nazlet el Seman, which borders the excavated areas. However, as Lehner's team has continued stripping the overlying sands from areas beyond the palace complex, the remains of modest irregular structures have begun to appear. Perhaps Lehner has finally found the elusive traces of the pyramid builders.

REFERENCE: *http://www.aeraweb.org*

▲ Excavation of a bakery in the area south of the Giza pyramids.

Mycerinus was the last king to build a pyramid at Giza, and his effort was more modest than those of his predecessors, reaching only 65 meters in height. The most impressive aspect of the Mycerinus pyramid is the fact that it was at least partially sheathed in polished granite. Some of the most beautiful Old Kingdom sculptures are figures of Mycerinus that were recovered from his valley temple. These figures convey the sense of quiet power that is the hallmark of Old Kingdom art.

**The Pyramids and the State.** The stepped pyramid of Djoser at Saqqara is cloaked in an enclosure wall. The great power of the pyramid complex was visible only to those allowed into the enclosure. The conception of the pyramid complex first developed by Snefru at Meidum and Dahshur and then brought to full fruition at Giza is radically different. At these sites, the pyramid complex sits on sacred ground, but the monumental pyramids are an inescapable presence visible to all. The Giza pyramids project the power of the king and make the power of the state an inescapably real part of the landscape. However, even at Giza, not all is visible: The king's body is wrapped in a shroud and placed in a stone sarcophagus in a chamber hidden in the mass of the pyramid.

The pyramid complexes made the power of the king visible while cloaking the body of the king in mystery. At the same time, the construction of the pyramids was an undertaking of such immensity that building pyramids became a substantial aspect of what the state did. One of the most fascinating questions in archaeology is how the early Egyptian state was able to mobilize the labor to build these spectacular monuments. Unfortunately, despite well over a century of archaeological excavation, little is known about the workers who built the pyramids. Extensive surveys and excavations in the areas directly surrounding the pyramids have produced little evidence of human habitation. Since pyramid building would have involved tens of thousands of people, this finding is surprising. Beginning in the 1980s, excavations to the south of the Great Sphinx have begun to pick up traces of the massive organization of labor involved in constructing the pyramids. Excavations directed by Mark Lehner have uncovered the remains of a massive structure which includes enormous galleries that might have served to house some of the workers. The structure also includes breweries and bakeries, as well as rooms for processing fish. This evidence indicates that at least some of the workers at the pyramids were paid in the form of food rations. The organization required in building the pyramids involved not only labor for constructing the structures, but also people to produce food for the labor force.

**S**tatue of Mycerinus and his wife from the Mycerinus Valley Temple at Giza. This sculpture has the quiet power characteristic of Old Kingdom sculpture. How does this representation of the king compare to the Narmer Palette?

# The City

The Egyptian king ruled over the entire Nile Valley. Egypt was a territorial state rather than a city–state. The fundamental expression of the Egyptian state was the unification of Egypt embodied by the figure of the king wearing the crowns of Upper and Lower Egypt. The monumental core of the early Egyptian state was not embedded in an urban center.

The largest settlements known from the Early Dynastic and Old Kingdom periods are best characterized as large towns rather than cities. However, it is possible that the picture of Egypt as a state without cities is partly the result of the limitations of archaeological recovery. At many sites, the Early Dynastic and Old Kingdom levels are far below the water table and cannot be reached by excavation. This is true of Memphis, the Old Kingdom capitol of Egypt, where excavations have not been able to penetrate below the New Kingdom occupation.

**Amarna.** A unique picture of an Egyptian city is preserved at the New Kingdom site of **Amarna** in Upper Egypt. Amarna was founded as a new capital city by the heretic king Akhenaten (1363 B.C.–1347 B.C.). **Akhenaten** put in place a reform of Egyptian religion, discarding much of the Egyptian pantheon in favor of a focus on the visible disc of the sun known by the Egyptians as Aten. Beyond religious reform and founding a new capital, Akhenaten developed a new art style in which he and his queen Nefertiti were depicted with oddly elongated features.

After his death, Akhenaten's religious reforms were abandoned, his monuments smashed, and his city at Amarna abandoned. Because Amarna was not subsequently reoccupied, it has provided archaeologists an opportunity to map extensive horizontal exposures of a fortified city stretching for over a kilometer along a major ceremonial road. Excavations of workshops, houses, and bakeries have provided unique insights into life in an Egyptian city. The question that lingers is whether there were cities like Amarna in earlier periods of Egyptian dynastic history or whether urban centers developed only during the New Kingdom.

> The city of **Amarna** was built by the New Kingdom ruler **Akhenaten** and was abandoned after his reign.

Statue of Akhenaten.

## Summing Up the Evidence

The Egyptian state challenges expectations archaeologists have of state societies. The most obvious challenge is that there is at present no evidence that the early Egyptian state was an urban society. No cities are known from the Old Kingdom. Indeed, not only are cities absent, but the focal point of the state was the construction of massive funerary monuments that were set out in the desert margins. However, there is also a more subtle challenge: What we know about social organization suggests that, in Egypt, kinship continued to play an important role long after the formation of the state.

The pyramids of Giza lead us to question the source of the legitimacy of this early state society. These monuments are spectacular feats of engineering, organization, and sheer human effort. We have begun to gain an understanding of how the labor was organized, but the question remains of how these people were motivated to participate in such an undertaking. Is it possible that the state was powerful enough to coerce such a massive labor force? There is no evidence to support such a hypothesis, although, undoubtedly, not everybody participated willingly. There is considerable reason to think that the belief in the king as the actual incarnation of divinity essential for the maintenance of *ma'at* played a key role in the creation of the Egyptian state. It is hard not to come to the conclusion that the people who built the pyramids at Giza did so, at least in part, because they believed that they were building the tomb of a living deity.

## 12.2 THE INDUS VALLEY

The Harappan civilization developed along the Indus Valley in modern-day Pakistan at approximately the same time that the Great Pyramids were built in Egypt. The Harappan civilization is in many ways the antithesis of Old Kingdom Egypt. The defining characteristic of the Harappan civilization is the presence of well-planned cities, notably the urban centers of Harappa and Mohenjo-Daro. However, monumental architecture is virtually absent from the Indus Valley, as is any evidence for the elaboration of the power of the ruler through intricate mortuary rituals. The Harappan civilization remains wrapped in enigma and mystery. The rulers remain largely faceless and nameless, and perhaps most intriguing, the Harappan script remains one of the few undeciphered ancient languages.

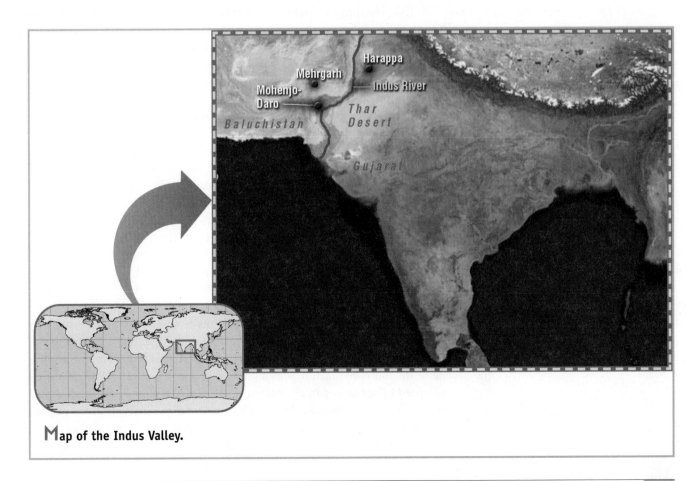

Map of the Indus Valley.

# The Setting and Chronology

The Indus River descends from the highlands of the Himalaya mountains and winds through 3,000 kilometers of modern Pakistan before flowing into the Arabian Sea. The Indus is among the most powerful rivers in the world, with twice the annual flow of the Nile and three times the combined flow of the Tigris and the Euphrates Rivers (Jarrige 1989). The Indus is also an unpredictable river that frequently changes its course. During the time of the Harappan civilization, the Ghaggar-Hakra River, which is now dry, flowed to east of the Indus.

The **Indus Valley** extends along the course of the Indus River and covers much of modern Pakistan and the Kutch and Gujarat provinces of India.

The rich agricultural lands of the **Indus Valley** are bounded on the east by the highlands of Baluchistan and on the northwest by the highlands of Afghanistan. To the east, the Indus Valley is bounded by the Great Thar desert. The Harappan civilization extended across the entire Indus Valley, covering an area of almost half a million square miles. In the southeast, Harappan sites are found along the coastal regions of Kutch and Gujarat (Allchin and Allchin 1982). Trade networks connected the Harappan civilization by sea to the Arabian Peninsula and Mesopotamia and overland into Iran and Afghanistan. Carnelian beads made in the Indus Valley are among the treasures discovered in the Royal Tombs at Ur. The Indus Valley has been identified as the land of Melluha, mentioned in Mesopotamian texts as an important trading partner.

Excavations at the site of Mehrgarh in the Baluchistan foothills to the west of the Indus Valley have produced important information on the Neolithic and later prehistoric societies of the region (Jarrige 1989). The agriculture of Mehrgarh was based on plants and animals first domesticated in the Middle East, including wheat, barley, sheep, goats, and cattle. These plants and animals continued to form the basis of agriculture during the Harappan period. In Level IIa at Mehrgarh, which dates to around 5500 B.C., buildings consisting of a series of square cells have been excavated. The excavators interpret these structures as silos for storing surplus crops.

The earliest evidence for extensive settlement of the Indus Valley comes from the Pre-Harappan period between 3300 B.C. and 2600 B.C. Sites dating to this period include large towns surrounded by fortification walls. It is unclear whether these walls were for defense from human invaders or for protection against river floods and erosion. During the Pre-Harappan period, there was an increase in the uniformity of material culture across the Indus Valley.

Urban centers developed in the Indus Valley during the **Harappan period** between 2600 B.C. and 1900 B.C.

The **Harappan period** lasted for 700 years, from 2600 B.C. to 1900 B.C. The beginning of the Harappan period is marked by the expansion of a small number of sites into major urban centers. The material culture of the Harappan period is extremely uniform across the entire Indus Valley. The end of the period is the subject of considerable debate. Some archaeologists believe that invading forces—perhaps even the Aryan invaders described in the sacred Hindu texts of the *Rigveda*—destroyed the Harappan civilization. The main evidence for this interpretation consists of groups of skeletons found in the final levels of Mohenjo-Daro. In one staircase thirteen skeletons of adults and children were found, while in another area the sprawled skeletons of three men, one woman, and a child were discovered (Agrawal 1985). A recent reanalysis of the skeletons from Mohenjo-Daro suggests that these people may have died from an outbreak of malaria, rather than as the victims of a conquering army (Bahn 2002). Many archaeologists today emphasize that the decline of the Indus civilization was a gradual process (Kenoyer 1998). Following the collapse of the Harappan civilization there was a decline in the size of sites in the Indus Valley and an increased diversity of material culture within the region. When large urban centers were reestablished in the Indian subcontinent over a century later, they were built along the Ganges river system in India.

# The City

In the 1850s, British railway engineers began construction of a railway link between Lahore and Multan in what was then the Punjab province of the British Empire (Kenoyer 1998). Searching for material for the railway beds, these engineers seized on the idea of using crushed brick rubble from mounds they found along the path of the railroad. Archaeologists were both powerless to stop the destruction and puzzled by the absence of Buddhist-period remains from the mounds. It took over fifty years until archaeologists understood that these sites were the remains of a previously unknown civilization (Marshall 1928).

Harappan cities have a number of common features. Houses and other structures are laid along a regular grid of streets that run through the city. The most striking aspect of Harappan cities is the sense of order and the emphasis on hygiene. Elaborate drains are found leading from the houses to covered channels that run through the streets and out of the city (Jansen 1989). Water was supplied to the city from wells lined with fired bricks, and structures were built of fired bricks of a uniform size. The normal brick size was 28 by 14 by 7 centimeters (Allchin and Allchin 1982).

Most of the Harrapan settlements were small villages. Only five large cities greater than 80 hectares in size are known. The largest Harappan cities were the sites of **Harappa** and **Mohenjo-Daro**.

> ▶ The largest Harappan cities were **Harappa** and **Mohenjo-Daro.**

Both Harappa and Mohenjo-Daro were built on a series of walled mounds. Most archaeologists argue that the cities consisted of an elite area on a high mound or citadel at the western side of the city that overlooked a lower town where the nonelite members of society lived. Excavations along the edge of the high mound at Mohenjo-Daro suggest that the citadel buildings were constructed on a massive mud brick platform.

Although the mounds that make up Harappa and Mohenjo-Daro were walled, it is not clear that the walls were designed for military defense. At neither site,

Reconstruction of the city of Harappa. A large street with a central drain runs from the gate through the city.

**V**iew down a street drain at Mohenjo-Daro, Pakistan.

with the possible exception of the Mohenjo-Daro skeletons, is there evidence of warfare.

At Mohenjo-Daro and Harappa, excavations uncovered large buildings that have been interpreted as granaries. At Harappa, the "granary" is a building measuring 40 by 50 meters, constructed on a mud brick foundation. The building consists of a series of two rows of six rooms built along a central passage. At Mohenjo-Daro, the "granary" is a building measuring 50 by 27 meters. The foundation of the building is divided into 27 square blocks separated (Kenoyer 1998). There is no evidence

**T**he Great Bath at Mohenjo-Daro, Pakistan.

that decisively supports the identification of these structures as granaries. However, the structures are clearly the remains of large public buildings of some kind.

The most impressive structure found on a Harappan site is the **Great Bath** of Mohenjo-Daro. At the center of the Great Bath is a brick-lined basin, sealed with gypsum mortar and asphalt, 12 by 7 meters in area and 3 meters in depth, surrounded by an impressive pillared gallery. A flight of stairs at both ends leads down to the bottom of the basin. A large well found in an adjoining room was the source of water for filling the Great Bath. Archaeologists have developed a wide range of interpretations of this structure, ranging from its serving as the site of sacred rituals of cleanliness to its being a nice place to cool off on a hot summer day.

▶ The **Great Bath** is an impressive structure built around a rectangular basin on the high mound of Mohenjo-Daro.

## Writing

The **Harappan script** is known mostly from small carved stone sealings used to mark vessels and bundles (Kenoyer 1998). Other inscribed objects include flat pieces of copper, a gold pendant, a bronze axe, and small incised tablets. The writing is limited to a small number of characters per inscription. Although over four hundred different signs have been identified, the longest-known inscription has a series of twenty-six signs. Given the large number of symbols, it appears likely that the writing system was either logographic (signs represent words) or ideographic (signs represent concepts). To date, the Harappan script has not been deciphered.

▶ The **Harappan script,** found mostly on sealings, has not been deciphered.

The unreadable inscriptions on the Harappan seals leave many unanswered questions. Are they the names of the owners of the seals? Or perhaps the inscriptions are the names of deities with whom the owner was identified? The unanswered questions increase when the depictions found on the seals are taken into consideration. The most common scene is of a bull, an elephant, or a rhinoceros, often shown standing in front of what appears to be an incense burner. But more fantastic creatures, including unicorns, three-headed animals, and what appears to be a horned tiger, are also found on Harappan seals. The most enigmatic seals show what appear to be deities. One type of deity appears as a three-headed horned person sitting in a lotus position. In a more complex scene, a figure wearing a crescent-shaped headdress is shown in front of a kneeling form and a bull. Below this scene is a procession of what appear to be people wearing bangles and headdresses.

**T**he script found on these seals has not been deciphered, and the significance of the scenes shown remains enigmatic.

The seals afford evidence of a complex administrative system. Carefully standardized stone weights offer further evidence for control over the flow of goods. These weights are usually plain cubes of rock carefully carved to adhere to a strict standard.

## Government

The people of the Harappan civilization lived in highly organized cities with a bureaucracy that used a writing system, seals, and weights. The influence of this bureaucracy was so pervasive that even bricks were made to a standard size. The power of the Harappan state is vividly expressed by its construction and maintenance of an urban sewage system unparalleled among other early state societies. Although the vitality of the Harappan state is evident, the structure of the state remains obscure. The identity of the elite, the basis of their claim to power, and their relation to other sectors of society remain largely unknown.

The Harappan elites appear not to have lived very differently from other members of society or to have expressed their power by constructing monuments or burying their dead with pomp and splendor. Only a handful of sculptures that can be considered depictions of royalty have been found on Harappan sites. The most impressive is a small steatite sculpture known as the "priest king." This expressive sculpture depicts a bearded man wearing a headband with a circular ornament at the center of his forehead and a similar circular ornament on a bracelet around his right forearm. He is dressed in a cloth adorned with a geometric pattern.

**S**culpture of the "priest king" from Mohenjo-Daro. Notice the diadems on his head and arm and the elaborate pattern on his cloak. These might be indicative of his high status in Harappan society.

## Summing Up the Evidence

The cities of the Harappan civilization remain deeply puzzling. These large population centers were exquisitely organized, down to the minute details of their sewage channels and standardized building materials. This degree of planning is unparalleled in the ancient world. Yet the leaders remain almost invisible. There are elite areas in the large cities of Mohenjo-Daro and Harappa, but impressive burials and palaces are stunningly absent. The only monumental architecture of note is, of all things, a bath! Were the Harappan cities based on an egalitarian form of social organization, different from that of any other known early state societies? If not, was it perhaps an ethos of equality that in fact cloaked a very real social *in*equality? Ultimately, we are left with the question of the identity of the person sculpted so powerfully into the figure of the "priest king." Was this the ruler of the city? If so, what was his power and on what was it based?

# 12.3 JENNE-JENO

The development of states in Africa was not restricted to the Egyptian Nile Valley. However, the formation of indigenous African states remains poorly understood (Connah 1987). In the Sudan, a series of complex societies developed along the Nile in what is known as Nubia. In the Ethiopian highlands, an impressive kingdom developed around the city of Axum, which flourished during the first millennium A.D. contemporary with the Roman Empire. Axum is famous for its standing stones carved in the shape of multistory buildings. The tallest of these monuments, carved from a single block of stone, rises 21 meters. Along the east African coast, stretching from Somalia in the north to Mozambique in the south, a series of cities developed along the coast of the Indian Ocean contemporary with medieval Europe. These cities were active in extensive trade networks connecting southern Africa with the Middle East and Asia.

When European explorers reached the coast of West Africa, they found well-established cities. One of the most impressive was Benin City in what is today Nigeria. Benin is celebrated for its remarkable brass plaques, many of which have been acquired by Western museums. Some have questioned whether cities such as Benin developed indigenously in West Africa or whether they emerged as the result of an external stimulus, first from Islamic North Africa and then from Europe.

> ▶ The site of **Jenne-Jeno** in Mali is a West African urban center that predates external contacts.

Excavations at the site of **Jenne-Jeno,** located in the Middle Niger valley in Mali, have demonstrated that urban centers in West Africa predate extensive external contacts (McIntosh and McIntosh 1993). The city of Jenne is known from historical sources as an important trade center for caravans coming from Timbuktu to the north. The region around Jenne is very fertile and the river is rich in a wide array of fish. Jenne-Jeno is a site 3 kilometers from modern Jenne. The mound at Jenne-Jeno rises 8 meters and covers over 330,000 square meters. Excavations have uncovered three major phases of occupation beginning around 250 B.C. and lasting through A.D. 800. By A.D. 300, the entire area of the site appears to have been

One of the monumental stelae at Axum, Ethiopia.

## The Trade in African Antiquities

The systematic looting of archaeological sites in Africa has been described as a "horror in the making" (Schmidt and McIntosh 1996). Nowhere is this problem worse than in Mali, around the ancient urban center of Jenne-Jeno, where sites are plundered for their terracotta and metal artifacts. The destruction of the cultural heritage of Mali is fueled by a lucrative market for antiquities in Europe and North America. Collectors are willing to pay very high prices for sculptures and other precious artifacts that serve as marks of prestige and wealth. But for archaeologists, the plunder of archaeological sites results in the irreparable loss of all contextual information. These objects, ripped from their context, lose much of their historical value.

In 1970, the UN agency UNESCO passed a historic legal convention to stem the illegal trade in antiquities (http://www .unesco.org/culture/laws/1970/html_eng/page1.shtml). This convention seeks to bar the export and import of cultural property without authorization from the country of origin. The burden of responsibility for stopping the looting of sites lies not only with local authorities, but also with the governments of countries into which the antiquities are transported.

The scale of the illegal trade in antiquities places a heavy ethical burden of responsibility on archaeologists. Archaeological expertise is often sought out by collectors and dealers who want to authenticate objects that are in their possession. Archaeologists are tempted to cooperate, not only out of financial self-interest, but also from a desire to see objects that otherwise will disappear into the hands of collectors without documentation. Increasingly, archaeologists have come to understand that it is important to resist this temptation (Schmidt and McIntosh 1996).

Stemming the trade in antiquities is imperative. The antiquities market has developed sophisticated methods for moving artifacts around the

world in violation of the UNESCO convention. International policing agencies such as Interpol are increasingly involved in trying to track and recover looted artifacts. How do archaeologists fit into this complex situation? Raising archaeological militias seems an unlikely strategy. One part of the answer is that archaeologists must work to raise awareness of cultural heritage as a fundamental human right.

REFERENCE: Peter R. Schmidt and Roderick J. McIntosh (Eds.) (1996). *Plundering Africa's Past*. Bloomington, Indiana: Indiana University Press.

► Rare example of terracotta figurines recovered from controlled archaeological excavations at the site of Jenne-Jeno. Because the provenience of this artifact is known it provides important information on the chronology and society of Jenne-Jeno. This information is lost for similar artifacts that have been looted from the site.

densely inhabited. Population estimates for the site range from 7,000 to 16,000. There is considerable evidence of local iron smelting and other specialized craft activity. The city was surrounded by a mud brick wall; however, there is no evidence that the houses were laid out along a regular grid. Surveys in the region around Jenne-Jeno have shown that the area was dotted with a range of sites of different sizes.

**T**he modern town of Jenne on the Middle Niger Valley in Mali.

Only a small area of Jenne-Jeno has been excavated, making it difficult to come to any conclusion about the social organization of the city. The excavators of the site, Susan Keech McIntosh and Roderick McIntosh, have found no evidence of either a clearly defined elite or a special elite area of the site. Roderick McIntosh has developed a picture of Jenne-Jeno as a city ruled by overlapping sources of authority, rather than the centralized authority found in other early state societies (McIntosh 1998).

# 12.4 BACK TO THE ROOTS OF POWER

We have now examined six case studies in early state formation and are in a secure position to answer a key question posed by Bruce Trigger. Given the biological similarities and the cultural diversity of human beings, how differently are they likely to behave under analogous circumstances (Trigger 2003)? We have seen that the institutional inequality characteristic of state societies was not arrived at through a single pathway; each case study we have examined is unique and must be understood on its own terms. Humanity emerges as a highly flexible species with wide-ranging variation among societies.

But putting aside the differences in the trajectories taken by these societies, striking regularities emerge in the end point of the process of state formation. The core of all the societies we have examined is power in its many manifestations. Internally, these societies were controlled by the immense power of their elites. The resulting achievements are staggering in their scale, even if they vary in their form. The achievements of early states range from establishing the ordered cities of the Indus Valley to constructing the massive pyramids of Old Kingdom Egypt. The material expression of the high status of the elites are highly variable. In the expression of their power, the Indus Valley elites left barely a discernible trace in the archaeological record, while the monuments of the Old Kingdom elites are virtually geological in scale. But regardless of the nature of the legitimacy that lay at the source of that power, whether based fundamentally on coercion or consensus, the fact of the power of a ruling elite is evident even in the most mundane aspects of the archaeological record, from bevel-rim bowls in Mesopotamia to sewer drains in the Indus Valley. The critical role of the power of the elites is most visible in periods when it weakens and the state societies collapse. The ancient Egyptians' recognition of the benevolent aspects of the power of their rulers is expressed in the concept of *ma'at*: the balance and justice that together keep the world in order.

The power of the early states was not only the internal power that the elites had over other members of their societies, but also the unprecedented power of these societies taken as a collectivity. The Old Kingdom Egyptians were able to raise mountains of rock in a feat of engineering and sheer brute force that has rarely been matched. The people of the Indus Valley lived in cities that brought together unprecedented numbers of people living and working in a single settlement. In some cases, the power of the early state was turned outwards, in warfare or territorial expansion. Uruk Mesopotamia expanded far up the Euphrates River Valley, and the Mayan cities fought wars of conquest. In the next chapter, we examine what happens when states harness their power and aim it at expansion, resulting in the formation of empires.

# CHAPTER SUMMARY

- The Nile Valley, a highly fertile agricultural land bounded by desert, is divided into Upper Egypt in the south and Lower Egypt in the north.
- The shift towards complex societies in Egypt began during the Predynastic period. Egyptian dynastic history can be divided into threes cycles of integration and collapse.
- The Egyptian king was the human incarnation of the god Horus and was responsible for preserving *ma'at*: balance and justice.
- Scribes played a critical role in maintaining the organization of Egyptian society.
- The earliest royal tombs are found at Hierakonpolis and Abydos. The stepped pyramid constructed by Djoser at Saqqara was the first Egyptian pyramid.
- The first true pyramid was constructed by Snefru at Dahshur. Pyramid building reached its apex in the three pyramids at Giza constructed during the Fourth Dynasty.
- No cities are known from the Old Kingdom of Egypt. The most completely documented Egyptian

city is the site of Amarna, built by the heretic New Kingdom king Akhenaten.
- The Harappan civilization developed along the Indus River Valley. The material culture of the Harappan civilization is essentially uniform across the entire region.
- The two largest Harappan cities are Harappa and Mohenjo-Daro. These cities are characterized by a regular grid of roadways and an impressive sewage system.
- There is little evidence of monumental architecture on Harappan sites. One exception is the Great Bath at Mohenjo-Daro.
- The Harappan script is found on a range of artifacts, including seals. The script has not been deciphered.
- There is little evidence for the concentration of wealth in the hands of the elites of Harappan cities.
- The site of Jenne-Jeno in the Middle Niger Valley was a large city occupied between 250 B.C. and A.D. 800.

## KEY TERMS

Abydos, 363
Akhenaten, 374
Amarna, 374
Cepheren, 370
Cheops, 370
First Dynasty, 363
Giza, 370
Great Bath, 379

Harappa, 377
Harappan Period, 376
Harappan Script, 379
Hierakonpolis, 363
Indus Valley, 376
Jenne-Jeno, 381
King Djoser, 369
Lower Egypt, 361

ma'at, 364
Mohenjo-Daro, 377
Mycerinus, 370
Narmer Palette, 362
Nile Valley, 360
Saqqara, 369
Upper Egypt, 361

## REVIEW QUESTIONS

1. How do the pyramids of Egypt compare with the Mayan pyramids discussed in Chapter 11?

2. Would it be proper to say that Harappan cities lacked a ruling elite? If so, how were these cities governed?

## FOR FURTHER READING

Barry Kemp. (1989). *Ancient Egypt: Anatomy of a Civilization*. London: Routledge.

J. M. Kenoyer. (1998). *Ancient Cities of the Indus Valley Civilization*. Karachi: Oxford University Press.

Mark Lehner. (1997). *The Complete Pyramids*. London: Thames and Hudson.

Roderick J. McIntosh. (1998). *The Peoples of the Middle Niger: The Island of Gold*. Malden, MA: Blackwell.

Greg Possehl. (2002). *The Indus Civilization: A Contemporary Perspective*. Walnut Creek, California: Altamira.

Bruce Trigger, Barry Kemp, David O'Connor, and A.B. Lloyd. (1983). *Ancient Egypt: A Social History*. Cambridge, U.K.: Cambridge University Press.

# Empires

EMPIRES ARE POLITICAL ENTITIES that bring together diverse societies under a single ruler. After reading this chapter, you should understand:

▶ The history of the rise and fall of the Inca and Aztec Empires.

▶ The economic and social organization of the Inca and Aztec empires.

▶ The power of the Aztec and Inca rulers.

▶ The role of violence in maintaining the power of the Aztec and Inca rulers.

Diego Rivera's painting of the Aztec capital of Tenochtitlan.

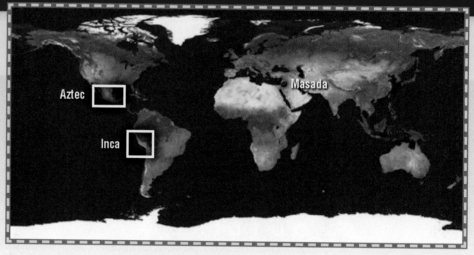

erched on a dramatically isolated rock overlooking the Dead Sea, Masada is
a seemingly impenetrable fortress. King Herod seized on this location to
build a fortified palace. Herod had reason to worry: He ruled at the whim of
the Roman Empire, and a change of heart in Rome could leave him in a precarious
position. Herod's palace at Masada is a masterpiece of engineering and of military
planning. The only approach to the summit is a series of precarious trails that are

Masada. The Roman siege ramp is visible leading up to the right side of the
summit.

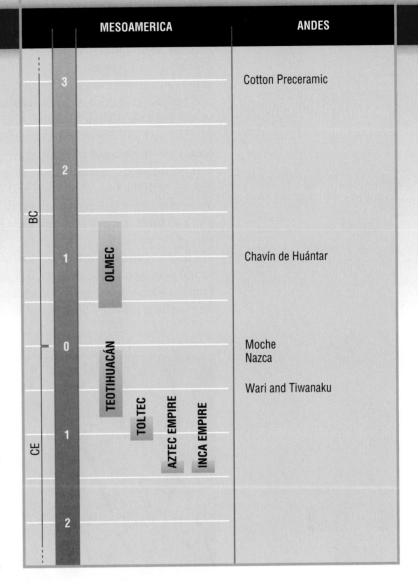

| MESOAMERICA | ANDES |
|---|---|
| | Cotton Preceramic |
| OLMEC | Chavín de Huántar |
| TEOTIHUACÁN | Moche / Nazca |
| TOLTEC · AZTEC EMPIRE · INCA EMPIRE | Wari and Tiwanaku |

BC 3 2 1 0 CE 1 2

easily defended. Herod excavated enormous cisterns and built an impressive complex of storehouses so that he would be able to withstand a prolonged siege. He also built a fabulous palace with baths, walls painted with frescoes, and mosaic floors. Even in retreat, he planned to live in style.

Herod never used the palace at Masada, but after his death a remnant group of rebels against the Roman Empire made a last stand at the site, building their makeshift homes amid Herod's glorious palaces. The fate of these rebels was never really in question. They were faced with an empire capable of projecting forces across an impressive geographical area stretching from Britain to Egypt. The rebels never had a chance. Standing on the top of Masada today, one can see the remains of the Roman siege camps ringing the site. Ultimately, the Romans built a ramp up to the summit of Masada. On the night before the assault, the rebels chose death over capture, committing mass suicide. The story of Masada recorded by the historian Josephus has become central to the military ethos of the modern state of Israel. The excavation and restoration of the site has resulted in one of the most visited archaeological sites in the world.

Masada offers a vivid picture of the ability of empires to expand their realm and control colonies through military might. Expansion is often the seemingly inevitable outcome of state formation. The need to control trade routes and to accommodate growing populations is among the reasons that early states often expand. In ancient Egypt, competition among states appears to have led to the consolidation of three kingdoms into a single state covering the entire Nile Valley. In Mesopotamia, sites such as Habuba Kebira suggest that the Uruk state began expanding northward up the Euphrates River valley soon after the appearance of the first urban center.

In some cases, states began aggressive campaigns of expansion, resulting in the formation of empires (Alcock et al. 2001). **Empires** are political entities that bring together a diverse and heterogeneous group of societies under a single ruler. Often,

▶ **Empires** are political entities that bring together a diverse and heterogeneous group of societies under a single ruler.

empires rely on the brutal use of military power to achieve domination. This aspect of empires is vividly depicted in the sculpture of the temples of the Assyrian empire, which expanded out of Mesopotamia to control a large part of the Middle East. Empires also require the development of methods of communication to allow for the rapid transmission of information. Communication enables the core of the empire to control events far from the center. The inequality between a core region and peripheral regions is characteristic of empires. The flow of goods and resources moves from the periphery to the core, usually in the form of tribute.

The archaeology of empires requires research covering an immense geographic area. One of the most interesting aspects of studying empires is exploring how the core maintained control and domination over the periphery. Archaeologists must look at both the sites at the core and sites at the periphery. Archaeologists working on empires must also pay attention to the two linchpins of the empire: communication and force. Excavations and surveys of roads and military camps are a common part of the archaeology of empires.

In many cases, empires are known from both archaeological remains and historical documents. The two empires we explore in this chapter—the Inca and Aztec Empires—are known from documents written after their collapse. The documents were written either by Spanish soldiers and administrators or by descendants of the

**R**elief showing the Assyrian attack of the town of Lachish.

rulers of the empires. It is important to emphasize that these two case studies offer only a sampling of the archaeology of empires.

# 13.1 THE INCA EMPIRE

The **Inca Empire** that was known as **Tawantinsuyu**, "The Four Parts Together," thrived for over a century, tying together a vast realm under the royal Inca in the capital city, Cuzco (D'Altroy 2002). At the peak of the empire, the Inca ruled over 12 million people in a region that stretched across 3,000 kilometers from northern Chile to Ecuador. Not only was the Inca Empire massive, but it also covered a highly heterogeneous region ranging from the river valleys of the Pacific coast to the high-altitude valleys of the Andean altiplano.

In 1533, the immense and powerful kingdom of Tawantinsuyu fell to a group of 168 Spanish soldiers under the command of Francisco Pizarro. Facing an army of 80,000 Inca soldiers, Pizarro was able to capture the Inca ruler Atawallpa and hold him for a ransom that reached $50,000,000 in melted gold and jewels. Despite the ransom paid, Pizarro executed Atawallpa on July 26, 1533. Atawallpa's murder touched off the rapid disintegration of the Inca Empire. Tawantinsuyu fell because of a combination of forces, including the ability of the European invaders to capitalize on internal divisions within Tawantinsuyu and the inability of the Inca rulers to comprehend the extent of the threat posed by the Europeans. The stunning rapidity of the collapse points to the fragility of an empire built around a divine ruler. When Atawallpa was murdered, the empire lost its very essence.

> The **Inca Empire** is known as **Tawantinsuyu,** which means "the four parts together."

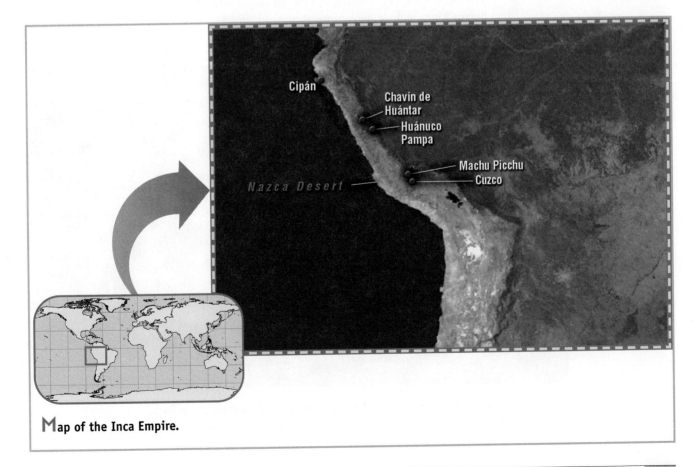

**M**ap of the Inca Empire.

# Before the Inca

The Inca were not the first Andean state or even the first Andean empire. Already during the Cotton Aceramic period, 5,000 years ago, monumental mounds were built on sites along the rich river valleys flowing along the Pacific coast. The establishment of a major ceremonial center at the highland site of **Chavín de Huántar** around 800 B.C. marked an important turning point in Andean society (Burger 1992). Chavín de Huántar was a large town perched in a steep valley at the confluence of two rivers. The ceremonial center consisted of a series of platforms and sunken courtyards. The structures at the site are elaborately carved with sculptures in what has become known as the Chavín style. One convention characteristic of this style is its use of symmetry to present a balanced image. The Chavín style spread rapidly beyond Chavín de Huántar and is found on sites covering a large area across central and northern Peru. It appears that the Chavín style was adopted as part of the spread of a system of religious beliefs or a cult, rather than as the result of military conquest.

Beginning two thousand years ago, the **Moche state** flourished along the Moche Valley, on the Pacific coast of Peru. The Moche built impressive mounds, including a massive structure known as the Pyramid of the Sun, made of more than 140 million mud bricks. Unfortunately, most of the Moche sites have been heavily looted for hundreds of years. The discovery of an intact tomb at the site of **Sipán** has given archaeologists a sense of the wealth and violence of Moche society. The burials at Sipán include an incredible range of ornaments made of turquoise and gold, along with sacrificial victims.

At the same time that Moche society flourished in the north, the **Nazca culture** developed along the Nazca River valley on the southern Pacific coast of Peru. The Nazca are best known for the large patterns they created on the desert floor. **Nazca Lines** include depictions of humans and animals, as well as a large number of

> **Chavín de Huántar** is a major ceremonial center in the Andean highlands constructed around 800 B.C.

> The **Moche state** that developed along the Moche Valley beginning two thousand years ago is known for the elaborate burials found at the site of **Sipán.**

> The **Nazca culture** that developed along the Nazca River valley beginning two thousand years ago is known for **Nazca Lines**—large patterns created on the desert floor.

The site of Chavín de Huántar located in a narrow highland valley in Peru.

straight lines that stretch for miles along the desert floor (Aveni 2000). To create the lines, the Nazca took black desert rocks and stacked them along the edge of a trail, leaving the lighter colored desert surface exposed. The purpose of this undertaking is a mystery that has intrigued archaeologists as well as UFO enthusiasts. Survey and aerial photography has shown that the lines are not randomly distributed across the desert floor; instead, they radiate out from a series of central points. Although some archaeologists argue that the lines served as astronomical observatories, it seems more likely that they were paths walked along in ritual processions, perhaps related to rain ceremonies.

By A.D. 400, a period of political expansion began in the Andes with the development of large urban centers at the highland sites of Tiwanaku on the shores of Lake Titicaca and Wari to the north. It appears that by A.D. 750 the Wari controlled a large empire that anticipated many features of the Inca Empire (Schreiber 2001).

## The History of the Inca

The early history of the Inca is shrouded in myth. The Inca believed that their ancestors were created by the creator god Wiraqocha and then journeyed until reaching the site where they founded their capital, Cuzco. The initial expansion of the Inca realm appears to have taken place during the reign of the eighth ruler, Wiraqoch Inka. The history of the remaining rulers in the Inca dynasty is a succession of wars of conquest punctuated by conflicts over succession to the throne. The most violent war of succession took place immediately before the arrival of Pizarro. Waskhar and his half-brother Atawallpa engaged in a long battle across much of the empire before Waskhar was captured and his family slaughtered.

## Inca Society

One of the most intriguing aspects of Inca society was the power exerted by deceased rulers. After death, the emperor was mummified as part of an elaborate collective ritual of mourning. The mummified ruler continued to play an active role in the ceremonial and political life of Cuzco. Food was burnt in front of mummies,

The Raimondi Stone shows the symmetry characteristic of Chavín art. The figure of a deity holding two staffs can be flipped to depict a series of animal heads.

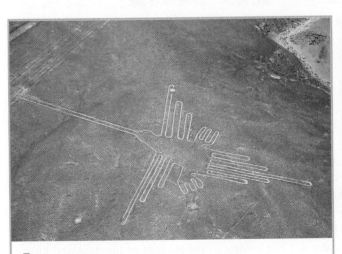

Aerial photograph of Nazca Line showing a hummingbird.

View along one of the paths creating the hummingbird.

## Excavating the Land of the Lines

by Lindsey Stoker

I was in my first year of graduate school in anthropology when our department hired an Andeanist, Dr. Christina A. Conlee. I took Dr. Conlee's course on Andean archaeology and was immediately intrigued by the rich culture history of the Andes. Dr. Conlee had been conducting her research in the Nazca region of Peru and was returning there to a site called La Tiza for a second excavation season. I accompanied her to investigate the initial settlement of the site.

La Tiza is a 28-hectare domestic site located 6 kilometers from the modern town of Nazca. The site is situated near the fertile banks of the Aja River and faces a sacred white sand mountain called Cerro Blanco. The site appears to have been continuously occupied for over a millennium, beginning around 200 B.C. until approximately A.D. 1476. My research suggests that La Tiza was established by local regional inhabitants, rather than migrants who were settling nearby during the Late Formative period. Over the years, the site was occupied by several different cultural groups, including the Nazca and the Wari, although its largest occupation dates to the Late Intermediate period (A.D. 1000–A.D. 1476). La Tiza appears to have then been abandoned due to the Inca conquest.

One of the reasons Peru is so fascinating is that it is so diverse ecologically. The coastal region is one of the driest deserts in the world. The desert pampa of the Peruvian South Coast is home to the enigmatic Nazca Lines, which have captured the imagination of scholars, as well as the general public, for many years.

Although many tourists visit Nazca to fly over the lines, there are actually very few archaeologists working in the region, and most of them are close colleagues of mine. I was fortunate that, through Dr. Conlee's connections, I was able to visit other formative sites, watch local potters in town who still use traditional manufacturing techniques, and discuss theories with scholars who are producing intriguing

▲ La Tiza dry river valley and Cerro Blanco in background.

new insights on the sociopolitical arena of the incipient Nazca culture.

Our team consisted of fourteen archaeologists and students, eight American and six Peruvian. Operating with a

---

> The property of the Inca emperor became the property of his descendants, known as his *panaqa*. ◀

and, through mediums, they were able to communicate their wishes. Nor was the role of the deceased emperor limited to ceremonial functions. The property amassed by the emperor during his life passed to his descendants, known as his *panaqa*. The son who became the new ruler did not belong to the *panaqa* of the deceased king. The new emperor had to go out and build his own fortune. This dynamic played an important role in the expansion of the Inca Empire, as each ruler was forced to carve out his own wealth.

bilingual crew was challenging, especially since only a few of us spoke both English and Spanish. However, after a few weeks of living, eating and working together, the language barrier virtually disintegrated.

Working with local archaeologists added a distinct cultural dimension to the project. For example, the first day of excavations was begun with a *pago*, or ceremonial offering. Each member of the team smoked tobacco, drank from a Peruvian alcoholic beverage called pisco, and then offered the items, along with coca leaves, to the local mountain deities. *Pagos* are intended to appease the gods for improved luck and to pay respects before disturbing the earth and its ancient contents.

Our crew stayed in a rented house in the town of Nazca that also operated as our laboratory. We woke at dawn to the incessant crowing of roosters and drove out to La Tiza early each morning. We removed and screened sand from archaeological structures for about six hours and then returned home for a

late lunch. After lunch, we spent the rest of the afternoon washing the recovered artifacts with toothbrushes. Another challenge we faced was water shortage. It rarely rains along the coast, but Nazca was suffering further from a three-year drought. Often, we had to pay to have a water truck come to pump water into our tank, yet we still usually ran out several days before its next visit. We had to start limiting showers to once every few days, and showering sometimes had to be sacrificed entirely in order to have water to wash the ceramics. Still, although fieldwork is obviously often unglamorous and accompanied by hardships, it is inevitably a very rewarding experience.

In my opinion, the most exciting aspect of participating in archaeology is that after years of learning through reading textbooks, one has the opportunity to discover something new and add to the current body of knowledge or, at the very least, experience the past in a tangible way that imbues it with newfound meaning.

▶ Excavating a structure at La Tiza.

The *panaqa* controlled considerable resources, including the royal estates of the former rulers. The royal estates provided physical support for the emperor and his descendants and included agricultural fields, pastures, forests, and mines (Niles 2004). In some cases, the estates served important ritual functions. The most famous of the royal estates is the site of **Machu Picchu.** Located on a high mountain peak at the western end of the **Urubamba Valley,** Machu Picchu was a royal estate built by Pachacuti Inca Yupanqui between 1450 and 1470 (Burger and Salazar

▶ The site of **Machu Picchu** is a royal estate on a high mountain peak at the western end of the **Urubamba Valley.**

Machu Picchu, Peru. This spectacular site seems to meld into its mountain landscape.

2004). Machu Picchu is a small walled settlement that includes royal and aristocratic complexes built in the classic Inca masonry style in which stone blocks are carefully fit together. There are also subsidiary buildings that appear to have housed the people who served the members of Pachacuti's *panaqa*, as well as a large number of shrines, some of which are built around striking natural rock outcroppings.

Analysis of burials recovered at *Machu Picchu* indicates that the people who served Pachacuti's *panaqa* were drawn from across the empire (Burger and Salazar 2004). One of the most unusual lines of evidence comes from the shape of skulls that had been deformed by either binding or wrapping the head during infancy. In the highlands the normal practice was to bind the head with cloth strips, while on the coast it was more common to flatten skulls by tying the head to a cradleboard. Both types of cranial deformation are found on skeletons from Machu Picchu, indicating that the people buried at the site came from both the coast and the highlands. The diversity of pottery vessels found with the burials offers further evidence for the ethnic diversity of the people buried at Machu Picchu.

Feasting and the exchange of gifts played a central role in Inca society. At state centers, the elite spent much time hosting feasts of corn beer, coca leaves, meat, and music for their subjects (Burger and Salazar 2004). Large feasting halls often adjoined open plazas. The large feasting hall at Machu Picchu is located outside the walls and was probably used to fête local farmers. At the large Inca center of **Hua'nuco Pampa,** over 600 kilometers north of Cuzco, two enormous halls and a series of subsidiary buildings were constructed alongside the main plaza of the site (Morris and Thompson 1985). Large jars and plates dominate the substantial quantities of pottery recovered from the buildings around the plaza. These vessels indi-

**Hua'nuco Pampa** was an Inca center 600 kilometers north of the capital, Cuzco.

cate that the plaza and the adjoining buildings were the site of large-scale feasting.

## Building Empire

The Inca engaged in constant military campaigns to maintain and expand their empire. Integrating and controlling the conquered territories required the development of effective mechanisms to administer a vast and heterogeneous territory. The Inca developed an impressive system of roads extending across their realm. These roads were critical for the movements of goods, people, and information. The Inca did not have a formal writing system; however, they did use an elaborate method for recording information in knotted ropes known as *khipu*. In bringing together the four corners of Tawantinsuyu, the Inca showed a great deal of flexibility. In some areas, they ruled through local elites with a minimum of interference; in others, they installed distinctive administrative centers to allow for direct rule.

**Warfare.** The Inca were able to field very large military forces consisting of tens of thousands of troops (D'Altroy 2003). These armies were drawn from the diverse ethnic groups belonging to Tawantinsuyu. The emperor often rode with the army, carried aloft on a litter. Weapons included arrows, sling stones, and javelins. The tactics of warfare were essentially massed frontal assaults followed by hand-to-hand combat using maces, clubs, and spears. Feigned retreats and similar tricks were often used to draw out an enemy, who could then be routed in a surprise counterattack. Forts and garrisons were built in particularly strategic locations. In Cuzco, the massive structure known as Saqsawaman appears to have served both as a temple to the sun and as a fortress. An early Spanish traveler described Saqsawaman as being built of "such big stones . . . as big as pieces of mountains or crags" (Hyslop 1990: 53). The outer walls of the fortress were built on three terraces in a zigzag pattern designed to deter a frontal assault.

**Roads.** Tawantinsuyu stretched over a vast and varied landscape. Control of the Inca Empire demanded a means for the rapid movement of information, military force, and tribute. The Inca built a network linking together approximately 40,000 km of roads (Hyslop 1984). Many of these were preexisting roads that the Inca brought into their system. The scale and construction methods of the roadways varied with the local topography and the importance of

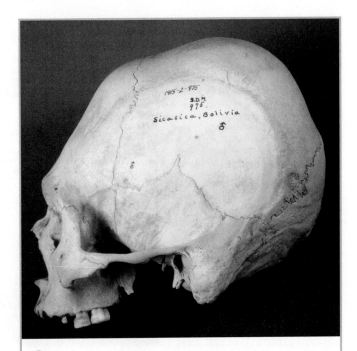

**S**kull showing cranial deformation.

**I**nca painted storage vessel.

Grass rope bridge spanning the Apurimac River, Peru.

the road. The width of the roads varied from 1 to 4 meters, and the construction ranged from a simple line of stones leading through the desert to elaborate stone-built roads with drains to control the flow of water. Bridges were erected in many places to allow the roads to cross bodies of waters. In some cases, the bridges were simple floating barges built of reeds; however, where the road needed to cross deep chasms, impressive suspension bridges were built out of reed cables woven together. The bridge built over the Apurimac River spanned 45 meters. The floor of the bridge was 1.5 meters wide and could support a line of people and animals. The Spanish conquistadores would even cross the bridges, riding their horses at a gallop. In some cases where a suspension bridge was not built, a cable was connected to the two sides of a chasm and a large basket was suspended from the cable. People or animals were then pulled from one bank to another by people hauling ropes attached to the basket.

One of the primary functions of the road system was its role as a conduit for rapid communication across Tawantinsuyu. Relay messengers were stationed every 6 to 9 kilometers. It is estimated that these messengers could cover 240 kilometers a day. Approximately 1,000 roadside lodging and storage areas known as *tampu* were also built along the roads. These installations served as Inca administrative centers.

**Khipu.** It would have taken over 350 transfers of information to get a message from the northern end of Tawantinsuyu to the capital in Cuzco. Because the messengers were drawn from the diverse cultures of the Inca Empire, they might well have not spoken the same language. Without written documents, the Inca road system would be more likely to resemble a game of broken telephone than an effective means for administering an empire. The transfer of information along the road system is only one example of the many situations in which a system for recording information would have been crucial for the Inca. However, the Inca did not develop a classic writing system. In place of signs impressed in clay or written on paper, the Inca used a system of knotted strings known as **khipu.**

**Khipu** was a system of knotted strings used by the Inca to record information.

A khipu consists of a series of colored pendant strings tied onto a main cord. Groups of knots are tied along the pendant strings. Khipu knots are of three basic types: a long knot with four turns, a single knot, and a figure-eight knot (see Figure 13.1A, B on next page). In addition to the main cord and the pendant strings, top cords were tied above the main cord and subsidiary cords were tied to the pendant strings.

Khipus are a highly complex system in which the number and placement of cords and knots can be manipulated into an endless set of configurations. When one considers that the color of the cords and even the way a cord was spun could also be controlled, the potential of khipus to code information seems almost limitless. Unfortunately, historic sources provide no glossary for translating or reading khipus. It is clear that khipus could code information, but the nature of the code behind the khipu remains the subject of debate. At one extreme is the argument that khipus were devices used to help jog the memory of individuals, known as khipu kamayuq, charged with keeping communal memory. According to this argument, khipus were personal memory devices. One khipu kamayuq could not read another's khipu. An alternative position holds that khipus were a form of writing or at least a coding system for language (Urton 2003). According to this position, khipus were records—administrative texts and even histories—that could be read by Inca administrators. A third position argues that khipus were indeed recording devices, but that they were used mostly for accounting and economic purposes (Ascher and Ascher 1981). In support of this position, some khipus did record numerical values by

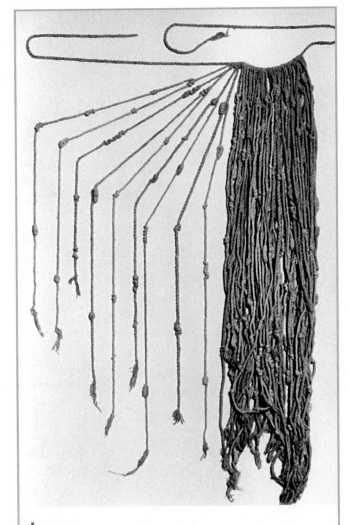

**I**nca khipu with knotted strings hanging from a main cord.

means of knots neatly arranged to represent numbers in decimal position. It is curious that the Inca responded to the need to manage information through the development of a code of knots rather than a script. One intriguing possibility is that the use of strings and knots to record information reflects the centrality of textiles in Andean society.

## Summing Up the Evidence

The Inca tied together an impressively large and heterogeneous geographic region through the use of military power, an extensive road system, and an administrative apparatus that made use of the khipu to keep records. It is important to emphasize that the Inca realms were not only geographically diverse, but also culturally and linguistically diverse. The expansionist dynamic of the Inca was driven in large part by a system of inheritance that passed the emperor's wealth on to his descendants, known as his *panaqa,* rather than to his successor. As a result, each new ruler had to accumulate his own wealth, often accomplished through military conquest. The Inca system of inheritance also resulted in frequent internal battles over inheritance.

## FIGURE 13.1A

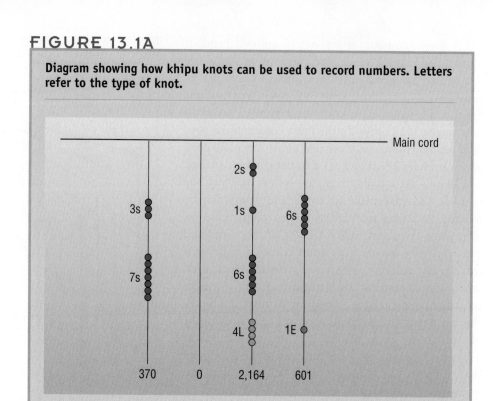

Diagram showing how khipu knots can be used to record numbers. Letters refer to the type of knot.

## FIGURE 13.1B

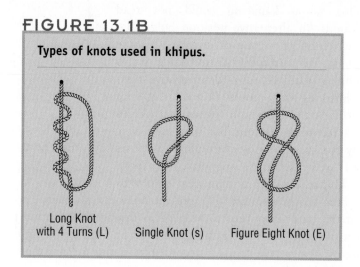

Types of knots used in khipus.

Long Knot with 4 Turns (L)    Single Knot (s)    Figure Eight Knot (E)

The final battle of succession between Atawallpa and his half-brother Waskhar fatally weakened the Inca Empire on the eve of the arrival of Pizarro.

# 13.2 THE AZTEC EMPIRE

In 1519, Spanish soldiers arrived at the city of **Tenochtitlán,** the capital of the **Aztec Empire.** Tenochtitlán was at that time one of the largest cities in the world and the largest city ever built in Mesoamerica. The soldiers were amazed by what they saw, writing that "some of our soldiers asked whether it was not all a dream" (Bernal Diaz del Castillo, quoted in Smith 2003). Tenochtitlán was built on an island in Lake Tetzcoco in the Valley of Mexico and was connected to the main-

**Tenochtitlán,** the capital of the **Aztec Empire,** was the largest indigenous city ever built in the Americas.

land by a series of causeways. At the center of the city rose the great twin pyramids of the Templo Mayor, the spiritual center of the Aztec universe.

The final conquest of Tenochtitlán took over two years of bloody and treacherous warfare (Townsend 2000). The end of the Aztec Empire came on August 13, 1521, when, at the close of a 93-day siege, the last Aztec king, Cuauhtemoc, was captured as he tried to escape the city by canoe. In a powerful symbolic act, the Spanish built their cathedral near the ruins of the Templo Mayor in the heart of what has become Mexico City.

Some of the priests who arrived on missions to convert natives to Christianity carefully documented Aztec history, religion, and society. Among the most important historical source is a series of books known as the **Florentine Codex,** compiled by the Spanish friar **Bernardo de Sahagún** (Brumfiel 2001). The Florentine Codex consists of the interviews Sahagún carried out with Aztec informants, both in the native language, Nahuatl, and in Spanish translation. This text is accompanied by extensive illustrations drawn by native artists. Illustrated books were also kept by the Aztecs themselves; however, few have survived. Archaeological research has brought the Florentine Codex vividly to life with spectacular discoveries at the site of the Templo Mayor in Mexico City. Archaeology has also extended our understanding of the Aztec Empire by throwing light on the states and empires that preceded the Aztecs and by uncovering evidence of the lives of the people living in areas beyond Tenochtitlán.

▶ The **Florentine Codex** compiled by the Spanish friar
▶ **Bernardo de Sahagún** is a major source of information on Aztec history and culture.

Khipu kamayuq with a khipu. Illustration from a sixteenth century Spanish manuscript.

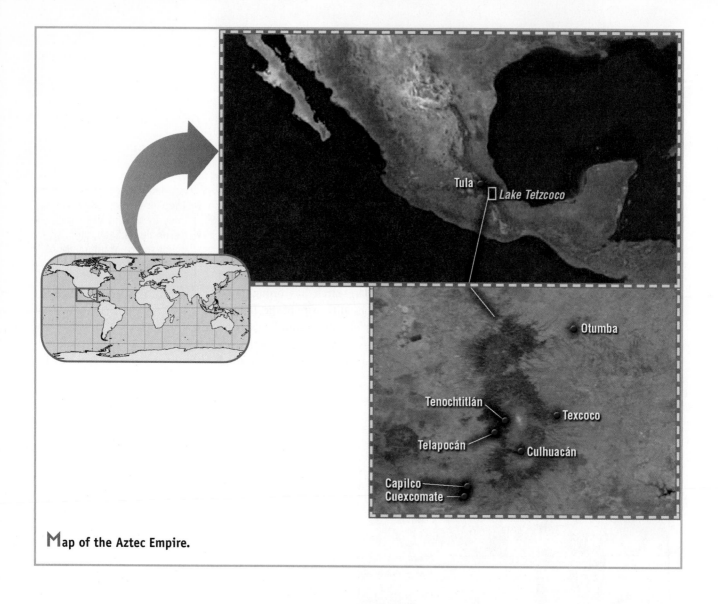

**M**ap of the Aztec Empire.

## Before the Aztecs

Political complexity in Mesoamerica can be traced back to the Olmec societies of the Gulf Coast, dated between 1200 B.C. and 300 B.C. By A.D. 100, the city of Teotihuacán, in the highland Valley of Mexico, had developed into a major city with a population of more than 80,000 people covering an area of 20 square kilometers. Subsequently, the Mayan city–states developed in the regions to the south.

The Aztecs were aware of both the Olmec and Teotihuacán and drew explicit connections to those societies. Among the precious objects found in ritual caches in the Templo Mayor was an Olmec stone mask (Moctezuma 1988). A number of objects from Teotihuacán were also found in excavations at the Templo Mayor, and Aztec architecture makes frequent reference to styles that originated in Teotihuacán. The name **Teotihuacán** is not the original name of the city, but rather the name used by the Aztecs, which, in the Aztec language Nahuatl, means "the place where gods (or rulers) are made."

Aztec kings traced their genealogy back to the rulers of the **Toltec Empire**, which developed between A.D. 950 and A.D. 1150 after the fall of Teotihuacán (Smith 2003). The Aztec kings depict the Toltec Empire as great and powerful; however, archaeology paints a rather more modest picture. The Toltec capital, **Tula**, was

> The Aztecs treated the city of **Teotihuacán** with reverence as "the place where gods are made."

> The Aztecs were preceded by the **Toltec Empire,** based in the capital city of **Tula.**

the largest city of its time, but its population of 50,000 was far smaller than those of both Teotihuacán and the Aztec capital of Tenochtitlán. It is also far from clear that Tula did actually control a large empire: There is little archaeological evidence for Toltec control of regions beyond Tula.

## The History of the Aztecs

The Aztecs, like the Inca, traced their origins to people who migrated from afar. The location of the Aztec homeland of Aztlán remains unknown and is perhaps mythical (Smith 2003). There was a series of migrations from Aztlán into the Valley of Mexico during the period between A.D. 1200 and A.D. 1250. All of these migrants are known as Aztecs, after the homeland of **Aztlán.** The first group of Aztec migrants settled in the Valley of Mexico, while the second wave settled in the surrounding valleys. The final group to arrive was the Mexica, who had to settle for a desolate area known as "grasshopper hill." Even in this setting, the Mexica faced attack by a coalition of Tepanecs (an earlier group of settlers from Aztlán) and their allies from the town of Culhuacán (Townsend 2000). The Mexica were roundly defeated and forced to resettle in yet a more desolate setting under the protection of Culhuacán. An alliance then developed between the Mexica and Culhuacán until an incredible incident led to the Mexica being forced to move yet again.

When the Mexica approached one of the leaders of Culhuacán and asked for a daughter as a bride for the chief Mexica deity, Huitzilopochtli, a daughter was sent,

> ▶ **Aztlán** is the homeland of the Mexica, who formed the Aztec Empire.

## FIGURE 13.2

Spanish map of the city of Tenochtitlán built on an island and reached by causeways. The sacred precinct of the Templo Mayor is located in the center of the city.

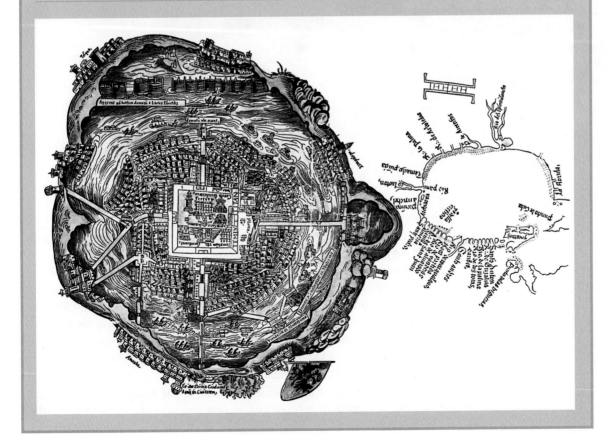

# TOOLBOX:
## Tuberculosis in the Americas

Because many diseases leave no traces on the skeleton, detecting the traces of disease in ancient skeletons is often extremely challenging. Even in cases where a disease does leave a clear trace on the skeleton, the interpretation of these skeletal pathologies can be ambiguous. Tuberculosis in the prehistoric Americas offers a good example of this problem. In severe cases, tuberculosis can lead to spinal deformities that can be identified on archaeological skeletons. But these same spinal deformities can be caused by infections other than tuberculosis. As a result, many researchers have been reluctant to accept skeletal evidence of tuberculosis in the Americas before European contact. It has long been thought that tuberculosis was a European disease that was only brought to the Americas by European settlers.

▶ **Piece of mummified lung tissue showing lesions characteristic of TB.**

Another way to trace disease in archaeological remains is to extract tissue and identify infectious agents directly. Unfortunately, this is rarely possible. However, in a pioneering study, DNA was extracted from mummified human remains that showed lesions consistent with a diagnosis of tuberculosis. This approach has succeeded in demonstrating that tuberculosis was present in the Americas before European contact.

The Chiribaya were an agricultural group that lived on the southern Peruvian coast between A.D. 1000 and A.D. 1300. The aforementioned DNA analysis was carried out on the spontaneously mummified body of a Chiribaya woman dated to A.D. 1040. DNA was extracted from a lesion on the right lung and then was amplified with the use of PCR (polymerase chain reaction). The results showed a clear match between the DNA recovered from the mummy's lung and the DNA of modern tuberculosis.

REFERENCE: Wilmar L. Salo, Arthur C. Aufderheide, Jane Buikstra, and Todd A. Holcomb. (1994). Identification of *Mycobacterium tuberculosis* DNA in a pre-Columbian Peruvian mummy. *Proceedings of the National Academy of Science* 91: 2091–2094.

paving the way for a further strengthening of the alliance between the two groups. The Culhuacán chieftain was then invited to festivities with the Mexica, only to recognize the flayed skin of his daughter on the body of the Mexica priest. The outraged Culhuacán chased the Mexica to uninhabited islands in Lake Tetzcoco. As the Mexica fled, one of their priests had a vision that they should settle at a sacred spot marked by an eagle perched on a cactus. When the Mexica found an eagle on a cactus the next day, they immediately built a crude temple, which developed over time into the Templo Mayor at the core of the great city of Tenochtitlán. Today, an eagle perched on a cactus is represented on the flag of Mexico in recognition of this significant turning point in the history of Mesoamerica.

How did the Mexica go from despised outcasts to the rulers of a great empire? First of all, one must take care to recognize that the origins of empires are often highly mythologized and this is clearly the case for the Mexica origin story.

Nonetheless, the rapid rise in the power of the Mexica is remarkable. The rise of the Mexica rested on a series of conflicts and alliances with neighboring groups and the consistent growth of Tenochtitlán as an urban center. In 1428, an alliance between the cities of Tenochtitlán, **Texcoco**, and **Telapocán** was established. The Triple Alliance formed the basis for the rapid expansion of the area dominated by the Aztec to cover regions far beyond the limits of the Basin of Mexico. Within the Triple Alliance, the Mexica rulers of Tenochtitlán were dominant, and their power grew along with the empire. Among the Aztec groups that migrated to the Valley of Mexico from Aztlán, the last to arrive, the outcast Mexica, came to rule over the entire Valley of Mexico and far beyond.

The Triple Alliance between the cities of Tenochtitlán, **Texcoco**, and **Telapocán** formed the basis of Aztec expansion.

## Aztec Economy

The rise of Tenochtitlán and the expansion of the Aztec Empire resulted in a dramatic increase in population in the Basin of Mexico. Archaeological surveys have shown that forty percent of the sites in the Basin of Mexico date to the period of the expansion of the Aztec Empire (Nichols 2004). Population estimates for the Basin of Mexico during this period range between 800,000 and 1.25 million, a fourfold increase over preceding periods. The large populations of the Basin of Mexico relied on an intensification of agriculture and a system for exacting tribute from conquered territories.

Tenochtitlán relied heavily on the expansion of raised agricultural fields, known as **chinampas,** within the swamps of the lakes of the Basin of Mexico (Smith 2003). The chinampa plots are artificial islands built up between long, straight drainage canals. By periodically scraping the muck out of the canals, the fertility of the plots was maintained. Archaeological surveys on the outskirts of Mexico City have uncovered the gridlike system of Aztec chinampa drainage canals and fields. In addition to farming chinampa plots, the Aztecs constructed extensive terrace walls to farm hillsides and dug large irrigation canals to open valleys to farming.

**Chinampas** are raised agricultural beds built in swamps.

Tributes from the conquered territories flowed into Tenochtitlán, supporting the growing population of the city and enriching the Aztec elite. An early colonial document known as the Codex Mendoza reproduces an Aztec list of tribute by province (see Figure 13.3 on the next page) (Smith 2003). All provinces provided textiles of cotton and maguey, as well as warrior costumes and shields. A variety of other goods, including tropical feathers, rubber balls, wooden beams, and incense, were also major tribute items. Notably, the only foods that were major tribute items were salt, honey, chili, and cocoa beans. The Aztecs lacked draft animals for transporting tribute, so all items had to be carried to Tenochtitlán by porters.

Archaeological excavations on sites outside the Basin of Mexico provide insight into the impact that the Aztec expansion had on what became the periphery of the empire. At the site of **Otumba** in the Teotihuacán Valley, an intensive survey, along with limited excavation, has provided evidence about the organization of craft production under the Aztecs (Charlton, Nichols, and Charlton 1991). On the basis of the artifacts recovered, craft workshops for production of obsidian blades, ceramic figurines, basalt grinding stone, and maguey fiber textile were identified at Otumba. One of the most spectacular discoveries provided evidence of specialized craft workshops for the production of ground stone artifacts from obsidian, including delicate earspools and lip plugs known as labrets. Because obsidian is volcanic glass, the production of ground objects requires considerable skill. It is not surprising that a large number of ground obsidian objects were found that had broken and been discarded in the process of manufacture. There is also evidence at Otumba for the production of cotton textiles and of censers (a special type of pottery vessel used in religious practices) within households rather than in specialized workshops.

Excavations at the site of **Otumba** in the Teotihuacán Valley have produced evidence about the nature of the Aztec organization of craft production.

## FIGURE 13.3

**Aztec Tribute List from the Codex Mendoza**

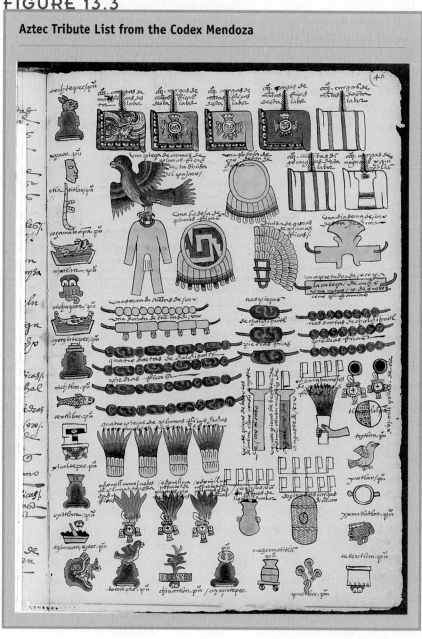

> Excavations at the sites of **Capilco** and **Cuexcomate** have produced insight into rural life under the Aztecs.

The research at Otumba shows the pressure to increase specialized craft production that the Aztec demand for tribute placed on the peripheral territories.

Excavations at the rural sites of **Cuexcomate** and **Capilco** in Morelos, to the south of the Basin of Mexico, have uncovered evidence of how people living in rural provincial settlements would have experienced the Aztec expansion (Smith 2001, 2003). Capilco is the smaller of the two sites, with a total of twenty-one houses; Cuexcomate has over 150 houses, as well as temples and storehouses. These sites grew significantly during the period of Aztec expansion, Capilco from an estimated population of 72 to 116, and Cuexcomate from an estimated population of 237 to 803. All of the houses excavated at these rural sites produced artifacts used in preparing food: blades, grinding stones, and large quantities of pottery. Spindle whorls and spinning bowls used in making cotton textiles were also found in every house, along with ritual artifacts, including figurines and incense burners. Surprisingly, all of the houses contained a large number of items that were traded over a distance, such as

# TOOLBOX:
## Metallurgy

In rare instances, metals are found in such a pure state that they can be hammered into tools or ornaments without any processing. Artifacts made of such a pure, or native, copper are found on prehistoric sites in eastern North America. However, most metals must first be smelted by heating ores to a high temperature. Once smelted, metals can be shaped by hammering or casting.

Copper can be smelted at relatively low temperatures. However, early metalworkers rapidly realized that copper could be strengthened by mixing it with other metals to create alloys. Bronze is a copper alloy produced by mixing copper and tin or arsenic. Both copper and tin are found in limited deposits, so bronze metal production often involved extensive trade. The Ulu Burun shipwreck found off the coast of Turkey provides vivid evidence of this trade: Both tin and bronze were recovered from the hull of the ship as stacks of "oxhide" ingots (Bass 1986).

Iron offers the advantage of being more widely available than copper or tin, but this advantage is counterbalanced by the need to reach very high temperatures in order to smelt iron. In the Americas, iron metallurgy did not develop indigenously. However, archaeologists have uncovered a fascinating record of the indigenous development of iron smelting in Africa (Schmidt 1997).

▶ **Spanish illustration of Aztec goldsmiths.**

Copper, bronze, and iron provided new and effective raw materials for the manufacture of both tools and weapons. However, archaeological metallurgists also stress the symbolic aspects of this technology. Dorothy Hosler (1995) has studied metal production in western Mexico under the Tarascan Empire. She found that western Mexican artisans emphasized the production of objects worn by elites and used in rituals, rather than the production of utilitarian tools. These artisans were most interested in two physical properties of the copper alloys they worked: sound and color. One of the most important types of artifacts produced were bells that were shaped by means of an elaborate technique known as the lost-wax method. For the production of high status or ritual objects, copper alloys were used that had high levels of arsenic or tin. Laboratory experiments have shown

that the amount of tin or arsenic found in these artifacts is far higher than is needed to enhance the mechanical properties of the resulting alloy. Moreover, utilitarian items were found not to have these high levels of arsenic or tin. Although the high levels of these metals do not alter the mechanical quality of the alloys, they do alter the color. High levels of tin or arsenic create increasingly golden or silvery hues.

Historical texts about the Tarascans indicate that they saw sound and color as connected. In one such connection, metallic sounds can create metallic color. As Hosler reconstructs the process, "Smelting, that is winning metal from its ore through heat, gives birth to sound (and song), and it also gives birth to the golden metallic colors" (Hosler 1995: 113). A consideration of Tarascan metallurgy points to the importance of not reducing the study of technology to an examination of the utilitarian functions of tools: Often, even the most elaborate technologies are shot through with symbolic elements.

elaborately painted pottery vessels. There was no difference in the amount of trade goods per house between Capilco and the larger town of Cuexcomate. It is interesting that the period of Aztec expansion actually saw a decrease in the quantity of traded goods found in the houses at those two sites. There also appears to have been an increase in the number of artifacts used in making cloth found in each house during the period of Aztec expansion.

The archaeological evidence from Otumba, Capilco, and Cuexcomate demonstrates the impact of the Aztec expansion on the people living beyond the Valley of Mexico. In many ways, the Aztec expansion acted as a stimulus, spurring the intensity of craft production at Otumba and leading to an increase in population at Capilco and Cuexcomate. However, the rise of the power of Tenochtitlán fundamentally rerouted the exchange of trade goods within the areas under Aztec rule. The need to provide tribute required increased specialization found not only at Otumba, but also in the peasant houses at Capilco and Cuexcomate, in the form of increased textile manufacture. At the same time that there was an increase in craft production, the access of the people living at sites like Capilco and Cuexcomate to trade goods actually decreased. The expansion of the Aztec Empire saw growth in the centralization of both wealth and power in the core of the empire in the city of Tenochtitlán.

## Ritual and Human Sacrifice

The **Templo Mayor** at the center of Tenochtitlán was the core of the Aztec world.

**Coyolxauhqui** was a goddess killed by the Aztec patron god **Huitzilopochtli** in a central event in Aztec mythology.

In 1978, workers were digging a trench for electrical cables near the cathedral in Mexico City when they hit a monumental stone sculpture. This fortuitous discovery led archaeologists to the core of the Aztec spiritual world: the **Templo Mayor** that once rose above the center of Tenochtitlán. The sculpture uncovered by the electric company workers is a spectacular rendition of the dismembered body of **Coyolxauhqui**, a goddess killed by the Aztec patron deity **Huitzilopochtli** in a central event in Aztec mythology (Moctezuma 1992). In this myth, a woman named Coatlicue living on the mountain of Coatepec was impregnated by a ball of feathers and became pregnant with the god Huitzilopochtli. When the four hundred children of Coatlicue learned of her pregnancy, they were enraged. Coyolxauhqui was one of these children, and she urged her siblings to kill their mother. At the very moment the siblings approached Coatepec to kill their mother, Huitzilopochtli was born full grown and immediately dressed for war. With a magical snake, Huitzilopochtli wounded Coyolxauhqui and cut off her head. As Coyolxauhqui's body fell down the mountain, it broke into pieces

**E**xcavation of Coyolxauhqui stone.

**T**emplo Mayor located in the center of modern Mexico City.

as is depicted on the sculpture discovered in Mexico City. Huitzilopochtli then chased down and killed the 400 siblings.

Excavations following the discovery of the Coyolxauhqui sculpture expanded rapidly until much of the sacred precinct was uncovered. The Coyolxauhqui sculpture was found to lie at the base of a double pyramid on the top of which were the dual temples of the gods Tlaloc and Huitzilopochtli. The pyramid represents the hill of Coatepec in the architectural retelling of the defeat of Coyolxauhqui and the victory of the Aztec patron Huitzilopochtli.

The excavation of the pyramid at Templo Mayor showed that, like other Mesoamerican pyramids, it had been built in stages, with each new pyramid encapsulating its predecessor. Within the body of the pyramid, more than one hundred ceremonial caches of artifacts were found (Moctezuma 1988). These caches often

Ceremonial cache found in the Templo Mayor excavations.

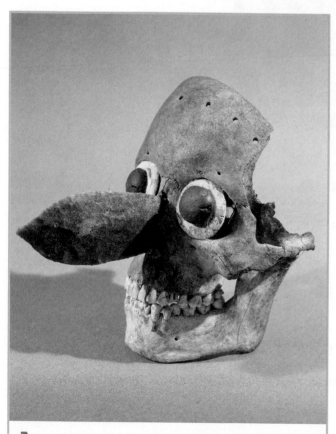

Aztec skull mask with a flint knife inserted in the nasal cavity.

bring together artifacts from across the domains controlled by the Aztec Empire. The symbolic meaning of the caches is often difficult to understand; however, many appear to express the placement of the Templo Mayor at the center of the Aztec spiritual world. Two of the offerings (offering 7 and offering 61) are particularly intriguing in that they are nearly identical. Both were placed in small stone walled chambers and consist of three levels. The lowest level has strombus shells oriented from north to south. Above this is a layer of crocodile remains, and above that are figures of a seated god. Coral was placed on the right side of the sculpture, and on the left a clay vessel was found depicting the god Tlaloc. The meaning of this arrangement is enigmatic, but might involve levels of creation, from the sea (the shells), the land (the crocodiles), and the heavens (the seated god).

Other caches in the Templo Mayor provide evidence of the important role human sacrifice played in Aztec ritual. Worked human skulls known as "skull masks" are found in a number of the offerings. The skull masks are the front part of the skull, with the eye sockets filled with white shell discs. Round pieces were placed at the center of the shell discs to represent the iris. Small holes were drilled along the top of the skull, perhaps for attaching other material. In some cases, carefully flaked flint knives are found inserted between the teeth or vertically into the nasal cavity.

Historic descriptions of the Templo Mayor mention racks with large numbers of human skulls. No such large concentration of skulls was ever found at the site; however, the excavations did uncover a large platform decorated with sculptures depicting 240 skulls. Human sacrifice played a critical role in Aztec ritual, and the sacrifice of war captives or slaves was an important part of the Aztec ritual cycle.

A detailed description of human sacrifice is found in the Florentine Codex. Four men stretched the victim out on the sacrificial stone. His breast was then cut open by the priest and his heart seized and dedicated to the sun. The victim's corpse was then sent toppling down the side of the pyramid. Finally, a priest removed the head for placement on the skull rack (Smith 2003). For the Aztecs, the sacrificial victim was transformed into a deity and was sacrificed in order to assure the continuation of the universe. However, as the Aztec Empire expanded, ritual sacrifice also came to play a role in projecting the power of the Aztecs and terrifying their opponents. In one case during the reign of Ahuizotl (1486–1502), a massive slaughter took place on the occasion of the rededication of the Templo Mayor. It appears that Ahuizotl was using ritual slaughter as a particularly brutal form of propaganda.

Archaeological research on sites outside the Basin of Mexico shows that the violent ritual found in the core of the empire did not have wide currency in the peripheral regions (Brumfiel 2001). Ceramic figurines are found on most Aztec-period sites, and it is likely that they were used in household rituals. During the period of Aztec dominance, female figurines outnumber male figurines by a ratio of three to one. Of the male figurines, few are of warriors. The women shown in Aztec art are usually depicted in a subservient, kneeling position. However, among the figurines, the women are usually standing and often holding two children. The rarity of figurines depicting warriors suggest that the ritual practices of rural people differed significantly from the ritual practices of Tenochtitlán. The question is raised, then, of who the audience was for the rituals enacted at the Templo Mayor. It is likely that the goal of these rituals was at least as much to inspire a spirit of warfare in the men of fighting age within the city of Tenochtitlán as to terrify the subjects of the Aztecs. Clearly, how one would have experienced these rituals would differ, given one's place in society. The elite and the warriors were active participants in the rituals. The masses of the city must have had difficulty avoiding the events taking place at the Templo Mayor. For people in the provinces, by contrast, the rituals practiced at the Templo Mayor would have been a terrifying rumor few would have personally experienced.

## Summing Up the Evidence

Empires are characterized by a degree of social heterogeneity such that different members of society have vastly differing experiences and world views. For this reason, it is important to take great care before making blanket generalizations about an empire such as the Aztecs or the Inca. Archaeology can often draw out the varied human realities that can be obscured by the narrow focus on the lives of elites found in historical texts. Archaeological excavations on rural sites have shown that although the impact of the Aztec Empire varied, it was invariably significant. Surveys in the Valley of Mexico demonstrate that there was a significant rise in population with the advent of the Aztec Empire. The Aztecs ruled through a triple alliance, but the city of Tenochtitlán was clearly the dominant party. Excavations in the Templo Mayor in the middle of modern Mexico City have brought archaeologists to the heart of the Aztec Empire. The evidence from these excavations vividly illustrates the ideology of warfare and human sacrifice that were essential to the Aztec Empire. But Aztec ideology was built not only on violence: The discoveries at the Templo Mayor also uncover the two paths the Aztecs took to connect themselves to an illustrious

**P**hoto of Aztec household figurine.

past. The symbolism of the sculptures connects the Aztecs to the mythological time of Huitzilopochtli. On a semimythological plane, the Templo Mayor was said to have been built on the actual spot where the Mexica refugees from Aztlán decided to make their last stand. But at the same time that the Aztecs rooted themselves in a uniquely Aztec mythical past, they also found connections with their Mesoamerican predecessors. The inclusion of Olmec and Teotihuacán objects speak to a reverence for antiquity that is strongly reminiscent of the interests of the Aztecs' European contemporaries in the antiquities of Greece and Rome.

The fall of the Aztec and Inca Empires is part of a global transformation that is still underway. The spread of Europeans, along with their culture and institutions, that began in the fifteenth century has had a dramatic impact on societies around the world, creating what anthropologists often refer to as a world system. The European expansion is richly documented in a wide range of written sources. Yet even here archaeology can play a critical role. This branch of the discipline is known as historical archaeology (Deetz 1996, Orser 2004). The written record is written largely by Europeans, leaving many indigenous societies as "people without history" (Wolf 1982). Archaeologists can contribute to giving a voice to these people and recovering a history that is otherwise lost. Examples of such research efforts include the archaeology of indigenous people around during the process of European contact and the archaeology of slave communities. Historical archaeologists also work in urban industrial centers examining the changing technologies and social relations that powered European expansion. Here again archaeologists can contibute to our understanding of aspects of society that are poorly represented in historical documents.

# CHAPTER SUMMARY

- Empires are political entities that bring together a diverse group of societies under a single ruler.
- The archaeology of empires often focuses on how the core of the empire maintained control over the periphery.
- The Inca Empire Tawantinsuyu covered an area that stretched over 3,000 kilometers and had a population of 12 million people.
- In 1533, the Inca Empire fell to a small group of Spanish soldiers under the command of Pizarro.
- The ceremonial center at Chavín de Huántar marks an important step in the development of social complexity in the Andes. Early Andean states include the coastal states that developed along the Moche and Nazca River valleys.

- The property of the Inca emperor was passed on to his descendants, collectively known as his *panaqa*. The site of Machu Picchu was an estate belonging to the *panaqa* of Pachacuti.
- Feasting and the exchange of gifts played an important role in Inca society. At the Inca center of Hua'nuco Pampa, two enormous halls used for feasting have been excavated.
- The Inca built an extensive network of roads to facilitate communication across the empire. The Inca used a system of knotted strings known as *khipu* to record information.
- The Aztec capital of Tenochtitlán was built on an island in Lake Texcoco in the Valley of Mexico and had a very large population.

- Tenochtitlán fell to the Spanish in 1521. Texts such as the Florentine Codex provide extensive documentation of Aztec history, religion, and society.
- Political complexity in Mesoamerica dates back to the Olmec. The Aztecs traced their genealogy back to the Toltec Empire, which developed after the fall of Teotihuacán.
- The Aztec migrated to the Valley of Mexico from a region to the north known as Aztlán.
- The formation of a triple alliance between Tenochtitlán, Texcoco, and Telapocán was a critical event in the formation of the Aztec Empire. Within this alliance, Tenochtitlán was the dominant force.

- The economy of Tenochtitlán relied on intensified agriculture, including the farming of raised fields known as chinampas.
- Excavations at the provincial sites of Otumba, Capilco, and Cuexcomate shed light on the effect of the Aztec expansion at the periphery of the empire.
- A chance discovery led archaeologists to the Templo Mayor, the massive pyramid temple that stood at the center of Tenochtitlán. Templo Mayor was the site of rituals involving human sacrifice.

## KEY TERMS

Aztec Empire, 400
Aztlán, 403
Bernardo de Sahagún, 401
Capilco and Cuexcomate, 406
Chinampas, 405
Chavín de Huántar, 392
Coyolxauhqui, 408
Empires, 389
Florentine Codex, 401
Hua'nuco Pampa, 396

Huitzilopochtli, 408
Inca Empire, 391
Khipu, 398
Machu Picchu, 395
Moche State, 392
Nazca Culture, 392
Nazca Lines, 392
Otumba, 405
Panaqa, 394
Sipán, 392

Tawantinsuyu, 391
Telapocán, 405
Templo Mayor, 408
Tenochtitlán, 400
Teotihuacán, 402
Texcoco, 405
Toltec Empire, 402
Tula, 402
Urubamba Valley, 395

## REVIEW QUESTIONS

1. How were the Inca able to maintain their dominion over the large territories that made up Tawantinsuyu?
2. What insight does archaeology yield about the impact of Aztec expansion on people living at the periphery of the empire?
3. How did Inca and Aztec beliefs about death and killing affect the nature of their empires?

## FOR FURTHER READING

Susan Alcock, Terence D'Altroy, Kathleen Morrison and Carla Sinopoli. (2001). *Empires*. Cambridge: Cambridge University Press.

Richard Burger and Lucy Salazar. (2004). *Machu Picchu: Unveiling the Mystery of the Incas*. New Haven: Yale University Press.

Terence D'Altroy. (2003). *The Incas*. Malden, MA: Blackwell.

Eduardo Matos Moctezuma. (1988). *The Great Temple of the Aztecs: Treasures of Tenochtitlan*. London: Thames and Hudson.

Michael Smith. (2003). *The Aztecs*. Malden, MA: Blackwell.

Richard Townsend. (2000). *The Aztecs*. London: Thames and Hudson.

# Bringing It Back Home

**A**s we arrive at the end of this book, a journey in a sense, we are filled with images from far away, both in place and in time. However, in closing, it is important to recall that archaeology is not only about exploring the unknown, but also about recognizing the traces of the past in our familiar world. Travel and archaeological research are invaluable experiences . At the same time, an increased awareness of the past that surrounds us in our daily lives can also profoundly alter our sense of the world in which we live.

The French historian Pierre Nora used the evocative term "Places of Memory" for locations or objects that become saturated with historical meaning (Nora 1996–1998). Places of Memory are critical touchstones for our connection with society, creating a visceral and real connection between present and past. The discovery of an African slave cemetery in Lower Manhattan in 1991 offers a vivid illustration of the emotional effect of the actual physical remains of the past (Mack and Blakey 2004). Although historians have known that slavery was widespread in early Manhattan, the discovery of the cemetery grounded this historical knowledge in a concrete physical presence. The effect was to dramatically alter the way we see the city of New York.

More recently, New York City was the site of a catastrophe of such a tragic scope that it bound the world in a sense of loss and grief. The events of September 11, 2001, transformed Ground Zero into one

**R**eburial ceremony at the African burial ground in Lower Manhattan.

**W**onderwerk Cave, Northern Cape Province, South Africa.

Ground Zero in New York is a powerful and tragic Place of Memory.

An archaeologist holds some of the household materials recovered from the excavation of a historical site.

of the most profound Places of Memory of our time, a place whose physical presence raises deep emotions.

Most of the traces of the past that enrich our world are neither as awful or as awe-inspiring as Ground Zero. The archaeologist James Deetz coined the phrase "In Small Things Forgotten," drawn from a seventeenth-century appraisal of the contents of a house in Plymouth, Massachusetts. At the end of the listing of the contents, the appraiser made a last entry: "In small things forgotten, eight shillings six-pence" (Deetz 1996: 4). One can imagine the various objects left behind that together came to a value of eight shillings six-pence. Small things forgotten are found all around us, even below our feet as we walk on roads, sidewalks, and even manhole covers. Recognizing and valuing these subtle traces of the past enriches the world we live in.

The social theorist Walter Benjamin developed a beautiful and harrowing image of the "angel of history" that might apply to archaeology. Benjamin writes of a painting by Paul Klee that shows an angel contemplating something he is about to move away from. For Benjamin, this is an image of the angel of history: "His face is turned toward the past. Where we perceive a chain of events, he sees one single catastrophe which keeps piling wreckage upon wreckage and hurls it in front of his feet" (Benjamin 1968: 257). Benjamin's angel would like to stay and heal the wreck before his eyes, but a "storm irresistibly propels him into the future to which his back is turned, while the pile of debris before him grows skyward. This storm is called progress" (Benjamin 1968: 258). Benjamin's vision is a horrifying idea of

**W**alter Benjamin based his vision of the Angel of History on Paul Klee's painting Angelus Novus.

progress that cautions us not to assume that progress implies improvement. Yet, as an archaeologist, I find something lacking from Benjamin's vision. In a sense, Benjamin is as guilty as those he wishes to criticize in seeing history as divorced from human experience. As we look back on the "wreckage of progress" that archaeologists have uncovered and continue to uncover, what do we see? There are many answers to this question, and it is largely a question of personal perspective. What I find lacking from Benjamin's vision is a sense of the humanity of the past. The archaeological record is profoundly human. A handaxe is not only a shaped stone, but also a stone that bears the traces of every blow used to sculpt a tool and the micro traces left as the tool is used. A pot bears the imprints of the hands of the person who made it and the paint strokes or incisions applied as decoration. Walls are not simply architectural spaces, but the remnants of structures in which people lived their lives.

Benjamin's vision can be balanced by a poem by the late Israeli poet Yehuda Amichai. In his poem, Amichai writes of sitting by David's Tower in Jerusalem after going shopping. He becomes the point of reference for a tour guide who says, "You see that man with the baskets? Just right of his head there's an arch from the Roman period." In the poem, Amichai looks to the day when the guide says, "You see that arch from the Roman period? It's not important: but next to it, left and down a bit, there sits a man who's bought fruit and vegetables for his family" (Amichai 1996: 137–138). So that is where we leave our journey, not with the gold of kings or the bones of early hominins, but with a person alive in a world saturated with the past. Wherever we live, some part of us is that person.

# Appendices

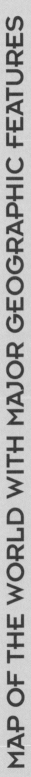

## MAP OF THE WORLD WITH MAJOR GEOGRAPHIC FEATURES

Beringia

Ohio R.

Mississippi R.

Mesoamerica

Amazon

Andes

Western Europe

Georgia

Nile Valley

Mesopotamia

Sahara

East African Rift Valley

Indus Valley

Yellow River

Yangtze River

New Guinea

Australia

AFGH. = Afghanistan
ALB. = Albania
ARM. = Armenia
AUS. = Austria
AZER. = Azerbaijan
BANG. = Bangladesh
BEL. = Belgium
B & H. = Bosnia and Herzegovina
BUL. = Bulgaria
BURK. FASO = Burkina Faso
C. AFR. REP. = Central African Republic
CAM. = Cameroon
CRO. = Croatia
C. V. = Cape Verde
CYP. = Cyprus
CZE. = Czech Republic
DEM. REP. OF THE CONGO =
    Democratic Republic of the Congo
DEN. = Denmark
EQ. GUINEA = Equatorial Guinea
EST. = Estonia
GAM. = Gambia
G.-B. = Guinea-Bissau
GER. = Germany
GUI. = Guinea
HOND. = Honduras
HUN. = Hungary
ISR. = Israel
KAMP. = Kampuchea
KRYG. = Kyrgyzstan
LAT. = Latvia
LEB. = Lebanon
LITH. = Lithuania
LUX. = Luxembourg
MAC. = Macedonia
MOL. = Moldova
MON. = Montenegro
MYAN. = Myanmar
NETH. = Netherlands
POL. = Poland
ROM. = Romania
RUS. = Russia
SER. = Serbia
SLO. = Slovakia
SLOV. = Slovenia
SWITZ. = Switzerland
SYR. = Syria
TAJIK. = Tajikistan
THAI. = Thailand
TURK. = Turkmenistan
UZBEK. = Uzbekistan
U.A.E. = United Arab Emirates

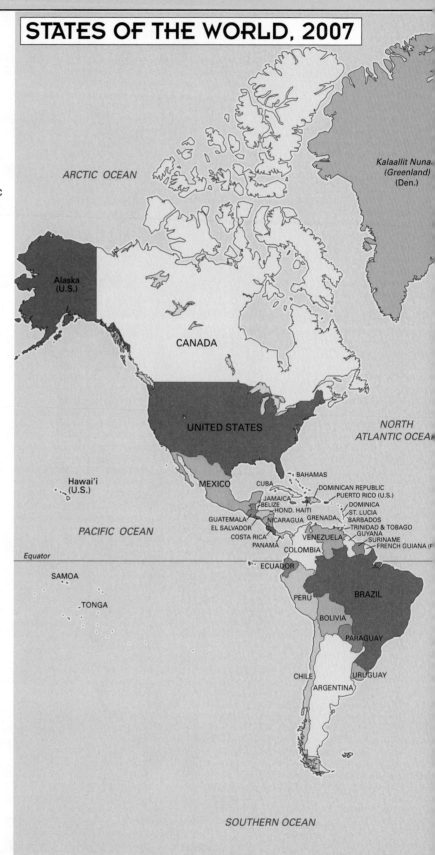

## STATES OF THE WORLD, 2007

# COMMONLY USED METRIC SYSTEM UNITS AND SYMBOLS

| QUANTITY MEASURED | UNIT | SYMBOL | RELATIONSHIP | | |
|---|---|---|---|---|---|
| Length, width, | millimeter | mm | 10 mm | = | 1 cm |
| distance, thickness, | centimeter | cm | 100 cm | = | 1 m |
| girth, etc. | meter | m | | | |
| | kilometer | km | 1 km | = | 1000 m |
| Mass ("weight") | milligram | mg | 1000 mg | = | 1 g |
| | gram | g | | | |
| | kilogram | kg | 1 kg | = | 1000 g |
| | metric ton | t | 1 t | = | 1000 kg |
| Time | second | s | | | |
| Temperature | degree Celsius | °C | | | |
| Area | square meter | $m^2$ | | | |
| | hectare | ha | 1 ha | = | 10 000 $m^2$ |
| | square kilometer | $km^2$ | 1 $km^2$ | = | 100 ha |
| Volume | milliliter | mL | 1000 mL | = | 1 L |
| | cubic centimeter | $cm^3$ or cc | 1 $cm^3$ | = | 1 mL |
| | liter | L | 1000 L | = | 1 $m^3$ |

## Conversion Table

| TO CONVERT FROM | TO | MULTIPLY BY * |
|---|---|---|
| acres | hectares (ha) | 0.4 |
| feet (ft) | meters (m) | 0.3 |
| inches (in) | centimeters (cm) | 2.54 |
| miles (mi) | kilometers (km) | 1.6 |
| ounces (oz) | grams (g) | 28 |
| pounds (lb) | kilograms (kg) | 0.45 or divide by 2.2 |
| yards (yd) | meters (m) | 0.9 |

*approximate, except for the inches-to-centimeter multiplier, which is exact.

# THE HOMININ WHO'S WHO

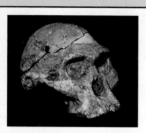

### Australopithecus

- 3.5–2.5 million years ago
- Brain size: 450–475 cc
- Found in East Africa, South Africa, and Chad
- Species include *Australopithecus bahrelghazali, Australopithecus afarensis,* and *Australopithecus africanus.*
- Bipedal and small canines

### Paranthropus

- 2.5–1.4 million years ago
- Brain size: 450–475 cc
- Found in East Africa and South Africa
- Also known as robust *Australopithecus.* Species include *Paranthropus robustus* and *Parathropus boisei.*
- Massive molars and muscles for chewing

**Hominoids are members of the biological family that includes humans, great apes, and gibbons.**

**Hominins are members of the human lineage after it split with the chimpanzee lineage.**

### Kenyanthropus

- 3.5 million years ago
- Brain size: 450–475 cc
- Only one species known, *Kenyanthropus platyops.*
- Similar to *Australopithecus*

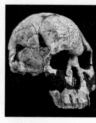

### Homo habilis

- 2.5–1.6 million years ago
- Brain size: 500–800 cc
- Found in East Africa and South Africa
- First member of genus *Homo*
- Increased brain size

### Homo erectus

- 1.9 million–45,000? years ago
- Brain size: 750–1,250 cc
- Found in Africa, Asia, and Europe
- Early *Homo erectus* is often referred to as Homo ergaster
- First hominin found out of Africa, increased brain size

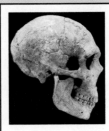

### Homo neanderthalensis

- 175,000–30,000 years ago
- Brain size: 1,200–1,700 cc
- Found in Europe and the Middle East
- Some anthropologists prefer to label this group of fossils as *Homo sapiens neanderthalensis.*
- Large brain size, muscular, and adapted to the cold

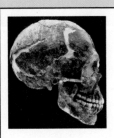

### Homo sapiens sapiens

- 160,000 years ago until today
- Brain size: 1,200–1,700 cc
- Found throughout the globe
- All living humans belong to this species, which is often referred to as "modern humans."
- Globular braincase, vertical forehead, decreased body mass

### Homo floresiensis

- 38,000–18,000 years ago
- Brain size: 380 cc
- Found only on the island of Flores
- Some anthropologists question whether this is in fact a distinct species.
- Small brain and body size

# DATING METHODS

## Radiocarbon Dating
**Toolbox on p. 131**

- Time range: Beginning 40,000 years ago.
- Material dated: Organic remains including charcoal, bone, wood, and shell.
- The death of an organism removes it from the carbon exchange reservoir and radioactive carbon-14 begins to decay at a steady rate. The concentration of carbon-14 relative to other isotopes of carbon is the basis for calculating the time since the death of the organism.
- Because of fluctuations in the concentration of carbon-14 in the global reservoir, carbon-14 dates have to be calibrated to derive a calendar date (see p. 178).
- Accelerator mass spectrometry (AMS) allows for the dating of very small samples (see p. 238).

## Paleomagnetic Dating
**Toolbox on p. 100**

- Effective for dating all periods of hominin evolution.
- Material dated: Sediments.
- Determines whether sediments were deposited in periods of normal or reversed polarity. Can be used to situate a stratigraphic context in the paleomagnetic timescale.

## Argon Dating
**Toolbox on p. 88**

- Effective for dating all periods of hominin evolution.
- Materials dated: Volcanic rock and ash, as well as meteoric glass (tektites).
- Measures the accumulation of argon-40 from the decay of potassium-40. The decay of potassium-40 takes place at a constant rate. The accumulation clock is zeroed at the time of a volcanic eruption because argon diffuses out of a material at high temperature. Consequently after an eruption there is no argon in lava and ash. Argon then begins to accumulate as a result of the decay of potassium.
- Can be used only in areas with volcanic deposits.

## Luminescence Dating
**Toolbox on p. 145**

- Most effective for the more recent periods of hominin evolution (since 200,000 years ago).
- Materials dated: Sediments (optically stimulated resonance, or OSL), Burnt Flint and Pottery (TL), Teeth (electron spin resonance, or ESR).
- Measures the accumulation of electrons in crystal lattices. The clock is zeroed when the material is heated (TL), when it is exposed to sunlight (OSL), or upon the initial growth of the crystal (ESR).
- The background radiation at the find must be measured with a dosimeter.

## Dendrochronology
**Toolbox on p. 309**

- Most useful for the last 10,000 years.
- Material dated: Wood.
- The ring pattern found in a piece of wood is matched to the fluctuations in a long-term chronology.

# ATTRIBUTES OF STONE TOOLS AND CERAMIC VESSELS

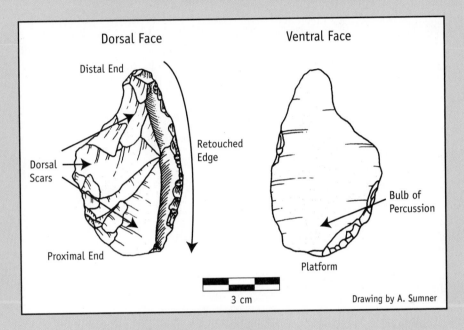

Dorsal Face      Ventral Face

Distal End

Retouched Edge

Dorsal Scars

Bulb of Percussion

Proximal End

Platform

3 cm

Drawing by A. Sumner

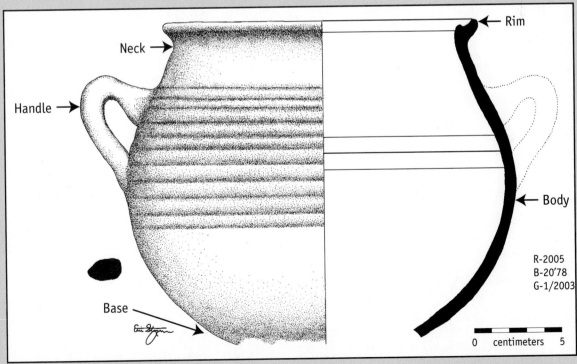

Neck

Handle

Rim

Body

Base

R-2005
B-20'78
G-1/2003

0    centimeters    5

# WRITING SYSTEMS

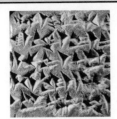

## Cuneiform  see pp. 330–331.
- Used for a wide range of Mesopotamian languages, including Sumerian, Akkadian, and Hittite.
- Documents include economic texts, legal codes, historical records, and myths.
- Developed from a pictographic to a syllabic script.

## Mayan Hieroglyphics  see pp. 344–345 and 348–349.
- Used on monumental inscriptions recording dynastic history. Also found in books known as codices.
- Combination of pictographic and syllabic script.

## Shang Chinese  see p. 351.
- Found on oracle bones used in divination and on bronze vessels.
- Related to modern Chinese script.

## Egyptian Hieroglyphics  see pp. 356–366.
- Used on monumental inscriptions and also on documents written on papyrus.
- Combination of logograms, phonograms, and determinatives.

## Indus Valley Script  see p. 379.
- Found mostly in short inscriptions on seals.
- This script has not been deciphered.

## Khipu  see p. 399.
- A system of knotted strings used by the Inca.
- The way this system worked and the kind of information it encoded is unclear.

# A

**Abrigo do Lagar Velho** The site in Portugal where the skeleton of a modern human child dating to 24,500 years ago was discovered. The discovery is thought by some to support the hybridization model.

**Abu Hureyra** A site on the Euphrates River in Syria that was occupied during the Natufian and the Neolithic periods.

**Abydos** The site of the royal cemetery of Egypt during the First and Second Dynasty of Egypt.

**Acheulian** One of the two major industries of the Lower Paleolithic. The Acheulian is characterized by bifaces and dates between 1.7 million and 200,000 years ago.

**Adena** A period of intensive mound building in the Ohio River Valley; corresponds to the early Woodland culture.

*Aegyptopithecus* One of the earliest hominoids; lived between thirty-five million and twenty-three million years ago.

**Agency Theory** A theory that emphasizes the centrality of individuals living in society as the basic unit of archaeology. It stresses the agency of individuals—the purposeful actions of the people who lived in the past.

**Aguateca** A site abandoned and burned, probably due to a military attack, leaving archaeologists with a unique record of the daily life of the Maya.

**Ain Afuda** A cave site in the Libyan Sahara that has produced the well-preserved remains of preagricultural occupation.

**Akhenaten** A religious reformer who built the city of Amarna. He shifted Egyptian religion to a focus on a single deity: the visible disc of the sun, known as Aten. This innovation was rejected after his death.

**Alpacas** A camelid animal domesticated in the Andean highlands.

**Amarna** A city built by the heretic king Akhenaten and abandoned after his reign. Excavation of this city has provided a unique horizontal exposure of an Egyptian urban center.

**AMS Radiocarbon Dating** A refined method of radiocarbon dating that makes it possible to date very small samples, including plant remains.

**Amud Cave** Location at which a Neanderthal child was found buried with the upper jaw of a red deer.

**An Yang** Site located in northern China; capital of the Shang Dynasty.

**Anthropogenic Deposits** Deposits that result from human activity. Human activities range from building fires on ephemeral hunter–gatherer campsites to erecting the palaces and fortifications of great cities.

**Archaeological Theory** A collection of ideas that archaeologists have developed about the past and the ways we come to know it.

**Arcy-sur-Cure** The site, located in Northern France, at which excavators discovered a rich collection of ornaments, bone tools, and Châtelperronian stone tools.

***Ardipithecus ramidus*** An early species in the hominin lineage. This species, which lived approximately four-and-a-half million years ago, is known from fossils originally discovered in 1992 at the site of Aramis in Ethiopia.

**Artifacts** Objects that show traces of human manufacture.

**Atapuerca** Location in Spain where stone tools and hominin remains dated to 800,000 years ago were found. These artifacts are the oldest reliable evidence of human occupation of western Europe.

**Aterian** A North African stone tool industry distinguished by the presence of points with a pronounced tang—a small projection located at the base of the point and used to secure the point to a spear or handle.

**Attribute** A particular characteristic of an artifact.

**Aurignacian** The earliest Upper Paleolithic period, industries of which have been found on sites across Europe and the Middle East.

**Australopithecine** A hominin genus that lived in Africa between four million and two-and-a-half million years ago.

**Aztec Empire** Large Mesoamerican Empire based in Tenochtitlán and located in the Basin of Mexico.

**Aztlán** The mythical homeland of the Aztecs.

# B

**Banpo** A large farming village located in the Yellow River Valley (China) dating to the Yangshou culture.

**Beringia** A land bridge that connected Asia and North America during periods of low sea level.

**Bernardo de Sahagún** The Spanish friar who compiled the Florentine Codex, a major source of information about Aztec history and culture.

**Bevel-Rim Bowls** Small, undecorated bowls made of coarse clay fabric that are ubiquitous on Uruk-period sites. Theories of the function of these bowls hold that they served to distribute rations and that they were molds for baking bread.

**Biache-Saint-Vaast** The site in France where the oldest-known fossil of a Neanderthal, dated to 175,000 years ago, was found.

**Bifaces** Characteristic tools of the Acheulian. Bifaces include handaxes and cleavers.

**Blackwater Draw** Site near Clovis, New Mexico, at which spearpoints were found in levels below Folsom points.

**Blombos Cave** The site in South Africa at which pieces of ochre with incised decoration was found in a Middle Stone Age level dated to 77,000 years ago.

**Bluestones** A ring of standing stones at the center of Stonehenge. The source of the stones is over 240 kilometers from Stonehenge.

**Border Cave** One of the South African sites where fossils of modern humans dated to between 120,000 and 70,000 years ago were discovered.

**Bose** Located in southern China, this site has produced a stone tool industry that includes handaxes dated to 800,000 years ago.

**Boxgrove** Among the oldest-known Acheulian site in Europe; located in England and dated to 500,000 years ago.

**Broad Spectrum Adaptation** Societies of complex hunter–gatherers that preceded the shift to agriculture, labeled "Archaic" in the Americas and "Epipaleolithic" or "Mesolithic" in other parts of the world are characterized by their exploitation of a broad spectrum of plant and animal resources.

# C

**Cahokia** A large settlement dating to the Mississippian Period and located just outside of St. Louis.

**Capilco** and **Cuexcomate** Sites located in Morales south of the Basin of Mexico at which excavations have produced insights into rural life under the Aztecs.

**Çatalhöyük** The Late Neolithic site in Turkey that includes rooms decorated with elaborate frescoes.

**Caverna de Pedra Pintada** Site in Brazil which shows that people were living in the tropical rain forests of South America between 13,000 and 11,500 years ago.

**Cepheren** Builder of the second pyramid at Giza. The Great Sphinx is located alongside the Cepheren Valley Temple.

**Cerro Juanaqueña** An early agricultural site in northern Mexico with extensive evidence of terracing and other stone built features.

**Chacoan Network** A road system that links Chaco Canyon with sites covering a large part of what is today the Four Corners region of the U.S. southwest.

**Châtelperronian** One of the industries in France and northern Spain identified as transitional between the Middle Paleolithic and the Upper Paleolithic.

**Chauvet Cave** The earliest-known painted cave, dated to between 38,000 and 33,000 years ago.

**Chavín de Huántar** A major ceremonial center in the Andean highlands constructed around 800 B.C.

**Cheops** Builder of the first and largest pyramid at Giza.

**Chesowanja** Site located in Kenya and dated to 1.4 million years ago that has produced tentative evidence for the use of fire by early hominins.

**Chinampas** Raised agricultural beds built in swamps and that were critical for Aztec agriculture.

**Clactonian** A simple flake tool industry contemporary with the Acheulian in England.

**Clovis** The period many North American archaeologists view as the initial human occupation of the Americas, dated to between 13,500 and 12,500 years ago.

**Coastal Migration** The route some archaeologists argue to have been used by the earliest people in Americas to move out of Beringia instead of through an ice-free corridor.

**Community** Term applied to characteristics of the transition to agriculture, which involved not only physical changes to the landscape through the construction of villages and monuments, but also a change in the way people viewed the landscape and the way ownership of the land was conceived.

**Copán** Copán was a large Mayan city with two large pyramids and an elaborate ball court at its center.

**Cotton Preceramic** Period beginning 5,700 years ago during which time sites with monumental architecture flourished on the coast of Peru.

**Coyolxauhqui**  A goddess killed by the Aztec patron god Huitzilopochtli in a central event in Aztec mythology.

**Cuneiform**  A writing system in which signs were impressed in clay. Cuneiform was used to write a range of languages, including Sumerian and Akkadian.

**Cylinder Seals**  One of the methods developed by Mesopotamian scribes to mark ownership.

# D

**Datum Point**  The linchpin for the control of an excavation. It serves as a reference point for all depth measurements on the site.

**David Rindos**  An archaeologist who saw agriculture as the result of a coevolutionary process involving a symbiotic relationship between plant and animal species.

**Deduction**  Drawing particular inferences from general laws and models.

**Depositional Unit**  The material deposited at a site at a particular point in time.

**Dhaka**  A mixture of clay and gravel that was used for building huts at Great Zimbabwe.

**Diachronic**  Relating to processes of change through time.

**Dispersal**  An event in which a single species expands its range dramatically.

**Djoser Pyramid Complex**  The first pyramid constructed in Egypt, a stepped pyramid built by Djoser at Saqqara and located within a walled complex.

**DKI**  The site at Olduvai Gorge where a stone circle was found, suggesting evidence of a temporary structure built on a home-base site.

**Dmanisi**  The oldest-known archaeological site outside of Africa, located in the country of Georgia and dated 1.7 million and 1.8 million years ago.

**Domestication**  Relationship between humans, on the one hand, and plants and animals, on the other, wherein the humans play an integral role in the protection and reproduction of the plants and animals.

# E

**East African Rift Valley**  A geological feature stretching from East Africa to the Middle East that is the richest context for the recovery of early hominin archaeological sites.

**Ecofacts**  Objects recovered from an archeological context that are either the remains of biological organisms or the results of geological processes.

**Egalitarian Society**  Society in which the only differences in status are based on skill, age, and gender.

**El Niño**  A severe reversal of the Humboldt Current that causes a massive decline in marine resources along the Andean coast.

**Empires**  Political entities that bring together a diverse and heterogeneous group of societies under a single ruler.

**Ester Boserup**  Economist whose research suggests that increased population size might have been the cause of the shift to agriculture among hominins.

**Eurasian Acheulian**  A stone tool industry found on sites throughout the Middle East and Europe beginning 500,000 years ago. The handaxe is the characteristic tool of this industry.

**Evolutionary Archaeology**  A range of approaches that stress the importance of evolutionary theory as a unifying theory for archaeology.

# F

**Feminist Archaeology** An approach to archaeology that both focuses on the way archaeologists study and represent gender and brings attention to gender inequities in the practice of archaeology.

**Fire-Stick Farming** A term used by Rhys Jones to describe the aboriginal use of fire in Australia.

**First Dynasty** Based in Hierakonpolis and Abydos in Upper Egypt.

**FLK North** The site in Olduvai Gorge where the remains of an elephant were found together with stone tools.

**Florentine Codex** A document that is a major source of information on Aztec history and culture; compiled by the Spanish friar Bernardo de Sahagún soon after the Spanish conquest of the Aztecs.

**Flotation** The process used to recover botanical material (wood and seeds) and which involves mixing sediments vigorously in water. In the process, charred remains of seeds and wood float to the surface while the mineral sediments settle to the bottom. The charred botanical material can then be skimmed off and dried for analysis.

**Frison Effect** The process through which, due to resharpening, the shape of stone tools changes during their useful life.

# G

**Geographical Information Systems** Software applications that allow spatial data to be brought together and consolidated.

**Giza** The site of the construction of the pyramids of Cheops, Cepheren, and Mycerinus—monuments representing the apex of pyramid construction in Old Kingdom Egypt.

**Gravettian** This second major Upper Paleolithic archaeological period in Europe. Venus figurines are found on Gravettian sites.

**Great Bath** Impressive structure built around a rectangular basin at the site of Mohenjo-Daro. One of the only monumental structures found on a Harappan site.

**Great Houses** Large multistoried structures located at Chaco Canyon, New Mexico, that became the center of a regional settlement network beginning around A.D. 800.

**Great Zimbabwe** A large settlement located in modern Zimbabwe that includes the remains of impressive stone enclosures and that was built between A.D. 1300 and A.D. 1400.

**Guilá Naquitz** A site in Oaxaca, Mexico, that has produced the earliest evidence of domesticated plants in the Americas.

**Guitarrero Cave** Site in the Andean highlands of Peru at which excavations uncovered the earliest evidence of domesticated beans dating to 4,300 years ago.

**Gunbilngmurrung** Site in Australia at which a beeswax figure of a turtle was found, radiocarbon dated to 4,000 years ago.

# H

**Habuba Kebira** An Uruk colony located on the upper reaches of the Euphrates River in Northern Syria.

**Hadar** Location in the East African Rift Valley where many important fossils, including the near-complete fossil of an Australopithicine, have been discovered.

**Harappa**  One of the two major urban centers of the Harappan period.

**Harappan Period**  Period from 2600 B.C. to 1900 B.C. during which urban centers developed in the Indus Valley.

**Harappan Script**  A script, found mostly on sealings, that has not been deciphered.

**Hemudu**  A well-preserved rice-farming village located in southern China.

**Hermeneutics**  A theory of interpretation that stresses the interaction between the presuppositions we bring to a problem and the independent empirical reality of our observations and experiences.

**Herto**  The site in Ethiopia where the oldest-known fossil of a modern human was discovered, dating to between 160,000 and 154,000 years ago.

**Hierakonpolis**  One of the two centers, along with Abydos, of Egypt during the late Predynastic period and the First Dynasty.

**Hohlenstein**  The site in Germany where a lion-headed figure was found in levels with an Aurignacian industry.

**Home-Base/Food-Sharing Model**  Model developed by Glynn Isaac that sees the sharing of meat at base camps as a fundamental part of the lives of early hominins.

**Hominins**  The members of the human lineage after it split with the chimpanzee lineage.

**Hominoids**  The biological family that includes humans, great apes, and gibbons.

*Homo erectus*  The first hominin found on sites outside of Africa. The earliest known *Homo erectus* fossils date to the period between 1.9 and 1.5 million years ago.

*Homo habilis*  This hominin is the earliest species to be assigned to the genus *Homo*.

*Homo sapiens*  The species name for modern humans.

**Hopewell**  A period of intensive mound building in the Ohio River Valley; corresponds to the Middle Woodland culture.

**Horizontal Excavation**  An excavation for which the goal is to excavate a broad area in order to expose the remains of a single point in time.

**Howieson's Poort**  Middle Stone Age industry found in southern Africa that is characterized by small crescent-shaped stone tools.

**Hua'nuco Pampa**  An Inca center 600 kilometers north of the capital, Cuzco.

**Huitzilopochtli**  The Aztec patron god.

**Humboldt Current**  Current that brings cool waters from the south up along the Andean coast and that accounts for the remarkable wealth of marine resources along that coast.

# I

**Ice-Free Corridor**  A potential migration route running between the Cordilleran and Laurentide ice sheets for populations expanding out of Beringia.

**In Situ**  Archaeological material is considered to be *in situ* when it is found in the place where it was originally deposited.

**Inca**  This empire thribed fro over a centruy. At it's peak the empire ruled over 12 million people from northern Chile to Ecuador.

**Induction**  Drawing general inferences on the basis of available empirical data.

**Indus Valley**  Area extending along the course of the Indus River and covering much of modern Pakistan and the Kutch and Gujarat provinces of India.

**Intersite** Comparison between two or more sites—for example, an analysis comparing the number of houses between sites in a region.

**Intrasite** Having to do with contexts within a single site—for example, an analysis comparing the sizes and contents of different houses to try to determine the social structure of a society.

**Isotope Analysis** The study of diet through the chemical signature of bones. Particularly effective in tracing the spread of maize agriculture.

# J

**Jenne-Jeno** The site of an urban center in Mali, West Africa, that predates external contact.

**Jerf el Ahmar** A Pre-Pottery Neolithic A site on the Euphrates River in Syria with the remains of communal structures.

**Jericho Tower** A 9-meter-high structure made of undressed stone and mud brick dating to the Pre-Pottery Neolithic A.

**Jomon** Japanese preagricultural societies that lived in large villages and produced elaborate pottery.

# K

**Katanda** Middle Stone Age site, located in the Democratic Republic of Congo, at which bone harpoons have been found.

**Kebara Cave** Site in Israel in which excavations have produced important evidence about the nature of Neanderthal occupation of cave sites, as well as one of most complete skeletons of a Neanderthal.

**Kennewick Man** Skeletal remains found at Kennewick, Washington and dated to 9,200 years ago. Control and ownership of the remains have been the subject of controversy.

**Kiva** Subterranean circular chambers found on sites in the U.S. southwest.

**Klasies River Mouth** A Middle Age site in South Africa that has produced remains of modern humans and that offers evidence of hunting and the intensive use of fire.

**Khipu** A system of knotted strings used by the Inca to record information.

**Kuk Swamp** A site in highland New Guinea that has produced early evidence of agriculture.

# L

**La Cotte de St. Brelade** Location on the Jersey Islands where evidence of Neanderthals hunting mammoths by stampeding them off of a cliff was found.

**Laetoli** Location in Tanzania where tracks of australopithecine footprints were found showing that australopithicines walked upright.

**Lake Mungo** One in a series of dried-out lakes located in southern Australia at which evidence of human occupation dates back to 40,000 years ago.

**Law of Superposition** In any undisturbed depositional sequence, each layer of sediments is younger than the layer beneath it.

**Legitimacy** Quality or status achieved when the right of a centralized authority to have power is accepted. Legitimacy can be based on consensus or coercion.

**Lepinski Vir** An impressive Mesolithic site located along the Danube River in Serbia at which structures, burials, and sculptures were found.

**Levallois Method** A particular prepared-core technology, used during the Middle Paleolithic, that often can be recognized on the basis of tortoise-shaped cores.

**Lewis Henry Morgan** Nineteenth-century American anthropologist who viewed the transition to agriculture as marking the boundary between the period of "savagery" and the period of "barbarism."

**Linear Band Keramik** The term referring to the earliest farming communities of Central and Western Europe; also known as the LBK culture.

**Llama** A camelid animal domesticated in the Andean highlands.

**Lokalalei** An archaeological site in Kenya dating to 2.3 million years ago. Analysis of refit cores from the site indicates that stone tool manufacture at this early date was more complex than anticipated.

**Lower Egypt** The northern part of the Nile River Valley, including the Nile Delta.

**Lower Paleolithic** The period when hominins began producing stone tools.

**Lunates** Tiny crescent-shaped stone tools characteristic of the Natufian.

# M

*ma'at* A concept that combines the virtues of balance and justice and that was of central importance to Egyptian society.

**Machu Picchu** An Inca royal estate on a high mountain peak at the western end of the Urubamba Valley.

**Mallaha** A Natufian site in northern Israel with the remains of oval stone structures.

**Marshall Sahlins** An anthropologist who has described hunter–gatherers as the "original affluent society."

**Mayan Hieroglyphs** Complex combination of pictographic and syllabic script used to record major events in the lives of Mayan rulers.

**Meadowcroft Rockshelter** Site in Pennsylvania at which evidence was found that supports Pre-Clovis occupation of the New World.

**Megafauna** Species of large animals that became extinct in many areas of the world, including the Americas and Australia, toward the end of the Pleistocene.

**Mesopotamia** The region along the course of the Tigris and Euphrates rivers centered in modern Iraq.

**Mezmaiskaya Cave** The location that has produced the most recent Neanderthal fossil, dated to 30,000 years ago.

**Mictochondrial DNA** DNA located outside of the cell nucleus and inherited exclusively from the mother.

**Middle Paleolithic** The archaelogical period during which Neanderthals occupied Europe.

**Middle Stone Age** The archaeological period of the earliest modern humans in Africa. The Middle Stone Age began between 300,000 and 200,000 years ago and ended around 40,000 years ago.

**Middle to Upper Paleolithic Transition** Period that saw the appearance of modern humans in Europe and that includes the development of new types of stone and bone tools and the dramatic appearance of a wide range of symbolic artifacts.

**Middle-Range Research** Research investigating processes that can be observed in the present and that can serve as a point of reference to test hypotheses about the past.

**Milagro Site** An early agricultural village located outside Tucson, Arizona.

**Millet** Cereal crop domesticated in northern China in the region around the Yellow River Valley.

**Miocene Era** The period twenty-three million to five million years ago when there was an explosion in the number of hominoid species.

**Moche State** Area along the Pacific coast of Peru that flourished beginning two thousand years ago and is known for the elaborate burials found at the site of Sipán.

**Modern Humans** Members of the species *Homo sapiens*, which includes all living humans.

**Mohenjo-Daro** One of the two major urban centers of the Harappan period

**Molecular Clock** Mechanism that allows the timing of the split between lineages to be calculated on the basis of the degree of genetic similarity.

**Monk's Mound** A massive earthen pyramid occupying the core of the ancient settlement of Cahokia.

**Monte Albán** Site of the oldest city in Mesoamerica, located in the Oaxaca Valley.

**Monte Verde** Site found in Chile where evidence of human occupation 15,000 years ago supports the argument that Clovis culture does not represent the first occupation of the Americas.

**Mound 72** Mound at Cohokia whose excavation uncovered an individual buried on a bird-shaped platform made of shells, as well as mass burials of apparently sacrificial victims.

**Mycerinus** Builder of the final and smallest pyramid at Giza. This pyramid was at least partially sheathed in polished granite.

# N

**Nabta Playa** An area in the Egyptian Western desert that was the location of a series of early agricultural and preagricultural sites located along the edge of a lake.

**Narmer Palette** Artifact discovered at the site of Hierakonpolis and whose two sides show the unification of Upper and Lower Egypt under king Narmer.

**Natufian** Period that has produced the earliest evidence of stone architecture found in the Middle East, although Natufian sites have not produced unambiguous evidence of plant and animal domestication

**Nawalabila I** Site offering the earliest evidence of human occupation in Australia, dating to between 53,000 and 60,000 years ago.

**Nazca Culture** Culture that developed along the southern pacific coast of Peru at the same time as the Moche society and that is known for Nazca lines.

**Nazca Lines** Large patterns created on the desert floor near the Nazca River on the Andean coast. The Nazca lines include depictions of humans and animals, as well as a large number of straight lines that stretch for miles.

**Neanderthal DNA** The recovery of DNA samples from Neanderthal fossils has provided a powerful new tool for determining the genetic relationship between Neanderthals and modern humans.

**Nenana** The earliest culture in Beringia, dating to between 14,000 and 12,800 years ago.

**Neolithic** The period in which there are polished stone tools. Also called the New Stone Age.

**Neolithic Revolution** V. Gordon Childe's term used to describe the transition to agriculture as an event that affected every aspect of human society.

**Netiv Hagdud** A Pre-Pottery Neolithic A site in the Jordan Valley that was a village of between twenty and thirty houses.

**New Archaeology/Processual Archaeology** An archaeology theory based firmly on scientific method and supported by a concerted effort aimed at its development.

**New Kingdom** The period between 1532 and 1070 B.C. when Egypt played an active role in trade networks connecting the lands of the Eastern Mediterranean.

**Ngandong** Site on the island of Java at which the most recent known fossil of *Homo erectus* was found, dating to between 46,000 and 27,000 years ago.

**Nihewan Basin** Location in Northern China where there is solid evidence of human occupation between 1.36 million and 1.1 million years ago.

**Nile Valley** Swath of lush vegetation descending from the Ethiopian highlands and standing in sharp contrast to the surrounding desert.

**Nuclear DNA** DNA located in the cell nucleus; combines DNA from each parent.

# O

**Ohalo** A Kebaran site in Israel with excellent preservation of organic remains; the site has shed new light on the Kebaran period.

**Oldowan** One of the two major industries of the Lower Paleolithic. It includes the earliest well-characterized archaeological industry dating between 1.9 and 1.15 million years ago.

**Olduvai Gorge** The most impressive and important location in the East African Rift Valley for the study of human evolution.

**Olmec** The earliest complex society in Mesoamerica. Olmec sites are located along the Gulf Coast of Mexico.

**Ontogeny** The growth and development of an individual organism.

**Optimal Foraging Theory** Theory based on the assumption that the choices people make reflect a rational self-interest in maximizing efficiency in collecting and processing resources.

**Oracle Bones** Oracle bones used in divination rituals are a major source of written evidence about the Chinese Shang Dynasty.

**Otumba** Site in the Teotihuacán Valley at which excavations have produced evidence about the nature of the Aztec organization of craft production.

**Oxygen Isotope Curve** The record of fluctuations in global climate during the Pleistocene produced by the analysis of deep-sea cores.

# P

**Paleoanthropologists** Scientists who study the evolutionary history of the hominoids.

**Paleolithic** The period during which humans lived with now-extinct animals. Also called the Old Stone Age.

**Palimpsest** An archaeological site produced by a series of distinct brief occupations.

**Paloma** A preagricultural village site on the coast of Peru.

**Panaqa** The collective descendants of the deceased Inca emperor. The new ruler was excluded from his father's panaqa.

*Paranthropus* Also known as robust *Australopithecus*, this hominin is characterized by massive molars and muscles for chewing. The earliest known *Paranthropus* dates to two-and-a-half million years ago.

**Pastoral Societies** Mobile societies with an economy based on herds of domesticated animals.

**Pedra Furada** Site in Brazil where highly controversial evidence of early human occupation that dates to 48,000–35,000 years ago was found.

**Pedra Pintada** A site located in the Brazilian Amazon which demonstrates that there were groups contemporary with the Clovis that were living in South America in a rain-forest environment.

**Pengtoushan** Site in southern China that has produced some of the earliest evidence of domesticated rice dating to approximately 9,000 years ago.

**Peştera cu Oase Cave** The site, located in Romania, where the oldest modern human remains in Europe, dating to 36,000 years ago, were found.

**Phylogeny** The evolutionary history of a species.

**Plastered Skulls** Skulls with faces modeled from plaster and found on Pre-Pottery Neolithic B sites.

**Pleistocene** Period beginning 1.8 million years ago characterized by periods with a significant buildup of ice sheets, known as glacial eras, and periods during which the ice sheet subsequently retreated, known as interglacial eras.

**Popol Vuh** Mayan epic tale of the battle between the hero twins and the lords of the underworld.

**Postdepositional Processes** Events that take place after a site has been occupied.

**Postprocessual Archaeology** A movement led by British archaeologist Ian Hodder which argues that archaeologists should emulate historians in interpreting the past.

**Poverty Point** A Late Archaic site in Louisiana with a series of six concentric embankments.

**Prepared-Core Technology** The dominant approach to tool manufacture during the Middle Paleolithic; a technique in which the person making the tools carefully shaped the core to control the form of the flakes produced.

**Pueblo Bonito** A massive 650-room complex, the largest Great House in Chaco Canyon.

*Purgatorius* The earliest-known primate; lived between ninety and sixty-five million years ago.

# Q

**Qafzeh Cave** One of the sites in Israel where modern human skeletons were found in a Middle Paleolithic context.

**Quantification** Methods ranging from the use of simple databases that provide counts of various types of objects to sophisticated statistical techniques used by archaeologists to represent the large quantities of material recovered in excavations and surveys.

**Quebrada Tacahuay** Site found in Peru dating to between 12,700 and 12,500 years ago that supports the pre-Clovis model.

# R

**Radiation** A period in which there is a rapid increase in the diversity of a single lineage. During the period between four million and two million years ago, there was a radiation in the hominin lineage.

**Ranked Society** Society in which there is a hierarchy of prestige not linked to age, gender, or ability.

**Rice** Cereal crop domesticated grass whose grain was domesticated in southern China in the Yangtze and Huai River Valleys.

**Royal Tombs at Ur** Tombs dating to the Early Dynastic period in which the dead were buried with a spectacular array of precious artifacts and sacrificial victims.

# S

**Sahara Desert** The most dominant feature of the North African landscape today. Between 14,000 and 4,500 years ago, there was increased rainfall in the area, allowing for human occupation.

*Sahelanthropus tchadensis* The earliest-known member of the hominin lineage. Fossils of the species were discovered in Chad in levels dating to seven million years ago.

**Sahul** The landmass that encompassed Australia, Tasmania, and New Guinea during periods of low sea level.

**Sangiran and Perning** Sites on the island of Java where fossils of *Homo erectus* dating to 1.8 million years ago were found.

**Sangoan/Lupemban** A Middle Stone Age industry found in Central and East Africa. Characterized by very crude heavy-duty tools, the Sangoan/Lupemban might be indicative of an adaptation to a heavily wooded environment.

**Saqqara** Location of the construction of the stepped pyramid, the earliest pyramid constructed in Egypt. In later periods, Saqqara continued to be used as a sacred burial area.

**Schöningen** The location in Germany where 400,000-year-old spears were discovered.

**Shell Middens** Sites built up of discarded shells.

**Sipán** Elite burial site on the coast of Peru that has given archaeologists a sense of the wealth and violence of Moche society.

**Skhul Cave** One of the Middle Paleolithic sites in Israel where modern humans skeletons have been found.

**Solutrean Hypothesis** The proposal that the origin of the Clovis culture was in the migration of groups from the Solutrean culture of southern France.

**Species** A group of intimately related and physically similar organisms that can produce fertile offspring.

**St. Césaire** The site in France where a Neanderthal was found dating to 36,000 years ago in a Châtelperronian context.

**Stable Isotope Analysis** *See* isotope analysis.

**State** Society in which power is organized on a supra-kin basis or by a bureaucracy that uses force.

**Stonehenge** A ring of massive standing stones on the Salisbury Plain, England, that was constructed beginning in the Early Neolithic and ending in the Early Bronze age.

**Strata** Discrete layers in a stratigraphic sequence.

**Stratified Society** Society in which access to key resources is linked to prestige.

**Sunda** The landmass that connected much of Southeast Asia during periods of low sea level.

**Survey** An archaelogical survey maps the physical remains of human activity.

**Synchronic** Relating to comparisons within a single period.

**Systems Theory** An archaeological theory which views society as an interconnected network of elements that together form a whole.

**Szeletian** An archaeological industry found in Eastern Europe during the transition between the Middle Paleolithic and the Upper Paleolithic. Bifacially retouched tools are characteristic of the Szeletian.

# T

**Taï Forest** Location where chimpanzees use stone hammers and anvils to break open hard nuts. The tools are not manufactured, but rather used as found.

**Talheim** A site in Germany were a pit containing a mass grave was discovered.

**Taphonomy** The study of the processes that affect organic remains after death.

**Tawantinsuyu** Inca Empire; the name means "the four parts together."

**Technology** The total of the tools used for daily tasks, including farming, food processing, and food storage.

**Tehuacán Valley** Site at which caves have produced some of the earliest evidence of domesticated plants in the Americas.

**Telapocán** Together with Texcoco and Tenochtitlán, formed the Triple Alliance that was the basis for Aztec expansion.

**Templo Mayor** Double pyramid at the center of Tenochtitlán that was the core of the Aztec world.

**Tenochtitlán** The capital of the Aztec Empire and the largest indigenous city ever built in the Americas; located in the Valley of Mexico.

**Teosinte** A wild grass found in the highlands of Mexico; the wild ancestor of maize.

**Teotihuacán** An enormous city with a population of over 80,000 people located in the highland Valley of Mexico.

**Texcoco** Together with Telapocán and Tenochtitlán, formed the Triple Alliance that was the basis for Aztec expansion.

**The Fertile Crescent** A ribbonlike area of Mediterranean climate that arcs across the Middle East.

**The Plaza** An artificially leveled area located just to the south of Monk's Mound.

**Three-Age System** A system developed by Danish antiquarian Christian Jürgensen Thomson that catalogues artifacts into relics of three periods—the Stone Age, the Bronze Age, and the Iron Age—based on the material of manufacture.

**Thunderstones** Objects such as ground stone axes that people in Medieval Europe believed were formed in spots where lightning struck the earth.

**Tigris and Euphrates Rivers** Rivers in modern Iraq bounding the ancient land of Mesopotamia.

**Tikal** One of the major Mayan urban centers.

**Tim Ingold** An anthropologist who views the shift from hunting to agriculture as a shift from trust to domination.

**Toltec Empire** An empire that preceded the Aztecs in the Valley of Mexico.

**Tough vs. Brittle Rachis** The rachis holds the seed of a cereal plant to the stalk. Domesticated plants have a tough rachis, wild grains a rachis that is brittle and shatters easily.

**Tula** The capital city of the Toltec empire.

**Typology** A list used to draw up an inventory of types of artifacts found by archaeologists in a particular archaeological context.

# U

**Uan Afuda** A preagricultural site in the Sahara which has yielded evidence that wild goats were penned in the back of the cave.

**Ubeidiya** One of the earliest archaeological sites outside of Africa, located in Israel south of the Sea of Galilee and dated between 1.4 and 1.0 million years ago.

**Ulluzian** An archaeological industry found in Italy during the transition between the Middle Paleolithic and the Upper Paleolithic. Arched backed knives are characteristic of the Ulluzian.

**Upper Egypt** The southern Nile River Valley ending in a series of cataracts, or rapids, in the area around the modern border between Egypt and Sudan.

**Upper Paleolithic** The archaeological period that saw the earliest occupation of Europe by modern humans.

**Urban Society** Society in which people live in large cities. V. Gordon Childe developed ten criteria defining an urban center.

**Urubamba Valley** The location of Machu Picchu, the most famous of the Inca royal estates.

**Uruk** The oldest known city in the world, located in southern Iraq.

**Uruk Period** Period between 4000 B.C. and 3200 B.C. during which the first cities in Mesopotamia were developed.

# V

**Vacant Center Theory** Theory according to which the Hopewell earthworks appears to be the empty core of a dispersed settlement system.

**Venus Figurines** Portable art objects found with the Gravettian industry and depicting the female body.

**Vertical Excavation** An excavation for which the goal is to excavate the entire depth of deposits in order to expose the record of a sequence of occupation.

**Vindija** The site in Croatia at which the discovery of Neanderthal remains, dated between 33,000 and 27,000 years ago, suggested that in at least these areas, Neanderthals survived long after the arrival of modern humans in Europe.

# W

**Wallace Line** The line that runs through Wallacea and separates the unique animals and plants of Australia from the animal and plant communities of Southeast Asia.

**Wet Screening** The process of spraying water onto a sieve to break up sediments and move them through the mesh to make sure that all artifacts are recovered during an excavation.

# Y

**Yangshao culture** A Neolithic culture in northern China that is particularly well represented at the village site of Banpo.

**Yangtze and Huai River Valleys** Area of Southern China where rice was domesticated.

**Yellow River Valley** The area in Northern China where millet was domesticated.

**Younger Dryas** A period of global climatic stress that had a significant impact on Natufian society.

# Z

**Zafarraya Cave** The site in Spain at which the discovery of Neanderthal remains, dated between 33,000 and 27,000 years ago, suggested that in at least this area, Neanderthals survived long after the arrival of modern humans in Europe.

**Zhoukoudian** A series of caves in Longgu-shan, or Dragon Bone Hill, outside of Beijing (Peking), China, where the remains of more than 40 *Homo erectus* individuals and over 100,000 stone tools, all choppers and flakes, were recovered.

**Ziggurat** Stepped pyramid found at the center of many Mesopotamian temple precincts.

# REFERENCES

Abu El-Haj, Nadia. *Facts on the Ground: Archaeological Practice and Territorial Self-Fashioning in Israeli Society.* Chicago: University of Chicago Press, 2001.

Adcock, G.J., et al. "Mitochondrial DNA Sequences in Ancient Australians: Implications for Modern Human Origins." *Proceedings of the National Academy of Sciences* 98.2 (2001): 537–42.

Adovasio, J.M., et al. "Meadowcroft Rockshelter 1977: An Overview." *American Antiquity* 43 (1978): 632–51.

Agrawal, D.P. *The Archaeology of India.* Scandinavian Institute of Asian Studies Monograph Series. Malmö, Sweden: Curzon Press, 1985.

Ahler, Stanley A., and Phil R. Geib. "Why Flute? Folsom Point Design and Adaptation." *Journal of Archaeological Science* 27 (2000): 799–820.

Aiello, Leslie C., and Peter Wheeler. "The Expensive-Tissue Hypothesis." *Current Anthropology* 36.2 (1995): 199–221.

Aitken, Martin J. *Science-Based Dating in Archaeology.* London: Longman, 1990.

Aitken, M.J., Chris Stringer, and Paul Mellars. *The Origin of Modern Humans and the Impact of Chronometric Dating.* Princeton, N.J.: Princeton University Press, 1993.

Akins, N.J. "The Burials of Pueblo Bonito." *Pueblo Bonito Centre of the Chacoan World.* ed. Jill E. Neitzel. Washington: Smithsonian Press, 2003. 94–106.

Alcock, Susan, et al., eds. *Empires.* Cambridge, U.K.: Cambridge University Press, 2001.

Algaze, Guillermo. *The Uruk World System: The Dynamics of Expansion of Early Mesopotamian Civilization.* Chicago: University of Chicago Press, 1993.

Allchin, F. Raymond, and Bridget Allchin. *The Rise of Civilization in India and Pakistan.* Cambridge World Archaeology. Cambridge, U.K.: Cambridge University Press, 1982.

Amichai, Yehuda. *Selected Poetry of Yehuda Amichai.* Trans. Chana Bloch and Stephen Mitchell. Berkeley, CA: University of California Press, 1996.

Andah, Bassey W. "Identifying Early Farming Traditions of West Africa." *The Archaeology of Africa: Food, Metals, and Towns.* ed. Thurstan Shaw. London: Routledge, 1993. 240–53.

Anping, Pei. "Notes on New Advancements and Revelations in the Agricultural Archaeology of Early Rice Domestication in the Dongting Lake Region." *Antiquity* 72 (1998): 878–85.

Arensburg, B. "A Middle Paleolithic Human Hyoid Bone." *Nature* 338 (1989): 758–60.

Arnold, Bettina. "The Past as Propaganda: Totalitarian Archaeology in Nazi Germany." *Antiquity* 64 (1990): 464–78.

Arsuaga, Juan Luis de, Andy Klatt, and Juan Carlos Sastre. *The Neanderthal's Necklace: In Search of the First Thinkers.* New York: Four Walls Eight Windows, 2002.

Ascher, Marcia, and Robert Ascher. *Code of the Quipu: A Study in Media, Mathematics, and Culture.* Ann Arbor, MI.: University of Michigan Press, 1981.

Asfaw, Berhane, et al. "Australopithecus Garhi: A New Species of Early Hominid from Ethiopia." *Science* 284 (1999): 629–35.

Aveni, Anthony F. *Nasca: Eighth Wonder of the World?* London: British Museum Press, 2000.

Bahn, Paul G. "The 'Unacceptable Face' of the West European Upper Paleolithic." *Antiquity* 52 (1978): 183–92.

———. *Written in Bones: How Human Remains Unlock the Secrets of the Dead.* Newton Abbot, Devon: David & Charles, 2002.

Ballard, Chris. "Writing (Pre)History: Narrative and Archaeological Explanation in the New Guinea Highlands." *Archaeology of Oceania* 38 (2003): 135–48.

Balter, Vincent, et al. "Ecological and Physiological Variability of Sr/Ca and Ba/Ca in Mammals of West Europe Mid-Wurmian Food Webs." *Palaeogeography, Palaeoclimatology, Palaeoecology* 186 (2002): 127–43.

———. "Les Néandertaliens Étaient-Ils Essentiellement Carnivores? Résultats Préliminaires sur les Teneurs en Sr et en Ba de la Paléobiocénose Mammalienne de Saint-Césaire." *Comptes Rendus de l'Académie des Sciences: Earth and Planetary Sciences* 332 (2001): 59–65.

Banning, E. B. *The Archaeologist's Laboratory: The Analysis of Archaeological Data. Interdisciplinary Contributions to Archaeology.* New York: Kluwer Academic/Plenum Publishers, 2000.

———. *Archaeological Survey. Manuals in Archaeological Method, Theory, and Technique.* New York: Kluwer Academic/Plenum Publishers, 2002.

Bar-Yosef, Ofer. *A Cave in the Desert: Nahal Hemar.* Jerusalem, Israel: Israel Museum, 1985.

Bar-Yosef, O. "The Walls of Jericho: An Alternative Interpretation." *Current Anthropology* 27.2 (1986): 157–62.

Bar-Yosef, Ofer, et al. "Netiv Hagdud: An Early Neolithic Village Site in the Jordan Valley." *Journal of Field Archaeology* 18 (1991): 405–23.

Bar-Yosef, O., et al. "The Excavations at Kebara Cave, Mt Carmel." *Current Anthropology* 33.5 (1992): 497–550.

Barlow, K. Renee. "Predicting Maize Agriculture among the Fremont: An Economic Comparison of Farming and Foraging in the American Southwest." *American Antiquity* 67.1 (2002): 65–88.

Barrett, John C. *Fragments from Antiquity: An Archaeology of Social Life in Britain, 2900–1200 B.C. Social Archaeology.* Oxford, U.K.: Blackwell, 1993.

Bartstra, Gert-Jan. "*Homo erectus*: The Search for His Artifacts." *Current Anthropology* 23.3 (1982): 318–20.

Bass, George. "A Bronze Age Shipwreck at Ulu Burun: 1984 Campaign." *American Journal of Archaeology* 90 (1986): 269–96.

Bednarik, Robert G. "Direct Dating Results from Australian Cave Petroglyphs." *Geoarchaeology: An International Journal* 13.4 (1998): 411–18.

———. "The Dating of Rock Art: A Critique." *Journal of Archaeological Science* 29 (2002): 1213–33.

Bell, Ellen E., et al. *Understanding Early Classic Copan.* Philadelphia: University of Pennsylvania Museum of Archaeology and Anthropology, 2004.

Bellwood, Peter, and Colin Renfrew, eds. *Examining the Farming/Language Dispersal Hypothesis.* Cambridge, U.K.: McDonald Institute, 2002.

Bellwood, Peter S. *First Farmers: The Origins of Agricultural Societies.* Malden, MA: Blackwell Pub., 2005.

Bender, Barbara. *Farming in Prehistory: From Hunter–Gatherer to Food-Producer.* London: J. Baker, 1975.

———. "Theorizing Landscapes, and the Prehistoric Landscapes of Stonehenge." *Man* 27.4 (1992): 735–55.

Benjamin, Walter. *Illuminations: Essays and Reflections.* Trans. Harry Zohn. New York: Schocken, 1968.

Benson, Elizabeth P., et al. *Olmec Art of Ancient Mexico.* Washington, DC: National Gallery of Art, 1996.

Benson, Larry, et al. "Ancient Maize from Chacoan Great Houses: Where Was It Grown?" *Proceedings of the National Academy of Sciences* 100.22 (2003): 13111–15.

Berger, Thomas D., and Erik Trinkaus. "Patterns of Trauma among the Neanderthals." *Journal of Archaeological Science* 22.6 (1995): 841–52.

Binford, Lewis. "Archaeological Perspectives." *New Perspectives in Archaeology.* eds. Sally Binford and Lewis Binford. Chicago: Aldine, 1968. 5–32.

Binford, Lewis. *In Pursuit of the Past: Decoding the Archaeological Record.* New York: Thames and Hudson, 1983.

Binford, Sally and Lewis, eds. *New Perspectives in Archaeology.* Chicago: Aldine, 1968.

Bird, M.I., et al. "Radiocarbon Analysis of the Early Archaeological Site of Nauwalabila I, Arnhem Land, Australia: Implications for Sample Suitability and Stratigraphic Integrity." *Quaternary Science Reviews* 21 (2002): 1061–75.

Blanton, Richard E. *Ancient Mesoamerica: A Comparison of Change in Three Regions.* New York: Cambridge University Press, 1987.

Blench, Roger. "Ethnographic and Linguistic Evidence for the Prehistory of African Ruminant Livestock, Horses, and Ponies." *The Archaeology of Africa: Food, Metals, and Towns.* ed. Thurstan Shaw. London: Routledge, 1993.

Blumenschine, Robert J., et al. "Late Pliocene Homo and Hominid Land Use from Western Olduvai Gorge, Tanzania." *Science* 299 (2003): 1217–21.

Bocherens, Hervé, et al. "New Isotopic Evidence for Dietary Habits of Neanderthals from Belgium." *Journal of Human Evolution* 40 (2001): 497–505.

Boëda, Eric. "Levallois: A Volumetric Construction, Methods, and Technique." *Definition and Interpretation of Levallois Technology.* eds. Harold Dibble and Ofer Bar-Yosef. Madison, WI: Prehistory Press, 1995. 41–68.

Boëda, Eric, et al. "A Levallois Point Embedded in the Vertebra of a Wild Ass (Equus Africanusafricanus): Hafting, Projectiles and Mousterian Hunting Weapons." *Antiquity* 73.280 (1999): 394–402.

Boesch, Christophe. "Animal Behaviour: The Question of Culture." *Nature* 379 (1996): 207–08.

Boesch, Christophe, and Hedwige Boesch-Achermann. *The Chimpanzees of the Taï Forest: Behavioural Ecology and Evolution.* Oxford, U.K.: Oxford University Press, 2000.

Boone, Elizabeth Hill. "Glorious Imperium: Understanding Land and Community in Moctezuma's Mexico." *Moctezuma's Mexico: Visions of the Aztec World.* eds. Eduardo Matos Moctezuma and David Carrasco. Boulder, CO: University of Colorado, 1992. 159–74.

Bordes, François. *A Tale of Two Caves.* New York: Harper & Row, 1972.

Boric, Dusan. "Body Metamorphosis and Animality: Volatile Bodies and Boulder Artworks from Lepenski Vir." *Cambridge Archaeological Journal* 15.1 (2005): 35–69.

Boserup, Ester. *The Conditions of Agricultural Growth.* London: George Allen and Unwin, 1965.

Bowler, James M., et al. "New Ages for Human Occupation and Climatic Change at Lake Mungo, Australia." *Nature* 421 (2003): 837–40.

Bowler, Peter J. *Theories of Human Evolution: A Century of Debate, 1844–1944.* Baltimore: Johns Hopkins University Press, 1986.

Brackenridge, Henry Marie. *Views of Louisiana Together with a Journal of a Voyage up the Missouri River, in 1811.* Chicago: Quadrangle Books, 1814 [1962].

Branch, Nick. *Environmental Archaeology: Theoretical and Practical Approaches. Key Issues in Environmental Change.* London and New York: Hodder Arnold; Distributed in the United States by Oxford University Press, 2005.

Brooks, A.S., et al. "Dating and Context of Three Middle Stone Age Sites with Bone Points in the Upper Semliki Valley, Zaire." *Science* 268 (1995): 548–53.

Brose, David S., James A. Brown, and David W. Penney, eds. *Ancient Art of the American Woodland Indians.* New York: Abrams, 1985.

Brose, David S., and N'omi Greber, eds. *Hopewell Archaeology: The Chillicothe Conference.* Kent, OH: Kent State University Press, 1979.

Brown, A.D. "Wetlands and Drylands in Prehistory: Mesolithic to Bronze Age Human Activity and Impact in the Severn Estuary, Southwest Britain." Ph.D. thesis. University of Reading, 2005.

Brown, James A. "Charnel Houses and Mortuary Crypts: Disposal of the Dead in the Middle Woodland Period." *Hopewell Archaeology: The Chillicothe Conference.* eds. David S. Brose and N'omi Greber. Kent, OH: Kent State University Press, 1979.

Brown, P., et al. "A New Small-Bodied Hominin from the Late Peistocene of Flores, Indonesia." *Nature* 431 (2004): 1055–61.

Brumfiel, Elizabeth. "Aztec Hearts and Minds: Religion and the State in the Aztec Empire." eds. Susan Alcock, et al. Cambridge, U.K.: Cambridge University Press, 2001. 283–310.

Brumm, A., et al. "Early Stone Technology on Flores and Its Implications for Homo Floresiensisfloresiensis." *Nature* 441 (2006): 624–28.

Brunet, Michel, et al. "The First Australopithecine 2,500 Kilometers West of the Rift Valley (Chad)." *Nature* 378 (1995): 273–75.

Brunet, M., et al. "New Material of the Earliest Hominid from the Upper Miocene of Chad." *Nature* 434 (2005): 752–55.

Bryan, Frank. "A Review of the Geology of the Clovis Finds Reported by Howard and Cotter." *American Antiquity* 2 (1938, 1939): 113–30, 43–51.

Buikstra, Jane, et al. "Tombs from the Copan Acropolis: A Life History Approach." *Understanding Early Classic Copan.* eds. Ellen E. Bell, Marcello A. Canuto, and Robert J. Sharer. Philadelphia: University Museum, 2004. 191–214.

Bulmer, Susan. *The Prehistory of the New Guinea Highlands.* microform/.[s.n.], Auckland, 1976.

Bunn, Henry T. "A Taphonomic Perspective on the Archaeology of Human Origins." *Annual Review of Anthropology* 20 (1991): 433–67.

Burger, Richard L. "An Overview of Peruvian Archaeology." *Annual Review of Anthropology* 18 (1989): 37–69.

———. *Chavín and the Origins of Andean Civilization.* London: Thames and Hudson, 1992.

Burger, Richard L., and Lucy C. Salazar. *Machu Picchu: Unveiling the Mystery of the Incas.* New Haven, CT: Yale University Press, 2004.

Cain, C.R. "Notched, Flaked and Ground Bone Artefacts from Middle Stone Age and Iron Age Layers of Sibudu Cave, KwaZulu-Natal, South Africa." *South African Journal of Science* 100 (2004): 195–97.

Cameron, Catherine. "Sacred Earthen Architecture in the Northern Southwest: The Bluff Great House Berm." *American Antiquity* 67.4 (2002): 677–96.

Cann, Rebecca L. "Tangled Genetic Routes." *Nature* 416 (2002): 32–51.

Carbonell, Eudald. "Out of Africa: The Dispersal of the Earliest Technical Systems Reconsidered." *Journal of Anthropological Archaeology* 18.2 (1999): 119–36.

Carbonell, Eudald, et al. "The Pleistocene Site of Gran Dolina, Sierra de Atapuerca, Spain: A History of the Archaeological Investigations." *Journal of Human Evolution* 37.3–4 (1999): 313–24.

———. "Les Premiers Comportements Funéraires Auraient-Ils Pris Place à Atapuerca, il y a 350,000 Ans?" *L'Anthropologie* 107.1 (2003): 1–14.

Carneiro, R.L. "A Theory of the Origin of the State." *Science* 169 (1970): 733–38.

Carr, Christopher, and D. Troy Case, eds. *Gathering Hopewell: Society, Ritual, and Ritual Interaction.* New York: Springer, 2006.

Carrasco, David. "Toward the Splendid City: Knowing the Worlds of Moctezuma." *Moctezuma's Mexico: Visions of the Aztec World.* eds. Eduardo Matos Moctezuma and David Carrasco. Boulder, CO: University of Colorado, 1992. 99–148.

Castelletti, Lanfredo, Michela Cottini, and Mauro Rottoli. "Early Holocene Plant Remains from Uan Afuda Cave, Tadrart Acacus (Libyan Sahara)." *Before Food Production in North Africa.* eds. Savino di Lernia and Giorgio Manzi. Forli, Italy: A.B.A.C.O. Edizioni, 1998. 91–102.

Castleden, Rodney. *The Making of Stonehenge.* London: Routledge, 1993.

Cauvin, Jacques, and Trevor Watkins. *The Birth of the Gods and the Origins of Agriculture. New Studies in Archaeology.* Cambridge, U.K.: Cambridge University Press, 2000.

Cessford, Craig. "A New Dating Sequence for Çatalhöyük." *Antiquity* 75 (2001): 717–25.

Chaloupka, George. *Journey in Time: The World's Longest Continuing Art Tradition: The 50,000 Year Story of the Australian Aboriginal Rock Art of Arnhem Land.* Reed, 1993.

Chang, Kwang-chih. *Shang Civilization.* New Haven, CT: Yale University Press, 1980.

———. *Art, Myth, and Ritual: The Path to Political Authority in Ancient China.* Cambridge, MA: Harvard University Press, 1983.

Chang, Kwang-chih. *The Archaeology of Ancient China.* 4th ed. New Haven, CT: Yale University Press, 1986.

———. "Ritual and Power." *China: Ancient Culture, Modern Land.* ed. Robert E. Murowchick. Norman, OK: University of Oklahoma Press, 1994. 60–69.

Charlton, Thomas H., Deborah L. Nichols, and Cynthia O. Charlton. "Aztec Craft Production and Specialization: Archaeological Evidence from the City–State of Otumba, Mexico." *World Archaeology* 23.1 (1991): 98–114.

Chase, P.G. "Relationships between Mousterian Lithic and Faunal Assemblages at Combe Grenal." *Current Anthropology* 27 (1986): 69–71.

Chen, Tie-Mei, et al. "ESR Dating of Tooth Enamel from Yunxian *Homo erectus* Site, China." *Quaternary Science Reviews* 16 (1997): 455–58.

Childe, V. Gordon. *What Happened in History.* Pelican Books; A108. Harmondsworth, U.K.: Penguin, 1942.

Chilton, Elizabeth. "Mobile Farmers of Pre-Contact Southern New England: The Archaeological and Ethnohistorical Evidence." *New York State Museum Bulletin* 494 (1999): 157–76.

———. "'Towns They Have None': Diverse Subsistence and Settlement Strategies in Native New England." *New York State Museum Bulletin* 496 (2002): 265–88.

Chilton, Elizabeth, Tonya Baroody Largy, and Kathryn Curran. "Evidence for Prehistoric Maize Horticulture at the Pine Hill Site, Deerfield, Massachusetts." *Northeast Anthropology* 59 (2000): 23–46.

Chippindale, Christopher, et al. *Who Owns Stonehenge?* London: Batsford, 1990.

Clark, David. *Analytical Archaeology.* New York: Columbia University Press, 1978.

Clark, J. Desmond, and Steven A. Brandt, eds. *From Hunters to Farmers: The Causes and Consequences of Food Production in Africa.* Berkeley, CA: University of California Press, 1984.

Clark, John E., and Mary E. Pye. *Olmec Art and Archaeology in Mesoamerica.* Washington, DC and New Haven, CT: National Gallery of Art 2000.

Clark, R.M., et al. "Pattern of Diversity in the Genomic Region near the Maize Domestication Gene Tb1." *Proceedings of the National Academy of Sciences* 101.3 (2004): 700–07.

Clarke, R.J. "First Ever Discovery of a Well-Preserved Skull and Associated Skeleton of an Australopithecus." *South African Journal of Science* 94.10 (1998): 1–6.

Cleal, Rosamund, K.E. Walker, and R. Montague. *Stonehenge in Its Landscape. Archaeological Report.* Vol. 10. London: English Heritage, 1995.

Clottes, Jean, Paul G. Bahn, and Maurice Arnold. *Chauvet Cave: The Art of Earliest Times.* Salt Lake City, UT: University of Utah Press, 2003.

Clutton-Brock, Juliet. "The Spread of Domestic Animals in Africa." *The Archaeology of Africa: Food, Metals, and Towns.* ed. Thurstan Shaw. London: Routledge, 1993. 61–70.

Coe, Michael D. *The Maya. Ancient Peoples and Places.* 5th ed. New York: Thames and Hudson, 1993.

Coe, Michael D. *Breaking the Maya Code.* New York: Thames and Hudson, 1999.

Coe, Michael D., Princeton University. Art Museum, and Houston Museum of Fine Arts. Houston. *The Olmec World: Ritual and Rulership.* Princeton, N.J. and New York: Art Museum. Cloth ed. distributed in 1996 by Harry N. Abrams, 1995.

Cohen, Claudine, and Jean-Jacques Hublin. *Boucher de Perthes, 1788–1868: Les Origines Romantiques de la Préhistoire. Un Savant, une Époque.* Paris: Belin, 1989.

Cohen, Mark Nathan. *The Food Crisis in Prehistory: Overpopulation and the Origins of Agriculture.* New Haven, CT: Yale University Press, 1977.

Coles, J.M. *Experimental Archaeology.* New York: Academic Press, 1979.

Conard, Nicholas. "Laminar Lithic Assemblages from the Last Interglacial Complex in Northwestern Europe." *Journal of Anthropological Research* 46.3 (1990): 243–62.

———. "Palaeolithic Ivory Sculptures from Southwestern Germany and the Origins of Figurative Art." *Nature* 426 (2003): 830–32.

Conkey, Margaret. "The Identification of Prehistoric Hunter–Gatherer Aggregation Sites: The Case of Altamira." *Current Anthropology* 21.5 (1980): 609–30.

Connah, Graham. *African Civilization: Precolonial Cities and States in Tropical Africa: An Archaeological Perspective.* Cambridge, U.K.: Cambridge University Press, 1987.

Conyers, Lawrence B., and Dean Goodman. *Ground-Penetrating Radar: An Introduction for Archaeologists.* Walnut Creek, CA: AltaMira Press, 1997.

Cordell, Linda. *Archaeology of the Southwest.* 2d ed. New York: Academic Press, 1997.

Coughlin, Sean, and Mark F. Seeman. "Hopewellian Settlements at the Liberty Earthworks, Ross County, Ohio." *Ohio Hopewell Community Organization.* eds. William S. Dancey and Paul J. Pacheco. Kent, OH: Ohio University Press, 1997. 231–50.

Cowan, C. Wesley, and Patty Jo Watson, eds. *The Origins of Agriculture: An International Perspective*. Washington, DC: Smithsonian Institution Press, 1992.

Crawford, Gary W., and Chen Shen. "The Origins of Rice Agriculture: Recent Progress in East Asia." *Antiquity* 72 (1998): 858–66.

Crawford, Gary W., and David G. Smith. "Paleoethnobotany in the Northeast." *People and Plants in Ancient Eastern North America*. ed. Paul E. Minnis. Washington, DC: Smithsonian Books, 2003. 172–257.

Crawford, Gary W., David G. Smith, and Vandy E. Bowyer. "Dating the Entry of Corn (Zea Mays) into the Lower Great Lakes Region." *American Antiquity* 62.1 (1997): 112–19.

Crawford, Harriet E.W. *Sumer and the Sumerians*. Cambridge, U.K.: Cambridge University Press, 1991.

Crown, Patricia L., W. James Judge, and School of American Research (Santa Fe NM). *Chaco & Hohokam: Prehistoric Regional Systems in the American Southwest. School of American Research Advanced Seminar Series*. Santa Fe, NM: School of American Research Press, 1991.

Cullen, Bob. "Testimony from the Iceman." *Smithsonian* 33.11 (2003): 42–45.

D'Altroy, Terence N. *The Incas. Peoples of America*. Oxford, U.K.: Blackwell Publishers, 2002.

D'Andrea, A.C., et al. "Late Jomon Cultigens in Northeastern Japan." *Antiquity* 69 (1995): 146–52.

D'Errico, F. "New Model and Its Implications for the Origin of Writing: The La Marche Antler Revisited." *Cambridge Archaeological Journal* 5.2 (1995): 163–206.

D'Errico, Francesco, and April Nowell. "A New Look at the Berekhat Ram Figurine: Implications for the Origins of Symbolism." *Cambridge Archaeological Journal* 10.1 (2000): 123–67.

D'Errico, Francesco, et al. "A Middle Palaeolithic Origin of Music? Using Cave-Bear Bone Accumulation to Assess the Divje Babe I Bone Flute." *Antiquity* 72 (1998): 65–80.

D'Errico, F., et al. "Neanderthal Acculturation in Western Europe?" *Current Anthropology* 39. Supplement (1998): S1–S43.

Dalan, Rinita A. *Envisioning Cahokia: A Landscape Perspective*. DeKalb, IL: Northern Illinois University Press, 2003.

Dancey, William S., and Paul J. Pacheco, eds. *Ohio Hopewell Community Organization*. Kent, OH: Kent State University Press, 1997.

———. "A Community Model of Ohio Hopewell Settlement." *Ohio Hopewell Community Organization*. eds. William S. Dancey and Paul J. Pacheco. Kent, OH: Ohio University Press, 1997. 3–40.

Dart, R.A. "The Predatory Transition from Ape to Man." *International Anthropological Linguistics Review* 1.4 (1953): 201–18.

Darwin, Charles. *The Origin of Species*. London: John Murray, 1859.

David, Bruno, et al. "New Optical and Radiocarbon Dates from Ngarrabullgan Cave, a Pleistocene Archaeological Site in Australia: Implications for the Comparability of Time Clocks and for the Human Colonization of Australia." *Antiquity* 71.271 (1997): 183–88.

David, Nicholas, and Carol Kramer. *Ethnoarchaeology in Action. Cambridge World Archaeology*. Cambridge, U.K.: Cambridge University Press, 2001.

Davis, Simon J.M. *The Archaeology of Animals*. New Haven, CT: Yale University Press, 1987.

Day, Michael H. *Guide to Fossil Man*. 4th ed. Chicago: University of Chicago Press, 1986.

Dayan, Tamar. "Early Domesticated Dogs of the Near East." *Journal of Archaeological Science* 21 (1994): 633–40.

De Heinzelin, Jean, et al. "Environment and Behavior of 2.5-Million-Year-Old Bouri Hominids." *Science* 284 (1999): 625–29.

De Lumley, Henry, et al. "Les Industries Lithiques Préoldowayennes du Debut du Pleistocene Inferieur du Site de Dmanissi en Georgie." *L'Anthropologie* 109.1 (2005): 1–182.

Deacon, H.J., and Janette Deacon. *Human Beginnings in South Africa: Uncovering the Secrets of the Stone Age*. Walnut Creek, CA: Altamira Press, 1999.

Deacon, Terrence William. *The Symbolic Species: The Co-Evolution of Language and the Brain*. New York: W.W. Norton, 1997.

Debaine-Francfort, Corinne. *The Search for Ancient China*. London: Thames & Hudson, 1999.

Deetz, James J.F. *In Small Things Forgotten: The Archaeology of Early American Life*. Garden City, N.Y.: Anchor Press/ Doubleday, 1996.

Defleur, Alban, et al. "Neanderthal Cannabalism at Moula-Guercy, Ardèche, France." *Science* 286 (1999): 128–131.

Demarest, Arthur Andrew. *Ancient Maya: The Rise and Fall of a Rainforest Civilisation. Case Studies in Early Societies, 3*. Cambridge, U.K.: Cambridge University Press, 2004.

Denham, Tim. "Archaeological Evidence for Mid-Holocene Agriculture in the Interior of Papua New Guinea: A Critical Review." *Archaeology of Oceania* 38 (2003): 159–76.

Denham, Tim, and Chris Ballard. "Jack Golsen and the Investigation of Prehistoric Agriculture in Highland New Guinea: Recent Work and Future Prospects." *Archaeology of Oceania* 38 (2003): 129–34.

Denham, T.P., et al. "Origins of Agriculture at Kuk Swamp in the Highlands of New Guinea." *Science* 301 (2003): 189–93.

Desmond, Adrian J., and James R. Moore. *Darwin*. New York: Warner Books, 1992.

Devries, T.J., et al. "Determining the Early History of El Niño." *Science* 276 (1997): 965–67.

Dhillon, N.P.S., and K. Ishiki. "Genomic Variation and Genetic Relationships in *Ipomoea* spp." *Plant Breeding* 118 (1999): 161–65.

Di Lernia, Savino. "Cultural Control over Wild Animals During the Early Holocene: The Case of Barbary Sheep in Central Sahara." *Before Food Production in North Africa*. eds. Savino di Lernia and Giorgio Manzi. Forlì, Italy: A.B.A.C.O. Edizioni, 1998. 113–26.

Di Lernia, Savino, and Giorgio Manzi, eds. *Before Food Production in North Africa*. Forlì, Italy: A.B.A.C.O. Edizioni, 1998.

Diamond, Jared. *Collapse: How Societies Choose to Fail or Succeed*. New York: Viking, 2005.

Dibble, Harold. "The Interpretation of Middle Paleolithic Scraper Morphology." *American Antiquity* 52 (1987): 109–17.

Dillehay, Tom D. *Monte Verde: A Late Pleistocene Settlement in Chile*. Washington, DC: Smithsonian Institution Press, 1989.

———. *The Settlement of the Americas: A New Prehistory*. New York: Basic Books, 2000.

Dixon, E. James. *Bones, Boats, and Bison: Archaeology and the First Colonization of Western North America*. Albuquerque, NM: University of New Mexico Press, 1999.

Dixon, James E. "Human Colonization of the Americas: Timing, Technology and Process." *Quaternary Science Reviews* 20 (2001): 277–99.

Dobres, Marcia-Anne, and John E. Robb. *Agency in Archaeology*. London and New York: Routledge, 2000.

Dominguez-Rodrigo, Manuel. "Hunting and Scavenging by Early Humans: The State of the Debate." *Journal of World Prehistory* 16.1 (2002): 1–54.

Domínguez-Rodrigo, Manuel, et al. "Woodworking Activities by Early Humans: A Plant Residue Analysis on Acheulian Stone Tools from Peninj (Tanzania)." *Journal of Human Evolution* 40 (2001): 289–99.

Duarte, Cidalia, et al. "The Early Upper Paleolithic Human Skeleton from the Abrigo Do Lagar Velho (Portugal) and Modern Human Emergence in Iberia." *Proceedings of the National Academy of Sciences* 96 (1999): 7604–09.

Duarte, C., et al. "The Early Upper Paleolithic Human Skeleton from the Abrigo Do Lagar Velho (Portugal) and Modern Human Emergence in Iberia." *Proceedings of the National Academy of Science* 94 (1999): 13367–73.

Duller, G.A.T. "Dating Methods: The Role of Geochronology in Studies of Human Evolution and Migration in Southeast Asia and Australasia." *Progress in Physical Geography* 25.2 (2001): 267–76.

Edwards, P. "Wadi Hammeh 27: An Early Natufian Site at Pella, Jordan." *The Natufian Culture in the Levant*. eds. O. Bar-Yosef and François Valla. Ann Arbor, MI: International Monographs in Prehistory, 1991. 123–48.

Elton, Sarah, Laura C. Bishop, and Bernard Wood. "Comparative Context of Plio-Pleistocene Hominin Brain Evolution." *Journal of Human Evolution* 41 (2000): 1–27.

Enloe, J.G. "Food Sharing in the Paleolithic: Carcass Refitting at Pincevent." *Piecing Together the Past: Applications of Refitting Studies in Archaeology*. eds. J.L. Hofman and J.G. Enloe. Vol. 578. Oxford: BAR International Series, 1992. 296–315.

Enloe, James G. "Food Sharing Past and Present: Archaeological Evidence for Economic and Social Interactions." University of Iowa, 2002. http://www.uiowa.edu/~zooarch/bffoodshare2003.pdf.

Eubanks, Mary. "An Interdisciplinary Perspective on the Origin of Maize." *Latin American Antiquity* 12.1 (2001): 91–98.

Evans, John G., and T.P. O'Connor. *Environmental Archaeology: Principles and Methods*. 2d ed. Stroud, U.K.: Sutton, 2005.

Eyre-Walker, A., et al. "Investigation of the Bottleneck Leading to the Domestication of Maize." *Proceedings of the National Academy of Sciences* 95 (1998): 4441–46.

Fagan, Brian M. *Eyewitness to Discovery: First-Person Accounts of More Than Fifty of the World's Greatest Archaeological Discoveries*. Oxford, U.K.: Oxford University Press, 1996.

Fajardo, D.S., D.R. La Bonte, and R.L. Jarret. "Identifying and Selecting for Genetic Diversity in Papua New Guinea Sweet Potato *Ipomoea batatas* (L.) Lam. Germplasm Collected as Botanical Seed." *Genetic Resources and Crop Evolution* 49 (2002): 463–70.

Fash, William Leonard. *Scribes, Warriors, and Kings: The City of Copán and the Ancient Maya. New Aspects of Antiquity*. London: Thames and Hudson, 1991.

Faupl, Peter, Wolfram Richter, and Christoph Urbanek. "Dating of the Herto Hominin Fossils." *Nature* 426 (2003): 621–22.

Fforde, C., J. Hubert, and P. Turnbull, eds. *The Dead and Their Possessions: Repatriation in Principle, Policy, and Practice*. Vol. 43. London: Routledge, 2002.

Fiedel, Stuart. "Artifact Provenience at Monte Verde: Confusion and Contradictions." *Scientific American Discovery Archaeology* 1.6 (1999): 1–14.

Fiedel, Stuart, and Gary Haynes. "A Premature Burial: Comments on Grayson and Meltzer's 'Requiem for Overkill.'" *Journal of Archaeological Science*. No. 31 (2004): 121–31.

Field, Judith, Richard Fullagar, and Garry Lord. "A Large Area Archaeological Excavation at Cuddie Springs." *Antiquity* 75.290 (2001): 696–702.

Field, Judith, et al. "Archaeology and Australian Megafauna." *Science* 294 (2001): 696–702.

Fladmark, K.R. "Routes: Alternate Migration Corridors for Early Man in North America." *American Antiquity* 44.1 (1979): 55–69.

Flannery, Kent. "Culture History V. Culture Process: A Debate in American Archaeology." *Scientific American* 217 (1967): 119–22.

———. "The Origins of Agriculture." *Annual Review of Anthropology* 1973 (1973): 271–310.

Flenley, John, and Paul G. Bahn. *The Enigmas of Easter Island: Island on the Edge.* 2d ed. Oxford, U.K.: Oxford University Press, 2003.

Ford, Richard I. "Corn Is Our Mother." *Corn and Culture in the Prehistoric New World.* eds. Sissel Johannessen and Christine A. Hastorf. Boulder, CO: Westview Press, 1994. 513–526.

Formicola, V., and A. Buzhilova. "Double Child Burial from Sunghir (Russia): Pathology and Inferences for Upper Paleolithic Funerary Practices." *American Journal of Physical Anthropology* 124.3 (2004): 189–98.

Fried, Morton H. *The Evolution of Political Society: An Essay in Political Anthropology.* New York: Random House, 1967.

Frison, George C. "Paleoindian Large Mammal Hunters on the Plains of North America." *Proceedings of the National Academy of Sciences* 95 (1998): 14576–83.

Fritz, Gayle J. "Gender and the Early Cultivation of Gourds in Eastern North America." *American Antiquity* 64.3 (1999): 417–29.

Gamble, Clive. *Timewalkers: The Prehistory of Global Colonization.* Stroud, U.K.: A. Sutton, 1993.

Gargett, Robert. "Grave Shortcomings: The Evidence for Neanderthal Burial." *Current Anthropology* 30.2 (1989): 157–90.

Garlake, Peter S. *Great Zimbabwe.* London: Thames and Hudson, 1973.

Gaudzinski, Sabine. "On Bovid Assemblages and Their Consequences for the Knowledge of Subsistence Patterns in the Middle Palaeolithic." *Proceedings of the Prehistoric Society* 62 (1996): 19–39.

Gebel, Hans Georg, et al. "Ba'ja Hidden in the Petra Mountains. Preliminary Results of the 1997 Investigations." *The Prehistory of Jordan II: Perspectives from 1997.* eds. Hans Georg Gebel, Zeidan Kafafi, and Gary O. Rollefson. Berlin: Ex Oriente, 1997. 221–62.

Geneste, Jean-Michel, and Hugues Plisson. "Hunting Technologies and Human Behavior: Lithic Analysis of Solutrean Shouldered Points." *Before Lascaux: The Complex Record of the Early Upper Paleolithic.* eds. Heidi Knecht, Anne Pike-Tay, and Randall White. Boca Raton, FL: CRC Press, 1993. 117–35.

Gero, Joan M., and Margaret Wright Conkey. *Engendering Archaeology: Women and Prehistory. Social Archaeology.* Oxford, U.K.: B. Blackwell, 1991.

Gibbons, Ann. "Ancient Island Tools Suggest *Homo erectus* Was a Seafarer." *Science* 279 (1998): 1635–37.

Gibson, Jon L. *The Ancient Mounds of Poverty Point: Place of Rings.* Gainesville, FL: University of Florida Press, 2000.

Gichuki, Simon Templar, et al. "Genetic Diversity in Sweet Potato (*Ipomoea batatas*)." *Genetic Resources and Crop Evolution* 50 (2003): 429–37.

Gifford-Gonzalez, Diane. "Early Pastoralists in East Africa: Ecological and Social Dimensions." *Journal of Anthropological Archaeology* 17 (1998): 166–200.

Glazko, Galina V., and Masatoshi Nei. "Estimation of Divergence Times for Major Lineages of Primate Species." *Molecular Biological Evolution* 20.3 (2003): 424–34.

Goebel, Ted, Michael R. Waters, and Margarita Dikova. "The Archaeology of Ushki Lake, Kamchatka, and the Pleistocene Peopling of the Americas." *Science* 301 (2003): 501–05.

Goldberg, P., et al. "Site Formation Processes at Zhoukoudian, China." *Journal of Human Evolution* 41.5 (2001): 483–530.

Golsen, J., and D.S. Gardner. "Agriculture and Sociopolitical Organization in New Guinea Highlands Prehistory." *Annual Review of Anthropology* 19 (1990): 395–417.

Gordon, Arnold L., Claudia F. Giulivi, and A. Gani Ilahude. "Deep Topographic Barriers within the Indonesian Seas." *Deep-Sea Research Part II* 50 (2003): 2205–28.

Goren, Yuval, et al. *Inscribed in Clay: Provenance Study of the Amarna Tablets and Other Ancient Near Eastern Texts.* Tel Aviv: Emery and Claire Yass Publications in Archaeology, 2004.

Goren, Y., A.N. Goring-Morris, and I. Segal. "The Technology of Skull Modelling in the Pre-Pottery Neolithic B (PPNB): Regional Variability, the Relation of Technology and Iconography and Their Archaeological Implications." *Journal of Archaeological Science* 28 (2001): 671–90.

Goren-Inbar, Naama, et al. "Pleistocene Milestones on the Out-of-Africa Corridor at Gesher Benot Ya'aqov, Israel." *Science* 289 (2000): 944–47.

Goring-Morris, A.N., and A. Belfer-Cohen. "The Articulation of Cultural Processes and Late Quaternary Environmental Changes in Cisjordan." *Paleorient* 23.2 (1998): 71–93.

Gould, S.J. "On Replacing the Idea of Progress with an Operational Notion of Directionality." *Evolutionary Progress?* ed. Matthew H. Nitecki. Chicago: University of Chicago Press, 1988. 319–38.

Gould, S.J., and R.C. Lewontin. "The Spandrels of San Marco and the Panglossian Paradigm: A Critique of the Adaptationist Programme." *Proceedings of the Royal Society of London* B 205 (1979): 581–98.

Gowlett, J., et al. "Early Archaeological Sites, Hominid Remains and Traces of Fire from Chesowanja, Kenya." *Nature* 294 (1981): 125–29.

Grayson, Donald K. *The Establishment of Human Antiquity.* New York: Academic Press, 1983.

Grayson, Donald K., and David J. Meltzer. "Clovis Hunting and Large Mammal Extinction: A Critical Review of the Evidence." *Journal of World Prehistory* 16.4 (2002): 313–59.

Grayson, Donald K., and David J. Meltzer. "North American Overkill Continued?" *Journal of Archaeological Science* 31 (2004): 133–36.

Green, Ernestene L. *Ethics and Values in Archaeology.* New York: Free Press, 1984.

Gremillion, Kristen J. "Early Agricultural Diet in Eastern North America: Evidence from Two Kentucky Rockshelters." *American Antiquity* 61.3 (1996): 520–36.

Gremillion, Kristen J. "Eastern Woodlands Overview." *People and Plants in Ancient Eastern North America.* ed. Paul E. Minnis. Washington, DC: Smithsonian Books, 2003. 17–50.

Griffin, James B. "Eastern North American Archaeology: A Summary." *Science* 156 (1967): 175–91.

Groube, Les, et al. "A 40,000 Year-Old Human Occupation Site at Huon Peninsula, Papua New Guinea." *Nature* 324 (1986): 453–55.

Guidon, N., et al. "Nature and Age of the Deposits in Pedra Furada, Brazil: Reply to Meltzer, Adovasio & Dillehay." *Antiquity* 70 (1996): 408–21.

Guilaine, Jean. *Premiers Paysans du Monde: Naissances des Agricultures. Collection des Hespérides.* Paris: Errance, 2000.

Guthrie, R. Dale. "Rapid Body Size Decline in Alaskan Pleistocene Horses before Extinction." *Nature* 426 (2003): 169–71.

Gutierrez, Manuel, et al. "Exploitation d'un Grand Cétacé au Paléolithique Ancien: Le Site de Dungo V a Baia Farta (Benguela, Angola)." *Comptes Rendus de l'Academie des Sciences: Earth and Planetary Sciences* 332 (2001): 357–62.

Haaland, Randi. "Sedentism, Cultivation, and Plant Domestication in the Holocene Middle Nile Region." *Journal of Field Archaeology* 22 (1995): 157–74.

Haberle, Simon G. "The Emergence of an Agricultural Landscape in the Highlands of New Guinea." *Archaeology of Oceania* 38 (2003): 149–58.

Hallo, William W., and William Kelly Simpson. *The Ancient Near East: A History.* New York: Harcourt Brace Jovanovich, 1971.

Hard, Robert, and John R. Roney. "The Transition to Farming on the Río Casas Grandes and in the Southern Jornada Mogollon Region." *The Late Archaic: Across the Borderlands.* ed. Bradley J. Vierra. Austin, TX: University of Texas, 2005. 141–86.

Harlan, Jack R. "The Tropical African Cereals." *The Archaeology of Africa: Food, Metals, and Towns.* ed. Thurstan Shaw. London: Routledge, 1993. 53–59.

——. *The Living Fields: Our Agricultural Heritage.* Cambridge, U.K.: Cambridge University Press, 1995.

Harris, David R., et al. *The Archaeology of V. Gordon Childe: Contemporary Perspectives.* London: UCL Press, 1994.

Harrison, Peter D. *The Lords of Tikal: Rulers of an Ancient Maya City. New Aspects of Antiquity.* London: Thames and Hudson, 1999.

Hastorf, Christine A. "The Cultural Life of Early Domestic Plant Use." *Antiquity* 72 (1998): 773–888.

——. "Recent Research in Paleoethnobotany." *Journal of Archaeological Research* 7.1 (1999): 55–103.

Hastorf, Christine A., and Virginia Popper, eds. *Current Paleoethnobotany: Analytical Methods and Cultural Interpretations of Archaeological Plant Remains.* Chicago: University of Chicago, 1988.

Haug, Gerald H., et al. "Climate and the Collapse of Maya Civilization." *Science* 299 (2003): 1731.

Hayden, Brian. "Nimrods, Piscators, Pluckers, and Planters: The Emergence of Food Production." *Journal of Anthropological Archaeology* 9 (1990): 31–69.

Haynes, C. Vance, Richard E. Reanier, and William P. Barse. "Dating a Paleoindian Site in the Amazon in Comparison with Clovis Culture." *Science* 275 (1997): 1948–52.

Haynes, C. Vance, et al. "A Clovis Well at the Type Site 11,500 B.C.: The Oldest Prehistoric Well in America." *Geoarchaeology: An International Journal* Vol. 14., No. 5 (1999): 455–70.

Haynes, Gary. *The Early Settlement of North America: The Clovis Era.* Cambridge, U.K.: Cambridge University Press, 2002.

Hedges, S. Blair. "A Start for Population Genomics." *Nature* 408 (2000): 652–53.

Heizer, Robert F. *Man's Discovery of His Past; Literary Landmarks in Archaeology.* Englewood Cliffs, N.J.: Prentice-Hall, 1962.

Hendon, Julia A., and Rosemary A. Joyce. *Mesoamerican Archaeology: Theory and Practice. Blackwell Studies in Global Archaeology* 1. Malden, MA: Blackwell, 2004.

Henshilwood, C.S., et al. "Emergence of Modern Human Behavior: Middle Stone Age Engravings from South Africa." *Science* 295 (2002): 1278–80.

Henshilwood, C.S., and J. Sealy. "Bone Artifacts from the Middle Stone Age at Blombos Cave, Southern Cape, South Africa." *Current Anthropology* 38 (1997): 890–95.

Hide, Robin. *Pig Husbandry in New Guinea: A Literature Review and Bibliography.* 2003. Canberra, Australia: Australian Centre for International Agriculture Research, 2003.

Higgs, E.S., ed. *Papers in Economic Prehistory.* Cambridge, U.K.: Cambridge University Press, 1972.

Higham, Charles, and Tracey L.-D. Lu. "The Origins and Dispersal of Rice Cultivation." *Antiquity* 72.278 (1998): 867–77.

Higham, Tom, Christopher Bronk Ramsey, and Clare Owen, eds. *Radiocarbon and Archaeology.* Oxford, U.K.: Oxford University School of Archaeology, 2004.

Hill, James. "Broken K Pueblo: Patterns of Form and Function." *New Perspectives in Archaeology.* ed. Sally Binford and Lewis Binford. Chicago: Aldine, 1968. 103–42.

Hodder, Ian. *Reading the Past.* Cambridge, U.K.: Cambridge University Press, 1986.

———. *The Domestication of Europe: Structure and Contingency in Neolithic Societies. Social Archaeology.* Oxford, U.K.: Blackwell, 1990.

———. *The Archaeological Process: An Introduction.* Oxford, U.K.: Blackwell, 1999.

Hodder, Robert Preucel and Ian, eds. *Contemporary Archaeology in Theory.* Oxford: Blackwell, 1996.

Holl, Augustin F. C. "Livestock Husbandry, Pastoralisms, and Territoriality: The West African Record." *Journal of Anthropological Archaeology* 17 (1998): 143–65.

———. "The Dawn of African Pastoralisms: An Introductory Note." *Journal of Anthropological Archaeology* 17.2 (1998): 81–165.

Hosler, Dorothy. "Sound, Color, and Meaning in the Metallurgy of Ancient West Mexico." *World Archaeology* 27.1 (1995): 100–15.

Houston, Stephen D. "Into the Minds of Ancients: Advances in Maya Glyph Studies." *Journal of World Prehistory* 14.2 (2000): 121–201.

Hovers, Erella, William H. Kimbel, and Yoel Rak. "The Amud 7 Skeleton—Still a Burial. Response to Gargett." *Journal of Human Evolution* 39 (2000): 253–60.

Howard, Edgar B. "An Outline of the Problem of Man's Antiquity in North America." *American Anthropologist* 38 (1936): 394–413.

Hublin, J.J., et al. "The Mousterian Site of Zafarrya (Andalucía, Spain): Dating and Implications on the Paleolithic Peopling Processes of Western Europe." *Comptes Rendus de l'Académie des Sciences,* Serie IIa 321.10 (1995): 931–37.

Huckell, Bruce B., and J. David Kilby, eds. *Readings in Late Pleistocene North America and Early Paleoindians: Selections from American Antiquity.* Washington, DC: Society for American Archaeology, 2004.

Huffman, O. Frank. "Geologic Context and Age of the Perning/Mojokerto *Homo erectus,* East Java." *Journal of Human Evolution* 40 (2001): 353–62.

Humle, Tatyana, and Tetsuro Matsuzawa. "Ant-Dipping among the Chimpanzees of Bossou, Guinea, and Some Comparisons with Other Sites." *American Journal of Primatology* 58 (2002): 133–48.

Hunt, Gavin R. "Manufacture and Use of Hook-Tools by New Caledonian Crows." *Nature* 379.6562 (1996): 249–51.

Hunt, Gavin R., and Russell D. Gray. "Diversification and Cumulative Evolution in New Caledonian Crow Tool Manufacture." *The Royal Society* 270 (2003): 867–74.

Hunter, John, and Ian Ralston. *The Archaeology of Britain: An Introduction from the Upper Palaeolithic to the Industrial Revolution.* London: Routledge, 1999.

Hyodo, Masayuki, et al. "Paleomagnetic Dates of Hominid Remains from Yuanmou, China, and Other Asian Sites." *Journal of Human Evolution* 43 (2002): 27–41.

Hyslop, John. *The Inka Road System. Studies in Archaeology.* Orlando, FL: Academic Press, 1984.

Hyslop, John, and American Council of Learned Societies. *Inka Settlement Planning.* Austin, TX: University of Texas Press. 1990.

Imamura, Keiji. *Prehistoric Japan: New Perspectives on Insular East Asia.* Honolulu: University of Hawaii Press, 1996.

Ingman, M., et al. "Mitochondrial Genome Variation and the Origin of Modern Humans." *Nature* 408 (2000): 708–13.

Ingold, Tim. *Hunters, Pastoralists, and Ranchers: Reindeer Economics and their Transformations.* Cambridge, U.K.: Cambridge University Press, 1980.

———. *The Perception of the Environment: Essays on Livelihood, Dwelling and Skill.* London: Routledge, 2000.

Inomata, Takeshi, and Laura R. Stiver. "Floor Assemblages from Burned Structures at Aguateca, Guatemala: A Study of Classic Maya Households." *Journal of Field Archaeology* 25.4 (1998): 431–52.

Isaac, Barbara. "Implementation of NAGPRA: The Peabody Museum of Archaeology and Ethnology, Harvard." *The Dead and Their Possessions: Repatriation in Principle, Policy and Practice.* eds. C. Fforde, J. Hubert, and P. Turnbull. London: Routledge, 2002. 160–70.

Jablonski, David. "Extinction: Past and Present." *Nature* 427 (2004): 589.

Janes, Robert R. *Archaeological Ethnography among Mackenzie Basin Dene, Canada.* Calgary, AB: Arctic Institute of North America, the University of Calgary, 1983.

Jansen, M. "Water Supply and Sewage Disposal at Mohenjo-Daro." *World Archaeology* 21.2 (1989): 177–92.

Jantz, R.L., and Douglas W. Owsley. "Variation among Early North American Crania." *American Journal of Physical Anthropology* 114 (2001): 146–55.

Jarrige, J.F. *Les Cités Oubliées de L'indus.* Paris: Musée National des Arts Asiatiques Guimet, 1989.

Jones, Rhys, and J. Allen. *Archaeological Research in Kakadu National Park.* Canberra, Australia: Australian National Parks and Wildlife Service, 1985.

Joyce, Rosemary A. "Academic Freedom, Stewardship and Cultural Heritage: Weighing the Interests of Stakeholders in Crafting Repatriation Approaches." *The Dead and Their Possessions: Repatriation in Principle, Policy, and Practice.* eds. C. Fforde, J. Hubert and P. Turnbull. London: Routledge, 2002. 99–107.

Juzhong, Zhang, and Wang Xiangkun. "Notes on the Recent Discovery of Ancient Cultivated Rice at Jiahu, Henan Province: A New Theory Concerning the Origin of Oryza Japonica in China." *Antiquity* 72 (1998): 897–901.

Kaessmann, H., and S. Paabo. "The Genetical History of Humans and the Great Apes." *Journal of Internal Medicine* 251 (2002): 1–18.

Kaplan, Lawrence, and Thomas F. Lynch. "Phaseolus (Fabaceae) in Archaeology: AMS Radiocarbon Dates and Their Significance for Pre-Columbian Agriculture." *Economic Botany* 53.3 (1999): 261–72.

Kappelman, John. "The Evolution of Body Mass and Relative Brain Size in Fossil Hominids." *Journal of Human Evolution* 30 (1996): 243–76.

Katzenberg, Anne M., et al. "Stable Isotope Evidence for Maize Horticulture and Paleodiet in Southern Ontario." *American Antiquity* 60 (1995): 335–50.

Keatinge, Richard W., ed. *Peruvian Prehistory.* Cambridge, U.K.: Cambridge University Press, 1988.

Keefer, David K., et al. "Early Maritime Economy and El Niño Events at Quebrada Tacahuay, Peru." *Science* 281 (1998): 1833–35.

Keeley, Lawrence. "Technique and Methodology in Microwear Studies: A Critical Review." *World Archaeology* 5 (2001): 323–36.

Keightley, David N. "Sacred Characters." *China: Ancient Culture, Modern Land.* ed. Robert E. Murowchick. Norman, OK: Oklahoma University Press, 1994. 70–79.

———. *The Ancestral Landscape: Time, Space, and Community in Late Shang China,* ca. 1200–1045 B.C. Berkeley, CA: University of California Center for Chinese Studies, 2000.

Kemp, Barry J. *Ancient Egypt: Anatomy of a Civilization.* London: Routledge, 1991.

Kenoyer, Jonathan M. *Ancient Cities of the Indus Valley Civilization.* 1st ed. Karachi and Islamabad, Pakistan: Oxford University Press and American Institute of Pakistan Studies, 1998.

Kenyon, K. *Excavations at Jericho, Vol. 3: The Architecture and Stratigraphy of the Tell.* London: British School of Archaeology in Jerusalem, 1981.

Kidder, Alfred Vincent, and Samuel James Guernsey. *Archeological Explorations in Northeastern Arizona.* Washington, DC: Govt. Print. Off., 1919.

Kimbel, W.H., et al. "Late Pliocene *Homo* and Oldowan Tools from Hadar Formation (Kada Hadar Member), Ethiopia." *Journal of Human Evolution* 289 (1999): 550–61.

Kinahan, John. "The Rise and Fall of Nomadic Pastoralism in the Central Namib Desert." *The Archaeology of Africa: Food, Metals, and Towns.* ed. Thurstan Shaw. London: Routledge, 1993. 373–85.

King, Maureen L., and Sergei B. Slobodin. "A Fluted Point from the Uptar Site, Northeastern Siberia." *Science* 273 (1996): 634–36.

Kislev, Mordechai, Anat Hartmann, and O. Bar-Yosef. "Early Domesticated Fig in the Jordan Valley." *Science* 312 (2006): 1372–74.

Klein, Richard G. "Whither the Neanderthals?" *Science* 299 (2003): 1525–26.

Klein, Richard G., and Blake Edgar. *The Dawn of Human Culture.* New York: Wiley, 2002.

Knecht, Heidi, Anne Pike-Tay, and Randall Keith White. *Before Lascaux: The Complex Record of the Early Upper Paleolithic.* Boca Raton, FL: CRC Press, 1993.

Kolata, Alan L. *Tiwanaku and Its Hinterland: Archaeology and Paleoecology of an Andean Civilization. Smithsonian Series in Archaeological Inquiry.* Washington, DC: Smithsonian Institution Press, 1996.

Kramer, Carol. *Village Ethnoarchaeology: Rural Iran in Archaeological Perspective.* New York: Academic Press, 1982.

Krings, Matthias, et al. "DNA Sequence of the Mitochrondrial Hypervariable Region II from the Neanderthal Type Specimen." *Proceedings of the National Academy of Sciences* 96 (1999): 5581–85.

Langbroek, Marco, and Wil Roebroeks. "Extraterrestrial Evidence on the Age of the Hominids from Java." *Journal of Human Evolution* 38 (2000): 595–600.

Larson, Edward J. *Summer for the Gods: The Scopes Trial and America's Continuing Debate Over Science and Religion.* New York: Basic Books, 1997.

Lauck, Rebecca Gonzalez. "La Venta: An Olmec Capital." *Olmec Art of Ancient Mexico.* eds. Elizabeth P. Benson and Beatriz de la Fuente. Washington, DC: National Gallery of Art, 1996. 73–82.

Lavallée, Danièle. *The First South Americans: The Peopling of a Continent from the Earliest Evidence to High Culture.* Salt Lake City, UT: University of Utah Press, 2000.

Laville, Henri, Jean Philippe Rigaud, and James Sackett. *Rock Shelters of the Perigord: Geological Stratigraphy and Archaeological Succession. Studies in Archaeology.* New York: Academic Press, 1980.

Leakey, Mary D. *Olduvai Gorge: Excavations in Beds I and II, 1960–1963. Olduvai Gorge; 3.* Cambridge: Cambridge University Press, 1971.

Leakey, Mary D., et al. "New Four Million Year Old Hominid Species from Kanpoi and Allia Bay, Kenya." *Nature* 393 (1995): 62–66.

Leakey, Mary D., and John Michael Harris, eds. *Laetoli, a Pliocene Site in Northern Tanzania.*

Oxford, U.K.: Clarendon Press and Oxford University Press, 1987.

Leakey, Meave G., et al. "New Hominid Genus from Eastern Africa Shows Diverse Middle Pliocene Lineages." *Nature* 410 (2001): 433–40.

Leakey, Richard E., and Alan Walker. *The Narioko-tome* Homo erectus *Skeleton.* Cambridge, MA: Harvard University Press, 1993.

Lebot, V. "Biomolecular Evidence for Plant Domestication in Sahul." *Genetic Resources and Crop Evolution* 46 (1999): 619–28.

Lee, Richard B. *The Dobe Jul'Hoansi. Case Studies in Cultural Anthropology.* 3d ed. South Melbourne, Australia: Wadsworth Thomson Learning, 2003.

Lehner, Mark. *The Complete Pyramids.* New York: Thames and Hudson, 1997.

Leone, Mark, Parker Potter, and Paul Shackel. "Toward a Critical Archaeology." *Current Anthropology* 28.3 (1987): 283–302.

Lepper, Bradley T., and Richard W. Yerkes. "Hopewellian Occupations at the Northern Periphery of the Newark Earthworks: The Newark Expressway Sites Revisited." *Ohio Hopewell Community Organization.* eds. William S. Dancey and Paul J. Pacheco. Kent, OH: Ohio University Press, 1997. 175–206.

Leroi-Gourhan, Arlette. "The Flowers Found with Shanidar IV, a Neanderthal Burial in Iraq." *Science* 190.4214 (1975): 562–64.

Leroi-Gourhan, André. *Pincevent: Campement Magdalénien de Chasseurs de Rennes. Guides Archéologiques de la France,* 3. Paris: Ministère de la Culture, Direction du Patrimoine, 1984.

Li, Xueqin, et al. "The Earliest Writing? Sign Use in the Seventh Millennium B.C. at Jiahu, Henan Province, China." *Antiquity* 77.295 (2002): 31–44.

Lieberman, Daniel E. "Another Face in Our Family Tree." *Nature* 410 (2001): 419–20.

Lillios, Katina. 1999. "Objects of memory. The ethnography and archaeology of heirlooms." *Journal of Archaeological Method and Theory* 6(2): 235–262.

Linares, O. "African Rice (*Oryza glaberrima*): History and Future Potential." *Proceedings of the National Academy of Science* 99.25 (2002): 16360–65.

Lloyd, Seton. *The Archaeology of Mesopotamia: From the Old Stone Age to the Persian Conquest.* London: Thames and Hudson, 1978.

Londo, J., et al. "Phylogeography of Asian Wild Rice, *Oryza rufipogen,* Reveals Multiple Independent Domestications of Cultivated Rice, *Oryza sativa.*" *Proceedings of the National Academy of Science* 103.25 (2006): 9578–83.

Lordkipanidze, David, et al. "The Earliest Toothless Hominin Skull." *Nature* 434 (2005): 717–18.

Loring Brace, C., et al. "Old World Sources of the First New World Human Inhabitants: A Comparative Craniofacial View." *Proceedings*

*of the National Academy of Sciences* 98.17 (2001): 10017–22.

Lourandos, Harry. *Continent of Hunter–Gatherers: New Perspectives in Australian Prehistory.* Cambridge, U.K.: Cambridge University Press, 1997.

Lu, Tracey L.D. "Some Botanical Characteristics of Green Foxtail (*Setaria viridis*) and Harvesting Experiments on the Grass." *Antiquity* 72.278 (1998): 902–07.

Lu, Tracey L.D. *The Transition from Foraging to Farming and the Origin of Agriculture in China.* Bar International Series. Vol. 774. Oxford, U.K.: BAR, 1999.

Lynch, Thomas F., ed. *Guitarrero Cave: Early Man in the Andes.* New York: Academic Press, 1980.

Mabry, Jonathan B. "Changing Knowledge About the First Farmers in Southeastern Arizona." *The Late Archaic: Across the Borderlands.* ed. Bradley J. Vierra. Austin, TX: University of Texas Press, 2005. 41–83.

MacGillivray, J.A. *Minotaur: Sir Arthur Evans and the Archaeology of the Minoan Myth.* New York: Hill and Wang, 2000.

Mack, M.E., and M.L. Blakey. "The New York African Burial Ground Project: Past Biases, Current Dilemmas, and Future Research Opportunities." *Historical Archaeology* 38.1 (2004): 10–17.

Magid, Anwar A., and Isabella Caneva. "Economic Strategy Based on Food-Plants in the Early Holocene Central Sudan: A Reconsideration." *Before Food Production in North Africa.* eds. Savino di Lernia and Giorgio Manzi. Forli, Italy: A.B.A.C.O. Edizioni, 1998. 79–90.

Mandryk, Carole A.S., et al. "Late Quaternary Paleoenvironments of Northwestern North America: Implications for Inland Versus Coastal Migration Routes." *Quaternary Science Reviews* No. 20 (2001): 301–14.

Marshack, Alexander. "Upper Paleolithic Notation and Symbol." *Science* 178 (1972): 817–28.

Marshall, Fiona, and Elisabeth Hildebrand. "Cattle before Crops: The Beginnings of Food Production in Africa." *Journal of World Prehistory* 16.2 (2002): 99–143.

Marshall, John. "A New Chapter in Archaeology: The Prehistoric Civilisation of the Indus." *Illustrated London News,* January 7, 1928.

Martin, R.D., et al. "Comment on 'the Brain of Lb1, *Homo floresiensis.*'" *Science* 312 (2006): 999.

Martin, Simon. "In Line of the Founder: A View of Dynastic Politics at Tikal." *Tikal: Dynasties, Foreigners, and Affairs of State.* ed. Jeremy Sabloff. Santa Fe, NM: SAR Press, 2003.

Matos Moctezuma, Eduardo. *The Great Temple of the Aztecs: Treasures of Tenochtitlán.* New Aspects of Antiquity. London: Thames and Hudson, 1988.

———. "Aztec History and Cosmovision." *Moctezuma's Mexico: Visions of the Aztec World.* eds. David Carrasco and Eduardo Matos Moctezuma. Boulder, CO: University of Colorado, 1992. 3–99.

Matos Moctezuma, Eduardo, and Michel Zabé. *Treasures of the Great Temple.* Eng. language ed. La Jolla, CA: ALTI Pub., 1990.

Matson, R.G. "The Spread of Maize Agriculture in the U.S. Southwest." *Examining the Farming/Language Dispersal Hypothesis.* eds. Peter Bellwood and Colin Renfrew. Cambridge, U.K.: McDonald Institute for Archaeology, 2003. 341–56.

Matsuoka, Y., et al. "A Single Domestication for Maize Shown by Multilocus Microsatellite Genotyping." *Proceedings of the National Academy of Sciences* 99.9 (2002): 6080–84.

Matthews, Roger. *The Archaeology of Mesopotamia: Theories and Approaches. Approaching the Ancient World.* London and New York: Routledge, 2003.

McBrearty, Sally, and Alison Brooks. "The Revolution That Wasn't: A New Interpretation of the Origin of Modern Human Behavior." *Journal of Human Evolution* 39.5 (2000): 453–563.

McCauley, J.F. et al.. "Subsurface Valleys and Geoarchaeology of the Eastern Sahara." *Science* 218 (1982): 1004–20.

McDonald, Mary M.A. "Early African Pastoralism: View from Dakhleh Oasis (South Central Egypt)." *Journal of Anthropological Archaeology* 17 (1998): 124–42.

McElhinny, M.W. "Paleomagnetism: Continents and Oceans." *International Geophysics Series* 73 (2000): 333–76.

McGovern, Patrick, et al. "The Archaeological Origin and Significance of the Dolphin Vase as Determined by Neutron Activation Analysis." *Bulletin of the American Schools of Oriental Research* 296 (1994): 31–43.

McIntosh, Roderick J. *The Peoples of the Middle Niger: The Island of Gold. Peoples of Africa.* Malden, MA: Blackwell Publishers, 1998.

McIntosh, Susan, and Roderick J. McIntosh. "Cities without Citadels: Understanding Urban Origins Along the Middle Niger." *The Archaeology of Africa: Food, Metals, and Towns.* ed. Thurstan Shaw. London: Routledge, 1993. 622–41.

McKeown, Francis P. "Implementing a 'True Compromise': The Native American Graves Protection and Repatriation Act after Ten Years." *The Dead and Their Possessions: Repatriation in Principle, Policy, and Practice.* eds. C. Fforde, J. Hubert, and P. Turnbull. London: Routledge, 2002. 108–32.

Mellaart, James. *Çatal Hüyük: A Neolithic Town in Anatolia.* London: Thames and Hudson, 1967.

Mellars, Paul. *The Neanderthal Legacy: An Archaeological Perspective from Western Europe.* Princeton, NJ: Princeton University Press, 1996.

Mellars, Paul, and Chris Stringer. *The Human Revolution: Behavioural and Biological Perspectives on the Origins of Modern Humans.* Princeton, NJ: Princeton University Press, 1989.

Meltzer, David J., James M. Adovasio, and Tom D. Dillehay. "On a Pleistocene Human Occupation at Pedra Furada, Brazil." *Antiquity* 68 (1994): 695–714.

Meltzer, David J., et al. "On the Pleistocene Antiquity of Monte Verde, Southern Chile." *American Antiquity* 62.4 (1997): 659–63.

Mercader, Julio, Melissa Panger, and Christophe Boesch. "Excavation of a Chimpanzee Stone Tool Site in the African Rainforest." *Science* 296 (2002): 1452–55.

Meskell, Lynn, and Peter Pels. *Embedding Ethics.* Oxford, U.K. and New York: Berg, 2005.

Metcalf, Mary. "Construction and Labor at Pueblo Bonito: Center of the Chacoan World." *Pueblo Bonito: Center of the Chacoan World.* ed. Jill E. Neitzel. Washington, DC: Smithsonian Institution Press, 2003.

Michab, M., et al. "Luminescence Dates for the Paleoindian Site of Pedra Pintada, Brazil." *Quaternary Geochronology* 17 (1998): 1041–46.

Miller, Gifford H., et al. "Pleistocene Extinction of *Genyornis newtoni*: Human Impact on Australian Megafauna." *Science* 283 (1999): 205–08.

Millon, Rene. "Teotihuacán: Completion of Map of Giant Ancient City in the Valley of Mexico." *Science* 170 (1970): 1077–82.

Milner, George R. *The Cahokia Chiefdom: The Archaeology of a Mississippian Society. Smithsonian Series in Archaeological Inquiry.* Washington, DC: Smithsonian Institution Press, 1998.

Milo, R.G. "Evidence for Hominid Predation at Klasies River Mouth, South Africa, and Its Implications for the Behaviour of Early Modern Humans." *Journal of Archaeological Science* 25 (1998): 99–133.

Minnegal, Monica, and Peter D. Dwyer. "Intensification and Social Complexity in the Interior Lowlands of Papua New Guinea: A Comparison of Bedamuni and Kubo." *Journal of Anthropological Archaeology* 17 (1998): 375–400.

Minnis, Paul E., ed. *People and Plants in Ancient Eastern North America.* Washington, DC: Smithsonian Books, 2003.

Miracle, Preston. "Through the Clovis Barrier." *Antiquity* 73 (1999): 944–47.

Mithen, Steven. "Technology and Society During the Middle Pleistocene: Hominid Group Size, Social Learning, and Industrial Variability." *Cambridge Archaeological Journal* 4.1 (1994): 3–32.

Montgomery, John. *Tikal: An Illustrated History: The Ancient Maya Capital.* New York: Hippocrene Books, 2001.

Moore, A.M.T., Gordon C. Hillman, and A.J. Legge. *Village on the Euphrates: From Foraging to Farming at Abu Hureyra.* Oxford, U.K. Oxford University Press, 2000.

Morgan, Lewis Henry. *Ancient Society: Or, Researches in the Lines of Human Progress from Savagery, through Barbarism to Civilization.* Chicago: C.H. Kerr, 1877.

Morlan, Richard E. "Current Perspectives on the Pleistocene Archaeology of Eastern Beringia." *Quaternary Research* 60 (2003): 123–32.

Morris, Craig, and Donald E. Thompson. *Huánuco Pampa: An Inca City and Its Hinterland.* London: Thames and Hudson, 1985.

Morris, Craig, and Adriana Von Hagen. *The Inka Empire and Its Andean Origins.* New York: Abbeville, 1993.

Morwood, M., et al. "Archaeology and Age of a New Hominin from Flores in Eastern Indonesia." *Nature* 431 (2004): 1087–91.

Muke, John, and Herman Mandui. "In the Shadows of Kuk: Evidence for Prehistoric Agriculture at Kana, Wahgi Valley, Papua New Guinea." *Archaeology of Oceania* 38 (2003): 177–85.

Murowchick, Robert E. *China: Ancient Culture, Modern Land. Cradles of Civilization.* North Sydney, Australia: Weldon Russell, 1994.

Murray, Tim. *Archaeology of Aboriginal Australia: A Reader.* St. Leonards, AUS: Allen & Unwin, 1998.

Muzzolini, A. "The Emergence of a Food-Producing Economy in the Sahara." *The Archaeology of Africa: Food, Metals, and Towns.* ed. Thurstan Shaw. London: Routledge, 1993. 227–39.

Nadel, D., ed. *Ohalo Ii-II: A 23,000 Year-Old Fisher–Hunter–Gatherers' Camp on the Shore of the Sea of Galilee.* Haifa, Israel: Hecht Museum, 2002.

Naveh, Danny. "PPNA Jericho: A Socio-Political Perspective." *Cambridge Archaeological Journal* 13.1 (2003): 83–96.

Neitzel, Jill E. *Pueblo Bonito: Center of the Chacoan World.* Washington, DC: Smithsonian Institution Press, 2003.

Nelson, D.E., et al. "New Dates on Northern Yukon Artifacts: Holocene Not Upper Pleistocene." *Science* 232 (1986): 749–50.

Nettle, Daniel. "Linguistic Diversity of the Americas Can Be Reconciled with a Recent Colonization." *Proceedings of the National Academy of Sciences* 96 (1999): 3325–29.

Neumann, Katharina. "New Guinea: A Cradle of Agriculture." *Science* 301 (2003): 180–81.

Nichols, Deborah L. "Rural and Urban Landscapes of the Aztec State." *Mesoamerican Archaeology: Theory and Practice.* eds. Rosemary A. Joyce and Julia A. Hendon. Oxford, U.K.: Blackwell, 2004. 265–95.

Nichols, Deborah L., and Thomas H. Charlton. *The Archaeology of City–States: Cross-Cultural Approaches. Smithsonian Series in Archaeological Inquiry.* Washington, DC: Smithsonian Institution Press, 1997.

Niles, Susan A. "The Nature of Inca Royal Estates." *Machu Picchu: Unveiling the Mystery of the Incas.* eds. Richard L. Burger and Lucy C. Salazar. New Haven, CT: Yale University Press, 2004.

Nissen, Hans. "Uruk: Key Site of the Period and Key Site of the Problem." *Artefacts of Complexity: Tracking the Uruk in the Near East.* ed. J.N. Postgate. London: British School of Archaeology in Iraq, 2002. 1–17.

Nitecki, Matthew H. *Evolutionary Progress.* Chicago: University of Chicago Press, 1988.

Nora, Pierre. *Realms of Memory: Rethinking the French Past.* New York: Columbia University Press, 1996–1998.

O'Connell, James, and Jim Allen. "When Did Humans First Arrive in Greater Australia and Why Is It Important to Know?" *Evolutionary Anthropology* 6.4 (1998): 132–46.

O'Sullivan, Paul B., et al. "Archaeological Implications of the Geology and Chronology of the Soa Basin, Flores, Indonesia." *Geology* 29.7 (2001): 607–10.

Odell, George. "Stone Tool Research at the End of the Millennium: Classification, Function, and Behavior." *Journal of Archaeological Research* 9.1 (2001): 45–100.

Oppenheim, A. Leo, and Erica Reiner. *Ancient Mesopotamia: Portrait of a Dead Civilization.* Rev. ed. Chicago: University of Chicago Press, 1977.

Orser, Charles. *Historical Archaeology.* Upper Saddle River, NJ: Prentice Hall, 2004.

Ovchinnikov, Igor V., et al. "Molecular Analysis of Neanderthal DNA from the Northern Caucasus." *Nature* 404 (2000): 490–93.

Owsley, Douglas W., and Richard L. Jantz. "Archaeological Politics and Public Interest in Paleoamerican Studies: Lessons from Gordon Creek Woman and Kennewick Man." *American Antiquity* 66.4 (2001): 565–75.

Panger, Melissa A., et al. "Older Than the Oldowan? Rethinking the Emergence of Hominin Tool Use." *Evolutionary Anthropology* 11 (2002): 235–45.

Parker Pearson, Mike, Josh Pollard, Chris Tilley, Julian Thomas, Colin Richards, and Kate Welham. 2005. *The Stonehenge Riverside Project Summary Interim Report 2005.* Published online at http://www.shef.ac.uk/content/1/c6/02/21/27/PDF-Interim-Report-2005-summary.pdf.

Partridge, T.C., et al. "Lower Pliocene Hominid Remains from Sterkfontein." *Science* 300 (2003): 607–12.

Pasquinucci, Marinella, Frédéric Trément, and POPULUS Project. *Non-Destructive Techniques Applied to Landscape Archaeology. Archaeology of Mediterranean Landscapes* 4. Oxford, U.K. and Oakville, CT: , USA: Oxbow Books; David Brown Book Co. [distributor], 2000.

Patty Jo Watson, Steven LeBlanc, and Charles Redman. *Archaeological Explanation: The Scientific Method in Archaeology.* New York: Columbia University Press, 1984.

Pauketat, Timothy R. "Resettled Farmers and the Making of a Mississippian Polity." *American Antiquity* 68.1 (2003): 39–66.

———. *Ancient Cahokia and the Mississippians. Case Studies in Early Societies* 6. Cambridge, U.K.: Cambridge University Press, 2004.

Pauketat, Timothy R., et al. "The Residues of Feasting and Public Ritual at Early Cahokia." *American Antiquity* 67.2 (2002): 257–79.

Pavlov, Pavel, John Inge Svendsen, and Svein Indrelid. "Human Presence in the European Arctic Nearly 40,000 Years Ago." *Nature* 413 (2001): 64–67.

Pearson, Richard. "Social Complexity in Chinese: Coastal Neolithic Sites." *Science* 213 (1981): 1078–86.

Pearson, Richard, and Anne Underhill. "The Chinese Neolithic: Recent Trends in Research." *American Anthropologist* 89 (1987): 807–22.

Peretto, Carlo. "The First Peopling of Southern Europe: The Italian Case." *Comptes Rendus Palevol,* 5. 1–2 (2006): 283–90.

Perlés, Catherine. *The Early Neolithic in Greece: The First Farming Communities in Europe. Cambridge World Archaeology.* Cambridge, U.K.: Cambridge University Press, 2001.

Perry, Linda. "Starch Granule Size and the Domestication of Manioc (*Manihot esculenta*) and Sweet Potato (*Ipomoea batatas*)." *Economic Botany* 56.4 (2001): 335–49.

Phillipson, David W. "The Antiquity of Cultivation and Herding in Ethiopia." *The Archaeology of Africa: Food, Metals, and Towns.* ed. Thurstan Shaw. London: Routledge, 1993. 344–57.

Pigeot, Nicole. *Magdaléniens d'Étiolles: Économie de Débitage et Organisation Sociale (l'Unité d'Habitation U5).* Paris: Editions du Centre National de la Recherche Scientifique, 1987.

Pikirayi, Innocent. *The Zimbabwe Culture: Origins and Decline in Southern Zambezian States.* Walnut Creek, CA: AltaMira Press, 2001.

Pineda, Rosa Fung. "The Late Preceramic and Initial Period." *Peruvian Prehistory.* ed. Richard W. Keatinge. Cambridge, U.K.: Cambridge University Press, 1988. 67–98.

Piperno, D. R., and K. V. Flannery. "The Earliest Archaeological Maize (*Zea mays* L.) from Highland Mexico: New Accelerator Mass Spectrometry Dates and Their Implications." *Proceedings of the National Academy of Sciences of the United States of America* 98.4 (2001): 2101–03.

Pitulko, V.V., et al. "The Yana RHS Site: Humans in the Arctic before the Last Glacial Maximum." *Science* 303 (2004): 52–56.

Plog, Stephen. *Ancient Peoples of the American Southwest.* London: Thames and Hudson, 1997.

Plug, I. "Resource Exploitation: Animal Use During the Middle Stone Age at Sibudu Cave, KwaZulu-Natal, South Africa." *South African Journal of Science* 100. 151–158 (2004).

Pollock, Susan. *Ancient Mesopotamia: The Eden That Never Was. Case Studies in Early Societies.* Cambridge, U.K.: Cambridge University Press, 1999.

Pope, Geoffrey. "Bamboo and Human Evolution." *Natural History* 98.10 (1989): 48–57.

Postgate, J. N. *Early Mesopotamia: Society and Economy at the Dawn of History.* Rev. ed. London and New York: Routledge, 1994.

———. *Artefacts of Complexity: Tracking the Uruk in the Near East.* Iraq Archaeological Reports; 5 [S.l]: British School of Archaeology in Iraq, 2002.

Potts, Richard. *Early Hominid Activities at Olduvai. Foundations of Human Behavior.* New York: A. de Gruyter, 1988.

Prentice, Guy. "Origins of Plant Domestication in the Eastern United States: Promoting the Individual in Archaeological Theory." *Southeastern Archaeology* 5 (1986): 103–19.

Preston, Douglas. "Fossils & the Folsom Cowboy." *Natural History* 106.1 (1997): 16–21.

Proskouriakoff, Tatiana. "The Lords of the Maya Realm." *Expedition* 4.1 (1961): 14–21.

———. *An Album of Maya Architecture.* New ed. Norman, OK: University of Oklahoma Press, 1963.

Quilter, Jeffrey. "Architecture and Chronology at El Paraíso, Peru." *Journal of Field Archaeology* 12 (1985): 279–97.

———. *Life and Death at Paloma: Society and Mortuary Practices in a Preceramic Peruvian Village.* Iowa City, IA: University of Iowa Press, 1989.

Quilter, Jeffrey, et al. "Subsistence Economy of El Paraíso, an Early Peruvian Site." *Science* 251 (1991): 277–83.

Radovanovic, Ivana. "Houses and Burials at Lepenski Vir." *European Journal of Archaeology* 3.3 (2000): 330–49.

Raymond, J. Scott. "A View from the Tropical Forest." *Peruvian Prehistory.* ed. Richard W. Keatinge. Vol. 279–302. Cambridge, U.K.: Cambridge University Press, 1988.

Reitz, Elizabeth J. "Faunal Remains from Paloma, an Archaic Site in Peru." *American Anthropology* 90 (1988): 310–22.

Renfrew, Colin. *Social Archaeology.* Edinburgh, U.K.: Edinburgh University Press, 1984.

Renfrew, Colin. *Archaeology and Language: The Puzzle of Indo-European Origins.* New York: Cambridge University Press, 1990.

Renfrew, Colin, Peter Forster, and Mathew Hurles. "The Past within Us." *Nature Genetics* 26 (2000): 253–54.

Richards, M.P., et al. "Stable Isotope Evidence of Diet at Neolithic Çatalhöyük, Turkey." *Journal of Archaeological Science* 30 (2003): 67–76.

Richards, Michael P., et al. "Neanderthal Diet at Vindija and Neanderthal Predation: The Evidence from Stable Isotopes." *Proceedings of the National Academy of Sciences* 97.13 (2000): 7663–66.

Rindos, David. *The Origins of Agriculture: An Evolutionary Perspective.* San Diego, CA: Academic Press, 1984.

Roberts, Mark, and Simon Parfitt. *Boxgrove: A Middle Pleistocene Hominid Site at Eartham*

*Quarry, Boxgrove, West Sussex.* London: English Heritage, 1999.

Roberts, Richard, et al. "Luminescence Dating of Rock Art and Past Environments Using Mud-Wasp Nests in Northern Australia." *Nature* 387 (1997): 696–99.

Roberts, Richard G., et al. "New Ages for the Last Australian Megafauna: Continent-Wide Extinction about 46,000 Years Ago." *Science* 292 (2001): 1888–90.

Roberts, Richard G., et al. "The Human Colonisation of Australia: Optical Dates of 53,000 and 60,000 Years Bracket Human Arrival at Deaf Adder Gorge, Northern Territory." *Quaternary Science Reviews* 13 (1994): 575–83.

Robertshaw, Peter. "The Beginnings of Food Production in Southwestern Kenya." *The Archaeology of Africa: Food, Metals, and Towns.* ed. Thurstan Shaw. London: Routledge, 1998. 358–71.

Robin, Cynthia. "New Directions in Classic Maya Household Archaeology." *Journal of Archaeological Research* 11.4 (2003): 307–56.

Roche, H., et al. "Early Hominid Stone Tool Production and Technical Skill 2.34 Myr Ago in West Turkana, Kenya." *Nature* 399 (1999): 57–60.

Rohling, E.J., et al. "Magnitudes of Sea-Level Lowstands of the Past 500,000 Years." *Nature* 394 (1998): 162–65.

Roksandic, M., et al. "Interpersonal Violence at Lepenski Vir Mesolithic/Neolithic Complex of the Iron Gates Gorge (Serbia-Romania)." *American Journal of Physical Anthropology* 129.3 (2006): 339–48.

Rollefson, Gary O. "Ritual and Social Structure Inat Neolithic 'Ain Ghazal." *Life in Neolithic Farming Communities.* ed. I Kuijt. New York: Plenum, 2000. 165–90.

Roosevelt, A.C., et al. "Paleoindian Cave Dwellers in the Amazon: The Peopling of the Americas." *Science* 272 (1996): 373–84.

Roth, A.M. *Egyptian Phyles in the Old Kingdom: The Evolution of a System of Social Organization. Studies in Ancient Oriental Civilization.* Vol. 48. Chicago: Oriental Institute of the University of Chicago, 1991.

Rothman, Mitchell S. *Uruk Mesopotamia and Its Neighbors: Cross-Cultural Interactions in the Era of State Formation. School of American Research Advanced Seminar Series.* Santa Fe, NM.: School of American Research Press, 2001.

———. "Studying the Development of Complex Society: Mesopotamia in the Late Fifth and Fourth Millennia B.C." *Journal of Archaeological Research* 12.1 (2004): 75–119.

Ruvolo, M. "Genetic Diversity in Hominid Primates." *Annual Review of Anthropology* 26 (1997): 515–40.

Ruvolo, Maryellen. "Molecular Phylogeny of the Hominoids: Inferences from Multiple Independent DNA Sequence Data Sets." *Molecular Biological Evolution* 14.3 (1997): 248–65.

Sabloff, Jeremy, and Gordon Willery. *A History of American Archaeology.* San Francisco: Freeman, 1980.

Sahlins, Marshall David. *Stone Age Economics.* Chicago: Aldine-Atherton, 1972.

Sandweiss, Daniel H., et al. "Variation in Holocene El Niño Frequencies: Climate Records and Cultural Consequences in Ancient Peru." *Geology* 29.7 (2001): 603–06.

———. "Quebrada Jaguay: Early South American Maritime Adaptations." *Science* 281 (1998): 1830–32.

Sandweiss, Daniel H., et al. "Geoarchaeological Evidence from Peru for a 5000 Years B.P. Onset of El Niño." *Science* 273 (1996): 1531–32.

Santos, G.M., et al. "A Revised Chronology of the Lowest Occupation Layer of Pedra Furada Rock Shelter, Brazil: The Pleistocene Peopling of the Americas." *Quaternary Science Reviews* 22 (2003): 2303–10.

Scarre, Christopher, and Geoffrey Scarre. *The Ethics of Archaeology: Philosophical Perspectives on Archaeological Practice.* Cambridge, U.K.: Cambridge University Press, 2006.

Schele, Linda, et al. *The Blood of Kings: Dynasty and Ritual in Maya Art.* New York and Fort Worth, TX: G. Braziller and Kimbell Art Museum, 1986.

Schick, Kathy D., et al. "Continuing Investigations into the Stone Tool-Making and Tool-Using Capabilities of a Bonobo *(Pan Paniscus)*." *Journal of Archaeological Science* 26 (1999): 821–32.

Schiffer, Michael B. *Formation Processes of the Archaeological Record.* 1st ed. Albuquerque, NM: University of New Mexico Press, 1987.

Schirmer, Wulf. "Some Aspects of Building at the 'Aceramic–Neolithic' Settlement of Cayonu Tepesi." *World Archaeology* 21.3 (1990): 365–87.

Schmidt, K. "Gobekli Tepe and the Early Neolithic Sites of the Urfa Region: A Synopsis of New Results and Current Views." *Neo-lithics* 10.1 (2001): 9–11.

Schmidt, Peter R. *Iron Technology in East Africa: Symbolism, Science, and Archaeology.* Bloomington, IN: Indiana University Press, 1997.

Schmidt, Peter R., and Roderick J. McIntosh. *Plundering Africa's Past.* Bloomington, IN: Indiana University Press, 1996.

Schmitz, Ralf W., et al. "The Neanderthal Type Site Revisited: Interdisciplinary Investigations of Skeletal Remains from the Neander Valley, Germany." *Proceedings of the National Academy of Sciences* 99.20 (2002): 13342–47.

Schnapp, Alain. *The Discovery of the Past.* New York: Harry N. Abrams, 1996.

Schreiber, Katharina. "The Wari Empire of Middle Horizon Peru: The Epistemological Challenge of Documenting an Empire without Documentary Evidence." *Empires.* eds. Susan Alcock, et al. Cambridge, U.K.: Cambridge University Press, 2001.

Schwartz, Jeffrey H., and Ian Tattersall. "Whose Teeth?" *Nature* 381 (1996): 201–02.

Scott, K. "The Large Mammal Fauna." *La Cotte de St. Brelade 1961–1978*. eds. P. Callow and J.M. Cornford. Norwich, U.K.: Geo Books, 1986. 109–38.

Sebastian, Lynne. *The Chaco Anasazi: Sociopolitical Evolution in the Prehistoric Southwest. New Studies in Archaeology*. Cambridge, U.K.: Cambridge University Press, 1992.

Semah, François, et al. "Did Early Man Reach Java During the Late Pliocene?" *Journal of Archaeological Science* 27 (2000): 763–69.

Semaw, S. "The World's Oldest Stone Artefacts from Gona, Ethiopia: Their Implications for Understanding Stone Technology and Patterns of Human Evolution between 2.6–1.5 Million Years Ago." *Journal of Archaeological Science* 27 (2000): 1197–214.

Semaw, S., et al. "2.5-Million-Year-Old Stone Tools from Gona, Ethiopia." *Nature* 385 (1997): 333–34.

Service, Elman. *Origins of the State and Civilization*. New York: Norton, 1975.

Service, Elman Rogers. *Primitive Social Organization: An Evolutionary Perspective*. 2d ed. New York: Random House, 1971.

Shanks, Michael, and Christopher Y. Tilley. *Social Theory and Archaeology*. Cambridge, U.K.: Polity Press, 1987.

———. *Re-Constructing Archaeology: Theory and Practice. New Studies in Archaeology*. Cambridge, U.K. and New York: Cambridge University Press, 1987.

Shea, John, Zachary Davis, and Kyle Brown. "Experimental Tests of Middle Paleolithic Spear Points Using a Calibrated Crossbow." *Journal of Archaeological Science* 28.8 (2001): 807–16.

Silverberg, Robert. *Mound Builders of Ancient America: The Archaeology of a Myth*. Athens, OH: Ohio University Press, 1968, 1986.

Sklenar, K. *Archaeology in Central Europe: The First 500 Years*. Leicester, U.K.: Leicester University Press, 1983.

Smith, Andrew B. "Keeping People on the Periphery: The Ideology of Social Hierarchies between Hunters and Herders." *Journal of Anthropological Archaeology* 17 (1998): 201–15.

Smith, Bruce D. "The Initial Domestication of *Cucurbita pepo* in the Americas 10,000 Years Ago." *Science* 276 (1007): 932–34.

———. *The Emergence of Agriculture*. New York: Scientific American Library, 1995.

———. "Low-Level Food Production." *Journal of Archaeological Research* 9.1 (2001): 1–43.

Smith, Bruce D., and C. Wesley Cowan. "Domesticated Crop Plants and the Evolution of Food Production Economies in Eastern North America." *People and Plants in Ancient Eastern North America*. ed. Paul E. Minnis. Washington, DC: Smithsonian Books, 2003. 105–25.

Smith, Colin, et al. "Not Just Old but Old and Cold?" *Nature* 410 (2001): 771–72.

Smith, Claire, and H. Martin Wobst, eds. *Indigenous Archaeologies: Decolonizing Theory and Practice*. London: Routledge, 2005.

Smith, C.E. "Plant Remains from Guitarrero Cave." *Guitarrero Cave: Early Man in the Andes*. ed. Thomas F. Lynch. New York: Academic Press, 1980. 87–119.

Smith, Fred H., et al. "Direct Radiocarbon Dates for Vindija G1 and Velika Pecina Late Pleistocene Hominid Remains." *Proceedings of the National Academy of Science* 96.22 (1999): 12281–86.

Smith, Michael Ernest. *The Aztecs. Peoples of America*. 2d ed. Malden, MA: Blackwell Pub., 2003.

Society for American Archaeology, SAA. *Principles of Archaeological Ethics*. 2005. Web Site. Available: http://www.saa.org/public/resources/ethics.html.

Soffer, O., J.M. Adovasio, and D.C. Hyland. "The 'Venus' Figurines: Textiles, Basketry, Gender, and Status in the Upper paleolithic." *Current Anthropology* 41.4 (2000): 511–37.

Solis, Ruth Shady, Jonathan Haas, and Winifred Creamer. "Dating Caral, a Preceramic Site in the Supe Valley on the Central Coast of Peru." *Science* 292 (2001): 723–26.

Sonett, Charles P. "The Present Status of Understanding of the Long-Period Spectrum of Radiocarbon." *Radiocarbon after Four Decades*. eds. R.E. Taylor, A. Long, and R.S. Kra. New York: Springer Verlag, 1992. 50–61.

Souden, David. *Stonehenge Revealed*. London: Collins & Brown; in association with English Heritage, 1997.

Spector, Janet. "What This Awl Means: Toward a Feminist Archaeology." *Engendering Archaeology: Women and Prehistory*. eds. Joan Gero and Margaret Conkey. Oxford, U.K.: Blackwell, 1991. 388–406.

Spindler, Konrad. *The Man in the Ice: The Discovery of a 5,000-Year-Old Body Reveals the Secrets of the Stone Age*. Toronto: Doubleday Canada, 1994.

———. *Der Mann Im Eis: Neue Funde Und Ergebnisse. Man in the Ice*, V. 2. Wien and New York: Springer-Verlag, 1995.

Spooner, N.A. "Human Occupation at Jinmium, Northern Australia: 116,000 Years Ago or Much Less?" *Antiquity* 72.275 (1998): 173–78.

Squier, Ephraim G., and Edwin Davis. *Ancient Monuments of the Mississippi Valley*. Washington, DC: Smithsonian Institution, 1848. Smithsonian Classics of Anthropology.

Stafford, C. Russel, and Steven D. Creasman. "The Hidden Record: Late Holocene Landscapes and Settlement Archaeology in the Lower Ohio River Valley." *Geoarchaeology: An International Journal* 17.2 (2002): 117–40.

Stafford, Michael D., et al. "Digging for the Color of Life: Paleoindian Red Ochre Mining at the Powars II Site, Platte County, Wyoming, USA." *Geoarchaeology: An International Journal* 18.1 (2003): 71–90.

Stanford, Craig. *The Hunting Ape: Meat Eating and the Origins of Human Behavior.* Princeton, NJ: Princeton University Press, 1999.

Stanford, Dennis, and Bruce Bradley. "The Solutrean Solution: Did Some Ancient Americans Come from Europe." *Discovering Archaeology* 2.1 (2000): 54–55.

Steele, James. "Stone Legacy of Skilled Hands." *Nature* 399 (1999): 24–25.

Stein, Gil. *Rethinking World-Systems: Diasporas, Colonies, and Interaction in Uruk Mesopotamia.* Tucson, AZ: University of Arizona Press, 1999.

Stiner, Mary C., et al. "Paleolithic Population Growth Pulses Evidenced by Small Animal Exploitation." *Science* 283 (1999): 190–93.

Stock, J.T., et al. "F-81 Skeleton for Wadi Mataha, Jordan and Its Bearing on Human Variability in the Epipaleolithic of the Levant." *American Journal of Physical Anthropology* 128.2 (2005): 453–65.

Storck, P., and A. Spiess. "The Significance of New Faunal Identifications Attributed to an Early Paleoindian (Gainey Complex) Occupation at the Udora Site, Ontario, Canada." *American Antiquity* 59 (1994): 121–42.

Storck, Peter L. *Journey to the Ice Age: Discovering an Ancient World.* Vancouver, BC: Published by UBC Press in association with the Royal Ontario Museum, 2004.

Stordeur, D., et al. "Les Bâtiments Communautaires de Jerf el Ahmar et Mureybet Horizon PPNA (Syrie)." *Paléorient* 26.1 (2000): 29–44.

Storm, Paul. "The Evolution of Humans in Australasia from an Environmental Perspective." *Palaeogeography, Palaeoclimatology, Palaeoecology* 171 (2001): 363–83.

Straus, L.G. "Solutrean Settlement of North America? A Review of Reality." *American Antiquity* 65.2 (2000): 219–26.

Stringer, Chris, and Robin McKie. *African Exodus: The Origins of Modern Humanity.* 1st Owl Books ed. New York: Henry Holt, 1998.

Stringer, C.B., and P. Andrews. "Genetic and Fossil Evidence for the Origin of Modern Humans." *Science* 239 (1988): 1263–68.

Sugiyama, Saburo. "Governance and Polity at Classic Teotihuacán." *Mesoamerican Archaeology: Theory and Practice.* eds. Julia A. Hendon and Rosemary A. Joyce. Oxford, U.K.: Blackwell, 2004. 97–123.

Sutton, Mark Q., Brooke S. Arkush, and Joan S. Schneider. *Archaeological Laboratory Methods: An Introduction.* 2d ed. Dubuque, IA: Kendall/Hunt Pub. 1998.

Suwa, Gen, et al. "The First Skull of *Australopithecus boisei.*" *Nature* 389 (1997): 489–92.

Swedlund, Alan, and Duane Anderson. "Gordon Creek Woman Meets Kennewick Man: New Interpretations and Protocols Regarding the Peopling of the Americas." *American Antiquity* 64.4 (1999): 569–76.

Swedlund, Alan, and Duane Anderson. "Gordon Creek Woman Meets Spirit Cave Man: A Response to Comment by Owsley and Jantz." *American Antiquity* 68.1 (2003): 161–67.

Swisher, C.C., et al. "Age of the Earliest Known Hominids in Java, Indonesia." *Science* 263.5150 (1994): 1118–21.

———. "Latest *Homo Erectus* of Java: Potential Contemporaneity with *Homo Sapiens sapiens* in Southeast Asia." *Science* 274 (1996): 1870–1874.

Tankersley, Kenneth B. "Sheriden: A Clovis Cave Site in Eastern North America." *Geoarchaeology: An International Journal,* Vol. 12., No. 6 (1997): 713–24.

Tattersall, Ian, and Jeffrey H. Schwartz. "Hominids and Hybrids: The Place of Neanderthals in Human Evolution." *Proceedings of the National Academy of Science* 96 (1999): 7117–19.

———. *Extinct Humans.* 1st ed. Boulder, CO: Westview Press, 2000.

Taylor, R.E., and Martin J. Aitken, eds. *Chronometric Dating in Archaeology.* New York: Plenum, 1997.

Taylor, R.E., et al. "Radiocarbon Analyses of Modern Organics at Monte Verde, Chile: No Evidence for a Local Reservoir Effect." *American Antiquity* 64.3 (1999): 455–60.

Taylor, R.E., A. Long, and R.S. Kra, eds. *Radiocarbon after Four Decades: An Interdisciplinary Perspective.* New York: Springer Verlag, 1992.

Taylor, Walter W. *A Study of Archaeology.* Carbondale, IL: Southern Illinois University Press, 1948.

Tchernov, Eitan, and Francois François Valla. "Two New Dogs, and Other Natufian Dogs, from the Southern Levant." *Journal of Archaeological Science* 24 (1997): 65–95.

Templeton, Alan R. "Out of Africa Again and Again." *Nature* 416 (2002): 45–47.

Thieme, Hartmut. "Lower Paleolithic Hunting Spears from Germany." *Nature* 385 (1997): 807–10.

Thomas, David Hurst. *Skull Wars: Kennewick Man, Archaeology, and the Battle for Native American Identity.* New York: Basic Books, 2000.

Thomas, Julian. *Rethinking the Neolithic.* Cambridge, U.K.: Cambridge University Press, 1991.

———. *Time, Culture, and Identity: An Interpretive Archaeology.* London: Routledge, 1996.

———. *Understanding the Neolithic.* Rev. 2d ed. London: Routledge, 1999.

———. *Archaeology and Modernity.* London: Routledge, 2004.

Thornton, Russel. "Repatriation as Healing the Wounds of the Trauma of History: Cases of Native Americans in the United States of America." *The Dead and Their Possessions: Repatriation in Principle, Policy, and Practice.* eds. C. Fforde, J. Hubert, and P. Turnbull. London: Routledge, 2002. 17–24.

Tieme, Chen, et al. "The Problems in ESR Dating of Tooth Enamel of Early Pleistocene and the Age of Longgupo Hominid, Wushan, China." *Quaternary Science Reviews* 20 (2001): 1041–45.

Tilley, Christopher and Michael Shanks. *Social Theory and Archaeology.* Albuquerque, NM: University of New Mexico Press, 1987.

Tobias, Phillip V. "Encore Olduvai." *Science* 299 (2003): 1193–94.

Tomasello, Michael. *The Cultural Origins of Human Cognition.* Cambridge, MA: Harvard University Press, 1999.

Toth, Nicholas, et al. "Pan the Tool-Maker: Investigations into the Stone Tool-Making and Tool-Using Capabilities of a Bonobo (*Pan paniscus*)." *Journal of Archaeological Science* 20 (1993): 81–91.

Townsend, Richard F. *The Aztecs.* London: Thames and Hudson, 2000.

Tozzer, Alfred M., et al. *Landa's Relación de las Cosas de Yucatán: A Translation. Papers of the Peabody Museum of American Archaeology and Ethnology,* Harvard University; V. 18. Cambridge, MA: The Peabody Museum, 1941.

Trigger, Bruce G. *A History of Archaeological Thought.* Cambridge, U.K.: Cambridge University Press, 1989.

———. *Understanding Early Civilizations: A Comparative Study.* Cambridge, U.K.: Cambridge University Press, 2003.

Trinkaus, Erik, et al. "An Early Modern Human from the Pestera Cu Oase, Romania." *Proceedings of the National Academy of Science* 100 (2003): 11231–36.

Trinkaus, Erik, and Pat Shipman. *The Neanderthals: Changing the Image of Mankind.* New York: Knopf, 1993.

Underhill, Peter A., et al. "Y Chromosome Sequence Variation and the History of Human Populations." *Nature Genetics* 26 (2000): 358–61.

Urton, Gary. *Signs of the Inka Khipu: Binary Coding in the Andean Knotted-String Records. The Linda Schele Series in Maya and Pre-Columbian Studies.* Austin: University of Texas Press, 2003.

Valdes, Juan Antonio, and Jonathan Kaplan. "Ground-Penetrating Radar at the Maya Site of Kaminaljuyu, Guatemala." *Journal of Field Archaeology* 27.3 (2000): 329–42.

Valdez, Lidio M., and J. Ernesto Valdez. "Reconsidering the Archaeological Rarity of Guinea Pig Bones in the Central Andes." *Current Anthropology* 38.5 (1997): 896–97.

Valladas, H., et al. "Thermoluminescence Dating of Mousterian Proto-Cro-Magnon Remains from Israel and the Origin of Modern Man." *Science* 331 (1988): 614–16.

Van den Bergh, Gert D., John de Vos, and Paul Y. Sondaar. "The Late Quaternary Paleogeography of Mammal Evolution in the Indonesian Archipelago." *Palaeogeography, Palaeoclimatology, Palaeoecology* 171 (2001): 385–408.

Van Schaik, Carel P., et al. "Orangutan Cultures and the Evolution of Material Culture." *Science* 299 (2003): 102–05.

Van Tilburg, JoAnne. *Easter Island: Archaeology, Ecology, and Culture.* Washington, DC: Smithsonian Institution Press, 1994.

Vandermeersch, Bernard. *Les Hommes Fossiles de Qafzeh, Israël. Cahiers de Paléontologie.* Paris: Editions du Centre National de la Recherche Scientifique, 1981.

Verhoeven, Marc. "Ritual and Ideology in the Pre-Pottery Neolithic B of the Levant and Southeast Anatolia." *Cambridge Archaeological Journal* 12.2 (2002): 233–58.

Vitelli, Karen D., and Chip Colwell-Chanthaphonh. *Archaeological Ethics.* 2d ed. Lanham, MD: AltaMira Press, 2006.

Vos, John de. "Dating Hominid Sites in Indonesia." *Science* 266 (1994): 1726.

Wadley, L. "Vegetation Changes between 61,500 and 26,000 Years Ago: The Evidence from Seeds in Sibudu Cave, KwaZulu-Natal." *South African Journal of Science* 100 (2004): 167–73.

Walker, C. B. F. *Cuneiform. Reading the Past;* V. 3. Berkeley, CA and London: University of California Press and British Museum, 1987.

Walter, R.C., et al. "Early Human Occupation of the Red Sea Coast of Eritrea During the Last Interglacial." *Nature* 405 (2000): 65–69.

Wanpo, Huang, et al. "Early *Homo* and Associated Artefacts from Asia." *Nature* 378 (1995): 275–78.

Wanpo, Huang, et al. "Whose Teeth?" *Nature* 381 (1996): 201–02.

Wasylikowa, K., et al. "Examination of Botanical Remains from Early Neolithic Houses at Nabta Playa, Western Desert, Egypt, with Special Reference to Sorghum Grains." *The Archaeology of Africa: Food, Metals, and Towns.* ed. Thurstan Shaw. London: Routledge, 1993. 154–63.

Watchman, A.L., et al. "Micro-Archaeology of Engraved and Painted Rock Surface Crusts at Yiwarlarlay (the Lightning Brothers Site), Northern Territory, Australia." *Journal of Archaeological Science* 27 (2000): 315–25.

Watchman, A.L., and R. Jones. "An Independent Confirmation of the 4 Ka Antiquity of a Beeswax Figure in Western Arnhem Land, Northern Australia." *Archaeometry* 44.1 (2002): 145–53.

Waters, Michael R., Steven L. Forman, and James M. Pierson. "Diring Yuriakh: A Lower

Paleolithic Site in Central Siberia." *Science* 275 (1997): 1281–84.

Watkins, Joe. "The Politics of American Archaeology: Cultural Resources, Cultural Affiliation, and Kennewick." *Indigenous Archaeologies: Decolonizing Theory and Practice.* eds. Claire Smith and H. Martin Wobst. London: Routledge, 2005. 189–206.

Watkins, Trevor. "The Origins of House and Home?" *World Archaeology* 21.3 Architectural Innovation (1990): 336–47.

Watson, Patty Jo, and Mary Kennedy. "The Development of Horticulture in the Eastern Woodlands of North America: Women's Role." *Engendering Archaeology: Women and Prehistory.* eds. Joan Gero and Margaret Conkey. Oxford, U.K.: Blackwell, 1991. 255–75.

Watson, Patty Jo, Steven A. LeBlanc, and Charles L. Redman. *Archaeological Explanation: The Scientific Method in Archaeology.* New York: Columbia University Press, 1984.

Wells, H.G. *The Time Machine and the The Invisible Man.* New York: New American Library,1984.

Wendorf, Fred, and Romuald Schild. "Nabta Playa and Its Role in Northeastern African Prehistory." *Journal of Anthropological Archaeology* 17 (1998): 97–123.

Wendorf, Fred, et al. "The Use of Plants During during the Early Holocene in the Egyptian Sahara: Early Neolithic Food Economies." *Before Food Production in North Africa.* eds. Savino di Lernia and Giorgio Manzi. Forli, Italy: A.B.A.C.O. Edizioni, 1998. 71–78.

Wetterstrom, Wilma. "Foraging and Farming in Egypt: The Transition from Hunting and Gathering to Horticulture in the Nile Valley." *The Archaeology of Africa: Food, Metals, and Towns.* ed. Thurstan Shaw. London: Routledge, 1993. 165–225.

Wheatley, David, and Mark Gillings. *Spatial Technology and Archaeology: The Archaeological Applications of GIS.* London and New York: Taylor & Francis, 2002.

Wheeler, Mortimer. *Archaeology from the Earth.* Harmondsworth, U.K.: Penguin Books, 1954.

White, Randall. "Husbandry and Herd Control in the Upper Paleolithic." *Current Anthropology* 30.5 (1989): 609–32.

———. "Beyond Art: Toward an Understanding of the Origins of Material Representation in Europe." *Annual Review of Anthropology* 21 (1992): 537–64.

White, Tim, Gen Suwa, and Berhane Asfaw. "*Australopithecus ramidus*, a New Species of Early Hominid from Aramis, Ethiopia." *Nature* 371 (1994): 306–12.

———. "Corrigenda: *Australopithecus ramidus*, a New Species of Early Hominid from Aramis, Ethiopia." *Nature* 375 (1995): 88.

White, Tim D., et al. "Pleistocene *Homo sapiens* from Middle Awash, Ethiopia." *Nature* 423 (2003): 742–52.

Whiten, A., et al. "Cultures in Chimpanzees." *Nature* 399 (1999): 682–85.

Whittle, Alasdair. *Europe in the Neolithic: The Creation of New Worlds.* Cambridge, U.K.: Cambridge University Press, 1996.

Willcox, George. "Measuring Grain Size and Identifying Near Eastern Cereal Domestication: Evidence from the Euphrates Valley." *Journal of Archaeological Science* 31 (2004): 145–50.

Williamson, B.S. "Middle Stone Age Tool Function from Residue Analysis at Sibudu Cave." *South African Journal of Science* 100 174–178 (2004): 174–78.

Wills, W.H., and Thomas C. Windes. "Evidence for Aggregation and Dispersal During the Basketmaker III Period in Chaco Canyon, New Mexico." *American Antiquity* 54 347–369 (1989): 347–69.

Windes, Thomas C. "This Old House: Construction and Abandonment at Pueblo Bonito." *Pueblo Bonito: Center of the Chacoan World.* ed. Jill E. Neitzel. Washington, DC: Smithsonian Press, 2003. 14–32.

Wittfogel, Karl. *Oriental Despotism: A Comparative Study of Total Power.* New Haven, CT: Yale University Press, 1957.

Wobst, H.M. "The Archaeo-Ethnology of Hunter–Gatherers or the Tyranny of the Ethnographic Record in Archaeology." *American Antiquity* 43.2 (1978): 303–09.

Wolf, Eric R. *Europe and the People without History.* Berkeley, CA: University of California Press, 1982.

Wolpoff, Milford H., and Rachel Caspari. *Race and Human Evolution.* New York: Simon & Schuster, 1997.

Wood, Bernard. "The Oldest Whodunnit in the World." *Nature* 385 (1997): 292–93.

Wood, B., and M.C. Collard. "The Human Genus." *Science* 284 (1999): 65–71.

Wood, Bernard, and Brian G. Richmond. "Human Evolution: Taxonomy and Paleobiology." *Journal of Anatomy* 196 (2000): 19–60.

Wood, Bernard, and Alan Turner. "Out of Africa and into Asia." *Nature* 378.6554 (1995): 239–40.

Wrangham, Richard, et al. "The Raw and the Stolen: Cooking and the Ecology of Human Origins." *Current Anthropology* 40.5 (1999): 567–94.

Wright, Henry T., and Gregory A. Johnson. "Population, Exchange, and Early State Formation in Southwestern Iran." *American Anthropologist* 77 (1975): 267–89.

Yamei, Hou, et al. "Mid-Pleistocene Acheulean-Like Stone Technology of the Bose Basin, South China." *Science* 287.5458 (2000): 1622–26.

Yellen, J.E., et al. "A Middle Stone Age Worked Bone Industry from Katanda, Upper Semliki Valley, Zaire." *Science* 268 (1995): 553–56.

Yesner, David R. "Human Dispersal into Interior Alaska: Antecedent Conditions, Mode of

Colonization, and Adaptations." *Quaternary Science Reviews* 20 (2001): 315–27.

Yi, Soojin, Darrell L. Ellsworth, and Wen-Hsiung Li. "Slow Molecular Clocks in Old World Monkeys, Apes, and Humans." *Molecular Biological Evolution* 19.12 (2002): 2191–98.

Yoffee, Norman. *Myths of the Archaic State: Evolution of the Earliest Cities, States, and Civilizations.* Cambridge, U.K.: Cambridge University Press, 2005.

Young, Biloine W., and Melvin L. Fowler. *Cahokia, the Great Native American Metropolis.* Urbana, IL: University of Illinois Press, 2000.

Zazula, Grant D., et al. "Ice-Age Steppe Vegetation in East Beringia." *Nature* 423 (2003): 603.

Zettler, Richard L., Lee Horne, and Donald P. Hansen. *Treasures from the Royal Tombs of Ur.* Philadelphia: University of Pennsylvania Museum of Archaeology and Anthropology, 1998.

Zhang, Juzhong, et al. "Oldest Playable Musical Instruments Found at Jiahu Early Neolithic Site in China." *Nature* 401 (1999): 366–68.

Zhijun, Zhao. "The Middle Yangtze Region in China Is One Place Where Rice Was Domesti-cated: Phytolith Evidence from the Diao-tonghuan Cave, Northern Jiangxi." *Antiquity* 72.278 (1998): 885–97.

Zhu, Rixiang, et al. "Magnetostratigraphic Dating of Early Humans in China." *Earth-Science Reviews* 61 (2002): 341–59.

Zhu, R.X., et al. "New Evidence on the Earliest Human Presence at High Northern Latitudes in Northeast Asia." *Nature* 431 (2004): 559–62.

Zilhao, J. "The Rock Art of the Coa Valley, Portugal: Significance, Conservation, and Management." *Conservation and Management of Archaeological Sites* 2.4 (1998): 193–206.

Zollikofer, C. P. E., et al. "Virtual Cranial Reconstruction of *Sahelanthropus tchadensis.*" *Nature* 434.7034 (2005): 755–59.

Zvelebil, Mark. "Demography and Dispersal of Early Farming Populations at the Mesolithic–Neolithic Transition: Linguistic and Genetic Implications." *Examining the Farming/Language Dispersal Hypothesis.* eds. Peter Bellwood and Colin Renfrew. McDonald Institute Monographs. Cambridge, U.K.: McDonald Institute, 2002.

Generalized hunter-gatherers, 197
Genetic traits (*see also* Evolution)
   cultural/human evolution and, 68–70
   DNA, 65, 148–149
   leadership based on heredity, 286
   Neanderthal DNA analysis, 117
   Neanderthals/modern humans and,
     115–116
   Out of Africa hypothesis and, 146–149
   possible mutation leading to modern
     humans, 162
Genus/species (*see specific name, i.e. Homo
   sapiens*)
*Genyornis newtoni*, 173
Geographical information systems, 11–12
Geological stratigraphy, 14–15
Geometric Kebaran, 205–208
Geophysical methods of excavation,
   344–345
Gesher Benot Ya'akov (Israel), 109, 113
Giza (Egypt), 370–373
Glacial chronology, 105–106
Göbelki Tepe site, 205
Gona (Ethiopia), 87–89
*Gorilla gorilla*, 66
Government (*see also* Social complexity)
   of Egypt, 364–366
     Indus Valley (Pakistan) and, 380
     Mayan civilization and, 340–342
     of Mesopotamia, 326–327
     sacrificial Mayan rituals and, 345–347,
     350
Gran Dolina site (Atapuerca), 107
Gravestones (Colonial America), 29–30
Gravettian industry, 151, 155–156
Great Bath, 379
Great Enclosure, 316–317
Great Houses, 302, 304–305, 308
Great Serpent Mound (Ohio), 234, 236
Great Zimbabwe, 294–295, 313, 316–318
Greek pottery vessels, 28
Grid, 19
Ground-penetrating radar (GPR),
   344–345
Group size/mobility of Neanderthals,
   131–132
Guilá Naquitz (Mexico)
   location, 234
   plant domestication and, 237, 239
Guiterrero Cave, 261, 271
Gunbilngmurrung, 166, 175
Günz glacial advance, 105

## H

Habuba Kebira (Syria), 333, 389
Hadar, 87–89
Hammath Tiberius (Israel), 17
Handaxes (*see also* Tools)
Harappan period, 375–380
Hard-hammer direct percussion, 84

Harris Matrix, 17, 214, 215
Hayonim Cave (Israel), 132
Hearths (*see* Fire)
Hemudu site (China), 261, 278
Hermeneutics, 54
Herto fossil, 138
Hierakonpolis (Egypt), 363, 367–368
Hieroglyphics (*see* Writing)
Hohlenstein-Stadel, 155
Home-base/food sharing model, 94
Hominins
   Acheulian sites/industries and, 108–113
   definition, 74–75
   initial occupation of Western Europe of,
     107–108
   Lower Paleolithic period and, 82–85
   tools and, 108–112
   use of fire by, 96
Hominoids
   definition, 64
   phylogeny of, 67
*Homo antecessor*, 107, 116
*Homo erectus*
   definition, 76–77, 79–80
   dispersal event and, 96–97
   earliest human occupation of
     Australia/Americas, 169–170
   Oldowan tools and, 82–83
   and possible fates of Neanderthals,
     146–149
   skeletal distinctiveness of, 116
   spread of, 97–99
*Homo ergaster*, 79
*Homo florensiensis*, 171–172
*Homo habilis*, 76–77, 79, 82–83
*Homo neanderthalensis*, 115
*Homo sapiens*
   definition, 64
   earliest human occupation of
     Australia/Americas, 167–168, 173
   living humans as, 115
   modern humans and, 137–138 (*see also*
     Modern humans)
   Paleoindian skeleton and, 185
Hopewell cultures, 248, 251
Horizontal excavation, 12–13, 18–21
Howieson's Poort industries, 139
Hsia dynasty, 350–351
Huange He (Yellow River), 261
Huánuco, 391
Hua'nuco Pampa, 396
Huitzilopochtlí, 408–409
Human sacrifices, 408–411 (*see also*
   Rituals)
Humboldt Current, 271, 275
Hunter-gatherers (*see also* Agriculture)
   Neanderthals as, 131–132
   of northwest North America, 287–288
   as original affluent society, 194–195
   types of, 197–198

Trade routes, 364
Training/resources, as principle of ethic, 4
Tribe societies, 285–286
Trilithons, 297
Tuberculosis, 404
Tuff, 87, 89
Tula, 402–403
Tumamoc Hill site (Arizona), 241
Typology
    Bordes, François and, 119
    definition, 28
    Frison effect and, 121–122

## U

Uan Afuda (Libya), 263, 266
Uan Muhuggiag (Africa), 266
Ubeidiya (Israel), 97
Ulluzian industry, 149
Upper Egypt, 361–363
Upper Paleolithic
    artwork of, 156–160
    chronology of, 147, 151–153
    human burials of, 154–156
    site structure of, 160
    stone/bone tools of, 153–154
    subsistence of, 161
Ur, 332–333
Uranium series dating, 170
Urban Revolution, 353
Urban societies, 286–287, 376–379 (see also specific society, i.e. Mayan civilization)
Urban states (see Mayan civilization; Mesoamerica; Shang China)
Urubamba Valley, 395
Uruk period, 325–326, 333, 389
Use-wear analysis of tools, 152

## V

V. Gordon Childe, 45–46, 48
Vacant center pattern, 250
Valtorta (Spain), 193
Venus figurines, 155–157 (see also Artwork)
Vértesszölös (Hungary), 110
Vertical excavation
    archeological stratigraphy and, 17–18
    control of, 18–21

definition/examples, 13–14
and formation of archeological sites, 16
geological stratigraphy and, 14–15
Vindija Cave (Croatia), 117, 151
Vogelherd (Germany), 155

## W

Wadi Mataha (Jordan), 205, 207–208
Wallace Line, 170–172
Wanlek, 261, 268
Warfare/expansion
    Aztec empire and, 411
    Inca empire and, 397–399
    Mayan civilization and, 345–349
    Mesopotamia and, 332–333
Wari culture, 393
Wet screening, 21
White Dog Cave (Arizona), 242
Wildebeest Kuil (South Africa), 162
Wisconsin glacial advance, 105
Wonderwerk Cave (South Africa), 414–415
Writing
    of Egypt, 364–366
    Epic of Gilgamesh and, 322
    of Inca/Aztec empires, 390
    Indus Valley (Pakistan) and, 379–380
    Mayan hieroglyphics, 343–345, 348–349
    Mesopotamian cuneiform tablets, 322, 330–332
    oracle bones of Shang China and, 351–352
    scribes of Mayan civilization, 343–345
Würm glacial advance, 105

## Y

An Yang (China), 351–353
Yangshou culture (China), 278
Yangtze River, 261, 276–277
Yax K'uk' Mo', 341–342
Younger Dryas, 211
Yuku (New Guinea), 267

## Z

Zafarraya Cave (Spain), 151
Zhou dynasty, 350–351
Zhoukoudian (China), 112–115
Ziggurats, 326

# FIGURE AND PHOTO CREDITS

## Part One

2, Demetrio Carrasco/Dorling Kindersley Media Library; 3, National Park Service; 4, National Geographic Image Collection

## Chapter 1

6, Kenneth Garrett/National Geographic Image Collection; 8, Naomi Rudov/Allyn & Bacon; 10, EENC; 11, PH ESM; 13, Corbis/Bettmann; 14, Dr. William Finlayson; 15, A. Ronen/Israel Exploration Society; 16, Courtesy of Dr. Parvinder S. Sethi; 17, Courtesy of Michael Chazan; 18 (bottom), Georg Gerster/Photo Researchers; 20, Figure 1.4 from *Village on the Euphrates* by AMT Moore, GC Hillman, and AJ Legge, p. 226, Figure 8.43. Copyright © 2002. Reprinted by permission of Oxford University Press, Inc.; 22, Courtesy of Michael Chazan; 23, Courtesy of Michael Chazan; 24, Dorling Kindersley Media Library; 25, Courtesy of Eric Stegmaier and Jodi Magness; 28, Courtesy of Harry N. Abrams; 30 (left), Courtesy of Michael Chazan; 30 (right), Figure 1.8 from *In Small Things Forgotten* by James Deetz, copyright © 1977 by James Deetz. Used by permission of Doubleday, a division of Random House, Inc; 33, James F. O'Connell; 34, Eurelios/Phototake

## Chapter 2

36, Hulton-Deutsch Collection/Corbis; 38 (top), Naomi Rudov/Allyn & Bacon; 38 (bottom), French School, (18th century)/The Bridgeman Art Library International; 39, Courtesy of Michael Chazan; 40 (top), Figure 2.1 from *Antiquity* 76(291):223–234. "Archaeological illustrations: A new development in 19th century science" by Serge Lewuillon, Figure 2. Reprinted by permission of Antiquity Publications Ltd; 40 (bottom), Johanes Sambucus *Emblemata*. Originally published in 1564 (Anverpiae: C. Plantini); 42, SuperStock; 43, Prehistoric/The Bridgeman Art Library International; 44, Figure 2.2, from Edouard Lartet and Henry Christy (1875) *Reliquiae Aquitanica*. PL XXIV; 45, Mansell/Time Life Pictures/Getty Images; 46, Hulton Archive/Getty Images; 47, Dmitri Kessel/Time Life Pictures/Getty Images; 49, Hillsman S. Jackson/Southern Methodist University; 51, Courtesy of Wessex Archeology; 52, Figure 2.3 from *The Emergence of Civilization* by August and Colin Renfrew, p. 486, Figure 21.1, © 1972. Published by Routledge, London. Copyright © 1972 by Routledge. Reprinted by permission of Thomson; 54, Figure 2.4 from *The Archaeological Process: An Introduction* by Ian Hodder, p. 39, Figure 3.3 (1999). Adapted by permission of Blackwell Publishing; 55, Courtesy of Ron Wise; 56, Courtesy of Peter Robertshaw; 57 (top), Courtesy of Peter Robertshaw; 57 (bottom), Courtesy of Peter Robertshaw; 58, Courtesy of Sophia Smith Collection, Smith College; 59 (top), Courtesy of Rissa M. Trachman; 59 (bottom), Courtesy of Rissa M. Trachman

## Part Two

66, The British Library/HIP/The Image Works; 67, Figure II.3 from "The Mosaic that Is Our Genome" by Svante Pääbo (2003). *Nature* 421: 409–412, Figure 1. Reprinted by permission from Macmillan Publishers Ltd; 68, Figure 2a-c from Moya-sola et al. *Science* 306:1339–1344 (2004). Reprinted with permission from AAAS; 69, Peter Hvizdak/The Image Works; 70, Cognitive Evolution Group/University of Louisiana at Lafayette

## Chapter 3

72, John Reader/Photo Researchers; 74, "Anthropology: The Earliest Toothless Hominin Skull" by David Lordkipanidze et al. (2005). *Nature* 434: 717–178, Figure 1 views a & e. Reprinted by permission from Macmillan Publishers Ltd; 76, "Virtual Cranial Reconstruction

of Sahelathropus Tchadensis" by Christoph P.E. Zolliker et al. (2005). *Nature* 434: 755–759, Figure 2. Reprinted by permission from Macmillan Publishers Ltd; 77, John Reader/SPL/Photo Researchers; 78, The Bridgeman Art Library International; 79, National Geographic Image Collection; 80, David L. Brill Photography; 81, John Reader/Photo Researchers; 82, Pictures of Record; 83, Courtesy of Michael Chazan; 84, Courtesy of Michael Chazan; 85, "Laterality in Tool Manufacture by Crows" by Gavin Hunt (2001). *Nature* 414: 707–707, Figure 1. Reprinted by permission from Macmillan Publishers Ltd.; 86, C. Bromhall/Animals/Earth Scenes; 88, Michael P. Doukas/Cascades Volcano Observatory, U.S. Geological Survey; 89, Figure 3.2 adapted from *Journal of Human Evolution* 31 W. H. Kimbel et al., "Late Pliocene Homo and Oldowan Tools from the Hadar Formation (Kada Hadar Member), Ethiopia," Figure 1, 549–561 (1996), with permission from Elsevier; 90, Philippe Plailly/Eurelios; 91, Philippe Plailly/Eurelios; 92, Ian Redmond/Nature Picture Library; 93, Figure 3.3 from M.D. Leakey, *Olduvai Gorge*, vol. 3, p. 65, Figure 32 (1971). Reprinted with the permission of Cambridge University Press; 94, Courtesy of Michael Chazan and Herve Monchot; 95 (left), M.D. Leakey, *Olduvai Gorge*, vol. 3, Plate 2 (1971). Reprinted with the permission of Cambridge University Press; 95 (right), M.D. Leakey, *Olduvai Gorge*, vol. 3, Plate 3 (1971). Reprinted with the permission of Cambridge University Press. Photograph by MacCalman and Grobbelaar; 98, HO/AP Images

## Chapter 4

102, John Reader/Photo Researchers; 104, Chris Hellier/Corbis/Bettmann; 106, Figure 4.1, adapted from "The Astronomical Theory of Climate and the Age of the Brunhes-Matuyama Magnetic Reversal," by F. C. Bassinot et al. (1994) in *Earth and Planetary Science Letters* 126(1–3): 91–108, Figure 7, with permission from Elsevier; 107, Javier Trueba/Madrid Scientific Films; 109, Courtesy of Harold L. Dibble; 110, Courtesy of Matthew Pope; 111, Courtesy of Carl Swisher; 112, Peter Pfarr/Hartmut Thieme; 113, *Cambridge Archaeological Journal* (2000) 10: 123–167, Figure 1, F. d'Errico and A. Nowell. Reprinted with the permission of Cambridge University Press; 114, Ken Mowbray/American Museum of Natural History; 116, John Wiley & Sons, Inc., Journals; 117, Reprinted by permission of Johannes Krause; 118, Courtesy of Harold L. Dibble; 119, Figure 4.4 from François Bordes, *Science* 134:803–810, Figure 6 (1961). Reprinted with permission from AAAS; 121, Figure 4.5 from *American Antiquity* 52:1 (1987). Reproduced by permission of the Society for American Archaeology and Harold Dibble; 123, Courtesy of Michael Chazan and Alexandra Sumner; 124, Figure 4.6 from P. Callow and J.M. Cornford (1986), *La Cotte de St. Brelade 1961–1978*. Norwich: Geo Books, Figure 18.2, p. 161; 125, "A Levallois point embedded in the vertebra of a wild ass" by Eric Boëda et al., *Antiquity* 73: 394–402, Figure 5 (1999). Reprinted by kind permission of Antiquity Publications Ltd; 126, Courtesy of Michael Chazan; 127, Courtesy of Paul Goldberg; 128 (top), Dorling Kindersley Media Library; 128 (bottom), *Journal of Human Evolution* 26, Y. Rak et al., Figure 2, 313–324 (1994), with permission from Elsevier; 129, Defleur et al. *Science* 286:128–131, Figure 2b (1999). Reprinted with permission from AAAS; 130, Courtesy of Lynne Schepartz

## Chapter 5

134, Kenneth Garrett/National Geographic Image Collection; 136, National Geographic Image Collection; 138, David L. Brill Photography; 139, Paul Mellars, *Science* 313:796–800, Figure 2

(11 August 2006). Reprinted with permission from AAAS; **140,** Yellen et al., *Science* 268:553–556, Figure 1 (1995). Reprinted with permission from AAAS. Photography courtesy of Chip Clark; **141,** Courtesy of Erlend Eidsvik; **142,** Courtesy of Tracy L. Kivell; **143,** Courtesy of Tracy L. Kivell; **145,** PhotoDisc/Getty Images; **148,** Instituto Portugues de Arqueologia; **150,** Courtesy of Randall White; **152,** Philippe Plailly/Eurelios; **153,** American Museum of Natural History; **154,** Gianni Dagli Orti/Corbis/Bettmann; **155,** "Triple Czech Burial" by Paul G. Bahn, *Nature* 332:302–303 (1988). Reprinted by permission from Macmillan Publishers Ltd; **156 (left),** Ulmer Museum; **156 (right),** Ira Block/National Geographic Image Collection; **157,** Figure 5.3 from F. d'Errico, "A New Model and Its Implications for the Origin of Writing: The La Marche antler revisited," in *Cambridge Archaeological Journal* (1994) 5(2), Figure 19. Reprinted with the permission of Cambridge University Press; **158,** American Museum of Natural History; **159,** Musee de l'Homme/Phototheque; **160,** Corbis/Sygma; **161,** Reprinted from *Current Anthropology* 30(5): 609–632 (b. redrawn by Bahn from Bahn 1978:190) with permission from The University of Chicago Press; **162,** Courtesy of Michael Chazan

## Chapter 6

**164,** Tony Heald/Nature Picture Library; **168,** Denver Museum of Nature & Science; **169,** Figure 6.1 from *Journal of Archaeological Science* 27:799820, "Why Flute? Folsom Point Design and Adaptation," Figs. 4c&d and 5d&e, (2001). Reprinted with permission of Elsevier; **170,** adapted from "Australian Prehistory: New Aspects of Antiquity" by J. Peter White and James F. O'Connell, Figure 1, *Science*, New Series, 203:21–28 (1979). Adapted with permission from AAAS and the authors; **171,** Courtesy of Dr. Peter Brown; **174,** Cary Wolinsky/Aurora & Quanta Productions; **175,** Steven David Miller/Nature Picture Library; **176,** Jacka Photography; **177,** Courtesy of the Texas Archaeology Research Lab; **179,** Reprinted by permission of Matt Duvall; **180,** Courtesy of Tom Dillehay; **181 (top),** A. C. Roosevelt et al., *Science* 272:373–384, Figure 7A (19 April 1996). Reprinted with permission from AAAS. Image courtesy of A. C. Roosevelt; **181 (bottom),** A. C. Roosevelt et al., *Science* 272:373–384, Figure 6A (19 April 1996). Reprinted with permission from AAAS. Image courtesy of A. C. Roosevelt; **182,** Figure 6.3, from A. C. Roosevelt et al., *Science* 272:373–384, Figure 5 (19 April 1996). Reprinted with permission from AAAS. Image courtesy of A. C. Roosevelt; **186,** Harry DiOrio/Syracuse Newspapers/The Image Works; **187,** Chase Studio/Photo Researchers; **188,** Joe Ben Wheat/University of Colorado Museum, Boulder

## Part Three

**193,** Courtesy of Berna Villiers; **194,** Jason Laure/The Image Works; **196,** National Geographic Image Collection; **197,** Jameson/American Museum of Natural History; **198,** Vroman/Peabody Museum, Harvard University; **200,** Danny Lehman/Corbis

## Chapter 7

**202,** Courtesy of Gary Rollefson/Whitman; **204,** Pictures of Record; **207,** *Ohalo II: A 23,000-Year-Old Fisher-Hunter-Gatherer's Camp on the Sea of Galilee,* curated by Dani Nadel. Haifa: Hecht Museum, University of Haifa. Reprinted by permission from Dani Nadel; **208,** Courtesy of Michael Chazan; **209,** Courtesy of Michael Chazan; **210 (top),** Philippe Plailly/Eurelios; **210 (bottom),** Courtesy of Dr. Joy McCorriston; **211,** Courtesy of Brigham Young University and Joel C. Janetski; **212 (top),** Courtesy of J. Perrot, Centre de recherche français de Jérusalem; **212 (bottom),** "Evidence for Domestication of the Dog 12,000 Years Ago in the Natufian of Israel" by Simon Davis et al. *Nature* 276: 608–610 (1978). Reprinted by permission from Macmillan Publishers Ltd; **213,** Courtesy of Gabi Laron/Kfar Hahoresh Archives and Nigel Goring-Morris; **216,** B. Arnaud/Eurelios; **217,** Frontispiece from *Village on the Euphrates* by AMT Moore, GC Hillman, and AJ Legge, p. 226, Figure 8.43. Copyright © 2002. Reprinted by permission of Oxford University Press, Inc; **218 (both),** Courtesy of Nigel Goring-Morris; **219,** Erich Lessing/Art Resource; **220,** Taiz & Zelger: Plant Physiology, Courtesy

of Sinauer Associates, Inc; **221,** Kislev et al., *Science* 312:1372–1374, Figure 1 (2006). Image by Y. Langsam. Reprinted with permission from AAAS; **223,** Courtesy of Ted Banning; **224,** Gianni Dagli Orti/Corbis; **226,** *Antiquity* 77 (295): 45–62. "Neolithic transition in Europe: The radiocarbon record revisited," Figure 7. Reprinted with permission of Antiquity Publications Ltd; **227,** Erich Lessing/Magnum; **228,** Corbis/Sygma; **229,** Gilles Tosello/Eurelios

## Chapter 8

**232,** The Bridgeman Art Library International; **236,** Tony Linck/Ohio Dept. of Natural Resources; **237,** Courtesy of Hugh Iltis/Doebley Lab/University of Wisconsin, Madison; **238,** Figure 8.1 from *Science-Based Dating in Archaeology* by Martin Jim Aitken, p. 83, Fig 4.3. Reprinted by permission of Pearson Education Limited; **239,** Smith, *Science* 276: 932–934, Figure 2 (9 May 1997); **240,** Hard & Roney, *Science* 279:1661–1664, Figure 2 (1998). Reprinted with permission from AAAS. Photo by Tom Baker; **241,** Courtesy of Desert Archaeology, Inc.; **242,** Courtesy of Desert Archaeology, Inc.; **244 (top),** National Museum of Women In the Arts; **244 (bottom left),** Hillel Burger/Peabody Museum of Archaeology and Ethnology; **244 (bottom right),** New Mexico Department of Tourism; **245 (top left),** New Mexico Department of Tourism; **245 (top right),** New Mexico Department of Tourism; **245 (bottom left),** New Mexico Department of Tourism; **245 (bottom right),** New Mexico Department of Tourism; **246,** J. Bird/American Museum of Natural History; **247,** Figure 8.2 from *The Ancient Mounds of Poverty Point* by Jon Gibson, p. 82, Figure 5.2. Copyright © 2000. Reprinted with permission of the University Press of Florida; **249,** Werner Forman Archive Ltd; **250,** The Ohio Historical Society; **252,** Figure 8.4 from American Antiquity 60:2 (1995). Reproduced by permission of the Society for American Archaeology and M. Anne Katzenberg; **254,** Courtesy of Elizabeth S. Chilton; **255 (top),** Courtesy of Elizabeth S. Chilton; **255 (bottom),** Courtesy of Elizabeth S. Chilton

## Chapter 9

**258,** National Geographic Image Collection; **262,** Jean-Loc Le Quellec/Eurelios; **263,** Jean-Loc Le Quellec/Eurelios; **264 (top),** Courtesy of A.F.C. Holl; **264 (bottom),** Courtesy of A.F.C. Holl; **265,** Courtesy of A.F.C. Holl; **267,** Adrian Arbib/Corbis/Bettmann; **268,** Figure 9.1 from Denham et al., *Science* 301:189–193, Figure 2 B, C & D (2003), published online 19 June 2003 (10.1126/science.1085255). Reprinted with permission from AAAS; **269 (top),** CAMR/A. B. Dowsett/Photo Researchers; **269 (bottom),** Andrew Syred/Science Photo/Photo Researchers; **270,** Figure 9.2 from *Chavin and the Origins of Andean Civilization* by Richard Burger, p. 21, Figure 11. Copyright © 1992. London: Thames and Hudson. Courtesy of Richard L. Burger; **271,** The Granger Collection; **272,** A. Ramey/Woodfin Camp; **273,** *Life and Death at Paloma* by Jeffrey Quilter, p. 59, Figure 41. Copyright © 1989. Iowa City: University of Iowa Press. Photograph by Jeffrey Quilter; **274,** Oscar Biffi/Latinphoto.org; **276,** P. Pleynet/Reunion des Musees Nationaux/Art Resource; **277,** "Oldest Playable Musical Instruments Found at Jiahu Early Neolithic Site in China" by Juzhong Zhang et al. (1999). *Nature* 401: 366–368, Figure 1. Reprinted by permission from Macmillan Publishers Ltd; **278,** "Fermented Beverages of Pre- and Post-Historic China" by McGovern et al., Figure 1, pp. 17593–17598, in *Proceedings of the National Academy of Sciences,* vol. 101 (Dec. 21, 2004). Copyright © 2004 National Academy of Sciences, U.S.A; **279,** Lowell Georgia/Corbis

## Part Four

**284,** Sarah Leen/National Geographic Image Collection; **286,** Image #32775. Photo by Thomas Lunt. Reprinted with permission from American Museum of Natural History Library; **287,** Photodisc/Getty Images; **288,** American Museum of Natural History; **290,** AP Images

## Chapter 10

**292,** Adam Woolfitt/Corbis/Bettmann; **294,** Steve Allen Travel Photography/Alamy Images; **296,** John Constable/The Bridgeman Art Library International; **297 (all),** Courtesy of English Heritage Photo Library; **298 (top),** Lawrence Mogdale/Photo Researchers; **298**

(bottom), Satellite image courtesy of GeoEye; **299**, Courtesy of Wessex Archaeology; **302**, Courtesy of the National Park Service; **303**, Courtesy of Joe Watkins; **304**, Richard A. Cooke/Corbis; **305**, Smithsonian/National Museum of Natural History; **306**, Image #2A6738. Photo by Rota. Reprinted with permission from American Museum of Natural History Library; **307** (top), Courtesy of NASA—Marshall Space Flight Center; **307** (bottom), Georg Gerster/Photo Researchers; **309**, Laboratory of Tree-Ring Research; **310**, Otis Imboden Jr/National Geographic Image Collection; **311**, *Cahokia: The Great Native American Metropolis* by Biloine Whiting Young and Melvin Fowler, p. 265, Figure 27 (2000). Urbana: University of Illinois Press. Courtesy of the Illinois Transportation Archaeological Research Program, University of Illinois at Urbana, Champaign, and the University of Illinois Press; **312**, *Cahokia: The Great Native American Metropolis* by Biloine Whiting Young and Melvin Fowler, Figure 15, p. 138. Urbana: University of Illinois Press (2000). Reprinted courtesy of the Illinois State Museum photographic archives; **313**, Pete Bostrom. Courtesy of Cahokia Mounds Historic Site, Collinsville, Illinois; **314**, Courtesy of John W. Rick; **315** (top), Courtesy of John W. Rick; **315** (bottom), Photo by Jason Selznick, Copyright: John W. Rick; **316**, Neil Beer/Stone/Getty Images; **317** (left), National Archives of South Africa; **317** (right), Federal Information/Department of Zimbabwe

## Chapter 11

**320**, Kenneth Garrett/National Geographic Image Collection; **322**, Trustees of the British Museum; **324**, Danita Delimont Photography; **325**, Corbis; **326**, Richard Ashworth/Robert Harding World Imagery; **327** (top), Erich Lessing/AKG-Images; **327** (bottom), Figure 11.1 from "Household Production at the Uruk Mound, Abu Salabikh, Iraq," by S. Pollock et al. (1996). *American Journal of Archaeology* 100: 638–698, Figure 4. Photograph courtesy of Susan Pollock; **328**, Image #150028 reprinted by permission of University of Pennsylvania Museum; **329**, Trustees of The British Museum; **330**, The Bridgeman Art Library International; **331**, *Early Mesopotamia*, Nicholas Postgate. Copyright 1992 Routledge. (P. Amiet, *Glyptique susienne*, Paris 1972, no 539) Reproduced by permission of Taylor & Francis Books UK; **332**, Dagli Orti/Kobal Collection/Picture Desk; **333**, Figure 11.2, from *The Uruk World System* by Guillermo Algaze, Figure 5b (1993). Chicago: University of Chicago Press. Reprinted by permission of the publisher; **335** (top), Courtesy of Fred Valdez; **335** (bottom), Courtesy of Fred Valdez; **336**, Robert Fried Photography; **337**, Elizabeth Barrows Rogers/Mexican Government Tourism Office; **338**, Courtesy of David Hyde; **339** (left), Courtesy of David Hyde; **339** (right), Courtesy of David Hyde; **340**, Peabody Museum/Harvard University; **341** (top), Figure 11.5, from *Scribe, Warriors, and Kings* by William Fash, Figure 48, p. 95. London: Thames and Hudson (1991). Reprinted by permission of William Fash; **341** (bottom), National Geographic Image Collection; **342** (top), Figure 11.6, from *Journal of Field Archaeology* 25 (1998): 431–452, Figure 6. Reproduced with permission of the Trustees of Boston University. All rights reserved; **342** (bottom), National Geographic Image Collection; **343**, *Journal of Field Archaeology* 25 (1998): 431–452, Figure 3. Courtesy of Vanderbilt University Press; **345**, *Journal of Field Archaeology* 27(3): 329–342, Figure 10 (Autumn 2000). Reproduced with permission of the Trustees of Boston University. All rights reserved; **346** (both), Trustees of the British Museum; **347** (top), Trustees of the British Museum; **347** (bottom), Peabody Museum/Harvard University; **348**, Figure 11.8 from *Expedition* 4(1), Figure 5, p. 17 (1961). Reprinted by permission of University of Pennsylvania Museum; **349**, *Expedition* 4(1), figs. 2–4a, p. 17 (1961). Reprinted by permission of University of Pennsylvania Museum; **350**, Figure 11.9, from *Ancient Maya* by Arthur Demarest, Figure 10.5, p. 251 (2004). Reprinted with permission of Cambridge University Press. Image courtesy of The Vanderbilt Institute of Mesoamerican Archaeology. Drawing by L. F. Luin; **351**, Lowell Georgia/Corbis/Bettmann; **352**, Richard Lambert/Reunion des Musees Nationaux/Art Resource

## Chapter 12

**356**, National Geographic Image Collection; **358**, Gustavo Tomsich/Corbis; **361**, Courtesy of Michael Chazan; **362**, Art Resource; **363**, Dagli Orti/Kobal Collection/Picture Desk; **364**, Institute of Nautical Archaeology; **365**, Dagli Orti/Kobal Collection/Picture Desk; **366**, Dagli Orti/Kobal Collection/Picture Desk; **367**, Figure 12.1, from *Ancient Egypt: Anatomy of a Civilization* by Barry Kemp, Figure 11. Copyright © 1989 Routledge. Reproduced by permission of Taylor & Francis Books UK; **368** (top), Dagli Orti/Kobal Collection/Picture Desk; **368** (bottom), Sylvia Cordaiy Photo Library/Alamy Images; **369**, Courtesy of Michael Chazan; **370**, Space Imaging Europe/Photo Researchers; **371** (bottom), Courtesy of Michael Chazan; **371** (top), Courtesy of Michael Chazan; **372**, Courtesy of Michael Chazan; **373**, *King Menkaure (Mycerinus) and queen*, Egyptian, Old Kingdom, Dynasty 4, reign of Menkaure, 2490–2472 B.C., Findspot: Egypt, Giza, Menkaure Valley Temple, Graywacke, Height x width x depth: 142.2 x 57.1 x 55.2 cm (56 x 22 1/2 x 21 3/4 in.); Museum of Fine Arts, Boston, Harvard University—Boston Museum of Fine Arts Expedition 11.1738, Photograph © 2008 Museum of Fine Arts, Boston; **374**, Dagli Orti/Kobal Collection/Picture Desk; **377**, Chris Sloan. Courtesy J. M. Kenoyer; **378** (top), J.M. Kenoyer/Doranne Jacobson International Images; **378** (bottom), Borromeo/Art Resource; **379**, Georg Helmes; **380**, Georg Helmes; **381**, Art Resource; **382**, Roderick J. McIntosh, 1981; **383**, Remi Benali/Panos Pictures

## Chapter 13

**386**, Charles & Josette Lenars/Corbis; **388**, Ted Spiegel/Corbis; **390**, Danita Delimont Photography; **392**, Charles Lenars/Corbis/Bettmann; **393** (top), Museo Nacional de Arqueologia; **393** (bottom left), David Nunuk/Photo Researchers; **393** (bottom right), David Nunuk/Photo Researchers; **394**, Courtesy of Lindsey Stoker; **395**, Courtesy of Lindsey Stoker; **396**, Pete Oxford/Nature Picture Library; **397** (top), San Diego Museum of Man; **397** (bottom), Peruvian School/The Bridgeman Art Library International; **398**, Robert Frerck/Odyssey Productions; **399**, The Granger Collection; **400**, Figures 13.1A and 13.1B from *Code of the Quipu: A Study in Media, Mathematics, and Culture*, Marcia Ascher and Robert Ascher, University of Michigan Press, 1981. Reprinted by permission of Marcia Ascher and Robert Ascher; **401**, The Granger Collection; **403**, The Granger Collection; **404**, Proceedings of the National Academy of Science: WL Salo, AC Aufderheide, J Buikstra, and TA Holcomb; **406**, Bodleian Library; **407**, Dorling Kindersley Media Library; **408**, David Hiser/Stone/Getty Images; **409**, Peter Wilson/Dorling Kindersley Media Library; **410** (top), David Hiser/Stone/Getty Images; **410** (bottom), Dagli Orti/Kobal Collection/Picture Desk; **412**, Courtesy of E. Brumfiel

## Epilogue

**414**, Courtesy of Michael Chazan; **415**, Courtesy of Nancy Siesel/New York Times; **416** (top), National Geographic Image Collection; **416** (bottom), Kevin Fleming; **417**, Collection of the Israel Museum/by David Harris

## Appendix

**422–423**, States of the World map from Barbara Miller, *Cultural Anthropology*, 4/e. Published by Allyn & Bacon, Boston, MA. Copyright © 2007 by Pearson Education. Reprinted by permission of the publisher.; **425**, Copyright © 1996–2007 U.S. Metric Association, Inc. www.metric.org; **426** (top left), Gallo Images/Corbis; **426** (top right), Meave Leaky, Fred Spoor/Kenya National Museum; **426** (bottom left), David L. Brill Photography; **426** (bottom right), David L. Brill Photography; **427** (top left), David L. Brill Photography; **427** (top right), David L. Brill Photography; **427** (bottom left), David L. Brill Photography; **427** (bottom right), National Geographic Image Collection; **431** (top), Courtesy of Michael Chazan; **431** (bottom), Courtesy of Eric Stegmaier and Jodi Magness; **432** (top to bottom): Dagli Orti/Kobal Collection/Picture Desk, Peabody Museum/Harvard University, Lowell Georgia/Corbis/Bettmann, Dagli Orti/Kobal Collection/Picture Desk, Georg Helmes, The Granger Collection